# *The*
# *Premature*
# *Baby Book*

# The
# *Premature*
# *Baby Book*

## A Parents' Guide
## to Coping and Caring
## in the First Years

*Helen Harrison*

with Ann Kositsky, R.N.

Illustrations by Anne Hawkins

*Cover photo by Al Thelin*

*Courtesy of the University of Utah*
*Intermountain Newborn Intensive Care Center*

ST. MARTIN'S PRESS
NEW YORK

*To Edward
and
to Colin, Kate, Lacey, Steven, Timothy, Ami, Paul, Rachel, John, Michael, Kiyomi, Keidi, Kenichi, Toshi, Tadashi, Anthony, Rosie, and their parents.*

THE PREMATURE BABY BOOK. Copyright © 1983 by Helen Harrison. All rights reserved. Printed in the United States of America. No part of this book may be used or reproduced in any manner whatsoever without written permission except in the case of brief quotations embodied in critical articles or reviews. For information, address St. Martin's Press, 175 Fifth Avenue, New York, N.Y. 10010.

*Design by Manuela Paul*

**Library of Congress Cataloging in Publication Data**

Harrison, Helen, 1946–
   The premature baby book.

   1. Infants (Premature) 2. Infants (Premature—Care and hygiene. I. Kositsky, Ann. II. Title.
RJ250.H28   1983       649'.122      83-3152
ISBN 0-312-63648-2
ISBN 0-312-63649-0 (pbk.)

10  9  8  7

# Contents

Acknowledgments     vii

Foreword     ix

Introduction     xi

Two Births     xiii

### 1   Coping with a Birth Crisis     1
Shock □ Denial □ Anger, Guilt, and Depression □ Bargaining □ Acceptance and Adaptation □ Suggestions for Coping □ Colin's Story

### 2   Why Me?     16
Pre-Term Delivery: Questions and Answers □ Facts About "Multiples" □ Kate's Story

### 3   Bonding and Attachment     28
Bonding at Birth: How Important? □ The Effects of Separation □ Obstacles to Attachment □ "Does the Baby Know I'm There?" □ The Beginnings of Affection □ Fathers and Attachment □ Siblings and Attachment □ Telling Your Children About the Baby □ Relatives, Friends, and the Premature Baby □ Long-Distance Bonding □ Lacey's Story

### 4   At First Sight     42
A Baby's Development from Conception to Week 24 □ Very Premature Babies: Babies Born from Week 25 to Week 30 □ Pre-Terms and Full-Terms Compared □ Moderately Premature Babies: Babies Born from Week 31 to Week 36 □ Very Premature Babies at 31 to 36 Weeks □ Borderline Prematures: Babies Born During Weeks 37 to 38 □ The Premature Baby at Term (40 Weeks) □ Babies Who Are Too Small □ Babies Who Are Too Large

### 5   The Problems of Prematurity     55
The Birth Transition □ Respiratory Distress Syndrome, Hyaline Membrane Disease, and Pulmonary Insufficiency of the Premature □ Complications of Respiratory Therapy (Bronchopulmonary Dysplasia, Air Leaks, Retrolental Fibroplasia) □ Patent Ductus Arteriosus (PDA, Open Ductus, Murmur) □ Steven and Timothy's Story □ Apnea and Bradycardia □ Controlling Body Temperature □ Nourishing the Premature Baby □ Necrotizing Enterocolitis □ Ami's Story □ Blood Disorders □ Jaundice □ Anemia and Polycythemia □ Rh and ABO Incompatibilities □ Clotting Problems □ Infections □ The Torch Syndrome □ Types of Newborn Infections (Pneumonia, Enteritis, Septicemia, Meningitis) □ Neurological Problems (Seizures, Intracranial Hemorrhage, Hydrocephalus) □ If Your Baby Has a Shunt □ Newborn Intensive Care: Parents' Rights and Medical Ethics □ Paul's Story

### 6   The Death of a Baby     107
When a Baby Dies at Birth or Soon Afterward □ Death in the Nursery □ Practical Decisions □ Saying Good-Bye □ A Special Grief □ Telling Your Children About the Baby's Death □ Back to Life □ Rachel's Story □ John and Michael's Story

### 7   The Premature Nursery, Past and Present     120
Premature Care Through the Ages □ Prematures Who Made Their Mark

on History □ The Premature Nursery Today □ Who Does What in the NBICU □ The Million Dollar Baby

**8   Nursery Parenting**                              131
Understanding Your Baby □ Your Loving Touch □ Your Baby Is Listening □ Eye to Eye □ Holding and Rocking □ Your Baby's Comfort □ Dressing Up □ Premature Baby Clothes by Major Manufacturers □ Homemade Premature Clothes □ Patterns for Prematures □ Diapers and Plastic Pants □ Playtime □ Ready to Go Home □ Taking Care of Yourself □ Kiyomi, Keidi, Kenichi, Toshi, and Tadashi's Story

**9   Feeding Your Baby**                              153
Breast-feeding the Premature Baby □ Breastmilk and Health □ How to Hand Express Your Milk □ How to Store and Transport Your Milk □ Sterilizing Collection Utensils □ Bottle-feeding in the Hospital and at Home □ How Much Does the Baby Need? □ From Bottle to Breast □ The Lact-Aid Nursing Supplementer □ Problems Nursing? □ The Decision to Bottle-feed □ Offering New Foods □ Beginning Solids

**10   The First Year**                               175
The Post-Nursery Letdown □ Getting Organized □ Getting Some Sleep □ Coping with a Difficult Baby □ Taking Precautions □ Bathing Your Baby □ A Homecoming Diary □ Your Baby's Health □ Cardiopulmonary Resuscitation □ Growth □ Development □ "You're Overprotecting That Child!" □ Anthony's Story

**11   Will My Baby Be Normal?**                       202
Follow-up Studies □ Testing Your Baby □ Ongoing Problems (Cerebral Palsy, Mental Retardation, Hearing Impairment, Visual Impairment) □ Professionals Who Can Help □ When a Child Has Ongoing Problems □ Edward's Story □ Rosie's Story

**12   Another Baby?**                                 226
Am I a High-Risk Mother? □ Choosing an Obstetrician □ Choosing a Hospital □ Tocolytic (Labor-stopping) Drugs □ Tests and Procedures That May Be Used in High-Risk Pregnancy □ Preparing □ Giving Your Baby the Best Chance □ Pregnancy Guide □ Nutrition Tips □ How to Eat Well When You Must Rest in Bed □ Learn to Relax □ Stay in Touch with Your Body □ Detecting Premature Labor □ Diary of a High-Risk Pregnancy

**Appendix A—Resources for Parents**                  241
Prematurity and Newborn Intensive Care □ Breastfeeding □ After the NICU: Health and Development □ Twins and Supertwins □ Continuing Health and Developmental Problems □ Death of a Baby □ High-Risk Pregnancy □ Parent-to-Parent Support

**Appendix B—Glossary**                               253

**Appendix C—Glossary of Trade Names**                263

**Appendix D—Conversion Tables**                      265

**Index**                                             267

# Acknowledgments

Special thanks to Sally Sehring, M.D., of Children's Hospital, San Francisco, for reviewing the medical sections of the book for accuracy, and for her help and encouragement throughout this entire project, and to Carolyn Lund, R.N., C.N.S., and Linda Lefrak, R.N., N.N.P., of Children's Hospital Medical Center of Northern California, for their numerous contributions to the book.

Thanks also to the following professionals who supported our efforts and gave freely of their time and expertise: Barbara Abrams, M.P.H., R.D., Nancy Akeson, Counselor for families of blind infants, Kathleen Auerbach, Ph.D., Roberta Ballard, M.D., Jan Berry, R.N., Charles Bookoff, M.D., C. F. Zachariah Boukydis, Ph.D., Jill Boxerman, M.Ed., T. Berry Brazelton, M.D., Mary Campisi, O.T.R., Ronald Clyman, M.D., Robert Creasy, M.D., Margaret Crosby, Staff Counsel, A.C.L.U. of Northern California, Marty Enriquez, R.N., Jan Epcar, M.A., Harriet Eskildsen, M.A., Joanne Figone, O.T.R., Kittie Frantz, R.N., C.P.N.P., Barbara Gaffield, R.D., Sandy Garrand, R.N., B.S.N., Anne Garrett, R.N., M.S.N., John Golenski, Ph.D., Peter Gorski, M.D., Kathleen Gray, R.N., Peter Haiman, Ph.D., John Herre, M.D., Marie Herron, R.N., Toshiko Hirata, M.D., Jane Hunt, Ph.D., Huntley R. Johnson, D.D.S., Marshall H. Klaus, M.D., Rowena Korobkin, M.D., Pamela Krell, M.A., Juliene Lipson, R.N., Ph.D., Pat Malmstrom, M.A., Janis Maxson, R.N., Nancy McCabe, M.A., Stephen H. Miller, Ph.D., Mary Molocavage, M.Ed., Jerri Oehler, R.N., M.S., Richard Oken, M.D., Leslie Osterweil, M.A., Roderic Phibbs, M.D., Barry Phillips, M.D., Robert Piecuch, M.D., Project I.C.N. Interact, Child Development Center, Children's Hospital Medical Center of Northern California, Oakland, California (Nancy Sweet, M.A., Project Director, Bette Flushman, M.A., Infant Educator, Kathleen VandenBerg, M.A., Infant Educator, and Diane Valentin, R.N., Follow-Up Nurse), Ruth Rice, R.N., Ph.D., Phillip Riedel, M.D., Martin P. M. Richards, Ph.D., Robert Roth, M.D., Sasha Smeink, M.A., Susan Sniderman, M.D., Earl Stern, M.D., Alison Walsh, Assistant Director, Whitney Clinic, Children's Hospital, San Francisco, Edwin J. Wilson, Attorney at Law, Hildred Yost, R.P.T.

And thanks to the parents: Terry Alexander, Dorothy Andrews, Elizabeth Augustyn, Joan and Albert Baker, Paulette Barry, Dorothy and Robert Bauer, Karen and Merrill Beeck, Catherine and Ken Berglund, Sandy and Ed Bielski, Ellen Block, Lisa Bornstein, Mr. and Mrs. Joseph Callahan, Jr., Anne Chaban, Connie Chance, Deborah Cherniss, Marion Cohen, Karen Cook, Donna Cowan, Terri Cruz, Katherine Degher, Gerri Dito, Alice and Robert Drake, Marcia and Chuck Driscoll, Gayla and Doug Edwards, Cathy Elias, Sandi and Ron Everett, Karen Fisher, Julie and Ed Flockens, Patty Freitas, Susan and Rich Fuller, Miriam Glaser, Marian Graney, Pat Hardy, Jacqui Harris, Pat and Bill Haseltine, Mr. and Mrs. Michael Hawes, Carolyn Highsmith, Linda and Neil Hodur, Margaret Hollingsworth, Joan and Jim Johnson, Sue and Steve Johnson, Tina Kauffman, Megan Kirschbaum, Teri and Bob Knepper, Gail and Michael La Motte, M. Jude Langhurst, Kathy and Bill Laurie, Pamela Lee, Laurie and David LeRoy, Juliene Lipson, Jasmine Locatelli, Lauri Lowen, Lucinda MacDonald, Chris and Bill MacDowell, Ceylon Mace, Sue Masio, Maririta McKenna, Chris McNamara, Molly Mills, Shirley Moore, Lenette Moses, Ann Mueller, Jean and Tony Mulvihill, Eleanor and Francis Myers, Kathie and Nao Noguchi, Sue Ellen O'Brien, Ann Ogilvie, Leslie O'Leary, Jackie and Allan O'Neil, Barbara and Ives Parrish, Bonnie Phair, Karen Pound, Caryl Pryor, Kathy Reed, Carolyn and Jack Reynolds, Charlene Richard, Betsy Ricks, Mary Rhodes, Nancy Samson, Sue Santos, Marsha Servetnick, Sandy Silver, Bonnie Slade, Jill Snow, Katherine Stimson, Peggy Stinson, Judy Stoddard, Kathleen Vasek, Kenn and Vicky Waters, Susan West, April Williams, Flora Williams, Jean Wilson, Linda and

Alan Zeichner, the members of Parent-to-Parent, San Francisco, the members of the UCSF Parent Support Group, the members of the Children's Hospital Parent Support Group, Oakland, California, the members of INSPIRE of Savannah, Georgia, the members of the Loyola Premature and High Risk Infant Parents' Association, Batavia, Illinois, the members of Christ Hospital Neonatal Parents' Support Group, Bridgeview, Illinois, the members of Parents of Preemies, Billings, Montana, the members of Lamorinda La Leche League, the members of Nursing Mothers Counsel, Inc., of Palo Alto, California, and to those parents who helped but who wish to remain anonymous.

Thanks also to: Dorothy Kenville and the Needlework Guild of the Piedmont Community Church, Piedmont, California for the premie bootie and cap patterns, and to Lyons Filmer, who designed the premie sweater pattern.

Thanks to those businesses and individuals who supplied product information or samples: Neonatal Corporation, Pearl River, New York, Medela, Inc., Crystal Lake, Illinois, Allied Healthcare Products, Inc., Buffalo, New York, Ora'Lac, Inc., Sitka, Alaska, Scientific Corporation, Farmingdale, New York, The William Carter Company, Needham Heights, Massachusetts, S. Schwab Company, Cumberland, Maryland, The Warren Featherbone Company, Gainesville, Georgia, Zona Lee, Inc., San Francisco, California, Paty, Inc., Houston, Texas, Toddle Tyke, Atlanta, Georgia, Anne Long, Greenville, South Carolina, Jenny Baarstad and Susan Edgar, Ventura, California, Judy Mickelsen, Wheaton, Illinois, Lora Whitemarsh, Puyallup, Washington, JoAnne Bock, Tacoma, Washington, Janet Thayer, R.N., Glendale, California, Patricia Silvers, Lopez Island, Washington, and Nancy Nelson, Renton, Washington.

Thanks to everyone who helped with the photographs, especially: Al Thelin, Salt Lake City, Utah, Thomas D. Coleman, M.S.W., Intermountain Newborn Intensive Care Nursery, Salt Lake City, Utah, Peggy Green, Children's Hospital Medical Center of Northern California, Oakland, California, Linda More, R.N., Mt. Zion Hospital and Medical Center, San Francisco, California, and Kathy and Bill Laurie, San Francisco, California.

Thanks to everyone who helped with the typing, editing, and proofreading: Catherine Elias, Margaret Hollingsworth, Lyons Filmer, Becky and Don Webster, and Pauline Harrison. And to our editor at St. Martin's Press, Barbara Anderson, for her enthusiastic support!

I would most especially like to thank my husband Alfred. Without his typing and editing skills, his constant help, encouragement, understanding, and endurance, this book could never have been written. Last, but not least, I would like to thank Amy, who had to spend her babyhood in sibling rivalry with a manuscript.

Helen Harrison
August 1982

# Foreword

Neonatology, the care of sick newborn infants, began as a pediatric subspecialty only two decades ago. Since then, this new branch of medicine has changed with incredible speed. The resulting knowledge and complex technology have not only increased the survival rate among premature infants, but also greatly improved the outcome. Many texts and articles on the medical conditions and management of sick newborns have been published for the specialists involved in research, clinical care, and subsequent growth and development of these infants. However, those most intimately affected by premature birth are the parents, and at last we have, in *The Premature Baby Book,* a volume addressed to their special needs and experiences.

Pregnancy and childbirth are among the "highs" of human existence. No doubt, the positive attitudes associated with the birth of a baby in our culture help strengthen family relationships, and no one would wish to cause anxiety among prospective parents or detract from their childbirth experience by overemphasizing the things that might go wrong. But premature birth is not a rare occurrence. In the United States, approximately a quarter-million infants are born each year at some degree of prematurity. Of these, 20% are very small infants weighing less than three pounds. The parents of these babies have not completed the developmental tasks of pregnancy when, suddenly, they are thrust into a situation in which their fantasies of a "perfect" normal child and a fulfilling childbirth are shattered. They are forced to cope emotionally, intellectually, physically, and financially with a stressful, sometimes catastrophic event. They find themselves abruptly dealing with a highly complex environment, a myriad of specialized staff, and, most difficult of all, an infant who appears tiny, sick, helpless, and beyond their reach to love and nurture.

*The Premature Baby Book* fills many needs for these families. In carefully researched detail, it presents the basic medical information about prematurity, the most frequently encountered conditions, underlying physiologic principles, and the current usual therapies employed. Even though the field is changing so rapidly that some of these therapies may soon be modified, the essential information is presented here in such a way that it will remain helpful to parents who wish to understand events leading to and comprising the intensive care nursery experience. There are descriptions of the problems that may occur as the natural accompaniment of the hospitalized premature's recovery. The knowledge that certain problems are to be expected and that we on the staff anticipate them and are prepared to deal with them should increase the equanimity of parents who might otherwise feel discouraged and overwhelmed by seeming setbacks. The book provides parents with answers to the many questions they may not have the opportunity to ask, and it addresses the concerns they may feel uncomfortable expressing.

The book also contains a complete guide for taking the premature infant home. Parents of prematures have special problems with aspects of caregiving that would seem commonplace to parents of full-term newborns. Matters such as breast-feeding, finding clothes, temperature control, and future health care needs are all discussed here.

A unique, especially effective facet of this book is the interweaving of parents' feelings into the fabric of the factual information to provide emotional support along with intellectual understanding. No one, no matter how empathetic or well-informed, can understand and communicate so well with parents of sick infants as others who have undergone the same experiences. Only other mothers and fathers of prematures can share a parent's depth of despair or height of euphoria over the many setbacks and advances the baby experiences on the road to recovery.

*The Premature Baby Book* fills an important void in the literature of prematurity. Certainly, I gained a great deal from reading it. I am convinced that parents of premature infants will be greatly helped and supported by it. I also feel it should be required reading for the staff who care for them. From it they will gain new insights into the feelings and needs of the families they serve. Helen Harrison and Ann Kositsky have done a monumental job in producing this book, which so sensitively integrates the facts and feelings accompanying premature birth.

—Roberta A. Ballard, M.D.,
  Chief, Department of Pediatrics
  and Director, Newborn Services,
  Mount Zion Hospital and Medical Center,
  San Francisco, California

# Introduction

When I became pregnant, I had no trouble obtaining information on normal pregnancy and delivery. But when things went wrong, I found no books to help me.

While my son, Edward, was a baby, there was plenty to read on the care and development of the normal child. But what about the child whose development is delayed as a result of prematurity? What of the tiny infant who might have suffered brain injury?

Although I had worked for three years as a paramedic, I was unprepared for the intensive care nursery where my son was treated. Here, up-to-the-minute medical techniques were being used, therapies so new that no one was entirely sure of their results or side effects.

I couldn't speak the language. Tongue-twisters like bronchopulmonary dysplasia and necrotizing enterocolitis were not to be found in my medical dictionary. Neither was the alphabet soup of RDS, NEC, and CPAP.

When I asked the doctors about Edward's eventual outcome, I was told, "We don't know. Babies this sick and this small have rarely survived."

I wondered whether anyone else had ever gone through the same isolation and despair that I felt after my son's premature birth. But there was nowhere I could go for an answer.

I promised myself, then, that if Edward lived, I would write the book I so badly needed, a book that would give other parents the information I had to search for in medical libraries, a book that could also help me and others like me make sense of the emotional devastation of a premature birth.

Edward has just turned seven. In the years since his birth, his intensive care nurse, Ann Kositsky, and I have interviewed scores of doctors—neonatologists, obstetricians, pediatricians—as well as the many other medical and nonmedical professionals who care for premature infants and their families. And we consulted the *real* experts, the mothers and fathers of premature babies. We met with parents in hospital nurseries, at follow-up clinics, at parent group meetings, and in their homes. Through personal interviews and through written questionnaires, we contacted over a hundred mothers and fathers around the country and abroad.

Their premature babies ranged from fourteen ounces to eight pounds and from 25 to 36 weeks gestational age at birth. The nursery stays varied from a few days to fourteen months; the medical costs ranged from the usual newborn nursery charges to over a million dollars. Our book relates the experiences of these families, it responds to their questions and concerns, and it shares the advice these mothers and fathers had to offer on coping with "premature" parenthood.

Although this book is written primarily for the parents of premature babies, we hope it will also be useful for concerned friends and relatives, as well as for the health professionals involved with premature babies and their families.

In the chapters that follow, we explore the special emotional difficulties that mothers and fathers face after the birth of a premature infant. We describe the premature baby, how he differs from a full-term baby in appearance, behavior and physiology.

Because we have found that parents want to participate, knowledgeably, in their child's hospital care, we have included a long chapter on the problems of prematurity—the special care needed to sustain the immature newborn, the diseases that threaten the tiny baby, and the therapies used to treat these conditions.

To help parents translate the language spoken by the nursery staff, a glossary of medical terms and metric conversion tables are provided. For mothers and fathers confused by the vast array of intensive care specialists, a guide to the nursery personnel has also been included. We discuss the parent-doctor relationship and ways to improve communication. We examine the rights of parents to consent to or refuse treatment for their child. We explore the agonizing moral and ethical issues involved in the use (or misuse) of "heroic measures" to sustain the life of a critically ill baby.

Suggestions are given for parenting in the nursery—for ways to observe, touch, hold, soothe, and stimulate the premature infant. There are also practical tips on breast- and bottle-feeding; bathing, diapering, and dressing the tiny baby; and advice on easing the difficult transition from hospital to home.

Once the baby is home, parents may still need special aid and information. During infancy and early childhood, the premature infant may continue to differ from the full-term baby in his behavior, growth, and development. We describe what parents might expect during the first year and beyond, ways they can cope with problems that may arise, and the types of help available to them and their child.

We have included two chapters on obstetrics. One explores the various conditions associated with pre-term delivery. The other gives practical advice to the high-risk mother contemplating another pregnancy.

Within most chapters are short accounts written by parents telling of their experiences with their premature babies. Our intent was *not* to provide typical case histories (there probably is no such thing), but to show how different parents and babies coped with a variety of difficult beginnings. Two of these babies

died. Several survived with ongoing problems. The majority are now normal healthy children.

We have chosen to pay special attention to the difficulties of the tiny prematures who require intensive care at birth, since it is their parents who have the greatest need for information and support. Not all prematures require this kind of care. Many "large," healthy prematures are kept in the regular newborn or premature nursery. Nevertheless, we think all parents whose premature babies require special care at birth, however briefly, will find something in common with the mothers and fathers who tell their stories in this book.

# About Pronouns

While writing the book, we experimented with different pronouns to use in referring to the premature baby. "S/he," "her/him" seemed awkward; "it" was dehumanizing; and switching pronouns arbitrarily was too disruptive. Finally, at the risk of appearing sexist, we settled on the traditional masculine pronoun. Since nature discriminates so harshly against premature baby boys (more of them die, more of the survivors have problems), readers may regard our use of the masculine pronoun as a small attempt at compensation. I hope the parents of baby girls will accept our rationale.

# Two Births

At a small community hospital two babies are being born.

In the alternative birth center, a cozy, dimly lit room, a woman lies in bed in the final stages of labor. Despite her exertions, she seems calm and confident as her husband directs her in the well-rehearsed breathing techniques. A feeling of happy expectation fills the room while the nurse-midwife prepares for the imminent birth. Gently the baby girl emerges, takes her first breath, and utters her first cry. She is placed on her mother's abdomen. She nuzzles at her mother's breast. The mother massages her daughter's still-moist body. The mother is radiant, ecstatic to see and touch her baby at last, grateful that pregnancy and birth are finally over and that all has gone well. Her husband severs the umbilical cord. The baby is bathed in warm water, wrapped in a heated blanket, and placed again beside her mother. She grabs her mother's forefinger in her small chubby fist. Both mother and baby seem alert and pleased with each other. That night the new parents will bring their daughter home, amid congratulations from friends and relatives, to begin their life together as a family.

Down the hall in another room, a second woman endures her labor without medication or breathing exercises. She has not yet taken a childbirth class, and painkillers would be too dangerous to her unborn child. She is six months pregnant. A nurse prepares her for a cesarean section. The baby is in a breech position, common in premature labors, and because the fetal heart rate indicates distress, surgical delivery must take place immediately. The father stands by helplessly.

The mother is unconscious as the tiny, limp baby is lifted from her womb. Under the harsh lights of the operating room, a team of doctors and nurses begins its efforts to revive the infant. A tube is inserted into the baby's mouth, between the vocal cords and into the windpipe. A nurse rhythmically compresses an oxygen bag to force air through the tube to the baby's lungs. Another tube is threaded through an artery in the end of the umbilical cord until it reaches a position near the baby's heart. This will be used to administer nutrients, blood, and medicine.

The doctors have done all they can. They wait for the ambulance that will transfer the baby to an intensive care nursery many miles away. Before the ambulance leaves, the baby is wheeled to his mother's room. Drowsy and disoriented, the mother looks at the mass of tubes and wires that all but obscure her son's miniature, seemingly lifeless body. She cannot make sense of his two-pound, eight-ounce birth weight. The father is invited to accompany the baby to the hospital, many miles away. At the wife's insistence, he agrees to go, grateful at last to have something to do.

The mother is alone to deal with her shock and sadness. Around her in the maternity ward she hears the cries of new babies being brought to their mothers to nurse. Her flattened, aching stomach seems unreal to her. She falls asleep, dreams happily that she is still pregnant, and awakens to experience her grief all over again.

The next day her husband returns, bringing a blurred Polaroid photograph and a pair of tiny footprints. For almost a week these will be her only tangible evidence of motherhood.

She spends the next five days in the hospital, recovering from surgery. Her friends who call seem awkward, not knowing whether to offer congratulations or condolences. The doctor's telephoned reports on her son's condition are confusing and discouraging to her. She prepares herself for her baby's death.

But when she leaves the hospital, her son is still alive. Though she doubts her emotional and physical strength, she makes the long trip to visit her son in the intensive care nursery. After scrubbing with disinfectant and putting on a surgical gown, she enters the nursery. She sees her son's face through two walls of plastic—an incubator and an oxygen hood. With the nurse's permission, she opens one of the incubator windows and timidly touches the baby's arm with her forefinger. His arm and her finger are the same size.

An alarm above the bed begins to buzz. A nurse rushes over and gives the baby a rap on the chest to remind him to breathe. The mother recoils in horror, but, with the nurse's encouragement, she reaches out again to touch her son. And so, the mother begins the slow and difficult process of coming to know and love her premature baby.

# 1
# *Coping with a Birth Crisis*

You have just had a baby—weeks, perhaps months, too early—and your child has been taken from you to be treated in a special nursery. Your baby's birth, which should have been a joyful event, has become an ordeal of anguish and uncertainty. In the maternity ward, surrounded by new mothers and their babies, you may feel isolated and bitter, angry to have missed the happy experiences of birth and motherhood you anticipated during pregnancy. Perhaps you are worried that something you did or did not do might have caused the premature birth. Possibly you feel someone else—your mate or your doctor—is to blame. But above all, your thoughts are of your child. "Will my baby live?" "Will my baby be normal?"

If your baby is quite premature, you may have been given a pessimistic report on the chances for survival and you may already have begun to grieve. You may doubt that such infants are "meant to live," having heard that they often survive with handicaps and retardation. You may not know whether to wish for your baby's life or death. You may be reluctant to see your baby for fear of becoming attached. You may want to withdraw from a situation you find overwhelming. Making matters worse is the guilt you feel about having such thoughts.

You are not alone. Approximately 250,000 infants are born prematurely (before the 37th completed week of pregnancy) in the United States each year, and many of their parents express these same thoughts and feelings. Few mothers and fathers ever face a more distressing situation than the one that confronts them as the parents of a tiny, high-risk baby. Many have found it helpful to realize that their painful emotions have been shared by others, that such feelings are natural under the circumstances, and that they can be resolved with time.

Psychologists have described the stages through which most people progress in reacting to a

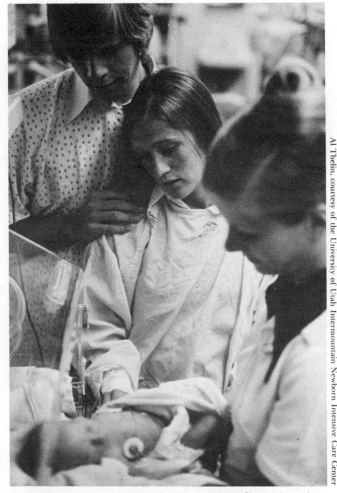

Al Thelin, courtesy of the University of Utah Intermountain Newborn Intensive Care Center

*Few mothers and fathers ever face a more distressing situation than the one that confronts them as the parents of a tiny, high-risk baby.*

traumatic, grief-producing event. In the following pages we will look at these stages—shock, denial, anger, bargaining, acceptance, and adaptation—as parents have experienced them following the birth of their premature baby.

# Shock

It may have happened suddenly: "My husband and I were shopping for a crib and the salesman asked when I was due. 'Oh, not for months,' I assured him. That night what I thought was indigestion turned out to be labor. Not until fifteen minutes before my son was born did I realize I was actually having the baby."

Perhaps there was warning: "I was in the hospital for a week with bleeding and contractions. They gave me drugs to help mature the baby's lungs. The nurse showed me pictures of premature babies so I would know what to expect. That helped a lot, but my daughter's birth and her fight for life were still a shock to me."

However it happens, it is always a shock—no one is ever really prepared.

A premature baby evokes, for many of us, the image of a slightly smaller than normal baby spending a few extra days warming in an incubator. For babies born only a few weeks before their due date, this is often how it is. Or perhaps we think of great uncle so-and-so who weighed three pounds at birth, was kept in a shoebox next to the stove, and lived to an obese old age. And it is true, some very tiny (and well-developed) babies survive without special medical care. But until recently, most very small premature babies died. Only in the past ten to fifteen years have sophisticated medical techniques made it possible for such babies to survive in relatively large numbers. And until very recently, there has been little public awareness of the many problems that afflict tiny newborns, of the medical advances that are saving so many of their lives, and of the special challenge these babies present to their parents. Few mothers have ever seen a premature baby or heard of an intensive care nursery. Most hospitals do not have such facilities; babies needing intensive care are transferred to large urban medical centers. Even if her hospital has an intensive care nursery, the mother-to-be is unlikely to have seen it. The premature nursery is rarely included on the hospital tours for expectant parents. It is too upsetting.

Between 6 and 8% of all births in the United States are pre-term,* making prematurity one of the greatest problems facing obstetricians, pediatricians, and parents today. Yet books on pregnancy, birth,

*Babies who are born at term (between the 38th and 42nd weeks of pregnancy) are often called "premature" when they weigh less than 5½ pounds. When these low-birthweight, high-risk babies are added to the statistics, the prematurity rate among whites is 10%; among blacks, 20%. Between 300,000 and 350,000 low-birthweight infants are born in the United States each year.

and childcare do little to prepare expectant mothers for this possibility. Recently, women in a prenatal class were asked if they were concerned about the possibility of premature delivery. "No such luck," was the typical response. "I'll probably be weeks overdue."

Almost every pregnant woman worries about having a baby that is not normal or about losing a baby through miscarriage or stillbirth. When an expectant mother thinks of her unborn child, she usually imagines the best and worst cases—a badly deformed or dead infant or the perfect "Gerber baby." But the gray in-between situation that confronts her after a premature delivery is one she is not likely to have considered. Here is a baby—far from the imagined ideal infant—who may still be intact and normal for its stage of development. Instead of the well-defined situations of her fantasies, the mother must cope with a long period of uncertainty.

Pregnant women are more likely to feel anxiety during the first three months of pregnancy when miscarriage is a threat, and again right before the term delivery. But the sixth, seventh, and eighth months—when a live premature birth becomes a possibility—are, for most expectant mothers, a relatively tranquil, happy time. They tend not to expect problems; they may be less aware of their bodies' danger signals. Whatever the reason, prematurity is usually low on the list of a pregnant woman's fears. "I really should have known better," said one mother. "Because I'm a nurse, I spent my pregnancy thinking of a thousand and one obscure, horrible things that could go wrong. But when my daughter arrived 10 weeks early, I was stunned. This was the one obvious possibility that hadn't occurred to me."

No matter how knowledgeable or well prepared a woman might be, a premature birth is still a uniquely upsetting experience. A special sort of psychological dislocation takes place when pregnancy is interrupted too soon. During the nine months of normal pregnancy, both mother and baby go through physical changes in preparation for birth. As the mother changes physically, she also changes psychologically, making a series of emotional adjustments that help her prepare for motherhood. During the first trimester she accepts the fact that she is pregnant, that a baby is growing in her body. By the second trimester she is obviously pregnant. She feels the baby move and recognizes that her infant has a real and separate identity. She begins to form a personal attachment to the unborn child. She and her mate may fantasize about the baby, about birth and parenthood. The last three months are filled with activity. It is the time to buy baby clothes, choose names, and furnish the nursery. An expectant mother often feels uncomfortable during this period, as her active and growing baby makes it increasingly difficult for her to eat, sleep, and breathe. She awaits the baby's arrival with impatience. She is now physically and psychologically ready for her pregnancy to end.

The mother who is headed for a premature delivery is at the most enjoyable phase of her pregnancy. She is just beginning the nesting activities of the final months. She hasn't fully experienced the last trimester discomfort, which makes full-term pregnant women eager for their babies to be born. She just isn't prepared. "When I went to the hospital," said one mother, "I kept thinking, 'This can't be labor—I haven't had my Lamaze classes . . . I can't be having a baby, we're still remodeling the nursery.' We hadn't even decided on names. My husband had just given me a beautiful maternity dress for my birthday and I hadn't had a chance to wear it." While the mother-to-be in her ninth month is likely to phone the obstetrician at the slightest twinge, a woman in premature labor tends to dismiss her symptoms until birth is imminent.

The psychological changes that occur during pregnancy may be influenced in part by chemical changes in the expectant mother's body. Researchers have found that pregnant animals close to the time of delivery experience hormonal changes that seem to affect the way the mother animal accepts and cares for her young. Rats that are induced to deliver prematurely, before these changes have fully taken place, show delays in assuming normal patterns of mothering. The premature animal mother eventually responds to the needs of the babies, but only after several days of exposure to them, and the earlier the pregnancy ends, the longer it takes the mother to begin caring for the litter. The theory that the hormones of late pregnancy might play a role in maternal behavior was further tested by transfusing virgin rats with blood from pregnant rats that were just about to give birth. As expected, the virgin rats began to display typical mothering behavior patterns. The chemistry involved is not entirely understood, but the hormone estrogen is thought to play a role. In the human female, there is a sharp rise in estrogen levels during the five weeks before a term delivery. It is possible that, as in lower animals, chemical factors help prepare a pregnant woman for motherhood. If so, premature delivery might in some way interfere with this process.

Whether from the psychological and physical factors just described or from the shock of delivering a tiny, strange-looking infant whose survival is in doubt, many women have negative or unmotherly feelings at first toward their premature babies. "I saw my baby right before he was transferred to the other hospital," one mother recounted, "and I have to admit my first reaction was totally unemotional. I talked

*"He didn't look like a real baby and I didn't feel like a real mother."*

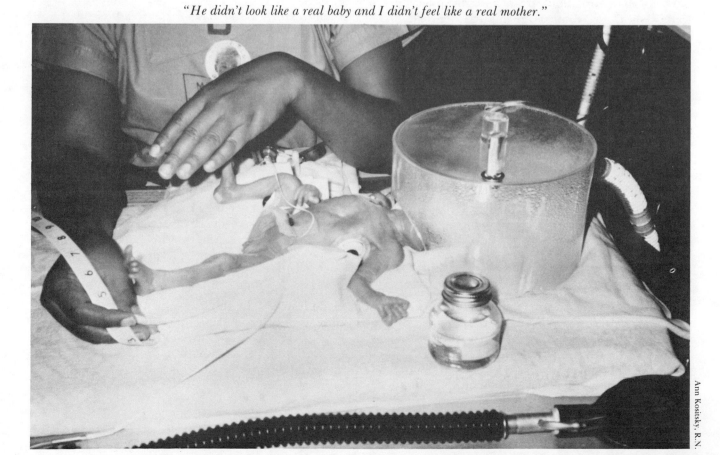

to the doctors about his weight, about the lanugo (hair) on his body, things like that. Then I looked at my husband. *He* was crying. It took a while for me to really relate to the baby as a human being. He didn't look like a real baby and I didn't feel like a real mother."

"For days I refused to name the babies," said a mother of twins. "Finally, my husband came to me with a pile of baby name books and yelled, 'Damn it!—The nurses are calling our kids Babies A and B. Either you help me name them or I'll do it myself!'"

Marna Cohen, a medical social worker at the University of California, San Francisco, has observed that mothers of premature babies tend to react differently from mothers whose full-term babies also need special hospitalization. Ms. Cohen studied two groups of women who had given birth to babies requiring intensive care. In one group were mothers of prematures; in the second group were mothers of full-term babies who were very small because of growth retardation in the womb. Both groups of babies were tiny and "at risk," yet the mothers' reactions were quite different. The premature mothers were distraught. Many expressed guilt and feelings of incompetence. One mother felt so inadequate to the task of caring for her baby that she feared she might accidentally kill the child if allowed to handle him. The mothers whose babies were full-term (though as small as the prematures) expressed only mild worry and loneliness at being separated from their hospitalized infants. For these women, an important process had been completed during the full nine months of pregnancy. They were able to relate to their babies' problems calmly and without the distress and guilt of the premature mothers.

Mothers we interviewed told of first reactions to their baby's birth that ranged from "overwhelming, shaking fear" to dazed numbness. "That first week," said one mother, "nothing and nobody could console me. I woke up each morning with fear in the pit of my stomach. I was afraid to call the nursery, afraid the baby had gotten worse or died during the night. I began to wonder about the limits of human endurance, both in terms of my baby's ability to survive, and my own ability to deal with this constant, horrible fear."

Many found the normal routines of daily life totally unmanageable: "I don't remember eating during those first days at home or taking a shower or changing my clothes. I was out of commission. If my mother hadn't come to stay with us, I don't know what would have happened."

Several women described unusual mental or physical sensations that accompanied their first feelings of shock: "My baby was born late at night and I was given something to help me sleep. When I woke up I didn't remember where I was or what had happened. My stomach felt peculiar and I thought 'Oh it's just the baby kicking.' I reached down. No baby! It was like waking up from surgery to discover a part of your body missing."

When her newborn daughter was taken to intensive care, one mother was literally paralyzed with fear: "I reached for the phone to call my family, but my entire right side was numb. For hours I couldn't move or speak."

Another said, "Everything seemed unreal. I felt like I had left my body and was watching myself do things."

And what of the shock to the premature baby's father? While sharing his wife's experiences, he has to contend with his own difficulties. "All of a sudden," said one father, "the weight of the world was on my shoulders. The baby was in intensive care at one hospital. My wife was recovering from a cesarean at a hospital 100 miles away, and we had a four-year-old at home. I also had my job to consider, especially with a hospital bill that was over $10,000 just for the first week. It was up to me to hold everything together, and I didn't see how I could do it. I was ready to panic."

The premature baby's father is also unprepared. A father recounted: "We'd been to one prenatal class and I fainted during the movie. Friends joked that when the baby arrived, *I'd* be the the one who'd need anesthesia. Peer group pressure was all that kept me from waiting the whole thing out in a bar somewhere. At the time my wife went into labor I knew next to nothing about birth and babies—much less premature babies. At the hospital, a nurse had to teach me how to help my wife breathe. I met the obstetrician for the first time in the delivery room. I'm really squeamish, as I said, but I watched my son's birth. I saw the doctors intubate and resuscitate him. I went with him to the intensive care nursery and I visited him every day. Soon I knew all about hyaline membrane disease, exchange transfusions, apnea, bradycardia. I surprised myself and everyone else. I guess you just do what you have to do."

Not all fathers cope so well with their introduction to the world of newborn intensive care. Said a neonatologist, "I remember a father who never once made it inside the nursery. Fortunately his baby was close to the door and he'd peek in on occasion. Then he'd get very pale and have to leave."

A young mother told how her year-old marriage dissolved the first time her husband came to the nursery: "He took one look at the baby, one look at the nursery, and one look at the medical bills, and asked me for a divorce. He just couldn't handle it."

The first trip to the nursery with its space-age technology, its unfamiliar vocabulary describing mysterious diseases, and its fetus-like infants hooked to large machines is a shock for anyone. "I didn't even know places like the intensive care nursery existed," said one parent. "I couldn't make any sense out of it. I might as well have been on Mars. The first thing that hit me was horrible fear—fear of the unknown, fear of death. The machines, the smell, the sounds, the incredible number of doctors and nurses per square inch all terrified me. The first three times I went to the nursery I literally passed out. The place scared the blood right out of my head."

# Denial

Denial, the second stage in adjusting to a trauma, is a temporary blocking out of reality. Denial can take several forms. It may be a brief accompaniment to the initial shock, the feeling of "Oh no, not me!"

"I wondered how on earth this could be happening," recalled one mother. "When we decided to have a baby, I got pregnant immediately. My pregnancy had been so easy. While I was still on the delivery table I asked the doctor when I could get pregnant again. I didn't want to have the baby like this. I hoped it would all go away like a bad dream so I could start over."

Denial may involve a refusal to believe the doctors, or a search for a specialist who will magically make the baby better.

Denial may also take the form of persistent and unwarranted optimism or pessimism along with an inability to comprehend any conflicting views.

"My husband was sure everything would turn out all right. I was frightened that the baby would die or be damaged. We would go together for conferences with the doctor and come away with totally different ideas about what he had said. For a long time we simply couldn't communicate. I did most of my grieving alone."

People often react to a crisis by assuming that "everything will be fine" or, on the contrary, that "all is lost." A fixed attitude, even an unrealistic one, seems to help in coping with an otherwise unbearable insecurity. "I just made up my mind that my daughter would live and be normal," one mother commented. "Denial was the only thing that got me out of bed in the morning and kept me functioning, at least on some level."

However, most of the parents we interviewed were overly pessimistic about their baby's survival, especially in the beginning. "When my milk came in," one mother said, "I was surprised and upset. All this milk for a baby who couldn't use it. I refused to believe that I had a baby who might live and have the same needs as other babies."

Some parents deliberately assume an attitude of pessimism in hopes that it will protect them emotionally. If the baby dies, they will be prepared; until the child's survival is certain, they try to stay detached. But the baby, whether he lives or dies, is an undeniable part of his parents' lives.

And the fact is, most premature babies do live. Intensive care nurseries report survival rates in the range of 80 to 90%. Even babies weighing two pounds or less who would surely have died a decade ago, now have a 50–50 chance for recovery. Optimism about the baby's survival is a realistic attitude for most parents to take.

Unwarranted pessimism is not always a matter of "denial" by the parents. Often it is fostered by doctors who give the new parents unduly negative or guarded reports. Many mothers we interviewed had been told by their obstetricians at the time of birth that their babies would surely die or at best have a very slim chance of survival. Later, at the nursery, the neonatologists had a much more optimistic prognosis. But for most of these mothers, the pessimism from the first forecast of doom was hard to erase.

Since a large number of specialists attend a tiny newborn, parents can receive mixed signals from different physicians with varied perspectives and personalities. "I remember my visit to the hospital on a morning after my baby had survived a difficult night," one mother recounted. "Doctor X approached me with a troubled frown and said: 'Your son had serious respiratory problems during the night, and while he appears to have stabilized for the time being, it is still too soon to make statements on his prognosis.' Soon afterward, Doctor Y bounded into the nursery, flashed a smile at my son's incubator, and exclaimed: 'What a fighter that boy is! He had a rough time last night, but this morning he pulled right out of it. You never know what these kids are going to do next!' The same information really, but the two doctors left me with totally different impressions."

To most parents the question is not so much "will my child live?" but "in what condition?"

Again, the physician's counseling greatly influences the parents' expectations. Mothers and fathers we interviewed whose children had ongoing problems often felt that doctors had given them an overly optimistic view of their child's probable outcome. In several cases the parents had simply not been told that their seriously ill premature might have future problems—an omission which delayed their seeking help for their child.

However, neurological problems and other handicaps can be difficult to predict during the time a baby is receiving intensive care. It has often been noted that of two babies with identical birth weights and complications after birth, one may grow up to be normal, while the other may be severely impaired. It may be months or years before parents have a clear idea of their child's outcome. Meanwhile, each stage in the baby's development presents a potential crisis. Denial may become a continuing strategy for the parent trying to cope with this long-term anxiety and uncertainty.

"I kept expecting the worst," one mother said. "Everything she did or didn't do seemed like evidence of brain damage. I blamed everything that happened on her prematurity. When she was a little older and had caught up with other kids her age, I finally relaxed a little."

Said another mother, "Every time we took him to the developmental clinic I would argue with the doctor. I wasn't ready to admit our baby had a problem."

Mothers and fathers often report that *their* parents also had trouble accepting a problem—or in some cases, the lack of one—in their premature grandchild. "My mother used to drive me nuts. She'd call and say, 'You mean you're taking him outside already?' That sort of thing. And she always wanted to know: 'Has he rolled over yet?' She seemed to feel he was on the brink of death and retardation." Said a mother whose baby was, in fact, handicapped: "Despite a good deal of evidence to the contrary, my mother-in-law refused to believe there was anything wrong. 'He's going to be fine,' she'd say. 'He's just been spoiled and overprotected. See how intelligent he looks.'"

## Anger, Guilt, and Depression

At some point most people experiencing a crisis stop denying, face reality and become angry. Like denial, anger has different forms. It may be expressed as a generalized bitterness towards God or an unjust fate.

"I tried for ages to get pregnant," one mother said. "We really wanted this baby. All I could think about was teenagers who get pregnant accidentally, or all those women in India and China. Why is it so easy for them and so hard for me? In the next incubator was a baby born to an addict. The baby was undergoing heroin withdrawal, but he was doing well and would go home soon. I hadn't taken so much as an aspirin while I was pregnant, but my baby was on a respirator. It seemed so unfair."

"When our son was at his worst," said a father, "one of the residents asked if we had any religious beliefs to help us in this difficult time. I told him I couldn't believe in a God who would allow this to happen to a tiny, innocent baby."

Anger may be directed at those perceived as more fortunate: "Every time I saw a pregnant woman or a new mother on the street I felt angry and envious. I couldn't face my friends who'd just had babies. The hospital social worker kept coming around to talk to me and I was terribly rude to her. How could she know what I was going through? She had two healthy kids at home."

A common target for the parents' wrath is the medical staff. "Our baby had an exchange transfusion for jaundice," said one father. "When I got an enormous bill from the hematologist, I called his office and vented all my accumulated rage on his poor secretary." Said another, "By the time our baby was ready to come home I had threatened to sue everyone from my wife's OB to the neonatologist to the head nurse."

Of course, incompetent and insensitive doctors and nurses *do* exist, so do unresponsive hospital bureaucracies and six-figure medical bills. Parental anger is often something quite apart from an irrational response to a birth crisis.

Some parents, seeking a scapegoat, may lash out and blame each other. "If only you hadn't insisted on taking that trip!" "If only you'd stopped smoking and taken better care of yourself!"

Relatives may join in the round of accusations. Typically, the wife's parents blame their son-in-law. "He couldn't earn enough money for her to quit her job while she was pregnant. Now look what's happened!" The husband's parents, of course, blame their daughter-in-law. "She was always too high-strung, not good stock!"

Anger may be directed inward as guilt and self-reproach—feelings that tormented many parents we interviewed. Mothers told of their preoccupation, to the point of obsession, with the events that preceded their babies' births. They wondered whether something they had done (or not done) might have caused the premature delivery. They wondered about some hidden physical or moral defect in themselves. Almost every mother felt that somehow, in some way, her baby's prematurity was her fault.

Fathers also expressed guilt. Some wondered if they had been helpful enough around the house. Others reproached themselves for not taking their wives' physical complaints more seriously. Several fathers asked, guiltily, whether arguments or sex could cause prematurity.

"Why me?" "Why my baby?" many parents still ask, even when the possible causes of prematurity have been explained. Secretly they reason, "I am being punished so I must have done something wrong." A single mother may feel she is being punished for having a child out of wedlock. The most "virtuous" of parents dredge their pasts for a minor wrongdoing or evil thought to "explain" why they and their child must suffer. When things go wrong, there is an unfortunate need in human nature to find *someone* to blame, even if that someone is oneself.

People who have difficulty expressing anger sometimes internalize their feelings as depression—an emotional state characterized by such symptoms as crying jags, loss of appetite, insomnia, lethargy, inability to concentrate, digestive upsets, headaches or chest pains. "I would cry until I was exhausted," a mother remembered, "but I still couldn't sleep. At four in the morning I'd get up and call the nursery. The only thing I could bring myself to eat was chocolate candy and then I found out it was bad for my breast milk."

Physical fatigue can worsen depression. While the mother of a full-term goes home with her baby to rest and recuperate, the mother of a premature begins an exhausting commute between her home and the hospital. And because she may not *feel* like a new mother, she may neglect her own postpartum care and become even more emotionally and physically run down. Several mothers we interviewed developed serious complications in the weeks following delivery, medical problems that they ascribed to their own unwillingness or inability to rest.

There is, in addition, the normal postpartum depression that can afflict any new mother with feelings of tension, anxiety and sadness. These emotions are thought to be caused by sudden hormonal changes accompanying delivery, and the prematurity of the birth in no way changes this postpartum chemistry. In fact, a mother with a premie, who already has reason to be upset, is all the more vulnerable. In the atmosphere of crisis, it may be difficult for her to realize that at least part of her emotional upset is hormonal in nature.

There is also a psychological element at work in postpartum depression. Few women in real life find themselves transformed by motherhood into the glowing, serenely competent madonnas of magazine and television ads. Newborn babies rarely match their mothers' prenatal fantasies. Even in the best of circumstances, birth and early motherhood often fall short of expectation.

For the mother of a premature baby the gap between expectations and reality is especially great. The baby is so different from her mental image that an occasional premature mother refuses to believe that the fetus-like infant she sees in the incubator is actually hers. She must return home with empty arms while her baby is cared for by strangers. The birth itself was far from the fulfilling experience she had hoped it would be.

The mothers we interviewed who had planned natural childbirths found their babies' high-risk, "high-tech" deliveries especially disappointing. Some mothers spent weeks hospitalized as they received drugs to try to stop labor. Many babies were delivered by cesarean section. All of these mothers and babies were separated after delivery, sometimes for a week or more. Meanwhile, the babies' needs were met, not by their parents, but by nurses, doctors, and life support equipment.

For parents today, the events surrounding childbirth have taken on a heightened, almost mystical, significance. Couples are having fewer and better-planned pregnancies. They want to make the most of what may be a once-in-a-lifetime experience. There has been a trend away from highly medicated and monitored deliveries, regulated for the convenience of doctors and hospitals, toward a more natural, family-centered birth in which parents actively participate and have free contact with their new baby. This effort to restore childbirth to its place as a natural function has changed modern obstetrics in many positive ways. But the natural childbirth movement has also given rise to certain exaggerated notions, which are as potentially tyrannizing as the old concepts of childbirth they replace. The mother who is unable to breastfeed is often made to feel she has failed her child in some permanently damaging way (despite the fact that many healthy adults born in the forties and fifties were bottle-fed). The woman who has had a home birth enjoys a great deal of status; the mother who needed a cesarean section may feel ashamed of her "failure." If her baby has not been "properly" initiated into the world (dim lights, warm bath) and "bonded" to her by the prescribed amount of skin-to-skin contact, a mother may fear for the future of her mother-child relationship. These anxieties are often expressed by mothers of full-term babies whose deliveries deviated in some small way from the births described in books for expectant parents. The social pressures on the mother-to-be for a certain type of delivery can greatly add to her distress if the baby is premature.

Wrote one mother, "As soon as I knew I was pregnant, I ran out to buy every book I could on natural birth—everything from Leboyer to prenatal yoga. By the end of the sixth month I was planning a home delivery and training for it like an Olympic event. The Great Earth Mother! Then I started having problems. I was put in the hospital with an IV and monitor. The baby was born, transferred to another hospital, and hooked to a million tubes and wires. So much of my ego was tied up in being a perfect performer in a perfect birth experience that I felt I had completely failed as a mother. I realize now that motherhood is so much more than just giving birth, but at the time I was horribly depressed and bitter."

# Bargaining

"After the baby was born, the most upsetting thing for me was the feeling that I had totally lost control. Despite everything I'd done to insure a healthy pregnancy, my baby was premature and sick. I had no real say in his care. There was nothing I could do to make him better. The situation had completely changed my relationship with my husband, and I had no idea what lay ahead for us as a couple. The bills were accumulating and our plans for the future were going down the drain. I felt I had lost control over my body, my baby, my marriage, and my life."

When there are no rational steps a person can take to influence events, often that person seeks refuge in the irrational. "Bargaining" is one such refuge.

"Bargaining," explains Marriage and Family Counselor Kathleen Levdar, "is when you promise you'll go back to church and start speaking to your mother again if only God will make everything all right."

Bargaining is an attempt to find a magical solution or just the right sacrifice to appease the angry gods. "I will be a perfect parent, a perfect person, if only. . . ."

An intensive care nurse remembers a father who sat by his tiny son's Isolette, telling about the baseball games they'd go to and the camping trips they'd take if he'd just pull through.

A mother who spent 10 to 12 hours a day at her baby's bedside said, "I felt that if I left my baby for a minute something awful would happen. It was as if I were somehow magically keeping him alive."

Bargaining can involve a superstitious search for signs and omens. "I had a lucky parking space at the hospital," recalls one mother. "If I drove up and it was empty, I knew I'd have good news about the baby."

The bargain frequently has religious overtones—such as the parents' vow to visit sacred shrines in exchange for their baby's recovery, or the case of the mother who remarked, "I think I would have sold my soul to the devil if it would have helped. It's a good thing I didn't have any offers."

Bargaining gives the person in crisis a brief, illusory sense of being in control: "If I can just do such and such, my baby will get well."

Like denial, bargaining is a temporary retreat from reality. And, like denial, it is a delaying tactic that lets an individual postpone facing a crisis in its entirety until he or she has marshalled sufficient strength for acceptance and adaptation.

# Acceptance and Adaptation

While shock, denial, anger, and bargaining are ultimately unproductive ways to cope, they do serve a temporary useful purpose. They give a person time to absorb a traumatic event in small, manageable doses. They are natural reactions that most people in a crisis experience before they are ready to accept their situation and adapt to it in a constructive manner.

A nurse, after the birth of her premature baby, remarked, "I used to counsel other parents. Because I knew all about the stages people go through, I guess I thought I would be exempt. But there I was having all the typical responses. My knowledge of psychology didn't really help except that I could step back and say to myself, 'Now you're at such-and-such a stage,' and I could reassure myself that what my husband and I were feeling was normal and, with any luck, temporary."

Nevertheless, there are great variations in the way each person progresses from shock to acceptance. The stages do not necessarily occur in order, they may overlap, some may be left out entirely. At any given time, mother and father may be in totally different stages, finding it difficult to communicate as a result.

The intensity of emotions is also different for everyone. The parents whose baby needs a little extra time to mature have a different experience from the parents whose child is critically ill, and they may not react as emotionally. Many do, however. Parents' perceptions of their baby's problems determine the way they respond. And few parents in the midst of even the most minor problems concerning their child have the perspective to judge what is and is not truly serious. The parents whose infant needs a few days of treatment for mild jaundice may be just as upset as the family whose child requires months of hospitalization and surgeries. Parents may feel grief and depression even if their premature baby is completely healthy, for they have lost the ideal pregnancy and birth experience they had hoped for.

Each parent brings to the situation his or her own strengths and vulnerabilities. A mother who has had a previous full-term baby and who has successfully nursed and cared for her child is less likely than the first-time mother to doubt her maternal abilities. Again, there are exceptions. Wrote one mother, "People would sometimes make me feel dumb because they knew this was my third child and I was supposed to know how to take care of babies. But dealing with a premie is different."

Mother and father almost always react in different ways. Since a mother is so much more intimately involved with her baby during pregnancy, her grief and sense of failure at the baby's premature birth is understandably more severe. She may stay longer in a state of shock. She is more likely to feel excessive pessimism and guilt—feelings her mate may not share or comprehend.

Even when one crisis has been accepted, the whole cycle may recur with each new difficulty. The birth and early life of a premature baby present not just a single crisis, but a series of them: the birth itself, the baby's medical course in the hospital, the baby's first feeding, the baby's homecoming, his first cold, and so on. At each new stage in the baby's development the parents are confronted with new potential problems.

Premature babies can be difficult to care for, especially those with ongoing health or developmental problems. The costs—financial and emotional—of the baby's care can be high. Under these trying circumstances some parents never do adapt successfully. Denial, anger, or guilt become permanent conditions, harming the parent's mental health, marriage, and relationship with the baby. This is reflected in the higher than normal divorce rate among parents who have had a sick or premature baby and in child abuse statistics showing that the prematurely born child is more often a target of abuse than his full-term counterpart.

The parents we interviewed all felt changed by their baby's premature birth. When we asked one mother for "before" and "after" pictures of her child, she replied that "before" and "after" pictures of the parents might be more to the point. Nevertheless, many mothers and fathers, especially those with some distance from the experience, said that they felt emotionally stronger and closer to their mate and child because of the ordeal they had survived together. As one mother put it, "I did more growing up in the three months my twins were hospitalized than I had done in my previous thirty years."

## Suggestions for Coping

Psychiatrists at Harvard and Stanford have studied the ways couples react to the birth of a premature baby to determine those factors that allow some mothers and fathers to adapt successfully, while others fail. The couples who adapted well, the doctors found, were those who freely expressed their feelings of anxiety, anger, depression, and frustration. They accepted help from each other and from friends, family, and the community in caring for their baby, and in handling the practical and emotional difficulties resulting from the birth. The successful parents actively sought information about their baby's current condition and care, and on his future needs.

Other researchers have found fewer divorces and fewer neglected or abused children among mothers who have early, frequent contacts with their babies in the nursery.

These same factors—expressing emotions, accepting help, seeking information and beginning an early relationship with the baby—were frequently mentioned by parents we interviewed. We asked mothers and fathers how they coped with their baby's premature birth, and what advice they would give others undergoing a similar experience. Here are some of their answers:

### On Handling Emotions

"Realize that you are in a situation that is highly stressful and that violates all your biological urges as a mother. The detached feelings, the angry feelings, the depressed feelings and especially the CRAZY feelings are quite normal under the circumstances."

*

"If you have mixed emotions about your baby at first, don't feel guilty about it. A lot of people do. There were times when my baby was very sick when I just wanted it all to be over. I wanted my baby to die. I never told anyone because it seemed so horrible. At a parents' group meeting one night we talked about our feelings towards our children and it turned out that a lot of others had similar thoughts at first, even though they loved their children very much."

"Don't blame yourself for your baby's prematurity. Guilt is a total waste of time. Feelings of guilt and failure can interfere with your relationship with your child."

*

"Repeat 100 times a day if necessary: 'Guilt is a worthless emotion.'"

*

"Talk! to each other, to your family, to the doctors and nurses. And cry, anytime, any place—it's a necessary release. Maintain open communication with your spouse about feelings of guilt and anger."

*

"Try to see this as a growth-producing experience."

*

"Be understanding when your friends try to comfort you but don't know how. Tell them what you're feeling. Let them know it's all right to talk about the baby. You may have to help them to help you."

*

"I found that while constantly reassuring my friends and relatives, I ended up reassuring myself."

*

"Get in touch with other parents of prematures. My solace was in talking out my fears with someone who really understood. You can be yourself with another premie parent."

*

"My self-esteem was very low after the baby was born. This hadn't happened to anyone else I knew. Several years later a Parents of Premies group started in our area. It was wonderful to meet others who'd been through it too. I felt stronger and better about myself knowing that I was not alone."

## On Accepting Help

"Accept counseling if it is offered. You'll need it more than you think."

*

"The social worker really helped me get my head together. He helped me understand and express the emotions I was trying to hide behind a brave facade. He helped me to cry."

*

"While the baby was in the hospital I couldn't deal with people who wanted to talk to me about how I was feeling. I wanted them to go away and leave me alone. After the baby came home— that's when I needed someone to talk to."

*

"When people want to help you, let them. Tell them specific things they can do to be helpful, as they often don't know—babysitting other children, driving you to visit your baby if you've had a cesarean and can't drive yourself, bringing in meals, etc."

*

"Our baby needed lots of transfusions so when friends asked what they could do, we suggested they donate blood."

*

"When you are feeling upset, ask someone to drive you to and from the nursery. There were times when I had absolutely no recollection of the drive to the hospital or home again. At other times, I would 'come to' en route and realize I'd just run the past three stoplights. It's a miracle I didn't kill myself or someone else. Don't drive in that condition. Don't compound the tragedy."

*

"Remember you've just had a baby and your hormones are out of balance. If you'd planned to have someone come and help with the baby, have that person come now to take care of you. Save your energy for visiting your baby."

*

"Although it's very difficult to come home without your baby, use this time to rest, regain your strength and get a full night's sleep. Premies may be more irritable at home than full-terms due to their immature nervous systems. Fatigued, strung-out parents don't handle this very well."

*

"It may be hard to think about money at a time like this, but check your insurance policy and contact the hospital's financial counselor as soon as possible. There are programs to help parents with the costs of intensive care. See if you're eligible. *And be sure to add your baby to your insurance policy right away; otherwise he will not be covered.*" (See page 128.)

*

"Check out community resources. We got a breast pump for home use and help with travel expenses through Easter Seals."

*

"If you want to breast-feed, contact other mothers who have successfully breast-fed premies. You'll need lots of advice and constant moral support. La Leche League is a wonderful resource."

## On Staying Informed

"As the baby's parents you have a right and a duty to know what's going on. We asked about the meaning of blood gases and respirator settings over and over and over again. We were lucky; our doctors encouraged that. But fight with them if you must to get the information you deserve."

"Don't be shy. Ask questions, even the ones you think are dumb. Usually they aren't. And be sure the doctors answer you in *your* language. The doctors came into my room, told me my child had hyaline membrane disease and then left. I lay there thinking my child would have a disease the rest of her life."

\*

"The more you know about your baby's condition, the better you'll be at dealing with it and with problems that may lie ahead. The more ignorant you are of the situation the more fear you have."

\*

"Don't be afraid to make observations and suggestions to the staff. You may not have the medical expertise, but you will be the only constant source of information through all the changes of shifts and rotations."

\*

"Keep a notebook of your baby's progress; it helps maintain your equilibrium when recovery is in slow, minute steps. The two steps forward, one step back pattern is reassuring once you've identified it."

\*

"We were often too frightened to talk or listen to the staff. When we left meetings with the doctors we couldn't always remember what had been said. We solved this problem by taking along a cassette recorder and, with the doctor's permission, taping the conferences."

## On Becoming Parents

"I empathize with anyone who is afraid to make an emotional commitment to a seemingly tentative life, but as soon as it is comfortable for you, get to know your child, for both your sakes."

\*

"Give your baby a name and use that name. I always felt sad to see a name tag that said 'Baby Girl Smith' or 'Baby Boy Jones.' Sometimes the nurses would make up a name of their own. They found it hard to relate to an unnamed baby."

\*

"Remember that your baby belongs to *you,* not the nurses and doctors. Don't be afraid to ask questions and make suggestions. Don't expect the nurses and doctors to *tell* you when you can hold your baby or feed your baby; *ask* them. I saw some parents who were afraid to assert themselves. They were afraid they might alienate the staff. They thought that if the nurses got mad at them they might not take good care of the baby. But I found that a *pleasantly assertive* attitude gets the baby better care. Let the staff know you want to be involved."

\*

"Take photographs. You don't recognize the progress until you actually see it in pictures."

\*

"You may think you won't want any souvenirs of this experience, but years from now you'll feel different. Save a premie Pamper or two; save those tiny clothes and take pictures—even with all the tubes and wires. Later on it will be hard to believe you and your baby actually went through all this. And keep a diary of both your baby's progress and your own feelings."

Bill Lauric

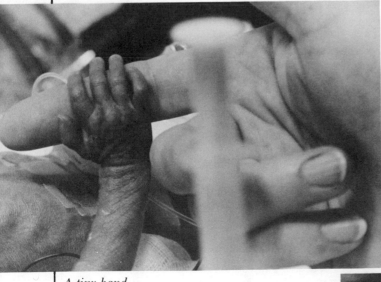

*A tiny hand . . .*

*. . . several months later.*

Bill Laurie

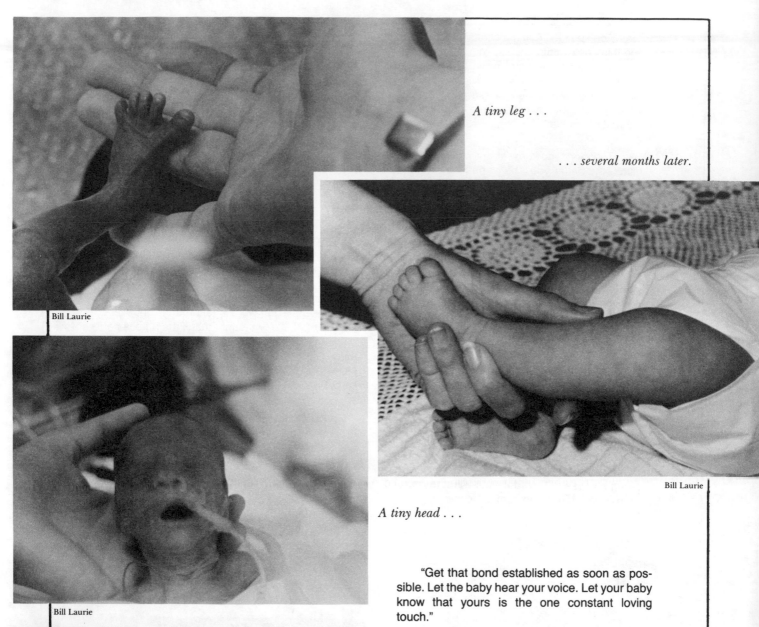

Bill Laurie

*A tiny leg . . .*

*. . . several months later.*

Bill Laurie

*A tiny head . . .*

Bill Laurie

Bill Laurie

"Get that bond established as soon as possible. Let the baby hear your voice. Let your baby know that yours is the one constant loving touch."

\*

"Express your breastmilk and bring it to your baby. This is one contribution no one else can make."

\*

"Plan for your baby's homecoming. I was superstitious at first about buying baby clothes or fixing up the nursery. But as soon as I started working on his bassinet, decorating his room, and buying him toys and clothes, I began to feel much, much better."

\*

"It is said that you learn from your children. Ours, who both needed intensive care at birth, brought us closer together and taught us courage."

*. . . the same baby, several months later.*

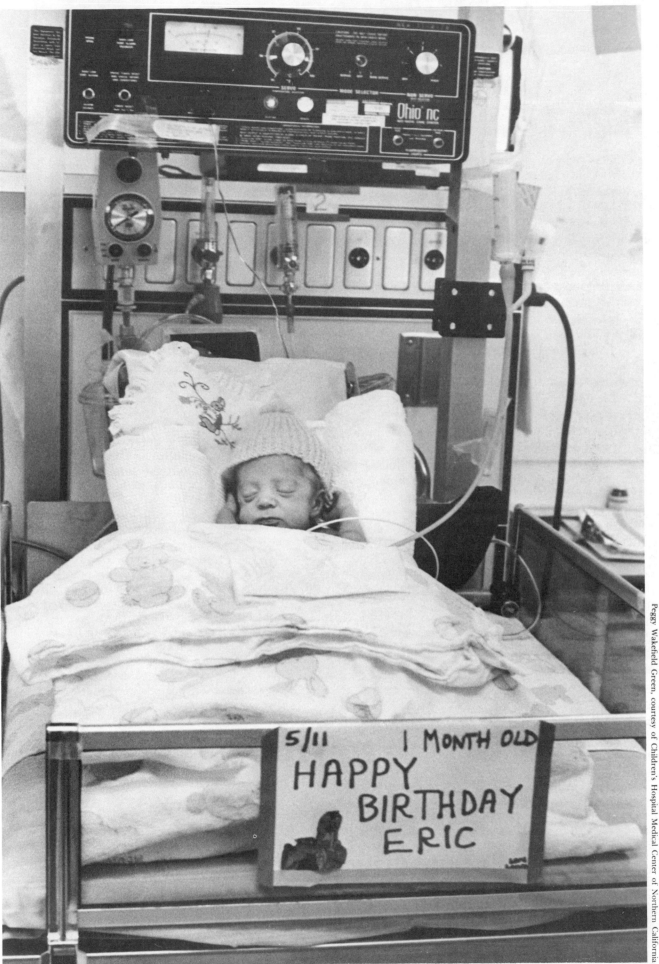

5/11     1 MONTH OLD

HAPPY BIRTHDAY ERIC

*"These babies are stronger than you think.     They have an inborn will for survival."*

## Colin's Story

### By Juliene Lipson

Colin is six months old, a charming and responsive baby. I have been experiencing a delayed depression over the circumstances of his birth, and it is time to look back on my feelings. I am very distressed by his fifth cold and the fact that his weight gain has slowed considerably because of the colds. Weight has assumed a disproportionate importance for me because Colin was such a skinny little chicken at birth. But most distressing to me is why he has to keep struggling with a stuffy nose and cough after he went through so much.

Colin was born by emergency cesarean when I went into labor unexpectedly at 30 weeks' gestation. My pregnancy had been easy and uneventful, except for a severe bout of flu 6 weeks before Colin was born. The obstetrician cannot give me a reason for my premature labor, except to say that the flu was not the cause. But I need a reason, and it seems the most logical one. Colin was big for his age—three pounds, nine ounces—but he had terrible lungs. He was on a respirator twice and spent a month under an oxygen hood. He had some lung damage, but he gained weight well and was discharged after 7 weeks.

During the time Colin was in the nursery, and in the period since, I learned a lot about myself and how I cope with stress. The most important lesson has been that I place too much importance on being competent, have difficulty admitting to feelings of being scared and helpless, and am reluctant to ask others for help when I need it. The following is an excerpt from my journal.

*October 30, 1979.* Colin was born 5 weeks ago. The staff say he is 36 or 37 weeks of gestation, but I know when I conceived; he's 35 weeks. How like doctors to profess to know better than mothers. I have finally realized another part of why I have been so distressed the past two weeks: AMBIVALENCE. I want Colin, but I don't want him; I want to be in the nursery, but I want to avoid the place. I know why I have not been able to bond with him yet, and I accept it as logical and self-protective, but I feel guilty as hell.

Yesterday was sad. Colin slept at my breast again after a few half-hearted sucks. The nurse handed me a bottle. The milk came too fast, and I was terrified that he'd choke. I became more and more anxious, and finally gave him back to the nurse, who fed him competently while I sat hand-expressing my breastmilk, close to tears. I

watch his color nervously. Two of the four times I tried to breast-feed him he stopped breathing and had a "brady" [bradycardia], complete with buzzing alarms. These experiences have taken a greater toll than I realized, and I am finding excuses to stay home: Trevor (my two-year-old son) needs me; it's a long trip and gas is expensive; I might have a cold (allergies?); I need more rest after surgery. All realistic excuses, but why do I feel so guilty?

It just hit me that I have been totally separating my feelings from my intellectual understanding of Colin's situation. Yes, I understand perfectly well that he's very young, that he needs more time to develop coordination between sucking and breathing. I nod my head and accept the staff's explanations. They seem to give me more information because I'm a nurse. But when I touch Colin, I'm awkward, afraid to do more than hold him and stroke his head. I'm embarrassed at my awkwardness and feelings of incompetence. I try to tell myself that I shouldn't be so uncomfortable. After all, I'm 35 years old, and I generally feel good about my abilities as an instructor in a nursing school, a psychotherapist, and a mother of a 2-year-old. I even have good manual dexterity. But I look to the nurses for an O.K. whenever I do anything for Colin: "Did I position him right?" "Did I disturb the lead?" And most telling, "Am I in your way?" I just realized that I feel like Colin belongs to the nurses rather than to me.

The nurses do not relay this message. They bend over backwards to get parents involved. My husband and I have been encouraged to hold Colin even when it appears that he cannot handle it. Once, after we held him for 10 minutes, it took him five hours to warm up again. And the monitor alarms keep going off. "Is it worth it?" we ask. "Yes," they answer, "babies do better when their parents hold them." On the other hand, perhaps they go too far. They don't really understand that I'm not quite ready to commit myself to Colin. It's hard to admit, but sometimes I'm in the nursery more so I'll be seen as a good mother than for the satisfaction of holding this small creature that mostly sleeps in my arms.

Looking back now, I see that I was clinging to my self-image as a professional woman because my self-esteem as a mother was at rock bottom. I coped by discussing my work with the staff and even managed to revise an article for publication in the hospital library while Colin slept between feedings. This kept me functioning at some level at the time. However, on another level, I felt I had failed this baby in utero, and I couldn't take care of him now.

But now, after a respite, all my sad feelings about Colin's birth and worries about his health have reemerged into my awareness. In spite of doing my share of crying in the hospital, the grieving process is not yet done. I put it aside, but it is nagging at me again. I must now be ready to face my feelings because I have finally bonded with Colin and am beginning to convince myself that he is going to survive (despite continuing fears of finding him dead in his crib some morning and worries that every little cough means pneumonia). In spite of his colds, it is now obvious that he is a strong little fellow and is developing well. Yet, the intellectual understanding of what is happening within me does not dispel the insomnia, the sad feelings, the worries. On the other hand, I can remind myself of a valuable lesson learned from Trevor—no matter how difficult things seem at the moment, "this too will pass."

*Colin at 7 days.*

*Colin at 22 months.*

*Update: 1982.* The first year was horrendous because of Colin's frequent respiratory infections. At one point he was rehospitalized with bronchitis. The infections slowed his weight gain and made breast-feeding difficult. Nevertheless, Colin nursed for 18 months. At age 2, his health is finally improving, though he's still rather allergic.

While Colin isn't as precocious or athletic as his brother Trevor, he is developing normally for his age (when corrected for prematurity). I'm very thankful that with all the things that *could* have gone wrong, he's an intelligent kid with a nice personality who seems to be essentially "all there."

It's hard to tell now that Colin was premature. He's handsome, chubby, and feeling his oats as a two-year-old. He's a real joy and the entire family is delighted with him.

# 2

# *Why Me?*

## Pre-Term Delivery: Questions and Answers

**Q:** What causes prematurity? Could this happen to me again?

**A:** Approximately half of all women who deliver too early go into premature labor for unknown reasons. The rest have diagnosed conditions such as toxemia, incompetent cervix, placenta previa, etc., which often result in premature delivery. Statistically, a woman who has had a premature baby runs a 25 to 50% chance of having another one (see page 226). Nevertheless, for many women the pre-term birth is a one-time event in an otherwise normal childbearing career.

**Q:** Was it my fault?

**A:** It is not useful to think about your baby's premature birth as being someone's fault, since nobody intentionally causes a baby to be born earlier than necessary. Some conditions that can cause prematurity involve the mother's body. Maternal high blood pressure, for example, increases the risk of prematurity. Other factors involve the baby: twins and other "multiples" are often born too soon, as are babies with congenital defects, or infants with defective or poorly positioned placentas (the placenta grows from fetal tissue). It has also been observed that some men repeatedly father premature babies by different women. Whether this is just a coincidence, or whether paternal factors might somehow play a role in prematurity, is unknown.

**Q:** I was in labor for days before I could convince myself or my doctor that it was for real. No one can explain why it happened. Doesn't anyone know what causes premature labor?

**A:** Premature labor may begin painlessly and is easily mistaken for the normal Braxton-Hicks "practice" contractions most women experience throughout pregnancy. Unlike Braxton-Hicks contractions, real labor contractions occur at fairly regular intervals and cause the cervix to shorten (efface) and open (dilate).

No one knows what causes full-term labor to start, so it is impossible to say for sure why it begins prematurely. However, researchers are investigating the hormones of pregnancy to see whether abnormal levels of these substances may be involved.

One of these hormones, progesterone, is thought to protect the fetus before birth. The baby, who derives half his genes from the father, is genetically different from his mother. Normally, the mother's immune system would expel the genetically "foreign" baby the way it might reject a transplanted organ. Progesterone may help suppress the mother's normal immune responses during pregnancy so that the baby can grow safely. Low levels of progesterone may allow premature labor to occur.

Other substances being investigated are prostaglandins, chemicals that stimulate labor and help the cervix soften and open. Prostaglandins may form from chemicals released when the uterine lining is stressed or injured. Any complication of pregnancy that unusually stresses the uterine membrane—anything from infection to the presence of more than one baby—might bring about the early production of prostaglandins and pre-term labor.

Premature labor might also be induced by cortisol, a hormone that a fetus under physical stress in the womb secretes in larger than normal amounts.

As the chemistry of labor is better understood, tests to sample an expectant mother's blood for hormone levels may help predict (and prevent) threatened premature delivery.

**Q:** In an attempt to stop my labor, I was given terbutaline and when that didn't work, I was given betamethasone. I had to sign a lot of scary forms before I was given the drugs, but at the time I was so frightened I would have signed anything. I wonder now if I made the right decisions. What effects will these drugs have on my baby?

**A:** Recently, certain drugs used to treat asthma have proven highly effective at stopping pre-term labor when labor is detected in its early stages. The drugs terbutaline (Brethine), ritodrine (Yutopar), and isoxsuprine (Vasodilan) relax the uterus much as they relax bronchial spasms in asthmatics. These drugs do have side effects. They speed up the heart rate of mother and baby. They may cause flushing of the mother's skin, nausea, headaches, and nervousness. Rare maternal complications include irregular heartbeat, very low blood pressure, and fluid accumulation in the lungs (pulmonary edema). Although terbutaline and similar drugs are new in the United States, at least for stopping labor, they have been used for this purpose in Europe for many years. European follow-up studies on children whose mothers were given the drugs, even for prolonged periods during pregnancy, have as yet revealed no long-term problems.

These drugs will not bring every pregnancy all the way to term, but delaying labor even for relatively short periods of time can be beneficial. An extra 48 hours allows the mother to receive betamethasone (Celestone), a type of cortisone that speeds the development of the baby's lungs. The safety of betamethasone has yet to be fully determined. Certain animal studies, using doses *many* times higher than those given to humans, suggest that the drug might interfere with proper growth and brain development. However, comprehensive testing of 139 prematurely born children whose mothers received betamethasone 6 or 7 years ago has so far revealed no adverse effects upon the children's health; on their mental, social or physical development; or on their academic achievement. Since respiratory distress syndrome (the disease betamethasone often prevents) kills many premature babies and causes a high incidence of intellectual and physical problems among the survivors, many feel it is worth taking a theoretical risk with the drug to avoid the *known* risks of respiratory distress syndrome.

**Q:** I was told I had uterine abnormalities and an incompetent cervix, a term I find insulting. What are the causes and treatments of these problems?

**A:** "Incompetent" cervix is the unfortunate name for a cervix that opens, often painlessly, in midpregnancy, leading to a miscarriage or premature birth. This condition usually results from damage to the connective tissue of the cervix during previous births or surgery involving the cervix. A weak or in-

competent cervix can also be caused by diethylstilbestrol (DES) exposure. Many DES daughters (daughters of women given the drug diethylstilbestrol during their pregnancies in the 1940s and '50s) have abnormalities of the cervix and uterus that make it difficult for them to carry babies to term.

An incompetent cervix can sometimes be repaired by a technique called cerclage, in which the cervix is stitched shut in early pregnancy. The stitches are removed before the baby is born. Since cerclage carries risks—the possibility of infection, even the stimulation of premature labor—doctors may be hesitant to perform this procedure unless they feel sure that the problem is actually an incompetent cervix. A reliable diagnosis is sometimes difficult to make, since a *normal* cervix can also open early as the result of undetected premature labor.

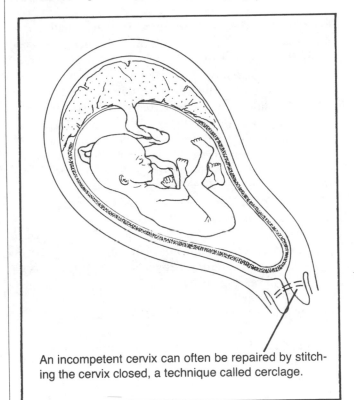

An incompetent cervix can often be repaired by stitching the cervix closed, a technique called cerclage.

Uterine abnormalities usually result from an incomplete fusion of two tubes, called Müllerian ducts, that grow together in the female embryo to form the uterus. When these tubes fuse improperly, a variety of malformations may result. Instead of the normal pear shape, the uterus may be indented at the top like a heart, or two separate wombs (bicornuate uterus) may form, or a single womb may be wholly or partially divided by a wall of tissue (septate, and subseptate, uterus.) These congenital abnormalities are not uncommon. Many affected women have no preg-

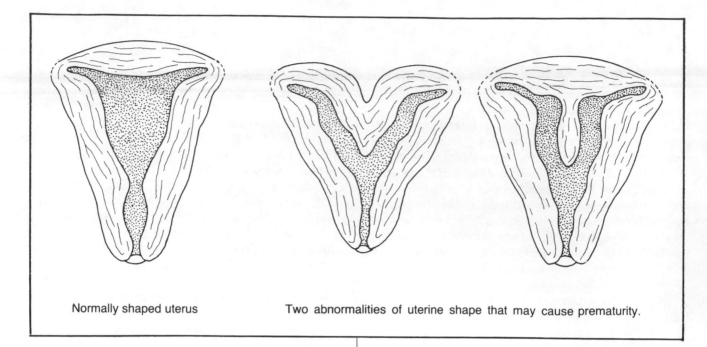

Normally shaped uterus                Two abnormalities of uterine shape that may cause prematurity.

nancy difficulties and are unaware that a malformation exists. Other women with these abnormalities repeatedly miscarry or deliver prematurely. When a uterine abnormality is suspected, a *hysterosalpingogram,* an x-ray of the reproductive organs, may be taken. During this test, a dye that is visible on an x-ray is injected through the cervix and into the uterus and Fallopian tubes. (The test is moderately painful and involves exposure to radiation.) If malformations are detected, they can often be surgically corrected to improve the outcome of future pregnancies.

*Fibroids,* benign (noncancerous) growths in the uterine wall that enlarge during pregnancy and distort the shape of the uterus, are also associated with prematurity. Large fibroids can sometimes be removed once pregnancy is over so that future pregnancies will be unaffected.

**Q:** My membranes ruptured prematurely. What could have caused it?
**A:** The membranes—the bag of amniotic fluid surrounding the baby—can rupture or leak at any time during pregnancy. If the membranes rupture *before* labor begins, they are said to have ruptured prematurely. Sometimes if the leak is small, it seals off on its own and the pregnancy continues. But usually, labor and delivery follow.

The membranes are more likely to rupture prematurely in women who have urinary tract, vaginal, or amniotic fluid infections. Premature rupture is also more common when the membranes are stretched by a multiple pregnancy or by polyhydramnios (too much amniotic fluid). *Amniocentesis,* the test in which a needle is inserted into the womb to withdraw fluid, involves a small risk of membrane rupture right after the procedure has been performed. The membranes

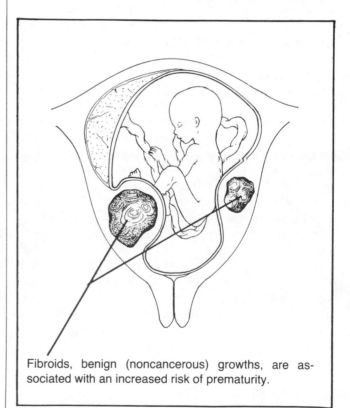

Fibroids, benign (noncancerous) growths, are associated with an increased risk of prematurity.

can also protrude and rupture when an incompetent cervix opens too soon. Some cases diagnosed as premature rupture of the membranes may actually be caused by undetected (painless) pre-term labor. It has been suggested that membranes that rupture early may be inherently weak. However, the late Dr. Alan Guttmacher, who studied membranes from both pre-term and full-term deliveries, reported that the membranes were of equal strength.

18

**Q:** What causes polyhydramnios?

**A:** Amniotic fluid is largely produced by the amnion, the innermost membrane surrounding the baby. Every hour, a third of the fluid is recycled. Some of it is reabsorbed by the membranes. About a pint a day is swallowed by the baby, absorbed through his digestive tract, and returned to the mother's bloodstream or excreted by the baby in his urine. If the delicately balanced production and absorption of fluid is off by even fractions of an ounce per day, abnormal amounts of fluid accumulate. Too much fluid (over two quarts) or too little fluid (less than a pint) may result from obstructions of the baby's digestive tract or urinary tract that leave him unable to swallow or urinate properly. Polyhydramnios also occurs more frequently in multiple pregnancies or in pregnancies complicated by diabetes or toxemia. But nearly one out of every three cases is of unknown origin. Both polyhydramnios and oligohydramnios (too little amniotic fluid) create an abnormal uterine environment that may lead to premature labor.

**Q:** I delivered three premature babies as a result of problems with the placenta. What are the causes?

**A:** Two common placental problems associated with prematurity are placenta previa and placenta abruptio (abruption).

Placenta previa refers to a placenta that implants low in the uterus, partially or entirely covering the opening to the birth canal. In the second half of pregnancy, as changes occur in the lower uterus, part of the placenta may dislodge. If excessive bleeding results, the pregnancy must be ended prematurely to save the lives of mother and baby. Placenta previa is most common among women who have had several babies already or among women who have had a cesarean section. Scarring of the uterus, poor circulation to the uterus, or fibroids may cause the placenta to implant too low. Placenta previa is also more likely to occur in multiple pregnancies, since the placentas must spread out to accommodate more than one baby. However, in many cases, the low position of the placenta seems to be simply an accident of nature.

Placenta abruptio refers to the detachment of a normally positioned placenta. If the edges of the placenta detach, painless vaginal bleeding (apparent hemorrhage) follows. If the bleeding is concealed behind the placenta, the mother may feel severe back or stomach pain. She may become faint from internal blood loss. Premature delivery of the baby is often necessary to save both mother and child. Abruption may be caused by a sharp blow to the womb or by sudden changes in blood pressure. This problem is most common among women suffering from high

### Placenta Previa

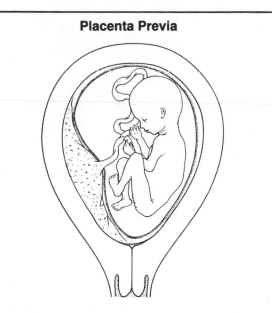

Partial placenta previa—the placenta covers only the edge of the cervix.

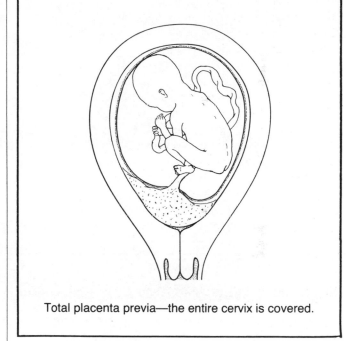

Total placenta previa—the entire cervix is covered.

blood pressure, kidney disease, malnutrition, or diabetes. Placental detachments also occur more frequently in multiple pregnancies or in pregnancies complicated by polyhydramnios. Women who smoke have a higher incidence of abruption (and of placenta previa). Nevertheless, well nourished, healthy nonsmokers with no other pregnancy complications can also have abruptions. A woman who has had an abruption has a 1 in 14 chance for a recurrence in a future pregnancy.

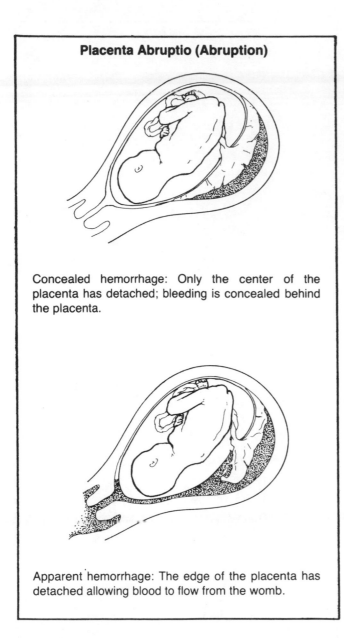

**Placenta Abruptio (Abruption)**

Concealed hemorrhage: Only the center of the placenta has detached; bleeding is concealed behind the placenta.

Apparent hemorrhage: The edge of the placenta has detached allowing blood to flow from the womb.

**Q:** I felt fine until the sixth month, when I developed toxemia. What causes it? Can it happen to me again?
**A:** Toxemia is a disease suffered by 5 to 7% of all pregnant women. The first stage of toxemia, called pre-eclampsia, is characterized by high blood pressure, protein in the urine, and rapid weight gain due to fluid retention. Untreated, pre-eclampsia can develop into eclampsia, a severe form of toxemia with symptoms including maternal seizures, brain hemorrhage, and coma. Because toxemia often involves a reduction in bloodflow to the fetus, the baby may be smaller than normal for gestational age. Toxemia can sometimes be managed by bed rest, nutritious diet, and blood pressure medications. When these measures fail, premature delivery is necessary to save mother and child. Toxemia occurs most frequently in first pregnancies. Later pregnancies are usually unaffected.

Toxemia has been called the "disease of theories." Since the time of Hippocrates, various causes have been proposed, as well as "cures" ranging from radical mastectomy to "properly" aligning a woman's body with the North Pole. Early in this century, toxemia was considered a disease of the well-fed upper classes. When protein was strictly rationed in war-time Europe, the incidence of toxemia declined. This observation led doctors to restrict the diets and weight gain of their pregnant patients, to deny them salt and protein, and to dose them with diuretics. But these treatments have not worked. In fact, mothers and babies may have been harmed by them. More recently, toxemia was linked to malnutrition, and doctors began recommending that women eat a nutritious diet and gain at least 25 pounds during pregnancy. Nevertheless, toxemia is still with us. It even strikes women who follow the high-quality diets designed to prevent the disease.

Other theories implicate poor uterine circulation as the underlying factor in the development of toxemia. Inadequate circulation to the womb could have numerous causes: pre-existing circulatory problems; narrow uterine blood vessels (in a first pregnancy); malnutrition; or stretching of the womb by twins, by excessive fluid, or by fibroids. Poor circulation to the uterus may impair the placenta's ability to produce substances that help regulate the mother's blood pressure, thus setting into motion a complicated chain of events that results in toxemia.

Recently, researchers reported isolating a previously unknown organism from the blood of women with toxemia. When this microorganism (*Hydatoxi lualba*) was injected into pregnant laboratory animals, they developed a toxemia-like syndrome. The medical community, however, is skeptical about these findings; and it remains to be seen whether the *hydatoxi lualba* theory is another false lead or a step forward in the understanding of toxemia, a disease that kills thousands of infants in the United States each year.

**Q:** There were days during my pregnancy when I was too nauseated to eat well. Could those days of poor nutrition have caused the prematurity?
**A:** The precise role nutrition plays in pregnancy is still not well understood. Studies have shown that good diet and weight gain are associated with healthier pregnancy outcomes. It is also known that women are more at risk if they begin their pregnancies weighing less than 100 pounds or if they fail to gain 12 pounds by the 32nd week of pregnancy. However, even the best nutrition cannot prevent certain complications or guarantee a trouble-free pregnancy. (Most of the women interviewed for this book had been

following nutritious diets designed to prevent pregnancy complications.)

Because of the current emphasis on nutrition and weight gain during pregnancy, many mothers who deliver early feel guilty about a skipped meal or vitamin pill. But nausea and loss of appetite are experienced by most pregnant women. If brief periods of less than perfect nutrition could cause prematurity, there would hardly be a population crisis in the world today.

**Q:** Can illness during pregnancy cause prematurity?
**A:** A mother's general health before and during pregnancy can affect pregnancy outcome. Pre-existing illnesses such as diabetes, kidney disease, hypertension (high blood pressure), and sickle cell anemia (even carrying the sickle cell trait) involve a substantial risk of pre-term delivery. Illnesses that arise during pregnancy such as urinary or genital infections, pneumonia, or flu are also associated with an increased incidence of premature labor. Pre-term labor often occurs following abdominal surgery during pregnancy.

Prematurity can also be the result of illness in the unborn baby. Although the membranes and placenta provide a barrier against many infections, certain organisms are still able to cross the placenta or enter the womb, possibly through weak places in the membranes. An infected baby may be born to a mother who has had only mild symptoms of illness or no symptoms at all. Many of the organisms that can infect an unborn baby normally live in the mother's body causing no apparent harm. For example, Group B streptococcus, a common cause of intrauterine infection, is carried by up to 30% of all pregnant women, but the majority of these women have healthy babies. Why some babies become infected while others do not is a mystery.

**Q:** Can sex during pregnancy cause prematurity?
**A:** A recent study of close to 11,000 pregnancies revealed *no* difference in the incidence of premature rupture of the membranes, intrauterine infection, or prematurity among women who engaged in intercourse throughout pregnancy compared to those who abstained.

However, sexual activity, even the nipple-toughening exercises practiced in preparation for breast-feeding, may release oxytocin, a hormone that stimulates uterine contractions. For a woman *already beginning labor,* sexual activity might speed things along. That is why doctors recommend that women abstain from these activities if they show actual signs and symptoms of premature labor. (See page 236.)

**Q:** Can a past abortion cause prematurity?
**A:** Abortion is associated both with a decrease and an increase in prematurity. In New York, a decline was reported in the prematurity rate following the legalization of abortion. Recent studies indicate that a woman who has had a single abortion performed during the first three months of pregnancy is at little or no increased risk for a future premature delivery. However, abortions carried out in the second trimester of pregnancy *do* increase the risk of a later premature birth. A woman who has had 3 or more abortions, whether performed in the first or second trimester of pregnancy, is at some increased risk for delivering prematurely. So is a woman who has had 3 or more miscarriages (called *spontaneous abortions* by physicians). No one knows why.

**Q:** Does the mother's age play a role?
**A:** Statistically, yes. Mothers under 18 and over 35 do have more than their share of premature babies. But a mother's age in itself does not cause her baby to be born early. Other factors associated with age may be more directly involved. A teenage expectant mother, still growing herself, might compete with her baby for needed nutrients. An older woman is more susceptible to hypertension and other health problems. First pregnancies and fourth or later pregnancies are at greatest risk to end prematurely, a fact possibly related to maternal age.

**Q:** My twins were diagnosed early. I'd already been taking good care of myself, but I started eating and resting even more. The boys were born almost four months early after a particularly restful week. How could I have prevented my babies' early birth? How usual is it for twins to be premature?
**A:** A multiple pregnancy is an abnormal situation that can impose great physical stress on mother and babies. Nutritious diet and bed rest do seem to help some mothers carry their infants to term, but even with the best prenatal care, many multiple pregnancies end early.

Pre-term labor is 10 times more common in a multiple pregnancy than in a single pregnancy. The incidence of toxemia is 3 times as high. Abruption, placenta previa, polyhydramnios, premature rupture of the membranes, and gestational diabetes (diabetes that arises during pregnancy) are also more likely to occur.

"Multiples" also tend to be born too small for their gestational age, possibly because of placental problems or competition among the babies for a limited supply of nutrients. Congenital defects are more common among identical twins, who develop from the accidental division of a single fertilized egg. If the babies share a single placenta, one twin may receive more than his share of blood and nutrients and may accumulate an excessive supply of red blood cells, a potentially dangerous condition called *polycythemia*. The other twin becomes undernourished and anemic. Perhaps because of these and other complications, over half of all multiple pregnancies end prematurely.

**Q:** Is there more prematurity in certain countries? In Spain, for example, premature babies seem to be very common—there is even a special word for a seven-monther, a *sietemesino*.

**A:** Infant mortality, largely the result of prematurity, tends to be highest among poor, socially disadvantaged populations. According to the 1981 World Population Sheet, Spain has 13 infant deaths per 1000 live births, the same as the United States. This is

### Facts About "Multiples"

One in every 90 pregnancies is a twin pregnancy. Triplets are born in 1 out of every 8100 (90 × 90) births, quadruplets in 1 out of 729,000 (90 × 90 × 90). Thirty percent of twins are identical, formed by the accidental division of a single fertilized egg. Seventy percent are fraternal, formed when two eggs are released and fertilized at the same time. Other multiples may include combinations of fraternal and identical twins. Over half of all multiple pregnancies end prematurely. The majority of very premature twins are undiagnosed prior to delivery.

Fraternal twins can be of the same sex or of opposite sexes. Except for being the same age, fraternal twins are no more alike than other brothers and sisters. In the womb they are always enclosed in separate membranes (the chorionic and amniotic sacs) and they have separate placentas, although sometimes the placentas fuse, or grow together. Fraternal twins are more likely to be born to women over 35, women who have twins in their families (the trait that influences twinning is passed from mother to daughter), to women who take fertility drugs, and to women who become pregnant soon after stopping the pill. Certain ethnic groups have high rates of fraternal twinning. In western Nigeria, twins account for 49 out of every 1000 births. In Japan, by comparison, they occur in 1 out of every 1000 deliveries. In the U.S., blacks have a 20% higher rate of twins, a 75% higher incidence of triplets, and an incidence of quadruplets that is 4 times higher than that of whites.

**Fraternal Twins**

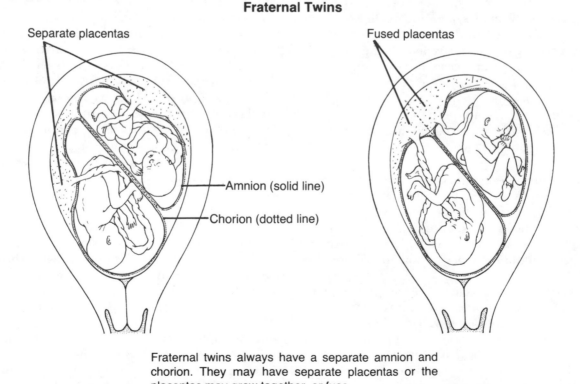

Separate placentas

Fused placentas

Amnion (solid line)

Chorion (dotted line)

Fraternal twins always have a separate amnion and chorion. They may have separate placentas or the placentas may grow together, or fuse.

*twice* the infant mortality rate of Sweden, where good social, educational, and medical services are available to the entire population.

Ethnically related health characteristics may also make some populations more vulnerable to prematurity. For example, blacks in the United States have twice the prematurity rate of other groups. Undoubtedly, this reflects the deprivations that blacks have suffered in this country. But American Indians, who also frequently live in poverty, have a relatively low prematurity rate. Lowest of all, is the prematurity rate for Japanese- and Chinese-Americans. Perhaps the prematurity rate among blacks can be partially explained by their high incidence of hypertension, fibroids, and multiple births—20% more sets of twins are born to blacks than to other groups. Sickle cell anemia and the sickle trait are also associated with prematurity.

---

### Identical Twins

Identical twins are of the same sex and genetic makeup, although one baby may be smaller than the other because of different growth rates in the womb. Before birth, the babies may share the same chorionic and amniotic sacs, as well as the same placenta. More commonly, like fraternal twins, they have separate sacs and placentas. Special genetic testing may be necessary in some cases to determine whether twins are identical or fraternal. Identical twins occur randomly in about 4 out of every 1000 pregnancies worldwide.

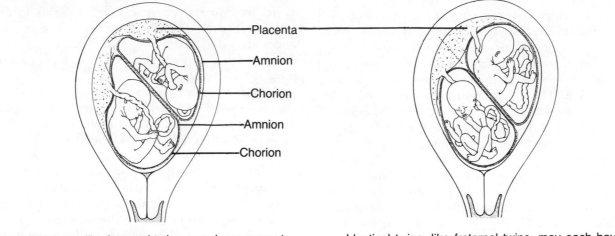

Placenta
Amnion
Chorion
Amnion
Chorion

Identical twins, like fraternal twins, may have separate amnions, chorions, and placentas.

Identical twins, like fraternal twins, may each have a separate amnion and chorion. Their separate placentas may fuse during pregnancy.

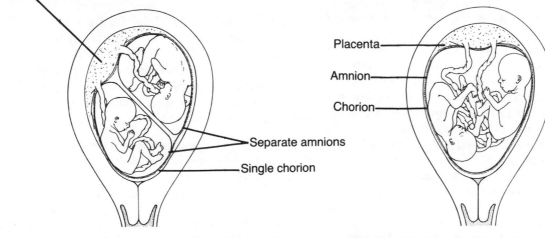

Single placenta

Separate amnions
Single chorion

Placenta
Amnion
Chorion

Identical twins may share a single placenta and chorion, but have separate amnions.

Identical twins may share the same amnion, chorion, and placenta.

Although the socially disadvantaged of all ethnic groups have higher prematurity rates, the much larger middle class in the United States produces a greater *number* of premature babies.

**Q:** I had a job I enjoyed, and I guess at some level I was ambivalent about having a baby. Could my emotions have caused the prematurity?

**A:** The demands of impending motherhood are always unsettling, even when the baby is clearly wanted and welcome. Pediatrician T. Berry Brazelton suggests that anxiety and ambivalence are a natural part of pregnancy. This emotional turmoil, he feels, helps an expectant mother mobilize her energies for her attachment to the new baby. When the pregnancy ends happily, these anxieties resolve. But when something goes wrong, the mother may suspect that her perfectly normal feelings of ambivalence somehow caused the unfortunate outcome of her pregnancy.

Several studies have tried to link emotional stress during pregnancy to premature birth. In most of these studies, premature mothers were questioned about stressful events in their lives that occurred before the birth. These responses were compared with those of mothers of full-term babies. The mothers of prematures generally had more stressful life events to report. But, concedes Jane Schwartz, the author of one such study, mothers who were already upset from the pre-term births of their babies "may have emphasized certain events less easily recalled by mothers of full-term infants whose joy in successful pregnancy tended to overshadow earlier life changes." So far, there is no good evidence to indicate that pregnancy can be interrupted by such emotions as anxiety, anger, grief, or fright.

**Q:** Can work, strenuous activity, or travel cause prematurity?

**A:** Nearly half of all women in the United States work during pregnancy. While some research indicates that physically demanding work increases the risk of prematurity, other studies do not confirm this. One investigation in Europe found a 3% rate of low-birth-weight infants among women who worked on farms, while women employed (less strenuously) in an urban hospital had a 10% rate. Says Marie Herron, R.N., at the University of California Preterm Labor Clinic, "Premature labor can happen to the active or the inactive woman, to the jogger or to the woman who spends her pregnancy in bed."

Travel, whether by airplane or other vehicle, does not cause prematurity. Women are advised against traveling in late pregnancy *not* to prevent prematurity, but to be sure they are close to the doctor when labor begins.

**Q:** What about alcohol, coffee, drugs, and cigarettes during pregnancy? Don't they cause prematurity?

**A:** Alcohol consumed in large quantities (more than six drinks a day) may cause a baby to be smaller than normal at birth. However, alcohol consumption is *not* associated with prematurity. In fact, the short-term use of alcohol is one of the methods used to stop premature labor. As for coffee, Harvard scientists who recently studied the coffee drinking habits of over 12,000 pregnant women concluded that consumption of the beverage "has a minimal effect, if any, on pregnancy outcome." Use of barbiturates and amphetamines has been associated with low-birth-weight babies but not specifically with prematurity. Marijuana use has *not* been linked to prematurity. Neither have such over-the-counter drugs as Tylenol or cold remedies. This is not to say that these substances are safe during pregnancy—they may cause other problems—only that they do not seem to cause prematurity.

Almost half the babies born to heroin addicts weigh less than 2500 grams as a result of prematurity, poor growth in the womb, or both. Whether these problems are directly caused by the drug or by other factors in the lives of heroin addicts is unknown.

Cigarette smoking has also been linked both to prematurity and to low-birth-weight infants. Heavy smokers have more pregnancy problems than light smokers. The University of California Preterm Labor Clinic does not consider smoking to be a significant risk factor unless the expectant mother smokes more than 10 cigarettes a day.

**Q.** I did everything right during my pregnancy. I even ate 100 grams of protein a day! A friend of mine was pregnant at the same time. She lived on diet soda and gained only nine pounds (I gained 25). She smoked, drank, used marijuana, and took Quaaludes. She had a healthy nine-pound baby. I had a two-pound premie. What I want to know is: Why me?

**A.** Statistically, women who eat well, avoid potentially harmful substances, and get good prenatal care do have better pregnancy outcomes than women who do not. However, there are always exceptions. Women who do all the "wrong" things can still have healthy term babies, and women who do everything "right" can still have premature babies. Some women, no matter how well they take care of themselves, are just more vulnerable to pregnancy complications.

**Q:** I feel my doctor is to blame. I think that with better care my baby's premature birth could have been prevented. Can I sue for malpractice?

**A:** Even if your baby's premature birth could have been medically prevented, it does not necessarily mean your doctor is guilty of malpractice. To establish malpractice, it must be demonstrated that the doctor violated accepted medical standards and that your baby was born prematurely as a direct result of this improper care. A doctor cannot be found guilty because of reasonable professional decisions that happened to be wrong. Reasonable decisions are ones that other competent physicians might have reached in a similar situation, given the same information.

Parents considering a malpractice suit should realize at the outset that the deck is stacked against them. Malpractice suits are expensive and hard to win. Lawyers are generally unwilling to take such cases unless they feel confident of a settlement of more than $100,000. Preparing the case and bringing it to trial takes years. It is difficult to find doctors who will testify against another physician. Of the cases that make it to court, nearly 80% are decided in the *doctor's* favor. If the parents win, a sizeable percentage of the award goes to the lawyer. On the other hand, the lawyer usually assumes the costs if the suit is lost.

If you still wish to sue, begin by asking a lawyer you know and trust to recommend a good medical malpractice attorney, or consult the lawyer referral service of your local Bar Association. The malpractice attorney can obtain your medical records and evaluate your chances for a successful suit. Most lawyers do not charge for this service.

**Q:** I've been told that it wasn't my fault that my baby was born early, but I still feel guilty. I suspect others think I did something wrong. My emotional state makes it hard for me to be a relaxed mother. What can I do to get over these feelings?

**A:** To achieve the peace of mind that you need to feel comfortable with your baby, confront your feelings of guilt on both a rational and an emotional level.

As a first step, you and your baby's father should meet with the obstetrician to discuss any aspects of your pregnancy or of your baby's birth that are unclear to you. Ask for a copy or a summary of your medical records and review them with your doctor. In many states, patients have a legal right to these documents. Tape the conference or take good notes that you can refer to later. Do not hesitate to ask any question, no matter how trivial it seems, and be sure to follow up on any additional questions that occur to you weeks, months, even years from now. You may also wish to consult a doctor who specializes in high-risk obstetrics—your baby's neonatologist can probably recommend a good one.

As a second step, become involved with a support group for parents of prematures. It may be a relief for you to realize that irrational guilt is felt by almost *every* mother of a premature infant. By sharing your feelings with others and by counseling new mothers of premature babies you may gain insights into your own emotional state that will help you put your guilt feelings behind you. Although you may never lose your irrational guilt feelings entirely (it has been said that guilt is an occupational hazard of motherhood), you can at least reduce them to manageable proportions.

If close relatives or friends seem to be blaming you, discuss your baby's birth with them openly and accurately. If possible, include them in your discussions with the doctor or invite them to attend a parents' group meeting. The sooner you, and those who are important to you, face and begin to resolve feelings of guilt and blame, the sooner you can get on with the happy, healthy upbringing of your baby.

## Kate's Story

# By Chris McNamara

Four days after we moved, I awoke early in the morning with strong, regular contractions, 20 minutes apart. What normally would have been a happy, exciting time was instead a nightmare. I was only seven months pregnant.

Leaving our two-year-old daughter with my mother, we rushed to the hospital. The ultrasound exam showed a 32-week fetus. At the hospital my contractions slowed by themselves to one every hour. Since my cervix hadn't effaced or dilated, I was sent home with instructions to stay in bed for 2 weeks.

But the contractions never entirely stopped. The next night, one very strong contraction was followed by heavy bleeding. We were off to the hospital again, this time to a hospital with a neonatal intensive care unit.

The doctor told me I had a placenta abruptio—that the placenta was pulling away from the uterus. I was now five centimeters dilated and they would not try to stop labor. We were going to have our baby—a baby who had, I was told, only a 50-50 chance of survival. The disappointment I felt at not giving birth at home as we had planned was eclipsed by the fear that the baby would die.

I was told I would need a deep episiotomy and

that forceps would be used to ease the baby's delicate head through the birth canal. We had wanted a home birth to avoid all this medical craziness, but now I had to put myself and my baby in the doctors' hands.

I am usually one who refuses aspirin, but I was tired and very scared. In the delivery room I asked for a block—I think I begged for it—but was told it would harm the baby. I had nothing. I screamed when the forceps were inserted, thinking at the same time, "My God! Is this really me?" Soon the baby's head was delivered and I felt her body slip into the world. "A girl," my husband John announced.

I heard Kate whimper but not cry. "That's okay," I thought, "some babies don't cry at all." I asked to hold and nurse her but was met with a resounding "No! She's too little!!" Somehow I didn't understand about Kate's prematurity. It wasn't sinking in at all. I called my mother from the delivery room and told her we had another beautiful little girl. I remember my mother crying on the phone. "A beautiful little girl," I kept repeating to all the doctors and nurses.

The neonatologist came to talk to me. At 4 pounds, 14 ounces, Kate was a good-sized baby. But she was being taken to intensive care. "Just to be checked," I assured myself.

When the other mothers were brought their babies to nurse I was puzzled when Kate was not brought in too. Instead, a nurse with a wheelchair came to take me to the nursery.

I scrubbed and gowned and was led to Kate's warmer. It was then that everything finally sank in. I felt sick and faint. In the warmer was a naked, frail, almost translucent little body hooked to tubes, IVs, and leads. She was under an oxygen hood and I could hardly see her face. She was breathing very rapidly and moaning with each breath. I remember sitting with her—just holding her little hand and crying.

The next three days would be the most dangerous, they told me. I made many promises to God if He would only let Kate live. John had been requested to sign all kinds of forms that allowed the hospital to take any emergency measures. He looked very shaken, and older. I wondered if he was blaming me for what Kate was going through. I was afraid to talk to him about it because I too was thinking back—what did I do to cause this? As a La Leche League leader, I was aware of the importance of good nutrition during pregnancy and my diet had been excellent. I did not smoke or drink, and during our move I'd been careful not to lift heavy objects or overexert myself.

The doctors cannot tell me why it happened, but I still feel, irrationally perhaps, that I must have done something wrong.

I left the hospital two days after Kate's birth. Before leaving I prayed to God to give me just a little sign so I could go home with more hope. I looked out the window at a bare tree outlined against the gray March sky. A robin—the first I'd seen that spring—landed on a near branch, stayed a few moments, then flew away. We said goodbye to Kate—it seemed so final. John and I drove home holding hands and not saying anything.

Erin, our two-year-old, was waiting at our house. We hadn't prepared her for my leaving since we had planned to have the baby at home. We cried together and I let her nurse. That evening my milk came in. I pumped and saved my milk to bring to Kate each day. I felt better knowing there was something I could do for her. John and I brought Erin along the next time we visited the hospital. The nurses encouraged us to let her look at Kate through the window. I was glad that they were aware how vital bonding is to the entire family.

On the fourth day I was allowed to hold Kate for the first time. She was so tiny; I felt as though I was holding only blankets. She opened her eyes for a second. They were beautiful—almost violet. I had never seen them before, though John said they were open when she was born.

Kate was rapidly improving. She had not developed hyaline membrane disease, and she no longer needed extra oxygen or intravenous feedings. The nurses and doctors who had predicted a two-month hospital stay for our baby were amazed. On the sixth day I was allowed to nurse her. I knew I shouldn't expect much the first time, and in fact, she slept in my arms for 2½ hours. Then she woke, turned to me, and latched on. She nursed for 13 minutes and fell asleep again at my breast. This was so much more than I had hoped for!

Nine days after Kate was born the neonatologist said she was healthy enough to go home. I brought doll clothes to dress her in and finally she was ours!

But at home I didn't know what to do with her. All Kate did was sleep, waking only to nurse. Sometimes I had to wake her myself. I felt alienated and detached from her. I felt I should be holding her and loving her more. In the nursery my feelings of worry and pity for Kate had been so all-consuming that I hadn't really considered the normal aspects of mother love. Now I realized that I didn't feel the emotional closeness for her that I had felt for her sister. Her cry didn't bring about that gut-level response in me that Erin's had.

It was about a week after Kate had come home. As I held her after a feeding, I saw her stop breathing and become ashen. At La Leche League, I had counseled a mother whose baby was home on an apnea monitor, and I remembered what she had done when her child stopped breathing. Slowly, I started counting. Before I reached 10, Kate took a breath on her own. My pediatrician advised me to watch Kate closely. If these spells became frequent or long, she, too, might need a monitor. Meanwhile, he suggested that Kate sleep on my stomach so that my breathing movements would stimulate her to breathe.*

The concern and extra attention I was giving Kate were hard on Erin. Overnight, she became a "terrible two"—whining, whimpering, throwing things, biting and hitting me, and climbing on my lap when I tried to nurse the baby. Occasionally, I let Erin nurse along with Kate, and at night I brought them both to bed with me—Kate sleeping on my stomach and Erin beside me.

Kate is now four months old. She hasn't had an apnea spell in over a month. Aside from anemia—her hematocrit dropped to 26 and she always threw up the iron drops I gave her—Kate has had no health problems. She has tripled her birth weight and weighs more than Erin did at the same age.

John and I do not talk much now about Kate's

*Author's note: Although this is an excellent method to soothe a fussy baby, it is not a recommended treatment for apnea. See page **188**.

*Kate at 4 months.*

birth and time in the hospital. He seems to have pushed it all out of his mind. But I live with those memories every day. Looking at my chubby, smiling, healthy baby, I still feel sad at times wondering why it had to happen and if it will happen again.

But Kate and I have bonded at last, and I can truthfully say that I feel the same love for her that I do for Erin. Erin, too, feels happier about her new sister. This morning I found them sound asleep in bed with their arms around each other.

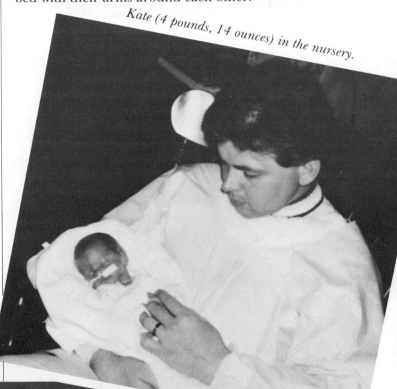

*Kate (4 pounds, 14 ounces) in the nursery.*

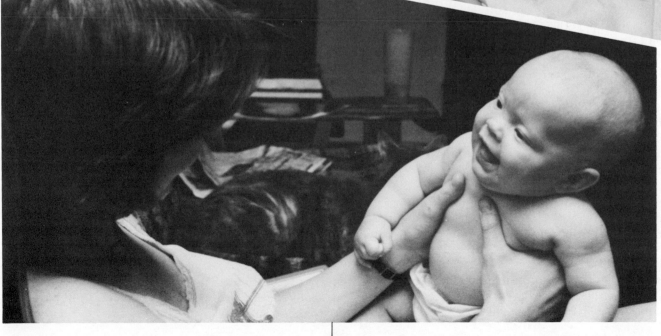

# 3

# Bonding and Attachment

## Bonding at Birth: How Important?

"In the past few years," says an intensive care nurse, "I've talked to a lot of mothers who are worried because they didn't hold or touch their premature babies right after birth. They're afraid that they haven't 'bonded.' These mothers ask me: 'How can I make it up to my baby? Will we ever be able to love each other?'"

"Bonding," a commonly used term in books and articles on birth and baby care, refers to the early interactions between parents and baby, especially between mother and baby, during a so-called sensitive period immediately after birth.

Bonding was first used to describe patterns of postpartum behavior in animals—special grooming, nursing, and caretaking activities that led the mother animal to form an attachment with her young. When this behavior is disrupted by separating mother and babies after birth, the mother may refuse, at least for a time, to accept her babies back or to care for them properly. Each species seems to have a certain period of time during which some separation can be tolerated. If mother and baby are kept apart longer than this sensitive or critical period, the consequences are likely to be irreversible—and the animal mother abandons her young.

For decades researchers have been studying the ways mothers and babies respond to each other after birth to see if a similar sensitive period occurs in humans. Films of mothers with their babies immediately following delivery show that during these early minutes, baby and mother are unusually alert and responsive to each other. During this time the mother and her baby become acquainted in a characteristic way. Typically, the mother begins touching her baby, at first with her fingertips, then with her whole hand.

She looks into her baby's eyes. She speaks to her baby in a high-pitched voice. The baby responds by turning toward his mother's voice in preference to others. The baby moves in the same rhythms as his mother's speech in what observers have called "a synchronized dance between mother and infant." Some researchers feel that a mother and baby who share this postpartum experience have an easier subsequent relationship, and that this improved mother-child relationship helps accelerate the baby's development.

In 1976, Drs. Kennell and Klaus of Case Western Reserve published their book *Maternal-Infant Bonding,* in which they expressed the theory that "there is a sensitive period in the first minutes and hours of life during which it is necessary that the mother and father have close contact with their neonate for later development to be optimal."

Their theory of bonding was reported in the media and widely accepted by parents and health professionals. Some began to view bonding as a sort of cure-all in the prevention of psychological problems. Parent-child difficulties such as child abuse were often blamed on improper bonding. Restrictive hospital policies that separated mother and baby were revised. The premature nursery, formerly off-limits to parents, was opened. Mothers and fathers were encouraged to visit and participate in their baby's care.

But the bonding phenomenon as Kennell and Klaus described it occurs in the first *minutes or hours* after birth. Separation of mother and premature baby during this period is often essential to save the baby's life. Does this mean that the relationship between mother and baby would inevitably suffer? Are those first minutes after birth really that critical to the future well-being of mother and baby?

Professionals began to take a closer look, and many had their doubts. After all, most mothers during the '40s, '50s, and '60s delivered their babies under anesthesia and were routinely separated from their infants after birth. Mothers were often kept in the hospital for a week or more while their babies were cared for in the nursery. Yet no epidemic of child abuse occurred. And how does the "bonding-at-birth" theory account for the majority of premature babies who have good relationships with their parents?

If bonding-at-birth is so crucial, how could adoptions ever succeed? Yet pediatricians report that adopted children are among the most loved and best cared for children in their practices.

Many professionals have now come to feel that the bonding-at-birth theory is too rigid and narrow to explain the highly individual and complex process by which a human mother and her baby come to love each other. "I don't like the concept of critical periods," comments Boston pediatrician T. Berry Brazelton, "because it mistakenly implies that you make it or you don't." While early contact is desirable, and pleasurable interactions between mother and baby after birth do seem to give a boost to their early relationship, the importance of this contact may have been exaggerated.

Dr. Peter Gorski of San Francisco's Mt. Zion Hospital puts it this way: "If you think of the mother-child relationship as a love affair, the early bonding that happens after birth is a first infatuation, but genuine attachment evolves over a long period of time."

Mothers of full-term infants who see and touch their babies right after birth often admit they do not feel the rush of emotion they had expected. Love for the baby develops later. Of close to 100 mothers inteviewed in a British study, only one mother in four felt her first feelings of love for her baby at birth.

Other studies have since cast doubt on the importance of bonding-at-birth. Doctors at the University of Pittsburgh, for example, studied 100 mother-baby pairs who were divided into two groups: one group had contact immediately after birth for an hour; the other group did not. At three days and at one month, *no difference* was detected between the two groups, either in the mothers' feelings about their babies or in their behavior with them.

UCLA researchers Cohen and Beckwith have written of their findings concerning mothers and their premature babies. They begin by listing some of the stresses experienced by a mother after her premature baby's birth: separation from the baby, depression over the failure to produce a normal baby in the normal manner, reluctance to become attached to a child who might not survive, the delay in assuming a normal maternal caretaking role with the baby, over-

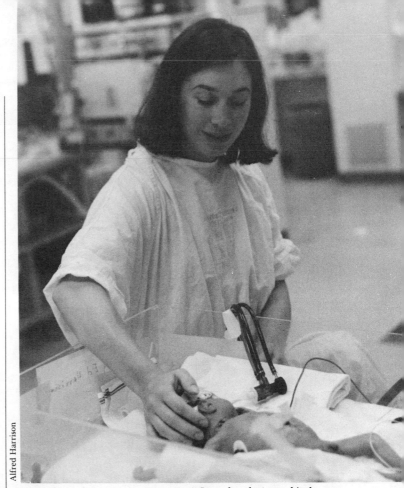

Alfred Harrison

*A mother who must be separated from her baby at birth may wonder about her ability to bond with her child.*

whelming hospital bills, and the inability of the premature baby to interact with his mother in the normal way.

In view of the bonding-at-birth theory, the trauma and separation these mothers and babies endured (the average hospitalization was 23 days; the longest stay, 88 days) should have predicted later difficulties between these mothers and their pre-term infants. Cohen and Beckwith found just the opposite to be true. In their study of these 123 mothers and babies, they found that the smaller and sicker the babies had been, the more care their mothers gave them. The babies were held more and their mothers made more of an attempt to interact with them than did mothers of full-term infants.

Cohen and Beckwith suggest that a psychological "self-righting" mechanism exists between mother and baby so that the more vulnerable the baby, the more attention he gets from his mother.

This "compensatory care," as they termed it, has important implications for the premature baby's future. Doctors are now beginning to realize that the attachments a parent forms with a high-risk baby may be as important to the child's eventual outcome as all the hospital's sophisticated medical technology. Even when a baby is very small or very sick at birth, *the single most important factor in predicting that child's later development is the quality of the home environment in which he will grow up.* This is not to say that a good home life will restore a baby's damaged vision or replace lost brain cells. But the parent's love and attention can help the child develop to his full potential—a potential medical experts often underestimate.

Tests have shown that a stimulating environment helps brain-damaged animals recover lost abilities. Additional stimulation may also help brain-damaged humans. Young children tend to recover more completely from brain injury than do adults. Because a child's brain is less specialized, one part can sometimes assume the functions that would have been carried out by the part that was damaged. Extra stimulation or training may help this transfer of function to occur. *All* children benefit from an enriched and loving family life, but for the premature baby who may have suffered brain injury, it can make a crucial difference.

While the actual importance of bonding-at-birth has yet to be determined, most parents and doctors would agree that the earlier a mother can be with her baby the better. The early attachments a mother forms with her child *do* seem to be important, but bonding—at least for most mothers and babies—is a *long term* process, not a single magical moment when their relationship is sealed with "super glue." Each mother and baby is unique. Their mutual love is unique, and it develops in its own way—at its own pace.

In their most recent book, *Parent-Infant Bonding* (1982), Drs. Klaus and Kennell offer these reassuring words to parents who must be separated from their baby at birth: "The human is highly adaptable and there are many fail-safe routes to attachment. Sadly, some parents who missed the bonding experience have felt that all was lost for their future relationship. This was (and is) entirely incorrect."

# The Effects of Separation

In our questionnaires and interviews we asked parents about their early relationship with their baby. Did the separation after birth cause problems? What if anything, kept them from feeling close to the baby? What helped them become attached to their child?

Approximately half the parents answered that separation from their baby after birth had *not* caused them any difficulties. A brief look or touch following delivery was enough to bond several mothers. Others told of feeling attached to their baby long before birth: "We tried for seven years to have our first child, and I loved him from the moment I knew I was pregnant." Some felt the crisis of the baby's birth had actually heightened their sense of attachment to their child. "Although I was afraid he would die," wrote one mother, "I immediately felt close to my son with a special kind of spiritual bond." Another couple wrote, "She was our little angel, just as if she'd been ten pounds and healthy. Maybe it was her fighting so hard to live that endeared her to us."

Several second-time mothers had a "normal" birth experience to compare to the birth of their premie. Their responses varied. Said one mother, "I had a quick glimpse of my premature daughter after delivery, then she was whisked away to be cultured. (My membranes had ruptured a week earlier and they feared infection.) When I saw her later in the nursery, I couldn't remember her face. I knew she was mine intellectually, but I didn't feel it. Even today my relationship with her is strained, unlike the one I have with my other daughter, the one I saw and held at birth. I'm sure other factors are also involved, but I think lack of bonding is part of it."

Wrote another mother, "I had more trouble bonding with my *full-term* baby. Before her birth I went from teaching to motherhood in just a couple of weeks with no time to prepare myself. Our full-term daughter was 'hyper' and colicky. The first three months were difficult, and I didn't feel attached to her until they were over. With Kevin, my premie, it was just the opposite. I felt a strong bond with him from the beginning. The night he was born I feared for both our lives, and hearing him cry after delivery and knowing that he was alive left me with a sense of closeness that he and I still share. His being in intensive care didn't hinder that at all. Up until his birth I took things for granted. The crisis we both experienced made me realize how fragile life is. I thought I had lost Kevin, and I feel he was given back to me for some very special reason."

And for a third opinion: "I was separated from my premature son after delivery and he wasn't able to breast-feed later. My 8½-pound daughter was nursing minutes after her birth. Before my daughter was born I tended to blame problems I had with my son on his prematurity and our lack of bonding. But with both babies I've had the same aggravations (neither sleeps worth a damn) and the same joys (both are lively and affectionate). I love my children equally and feel that the separation in one case and the lack of it in the other made no ultimate difference."

# Obstacles to Attachment

Those parents who did find the early attachment process difficult gave a number of reasons why.

"I was at work when I went into labor," one mother wrote. "I had planned to start my leave of absence the next day and go home for seven weeks of mental and physical preparation. I was unprepared for *any* baby, much less an utter snip of a thing that I could practically hold in one hand." A mother of twins wrote, "The fact that it was *two* instead of one was overwhelming and upsetting. And I didn't feel prepared—I needed that last month."

Feelings of guilt toward the baby were a common barrier: "In my mind I knew I was not to blame, but I still felt responsible for my son's prematurity and for the problems it had caused. I was reluctant to get close to him for fear I might inadvertently harm him again."

Fear of the baby's death was the most frequently mentioned impediment to bonding: "I felt that if I got too excited and loved him too much he would be taken away from me." (It is interesting to note that in some primitive societies where infant mortality is high, parents postpone naming or even establishing eye contact with their baby until survival seems certain.) Fathers appeared to be less affected by this fear than mothers. Several women said that their husbands had to help them make their first difficult contacts with the baby. "I was afraid Leah would die," wrote one mother, "and I didn't want to bond and then lose her. But after several days with my husband's constant help and support, I was finally able to see her."

In the sterile, emergency-charged atmosphere of the intensive care nursery, motherly and fatherly emotions are often slow to blossom. A common difficulty for many parents is getting past the tubes and wires, not to mention the other barriers that separate them from their baby. As one mother put it, "No matter how hard you try, the incubator is a real wall."

On the other hand, nursery technology can give a sense of security. Some parents later feel uncomfortable without it: "Two months after my baby was born I was finally able to carry him around the nursery with *nothing* attached to him. It was absolute euphoria—for about five minutes. Then I got terrified that he'd have an apnea spell and I

*"No matter how hard you try, the incubator is a real wall."*

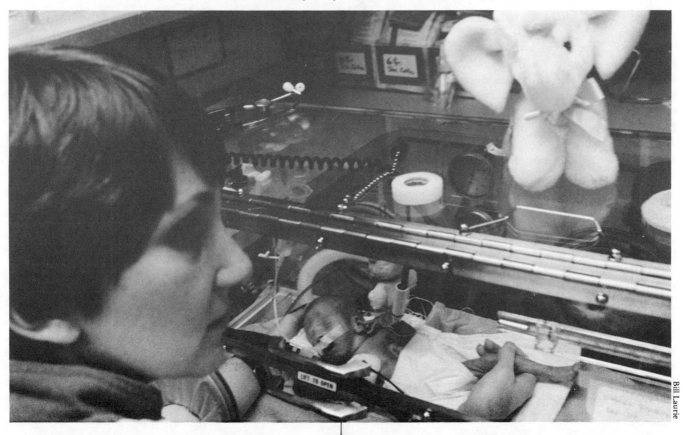

Bill Laurie

## "Does the Baby Know I'm There?"

Until recently, premature babies had been considered by parents and doctors alike to be passive, inert, and unaware of their environment. This view is now changing. At Mt. Zion Hospital, San Francisco, Dr. Peter Gorski, Director of Behavioral Pediatrics, has been studying premature behavior in a careful and comprehensive way. Dr. Gorski selects certain babies in the nursery for special observation. Around the clock, the heartbeats, temperatures, breathing rates, and blood oxygen levels of the infants are followed by mechanical monitors. A trained observer sits by each baby's bedside and makes notations every 30 seconds on the infant's level of alertness, movement, skin color, and any other significant details of appearance or behavior. The observer also records any treatments the baby receives and notes other environmental factors that may be influencing the baby—a parent's visit, for example.

Far from being inert and unresponsive, the premature babies studied seemed acutely sensitive to their environment, though they often responded in ways too subtle for a *casual* observer to notice. Each baby was found to have his own personality—a pattern of highly individualized responses to his environment. The baby's ability to heal and grow were greatly enhanced when doctors and parents understood and respected these individual differences.

One of Dr. Gorski's most interesting observations was of a very sick premature baby and his reaction to his mother. The mother, a single parent, lived and worked hours away from the hospital where her son was treated. She visited when she could, but the long trip was difficult. The baby was on a respirator with bronchopulmonary dysplasia (chronic lung disease). It was repeatedly noticed that during the mother's visits, the baby's heart rate and blood oxygen levels made dramatic improvements. And so Dr. Gorski soon suggested that the mother come stay in the hospital to be near her son. With Dr. Gorski's help, the mother arranged for a leave of absence from work. She came to San Francisco and lived in a room at the hospital. With his mother nearby, the baby made steady progress toward recovery.

Nurses often comment that babies seem to know when their parents are present. They behave differently, tolerate feedings better, and generally improve. Researchers have found that when parents come to the nursery at a specific time each day, the baby often becomes active right before the visit as if anticipating their arrival.

---

wouldn't notice it. I gave him right back to the nurse."

The constant focus on the baby's medical condition can be depersonalizing. Said one mother, "Doctors were in and out of my room that first day telling me what was wrong with my baby and what complications they expected. Then a nurse from the NBICU (Newborn Intensive Care Unit) came in smiling and said, 'Congratulations, you have a lovely little girl!' She gave me a picture of Katy and a copy of her footprints. For the first time I felt like I'd really had a baby and not just a medical problem." Said another mother, "My way of coping was to immerse myself in the medical details of my son's care. One day a resident commented to me, 'He really is a little *person*, you know.' I realized then how I'd been using the medical aspects to keep my distance from the baby."

When mother and father must ask the staff before touching their baby, their role as parents is compromised. Lack of control over the baby, and the lack of confidence that accompanies it, delays the attachment process. Mothers often told of looking to the nurses as role models and adopting the same caretaking techniques they'd seen in the nursery: "When our son came home I was still feeding, bathing, and weighing him just the same way they had in the hospital. I even kept a nurse's log. It was several months before it occurred to me that there might be other ways to do these things."

Lack of privacy was a problem for many parents. While full-term babies and their parents go through the trial-and-error stage of getting acquainted at home, mothers and fathers of premies have their parental behavior on public display. Under the watchful eyes of the nursery staff, they may become too nervous and inhibited to relate to their baby spontaneously: "Sometimes I wanted to have long conversations with the baby or sing to her, but I was afraid people would think I was nuts. Besides my singing voice isn't that great."

Several mothers and fathers told of their need to "make it socially" with the nurses and doctors, the baby's surrogate parents: "My husband spent most of his time chatting with the staff. He felt it was very important for them to like us." Said another mother, "I don't know why, but I always got dressed up to go to the hospital as if I were going to work. I'm not sure whom I was to impress."

A major barrier, perhaps *the* major barrier, is the behavior of the premature baby himself. The parent-infant relationship is a two-way street. The baby as well as the parent is responsible for the quality of that relationship. A lively responsive baby stimulates the parent to act in a similar manner. But the premature baby, especially the sick premature baby, cannot respond in ways most parents find rewarding. He needs to conserve energy in order to regain health, grow, and mature. He may spend much of his time asleep. For certain treatments he must be restrained and sedated, which further limits his ability to respond: "I'd come to the nursery and find the baby blindfolded under the 'bili' lights. There wasn't much for me to do except talk to the nurses and watch the monitors go up and down. I wondered if I really needed to come in to see him so much. He didn't even know I was there, what difference did it make?"

## The Beginnings of Affection

The parents we interviewed described the various ways in which they came to feel affection for their babies.

Most mothers needed to feel confident of their child's survival before attachment began in earnest. Some had to face up to negative emotions or relin-

quish unrealistic expectations as a first step. "I began to feel close to my baby," one mother wrote, "once I finally *accepted* my *not* wanting to bond in case he didn't survive." Wrote another mother, "One day as I stood by Matthew's Isolette, I thought how difficult it was for him to go on, how every minute was a fight. I told him to do whatever it was he needed to do and I would be O.K. I accepted that he was in charge of his life, and in doing so, I stopped imposing my previous expectations on him."

It helped many parents to discover the positive, but often subtle, ways in which the baby acknowledged their presence: "My baby was on a transcutaneous oxygen monitor, and I can't tell you what an ego boost it was to cradle him in my hands and see the numbers on his monitor go up and up."

Decorating the baby's Isolette with toys and family pictures, adding a personal touch to the baby's environment and care gave many parents their first feelings that the baby was truly theirs. Almost every mother mentioned the importance of close physical contact, of holding her baby and looking into her baby's eyes. Supplying breastmilk for the baby and later nursing also gave many mothers an enormous feeling of accomplishment and a deep sense of attachment to their babies.

*Each parent and baby is unique; their mutual love develops in its own way, at its own pace.*

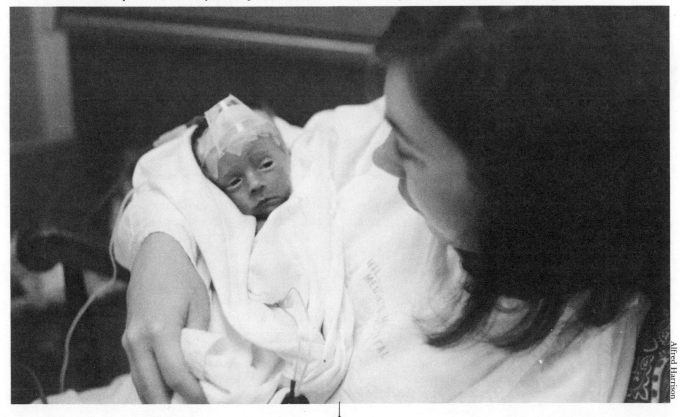

Alfred Harrison

Bonding was always easier once parents became comfortable with their baby, once they learned that the baby was a hearty little creature who would not break if touched. Wrote one mother, "On a home visit the pediatrician saw how terrified I was of handling Brian. 'I don't recommend that *you* try this,' he cautioned, 'but I want to show you something.' He picked Brian up by the heels and swung him upside down like a pink pendulum. My heart dropped to my feet, but Brian didn't seem to mind. The doctor had made his point!"

The bond strengthened as parents assumed greater and greater control over their baby's care: "At first I felt like a helpless bystander. The doctors and nurses were all-powerful. But as time went on I gained confidence in my ability to take care of my baby. I was often the first to notice a change in his condition. The doctors came to trust my observations and often asked my opinion. Dressing my son in clothes I had chosen for him, bringing him my breast-milk, bathing him, diapering him, gavage-and-bottle-feeding him, and later on nursing him, all made me feel that I was his mother."

For some women the feeling of being a mother began in the nursery, for others it didn't start until well after the baby was home. "The first weeks he was home I felt I was babysitting for someone else's baby (even though I was up half the night with him). But I finally realized that he really was mine and no one was going to take him away," one mother related. "The attachment came slowly," wrote another, "because I did not take full charge of my daughter for two months. First she was cared for by the hospital staff and then for several weeks by my mother, which didn't allow me to face up to the situation. But our closeness grew when breast-feeding was established and when I was finally left alone to care for her."

Although the attachment process was different for every parent we interviewed, almost all felt that at some point a bond or connection had been made. The most important elements in forming the attachment were, as one mother put it, "simply lots of physical closeness, patience, and time."

## Fathers and Attachment

The father of a premature baby often has a head start at bonding. He may be the first to visit the baby while the mother recovers from delivery. If his wife has had a cesarean or is in a separate hospital, he may have days of exclusive contact. Men sometimes find it easier to relate to the high-tech nursery environment. One father, an engineer, became so proficient with the machinery that he began adjusting his child's respirator settings, much to the staff's dismay!

Because the mother is unable to nurse her baby—at least at first—both mother and father begin on equal footing as the baby's care-givers. And during the postpartum period, the father usually has more emotional and physical energy to devote to the attachment process. An extraordinary closeness between father and baby may result.

"My wife and I had been married for many years," one father recounted, "and I was ambivalent about having children and losing our freedom. Mostly, I wasn't sure about my abilities as a father. But when our son was born prematurely, I was with him from the start. I was amazed at the incredible love I felt for that tiny little creature with a head no bigger than a baseball. I went to see him every day. I gave him his first bottle-feeding—the first of many. Since then I've done at least 50% of his child care, sometimes more. We are very, very close. I can't imagine life without him."

Some mothers have mixed feelings about the father's special ties to the baby: "I was so devastated by the baby's birth that there were times I couldn't bring myself to visit the hospital. My husband would go alone, I was glad one of us could go, but it also made me feel more of a failure because he was taking over and doing the things I felt I should have been doing." Said another mother, "My husband saw our daughter long before I did, since I was in another hospital for almost a week after a cesarean. They have a beautiful relationship even now. It makes my life easier in many ways, but sometimes I feel envious." The envy can go both ways. A father may feel left out once his wife begins to breast-feed. Nurses note that paternal visits often become less frequent once the mother is in charge of feedings.

Both mother and father have special contributions to make to their baby's care and upbringing. Observers note that when mother and father play with their baby *together*, they are each more animated and positive than when either one plays with the baby alone. It is when both mother and father are actively involved that the baby has the highest quality family life.

While many fathers in the families we interviewed became attached to their baby in the nursery, there were exceptions. "My husband rarely went to see our son," one mother said, "and whenever he did, he was very uneasy. He'd leave at the first opportunity. At home he hardly mentioned the baby. I knew he was a man who had difficulty expressing emotions, and I made excuses for him to the nurses who thought he was a terrible husband and father. Still, it

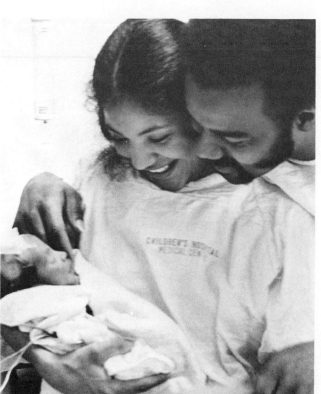

Peggy Wakefield Green, Courtesy of Children's Hospital Medical Center of Northern California

*It is when both mother and father are actively involved that the baby has the highest quality family life.*

was hard on me. I felt like I was in this entirely alone. Then one day before driving to the hospital, I went out to the backyard where my husband was pruning roses. Tears were streaming down his face. I realized then that his problem was not caring too little, but caring too much." Once the baby was home from the hospital the father began to spend more time with his infant son and slowly, but surely, an attachment grew.

## Siblings and Attachment

Brothers and sisters also need to form attachments to the new baby. This is all the more important when the baby needs special care at birth. Even in the best of circumstances, the arrival of a new baby is a time of great emotional upheaval for the other children in the family. If the baby is premature, the experience can be especially disturbing to them.

The early birth catches everyone by surprise. Sometimes the siblings haven't been informed yet that a new baby is on the way. They are not prepared for their mother's sudden trip to the hospital. They may be confused and frightened to see their parents upset. They may feel angry or rejected when their

*Brothers and sisters also need to form attachments to the new baby.*

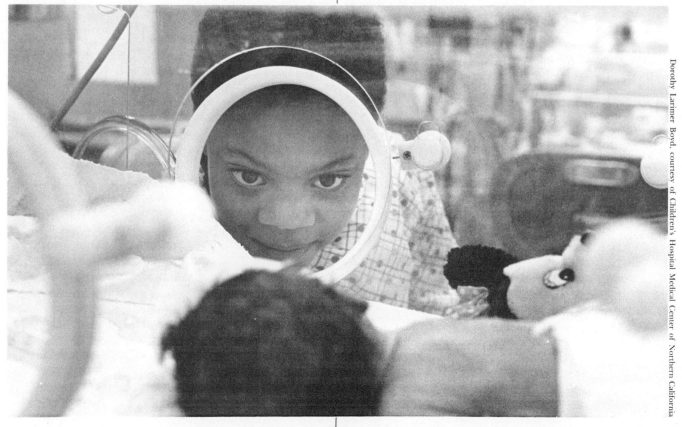

Dorothy Larimer Boyd, courtesy of Children's Hospital Medical Center of Northern California

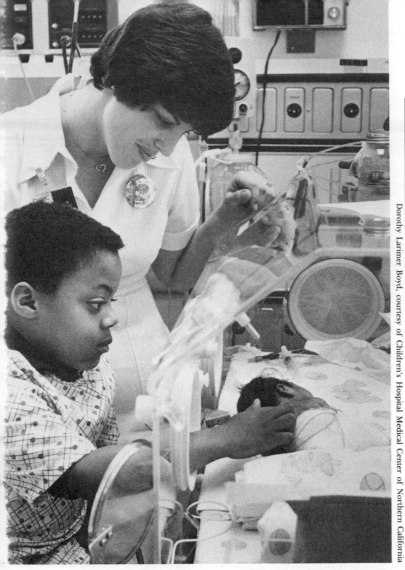

*Dominic Williams visits baby sister Danielle in the intensive care nursery.*

parents are physically absent or emotionally preoccupied with the hospitalized baby. Like their parents, children may have irrational guilt feelings about the baby's premature birth. Most children are ambivalent at the very least about a new baby in the family. When the baby is sick or endangered, the sibling, with his child-like view of cause and effect, may fear that his negative thoughts actually caused the problems to happen.

Children express their guilt or resentment in various ways. Some become depressed and withdrawn. Some engage in attention-getting misbehavior. Others develop psychosomatic ailments.

Parents can help ward off these problems by including their children as much as possible in the family experience, even though that experience is an upsetting one. Often the parents' first impulse is to protect their children by keeping up a brave front, by not telling the children what has happened, or by sending the children off to calmer surroundings with a relative or babysitter. Unfortunately, the message this may give a child is that something dreadful and secret has happened that he is too little or too unim-

portant to share. Even the youngest toddler can sense the tension behind his parents' cheerful facade, and the resulting fantasies or feelings of distress may harm him more than the reality his parents are trying to hide. A parent's honest tears and straightforward explanations are usually easier for a child to accept than repressed emotions and evasions.

The children need to be told simply, but honestly, about the baby's birth and problems. In discussing the baby's condition, parents should be aware of some nonlogical concerns children often have about illness. For example, a young child hearing about his sick newborn sibling may worry that he or his parents will also become ill. The child may have questions or anxieties about his own birth and babyhood. He may need reassurance that his own thoughts and wishes cannot make bad things happen to the baby.

Involving the other children in projects for the baby can give them a sense of pride and participation at a time when they might otherwise feel jealous or neglected. Children of all ages can help select clothes and toys for the baby. A young child can make drawings and get well cards to decorate the baby's Isolette. Older children can sew baby clothes or stuffed animals. The children might also enjoy making a tape recording of their voices to help acquaint their hospitalized sibling with the sounds of home.

The children can accompany their parents to the hospital to see the baby through the nursery window. Some hospitals allow siblings inside the nursery where they may touch or hold the baby. Sibling visits may be limited to certain hours on a weekend day when both parents, or a parent and a sitter, can come along to help supervise. The children may wish to bring a present to the new baby (check with the nurses in advance to find out what toys are permitted), and it may help the attachment process if the new baby has some presents for his brothers and sisters—preferably ones that will keep them quietly occupied in the waiting room before and after their visit.

Parents often wonder if it is advisable to bring children into an environment like the intensive care nursery that most adults find upsetting. Although no studies have yet been done to evaluate the effects of such visits, parents, nurses, and doctors we interviewed were almost unanimously enthusiastic. They told of nursery visits curing siblings of behavior problems that had arisen following the baby's birth—problems that ranged from a three-year-old's nighttime tantrums to an eight-year-old's fire-setting. However, what works well for most children may not work for all. Parents concerned about their child's possible reaction to the nursery may wish professional

### Telling Your Children About the Baby

To help parents discuss the premature baby with their other children, Jerri Oehler, R.N., M.S., of Duke University Medical Center, and artist Katherine Shelburne have created a story-coloring book entitled *The Frogs Have a Baby, a Very Small Baby.* A frog family was chosen because Katherine Shelburne, in illustrating other children's books, had discovered that frogs are popular with children of all ages. Children, regardless of age or sex, can identify easily with the frog "child." Blanks provided in the text for the child's name, the new baby's name, and the baby's problems allow parent and child to structure the story to fit their own situation. The 13-page, 8½ × 11-inch coloring book is available for $1.50 from Jerri Oehler, R.N., Ph.D., Box 3362, Duke University Medical Center, Durham, North Carolina 27710.

**Three sample pages from *The Frogs Have a Baby, a Very Small Baby,* by Jerri Oehler, R.N.**

RIGHT NOW THE BABY NEEDS SPECIAL DOCTORS AND NURSES AND SPECIAL EQUIPMENT TO GET WELL AND GROW.

IT IS HARD FOR _____ TO SHARE MOTHER AND DADDY. HOWEVER, EVEN THOUGH MOTHER AND DADDY HAVE TO DO MANY THINGS FOR THE BABY, THEY STILL PLAY WITH _____, WHO IS LOVED AND IMPORTANT, TOO. AS THE BABY GROWS BIGGER AND DOESN'T NEED AS MUCH OF MOTHER AND DADDY'S TIME, THE NEW FAMILY WILL BE ABLE TO DO MORE THINGS TOGETHER.

advice from their pediatrician, neonatologist, or hospital social worker before bringing the child to see the hospitalized baby.

Like adults, school-age children and adolescents are sometimes distressed by the nursery; however, many handle their visits to the baby quite well. Toddlers, parents reported, were seldom emotionally affected by the nursery or the baby. Most were much more interested in the machines. A few young children developed strange misconceptions about what they saw. One little boy, looking through the nursery window, could only glimpse his brother's leg kicking in the incubator. Until he was later allowed into the nursery to see the baby, he imagined his brother as a tiny, disembodied foot. A three-year-old who first saw her baby brother under an oxygen hood remarked matter-of-factly, "The baby doesn't have a head." (Neither child seemed particularly disturbed by these bizarre misconceptions.) To discover and correct similar erroneous notions, parents should encourage their children to talk about the baby and the nursery and to draw pictures of what they saw at the hospital.

On the whole, the parents we interviewed felt that early exposure to the baby and the nursery had helped their other children begin a healthy attachment to their prematurely-born sibling.

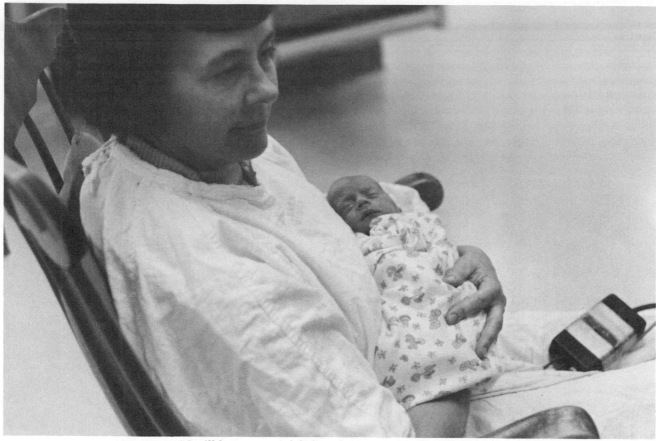

Alfred Harrison

*"I still have a special feeling for my premature grandson."*

## Relatives, Friends, and the Premature Baby

The birth of a baby is a family affair and that includes the extended family. Grandparents, relatives, and friends who are close to the parents are also important to the baby. Some nurseries now encourage relatives and "significant others" to visit and bond with the hospitalized premature baby.

Adults, seemingly more so than children, are emotionally affected by what they see in the nursery. A friend or relative who wishes to visit should be well prepared in advance. "After several weeks," recounted one mother, "I asked my best friend to come see the baby. I guess I hadn't told her enough about what to expect. She tried to hide it, but she was visibly shocked by the nursery and the baby. I had become quite used to my baby's appearance by that time; in fact, I thought he was rather cute. But her reaction made me experience my own first shock feelings all over again."

But shock usually gives way to involvement and warmer emotions. Said a grandmother, "My son-in-law warned me that it would be gruesome and he was

right. When I saw the baby, my first thought was, 'What a pathetic creature!' Then, after I visited a few times, I began to see him as a real little person with his own personality. I still have a special feeling for my premature grandson because I helped see this little boy through his early bad times."

"My five children were all full-term and healthy," said another grandmother, "and I had no idea of the complications and problems of premature babies. If I hadn't been allowed in the nursery, I don't think I could have ever understood what my daughter and son-in-law were going through."

New babies usually bring parents closer to their own parents and in-laws, but the birth of a baby, especially a sick or premature baby, can also stir up existing family tensions. Involving the grandparents with the baby may help, but it is not the answer for everyone.

One nurse cautions, "I've seen grandparents come in here and react a lot more emotionally than the parents themselves. They may have misinformation about the causes of prematurity and outdated advice about the ways a premature baby should be handled. While most grandparents are helpful, some really add to their children's misery. Even a well-meaning grandmother will come in and 'take over' with the baby, thinking she's doing the parents a favor. But this is absolutely the wrong way—the parents need their confidence boosted, not undermined. I'm all for grandparent visits, but I think the parents should decide whether these visits will help or hurt them emotionally before issuing invitations."

# Long-Distance Bonding

One of the unfortunate aspects of regionalized infant intensive care is that the premature baby must often be cared for far from the parents' home. The complicated technology for infant life support is expensive and limited to a few large hospitals. The medical personnel needed to staff an intensive care nursery must be highly trained, and their skills must be kept up-to-date by the constant experience they can get only in large urban medical centers.

Hospitals make efforts to help out-of-town parents visit their hospitalized infants. Some provide rooms and meals at the hospital or in nearby facilities so parents can make overnight visits. Playrooms and babysitting may be available for the other children in the family. Members of parent groups may take new parents into their homes or help them find other lodging. The nursery social worker can give information on any such services provided by the hospital.

The nursery staff usually makes an effort to keep out-of-town parents in touch with their baby. Parents are often sent snapshots of the baby or a set of the baby's footprints or even videotapes. A nurse or doctor may call daily with reports on the baby's condition.

The intensive care staff realize how difficult it is when parent and baby are separated, and they make every effort to discharge the baby as soon as his medical condition permits. When the baby has stabilized, he is transferred to the nursery of a community hospital closer to the parents' home, where he will stay until he reaches the discharge weight of 4½ to 5 pounds. In the community hospital, parents can visit more often and learn to care for their baby in a comfortable, supportive setting.

Meanwhile, there are several steps parents can take to help them feel involved with their baby. The mother who wishes to breast-feed can begin expressing and freezing her breastmilk to keep her milk flowing and to build up a supply that can later be given to her baby. Parents might ask a local nurse or pediatrician or social worker to put them in contact with other parents who have had premature babies, parents who can give them moral support at this difficult time.

Many parents have been helped by a spiritual sort of bonding. One mother, when she was unable to visit, would hold her baby's picture and send "loving, healing thoughts." Another said, "I felt energy flowing from my body to the baby. Even though I wasn't with her, I felt we had bonded and I became very optimistic for her recovery." Distance is no barrier here.

# *Lacey's Story*

## By Gayla Edwards

Early in my pregnancy I felt something was wrong. In my fourth month I began having severe headaches at night. I was gaining weight rapidly even though I was careful about my diet. Occasionally my eyes would blur and my ears would ring. I had to quit my swimming classes because I was afraid of fainting. I was changing doctors at this time, and my new doctor was out of town for a month. The nurse told me to restrict my salt intake, which I was already doing.

One night after a strenuous evening of shopping, I woke up with an intense headache. I felt swollen—as if my sides were going to burst. Early the next morning, in a state of panic and confusion, I left without waking my husband or my son and drove myself to a nearby hospital. I knew something was terribly wrong, and I was frightened about the effect it would have on my baby. The doctors diagnosed pre-eclampsia (toxemia). My blood pressure was extremely high and my kidneys were not functioning properly. I would have to be hospitalized and they might have to deliver my baby. I was 6½ months pregnant.

My second night in the hospital I lost my eyesight. For the next 24 hours I was almost completely blind. I felt as if this could not be my body. So much was happening that was beyond my control.

The next day I was attached to monitors as the doctors tried to induce labor. After six hours I still hadn't dilated; a cesarean would be necessary. The baby would be extremely small, I was told, and probably would not survive. The baby would have to go to a hospital with an intensive care unit 70 miles away. I would be taken there to give birth and the baby could go right into the nursery. But just then the monitors showed that my condition was suddenly becoming quite serious. There was no time to lose. My doctor left to scrub for an emergency cesarean. I cried as I was wheeled into the operating room, fearing for my own life and the life of my baby. Through the anesthesia I felt an intense burning as they began the incision. I kept telling myself to be strong. Then I lost consciousness.

I first saw Lacey in the recovery room. They wheeled her to me in a transport Isolette. "She weighs two pounds, six ounces," said my husband Doug who had been with her the entire time. "Would you like to touch her?" I was helped to roll over so I could see her. I didn't touch her though. I felt it was wasting precious time, and I wanted her to go immediately to where she could be saved. Doug went along to be near her.

I kept hoping it was just a bad dream and that I would wake up. But once I was in my room the sadness came more strongly than ever. I felt as if my heart were being torn out. My baby, where is she? Is she all right?

I was kept in our community hospital for the next eight days. I had successfully breast-fed my son Robby, and I had planned to breast-feed the new baby. I told this to a nurse, who taught me how to use a breast pump. The first day I pumped two ounces, but after that I got less and less. I started out pumping twice a day, but soon my breasts became sore and I began to get discouraged. Each trip to the pump room was an emotional ordeal. I was almost always alone, and this was the time I missed my baby the most. One night my husband went with me to the pumping room. I felt embarrassed and sad for him to watch me using a machine instead of nursing our baby. It seemed so cold.

Although I knew my breastmilk could not be used because of the drugs I was being given for hypertension, I sent the milk to Lacey's hospital anyway. It was a gesture of my love and concern, the only one I could make at the time.

My breastmilk soon slowed to a trickle, but I was reassured by a woman from La Leche League. She said that fatigue and depression could hold the milk back, but that the milk was still there, and when the time came I would be able to nurse. She was right.

Meanwhile, I was receiving good news about Lacey's condition, accompanied by photographs, a set of footprints, and a note that said, "I'm not as small as you think, Mom." This helped me so much.

Then, the day I was released from the hospital, Lacey's doctor called to say that she had suffered a setback. A spinal tap showed meningitis and she also had a heart murmur. I was afraid to talk to him. I could only cry. Against my doctor's orders I decided to make the trip to Lacey's hospital. I knew I couldn't get better until I had seen my baby. It was a two-hour drive and I cried all the way. I was afraid she would die before Doug and I arrived.

I entered the nursery still weak from toxemia and shaking with fear, but when I saw Lacey in her Isolette I felt only warm and loving feelings for my precious baby girl. She seemed so skinny and fragile. Her largest features were her nose and her feet—my nose, Doug's feet. But I adjusted to her size immediately. Wearing gloves, I was able to touch Lacey. I talked to her and felt she could hear me. After my first visit she began to gain weight. I like to think it was because of mother-child bonding.

However, there was much that disturbed me. The monitors were frightening. I could hear them beeping long after I'd left the nursery. And many of the treatments Lacey received seemed cruel to me. Sometimes she would turn blue during spells of apnea and bradycardia. Though I handled my anxieties well when I was with her, I worried that when we left the hospital, the nurses wouldn't notice her monitor when she was in distress. One nurse in particular seemed inattentive. We complained to the doctor and then worried that we would be seen as troublemakers. At this point, I knew I needed help in dealing with my fears. I talked to another nurse, a male nurse, who had been especially nice to us, and he told me about the hospital's parent group.

Soon I was in touch with JoAnn from the parent support group, whose two children had been premature. I asked many questions about premies. We discussed my fears. She listened to me, gave me good advice and moral support.

Often I had to deal with the insensitive reactions of the people around me, such as the friend who came to the hospital but refused to look at the tiny premature babies, saying, "You're the one who wanted a baby, not me." Or the close relative who called at a time when Lacey was in especially critical condition to say, "We don't want her if she's not all there, honey. You know what I mean?" I didn't know. I wanted Lacey to live, no matter what. It was times like these when the support of caring people helped the most.

Soon I was visiting Lacey all day every day, holding her as much as I could, massaging her, changing her, dressing her in doll clothes, decorating her Isolette with toys and mobiles. It was difficult to leave each evening, especially if she was crying. I often left in tears, torn between Lacey and my husband and son at home. I felt better being able to discuss these feelings with JoAnn.

The nurses were very supportive, too, especially in my attempts to breast-feed. My milk supply was still very low. One nurse taught me to massage my breasts to encourage the milk to come in. I also found that hand expressing the milk was easier and less painful than using the pump. I was soon able to try nursing Lacey, but only a couple of minutes each shift so she wouldn't tire. After three days of this beautiful closeness, Lacey became jaundiced. The doctors didn't want her to have breastmilk until the cause of her jaundice was discovered. She was unable to nurse for the next 10 days, a terrible setback. Another barrier to breast-feeding, a psychological one, was that Lacey gained weight more slowly on breastmilk than on the higher-calorie formula. I wanted her to gain quickly so she could come home as soon as possible. But it was explained to me that the rapid weight gain in formula-fed babies wasn't necessarily desirable and could contribute to other problems such as anemia.

*Lacey at age 3.*

A week before Lacey came home from the hospital, I began working with her again to get her to breast-feed. An hour before each feeding I would begin talking to her, while rubbing her hands and feet to wake her. After she had nursed, I would give her a bottle and later express my breastmilk to add just a little more to her formula. We continued this technique once Lacey was home. Finally, two weeks after she had come home, ten weeks after her birth, Lacey was fully breast-feeding. Although I know I would be just as close to Lacey if I were bottle-feeding her, I feel that the psychological rewards I received from my breast-feeding her have been great. It is hard for me to look at my nursing six-month-old-baby and believe she is the baby in those early pictures. We've both come a long way.

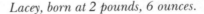

*Lacey, born at 2 pounds, 6 ounces.*

*Update: 1982.* Lacey nursed until a week before her first birthday, when she weaned herself to a cup. She's always been a very independent child but at the same time quite lovable and friendly. It's hard to believe that someone who began life in such a difficult way could be this trusting and cheerful. She recently started nursery school and made friends with everyone immediately. Her development is normal. She's had the usual babyhood ailments, but her health wasn't adversely affected by her prematurity. Although she is still somewhat small at age three, she's finally "made the chart" and is growing fast.

# 4

# *At First Sight*

"I really didn't know what to expect, a blob of protoplasm I guess, but our (28-week) daughter had arms, legs, fingers, and toes. She cried when she was born and pee'd all over the doctor."

*

"I expected a smaller version of a full-term baby. Instead, she looked like a spider monkey."

*

"The premies took some getting used to. At first they seemed painfully frail. But after a while I couldn't walk past the regular newborn nursery without thinking how fat and ugly all those *full-term* babies looked."

*

"The doctors asked if I wanted to see the twins. On the table lay a small red thing that reminded me of pictures I'd seen of concentration camp victims. This was 'Baby A'—my oldest son. There was a tube in his mouth and another in his navel, and there were wires attached to his body. 'Baby B' looked even worse. He was smaller and badly bruised. I thought they were beautiful. Tentatively I touched the inside of Baby A's hand. It was a reflex, I'm sure. He didn't know what he was doing, but he did it. He grabbed my finger. I was a father."

***

A premature baby, at first sight, evokes both distress and amazement. Compared to a full-term baby, he presents an alarming picture. His small scrawny body is limp. His arms and legs stretch straight out or are contorted in bizarre positions. His head seems too large for his body. His reddish, translucent skin hangs in folds from his arms and legs. The protruding stomach, out of proportion to the baby's tiny chest, makes him resemble malnourished infants in news photographs. And yet, the baby is completely formed, a miniature person. Mothers and fathers marvel that their baby, even their *extremely* premature baby, has arms, legs, genitals, fingers, and toes, not to mention the wondrous details of hair, eyebrows, nails, and lashes. The baby can open his eyes. He blinks at a bright light. He startles at a loud noise. He stretches and yawns, sneezes, and

hiccups. If not intubated, he can cry. Some premature babies are already sucking their thumbs, a skill they acquired *before* birth.

In this chapter we look at the premature baby and see how he develops in the nursery during the time he would normally be in his mother's womb. And because so many parents are surprised at first—in both negative and positive ways—by their premature baby's appearance and behavior, we look at how the baby was developing *before* his premature delivery.

## A Baby's Development from Conception to Week 24

Let's start at the beginning—or rather two weeks before the beginning—on the first day of the mother's last menstrual period. Few women can be certain of the exact day they conceived, but most mothers know when they last menstruated. For this reason doctors use the first day of the mother's period as day 1 of the baby's gestation, even though the egg is actually fertilized about 14 days later.* This is why a baby who is, for example, 27 weeks old from *conception* is said to have a *gestational age* of 29 weeks. By this method of reckoning, a term pregnancy lasts 40 weeks or 10 lunar months (about 9 calendar months). A premature birth occurs before the 37th completed week.

## *Weeks 1 to 4 of Gestation*

Around the end of the second week, egg and sperm unite to begin a new life. Two weeks later the fertilized egg has divided into many smaller cells to

*This method has its drawbacks. It is not accurate for women whose periods are irregular or for mothers who experience breakthrough bleeding (which may be mistaken for a period) during early pregnancy. Doctors use many other criteria, discussed in this chapter, to determine a baby's gestational age.

form a hollow ball. Inside the ball is a disc two cell layers thick that will soon be recognizable as a human baby. The other cells form the placenta and chorion, which nourish and protect the growing fetus. By the time the mother has missed her first menstrual period, the fertilized egg has quadrupled in size. It is now as big as the head of a pin and is nestled securely in the wall of her womb.

## Weeks 5 to 12

By the third week after fertilization, the fifth week of gestation, the disc of cells has begun to curve and grow. A third cell layer emerges. From these three layers the various tissues of the baby's body begin to form. Soon the baby has a head, tail, and primitive umbilical cord. A tube-like heart begins to beat. The brain develops two lobes, and a spinal cord is visible. By the eighth week (when the mother may already have had a positive pregnancy test), the baby's tiny heart is beating 65 times a minute. Arms, legs, fingers, toes, and facial features are beginning to take shape. The eyes appear as large dark spots on the head. Heart, brain, and liver are visible through the baby's transparent skin. A skeleton of cartilage is forming. Ovaries or testicles are developing. In males the penis now appears. The baby weighs about one gram (1/28th of an ounce) and is almost an inch long.

## Weeks 13 to 16

After 13 weeks of gestation the baby's arms, legs, fingers, and toes are formed. Fingernails and toenails start to grow. Markings begin to appear on the palms of the hands and soles of the feet. (By the sixth month the baby will have fingerprints and footprints.) The facial features are assuming more normal proportions. The ears are taking shape, and eyelids cover the eyes. The eyelids fuse shut and will remain sealed until sometime between the 24th to 26th week. The heart is beating 117 to 157 times a minute, the stomach is producing digestive juices, the liver is making blood cells, and the kidneys are producing urine, which the baby excretes into the amniotic fluid. The muscles respond to stimulation. The baby becomes active—kicking, moving his arms, wiggling fingers and toes. He can make a fist, open his mouth, move his lips, and swallow. Because the baby is still quite small (three inches in length, 30 grams or so in

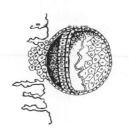

Weeks 1–4. Two weeks after fertilization, the egg has divided into a many-celled hollow ball. Inside are two cell layers that will soon be recognizable as a human baby.

Soon the baby has a head and tail. A tube-like heart begins to beat. The brain develops two lobes; a spinal cord is visible.

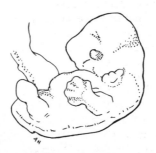

Weeks 5–12. Arms, legs, fingers, toes, and facial features are forming. The eyes appear as dark spots on the sides of the head.

Weeks 13–16. At this stage, all the baby's organs and physical features are present. From now on the changes that take place are ones of growth, maturation, and refinement.

weight), the mother may not feel motion in her womb for another month. *At this stage all the baby's major organs and physical features are present. From now on, the changes that take place will be ones of growth, maturation, and refinement.*

## Weeks 17 to 24

From the 13th to the 20th week of gestation the baby undergoes a rapid growth spurt. By the end of the 20th week he is 10 to 12 inches long, or half his length at (full-term) birth. Although the baby is still very skinny, fat is beginning to be deposited under the skin. The baby weighs about a pound now. Although he is half as long as he will be at term (40 weeks), he is only an eighth as heavy. A downy fur called *lanugo* covers his body. Eyebrows and eyelashes appear. Flat, pink nipples develop on the chest. Bone is replacing the cartilage skeleton. The heart pumps about 25 quarts of blood a day.

Sometime between the 16th and 20th weeks, most mothers feel the kicks of their increasingly strong and active baby. During these weeks the baby begins to practice skills that he will need after birth. He tries out breathing motions by inhaling and exhaling amniotic fluid (this does no harm, since he receives all his oxygen through the umbilical cord). The baby's sense of hearing is also developing. He can hear his mother's internal organs and her voice as well as sounds from the outside world. He may react to a sudden loud noise. He spends a great deal of his time sleeping and probably has a favorite position for napping. He has an individual sleep-wake cycle, which, if his mother is lucky, coincides somewhat with her own.

Between the 21st and 24th week, the baby's skin begins to secrete a greasy white substance called *vernix*, which coats the delicate skin like protective ointment.

Sometime between the 24th and 26th weeks, the baby's eyelids, fused since the third month, open. In the past, babies born with fused eyelids were thought to be too immature to survive. But recent efforts to save some of these babies have been successful. Survival depends more on the maturity of their other organs than on whether or not the eyelids are fused.

The 24th week is also a legal turning point for the fetus. After the 24th week, usually between the 24th and 28th weeks, the fetus becomes viable, or capable of life outside the womb. At this point, abortion may be prohibited except when necessary to preserve the life or health of the mother.*

# Very Premature Babies: Babies Born from Week 25 to Week 30

## Vital Statistics

Every year in the United States 35,000 to 39,000 very premature babies are born, comprising slightly over 1% of all live births. These babies range in length from 11 to 18 inches and in weight from 2 to 3½ pounds, although a 25-weeker may weigh as little as 600 grams (1 pound, 5 ounces) and a thirty-week baby can weigh as much as 1750 grams (3 pounds, 14 ounces) and still be within normal limits.

Factors besides age influence a premature baby's size. If his mother has eaten very well during pregnancy, he may be on the large side. If his parents were large (or small) as babies, he may be large (or small) too. Infants born at high altitudes generally weigh a bit less than those born at sea level. Black premature babies are, on the average, 80 grams (almost three ounces) heavier than white babies of the same gestational age up until the 30th week of pregnancy; after that, white babies are heavier. Later in this chapter we discuss babies who are *abnormally* large or small for their gestational ages.

A few extra ounces (and the extra maturity these ounces represent) can make a big difference in the very premature baby's ability to survive. While babies under two pounds have a slightly better than 50-50 chance, babies who weigh 3½ pounds have a 90% survival rate. The baby's sex and race also influence survival. Girls have a better chance to survive than boys. Blacks, born prematurely, survive at higher rates than whites. Presumably, females and blacks mature earlier in pregnancy. Black females have the best survival statistics, followed by black males, white females, and white males. But every baby is an individual. Two infants of the same sex, race, birth weight, and gestational age may be very different in their level of maturity and their abilities to cope with the world outside the womb.

---

*In a 1979 decision (Colautti v. Franklin), the Supreme Court ruled that the precise moment of viability for an individual infant could not be established by law, but must be left to the determination of the attending physician.

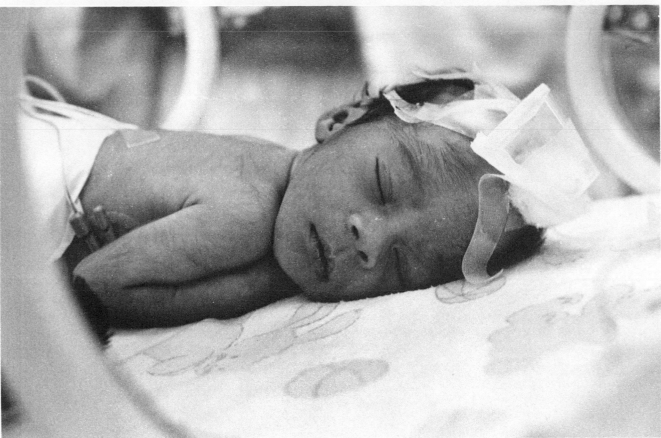

*Fetal hair, lanugo, can be quite heavy or it may merely give a peach-fuzz-like covering to the skin.*

## Appearance

A very premature baby is born with a thick coating of white vernix. This is washed off after birth, revealing the red, wrinkled folds of the baby's skin. The skin is translucent. Tiny veins are visible below the surface. Sometimes the baby's tissues have filled with fluid, a condition called *edema*, which gives him a deceptively chubby appearance. Premature babies of all ethnic groups have the same dusky red skin color when they are born. Their natural skin color or pigmentation develops three to six weeks later.

During the final four weeks of pregnancy, a *full-term* baby gains a pound or more each week. The premature infant misses out on this baby fat. It is this lack of fat filling out his skin folds that gives the premie his wrinkled appearance and makes his fingers, toes, and nose seem so disproportionately long.

The premature baby's facial features are well developed except for his outer ears, which are still very soft and limp. They lie flat against his head; when folded over, they do not spring back. As the baby matures, the cartilage becomes firmer and his ears take on their regular shape.

Since the 20th week of gestation, the baby's hair has been growing. By the time of his premature birth it covers his head. A premature baby's hair is fine and fuzzy; it tends to clump togehter like bits of down. The baby also has eyebrows and eyelashes and hair on much of his body. This fetal hair, or lanugo, can be quite heavy (especially around the shoulders) or it may merely give a peach-fuzz-like covering to the skin. During the final weeks of pregnancy, the term baby sheds most of his lanugo. The prematurely born baby loses most of his fetal hair by his due date.

Even the very premature baby has fingernails and toenails, which usually reach the ends of the fingers (or toes) by 35 weeks. At term (40 weeks), the baby can give himself and others a nasty scratch if his nails aren't trimmed.

A premature baby's bones are quite soft and easily molded, especially the bones of the skull. Before birth, amniotic fluid surrounds the baby's head and exerts equal pressure on all parts. But once the baby is born, his nicely symmetrical, rounded head begins to flatten from the firm surfaces on which he lies.

This elongation and flattening of the skull bones are temporary. Once the baby is older and able to hold his head up for most of the day (air, like amniotic fluid, exerts equal pressure), his head begins to assume its normal shape. Although the baby's head may never be quite as round as it would have been if he'd gone to term, by the age of two or three this effect of prematurity should be almost unnoticeable.

Both boys and girls have immature genitals, which look unusual in comparison with those of a term baby. In premature baby girls, the outer vaginal tissues, the labia majora, are widely spread and small.

45

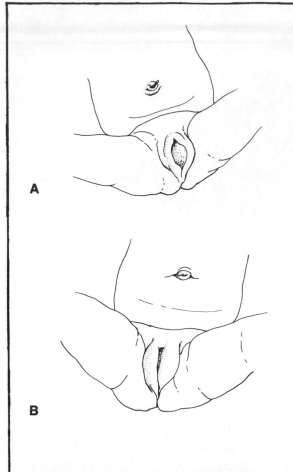

The premature baby girl's inner vaginal tissues are not yet covered (A) as they will be at term (B).

The premature baby boy's testicles have not yet descended (A) as they will at term (B).

The inner tissues, the labia minora and the clitoris, are large and prominent. At about 40 weeks the labia majora completely cover the inner tissues, giving the vagina its normal appearance.

In very premature boys the testes are still inside the body and have not yet descended into the scrotum, the sac behind the penis. The scrotum itself is small and smooth. Sometime between the 36th and 40th weeks, the testes descend and fill the scrotum, which has now become covered with wrinkles (rugae).

The very premature baby has almost no muscle tension or tone. He lies passively. If his arms or legs are lifted and then dropped, they fall heavily. Muscle tone starts to appear around the 30th week. It first appears in the legs and proceeds upward toward the head. The first sign the baby shows of this developing tone is a slight bending of the legs at the knees and hips caused by the contraction of his leg muscles. The degree of bending increases over a period of weeks as the baby gains greater control over his muscles.

Because he lacks muscle tone, the premature baby is very limp and flexible. When his arm is draped across his neck like a scarf or his heel is raised to touch his ear, he offers no resistance. These maneuvers are used by doctors to test the baby's gestational age—the more resistance from muscles and connective tissue, the older the baby. Although these positions look very uncomfortable to an adult, they cause the baby no pain or harm. In fact, some premature babies like to sleep with their feet tucked up next to their heads in a position they may have enjoyed in the womb.

The premature baby's posture reflects his limp muscle tone. When he is held under his stomach, his arms, legs, and head dangle loosely. When pulled to a sitting position, his head lags backwards, and he is unable to raise it. In a sitting position, his head slumps forward. When held upright under his arms, he slips through the holder's grasp. The premature baby *does* have a gripping reflex with his fingers, but unlike the full-term baby his muscles are too weak for him to maintain his grip when lifted by his hands.

## Pre-Terms and Full-Terms Compared

Doctors cannot always tell by size alone if a baby is premature. Some full-terms are born smaller than normal and some prematures, especially infants of diabetic mothers, are unusually large. But prematures differ from full-terms in various other aspects of appearance and behavior. Here are a few of the characteristics physicians use to determine whether or not a baby is premature and, if the baby *is* premature, to what degree. Using these and other criteria, tests of newborn maturity such as the Dubowitz scoring system can determine a baby's gestational age at birth with an accuracy of plus or minus two weeks.

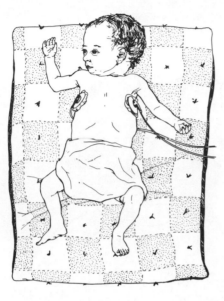

A premature baby has little muscle tone. He lies with his arms and legs straight out or slightly bent. The baby's muscle tone and the degree of bending in his arms and legs increases somewhat as he gets older. This baby's posture is that of a 34–36 week gestational-age premie.

A newborn full-term, by contrast, keeps his arms and legs drawn up close to his body. This very tight muscle tone relaxes in the weeks following delivery.

A premature has a grasping reflex with his fingers, but too little strength to be lifted by his grasp.

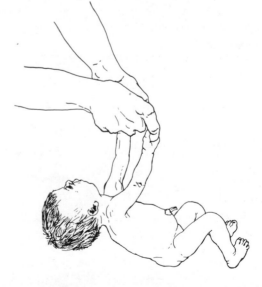

A full-term can grasp the examiner's finger tightly and exert enough pull to lift himself off the table.

## Pre-Terms and Full-Terms Compared

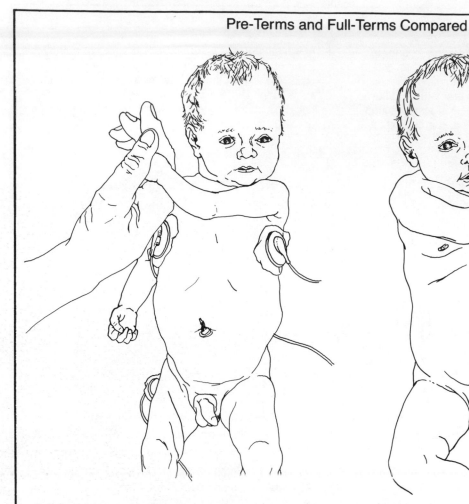

A premature baby's elbow passes the midline of his body when his arm is pulled across his neck like a scarf. This baby shows a degree of flexibility typical of a 30–36-week gestational-age premie.

A full-term baby's arm is less flexible. The elbow cannot be pulled as far as the midline of the baby's body.

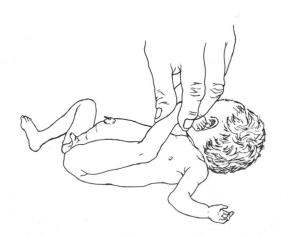

A young premature's leg is so flexible that the foot can easily be raised to touch the ear. The degree of flexibility shown here is typical of a baby of 30 weeks gestational age, or younger.

The heel-to-ear maneuver is impossible with a full-term.

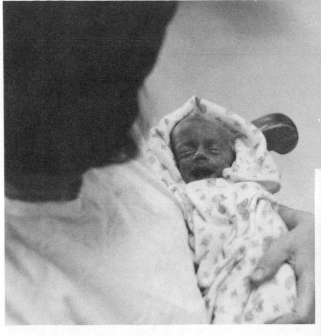

*This newborn premie's reflex smiling . . .*

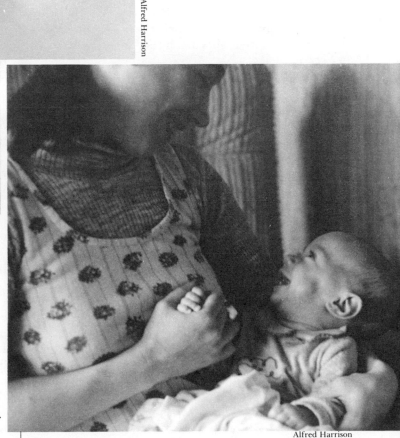

Alfred Harrison

*is different from his social
smiling several months later.*

## Behavior

The very premature baby's nervous system is still in a delicate stage of growth and differentiation. The nervous system of a *full-term* baby has developed to the extent that the infant can focus selectively on elements of his environment while his brain regulates his bodily functions automatically. This is not always possible for a premature baby, who may have difficulty looking, listening, and remembering to breathe all at the same time. His neurological "circuits" are easily overloaded by the constant bombardment of sights, sounds, and sensations of the world outside the womb. When he is tired or overly excited, he may have spells of forgetting to breath (apnea) and of lower than normal heart rate (bradycardia).

Because of his immature nervous system and poor muscle tone, the baby's movements are weak and poorly controlled. His arms and legs flail about in a disorganized way with lots of jerks and startles. This is normal behavior for a premie. As he matures, his movements become smoother and more purposeful.

Before the age of 28 weeks, the baby sleeps almost constantly. At times, he is in a calm, quiet sleep, consuming little oxygen, with a stable heartbeat and breathing rate. More often, he dozes restlessly in what is called "active" sleep. He breathes unevenly, his heartbeat is irregular, his eyes move rapidly back and forth under closed lids. This active sleep is also called REM, or rapid eye movement, sleep. When an adult in REM sleep is awakened, he usually says that he has been having a dream. It is not known whether the premature baby dreams during REM sleep (or what he could be dreaming about), but his behavior is similar to a dreaming adult. He may gasp, cry out, or smile and grimace in rapid succession.

Reflex smiling is common among very premature babies. It is not the same as social smiling that begins two to three months after term. Girl babies, who smile socially more than boy babies, also do *twice* as much reflex smiling.

During REM sleep the premature baby may move his mouth in a rhythmic sucking or chewing fashion, referred to as "non-nutritive sucking." Nutritive sucking, used to obtain food, is a skill the baby acquires around the 29th or 30th week. It differs from non-nutritive sucking by its steady one-suck-per-second pace.

Another reflex—the startle—occurs most frequently during quiet, or non-REM, sleep and seems to act as a discharge of energy. The baby will suddenly fling arms and legs apart. Boys startle more than girls.

The 28-week baby spends almost 100% of his time asleep; approximately 85% of that sleep is of the restless REM variety, while 15% is quiet sleep. As he matures, the total amount of time he sleeps will decrease, as will the amount of time he spends in REM sleep. The full-term newborn, by comparison, sleeps about 75% of the time, with less than 50% of that sleep being REM sleep.

The baby in the womb becomes accustomed to his mother's biorhythms, her normal times for sleeping and waking. Doctors (and parents) have wondered what effects the nursery's constant light and activity might have on the premature baby. In one experiment at the Child Development Unit of Boston's Children's Hospital, doctors began covering the babies' Isolettes at night to simulate the normal cycle of day and night. Four days later, the babies in the experiment were eating better and gaining more weight.

After 28 weeks, the baby begins to have increasingly longer periods of alertness in which to interact with his environment. But to what extent is he capable of sensing his environment?

## What the Baby Can Feel, Taste, Smell, See, and Hear

Even the very premature baby knows the difference between a pleasurable and painful touch. The baby is calmed by his mother's gentle massage, by being held and rocked, or by being swaddled in a warm blanket. He may react to a painful stimulus, like a heel stick, with a spell of apnea and bradycardia or he may "tune it all out" by drifting off to sleep. Most very premature babies enjoy being covered, firmly wrapped, or contained. They may nestle against the side of the Isolette or cuddle up to a rubber glove filled with warm water (which some nurseries use as an additional heat source) as if they miss the warm, watery enclosure of the womb.

The very premature baby can taste the difference between something sweet and something salty. Like most children, he tends to prefer the former.

A *full-term* baby has a sense of smell so well developed that he can recognize his mother by her scent alone. No one knows for certain what a premature baby can smell, but some nurseries place an article of the mother's clothing in the baby's Isolette in hopes that it will give him a sense of her comforting presence.

Between the 24th and 26th weeks the baby can open his eyes. He blinks or closes his eyes tightly in a bright light. As the premature baby matures and recovers from illness, he may begin to have brief periods of visual responsiveness. Healthy prematures as young as 29 weeks have been seen to follow, or track, a moving object with their eyes. By 30 weeks some prematures are able to respond selectively to patterns. By 35 to 36 weeks the baby, if healthy, has visual abilities similar to those of a full-term baby; like the full-term, he seems to show an innate preference for the human face.

The baby's eyes mature rather early. By the eighth month, they are ready to see. But seeing is not merely a function of the eye; it also involves the brain. Like a camera, the eye "takes" the picture, but it must be transmitted to the brain to be "developed."

There is now a way to test how quickly the visual centers of the brain receive and decode, or make sense of, that picture. A light is flashed before the baby's eyes. Electrodes placed on the baby's head pick up electrical activity from the visual centers of the brain. The time it takes for the light impulse to travel from the eye to the brain can therefore be measured. This interval between stimulus to the eye and response in the brain is called the latency period. The shorter this latency period, the quicker the picture "develops" and, presumably, the better the baby can see. Before 34 weeks, most babies have a long latency period. As they mature, the latency period becomes shorter and shorter.

The premature baby, like the full-term newborn, has poor control of his eye movements. His eyes do not work together most of the time and may appear to be crossed or out of alignment. Babies usually learn to keep their eyes centered and moving together by four to six months after term.

The very premature baby may startle at a loud noise, but often his response to sound is more subtle. He may stop moving, he may open his mouth or widen his eyes. His breathing pattern may change. When noise is irritating, he may react with a spell of apnea or bradycardia. Dr. Peter Gorski recounts the case of a premature infant whose vital signs would plummet every time the doctors made their rounds. It seems that their discussions close to bed disturbed him. When the doctors moved their conferences to the other side of the room, the baby improved.

Sometimes the baby reacts to annoying sounds by shutting them out entirely. This is called *habituation*. It is a normal way for newborns to cope with a stressful environment. One mother related, "Our baby was on a warming table next to the lab phone. It was very loud. Every time that phone rang, *I* jumped a mile, but the baby just lay there. I was sure he was deaf. Then one day a nurse dropped a hemostat next to his bed. It fell to the floor with a loud clatter, and our baby practically leapt off the mattress. He had been tuning out the constant ring of the lab phone, but this new noise really startled him."

Impulses from the ear, like those from the eye, must be processed by the brain. Brain wave tracings show that very premature babies have long latency periods between the time a sound is picked up by the ear and the time it is received by the brain. The latency periods become shorter as the baby matures. Once again, no one is certain how well the very premature baby can hear, but if there is any sound he might recognize, it would be his mother's voice, which he heard in the womb before birth. Premature babies, like full-terms, usually turn toward their mother's voice in preference to others. Several studies have shown enhanced development and greater attentiveness in prematures who regularly heard recordings of their mother's voices during their stay in the nursery.

The baby is also accustomed to hearing his mother's internal organs—her heartbeat, the pulsations of her arteries, the churning noise of the placenta. Scientists have recorded these sounds from the womb, and they are being played in nurseries throughout the country to calm "homesick" full-term and premature newborns.

# Moderately Premature Babies: Babies Born from Week 31 to Week 36

Each year in the United States between 150,000 to 200,000 babies are born 4 to 9 weeks too early. These moderately premature babies are generally 16 to 19 inches in length and range from 1500 to 2500 grams in weight. Survival rates among these infants are an excellent 90 to 98%, although respiratory dis-

tress syndrome (see page 58) and infection still pose a small, but significant, threat. *Contrary to widespread myth, babies born in the eighth month do not have a poorer prognosis than babies born in the seventh month. The older the baby, the greater the chance for survival.*

The moderately premature baby is plumper and sturdier in appearance than the very premature baby. He is not as flexible as the younger premature. For example, when his arm is pulled across his neck (the scarf sign), his elbow will not pass much further than the midline of his body. He offers increasing resistance when his heel is brought to his ear, and after the 34th week this maneuver becomes impossible. His increased muscle tone is evident in his resting posture. He keeps his arms and legs slightly bent. When placed on his stomach, his arms and legs go out to the side in a froglike position. Nevertheless, he still has far less tone than the full-term baby. Even at 36 weeks, he does not present the same compact bundle as the 40-week-old infant, who lies with his arms tight against his body and legs drawn up under his abdomen.

A moderately premature baby's skin is thicker and more opaque than that of the very early premature. Lanugo is less evident on his face and body. His ears have more shape and resilience. When the outer ear is folded over, it slowly returns to its normal position. The baby's fingernails may now reach his fingertips. By the 36th week, the baby boy's testicles are beginning to descend into the scrotum, and the baby girl's outer vaginal tissues are growing to cover the clitoris.

The moderately premature baby has brief periods of spontaneous alertness, periods that lengthen and become more frequent with increasing age. At times he seems to be actively taking in the world around him. He may make eye contact with his parents, the nurse, or doctor, or he may focus on a colorful mobile or toy.

He still spends much of his time asleep, but the nature of his sleep is changing. REM sleep is declining in proportion to quiet sleep. The jittery motions, frequent startles, and reflex smiling and frowning are still present—even full-term newborns display this behavior—but they are less evident than with the younger prematures. Compared to the very premature baby, the older infant is definitely more in control. His movements are smoother and seem more purposeful. He may bring his hand to his mouth or move his arms and legs in an alternating pattern. When pulled to a sitting position, he makes an effort to hold up his head.

He is also in better control of his physiological processes. He may still have spells of apnea and bradycardia, especially when fatigued, but he can handle more stimulation without forgetting to breathe than can younger babies. When he reaches a weight of 1750 grams, he may be able to control his body temperature in an open crib.

By the 34th week the baby may have coordinated the skills needed to nipple-feed. Since his early days in the womb, the baby has practiced his sucking. By the 30th week he will consistently turn his head and mouth in the direction of anything that touches his cheek, as if searching for a nipple. This is called the *rooting reflex*. About the same time, the baby may start to gag on his gavage tube. This *gag reflex*, which helps keep the baby from choking, must appear before nipple-feeding can begin. The baby may also begin to chew or suck on the gavage tube during feedings. He may frequently bring his hand to his mouth. All these are signs of readiness for the nipple.

## Very Premature Babies at 31 to 36 Weeks

At 31 to 36 weeks of age, a baby who was born very prematurely is rarely the same in appearance or behavior as the baby *born* at this stage. He will almost certainly be smaller. A typical 29-week baby might weigh 1200 grams at birth. Like most newborns, he immediately loses weight—usually between 150 to 200 grams. It may take the baby 2 to 3 weeks just to regain his birthweight. If he is quite ill, it may take even longer. Once the baby has regained his birthweight and is on the road to recovery, he gains, ideally, at a rate of 10 to 20 grams a day. Under the best of conditions, he then weighs only 1750 grams at 36 weeks. By contrast, babies *born* at 36 weeks weigh an average 2500 grams.

The very premature baby who reaches 31 to 36 weeks may also be less mature in his behavior than the baby born at this age. He may be less alert and less in control of his body. He may not be ready to nipple-feed or sleep in an open crib. A baby who was seriously ill after birth may take an especially long time to catch up.

## Borderline Prematures: Babies Born During Weeks 37 to 38

Between 600,000 and 700,000 babies are born in the United States each year during the 37th or 38th week of pregnancy. Their appearance and weight are usually similar to those of a 40-week baby. Technically speaking, a 38-week baby is not premature. But even this close to term, each day in the womb is important. Babies born 2 to 3 weeks before their due date may still be vulnerable to such problems of immaturity as excessive jaundice, unstable body temperature, or feeding difficulties. The survival rate for the 37- to 38-week infant is well above 98%. However, respiratory distress syndrome still poses a slight threat, and a baby of any age with this disease is seriously ill. As one parent put it, "No matter what the statistics, when it happens to *your* baby, it's 100%."

## The Premature Baby at Term (40 Weeks)

A premature baby at 40 weeks is different from a full-term newborn. Premature birth and the illnesses that accompany it slow the baby's growth. Our hypothetical 29-week baby with a 1200-gram birthweight weighed 1750 grams at 36 weeks. By 40 weeks he will weigh around 2500 grams or five pounds, eight ounces. This is assuming an optimal growth pattern. Many such babies weigh a great deal less.

The premature baby has also been set back in his development. At 40 weeks his behavior is not as advanced as that of a full-term baby. His brain wave patterns are less mature. He is not as visually responsive. His sleep-wake cycle is not as well organized or predictable as that of the term infant. He may be irritable and difficult to soothe. Though he is often more active than the full-term newborn, the premie at 40 weeks generally does not do as well as full-terms in tests of neurological development.

Drs. Peter Gorski, Martha Davison, and T. Berry Brazelton have proposed a list of abilities that reflect a newborn's level of neurological maturity. The most basic ability is the control of bodily functions such as respiration and heartbeat that are necessary for life. The second is the capacity to maintain muscle tone and perform certain controlled movements such as bringing the hand to the mouth. Third, the baby must be able to remain alert for positive stimulation. Finally, the baby should show a consistent reaction to pleasant sights and sounds in his environment; he should "respond reliably and selectively in a social interaction with a nurturing adult."

Most premature babies achieve the first two stages of neurological maturity while still in the nursery. But at about 40 weeks, when many prematures go home from the hospital, they often have not mastered the final two stages. As a result, parents may bring home a baby whose behavior is inconsistent, puzzling, and distressing.

Their baby may not give them clear signals when he wants to eat or sleep, when he has had too much stimulation or not enough. He may be excessively fussy or spend most of his time asleep.

Many parents wrongly blame themselves for their baby's temporarily immature behavior patterns. The guilt they feel about their "hyper" or "unresponsive" baby can have a snowballing negative effect on their relationship with the child. They may avoid or overstimulate the baby, further worsening his behavior and their own frustration.

Later we will look at the behavior of the premature baby in the hospital and at home and give suggestions on interpreting the baby's cues and responding appropriately to his needs.

# Babies Who Are Too Small

Any baby with a birthweight below 2500 grams (five pounds, eight ounces) is a *low-birthweight* baby (LBW). For a 35- or 36-week premie, a 2500-gram birthweight is *appropriate* for his *gestational age* (AGA). But a full-term baby who weighs 2500 grams is *small* for *gestational age* (SGA). His weight falls below the 10th percentile for full-term babies. A low birthweight is normal for a premie; for a full-term baby, it is abnormal, indicating that he may have suffered disease or deprivation in the womb.

A premature baby can also be small for gestational age. A 35-week baby who weighs 1500 grams at birth is both LBW (weight below 2500 grams) and SGA (below the 10th percentile in weight for babies his age). Such conditions as uterine or placental malformations can cause the baby to be born too small (SGA) as well as too soon (premature).

If a baby's growth is retarded early in pregnancy, the baby is uniformly small but has fairly normal body proportions. Causes of early growth retardation—that is, causes that begin affecting the baby before the 24th week of pregnancy—include chromosomal abnormalities such as Down's syndrome, and fetal infections such as herpes, German measles, cytomegalovirus, or toxoplasmosis. If the mother is a heavy user of drugs or alcohol, her baby's growth can be affected quite early in pregnancy.

When growth slows later in pregnancy, the baby's length and head circumference may be close to normal, but he will lack fat, and some of his organs may be abnormally small. Growth retardation after the 24th week may be caused by such diseases in the mother as heart, kidney, or lung problems; toxemia; high blood pressure; or sickle cell anemia. Malforma-

**Growth Rates for Infants in the Womb**

LENGTH ____ cm

WEEK OF GESTATION

WEIGHT ____ gm

PRE-TERM | TERM | POST TERM

Above the 90th percentile = large for gestational age (LGA).

Between the 10th and 90th percentiles = appropriate for gestational age (AGA).

Below the 10th percentile = small for gestational age (SGA)

tions of the uterus or placenta may decrease circulation to the baby, partially depriving him of food and oxygen.

Multiple pregnancies tend to end early and produce babies of lower than normal birthweight. Twins, for most of the pregnancy, grow at a rate similar to that of a single baby. But after the 34th week they may begin to crowd each other out. Triplets begin to slow in growth by the 30th week, quadruplets by the 26th week.

Maternal malnutrition may also cause low birthweight. Animal studies show that poor diet during pregnancy results in smaller offspring. Human mothers living in poverty have a higher incidence both of premature and low-birthweight babies. Nevertheless, the actual amount of harm to the baby from a poor diet during pregnancy remains a subject of controversy. During World War II, inhabitants of Nazi-occupied Holland were subjected to severe starvation, yet birthweights of their infants fell only by an average 200 grams (seven ounces). And the fact remains that most mothers who deliver infants small for gestational age show no evidence of malnutrition.

Smoking is another possible cause of intrauterine growth retardation. Nicotine, cyanide, and other ingredients found in cigarette smoke may be directly toxic to the fetus. Carbon monoxide from cigarette smoke displaces oxygen circulating in the mother's and baby's bloodstream. Chronic oxygen deprivation may result. Smoking may have an adverse effect on protein and carbohydrate metabolism, and it may also cause vitamin $B^6$, $B^{12}$, and C deficiencies in both mother and fetus.

Some babies are small for normal genetic reasons. Their parents were small. It runs in the family.

For many SGA babies, no cause can be found to explain their smaller than normal size.

SGA babies are often alert and anxious-looking. Parents and hospital staff note that these babies are likely to be exceptionally irritable and hard to soothe. Many dislike being held or cuddled.

The SGA baby is particularly vulnerable during delivery. Because he has been undernourished and deprived of oxygen during gestation, he may not be strong enough to withstand the birth process. He may be born with hypoglycemia (low blood sugar) and require special monitoring and intravenous feedings.

The premature baby who is SGA has all the normal problems of prematurity plus the added disadvantages that result from abnormal growth before birth.

# Babies Who Are Too Large

A baby who is above the 90th percentile in weight is considered large for gestational age (LGA). He may be premature, overdue, or born at term. The LGA baby may simply be large because of an inherited tendency—his parents were probably also big at birth. Such babies are normal, although they are at higher risk for birth trauma during a vaginal delivery. Many are more safely delivered by cesarean section.

Maternal diabetes is the other common cause of LGA babies. In the womb, the baby of a diabetic mother receives greater than normal amounts of glucose, or blood sugar. The baby grows accordingly. At birth, the baby often has difficulties maintaining proper blood sugar levels. The baby is also quite vulnerable to respiratory distress syndrome and to a condition called *polycythemia*, sluggish circulation of the blood caused by an overabundance of red blood cells.

Diabetic pregnancy is associated with a high incidence of toxemia, polyhydramnios, and congenital defects. Because of the high fatality rate among infants of diabetic mothers who are allowed to go to term, many of these babies are delivered prematurely on purpose, either by inducing labor or by performing a cesarean section. Many diabetic mothers go into pre-term labor on their own. The pre-term LGA infant of a diabetic mother may weigh nine pounds or more, yet still be immature and vulnerable to the usual complications of prematurity.

# 5

# The Problems of Prematurity

## The Birth Transition

### The Full-Term Baby at Birth

A newborn baby takes his first gasping breath and begins to cry. It seems so simple. And yet complex changes are happening in the baby's body at this very moment—changes crucial to his survival outside the womb.

Birth is a stressful process for any baby, but some of the stresses of birth actually benefit the full-term infant by helping him begin to breathe. Labor contractions, which bear down on his body with a force of 30 pounds or more, squeeze his chest and clear his lungs of fluid. The stresses of labor also leave the baby *slightly* hypoxic, or oxygen-deprived. Low levels of oxygen in the blood act on respiratory centers in the brain to induce the baby to make breathing motions. The new, startling sensations of cold, light, and noise also seem to stimulate the baby to begin and continue breathing.

The first breath is the hardest. The baby must inhale a large volume of air to inflate his lungs. Then, when he exhales, some of the air from that first breath stays in his lungs so that they always remain partially open. The full-term infant produces a fatty substance in his lungs called *surfactant*. Surfactant lines the *alveoli* (the lung's tiny air sacs) and prevents their thin, wet walls from collapsing and forcing out this residual air. With the lungs partially expanded, the baby needs to inhale less air with his subsequent breaths. Breathing becomes easier, much as inflating a balloon becomes easier after the first difficult puff.

As the baby begins to breathe, the pattern of blood flow through his body changes dramatically. Before birth, the baby's blood received oxygen in the placenta. The baby's heart circulated the blood from the placenta, through his body, and back to the placenta again. Most of this blood bypassed the baby's own tightly closed lungs and flowed instead through the *ductus arteriosus,* a short fetal blood vessel connecting the pulmonary artery (the artery leading from the heart to the lungs) with the aorta—the artery that originates in the heart and supplies the body's tissues with oxygenated blood. Only the small amount of blood needed to nourish the developing lung tissue entered the baby's lungs; the rest was channeled through the ductus.

But once the umbilical cord is severed at birth, *all* the baby's blood must begin to circulate through the lungs to receive oxygen. As the baby inflates his lungs for the first time, pressure is released on the lungs' blood vessels. Blood rushes into these expanded vessels, and circulation to the lungs suddenly increases tenfold. Since the newly opened lung blood vessels offer the line of least resistance, blood is no longer diverted through the ductus arteriosus; it enters the lungs to take on oxygen.

---

### A Note to Parents

In a medical field as new and rapidly changing as neonatology, there are bound to be variations from hospital to hospital in terminology, technology, and treatments. Your doctor may use slightly different terms to describe some of the problems and therapies discussed here. Equipment such as the monitor and respirator illustrated in this chapter may differ in certain details from those at your nursery. New methods to treat the problems of prematurity are also constantly evolving. The purpose of this chapter is to provide a basic understanding of the problems of premature babies and of the principles involved in managing those problems. We hope that with this basic information you will be better able to discuss the specifics of your baby's care with your neonatologist and pediatrician.

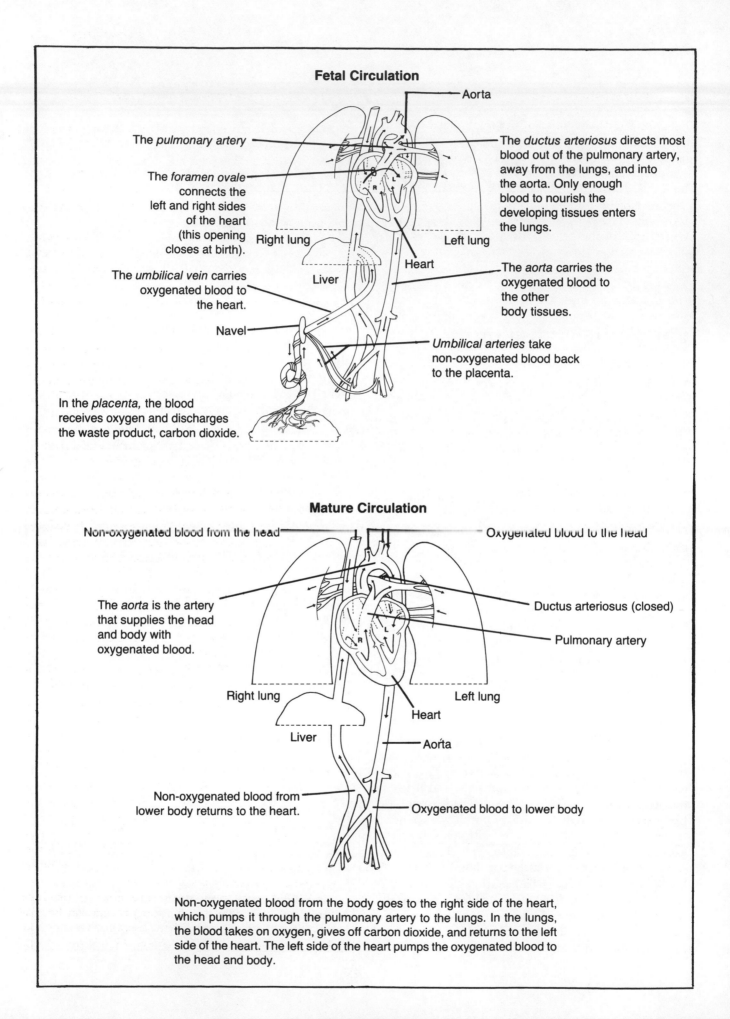

## Fetal Circulation

Aorta

The *pulmonary artery*

The *foramen ovale* connects the left and right sides of the heart (this opening closes at birth).

The *ductus arteriosus* directs most blood out of the pulmonary artery, away from the lungs, and into the aorta. Only enough blood to nourish the developing tissues enters the lungs.

Right lung

Left lung

Heart

Liver

The *umbilical vein* carries oxygenated blood to the heart.

The *aorta* carries the oxygenated blood to the other body tissues.

Navel

*Umbilical arteries* take non-oxygenated blood back to the placenta.

In the *placenta,* the blood receives oxygen and discharges the waste product, carbon dioxide.

## Mature Circulation

Non-oxygenated blood from the head

Oxygenated blood to the head

The *aorta* is the artery that supplies the head and body with oxygenated blood.

Ductus arteriosus (closed)

Pulmonary artery

Right lung

Left lung

Heart

Liver

Aorta

Non-oxygenated blood from lower body returns to the heart.

Oxygenated blood to lower body

Non-oxygenated blood from the body goes to the right side of the heart, which pumps it through the pulmonary artery to the lungs. In the lungs, the blood takes on oxygen, gives off carbon dioxide, and returns to the left side of the heart. The left side of the heart pumps the oxygenated blood to the head and body.

The new pattern of blood flow also causes a flap of tissue to cover an opening called the *foramen ovale* that connected both sides of the fetal heart. Now the heart begins to function as two separate pumps working side by side. The right side of the heart receives non-oxygenated blood from the body and pumps it to the lungs. In the lungs, the blood gives off the waste product carbon dioxide and takes on a fresh supply of oxygen. The newly oxygenated blood then flows to the left side of the heart and is pumped through the aorta to the body tissues. The full-term baby's ductus arteriosus closes off soon after birth so that non-oxygenated blood flowing to the lungs cannot mix with oxygenated blood flowing to the body. The mature pattern of circulation has then been established.

These respiratory and circulatory changes occur so rapidly that doctors begin measuring their effects when the baby is only a minute old. At one minute after birth, and again four minutes later, the baby is given the *Apgar evaluation,* which indicates how well he is handling his transition to the outside world. Five different observations are made on the baby, and he is given a score on each item ranging from 0 to 2. The ratings are added up to give the baby's Apgar score. A perfect score is 10. A score below 6 indicates that the baby is suffering moderate to severe distress. Full-term babies normally score 6 or 7 on the test at one minute and 8 or 10 at five minutes.

## THE APGAR SCORING CHART

| SIGN | SCORE 0 | SCORE 1 | SCORE 2 |
|------|---------|---------|---------|
| 1. Heart rate | Absent | Below 100 beats/min. | Over 100 beats/min. |
| 2. Breathing effort | Absent | Slow, irregular | Good, crying lustily |
| 3. Muscle tone | Limp | Some bending of arms, legs | Active motion |
| 4. Reflex irritability (baby's reaction when soles of feet are flicked) | No response | Cry, some motion | Vigorous cry |
| 5. Color | Blue, pale | Pink body; blue hands and feet | Completely pink |

## The Premature Baby at Birth

When a baby is born three or more weeks too early, the birth transition carries many potential risks and difficulties. The baby's organ systems are often unready to make the rapid readjustments necessary for independent life. The stresses of birth that a sturdy full-term handles with ease are not so well tolerated by the tiny pre-term infant.

Ideally, a baby is born slowly, head first. During the hours of a labor of normal length, the baby's head is gently and gradually molded to fit the birth canal. A slow delivery minimizes trauma to the baby's head. But the premature baby, who may not yet have settled into the head-down position, is often born breech—bottom first. Whatever the birth position, a small baby tends to be delivered rapidly, with little time for head molding, and subjected to abrupt changes in pressure. The premature baby is highly vulnerable to the physical forces of birth; his fragile capillaries can break easily and cause bruising or internal bleeding.

It takes stamina for a baby to make a successful birth transition. While the full-term is well supplied with reserve calories for energy and endurance, the premature, who has low caloric (energy) reserves, tires easily. He may develop hypoglycemia, a serious condition in which the cells have too little glucose (blood sugar) to fuel their life-sustaining functions. The same stresses of labor that leave a term baby *mildly hypoxic* and *stimulated* to breathe, may cause the premature to be born *asphyxiated*—badly deprived of oxygen—and *unable* to begin breathing on his own.

Outside the warmth of his mother's womb, the *full-term* baby has an ample supply of calories that his body can use to produce heat; his extra pounds of baby fat help insulate him from the cold. The scrawny, calorie-depleted premature, however, is dangerously susceptible to chilling (hypothermia).

But the most common serious problem facing a newborn premature is the immaturity of his lungs, specifically an inability to produce enough surfactant to keep his lungs expanded as he breathes—a condition known as respiratory distress syndrome (RDS).

The baby with RDS has difficulty making the switch from the fetal pattern of circulation to the mature pattern, since pressure in his poorly expanded lungs forces blood away from the lungs and back through the fetal blood vessel, the ductus arteriosus. Non-oxygenated blood then circulates to the body, and the baby's tissues become oxygen-deprived.

While many prematures are able to produce some surfactant, the production process can be disrupted by stresses during birth—problems such as asphyxia (an Apgar of 5 or lower), blood loss or low blood pressure, hypothermia (chilling), or hypoglycemia (low blood sugar level). Because these stresses increase the infant's vulnerability to RDS and other dangerous conditions, everything possible is done to make the birth process easy on the baby. Pain-relieving drugs are rarely given to a mother in pre-term labor for fear of overly sedating the infant. Mother and baby are closely monitored during labor and delivery, either with an external monitor wrapped around the mother's abdomen, or by an internal monitor inserted into the baby's scalp. These devices measure the effects of contractions on the baby's heart rate. If the infant becomes tired or stressed, the monitor sounds the warning and the baby is immediately delivered by cesarean section. Many doctors also consider a cesarean to be the safest method to deliver a very young (under 30-week) premature or a pre-term infant in the breech position. When a premature baby is delivered vaginally, the special precautions of a deep episiotomy and the use of forceps (as a protective helmet) help avoid compression of the baby's delicate head.

Once the baby is born, he is immediately dried, placed on a warming table, and vigorously rubbed to stimulate breathing. If the baby has trouble breathing, he is resuscitated—mechanically helped to begin and continue breathing. A mask is placed over the baby's face. A doctor or nurse rhythmically compresses a bag attached to the mask to send highly oxygenated air in and out of the baby's lungs, a procedure referred to as *bagging*.

The newborn who cannot be stimulated to breathe by this method is quickly *intubated*. A thin, curved instrument called a *laryngoscope* is used to view the back of the baby's throat. When the vocal cords are visible, a flexible tube, smaller around than a drinking straw, is gently inserted into the baby's mouth or nostril, between the vocal cords and into the trachea (windpipe). The *endotracheal (ET)* tube comes to rest just above the area where the bronchial tubes branch off to the lungs. Because the tube goes between the vocal cords, the intubated baby is temporarily unable to make noise when he cries. The endotracheal tube is attached to a bag that supplies warm, humid oxygenated air. A nurse or doctor pumps the bag by hand until the baby can be put on a *respirator,* a machine that performs this breathing function automatically.

Depending on his needs, the baby may be given air with concentrations of oxygen ranging from 21%—the amount in room air—all the way up to 100%.

A baby receiving oxygen therapy must have his blood tested frequently to determine the actual amount of oxygen reaching his bloodstream. For easy blood withdrawal, a thin tube, or catheter, is placed in the end of the infant's umbilical cord and threaded through the umbilical artery into the aorta, the main artery supplying the body with oxygenated blood. Since there are no nerve endings in the umbilical cord, inserting the catheter is not a painful procedure for the baby. The catheter is left in place as long as it is needed for frequent blood sampling. Fluids, nutrients, blood, and medications can also be given through the *umbilical catheter.* A device attached to the catheter constantly monitors the baby's blood pressure. Other vital signs—heartbeat, temperature, and breathing rate—are measured by separate electronic monitors.

Even the premature who begins breathing normally at birth needs careful observation. If the baby continues to breathe well for the first two or three days after delivery, it is unlikely that he will develop respiratory distress syndrome. But he is still vulnerable to such problems of prematurity as jaundice, feeding difficulties, infection, unstable body temperature, and irregular breathing or heart rate patterns. The special level of care involved in monitoring and treating these problems requires mother and baby to be separated at birth.

# Respiratory Distress Syndrome, Hyaline Membrane Disease, and Pulmonary Insufficiency of the Premature

## Who Is Vulnerable and Why?

Respiratory distress syndrome (RDS), also known as hyaline membrane disease (HMD), is a breathing disorder of premature babies. It is caused by the baby's inability to produce surfactant, the fatty substance that coats the alveoli—the lungs' tiny air sacs—and prevents them from collapsing.

An unborn baby's lung tissue begins making small amounts of surfactant in the early weeks of pregnancy, but most babies are not producing enough surfactant for efficient breathing until the 35th week of gestation. However, babies vary greatly in their rates of lung development. Some very premature infants have enough surfactant to breathe without difficulty, while some (very few) full-terms do not.

Linda More, R.N.

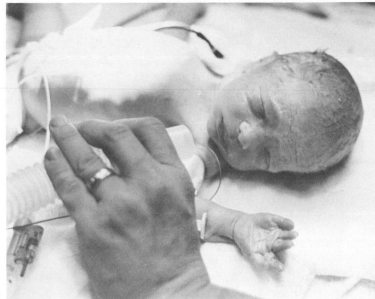

In general, the more premature the baby, the greater the likelihood he will develop RDS. While approximately 35% of all prematures develop the disease, almost every infant weighing 1000 grams or less is afflicted. In prematures under 30 weeks gestational age, respiratory distress results not only from a lack of surfactant, but also from an immaturity of the alveoli and poor connections between the alveoli and the surrounding capillaries. The term *pulmonary insufficiency of the premature* (PIP) may be used to refer to this serious form of RDS. It differs from respiratory distress in older prematures by its late onset (sometimes two to three days after delivery) and its longer, more difficult course.

*The newborn premature who cannot be stimulated to breathe . . .*

*. . . is quickly intubated and weighed . . .*

*. . . then placed on a respirator.*

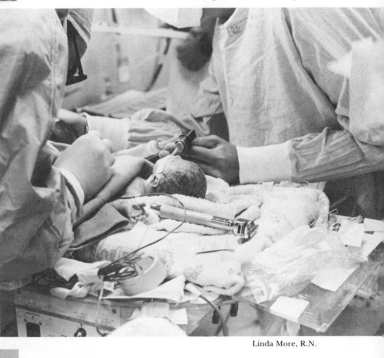

Linda More, R.N.

Linda More, R.N.

## Your Baby's Lungs and How They Mature

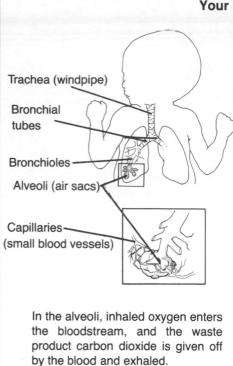

Trachea (windpipe)

Bronchial tubes

Bronchioles

Alveoli (air sacs)

Capillaries (small blood vessels)

In the alveoli, inhaled oxygen enters the bloodstream, and the waste product carbon dioxide is given off by the blood and exhaled.

**3 weeks after conception:** Lung tissue buds out from the embryonic digestive tract and begins to grow like an upsidedown tree. From the trachea, or windpipe, two bronchial tubes branch off and subdivide into smaller tubes called bronchioles. By the 24th week, most of the bronchioles have formed.

**11 weeks** after conception: the baby begins to practice "breathing" by inhaling and exhaling amniotic fluid.

**22 weeks:** the lungs are producing small amounts of usable surfactant.

**26–28 weeks:** Each bronchiole ends with a cluster of bubble-shaped air sacs called alveoli. Tiny blood vessels (capillaries) touch the porous walls of the alveoli, making possible the exchange of oxygen and carbon dioxide between the lungs and the bloodstream.

**30 weeks:** Respiratory centers in the brain may be mature enough to properly coordinate the baby's breathing.

**35 weeks:** The baby produces enough surfactant to prevent the alveoli from collapsing and sticking together when he breathes.

**40 weeks** (term): Only 10% of the baby's lung tissue is present. Growth of healthy new lung tissue continues until age six, a reassuring thought for parents whose baby has sustained lung damage.

*(This timetable is an approximation. Each baby matures at his own rate.)*

---

Other factors besides the degree of prematurity predispose certain babies to RDS. Between the ages of 28 to 38 weeks' gestational age, boys are more susceptible than girls; earlier than 28 weeks, both sexes are equally at risk. Infants of diabetic mothers, even those very close to term, have a special vulnerability. It is thought that fluctuating insulin levels in the womb reduce the ability of these babies to make surfactant. Babies who have had difficult deliveries are quite susceptible, since extreme physical stress can temporarily stop surfactant production. The second-born of twins, whose birth is generally more complicated than that of the first born, is also the more likely of the two to develop RDS.

While extreme stress during delivery can lead to RDS, *mild, prolonged* stress before birth can actually help prevent the disease or reduce its severity. Certain complications associated with prematurity—conditions such as toxemia, maternal high blood pressure, prematurely ruptured membranes, mild fetal infection, and maternal heroin addiction—all exert moderate stress on the unborn baby. These conditions may increase the baby's exposure to steroid hormones, which speed up lung development and surfactant production. In this way, the potentially premature baby is given a degree of natural protection against one of prematurity's most dreaded diseases.

In certain cases, doctors can artificially induce an unborn baby to produce surfactant by giving the mother injections of the synthetic steroid betamethasone 48 hours or more before delivery. Girls are more likely to respond to the drug than boys.

Before a baby is born, doctors can assess the maturity of the lungs by removing some amniotic fluid by amniocentesis and checking the fluid for two components of surfactant, *lecithin* (L) and *sphingomyelin* (S). If there is twice as much lecithin as sphingomyelin (an *L/S ratio* of 2:1), the baby is usually producing enough surfactant to breathe well on his own. (With infants of diabetic mothers, more sophisticated tests are needed to determine lung maturity.) Doctors use the L/S ratio test in deciding when to try to stop pre-term labor, when to give betamethasone, and when to schedule an elective cesarean section in order to avoid accidental delivery of an immature infant.

## How RDS Develops

A baby who is born without enough surfactant may take his first breath and inflate his lungs just like the full-term baby. The problem begins when he ex-

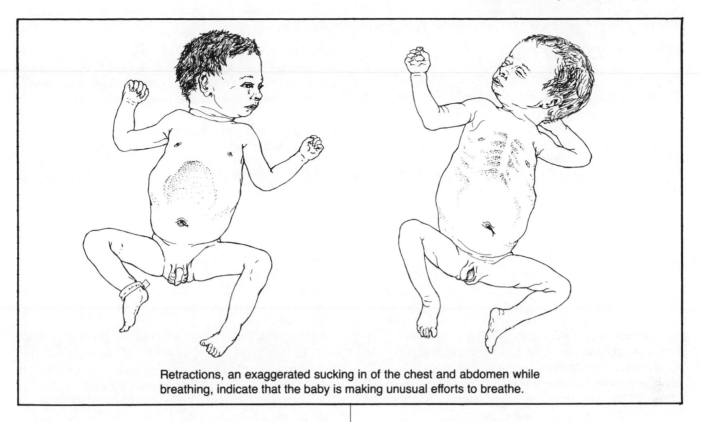

Retractions, an exaggerated sucking in of the chest and abdomen while breathing, indicate that the baby is making unusual efforts to breathe.

hales. His alveoli collapse, and all the air is forced out of his lungs. The next breath is just as hard as the first one. Each time the baby inhales, he must completely refill his lungs. Each time he exhales, his lungs collapse again. By contrast, a baby with enough surfactant is able to keep some residual air in his lungs when he exhales. With partially expanded lungs, breathing requires less effort.

The baby with insufficient surfactant shows signs of fatigue within minutes or hours of birth. His breathing becomes rapid and labored. The baby's chest *retracts*, or sucks in deeply, with each breath. When the baby exhales, he makes grunting noises as he tries to close off the back of his throat to prevent all the air from leaving his lungs.

Each time the baby inhales, fewer of the alveoli reopen, the collapsing air sacs begin to stick together, and the baby must make progressively greater exertions to obtain progressively less oxygen. He may use up his limited supplies of calories and oxygen just to provide the energy to continue breathing.

As less oxygen enters the baby's bloodstream and more is used up in his efforts to breathe, the baby's blood oxygen level falls and his blood carbon dioxide level rises. Too much carbon dioxide and too little oxygen cause the blood to become acidic. Excess acid in the blood constricts the blood vessels in the lungs and blood is forced away from the lungs back through the ductus arteriosus. The fetal pattern of

circulation persists; blood bypasses the lungs and the baby's tissues do not receive enough oxygen.

Poor circulation to the lungs also makes it difficult for the baby to produce new surfactant. Without surfactant, the alveoli continue to collapse and stick together, a condition called *atelectasis*. The stuck-together, or atelectatic, areas can be seen on an x-ray as grainy looking patches in the lungs. Some of the oxygen-deprived lung cells die and combine with fluid leaking from the capillaries to form thick membranes. These so-called *hyaline membranes* stiffen and clog the lungs, providing still another barrier to oxygen trying to enter the bloodstream.

As the baby's condition worsens, his breathing rate becomes irregular, and he may have spells of *apnea*—periods during which he stops breathing entirely.

There is no cure for RDS. The baby can only be given medical treatment to aid his breathing and circulation until he is able to produce surfactant and cure himself. After the first three or four days, the baby's lungs may begin to produce enough surfactant for him to breathe normally. But without vigorous and sophisticated medical support, many babies would not survive this critical period. Before the days of modern infant intensive care, approximately 40,000 babies died of this disease in the United States each year. Now, of the 30,000 to 60,000 babies afflicted in this country annually, over 85% survive.

## How RDS Is Treated

### Respiratory Therapy

In the nursery, the baby can receive oxygen and various types of mechanical help with the breathing process.

**Oxygen.** Oxygen can be piped directly into the baby's incubator, but if high or precisely measured doses of oxygen are required, a plastic dome called an oxygen hood is fitted over the baby's head. Warm, moist oxygenated air flows into the hood; an oxygen analyzer, placed beside the baby's head, double-checks the amount of oxygen he is receiving.

**Continuous Positive Airway Pressure.** A baby who cannot keep his lungs expanded is treated with continuous positive airway pressure (CPAP, pronounced "see-pap"), which delivers a steady stream of pressurized air into the baby's lungs to keep them partially inflated at all times. This air can be normal room air (21% oxygen), or it can contain higher levels of oxygen if the baby needs it. The pressurized air can be delivered through a face mask, through small tubes placed just inside the baby's nostrils, or through an endotracheal tube, a tube inserted through the nostril or mouth and into the trachea.

**The Respirator (Ventilator).** A baby who is having frequent apnea spells or a baby who is too weak to make good breathing motions is intubated, and his endotracheal tube is attached to a respirator—a machine that does his breathing for him. The baby may be given the drugs curare or pancuronium (Pavulon) to paralyze his breathing muscles *temporarily*. This is to keep the baby from trying to breathe at cross-purposes with the machine. Although the drugs leave the baby temporarily unable to use his muscles for breathing, or other movement, he can still hear and feel things around him.

The respirator performs several functions. It delivers a measured amount of oxygen to the baby's lungs. It provides a constant basic pressure to keep the lungs open. This pressure, referred to as *positive end-expiratory pressure* (or PEEP), is quite similar to CPAP. At regular intervals the machine inhales for the baby by pushing in additional air at a higher pressure called the *inspiratory pressure*. The oxygen content of the air, the inspiratory pressure, the end-expiratory pressure, and the number of breaths per minute can all be adjusted to the baby's needs. Doctors determine these needs by observing the baby and by constantly measuring the oxygen, carbon dioxide, and acid levels in the baby's bloodstream.

### Blood Gases

A seriously ill baby has his blood gases checked several times each hour. A baby in more stable condition might be tested several times each day. These very important tests indicate how well the gases oxygen and carbon dioxide are being exchanged between the lungs and the bloodstream, and what effect the baby's illness is having on the acid content of his blood. The tests are repeated often because changes in the baby's blood chemistry can occur rapidly. Test results are reported to the doctor or nurse within minutes, so that any abnormalities can be quickly corrected.

Oxygen levels in the blood must be sufficient to keep tissues alive and functioning, but not so high as to produce toxic side effects. Carbon dioxide levels must also be kept in balance. Too little carbon dioxide gives insufficient stimulation to the respiratory centers—those areas of the brain that signal the baby to breathe; too much carbon dioxide causes the blood to become acidic.

Many sick newborns experience abnormal acid levels in the blood as a side effect of their illness. At times the acid imbalance causes more problems than the original illness itself. Too much or too little acid in the blood disrupts the body's vital chemical processes. High acid levels in the blood also constrict the blood vessels in the lungs, causing or worsening respiratory distress.

The balance between an acid (like vinegar) in solution and its opposite, a base (like baking soda), is measured on the pH scale. Pure water, taken as a neutral midpoint, has a pH of 7.0. Addition of acid *lowers* the pH; addition of a base *raises* it. In other words, the lower the pH number, the more acidic the solution. The normal pH range of the blood is 7.35 to 7.45 (which is slightly alkaline), although life is possible within the range of 6.8 to 7.8.

There are two ways that excess acid can build up in the blood. If the baby is having difficulty breathing, he may be unable to exhale enough carbon dioxide. Carbon dioxide in the blood forms carbonic acid. Accumulation of acid in the blood from respiratory problems *(respiratory acidosis)* can occur very quickly. For example, by holding your breath for one minute you can lower your blood pH (increase its acidity) from a normal 7.4 to a very acidic 7.1.

The second type of acidosis, called *metabolic acidosis,* results from an accumulation in the blood of lactic acid—a waste product formed when the cells must function with insufficient oxygen. A baby with severe acidosis (a very low blood pH) can be treated with intravenous administration of bicarbonate or other acid-neutralizing medications.

Samples of blood to be tested for oxygen, carbon dioxide, and acid may be taken from the baby's arteries, since it is arterial blood that supplies the body

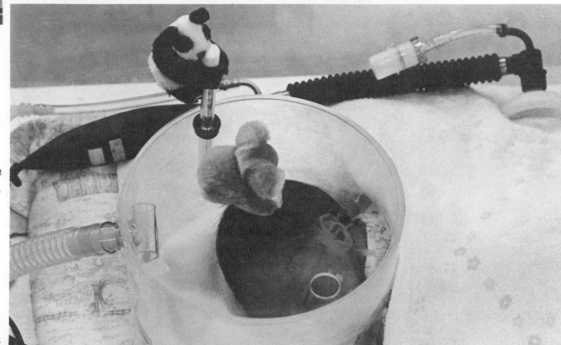

*Oxygen can be delivered directly into the incubator . .*

*. . . or through an oxygen hood . . .*

*. . . or through a respirator.*

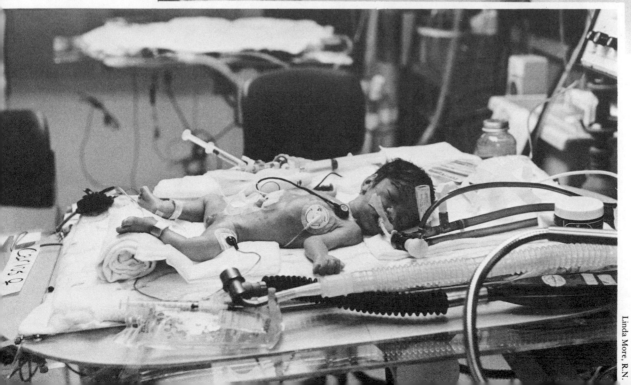

## An Infant Respirator

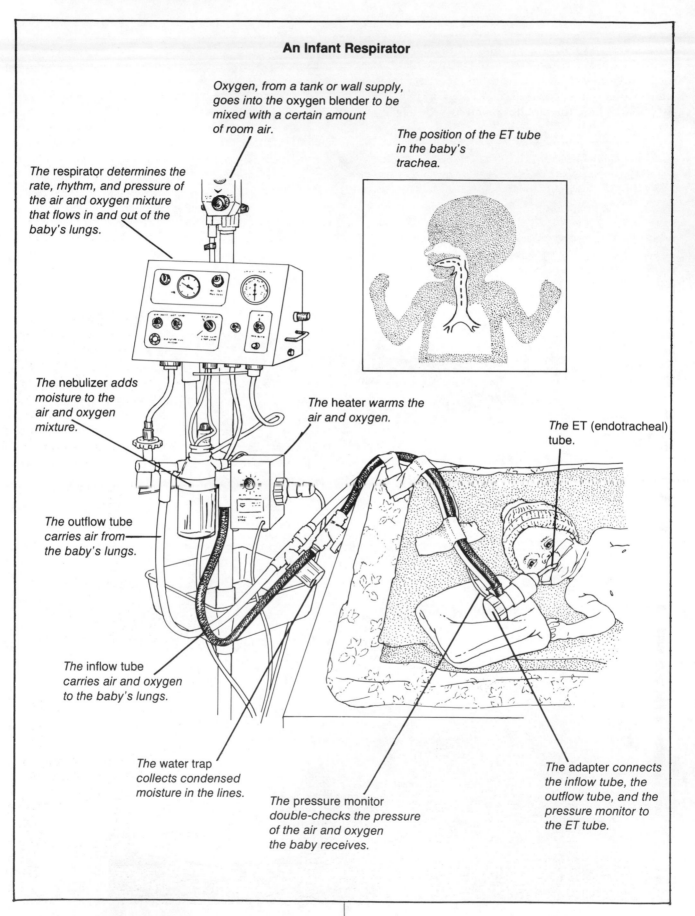

Oxygen, from a tank or wall supply, goes into the oxygen blender *to be mixed with a certain amount of room air.*

The position of the ET tube in the baby's trachea.

*The* respirator *determines the rate, rhythm, and pressure of the air and oxygen mixture that flows in and out of the baby's lungs.*

*The* nebulizer *adds moisture to the air and oxygen mixture.*

The heater *warms the air and oxygen.*

*The* ET (endotracheal) tube.

The outflow tube *carries air from the baby's lungs.*

*The* inflow tube *carries air and oxygen to the baby's lungs.*

*The* water trap *collects condensed moisture in the lines.*

The pressure monitor *double-checks the pressure of the air and oxygen the baby receives.*

*The* adapter *connects the inflow tube, the outflow tube, and the pressure monitor to the ET tube.*

tissues with oxygen. Arterial blood can be withdrawn from the aorta (through the umbilical artery catheter), or from arteries on the baby's wrist, foot, or scalp. Sometimes a sampling of capillary blood is sufficient. Then, the blood is taken by puncturing the baby's heel, a procedure called a *heel stick*. Blood gases can also be monitored by *transcutaneous* (across the skin) *monitors*. These electronic monitors do not break the skin or come into direct contact with the blood. They greatly reduce the need for frequent blood-drawing, although blood samples are still taken occasionally to double-check the monitor. The transcutaneous (TC) monitor must be kept at a temperature of 109 to 113° F. (43 to 45° Celsius) to operate accurately. Consequently, the monitor is frequently repositioned to avoid burning the baby's delicate skin. The tiny red marks the monitor leaves usually disappear in a day or two, although some babies retain faint white scars from skin irritation caused by the heated monitor.

### X-Rays

The baby with respiratory problems is x-rayed as often as several times a day to assess the condition of the lungs and other organs, and to check the positions of any tubes or catheters inside the body.

Mothers who have been warned against so much as a dental x-ray during pregnancy are understandably concerned about these procedures. "Every time the x-ray machine was wheeled into the nursery," said one parent, "the staff would run for cover. If they were so scared of the radiation, what about the poor baby being x-rayed or the babies nearby who couldn't move out of the way? I wondered if my baby would be sterile or would develop cancer later on. I asked about this, but no one ever gave me a straight answer."

Radiation is measured in units called rads. Every year the average person is exposed to more than 0.1 rad from natural sources such as cosmic rays that penetrate the earth's atmosphere. And while the safety of x-rays for prematures is still a subject of debate, Dr. Arnold Vinstein, Director of Pediatric Radiology at Cedars-Sinai Medical Center in Los Angeles, feels that fears of nursery personnel and parents are largely unjustified because only tiny doses of radiation are needed to x-ray sick babies: "If 100 portable chest x-rays were performed on a single infant [the baby would receive] no more than 0.1 rad, or in other words, no more radiation than received yearly from background sources." Such low doses of radiation have not been found to cause sterility or

*The baby may be x-rayed several times a day.*

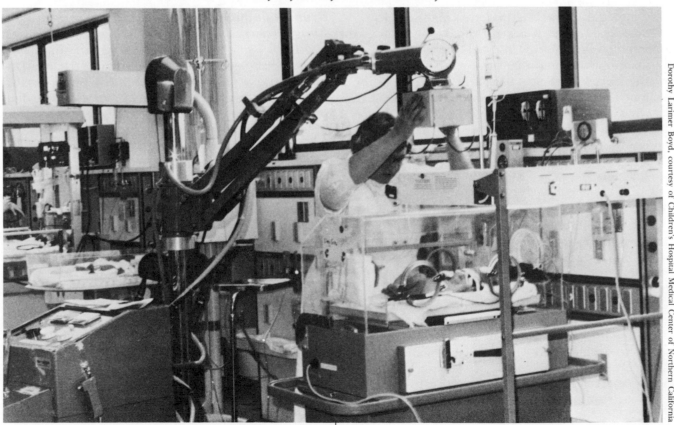

genetic problems in humans. This small amount of radiation would increase the child's cancer risk by only a miniscule 0.00005%.

As for scatter radiation received by neighboring babies or nursery personnel, it is too small to be measured. However, to be extra safe, nurseries may provide lead shielding to protect the baby's genitals and to reduce exposure of nearby babies. The nursery staff often leave the area since even small amounts of scatter radiation can become significant to the person exposed all day, every day, for many years.

### Suctioning

The baby with breathing problems cannot cough up the mucus that accumulates in his lungs. These secretions must be removed for him by a process called *percussion, vibration, and suctioning,* which may also include *postural drainage*—tilting the baby in various positions to facilitate drainage of lung secretions. Congestion in the lungs can be detected by x-ray. It is loosened by applying a vibrator (yes, the adult bookstore variety!) to the baby's chest or back, and by vigorously thumping on the affected areas. The thumping procedure looks rather violent, but as one mother remarked, "It sure got me over my fear of handling the baby. He even seemed to enjoy it. Later at home when he had colic, I would thump on his back. It was the only way to quiet him."

Once the mucus has been loosened, the baby's endotracheal tube is detached from the respirator. A suctioning tube is quickly inserted through the endotracheal tube and into the baby's trachea to vacuum up any secretions. Since oxygen in the lungs is also suctioned out, the baby may have a brief spell of duskiness and slow heart rate *(bradycardia).* Babies on the drugs Pavulon or curare also need to have their mouths suctioned frequently, since the drugs cause them to salivate but leave them temporarily unable to swallow.

### Weaning

Although the critical period of respiratory distress syndrome lasts only three to four days, many babies continue to need oxygen and/or pressure to the lungs for longer periods. But as soon as possible, the baby's dependence on artificial breathing aids is reduced to avoid harmful side effects of oxygen and respirator therapy.

Some babies are quickly weaned from the respirator and from oxygen. For others the weaning process involves weeks or months of two steps forward, one step back. (Hourly variations in the baby's oxygen needs are quite normal—they usually reflect the baby's cycle of rest and fatigue. These constant minor ups and downs are less significant than the larger pattern of recovery.) As the baby tolerates it, the various respirator settings are lowered and oxygen levels decreased. The breaths per minute may be reduced so that while the respirator occasionally breathes for the baby, he must take some breaths for himself.

Next, the baby graduates to CPAP, which provides constant pressure to the lungs but does not inhale or exhale for him. This is followed by extubation—removal of the baby's endotracheal tube. Once he is extubated, the previously silent infant will make his presence known. Mother and father hear their child's voice for the first time. (Several parents found it helpful to recall this wonderful moment later on when responding to their little one's nocturnal howls.) For a while the baby's cry is weak and hoarse, while his vocal cords, stretched by the endotracheal tube, reassume their normal shape.

After extubation, the baby may still need days or weeks in oxygen. Slowly, the oxygen levels are reduced until the happy day arrives when he is breathing room air.

## Complications of Respiratory Therapy

### Bronchopulmonary Dysplasia or Chronic Lung Disease

The oxygen and pressure to the lungs that help save the baby's life during the critical phase of RDS can, paradoxically, also delay recovery. Some babies, on a respirator for a week or more, develop damage to the lungs and bronchioles from high oxygen doses or high respirator pressures—a disease known as bronchopulmonary dysplasia (BPD) or chronic lung disease (CLD). The damaged tissue dies and forms scars that impede the passage of air in and out of the lungs and obstruct the exchange of oxygen and carbon dioxide between the lungs and bloodstream.

Unlike an adult with lung disease, a baby with BPD can grow healthy new lung tissue. And while scarring in the bronchioles is permanent, the bronchioles eventually grow and expand to the point where the scar tissue no longer hampers airflow to and from the lungs.

But until the lungs have healed sufficiently, the baby continues to be dependent on the respirator and/or supplemental oxygen—a dependency that may take weeks or months to resolve.

A baby who must be intubated for many months may be given a tracheostomy, a surgically created opening in the neck that allows insertion of the endotracheal tube directly into the trachea below the vocal cords. A tracheostomy avoids damage to the vocal cords from prolonged presence of the tube. Once the baby is ready to be extubated, the tracheostomy is repaired.

The baby with BPD often suffers from excessive fluid accumulation in his lungs and other body tissues. He may be treated with diuretics such as furosemide (Lasix) to help him excrete these fluids. And although the baby needs extra calories to fuel his difficult breathing efforts, his intake of liquids must be restricted to prevent fluid buildup in the lungs. High-calorie supplements are added to his breastmilk or formula to give him the most concentrated nutrition in the least amount of liquid.

Weaning the BPD baby from oxygen can be such a slow process that some hospitals allow these babies to go home while still in oxygen. Other hospitals do not permit this, since they feel the home care of an oxygen-dependent baby would be too difficult for the parents.

Babies who have had BPD, whether they come home in oxygen or not, often have continuing respiratory problems that require special care. They are highly vulnerable to colds and other respiratory infections. As many as 85% of these infants develop pneumonia or bronchitis in the first year, usually requiring rehospitalization.

During early infancy the baby may still find it hard to breathe. He may have retractions—a sucking in of the chest above, around, or below the breastbone when he breathes. He may develop an overly large chest (barrel chest) from air trapped in the alveoli that he cannot completely exhale. He may make wheezing noises—humming sounds produced when air passes through the scarred bronchioles. Because of these breathing problems, BPD babies can be excessively irritable, easy to tire, hard to feed, and slow to gain weight. Despite the many difficulties BPD infants (and their parents) endure in the early months and years, most outgrow their respiratory symptoms in infancy or early childhood, and by school age, almost all are able to participate in normal vigorous physical activity.

### Air Leaks: Pulmonary Interstitial Emphysema and Pneumothorax (Collapsed Lung)

Pressure from the respirator or CPAP occasionally causes air to leak from the lungs. Tiny air bubbles may be forced out of the alveoli and in between layers of lung tissue. This condition, called pulmonary in-

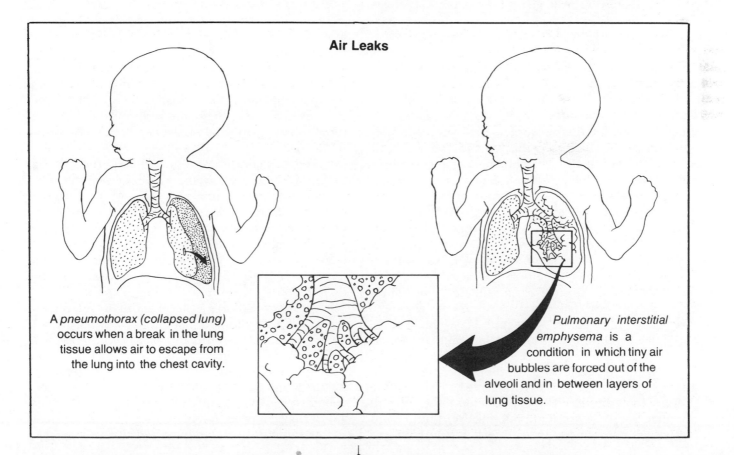

**Air Leaks**

A *pneumothorax (collapsed lung)* occurs when a break in the lung tissue allows air to escape from the lung into the chest cavity.

*Pulmonary interstitial emphysema* is a condition in which tiny air bubbles are forced out of the alveoli and in between layers of lung tissue.

terstitial emphysema (PIE), usually subsides as the baby's respiratory problems improve and respirator pressure to the lungs can be reduced.

When a baby receives high respirator pressures, especially if he is trying to breathe against the respirator, one or more of the alveoli in his lungs can burst, leaking air into the surrounding chest spaces and causing the lung to collapse—a medical emergency called pneumothorax. A rapid deterioration is the first symptom to be observed. To check for pneumothorax, doctors place a bright light against the baby to transilluminate the chest. Pockets of air can be seen as light areas. An x-ray confirms the diagnosis, and emergency surgery is performed in the nursery. Under local anesthesia, a tiny incision is made in the baby's chest and a tube is inserted to suction off the air between the lung and the chest wall, and allow the lung to reinflate. The suction around the outside of the lung is continued for days or weeks until the lung heals. Meanwhile, high respirator pressures must be continued to keep the lung inflated. This in turn can cause more air leaks, requiring more chest tubes.

When a chest tube is in place, the baby is moved as little as possible. He may be sedated or given pain medication. Although pneumothorax is a temporarily life-threatening emergency, long-range recovery is usually good. One little girl, whose parents we interviewed, had 44 chest tubes during her hospital stay. She is now a bright, normal, healthy three-year-old.

## Retrolental Fibroplasia or Retinopathy of Prematurity

Retrolental fibroplasia (RLF), also called retinopathy of prematurity (ROP), is an eye disease associated with the use of supplemental oxygen in premature infants. It is thought that the disease begins when a higher than normal blood oxygen concentration constricts the growth of blood vessels in the baby's developing retina (the lining of the back part of the eye that receives visual images). Several days or weeks after oxygen therapy has stopped, the vessels of the retina begin to grow again. Sometimes they grow abnormally: instead of growing toward the edges of the retina, they turn and start growing toward the center of the eye, into the fluid-filled vitreous body. These abnormal blood vessels are quite weak and vulnerable to leakage.

The blood and fluid that leak from these vessels into various parts of the eye sometimes form scar tissue. Over a period of weeks or months, the scar tissue shrinks; and in the process, it may tear or detach the retina. In addition, scar tissue may block the lens and impede the passage of light into the eye. The amount of visual impairment that results depends on the amount of scarring and the extent to which the scar tissue damages the retina. If the retina detaches entirely, blindness results.

Approximately one out of six prematures who need supplemental oxygen develop the early signs of RLF—constriction of the retinal blood vessels followed by abnormal regrowth. For most of these babies (well over half), the abnormal blood vessel changes are not accompanied by damage from scarring in the eye. The rest have varying degrees of visual impairment such as myopia (nearsightedness) or loss of part of the field of vision. Total blindness is relatively rare.

Very tiny prematures (under 1000 grams) are more likely to develop RLF-related eye damage than are bigger, more mature infants. An estimated 22 to 42% of these infants suffer visual impairment from RLF, and 5 to 11% are blinded by it. By comparison, eye damage from RLF afflicts only 2% of babies with birthweights between 1000 and 1500 grams; of these children, 0.3 to 1% are blind. As more and more very tiny prematures are being saved, the number of babies with RLF-related blindness and visual impairment is, unfortunately, on the rise.

Retrolental fibroplasia was first noticed in the 1940s and '50s, at a time when many premature babies were being saved by the use of oxygen. In the '50s it was suggested that the eye disease was caused by high doses of oxygen, and physicians began to limit their use of the gas to levels thought to be safe for the babies' eyes—concentrations of 40% or less. While oxygen restriction did reduce the number of cases of RLF, it also reduced the number of surviving prematures. (Some doctors feel that the apparent decline in RLF was actually the result of the deaths of those infants who would have been most susceptible to the disease.)

Today, many doctors question the notion that oxygen is the cause, or at any rate the only cause, of RLF. They point out that even the most careful monitoring of oxygen doses and blood oxygen levels cannot predict which baby will develop eye damage. Some babies with consistently low blood oxygen levels have sustained visual impairment, whereas other infants with high blood oxygen levels have escaped the disease.

The degree of eye damage an infant suffers also seems unrelated to the amounts of oxygen he was given. There are even a few babies with RLF who never received oxygen at all. Factors that cause the baby to need oxygen in the first place—extreme immaturity and stressed physical condition—may contribute at least as much to the progression of the disease as oxygen use.

It should also be emphasized that it is oxygen

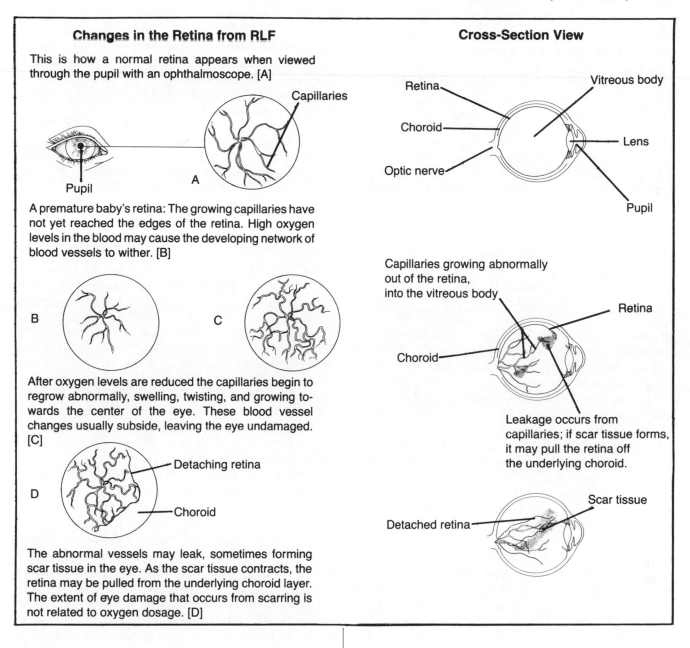

**Changes in the Retina from RLF**

This is how a normal retina appears when viewed through the pupil with an ophthalmoscope. [A]

Capillaries

Pupil

A

A premature baby's retina: The growing capillaries have not yet reached the edges of the retina. High oxygen levels in the blood may cause the developing network of blood vessels to wither. [B]

B

C

After oxygen levels are reduced the capillaries begin to regrow abnormally, swelling, twisting, and growing towards the center of the eye. These blood vessel changes usually subside, leaving the eye undamaged. [C]

D

Detaching retina

Choroid

The abnormal vessels may leak, sometimes forming scar tissue in the eye. As the scar tissue contracts, the retina may be pulled from the underlying choroid layer. The extent of eye damage that occurs from scarring is not related to oxygen dosage. [D]

**Cross-Section View**

Retina

Vitreous body

Choroid

Optic nerve

Lens

Pupil

Capillaries growing abnormally out of the retina, into the vitreous body

Retina

Choroid

Leakage occurs from capillaries; if scar tissue forms, it may pull the retina off the underlying choroid.

Scar tissue

Detached retina

levels in the *bloodstream* that are thought to be associated with RLF, not high oxygen levels delivered through a respirator or oxygen hood. A baby may receive 100% oxygen, but still have low or normal blood oxygen levels. Oxygen that touches the outside of the baby's eyes does no harm.

Although there is as yet no way to prevent or cure RLF, there are some experimental treatments that may prove to lessen the severity of the disease. At some nurseries, large doses of vitamin E are being given to infants in hopes of reducing their susceptibility to eye damage. And at certain medical centers, babies with detaching retinas are treated surgically to help prevent total retinal detachment and blindness. The difficult and delicate procedure involves freezing

tissue in the back of the baby's eye to form new scars that counteract the pull of scar tissue in other parts of the eye and help to hold the retina in place.

Any baby who receives oxygen therapy should be examined by an ophthalmologist (eye doctor) as soon as the oxygen therapy has ended. The baby who has abnormal changes in the retina at this time should be reexamined regularly in future weeks for any additional changes. Some doctors feel that all tiny prematures, whether they receive oxygen or not, should have similar examinations.

The baby with visual impairment from RLF remains vulnerable to further eye problems and should be seen throughout childhood by an ophthalmologist. (See page 212.)

# Patent Ductus Arteriosus (PDA, Open Ductus, Murmur)

The ductus arteriosus is the short, wide tube connecting the pulmonary artery (the artery leading from the heart to the lungs) with the aorta (the main artery leading from the heart to the body). In the unborn baby, the ductus directs much of the infant's blood flow away from the still-developing lungs to the rest of the body. Once the newborn baby starts using his lungs to breathe, the ductus must close for efficient circulation to take place.

The mature newborn's ductus usually closes within hours of delivery, but for two-thirds of premature babies weighing under 1750 grams (about four pounds) the ductus remains open for a significant period after birth. No one is sure why. Perhaps the immature ductus is less responsive to the chemical changes in the blood that seem to cause the mature baby's ductus to constrict.

An open ductus, writes neonatologist John Scanlon, "complicates or is complicated by almost all the ills that befall the tiny premature infant." During RDS the ductus channels blood away from the baby's constricted lung vessels, leaving much of the blood poorly oxygenated. The blood travels through the ductus from the pulmonary to the aortic artery as it did before the baby was born. This problem is called *persistent fetal circulation* (PFC) or a *right-to-left shunt.*

Later, as the baby recovers from RDS and his lung compliance—the lungs' ability to expand—improves, the capillaries that surround the lungs open up and allow blood to enter more easily. Blood going to the lungs is no longer diverted to the aorta through the ductus. But if the ductus remains open, blood from the aorta may flow back through the ductus into the pulmonary artery, causing a *left-to-right shunt.* As a result, oxygenated blood that should be going to the body tissues reenters the circulation going to the lungs and the heart. Blood flow to the stomach, intestines, and kidneys is reduced, causing them to function poorly. And now, instead of *too little* blood going to the lungs, there is *too much.*

Both lungs and heart can be strained by the overload. Fluid may leak out of the capillaries into the lung tissues, a condition called *pulmonary edema.* The left half of the heart may enlarge to handle the lopsided circulation. The baby's throbbing pulses and pounding heartbeat indicate circulatory strain. Blood returning to the heart from the body has difficulty entering the heart. The blood flow may back up in the baby's liver, causing it to swell. These symptoms of stress to the heart from an overload of fluid are referred to as *congestive heart failure.* (The term congestive heart failure describes a type of circulatory stress on the heart. It does not mean the baby's heart has actually stopped.)

The ductus is never large enough to rechannel *all* the baby's blood. Some blood will continue to circulate normally to the tissues of the body. In some babies the ductus opening is so small that it causes only minor problems or none at all. Treatment is then unnecessary, and the ductus closes by itself as the baby matures.

The baby with a large patent ductus may begin to experience difficulties several days, sometimes weeks, after birth. The sick baby who was improving in oxygen or on the respirator may suffer a setback or fail to make progress. A healthy premature who had no initial lung problems may stop gaining weight.

To diagnose a patent ductus, doctors listen for the turbulent sound or murmur that the blood sometimes makes as it flows through the ductus. They may perform *echocardiography*, testing in which sound waves are painlessly bounced off internal body tissues. The waves produce a picture of the ductus in the same way that an ultrasound or sonogram produces pictures of the fetus during pregnancy. X-rays of the ductus may also be taken.

Ductus problems can be treated by fluid restriction and diuretics. This treatment diminishes the fluid content of the circulatory system, thus reducing swelling in the lungs and strain on the heart.

An aspirin-like drug called *indomethacin* may be used to try to make the ductus close. Several doses of the drug, given intravenously or in a gavage-feeding, may be necessary. The drug is still experimental, and it can have side effects—such as temporary disruption of the baby's kidney function. Indomethacin, like aspirin, increases the tendency to bleed, so it is generally not used if a baby already has bleeding in the intestinal tract or has clotting problems. It is also not used if the baby has a high bilirubin level (jaundice, see page 86), since the drug may cause the bilirubin to circulate in a more toxic form.

Although indomethacin successfully closes the ductus for many babies, some infants require surgery to tie off, or *ligate*, the fetal blood vessel. Surgery is always a risk, but babies usually tolerate the operation well. The surgery is performed in an operating room by a pediatric thoracic surgeon—one whose specialty is chest surgery in children. The baby is given general anesthesia by an anesthesiologist who has special experience with infants. The operation takes about one hour. A two-inch incision is made on the left side of the baby's chest. His ribs are carefully spread apart

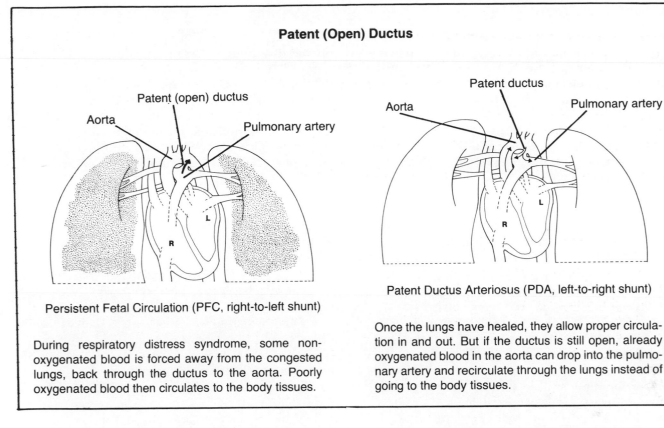

**Patent (Open) Ductus**

Patent (open) ductus

Aorta

Pulmonary artery

Persistent Fetal Circulation (PFC, right-to-left shunt)

During respiratory distress syndrome, some non-oxygenated blood is forced away from the congested lungs, back through the ductus to the aorta. Poorly oxygenated blood then circulates to the body tissues.

Patent ductus

Aorta

Pulmonary artery

Patent Ductus Arteriosus (PDA, left-to-right shunt)

Once the lungs have healed, they allow proper circulation in and out. But if the ductus is still open, already oxygenated blood in the aorta can drop into the pulmonary artery and recirculate through the lungs instead of going to the body tissues.

until the ductus is visible. The ductus is tied off in one or two places and the incision is closed.

Although the incision may seem huge on the very tiny baby, it becomes much less noticeable as the child grows. The surgery is *not* heart surgery, and it does *not* mean that the baby has a heart weakness or defect or that the baby will be vulnerable to heart problems. Negative side effects from the surgery are rare.

Recovery takes a day or two. The baby may be given pain medication during this time. Then, with the ductus closed and the circulatory pattern brought back to normal, an improvement in the baby's condition usually begins.

## Steven and Timothy's Story

### By Kathy Swinbank Laurie

"Here's the baby's head and body," said the nurse pointing to the ultrasound picture, "and over here is the other head and . . ."

*"What do you mean the other head?"* I yelled.

Six weeks ago I was just outgrowing my jeans as I left for a long business trip abroad. When I stepped off the plane after a month's absence I saw my husband's jaw drop. "Good God!" Bill exclaimed, "Are you ever pregnant!" My doctor agreed. At 22 weeks I was the size of most women at term.

Now we had the ultrasound diagnosis. Bill, who had once described himself as a "confirmed bachelor and child hater," and I, who scarcely knew which end of a baby to diaper, were to be parents of twins.

Nervously we began devising a list of twin names—Fric and Frac, Abbott and Costello, Bambi and Thumper.

We didn't have long to prepare ourselves. At a regular doctor's visit three weeks later I was found to be four centimeters dilated. I was rushed to the hospital in an ambulance. Forty-five minutes later 2-pound Steven was born. I heard him cry before I was put to sleep for the breech delivery of 1-pound, 13-ounce Timothy. Bill made it to the hospital just in time for their births.

While I recovered from the anesthesia, Bill went to the nursery to see the babies. Friends who had heard the news arrived as Bill returned, transformed, from the intensive care unit. As they told it later, "He was no longer the gruff, unsentimental Bill Laurie we'd always known and loved. In five minutes he had become Steven and Timothy's father."

The doctors and the labor room nurses all told me the twins would die. But to Bill, that was all irrelevant conversation; the boys would be fine. He insisted we name them, he took hundreds of pictures. I thought he was nuts.

Bill was certain they'd live, but I couldn't see

how that was possible. I didn't want to see the babies or think about them, I just wanted to curl up in my bed and be left alone. But a day later, at Bill's urging, I finally made it to the nursery. From then on I was hooked too, and we both became totally involved with our babies and their fight to survive.

For the next three months, Bill and I lived with a level of fear that only a parent of a very sick child can understand. Our mornings began with an anxious call to the nursery, we visited the boys before Bill went to work, I came in alone during the day, and we returned for another visit after dinner. Then home to sleep unless, as was often the case, we were awakened by a late night phone call. We would answer, our hearts in our throats, to be informed of some new complication or asked to consent to some new test or procedure.

As our boys battled respiratory distress syndrome, bronchopulmonary dysplasia, hyperbilirubinemia, and so on, we learned the language of the NBICU. Sometimes we learned the hard way. A doctor once took us aside to say the boys had heart murmurs and might need surgery. We translated this to mean, "Your babies are dying." Moments later, a second doctor breezed in and remarked on how well Steven and Timothy looked. We were astonished. Hadn't she heard? They were going to die—they had heart murmers! "Oh, that's no big deal," said the doctor. She took us on a tour of the nursery to see all the babies with scars from ductus surgery.

A dose of indomethacin closed the boys' ductuses, and they escaped surgery. (Steven's reopened two weeks later, but closed again after a second dose of medication.)

People sometimes ask if it was harder for us with two babies to worry about, or if having two somehow diluted the anxiety. I don't know. I have nothing to compare it with. But we never really had a rest. As soon as we finished being hysterical about one child, the other would develop a problem. At least they had the decency not to become seriously ill at the same time.

My few hours at home were spent with the electric breast pump we'd rented. It was a far cry from my pregnancy visions of nursing. Never have I known such intense hatred as that which I came to feel towards the machine. I had fantasies of smashing the damn thing to bits once the boys were nursing on their own. Since the pumps cost over a thousand dollars, I knew this fantasy was too expensive to fulfill.

I pumped three to four times a day, freezing the milk and bringing it in when the boys were able to use it. But as the twins' appetites increased, my supply was dwindling to less than an ounce each time I pumped. The frozen milk was just about gone, and the doctors were going to use donated milk from the milk bank unless I produced more. Since this was the one unique contribution I could make, I became determined. I increased my pumping time, alternating five minutes on one side, five minutes on the other side, back and forth, until I was too sore to go on. Soon I was getting four to five ounces at a time.

Two months after the boys' birth, I had my first try at nursing Steven, the bigger, healthier twin. He snuggled into my arms but didn't seem to understand he was there for a reason. He'd take the nipple in his mouth, then drop it. By the time he got around to some productive sucking, he was so worn out that he fell asleep. The next day was easier. He nursed well for 10 minutes.

Timothy had to wait another two weeks to nurse, but I swear he'd been lying there in his incubator watching Steven and taking notes. When his turn came, he knew exactly what to do. He lunged at me like a shark in a feeding frenzy. I was glad he didn't have teeth.

Although Timothy was progressing more slowly, both boys were recovering and growing, and soon we'd have to make decisions about taking them home. Did we want to bring Steven home alone when he reached the five-pound discharge weight, or did we want to wait and bring both boys home together? We chose to bring Steven home first, figuring the transition to twin parenthood would be easier and more gradual this way.

As it turned out, Steven's homecoming was anything but easy and gradual. Late one afternoon while I visited the boys, a doctor asked if I wanted to take Steven home *that night*. The nursery was overcrowded, and four-pound, three-ounce Steven was the healthiest baby there.

Panic! The house was a mess, the cribs were still unassembled, I didn't even have a car seat. I purchased one on the way home and went to work— madly vacuuming, dusting, and scrubbing away three months of accumulated dirt. I couldn't bring a baby with breathing problems home to a dusty house! I was still bouncing off the walls from adrenalin when Bill and I arrived at the hospital to get Steven. We must have taken 100 pictures, 50 as we left the nursery, 50 more when we arrived home.

We kept Steven in with us that night, and I didn't sleep for a second. In our dark, quiet room, Steven fussed and fretted. With every whimper I was up to check on him; and when he was quiet, I was up checking him even more. The next night we put him in his own room with a ticking clock, a radio, and a night light, and everyone got some sleep at last.

During the next three weeks we took Steven with us on our daily visits to the hospital. Back in familiar surroundings, Steven would doze off while I nursed and played with Timothy.

We thought that once both boys were home our troubles would be over. They weren't. Three days after Tim's homecoming, I was nursing Steven when I glanced down and saw he had turned completely gray. He wasn't breathing at all. Luckily, my sister, who is a nurse, was there. She grabbed Steven and worked on him until he revived. Although it seemed an eternity, she had him breathing again in less than a minute. We rushed Steven to the hospital. I'm still amazed I had the presence of mind to bring Timothy along; as it was, I'd left the house without my shoes.

Steven was readmitted to intensive care and checked for everything imaginable. He was given a sleep study, a test in which his breathing was monitored during sleep while carbon dioxide levels were raised and oxygen levels were lowered to what is normally found at 8000 feet. Steven flunked the test and was sent home with an apnea monitor and instructions to stay away from mountains and airplanes. I figured if this could happen to big, healthy Steven, it could also happen to his brother. For my

*Steven at 2 pounds.*

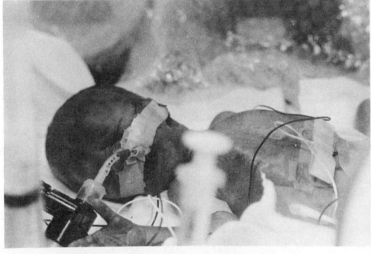

*Timothy at 1 pound, 13 ounces.*

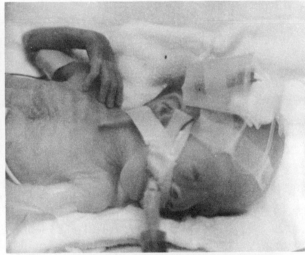

*Steven at 9 months.*

*Timothy at 9 months.*

peace of mind more than anything else, the doctors agreed to give Tim a monitor, too.

I understand doctors are very hesitant to put a baby on a home monitor because they think it will frighten the parents. But no ICU parent is frightened of an apnea monitor, quite the contrary. What frightens us is the possibility of an unnoticed apnea spell. I was furious that no one had warned us this might happen, angry that no one had taught us CPR (cardiopulmonary resuscitation)—a lifesaving technique *every* parent should know. I hate to think what might have happened if my sister had not been there that day.

With the monitors I was finally able to relax and sleep a bit at night. During the day, when we could watch the boys, we unhooked them for outings. There were occasional false alarms, but the boys never again stopped breathing. At the age of six months, Steven had another sleep study. This time he passed, and we stopped the monitoring. Over a period of weeks I'd begun using the monitors less and less in an attempt to "wean" myself. When the time came to give the monitors back, I was confident and comfortable without them.

The boys had other problems during their early months at home. Steven was rehospitalized to repair a hernia. Both boys were circumcised and then recircumcised under general anesthesia when complications developed from the first attempt. The boys had continuing respiratory difficulties from RDS (respiratory distress syndrome) and BPD (bronchopulmonary dysplasia). They wheezed, had frequent colds and bouts of pneumonia. I soon learned to recognize the first signs of pneumonia and to call the doctor at the slightest hint of trouble. Once, it took four phone calls to get someone to see us at midnight, but when the doctor looked at Tim's x-rays, she said it was good I had insisted. We discovered the pneumonia before it was serious. I've learned how important it is to trust my ability to "read" my children and to be assertive when necessary.

But even with all their early health problems, Steven and Timothy have always been remarkably easygoing, good-natured babies. I know prematures are supposed to be difficult infants, but that hasn't been our experience (or the experience of other parents of prematures we know). Perhaps it's all the attention these kids get or perhaps they're just happy to be out of intensive care.

At the age of six months, both boys weaned themselves from the breast—much to my relief. Before they were born I had the same visions all pregnant women have of the love, serenity and satisfaction that is supposed to accompany nursing. This was not how it was for me. I found nursing uncomfortable, time-consuming, exhausting, and generally a nuisance. Within days of weaning I felt happier and less tired. I had pumped for three months and nursed for three months. I had done my best. Enough already!

We took the boys back to the unit to celebrate their six-month birthday with the doctors and nurses who'd become such a part of our lives. During the festivities one of the doctors picked up our now healthy, chubby twins and marched them over to Obstetrics "to show those labor room nurses what *really* happens to the babies they always say are going to die."

Friends who come to our house sometimes find it hard to look at the early pictures of Steven and Timothy that we keep in our family albums. They ask if we're actually going to let the boys see those pictures when they're old enough to understand.

You bet we are! Steven and Timothy are *survivors*. We are proud of them and we'll always let them know it. While medical care and parental love certainly helped, the boys had to have an incredible inner strength to make it.

Bill and I feel like survivors, too. We've been through a hell of a lot. People ask us, "How did you do it? How did you stand the pressure?" Well, I don't recall anyone giving us any options. You stand what you have to stand, that's all.

And it was worth it, every minute of it. Steven and Timothy are nine months old now. Each weighs over 15 pounds. They are healthy, happy, beautiful, active, *normal* baby boys. We feel very lucky indeed.

# Apnea and Bradycardia

Apnea—the absence of breathing for more than 15 seconds—occurs commonly in premature babies. About 45% of babies weighing less than 5½ pounds and 85% of those under 2½ pounds have apnea spells during the early weeks of life. Apnea is often accompanied by bradycardia—a lower than normal heart rate. For the tiny infant this means the heart is beating fewer than 100 times a minute—slow for a baby, even though the adult heart rate is normally much slower.

In the nursery premature infants are closely watched for signs of apnea and bradycardia with the aid of electronic monitoring. Small adhesive monitoring pads are placed on the baby's skin to detect chest movements as he breathes and to pick up the impulses of his heartbeat. Wires attached to the pads transmit this information to a machine next to the baby's bed. Here, variations in heart or breathing rate are displayed as changes in a line on a television screen or they are broadcast as beeps. If the baby's vital signs become abnormal, an alarm sounds. These monitoring machines only record the baby's heart and breathing rates; they do not control them in any way.

While monitors are a useful aid, they cannot re-place the nursery staff's close personal observation of the baby. Monitors tend to give false alarms, some-times because of a loose monitor pad or faulty con-nection, sometimes in response to *normal* changes in the baby's breathing. The premature baby, like the full-term newborn, can have temporarily irregular breathing patterns. He may take several deep breaths and stop breathing for 10 seconds or longer. Then he begins breathing again on his own. During the time

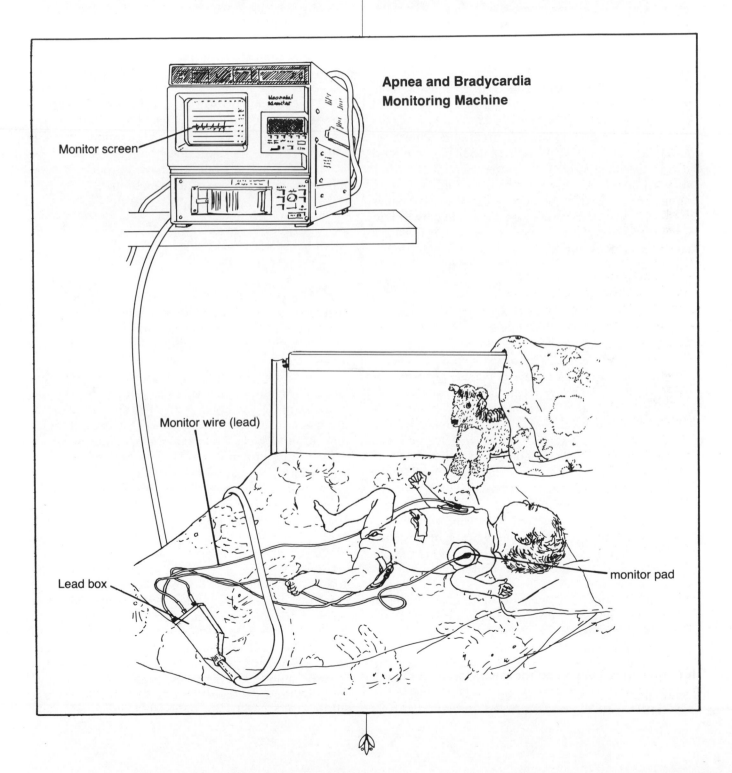

**Apnea and Bradycardia Monitoring Machine**

Monitor screen

Monitor wire (lead)

Lead box

monitor pad

he stops breathing, his color, muscle tone, and heart rate remain normal. This phenomenon is known as *periodic breathing*. Periodic breathing may trigger the apnea alarm, but it is not necessarily a cause for concern. The baby's appearance is the best indication of the existence of a problem.

The more worrisome form of apnea is accompanied by a change in the baby's color. The infant becomes a dusky blue-gray (cyanotic) color in response to a drop in his oxygen level. *Cyanosis* is usually first seen around the baby's lips. The infant becomes very limp; his heart rate slows; and about 30 seconds after he stops breathing, he begins to have bradycardia.

The premature baby is thought to be vulnerable to apnea because the centers in his brain that control respiration are still immature and poorly coordinated. Normally, the brain's breathing centers respond to the levels of oxygen, carbon dioxide, and acid in the bloodstream. When oxygen levels are low and carbon dioxide and acid levels are high, the brain signals for the body to breathe faster. When oxygen is high and carbon dioxide and acid are low, the brain signals for breathing to slow down. This feedback mechanism does not always work well in the premature baby. Low blood oxygen, instead of stimulating him to breathe, can depress the respiratory centers and bring on apnea.

Apnea may accompany respiratory problems or a patent ductus. Low levels of blood sugar or of calcium may cause apnea. Apnea may also be a symptom of infection or of a central nervous system disorder.

But most apnea spells are not associated with disease. Almost any change in the baby's status quo can affect his vulnerable breathing centers. If the baby becomes slightly too hot or too cold, he may become apneic. Stress or fatigue, even normal feeding and handling, can bring on an episode of apnea.

The baby may pull out of the apnea spell on his own; perhaps the alarm reminds him to breathe again. Usually gentle stimulation—rubbing the baby's arm or leg—revives him. The baby who remains unresponsive is bagged with room air or given oxygen. If his apnea is frequent or persistent, the baby is put on a respirator and checked for underlying problems such as infection.

Some hospitals have found that babies placed in rocking hammocks or on undulating waterbeds have fewer apnea episodes. It is believed that irregular rocking motions provide stimulation to various parts of the brain, including those controlling respiration. The stimulants caffeine and theophylline are sometimes given to babies to help reduce apnea.

The breathing and heart rate monitors are also used to be sure the baby's breathing and heartbeat rates do not become too rapid. A breathing rate of over 60 breaths per minute—too fast—is called *tachypnea*. A heartbeat rate of over 180 to 200 beats per minute—also too fast—is called *tachycardia*. Tachypnea and tachycardia normally occur when the baby is upset or excited.

If tachypnea and tachycardia are persistent, the baby is tested for an underlying cause, such as infection or respiratory problems; meanwhile, the rapidly breathing baby is given oxygen or other respiratory assistance to keep him from becoming too tired.

When the baby is healthy, more mature, and in control of his breathing, the monitors are disconnected.

The great majority of premature babies stop having apnea spells when they reach 36 to 37 weeks' gestational age, but occasionally a baby continues to have apnea spells for weeks or months longer. A baby who is otherwise healthy but still having apnea may be allowed to go home on an apnea monitor.

# Controlling Body Temperature

From conception, the developing baby has been nurtured in the warmth of his mother's body. At birth, he emerges wet into a cold world where he must suddenly begin to regulate his own body temperature.

The baby loses heat from his exposed body surfaces. The chubby full-term, who gains a pound of fat a week during the last month of pregnancy, is relatively well insulated; his curled up posture also helps him conserve heat. The premature baby, however, is dangerously vulnerable to chilling as a result of his open posture and large body surface area relative to his weight. Because of the greater exposure of his body surfaces, a 1500-gram baby loses five times the amount of heat per unit of body weight as an adult does.

The premature baby, especially the baby with breathing problems, is poorly supplied with calories and oxygen—the fuels he needs to heat his body. If the baby must burn his limited calorie supply for warmth, he has none left to grow. The chilled baby struggling to heat himself may become so depleted of oxygen and calories that lactic acid—a byproduct of low oxygen metabolism—accumulates in his blood in harmful amounts. This excess acid temporarily constricts the lungs' blood vessels and reduces blood flow through the lungs—a situation that can cause or worsen respiratory distress. The cold- or heat-stressed baby is also likely to have attacks of apnea and bradycardia. Once a baby becomes too cold or too hot, he must be brought back to a normal temperature slowly, since abrupt temperature changes can be hazardous.

Because of these potential dangers, a primary objective of the baby's care is to keep him warm—but not too warm. On a table heated by radiant lamps or in an incubator, the baby's temperature is carefully controlled. A probe taped to the baby's abdomen constantly records the baby's temperature and regulates the surrounding temperature. If the baby becomes chilled, the probe signals for more heat; if the baby becomes too warm, the heat is reduced. The infant's axillary (under the arm) temperature is frequently checked as well.

The goal is to keep the baby as close as possible to the normal body temperature of 98.6° Fahrenheit, or 37° Celsius—the temperature at which the baby conserves the most oxygen and calories and gains the most weight.

The tiny premature has difficulty with temperature control not only because he lacks energy reserves and insulating fat, but also because he is limited in the ways he can cope with temperature changes. Like other newborns, he cannot shiver to generate heat when he is chilled; and when he is too warm he cannot sweat to cool off because his sweat glands are still poorly developed.

Until the tiny premature grows and matures, he is at the mercy of his environment. Even slight temperature changes can affect him. The baby may become chilled by the minor temperature drop that occurs when the incubator door is opened. On the warming table the baby is vulnerable to drafts. Through a process of radiant heat loss, the baby can be chilled by cool objects around him, even when these objects do not actually touch him. If the baby's incubator is close to a sunny window, he may become too warm as a result of radiant heat gain—a "greenhouse effect."

A higher than normal temperature in a young premature is rarely a fever or sign of illness the way it is in an older child. Usually it is the result of too warm an environment. However, a *fluctuating* temperature that cannot be explained by environmental factors *can* be a symptom of infection or other illness.

Usually chilling, rather than overheating, poses the greatest problem for the baby. Even in a heated incubator, he often needs additional protection. He may be dressed in a cap and booties and wrapped in a transparent blanket (which allows the staff to observe him). He may be covered with a plastic dome called a heat shield, or his incubator may be lined with foil to provide a second insulating wall and prevent radiant heat loss.

When a baby reaches 35 to 36 weeks' gestational age, weighs over 1800 grams, and is medically stable, he is slowly weaned from the artificially heated environment. At first, the baby is dressed and bundled. Then the heat in his incubator is reduced. If the baby's temperature remains stable, he is moved to an open bassinet and carefully observed. Weaning from artificial heat often follows the two steps forward, one step back pattern. After a few hours in the open the baby may become too cool. Even if the baby can maintain his temperature, he may use up all his calories doing so and fail to gain weight. He is then returned to the incubator for a few more days before being tested again in a bassinet. Before the baby leaves the hospital, he must achieve the ability to control his body temperature and gain weight at the same time.

# Nourishing the Premature Baby

Before birth, the baby receives a steady flow of ideally selected, predigested nutrients that cross the placenta from his mother's bloodstream into his own. The premature baby is often removed from that perfect food source before he is ready to eat, digest, and assimilate food by himself.

No one has yet learned to recreate a formula like the one that nurtures the unborn baby. But pre-term nutrition is receiving increased attention at neonatal centers around the country. Knowledge of the premature's special needs is growing. Each hospital has its own feeding plan, one that is further tailored to meet the individual requirements of each baby.

## *Intravenous Feedings*

A very young premature, or a baby with breathing problems, cannot be given anything by mouth at first. The baby's immature digestive tract must be slowly and cautiously initiated into its new nourishing role. In addition, a baby who is sick or stressed has poor circulation to his digestive tract. This is because the body reacts to stress by diverting blood from temporarily less essential organs such as the stomach and intestines to those organs needed for immediate survival such as the heart, brain, kidneys, and lungs. Anything given by mouth is unlikely to be properly digested by a baby who is using most of his energy just

## The Umbilical Artery Catheter

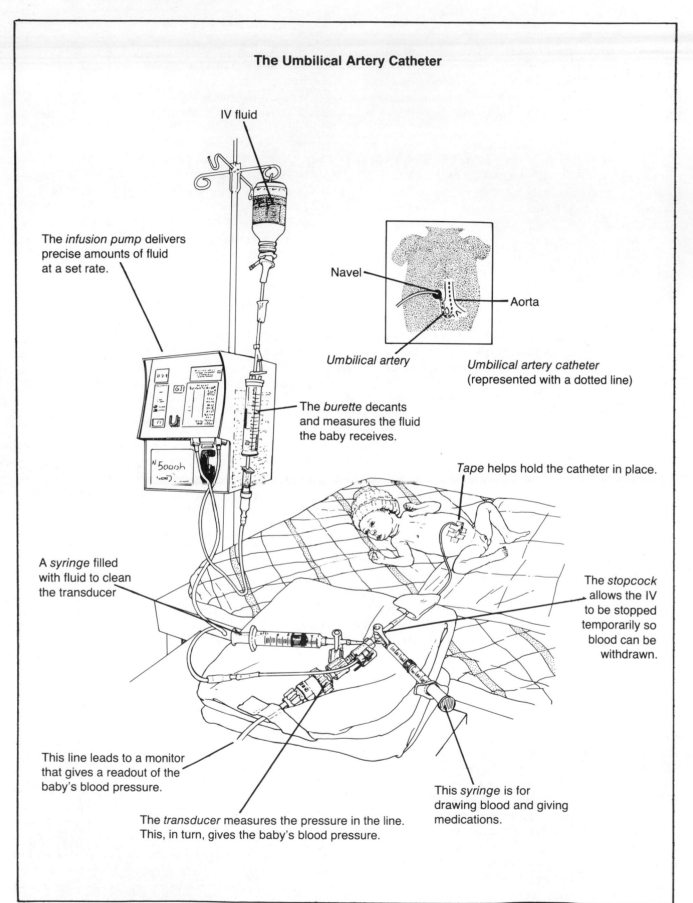

IV fluid

The *infusion pump* delivers precise amounts of fluid at a set rate.

Navel

Aorta

*Umbilical artery*

*Umbilical artery catheter* (represented with a dotted line)

The *burette* decants and measures the fluid the baby receives.

*Tape* helps hold the catheter in place.

A *syringe* filled with fluid to clean the transducer

The *stopcock* allows the IV to be stopped temporarily so blood can be withdrawn.

This line leads to a monitor that gives a readout of the baby's blood pressure.

This *syringe* is for drawing blood and giving medications.

The *transducer* measures the pressure in the line. This, in turn, gives the baby's blood pressure.

to breathe. Oral feedings can even create new medical problems. Therefore, many prematures receive their first feedings intravenously—through a needle or tube inserted into an artery or vein.

Intravenous (IV) solutions must be given to the baby in minute, precisely measured amounts. An infusion pump attached to the baby's IV line carefully regulates fluids flowing into the baby's bloodstream.

There are three main types of intravenous lines: the *umbilical artery catheter* (UA catheter or UA line), the *superficial IV,* and the *central line.* Each has its special advantages and drawbacks.

### Umbilical Artery Catheter*

The umbilical catheter, inserted through an umbilical artery into the aorta, provides a convenient, painless way to draw the baby's blood and give him food and medication. But it does pose risks. The catheter is a foreign object deep inside the body. If bacteria grow in the line, infection can spread rapidly throughout the baby's bloodstream. Other complications include circulatory disturbances and the formation of blood clots that may affect the legs and feet and occasionally the kidneys and intestines. Because of these potential hazards, the UA catheter is withdrawn as soon as it is no longer needed for frequent blood sampling.

### Superficial IV

The superficial IV is inserted into a superficial vein (one close to the skin's surface) with a small gauge "butterfly" needle—so called because of the plastic "wings" that help hold it in place. If the IV is in an arm or leg, the limb may be splinted with a padded tongue depressor and restrained with a piece of gauze so that the baby cannot dislodge the needle. If the IV is in the baby's scalp—an area rich in superficial veins—some hair must be shaved (it grows back!). A scalp IV allows the baby to move his arms and legs freely.

Nutrients, medication, and blood can be *given* through the superficial IV, but blood cannot be withdrawn; the superficial veins are too fragile. A baby who needs frequent blood sampling may have two IV lines: an umbilical catheter for blood drawing and a superficial IV or central line for feeding and medication.

---

*Arterial catheters may be placed in arteries other than the umbilical arteries. Some physicians prefer the use of radial artery catheters, catheters inserted into the radial artery of the arm, or temporal artery catheters inserted into the temporal artery of the scalp.

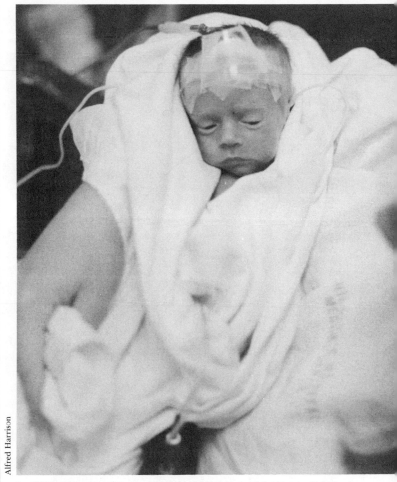

Alfred Harrison

*An IV may be placed in the baby's scalp, an area rich in superficial veins.*

The superficial IV is relatively free of side effects such as clotting and infection. However, high concentrations of nutrients or medication cannot be given since they irritate the delicate superficial veins. Superficial IVs also frequently *infiltrate*—that is, the needle moves out of the vein and allows IV fluid to collect in the surrounding tissues. IV sites are closely observed for swelling indicative of an infiltration. When an IV infiltrates, it is quickly removed, and the fluid is usually reabsorbed into the tissues without causing damage.

### Central Line

When a baby needs IV feeding for an extended period of time, a thin intravenous tube called a central line may be placed in one of the larger veins of the arm, leg, scalp, or neck. The central line can be installed in the vein through a small hollow needle. Once the tube is in place the needle is removed. The line may also be inserted by a minor surgical technique referred to as a *cut down,* which is performed in the nursery by a pediatric surgeon. Under local anesthesia, a tiny incision is made over the baby's vein and the tube is threaded through the vein until it reaches a position as close as possible to the baby's heart. With the intravenous line in a large central vein, higher concentrations of nutrients and medication can be given. The central line is much less likely than a superficial IV to infiltrate, and it is not as likely as an umbilical catheter to disrupt circulation or form clots. However, like the umbilical catheter, it is a foreign object deep inside the body and a possible site for infection. At the first indication of infection the line is removed.

## The Intravenous "Formula"

Preparing the intravenous formula best suited to the baby is a process of constant monitoring and fine tuning. The baby must receive a balance of nutrients—enough to recover and grow, but not so much as to strain his system. The baby on IV feedings is frequently tested to be sure that his body responds properly to each substance that is given.

The first intravenous feeding that the baby receives is sugar (glucose, also called dextrose) and water. Sugar water supplies the baby with vital calories and fluids.

The amount of fluid the baby takes in is carefully measured. His urine output is measured too, by weighing his diapers after he urinates. On the nursery's sensitive scales, even a drop of urine can be detected. By comparing the amount of fluid the baby is given with the amount he excretes, it is possible to tell if the baby is retaining or losing too much water. The urine is also examined. If the baby produces small amounts of highly concentrated, dark yellow urine, he probably needs more fluids. If he urinates very frequently and his urine is quite dilute, he may need to have the amount of fluids reduced.

Both the baby's blood and urine are checked for the presence of sugar. Normally, sugar does not enter the urine. When it does, it may mean the baby's blood sugar level is too high—a condition called *hyperglycemia*. Hyperglycemia is corrected by reducing the baby's sugar intake. The baby may also be given a dose of insulin to help him metabolize the extra sugar. If levels of sugar in the blood are low *(hypoglycemia)*, more glucose is added to the intravenous formula.

A simple test for blood sugar frequently performed in the nursery is called a *Dextrostix*. It involves placing a drop of blood on a chemically treated strip. The resulting color change indicates the amount of sugar present.

Sodium and potassium—minerals referred to as *electrolytes*—are added, along with calcium, to the sugar-water solution. These minerals play vital roles in many of the body's chemical processes. They conduct nerve impulses, allow the tissues to maintain a proper fluid balance, and help keep the body from becoming too acidic or too alkaline. Premature babies, especially when sick or stressed, are vulnerable to imbalances of these important minerals. The baby's blood may be checked several times each day for calcium and electrolyte levels so that the amounts given intravenously can be properly adjusted.

The baby also needs protein for building new tissue and repairing tissues damaged by illness. Sometime during the first week after birth, protein in the form of essential amino acids is added to the baby's IV solution. Once protein has been added to the solution, the baby is said to be receiving *hyperalimentation* (HA) or *total parenteral nutrition* (TPN).

At first, the protein is highly diluted, since too much can stress the baby's liver and kidneys. As the baby's toleration increases, protein levels are increased. Every few days while the baby is on hyperalimentation, he is tested for signs of strain to his organs. A blood test for *creatinine* levels indicates how well the kidneys are functioning. A test for blood urea and nitrogen *(BUN)* checks the liver and kidneys. Tests for the enzymes *SGOT* (serum glutamicoxaloacetic transaminase) and *SGPT* (serum glutamic pyruvic transaminase) show when organ damage is occurring from a protein overload. The baby's urine and blood are also examined for ammonia, which accumulates in excessive amounts if too much protein is given.

Tiny prematures have greater requirements than full-terms for certain vitamins because of their rapid growth, low nutrient stores, and the stresses they encounter after birth. Prematures often need extra vitamin D to insure proper bone growth. Large amounts of vitamin E may be given to help prevent anemia and to counteract the toxic effects of oxygen on the lung and eye. (There is controversy, however, about whether vitamin E is actually effective in this role.) Additional vitamin K, for proper blood clotting, may be given if the baby is on antibiotic therapy. Normally, vitamin K is manufactured by intestinal bacteria, but these bacteria are killed off by antibiotics. Vitamins A and C and the B complex vitamins are also part of the hyperalimentation formula. It is the B vitamins that give the solution its yellow color. In addition, the hyperalimentation formula contains folic acid, a nutrient needed for growth, along with the trace elements zinc, magnesium, copper, and iron. *Intralipid,* a white, fatty liquid derived from soybeans, may be mixed in to provide the baby with a concentrated calorie source. The baby's blood is checked frequently to be sure the fat leaves the bloodstream and is properly used by the body.

For reasons that are still poorly understood, some babies develop vitamin and mineral deficiencies when they are fed intravenously for long periods of time. Copper deficiency may play a role in *osteopenia*, a condition similar to rickets, in which the baby's bones lose minerals (become demineralized) and fracture easily. Some babies have hair loss or skin peeling, possibly from a zinc deficiency. It is not yet known if these deficiencies have any long-range effects, but the immediate problems they cause can often be reversed by giving the baby extra vitamins and minerals. As soon as possible, the baby is started on oral feedings, since such nutritional problems are much less likely to occur in babies fed by mouth.

## Gavage Feeding

The transition from intravenous to full oral feedings is made gradually and carefully. There is usually an overlap period during which the baby receives both intravenous nourishment and feedings through a gavage tube—a small flexible tube inserted into the baby's mouth (or nose) and into the stomach. Young prematures who have not developed the gag reflex do not seem to find the gavage tube uncomfortable. The tube may be left in place for continuous feeding or inserted and withdrawn for periodic meals. Although the food goes directly from the tube to the stomach, gavage is considered an oral feeding method.

The gavage-fed baby *is* able to suck and has been doing so in utero since the early months of gestation; but he cannot nipple-feed until he learns to suck, swallow, and breathe in the right sequence. In the meantime, sucking remains an important activity for the baby. Gavage-fed babies, even those on respirators, are often given pacifiers to suck during their gavage meals. Practice with a pacifier gives the baby a stronger suck for later nipple-feeding. Researchers have also found that babies who suck on pacifiers during gavage feedings digest their food better and gain more weight than do babies who are not given this sucking experience.

As gavage feedings are increased, intravenous feedings are tapered off and stopped altogether once the baby is receiving sufficient calories by gavage.

The baby's first gavage meal is dilute sterile glucose water. The sugar water is usually given in continuous tiny doses at first, as little as one cc. (cubic centimeter) per hour for 24 hours. (One cc. is the same as one milliliter or ml. It equals 20 drops.) If the baby digests the glucose water, he is given half-strength formula or breastmilk for a day or two. Then if all goes well, he is started on full-strength breastmilk or formula. Some hospitals like to begin with a formula specifically designed to meet the needs of low-birthweight infants. They may wish to give this formula instead of breastmilk, at least until the baby regains his birthweight. Breastmilk can be given later, and mothers are encouraged to keep up their milk supply.

The baby's feedings are increased until he is taking and digesting relatively large meals (30 to 45 cc.'s) every two to three hours.

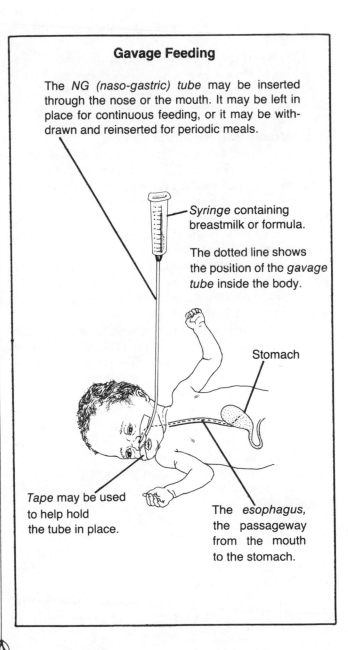

**Gavage Feeding**

The *NG (naso-gastric) tube* may be inserted through the nose or the mouth. It may be left in place for continuous feeding, or it may be withdrawn and reinserted for periodic meals.

*Syringe* containing breastmilk or formula.

The dotted line shows the position of the *gavage tube* inside the body.

Stomach

*Tape* may be used to help hold the tube in place.

The *esophagus*, the passageway from the mouth to the stomach.

## Feeding Complications

Digestion is a new task for the baby, and many prematures have difficulties at first. A swollen abdomen, spitting up, and apnea are common symptoms of feeding problems. The baby's *residuals*—undigested food in the stomach—are frequently checked by applying suction to the gavage tube and withdrawing the contents of the stomach. Large residuals or the presence of bile in the stomach indicate that the baby's digestive tract needs a rest. Oral feedings are stopped or reduced, and IV feedings are resumed. If abdominal bloating becomes severe, the baby's stomach is *decompressed*, a process in which continuous suction is applied to the gavage tube to draw off stomach contents and air. Decompression reduces abdominal swelling and gives the intestinal tract time to recuperate.

X-rays of the baby's stomach and intestines may be taken to detect any thickenings or air pockets in the baby's intestinal walls that can be early signs of the disease called *necrotizing enterocolitis.*

### Necrotizing Enterocolitis

Necrotizing enterocolitis (NEC) is a disease first described in prematures in the late 1960s, about the time doctors began saving relatively large numbers of very tiny and severely stressed infants. It is these babies whom the disease most often strikes. The precise cause of NEC is still unknown. Early feeding may complicate, but does not seem to cause, the disease. Breastmilk was once thought to provide protection. If it does, that protection is not absolute. Babies fed breastmilk have developed NEC, and so have babies who have never had oral feedings at all.

Doctors suspect that the disease begins when circulation to the intestines is interrupted during an episode of hypoxia (oxygen deprivation) or from chronically poor intestinal circulation resulting from an open ductus. Poor circulation weakens the intestinal wall and disrupts the production of protective mucus. Normally harmless bacteria that live in the intestinal tract then invade the tissue layers of the intestinal wall. The bacteria form gas bubbles that cause swelling and further disruption of intestinal circulation. Left untreated, intestinal tissue may die and break open, or *perforate*, spreading infection through the abdominal cavity.

At the first sign of NEC the baby is given antibiotics. His stomach is decompressed, and feedings are stopped until the intestine has recovered. Occasionally, surgery is necessary to remove dead intestinal tissue. If a small area of intestine is affected, it is removed and the healthy ends are joined. In rare

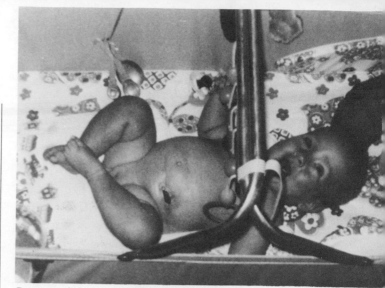

*Prematurely born Ami Everett at 8½ months with colostomy (see story, page 84).*

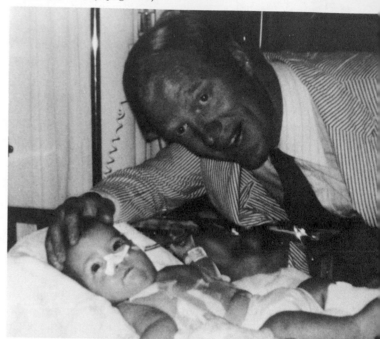

*Ami rehospitalized for colostomy repair, shown with her surgeon, Michael Harrison.*

*Ami at 2 years, 8 months, with her friend Christina.*

cases, a large portion of the intestine must be removed. The surgeon then performs a temporary *ileostomy* or a *colostomy,* operations in which the healthy upper end of the intestine is brought through the abdominal wall to the outside. The damaged sections are removed, and the lower part of the intestinal tract is left inside the body to rest and grow. The baby's digestive tract now empties through the surgically created opening in the abdominal wall. Six months to a year later, when the baby is older and chances for successful surgery are greater, the two healthy ends of the intestines are rejoined, and the child has a normally functioning digestive tract.

## Urination and Bowel Movements

The developing fetus swallows amniotic fluid and produces urine. Even the very tiny premature baby can urinate at birth, and often does. Because of his tiny bladder size, the premature urinates frequently, commonly wetting a diaper or two every hour.

But during illness or episodes of stress, the baby may urinate much less frequently and retain fluid because of a temporary kidney malfunction.

A baby who has been given curare, pancuronium (Pavulon), or sedatives has difficulty emptying his bladder. The nurse may press gently on the baby's lower abdomen, the area above the bladder, to help him urinate.

Sometime during the first two days after birth, the baby usually has a bowel movement. Until oral feedings are begun, the baby passes blackish-green meconium, a substance produced in the intestinal tract during gestation. The baby may normally move his bowels several times a day or as infrequently as once every two days.

As the baby begins to take formula or breastmilk, his stools become lighter in color and more frequent. Breastmilk has a laxative effect, and some breast-fed babies have a bowel movement with each feeding. The breast-fed baby has loose, yellowish stools that are smooth or curdlike in consistency. Formula-fed babies have fewer stools than babies fed breastmilk. Their stools are light brown in color, with a smooth or grainy consistency.

A baby receiving phototherapy for jaundice often has diarrhea as his body excretes toxic bilirubin (see page 86). Diarrhea may also be caused by antibiotics, since in addition to killing the disease-causing germs, they also destroy the helpful bacteria that normally aid digestion. The diarrhea stops once the antibiotic course is over.

If a formula-fed baby develops diarrhea, it may be a sign of formula intolerance. Switching formulas may help. Babies fed breastmilk normally have loose, frequent stools, but if the stools are very frequent and watery, the mother may wish to eliminate foods such as fruit juices, chocolate, or cabbage-type vegetables from her diet. Since diarrhea can also be a sign of infection, a baby with very loose, frequent stools is closely examined and tested. A sick or sedated baby tends to become constipated and may be given suppositories to keep his bowel movement regular.

## The Ups and Downs of Weight Gain

Regaining birthweight is an important milestone on the premature's road to recovery. Almost all babies, full-term and premature, lose some weight after birth. The healthy full-term is usually back to his birth weight in a matter of days, but the premature baby, especially if he has been sick, may take a month or longer to make up the 200 to 500 grams (or more!) that he lost in the beginning.

Illness, surgery, or other complications may cause temporary setbacks in the baby's weight gain. Babies with bronchopulmonary dysplasia are especially slow to gain, since they use up so many calories struggling to breathe but cannot be fed much without risking metabolic disturbances or fluid overload.

To gain, a baby needs around 90 to 120 calories from oral feedings for each kilo (2.2 pounds) of body weight. If the baby is fed intravenously, calories are used more efficiently and fewer need be given. Ideally, a baby who gets enough calories gains 10 to 20 grams a day. In reality, most babies grow in lags and spurts, staying near the same weight for days or weeks, then making a rapid gain of 30 to 60 grams a day. Most hospitals allow a healthy premature to go home once he weighs 4½ to 5 pounds.

## Ready to Nipple

At about 34 weeks of gestational age, the baby may resist the gavage tube, perhaps suspecting that there are better ways to be fed. The baby may gag a bit as the tube is inserted. He may actively suck on the tube during feedings. The appearance of the baby's gag reflex along with his strengthening suck are signs that he is ready to try the nipple.

Before a baby is started on breast- or bottle-feedings, he must be medically stable and gaining weight. A baby on a respirator is too sick to nipple-feed, but a baby in oxygen can usually be nursed or bottle-fed.

Nipple-feeding is a new skill for the baby. He must learn to suck, swallow, and breathe in the right sequence; he also uses up a larger amount of energy to get his food. Until he acquires the strength and coordination for exclusive nipple-feedings, his sessions with the breast or bottle are supplemented by gavage. See Chapter 9, page 153 for information on breast- and bottle-feeding in the nursery and at home.

## Ami's Story

### By Sandi Everett

As I write, we're having a quiet morning under our grape arbor. Ami with garden hose in hand is carefully watering the patio furniture. She sees that her socks look a little too dry and proceeds to remedy the matter. Her sister Anya is sleeping peacefully in her basket, making the little squeaking, stretching sounds that three-week-old babies often make. After one such squeak, Ami stops her work, gazes with concern toward the basket, and announces, "Baby seepin."

Ami is a very average, beautiful 2½-year-old. Nobody would ever guess what she has been through, but those of us who do know will never forget.

I was just six months into what had been a normal, comfortable pregnancy, when I awakened one night to find my waters had broken. Sick with fear, I phoned my doctor and sobbed the details. He said he was sorry, but my baby was just too early to survive.

We left for the hospital, my eyes nearly swollen shut from crying as I felt my baby kick and squirm inside me. At the hospital I was given two shots of betamethasone to help the baby's lungs mature on the outside chance that our child might actually live.

Despite the possibility of infection from my broken membranes, my doctor wanted to keep the baby inside me as long as possible. But Ami had her own plans. After four days in the hospital I began hard labor. My husband Ron held me as I gave the one push that brought our daughter into the world. We were so afraid, expecting to have to watch our tiny fetus struggle and die.

Ami surprised us all. She was beautiful, so teeny and red, a perfect little baby crying the softest cry I'd ever heard. She was whisked away as her father followed, bewildered. That was the beginning of the longest three months of our lives.

Born at 27 weeks, Ami weighed two pounds, five ounces, but was amazingly alert and active. She had no trouble breathing at first and was able to drink my milk through a feeding tube. She had been born on November 7th (her due date was February 10th), and we expected to have her home by Christmas. We were so, so happy. I watched the doctor who had predicted her death as he stood by her Isolette shaking his head in amazement. "It's a miracle," he repeated over and over again.

We visited Ami every day, rocking her, diapering her, and rubbing vitamin E oil on her tender skin. I pumped my breasts using a bicycle-horn-shaped pump at home and an electric pump at the hospital. I pumped every four hours just as if Ami were home on a regular feeding schedule. If I couldn't carry her the full nine months, at least I could give her the best possible food, something all the doctors and nurses in the world couldn't do.

Three days after birth she became jaundiced and was placed under the bilirubin lights. On the fifth day she seemed especially tired and listless to me. I was holding her when suddenly she became very still and gray. Her monitor began to alarm. The nurse thumped on her foot to start her breathing again, as I fought back my tears. Oxygen was added to Ami's Isolette but it didn't help. She was developing pneumonia.

Soon she was on a respirator. She was given antibiotics through an IV in her scalp. She looked pretty sad with patches of her hair shaved, a respirator mask taped to her face, and her arms tied down to prevent her from pulling out the tubes. We were no longer able to hold her.

After a couple of days she responded to the antibiotics and was taken off the respirator. Things were looking up again when Ami began having bloody stools. Necrotizing enterocolitis, the doctors called it. She had an open ductus, which caused a backflow of blood to her lungs. While her lungs got too much blood, her intestines were becoming damaged from poor circulation.

Ami's feedings were stopped for a few days. Then, slowly, she was given food again. She took my milk in a bottle for the first time when she was only two weeks old. The next day I ordered baby announcements and bought Ami some doll clothes. But when I arrived at the nursery, the doctor told me Ami was being transferred to Moffitt Hospital in San Francisco. Her intestines were bleeding again, and they wanted her to have immediate surgery to close her ductus.

We followed the ambulance, our hopes sinking. She weighed less than two pounds now, and it seemed impossible that she could survive an operation. She went into surgery at one in the morning on Thanksgiving day. The ductus operation went well, and we were told she would be at Moffitt Hospital only a few more days. But those days turned into weeks. She was put on a respirator and fed by a tube in her jugular vein. At five weeks she contracted viral meningitis. We were told she might be handicapped as a result—hearing loss, cerebral palsy, and retardation were all possibilities. But she was such a little fighter! She quickly recovered with no lasting effects.

By Christmas Eve Ami was off the respirator. After a month of wanting to, we were able to hold her at last.

*Ami at 4 weeks.*

*Ami with newborn sister Anya.*

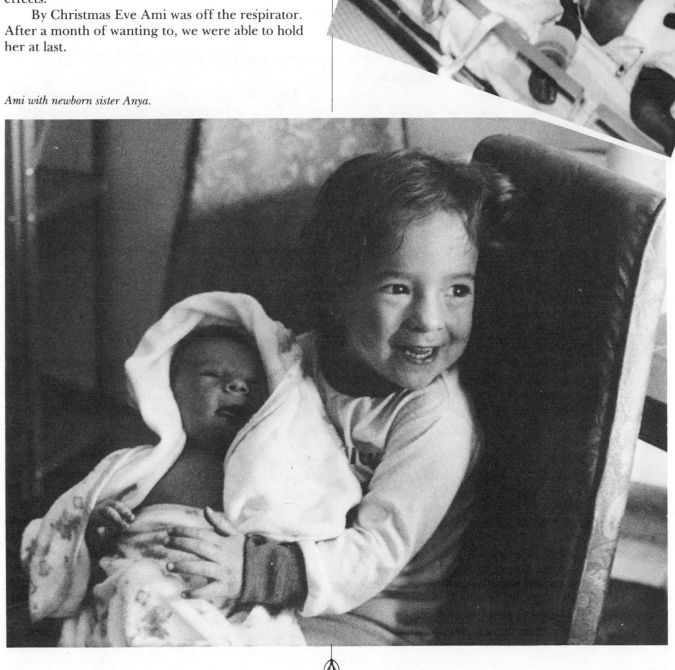

But her intestinal problems continued: her stomach was swollen, her color was terrible, she was unresponsive and listless. On January 3rd she again had surgery, this time to remove a part of her colon that had been damaged by the necrotizing enterocolitis. A colostomy was made on her lower abdomen. The surgery was long and hard on her. When I came to visit the next day, I hardly recognized her. I thought at first that her hat had been put on another baby. She had swollen to twice her normal size.

This was the lowest point for Ron and me. "Would she ever come home?" we asked ourselves. "How long can she stand all that pain and misery, all the wires and tubes? How long will we have to ask permission to hold our baby? How long will we have to drive 100 miles a day to look at her through the glass of an Isolette?"

Well, the colostomy did the trick. It was kind of strange seeing her poop from a little hole on her belly, but the difference it made was incredible. She began eating and gaining weight. Ten days after the operation I was able to nurse Ami for the first time, and there just aren't words to describe how I felt. Those months of pumping were certainly worth it!

She was transferred to our community hospital to convalesce and grow. I was able to nurse her for all of her daytime feedings, and she was given my milk in bottles at night. The doctors encouraged me to nurse, since breastmilk was the easiest food for her digestive tract to handle.

On February 4th, six days before her due date, Ami left the hospital weighing four pounds, five ounces. That was *some* day! Our little girl was finally home. She had come from a world of 24-hour-a-day lights, beepers, doctors, and nurses, and we expected her to have trouble adjusting to our quiet house. The first night we even left the lights and radio on. But Ami was used to taking things in stride. She was an easygoing baby who seemed as happy to be home as we were to have her there. Nursing went smoothly (I weaned her at 15 months).

A case of retrolental fibroplasia that had been diagnosed while she was in the hospital resolved completely. Her eyes were all right. The colostomy was no problem, either. She simply dirtied the front of her diaper instead of the back. At 8½ months she returned to Moffitt Hospital, and her bowel was reconnected and her tummy patched up. Except for a few scars, which will later be fixed by cosmetic surgery, Ami was normal.

And now? Things have been fine ever since. As I nurse little Anya, Ami snuggles in next to us, patting her newborn sister's head as gently as a 2½-

year-old can. On mornings like this, those hospital days seem very far away.

# Blood Disorders

Many of the illnesses that can accompany prematurity involve temporary abnormalities in the baby's blood. Blood, or certain components of blood, may be given to the baby to help correct such conditions as *jaundice (hyperbilirubinemia)*, anemia, *polycythemia*, clotting problems, low blood volume *(hypovolemia)*, and infection.

## *Jaundice (Hyperbilirubinemia)*

The cells that circulate in the blood are constantly dying and being replaced by new cells. When red blood cells die, the hemoglobin in the cells breaks down into iron, protein, and a yellow pigment called *bilirubin*. Bilirubin, a potentially toxic substance, is transported in the blood attached to the protein albumin. In this combined form, bilirubin is transported to the liver, where it is detoxified by a process known as *conjugation*. Conjugated bilirubin, also called *direct bilirubin*, is harmless and is excreted through the urinary and intestinal tracts.

Babies are born with a large number of fetal red blood cells. Soon after birth these cells begin to break down and release bilirubin. However, the enzyme systems in the liver that normally detoxify (or conjugate) bilirubin are not yet working efficiently. As a result, harmful concentrations of bilirubin can accumulate in the baby's blood.

When bilirubin levels rise in the blood, some of the pigment enters body tissues, where it causes temporary yellowing of the baby's skin and the whites of the eyes—the condition called jaundice. If concentrations in the blood become very high, bilirubin can penetrate and damage brain cells. Central nervous system damage caused by bilirubin is called *kernicterus*.

Three to seven days after birth, almost every baby has some degree of hyperbilirubinemia (bilirubin in the blood). This is normal and not a cause for concern as long as levels remain relatively low. But some babies are likely to develop the higher bilirubin levels that require medical treatment. A baby who has experienced bruising or internal bleeding during delivery has an especially large number of red cells breaking down and releasing bilirubin. The baby with

## The Composition of Blood

### Red Blood Cells (RBCs, Erythrocytes)

Red cells, formed in the bone marrow, make up nearly half the blood's volume. These cells contain the red substance *hemoglobin* that transports oxygen and carbon dioxide to and from the body tissues. The percentage of red cells in the blood (normally 40 to 50%) is called the *hematocrit.*

### White Blood Cells (WBCs, Leukocytes)

The various types of white blood cells produced by the bone marrow help the body fight disease. During a brief life span of several hours to several days, a single white blood cell can devour as many as 25 bacteria. Different types of white cells are constantly produced in response to the body's needs. An analysis of the number and type of white blood cells in circulation gives important information about disease conditions the body is trying to combat.

### Platelets (Thrombocytes)

Platelets are cell particles that help the blood to clot and prevent excessive bleeding.

### Plasma

Plasma is the clear liquid in which the red cells, white cells, and platelets circulate. Plasma contains water, protein, glucose, and other substances that nourish the cells. In addition, plasma contains disease-fighting proteins called *antibodies* that lock into specific germs and toxins to make them harmless. Other proteins in plasma called *clotting factors* act together with the platelets to form clots. When clotting factors are removed from the plasma, the resulting liquid is called *serum.*

### Proteins That Determine Blood Type

Depending on the type of protein present in the blood cells, each person is said to belong to a specific blood group or type—either *type O, type A, type B,* or *type AB.* Another sort of protein known as the *Rh factor* is present in the red blood cells of 85% of the population. Those without the Rh factor are said to be *Rh negative;* those with it, *Rh positive.* Bloods of different groups when mixed together can attack each other's cells. Before a transfusion is given, the patient's blood and the donor's blood are *crossmatched,* that is they are mixed together in the laboratory and observed under a microscope to make sure they are compatible. Blood problems in newborns can be caused by certain incompatibilities between the mother's and the baby's blood.

---

an infection at birth also tends to have high bilirubin levels as a result of red blood cell breakdown, and so does the baby who has an Rh or other incompatibility with his mother's blood. If a large amount of placental blood entered the baby's body before the cord was clamped, he too may have jaundice problems.

The premature baby is likely to develop high bilirubin levels, and he is more vulnerable than the full-term to bilirubin's toxic effects. The premature baby's liver is even less ready to begin detoxifying bilirubin, and the bilirubin in the baby's blood may have difficulty even reaching the liver. If the baby is cold, acidotic, or under stress, the bond between albumin and bilirubin may break, freeing the bilirubin to enter body tissues. The premature baby's cells are weaker and more permeable than those of the full-term infant; bilirubin seeps into his tissues more easily.

At birth, babies are given injections of vitamin K to help reduce the possibility of bleeding, red cell breakdown, and resulting jaundice. After birth, all babies—prematures especially—are closely watched for signs of hyperbilirubinemia. Besides yellowing of the skin and eyes, symptoms include lethargy, a high-pitched, irritable cry, feeding difficulties, and temperature instability. The baby's blood is frequently checked for bilirubin. If levels threaten to rise above those considered safe, the baby is treated by phototherapy or transfusion.

### *Phototherapy*

Phototherapy—exposing the baby's skin to special bright lights—often helps reduce bilirubin levels. Blue light waves from the *bililights* change the molecular structure of bilirubin so that it binds more easily with albumin for transport to the liver, detoxification, and excretion. The baby's eyes are covered with a mask during the treatment, since prolonged exposure to the lights might damage them. Although the lights can temporarily disrupt a baby's day and night cycles—a problem for any infant in intensive care—no long-term side effects have yet been reported from their use, and parents and nursery staff are unaffected by exposure to the lights. Phototherapy is continued for 3 to 10 days until bilirubin levels are reduced. (Since the lights tan the baby's skin, it may be hard to see the jaundice fading.)

Sunlight also reduces bilirubin levels, although it is less effective than the intense lights used in the nursery. North American Indians long ago discovered the value of exposing jaundiced infants to the sun. Modern medicine made a similar discovery 30 years ago, when nurses in a British hospital

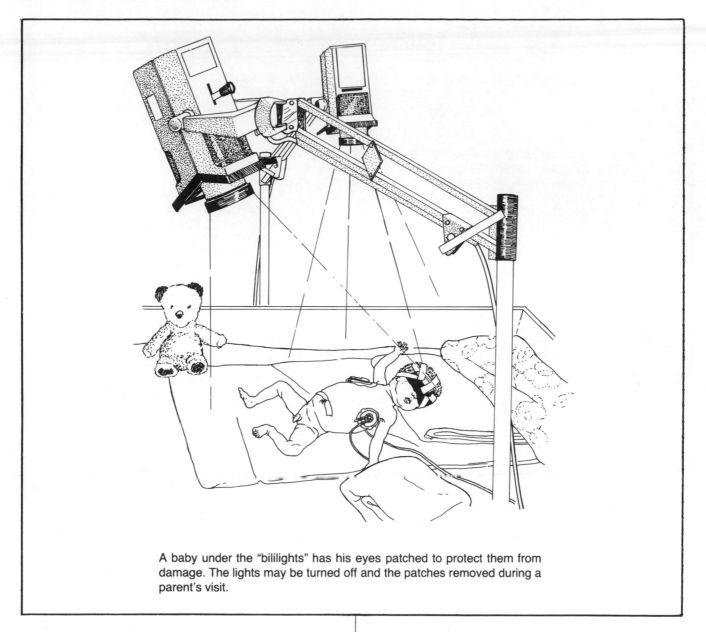

A baby under the "bililights" has his eyes patched to protect them from damage. The lights may be turned off and the patches removed during a parent's visit.

noticed that fewer babies on the sunny side of the nursery had jaundice.

The baby receiving phototherapy is given plenty of fluids to help dilute the bilirubin and aid its excretion. During phototherapy the baby may have frequent dark green or black, watery stools as his body eliminates bilirubin.

A mother may be asked not to breast-feed or supply breastmilk to her baby with jaundice. In very rare cases—an estimated 0.5% of all breast-fed babies—a substance in the breastmilk has been found to cause or contribute to jaundice (so called, *breastmilk jaundice*). Although 99.5% of the time breastmilk is *not* the culprit, doctors may wish to be extra cautious. Once the baby's bilirubin levels have fallen and the doctor has given the O.K., nursing can safely resume.

## Exchange transfusions

If the baby's bilirubin levels are very high, or continue to rise despite phototherapy, he is given an exchange blood transfusion. An exchange transfusion is done by slowly removing small quantities of the baby's blood while replacing it with a similar amount of donor blood. The baby's blood volume remains fairly stable throughout the procedure.

Babies have about 85 milliliters of blood per kilogram (2.2 pounds) of body weight. During the exchange transfusion the baby may receive up to two to three times this amount of blood (an equal amount is removed at the same time) in an attempt to dilute the bilirubin concentrations in his system.

The blood is given and removed through the umbilical catheter in the baby's navel. Rarely, complications such as bradycardia, acidosis, and low calcium or glucose levels can accompany the procedure. The baby is carefully monitored throughout the transfusion to be sure his heart is able to tolerate the slightly fluctuating blood volumes and to be sure his blood chemistry remains normal.

It is not unusual for bilirubin levels to rise again soon after an exchange transfusion, since more bilirubin leaves the body's tissues and reenters the bloodstream. Several exchange transfusions may be needed to rid the body of bilirubin before the liver is ready to function normally and remove bilirubin on its own.

## Anemia (Too Few Red Blood Cells) and Polycythemia (Too Many)

When the hematocrit, the percentage of red cells in the blood, drops below 40%, the resulting condition is called anemia. Red blood cells carry oxygen and carbon dioxide between the lungs and the body's tissues. When too few red cells are in the blood, the cells of the body may not receive the oxygen they need.

Anemia can result from blood loss, poor red blood cell production, or certain illnesses that destroy red blood cells. Before birth, the baby can lose blood through a detached placenta and develop anemia. When identical twins share a placenta, one baby may become chronically anemic in the womb, while his twin receives more than his share of the blood supply. Differences in blood types between mother and baby can cause the baby to be born anemic because of red blood cell destruction. Intrauterine infections can disrupt blood clotting mechanisms and lead to bleeding problems and anemia. During a difficult delivery a baby may lose blood from internal bleeding, and he may later become anemic. In the nursery, babies who have blood removed frequently for testing develop anemia if the blood is not replaced. Anemia can be corrected by giving the baby whole blood or a solution containing concentrated red blood cells (sometimes called *packed cells* or "*sed*" *cells*).

Many babies, both full-term and premature, experience a normal, or *physiological* anemia about six to seven weeks after birth. This is the time when most of the fetal red blood cells present at birth have broken down. However, the bone marrow has not yet started producing enough new red cells to meet the baby's needs. The anemia that results helps to stimulate the baby's bone marrow to begin making new red cells.

Sometimes the baby's hematocrit drops as low as 20% before his body begins to manufacture the needed red blood cells.

Premature babies often experience an exaggerated form of this physiological anemia. The premature grows proportionally faster after birth than does the full-term, and his body's red cell production may fail to match his rapid growth. Prematures also lack the stores of iron that the full-term baby acquires in the last weeks of pregnancy. Iron is essential for red blood cell production, as is vitamin E—another nutrient in which the premature may be deficient. Iron and vitamin supplements are usually given to prematures to prevent or lessen the severity of anemia.

Late anemia in prematures can also result from blood transfusions given weeks earlier. A blood transfusion artificially raises the baby's red blood cell count, inhibiting the mechanism by which the baby begins making red cells on his own. About six weeks after a transfusion, when the transfused cells die off in large numbers, the baby has a rapid drop in hematocrit. *Many babies are home from the hospital at this time. It is important that parents and the baby's pediatrician be aware of the increased potential for anemia during the two months following a transfusion.*

Polycythemia—a hematocrit over 65—occurs in certain prematures right after birth. If one identical twin is born anemic, the other may suffer the opposite problem—too many red blood cells. Babies born to diabetic mothers also tend to be polycythemic, as do some babies who are small for gestational age. Too many red blood cells thicken the blood and cause sluggish circulation. Left untreated, this condition can lead to tissue damage from lack of proper blood supply. The problem is easily corrected, however, by removing some of the baby's blood and diluting the remaining blood with albuminated saline, a solution closely resembling blood serum.

## Rh and ABO Incompatibilities

If a mother with an Rh-negative blood type carries a baby with Rh-positive blood, she may previously have developed antibodies that will attack the baby's red blood cells during pregnancy. Rh incompatibility, also known as *erythroblastosis fetalis,* can vary greatly in seriousness. Some babies die or are damaged before birth. Others are born, often prematurely, with moderate to severe anemia and jaundice caused by red blood cell breakdown.

Unless a mother has developed Rh-positive antibodies from a blood transfusion or an earlier abortion or miscarriage, she is unlikely to have problems during a first pregnancy. But during delivery of the first Rh-positive baby, some of the baby's blood enters the mother's body and causes antibodies to form. These antibodies will then attack the red blood cells of any future Rh positive baby the mother might conceive. Erythroblastosis fetalis was once a common cause of prematurity, infant death, and damage. Now RhoGAM shots given to the mother after delivery of an Rh-positive baby keep her from forming antibodies that could harm future babies. This treatment has greatly reduced, but not entirely eliminated, the problems of Rh incompatibility.

Incompatibilities among the blood groups O, A, B, and AB are more common but less serious than erythroblastosis fetalis. ABO problems can occur in any pregnancy in which an infant with type A or B is born to a mother with type O blood. About 20% of all pregnancies have the potential for ABO incompatibility problems to develop. Soon after birth the baby with ABO incompatibility is likely to develop anemia and jaundice serious enough to require phototherapy or transfusions.

## Clotting Problems, Thrombocytopenia, and Disseminated Intravascular Coagulation

Platelets, or thrombocytes, are cells that help the blood to clot. Thrombocytopenia (an abnormally low platelet count) occurs when platelets are produced in insufficient numbers, or when they are destroyed by infection, injury, blood incompatibilities, or by certain drugs. Disseminated intravascular coagulation (DIC) is a related problem in which both platelets and other clotting factors in the blood are overly consumed, usually as a result of severe infection, injury, asphyxia, or acidosis.

Both of these conditions can cause the baby to bleed excessively. The baby may bruise or bleed internally. Heel sticks may bleed for an unusually long time, and in some cases the baby develops a pin-point-like rash called petechiae caused by tiny hemorrhages from the blood vessels close to the surface of the skin.

The baby with clotting problems may be given transfusions of platelets, or of whole blood containing platelets, to help correct these disorders.

# Infections

Throughout pregnancy, disease-fighting proteins called antibodies pass from the mother's blood into the unborn baby and give the infant temporary immunity against many illnesses to which the mother has been exposed. Babies born prematurely miss out on most of these antibodies. As a result, they are highly vulnerable to infection. Even with the partial protection of maternal antibodies, newborns—full-terms and prematures alike—have special susceptibilities to infectious disease. Because their own defenses against infection have not yet fully matured, newborns are vulnerable to serious infections from germs that cause only mild illness or no illness at all in older children or adults. Male infants are twice as likely to develop infections as females. According to one theory, factors regulating the immune system that are found on the X chromosome give baby girls a double-dose of immunity. (Females result from the union of two X chromosomes, males from an X and a Y.)

Before birth, a baby can be infected by organisms that either cross the placenta or ascend from the mother's genital tract and enter the womb—possibly through a weak place in the membranes. A baby can also acquire an infection between the time the membranes rupture and the time of birth.

Intrauterine infection is suspected if a mother has a fever at the time of delivery; if the infant is premature or in distress for unknown reasons; if the amniotic fluid appears infected or is stained with meconium; if the baby has anemia, a low platelet count, enlarged liver or spleen; if the baby has a rash at birth; or if the infant displays symptoms characteristic of the TORCH syndrome infections (see box, page 92).

After birth, the baby is exposed to hospital germs. Despite the "sterile" environment of the nursery, true sterility—the total absence of germs—is next to impossible to achieve. Germs are everywhere—in the air, on floors and counter tops, on medical equipment, and even in antiseptic solutions.

A premature baby who becomes infected in the first weeks or months after birth may show such symptoms as persistent apnea and bradycardia; persistent tachypnea and tachycardia; irritability or lethargy; unexplained jaundice, anemia, or thrombocytopenia (low platelet count); feeding problems, abdominal swelling or diarrhea; a rash; or temperature instability (but rarely fever).

A baby displaying any of these symptoms may be isolated from other infants in the nursery and given a series of tests for infection referred to as a *septic workup.* Since prematures experience the symptoms listed above for many reasons other than infection, septic workups are done frequently, often giving the baby a clean bill of health. As one mother recalled, "I came into the nursery to find a quarantine sign on Brian's incubator. For two days I was not allowed to touch him while they ran tests to determine the nature of a suspicious reddening of the skin. The final diagnosis? Diaper rash!"

## Septic Workup

A septic workup is done to check for the presence of infectious organisms and for signs that the body's immune system is fighting a disease. The following tests and procedures may be included.

### Gram Stains, Cultures and Sensitivities

To treat an infection properly, it is important to know whether it is caused by a virus or by bacteria, and, if by bacteria, what variety, since each strain of bacteria responds differently to each of the available antibiotics. Antibiotics do not work at all against viruses.

To test for bacteria, a sample of blood, urine, or other body material is put on a laboratory slide and treated with dyes known as Gram stains, which color bacteria in characteristic ways. This simple, quick test allows the observer to make a rough guess about which bacteria is causing the infection. But since many types of bacteria look alike, more complicated identification procedures called *cultures and sensitivities* are also performed. Swabs of blood or other body material are placed in culture plates containing nutrients on which bacteria thrive. The cultures are kept warm for several hours to several days and then checked for bacterial growth. Any bacteria that grow are then identified through a variety of tests, and the sensitivity of the bacterial strain to various antibiotics is determined.

Doctors rarely wait for the results of the culture before beginning to treat a premature suspected of having a bacterial infection—delay is too dangerous. They may guess at the organism on the basis of the Gram-stain slide and use the appropriate antibiotic, or they may use a combination of antibiotics known to affect the most common infectious organisms. Once the culture results are known, the antibiotic can be changed if necessary.

If bacteria cannot be found and if other clues point to a viral infection, viral cultures are taken. Vi-

## What Is a Germ?

The tiny organisms that cause disease, commonly referred to as "germs," can be classified into several different categories. Most germs involved in newborn infections belong to one of the three following groups.

*Bacteria,* one-celled organisms belonging to the plant kingdom, are found throughout the environment and throughout much of the human body. Most are harmless; a few are helpful, like the *Lactobacillus* bacterium that aids in digestion. Only 1% of bacteria cause disease, and even these potentially harmful varieties often live in the human body in an ecological balance with harmless bacteria. Infection occurs when the body's ecology is disturbed in a way that allows the overgrowth of harmful bacteria or when the body's natural defenses—the antibodies and white blood cells—are overwhelmed by a massive bacterial invasion. Bacteria can be killed or controlled with antibiotics, drugs such as penicillin, ampicillin, gentamicin, or kanamycin. Bacteria that cause newborn infections include: "staph" (Staphylococcus), Group B "strep" (Streptococcus), E. coli *(Escherichia coli)*, *Pseudomonas,* pneumococci, *Listeria,* and *Klebsiella.*

*Viruses* are very tiny fragments of living matter that exist parasitically *inside* body cells. Unlike bacteria, which live *outside* body cells, viruses are extremely difficult to reach and destroy. While a number of drugs are being tested for use against viruses, no proven antiviral drug is yet available. Vaccines can provide immunity against certain viruses by stimulating antibody production, but the vaccine must be given *before* the disease strikes. *Antibiotics do not work against viruses.* Viruses are responsible for such infections as colds, flu, chicken pox, measles, hepatitis, and herpes.

*Funguses* that cause disease are microscopic members of the plant kingdom. The fungus *Candida albicans,* also known as Monilia or "yeast," frequently infects infants, causing a severe, persistent diaper rash, or red and white sores in the mouth known as "thrush." Certain funguses normally live on or in the human body in a balance with other microorganisms. Fungal infections often occur following a course of antibiotics that kills off the bacterial competition and allows the fungus to overgrow. Fungal infections are treated with application of antifungal drugs such as nystatin (Mycostatin) directly to the affected areas.

ruses are much more difficult than bacteria to identify. They must be grown in cultures of living cells, a procedure that may take a week to a month. Since there are no available antiviral drugs, a baby with a viral infection can be treated only to alleviate the symptoms of the illness, not to kill the virus itself. However, the baby may receive antibiotics to prevent bacteria from causing an additional infection while his resistance is low as a result of the viral infection.

### Complete Blood Count (CBC)

A complete blood count (CBC) is done to determine the number and types of cells in the blood. A low red blood cell count (a low hematocrit) or a low platelet count may be a sign of an infection. White blood cells, which combat infectious organisms, are also counted. Both very high and very low counts can mean infection. An abnormally high count indicates the body is mobilizing to fight an infection. An abnormally low count may mean the white cells are being overwhelmed by the infectious organisms. If these organisms are bacteria, a certain type of white blood cell, the *polymorphonuclear cell (PMN)* is most abundant. If the infection is viral, other white cells called *lymphocytes* predominate.

### Urinalysis

A sample of the baby's urine may be taken by inserting a needle through the lower abdomen directly into the bladder and withdrawing the urine. This procedure, known as a *bladder tap*, is done to prevent the urine from being contaminated by bacteria that normally live in the lower urinary tract or outside the body. Urine taken directly from the bladder should be sterile. If organisms can be seen under the microscope or if they can be grown in a culture, a urinary tract infection probably exists. The urine is also checked for white blood cells, blood, and protein, which can also indicate infection.

### Spinal Tap or Lumbar Puncture

A spinal tap, also called a lumbar puncture, is done to check for infectious organisms and other abnormalities in the *cerebrospinal fluid (CSF)*, the fluid that circulates around the brain and spinal cord. The baby is held in a curled-over sitting or lying position, and a thin needle is inserted between the fourth and fifth lumbar (lower back) vertebrae into the fluid-containing space of the spinal column (see page 97). A sample of spinal fluid is then removed. When done properly, there is no danger of striking the spinal

## The Torch Syndrome

TORCH is an acronym derived from the first letters of the diseases *toxoplasmosis, rubella, cytomegalovirus,* and *herpes*—nonbacterial illnesses that can infect babies during pregnancy. The baby with one of these infections may be born with birth defects, an abnormally large or small head, enlargement of the liver or spleen, rashes or sores, anemia, thrombocytopenia, or jaundice. The baby is usually small for gestational age and may be premature as well. TORCH infections occur in up to 5% of all newborns.

*Toxoplasmosis* is a one-celled parasite spread by eating undercooked meat and by contact with soil, or the feces of house cats. About 50% of the U.S. population has contracted the disease at some time. In France, where rare meat is part of the national diet, 90% of the population has been exposed. Infected adults have mild flu-like symptoms or no symptoms at all. A woman who becomes infected during pregnancy can transmit the parasite to her unborn baby, who may suffer brain and eye damage as a result. Over 3000 infants are born with the disease in the United States each year. When toxoplasmosis is diagnosed in a newborn, prompt drug therapy can often halt continuing damage from the disease.

*Rubella* (German measles), a mild infection in children or adults, causes birth defects, brain damage, vision and hearing impairments, and growth retardation in the fetus. Widespread immunization against rubella has greatly reduced the number of infants born with this serious, untreatable disease.

*Cytomegalovirus* (CMV) is the most common intrauterine disease, afflicting up to 8000 infants in the United States annually. Nearly one-third of all young adults have had CMV—a mild, flu-like illness—and many still carry the virus in their bodies. A baby infected in the womb can be born with multiple birth defects, brain damage, and other health problems. Babies who contract the disease after birth (sometimes through a blood transfusion) become quite ill but do not suffer the same damage as babies who acquire the disease in utero. Studies are currently underway to discover any long-range problems of infants who contract CMV after birth. Although work on a vaccine continues, no prevention or treatment now exists.

*Herpes*, both oral herpes (type 1) and genital herpes (type 2) are widespread among the childbearing population. In adults, the disease causes annoying fever blisters or genital sores, but the virus is fatal for over half of all infected newborns. Most of those who survive are brain-damaged. Despite the common occurrence of herpes among adults, newborn herpes is relatively rare—about 1 case in every 3000 births. The only precaution that can be taken to avoid newborn herpes is cesarean delivery of the baby when the mother has an active infection at the time of birth.

cord, which ends higher up in the spine. It is much easier to perform a spinal tap on a flexible premature infant than on an older child or adult. The premature baby also seems less bothered than older people by the procedure.

The spinal fluid is cultured and examined microscopically for bacteria. The fluid is also analyzed for protein and sugar content; abnormal amounts suggest an irritation or infection. The presence of white blood cells in the spinal fluid is a sign of infection. Red blood cells in the spinal fluid indicate bleeding either from an infection or an injury to the central nervous system, although minor bleeding into the spinal fluid can result from the tapping procedure itself.

# Types of Newborn Infections

## Pneumonia

Pneumonia, an infection of the lungs, is the most common of serious newborn infections. It can be caused by viruses or bacteria. Pneumonia can be acquired before birth from organisms present in the womb, and babies with this congenital pneumonia tend to be more seriously ill than those who develop the disease later. Coughing and fever, symptoms of pneumonia in older children, are usually not seen in the newborn baby. Rather, the symptoms are similar to those of respiratory distress syndrome. Diagnosis of lung infection can usually be made on the basis of chest x-rays, blood counts, and cultures of lung secretions. The baby is given antibiotics if the pneumonia is bacterial. Otherwise, the treatment is the same as that for RDS. The baby receives oxygen or is put on a respirator if necessary.

## Enteritis

In the past, outbreaks of enteritis—diarrhea caused by viral or bacterial infection—accounted for a large number of infant deaths. Fear of hospital epidemics led doctors to declare premature (and fullterm) nurseries off limits to visitors. Although enteritis is highly contagious and still a cause for concern, infants today are not likely to die from it, thanks to antibiotic therapy and IV feedings to prevent dehydration.

## Septicemia (Sepsis)

Septicemia, or sepsis, is an infection of the bloodstream that can affect the entire body. Early signs of sepsis include symptoms such as apnea, lethargy, and temperature instability. A positive blood culture in which a disease-causing organism has been identified is diagnostic of sepsis. Bacterial sepsis is treated with antibiotics. Exchange transfusions may be used to help flush infectious organisms and toxins from the baby's system and to help strengthen the baby's immunity.

## Meningitis

A third of all sepsis cases develop into meningitis—an infection of the brain and spinal column. Meningitis occurs most frequently in the first year of life, and the neonatal period, the first 28 days after birth, is a time of special vulnerability. Prematures are more susceptible than full-terms.

A newborn with meningitis has the usual signs of infection—apnea, tachypnea, irritability, lethargy, temperature instability, and feeding problems. The baby's soft spot, or fontanel, may bulge from increased pressure in the brain. The baby with meningitis may also have seizures.

Meningitis can be caused by viruses or bacteria. It is diagnosed by abnormalities in the spinal fluid obtained by a spinal tap. Several weeks of antibiotic therapy may be needed in cases of bacterial meningitis. Neonatal meningitis is a serious disease with a 30 to 50% mortality rate. Of the babies who survive, approximately half sustain some degree of brain damage.

# Preventing Infections

## What You Can Do

Before the 1970s, doctors who feared the spread of infection barred parents from the newborn nursery. Prematures, especially, were isolated from human contact and handled as little as possible to limit their exposure to germs.

A study at Stanford in the mid-60s helped change all that. In the experiment, parents were allowed to enter the premature nursery to see, touch, and hold their babies. Frequent tests were performed to check the babies for infectious organisms. No increase in infectious organisms occurred with the new policy. On the contrary, harmful bacteria actually decreased when parents were allowed to hold and touch their babies! Perhaps, thought the researchers, parents transmitted harmless bacteria to their infants and these organisms helped protect the babies from dangerous hospital germs.

Even though parents are now allowed into most nurseries, the intimidating sterile atmosphere can make them fearful of handling, and possibly infecting, their babies. But babies, even premature babies, must get used to the organisms their parents normally carry. Unless you are ill, there is no reason not to enjoy close contact with your premature baby.

Massaging your baby's delicate skin with creams or oils is one form of close contact that helps your baby resist infection. Normally, the skin provides a barrier against infectious organisms, but a premature's skin is thin and permeable. Many substances, including bacteria, easily pass through the baby's skin, especially if it has become dry and irritated. Frequent massage, at least once every eight hours, helps keep the baby's skin moist, healthy, and better able to resist bacteria. (Use *unscented* creams or oils—the perfumes in some skin care products can be absorbed by the baby in toxic amounts.) And to prevent chafing, make sure your baby is frequently repositioned and placed on the softest possible bedding.

Breast-feeding helps too. Your breastmilk contains disease-fighting substances that you continually produce in response to your baby's individual needs (see Chapter 9, page 153).

### Some Sensible Precautions

The two-minute hand scrub required by most nurseries gets rid of most infectious organisms on your skin. The surgical gown that is required keeps germs on your clothing from touching the baby.

Do not come into the nursery if you have a cold,

*Unless you are ill, there is no reason not to enjoy close contact with your premature baby.*

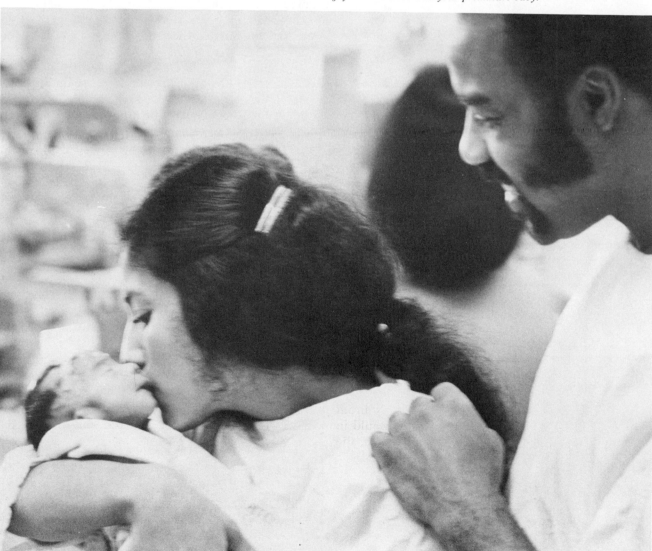

Peggy Wakefield Green, courtesy of Children's Hospital Medical Center of Northern California

the flu, diarrhea, open sores, or fever blisters. Stay home while ill, and consult with the neonatologist before reentering the nursery.

Some nurseries allow parents and staff members with slight colds into the nursery if they wear face masks. These masks quickly become wet from exhaled moisture and should not be touched, since the moisture contains viruses. The mask should be changed every 20 minutes.

Clothing, blankets, and toys brought to the baby should be clean.

Small children should not come into the nursery unless they are absolutely free of runny noses, diarrhea, or recent exposure to contagious diseases.

# Neurological Problems

The fourth, fifth, and sixth months of pregnancy are a time of rapid cell division in the baby's brain. By the end of this second trimester, most of the baby's nerve cells, or neurons, have been created. Brain tissue is differentiating into specific areas with specific functions. The cerebral cortex—the outer layer of the brain associated with thought, memory, and other higher functions—is now fairly well established.

During the last trimester, the neurons send out billions of branches, or dendrites, to connect with other nerve cells. The richness and complexity of these interconnections greatly influence the child's later abilities and intelligence. The long connecting nerve fibers are becoming insulated with a fatty substance called *myelin*, which aids the rapid conduction of electrical nerve impulses. Brain growth, myelination, and the interconnecting of nerve cells continue long after birth. Although the child's brain is very close to its adult size by the age of two, the process of brain development goes on to some extent even into adulthood.

## Possible Causes of Brain Injury

When a baby is born prematurely, his brain should continue to develop and grow as it would in the womb. But in the world outside the womb, the infant's immature nervous system may be exposed to a number of abnormal or harmful conditions.

### Abnormal Environment

Usually an infant spends the months of pregnancy being gently rocked in the dark, liquid isolation of the womb. In the hospital nursery, the prematurely born baby may be overstimulated by bright lights, loud noises, and uncomfortable handling. At the same time, he may be understimulated by lying on a flat, motionless surface for days or weeks on end. Prematures often respond to stressful over- or understimulation with jittery, hyperactive behavior or spells of apnea and bradycardia. The long-term effects of the nursery environment on the baby's sensitive nervous system are not yet known. Researchers are finding, however, that babies recover and develop better when protected from unpleasant sensations while being provided with stimulation (rocking, for example) that is appropriate for the infant's level of maturity. Efforts are being made in hospitals across the country to humanize the nursery in ways that reduce environmental stresses on vulnerable prematures. (See Chapter 8, page 131, Nursery Parenting, for ways parents can help.)

### Poor Nutrition

The nutritional needs of the premature baby are not fully understood; and it is not always possible to meet those needs that *are* understood. Only certain amounts of nutrients can be given intravenously, and oral feedings may not always be well absorbed and metabolized. What are the effects of less than optimal nutrition on the baby's growing brain? Again, no one is certain. It may be that early deficiencies can be compensated for later on with excellent nutrition. When prematures are examined later in follow-up clinics, their head circumferences are usually the first measurement to catch up to normal. Rapid, catch-up brain growth is thought to be the reason.

### Lack of Oxygen

When brain cells are deprived of proper blood flow and oxygen, lactic acid, a byproduct of low-oxygen metabolism, accumulates in the cells. In large quantities, the acid weakens or kills the cells. Once the cells are injured, they absorb fluid and expand. The swelling of brain tissue, called *brain edema*, further cuts off circulation to other parts of the brain and causes more cells to die. A baby who is asphyxiated at birth or who later suffers from a prolonged lack of oxygen may be treated with cortisone-like drugs such as dexamethasone (Decadron) to reduce brain tissue swelling and limit further injury.

### Metabolic Imbalances

Premature babies are highly susceptible to imbalances of certain vital nutrients and minerals. If these imbalances are severe and prolonged, injury to the brain can result. Too little blood sugar (hypoglycemia) deprives brain cells of their necessary fuel and may cause tissue death. Too much sugar (hyperglycemia) may cause brain edema. Too little sodium (*hyponatremia*) also leads to brain edema, while too much sodium (*hypernatremia*) pulls fluid out of the brain cells and into the blood vessels. The fragile blood vessels of the brain may burst from fluid overload and bleed into the brain tissue. Too little calcium (*hypocalcemia*) may bring on seizures, but this condition is easily corrected and does not seem to cause permanent injury. Because infants in intensive care are very closely monitored for imbalances of these vital elements, problems are usually corrected before they lead to brain injury.

## Kernicterus

Kernicterus, brain damage caused by high levels of bilirubin, may result in retardation, hearing loss, and *choreoathetosis*, a type of cerebral palsy characterized by involuntary, purposeless muscle movements. Severe kernicterus is now rare because of the vigorous measures taken to keep the infant's bilirubin at levels thought to be safe.

## Infection

Meningitis, infection of the tissues lining the brain, is a special threat to prematures. The disease is fatal for 30 to 50% of prematures in whom it develops, and approximately half of the survivors have some degree of brain injury.

## Seizures

Seizures are a short-circuiting of the brain's electrical impulses. They may occur when brain tissue is irritated or injured. Seizures may accompany metabolic imbalances, bleeding in the brain, meningitis, and brain edema.

In premature babies, seizures are hard to detect since they are characterized by subtle variations of normal premature behavior, such as trembling of the mouth, fluttering of the eyelids, rolling of the eyes, flailing of the arms and legs, and, of course, apnea and bradycardia. *Normal* premature jittery behavior can usually be stopped by calming or restraining the baby; seizure activity cannot. Nevertheless, even the trained observer may have difficulty identifying seizures in a premature infant. To aid in the diagnosis, the baby's brain waves may be studied. The brain wave tracing is called an *electroencephalogram* or *EEG*. Monitoring pads are placed on the baby's scalp to detect electrical impulses in the brain below; an ab-

normal pattern of electrical discharge indicates seizure activity.

Seizures need to be treated, since they can disrupt the baby's breathing and heart rate. During seizures, brain cells also require tremendous amounts of sugar and oxygen, and when these needs are not met the cells may die.

Seizures can be controlled by drugs such as phenobarbital or phenytoin (Dilantin). Seizure-controlling drugs may be given for several days, several months, or indefinitely if the child continues to need them.

A baby who has had seizures in the newborn period does not necessarily have brain damage or a permanent seizure disorder (epilepsy). The baby's eventual outcome depends more on what caused the seizures in the first place. For example, low calcium levels (hypocalcemia) may bring on seizures, but the condition does not seem to cause any later neurological problems. However, seizures accompanying meningitis, brain bleeding, and hypoglycemia (low blood sugar levels) are often associated with subsequent neurological abnormalities.

## Intracranial Hemorrhage (Intraventricular Hemorrhage, Subarachnoid Hemorrhage)

The tiny blood vessels in the premature baby's brain have fragile walls that can weaken to the breaking point if deprived of oxygen and proper blood flow. Abrupt fluctuations in the baby's blood pressure or pressure to the head during delivery may also cause these delicate vessels to rupture and bleed into the brain.

Brain bleeding usually shows up within two days after the baby has had an episode of asphyxia or severe lack of oxygen. Symptoms of brain bleeding may include apnea, bradycardia, seizures, lethargy, fluctuating temperature, low blood pressure and anemia (from blood loss), and a bulging fontanel or soft spot (because of increased pressure in the brain). Often, however, babies with brain "bleeds" develop no symptoms at all.

Until recently it was thought that bleeding into the brain always meant a very bad outcome—death or severe disability—for the affected infant. But that was because only the most serious cases were ever identified. New x-ray and ultrasound techniques are now showing that brain bleeds are much more common than previously thought. From 40 to 90% of babies under 1500 grams have some degree of brain bleeding after birth, but most under-1500-gram babies survive without major handicaps. The location and amount of the bleeding and the extent of the asphyxia that caused the bleeding have more to do with the baby's outcome than the mere fact that bleeding has taken place.

Bleeding can occur in many different parts of the brain, but prematures have special areas of vulnerability. Most bleeding and brain injury in prematures occur in the tissue surrounding the *ventricles*—the spaces in the center of the brain that produce cerebrospinal fluid. In prematurely born infants, the tissue around the ventricles is undergoing rapid growth and differentiation. The area is richly supplied with blood vessels that are still poorly supported by connective tissue. When the brain's blood flow and oxygen are reduced, the weakly supported blood vessels around the ventricles are likely to rupture. This area around the ventricles is crossed by nerve fibers descending from the cerebral cortex to the legs. Stiffness and increased muscle tone *(spasticity)* in the legs are frequently seen among those prematures who have neurological problems.

Bleeding into or near the ventricles occurs in different degrees or grades. The bleeding may be limited to a small area and contained within the tissue. This is called a *subependymal hemorrhage*—a grade I bleed. If the subependymal hemorrhage ruptures and spills blood into the ventricles, the bleeding is called an *intraventricular hemorrhage* (IVH) or grade II bleed. A grade III bleed is one in which the ventricles are so full of blood that they expand and push out against the brain tissue. A grade IV bleed occurs when blood from the dilated ventricles is forced back into the brain tissue itself. Babies with grade IV bleeds almost always have serious ongoing neurological problems. Babies with grades I, II, or III bleeds have a somewhat more optimistic prognosis. Although these infants have a relatively high incidence of such problems as hydrocephalus, retardation, cerebral palsy, vision loss, and hearing impairment, follow-up studies indicate that many escape these handicaps, and, in early infancy at least, develop normally. Studies are currently underway to determine the long-range outcomes of babies with these mild to moderate bleeds.

Premature babies may also bleed into the *subarachnoid space*—the fluid-filled space between the membranes that cover the outside of the brain. The outlook for babies with this type of bleed is good. Approximately 90% are reported to be normal.

When bleeding has occurred in the ventricles or subarachnoid space, the blood circulates with the cerebrospinal fluid around the brain and spinal cord. That is why a lumbar puncture or spinal tap that removes fluid from a space low in the baby's spine can

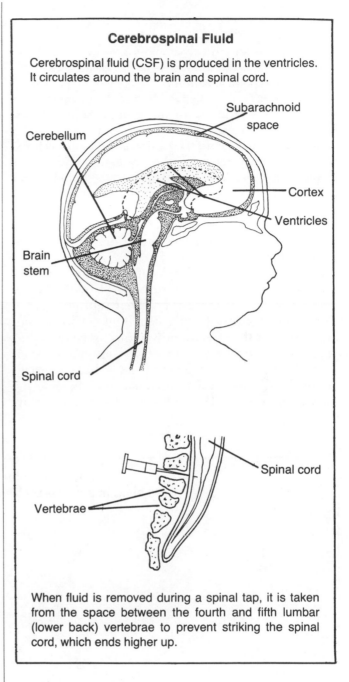

### Cerebrospinal Fluid

Cerebrospinal fluid (CSF) is produced in the ventricles. It circulates around the brain and spinal cord.

Subarachnoid space

Cerebellum

Cortex

Ventricles

Brain stem

Spinal cord

Spinal cord

Vertebrae

When fluid is removed during a spinal tap, it is taken from the space between the fourth and fifth lumbar (lower back) vertebrae to prevent striking the spinal cord, which ends higher up.

reveal bleeding that took place in the center of the brain.

A recently developed x-ray technique, *computerized axial tomography*, also called a *CAT* or *CT scan*, is now commonly used to diagnose brain bleeding. This combination x-ray machine and computer aims a very narrow beam of radiation at a specific layer of body tissue and produces a horizontal or cross-sectional picture. The baby must be taken to the x-ray department for a brain scan because the machine itself is much too large to move. The procedure takes several minutes, and the baby—who must be completely still during this time—is usually sedated. A brain scan usually involves about one to two rads of radiation, although amounts can be greater depending on the type of machine.

A newer and simpler method of diagnosing brain bleeds involves the use of ultrasound. Sound waves are directed through the infant's soft spot (fontanel). The sound waves send back different types of echoes that indicate the density of the tissues they encounter. A picture can be constructed of the baby's brain from the sound wave echoes. Ventricle size and areas of bleeding can be seen. Ultrasound scans can be performed at the baby's bedside; no sedation is needed. It is a painless, noninvasive procedure that involves no radiation.

About two to three weeks after a brain bleed occurs, most of the blood is reabsorbed by the body. Meanwhile, the baby may be given repeated spinal taps to remove the bloody spinal fluid. There is controversy over the effectiveness of this procedure. But it may be done with the aim of preventing the blood from further irritating the brain tissue, because when those tissues that reabsorb spinal fluid become irritated and scarred, large amounts of spinal fluid may accumulate in the ventricles. This dangerous condition is known as *hydrocephalus*.

## Hydrocephalus

Cerebrospinal fluid, constantly produced in the ventricles of the brain, circulates around the brain and spinal column to cushion the delicate nervous tissues. The fluid is reabsorbed in the same amounts as produced by membranes that cover the outside of the brain.

Blood in the spinal fluid may damage and scar these fluid-absorbing membranes. If the narrow channels connecting the ventricles become obstructed with scar tissue, or if the tissues in the subarachnoid space become too scarred to reabsorb spinal fluid properly, the fluid backs up and accumulates in the ventricles. The ventricles expand with fluid and compress the surrounding brain tissue.

The infant's skull bones, which have not yet fused together, are also pushed out by the increasing pressure, and an abnormal rate of head growth occurs. If the pressure inside the brain continues to increase, the head grows larger and there is a pro-

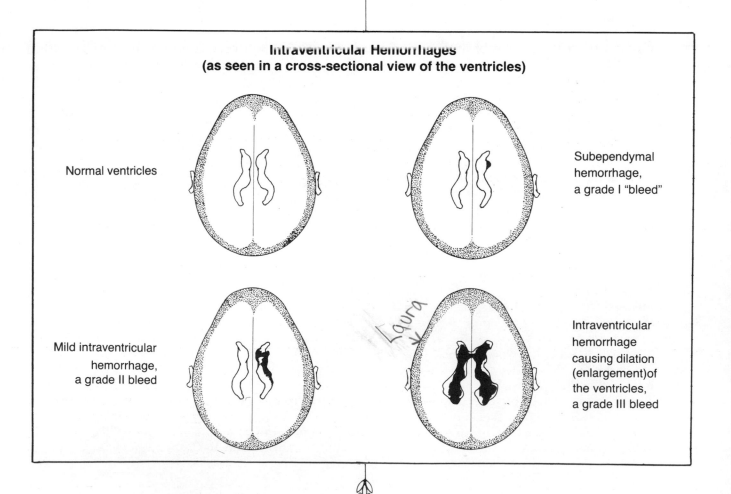

**Intraventricular Hemorrhages**
**(as seen in a cross-sectional view of the ventricles)**

Normal ventricles

Subependymal hemorrhage, a grade I "bleed"

Mild intraventricular hemorrhage, a grade II bleed

Intraventricular hemorrhage causing dilation (enlargement) of the ventricles, a grade III bleed

gressive loss of brain tissue. Hydrocephalus sometimes stops, or *arrests*, on its own. The ventricles may stay larger than normal, but the pressure remains stable.

Surgery is necessary for those cases in which the pressure in the brain continues to rise. A thin tube called a *shunt* is inserted into the side of the head, through the brain, and into the ventricle. The other end of the shunt is passed beneath the skin and into the abdominal cavity (the *peritoneum*). When pressure from accumulated fluid builds up in the brain, the one-way valves in the shunt tube open and allow the spinal fluid to drain into the abdominal area, where the fluid is reabsorbed by the body. This shunt, called the *ventriculo-peritoneal (VP) shunt,* is the type most commonly used in infants. Other types of shunts include the *ventriculo-atrial (VA) shunt* that empties into the heart, and the *lumbar-peritoneal (LP) shunt* that drains fluid from the spinal canal into the peritoneum.

With a shunt in place and operating properly, ventricle size often returns to normal. To keep pace with the growing child, the shunt tubing must be lengthened periodically, generally every two to four

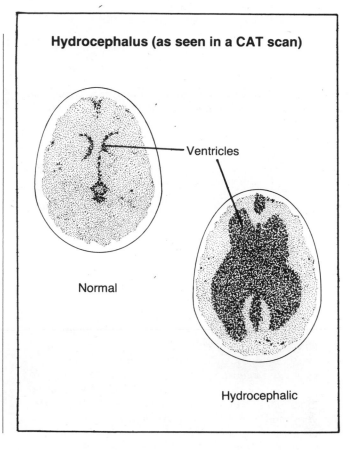

**Hydrocephalus (as seen in a CAT scan)**

Ventricles

Normal

Hydrocephalic

*Baby with a shunt (sucking on mother's finger).*

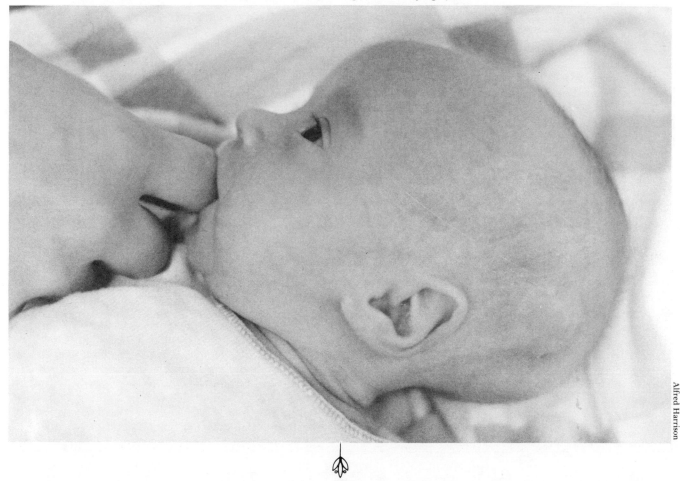

Alfred Harrison

## Ventriculo-Peritoneal Shunt

The shunt tubing extends from the ventricles in the center of the brain into the peritoneal, or abdominal, cavity. The tube runs under the skin behind the ear, down the neck, chest, and abdomen. Once the shunt is installed, all that is visible is a small raised area of skin about the size of a nickel behind the ear. This is where the pump or reservoir is located. Also visible are scars from the scalp and abdominal incisions. Sometimes an incision on the neck is also made. The shunt tubing under the skin looks somewhat like a large vein for a while, but, after the baby gains weight, it is scarcely noticeable. The reservoir and the scalp incisions are soon hidden by the baby's growing hair.

### If Your Baby Has a Shunt

1. Learn the signs and symptoms of *shunt infection* and of *shunt failure*. The shunt, a foreign object inside the body, is highly vulnerable to infection. Signs of a *shunt infection* may include: a rectal temperature of 101° F. or higher; inflammation and swelling along the shunt tubing; abdominal distress (loss of appetite, vomiting, diarrhea, swelling); lethargy; or seizures. Signs of increased pressure in the brain that accompany *shunt failure* include: lethargy, unusual irritability, repeated vomiting, and (in an infant) a bulging fontanel when the baby is upright. An older child may complain of severe headache or double vision. If your child is having symptoms of shunt infection or failure, do not assume that it is just the flu. Call your doctor at once. Shunt problems can occur at any time, and when they do, they are medical emergencies.

2. There are several different types of shunts. Before you take your baby home, have the neurosurgeon give you a full written description of your child's shunt and a copy of your child's brain scan taken when the shunt is in place and working. These two items provide important information to any doctor who may treat your child. Since shunt failure occurs unexpectedly, you cannot always count on having your child's regular doctor available. Be sure to take the scans and shunt description (along with the name of a good local neurosurgeon) whenever you travel with your child.

3. Infants with shunt failure may not show dramatic symptoms, however. Because their skull bones have not yet fused, fluid accumulation in the brain may simply cause a rapid growth in head circumference. During infancy, your child should have his head circumference measured frequently. If you wish to do this yourself, ask your doctor for a chart showing the normal rate of head growth. Learn to measure your baby's head circumference and plot this information on the chart. (Dots of ink on the front and back of your baby's head can help you align the tape the same way each time for more accurate measuring.)

4. If your baby's shunt has a pump or reservoir, find out if, when, and how you should pump it.

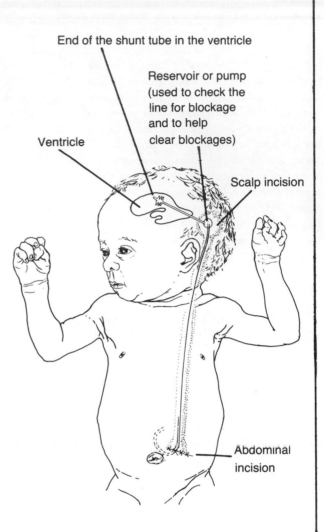

End of the shunt tube in the ventricle

Reservoir or pump (used to check the line for blockage and to help clear blockages)

Ventricle

Scalp incision

Abdominal incision

5. To prevent the shunt from becoming infected, be sure that your baby's health problems—such as ear infections, strep throat, boils, or other skin infections—are promptly treated. Your child may need antibiotic treatment before having dental work such as teeth cleaning or extractions, since these procedures release many bacteria into the bloodstream. (Normal teething and loss of baby teeth do not cause problems.) Discuss this with your neurosurgeon, your pediatrician, and your baby's dentist.

6. If your child becomes badly constipated, the intestines can press against the lower end of the shunt and obstruct the flow of fluid through the shunt. Consult your pediatrician for advice if your child fails to have a bowel movement for three days or more.

7. Do not be afraid to play vigorously with your baby. Holding him upside down or bouncing him will not cause a backflow of fluid and should not dislodge the shunt. Your baby can enjoy as active a life as any other child.

years (and replaced altogether if it becomes infected or obstructed). The surgery involved requires a hospital stay of a week or two. Although a small number of children shunted for hydrocephalus eventually outgrow their condition and no longer need the shunt, most remain shunt-dependent for life.

While many hydrocephalic children have neurological problems, some are normal. Recently, British neurosurgeon John Lorber examined a number of people with severe untreated hydrocephalus—up to 95% of their brain tissue had been replaced by fluid. He reported startling findings: over half of the severely hydrocephalic individuals he examined had normal IQs and were functioning well in society. One man was a university honors graduate in mathematics!

# Newborn Intensive Care: Parents' Rights and Medical Ethics

## *Your Right to Informed Consent*

As parents of a hospitalized baby you have the right to be fully informed of your child's condition and medical treatment throughout his hospital stay. In some states this includes the right to read and copy the baby's chart. In other states, legal action may be needed to gain access to these records. You will be asked to sign forms when your child is transported and/or admitted to the hospital. Later you may be asked to sign papers giving your consent to specific procedures, and in some cases to experimental methods of treatment. These forms in no way remove the responsibility of the hospital and staff to provide proper care or to keep you fully informed. They do not preclude malpractice suits for improper care. You do not surrender your rights as parents by signing these forms. You may refuse to sign the forms and you may revoke a form you have already signed.

The papers you sign when your child enters the nursery give your consent for admission and routine care, and establish your financial responsibility for that care, permitting the hospital to bill your insurance company. Routine care refers to the blood tests, x-rays, and others tests or treatments considered routine by the hospital (this may include putting your child on a respirator).

In addition to the admission forms, you may be asked to sign papers giving your informed consent to procedures such as surgical operations or spinal taps.

The medical procedures that require informed consent vary from hospital to hospital; generally they are procedures that invade body spaces or the central circulation. Insertion of an IV line does not require a signed consent form, but installing a central line may. Before you sign the consent form, the physician is obliged to discuss with you the risks and benefits of performing the procedure, as well as the risks and benefits of *not* performing it. If you wish further explanations or second or third opinions, it is your right to receive them before you sign.

You may refuse to sign the form. If the physician proceeds without your consent, he or she is technically guilty of assault. But if the doctor feels the treatment is necessary for the child's life and health, a court order may be obtained to override your objection. This might happen, for example, if parents refuse a blood transfusion for their child on religious grounds. In such cases, the courts usually rule in favor of the doctor, but if the life or health of the child is not seriously threatened by forgoing treatment, the courts may support the parents' right to refuse.

In an emergency, however, the doctor can do whatever he or she feels is necessary without your consent. An emergency is broadly defined as any event that puts the child's life or health in immediate danger. If a baby has a pneumothorax (a collapsed lung), this is an emergency, and the surgery for a chest tube insertion to treat this condition could be done whether or not you were available to give consent.

While your child is in the hospital, you may be asked to allow him to take part in the study of a new treatment. The doctors doing the research are legally required to inform you of the nature of the study *fully, in great detail,* in language you understand. You are under *absolutely no obligation* to have your child participate.

Most of these studies involve the assignment of the child either to a group that receives a standard treatment or to one that receives an experimental treatment. Assignments are made by lot. You cannot choose which group your child will be in if you decide to allow your child to be part of the study. The random assignment of children to treatment or nontreatment groups may disturb you. Perhaps you want your baby to receive the new treatment. Although your child may well benefit from receiving the treatment, he may also benefit from *not* receiving it. When the drug DES (diethylstilbestrol) was being tested, those in the control group, who did *not* receive the drug, were better off.

Although the idea of experimentation may seem

repugnant to you, this is a time-honored method of proceeding in the face of uncertainty, and many of the treatments used or proposed for use in infant intensive care involve uncertainties about their short-term effects and long-range consequences.

## Stopping Life Support

*"First, do no harm."*
—HIPPOCRATES

There may come a time in the medical course of a very ill or extremely premature baby when physicians or parents feel that medical intervention is doing the baby harm. That is, instead of saving the baby's life, treatment is postponing the baby's inevitable death or, at best, keeping alive an infant who will never have a full or meaningful existence. Parents and doctors together may then agree that it is in the best interests of the baby and his family to stop artificial life support and allow the child to die a natural death.

"We have the technology now," says pediatrician Peter Gorski, "to prolong, at least, almost any baby's life. This leaves us with some hard choices to make and difficult questions to answer: like when and why do you call a halt to the heroics?" The decision to stop or continue treatment is never an easy one. It must be made on a case-by-case basis in the absence of clear legal, ethical, religious, or medical guidelines. Ideally, it is the result of open and honest dialogue between the parents and their baby's doctors and is consistent with the ethics and rational judgments of everyone involved.

The decision-making process is agonizing for physicians and parents alike. Says neonatologist Sally Sehring, "It's extremely hard to give up on a baby, but I worry about keeping alive a baby who will impose such a devastating emotional and financial burden on his family that *their* lives are destroyed by it. What right do I have to make decisions like this and then go home at night and walk out of their lives?" Said a father whose critically ill son was taken off the respirator, "The choice as we saw it was one of prolonging his suffering or consenting to his death. Either way we knew we would feel guilt."

Some parents feel emotionally unable to participate in life-and-death decisions concerning their child. But even a nondecision is a decision of sorts, for doctors consider themselves obligated to use every possible means to keep a baby alive unless parents give their active consent for medical intervention to stop. "Only parents," writes Dr. Michael Garland,

"can exercise the prudence that weighs the continued life of the infant against the impact on their family. Physicians should not substitute their judgment for that of . . . the absent parents. They must secure whatever treatment is necessary."

Few mothers and fathers have considered these painful, difficult issues before being forced to, and they may legitimately wish religious, psychological, medical, or legal counseling before they decide. They should not hesitate to seek second, third, and fourth opinions. Writes Dr. David Abramson, "These are human, not godly decisions. Not confronting them is far more disastrous than making them in good faith."

Parents may be the first to raise the issue of stopping life support for their infant. But for a number of reasons, physicians may be reluctant to stop treatment. People in the medical professions are trained to preserve life whenever possible, regardless of the outcome. And the eventual outcome for a particular baby in intensive care is hard to predict. While one child may be seriously handicapped, another with identical perinatal problems may survive to be normal. One neonatologist asked, "How do you decide? Where do you draw the line? Do you stop life support for a child who might be blind, retarded, or have a learning disability?" Faced with these uncertainties, some doctors feel that virtually every baby should be treated.

Doctors may also go against parental wishes because they feel the distraught mother and father are overreacting. Said one neonatologist, "I've had parents become quite upset and want to pull the plug on a baby with a minor brain bleed, a baby I thought had an excellent prognosis. Of course, I could not do this, ethically or legally."

The legal criteria for stopping the life support of a patient vary from state to state. Generally, brain death (absence of brain wave activity on an electroencephalogram—EEG) must be documented. But in reality, life and death decisions in the nursery seldom conform to strict legalities. Infants are generally removed from respirators not because they are legally dead, but because they have suffered a brain injury— a massive intraventricular hemorrhage, for example—that makes a normal outcome unlikely. Legal action is usually not taken against parents or physicians who decide not to treat infants with lethal or seriously damaging conditions, because, to quote Dr. Raymond Duff, "few believe that any other alternative makes sense." Dr. Duff, who has written extensively on the ethics of newborn intensive care, states, "Choosing death is sometimes viewed as an act of love because some life can only be wrongful."

Nevertheless, doctors (and parents) have occasionally been prosecuted for stopping life support for terminally ill or defective babies. An obstetrician in Los Angeles was charged with murder for not actively resuscitating a severely damaged fetus who might have survived briefly following a therapeutic abortion. In Danville, Illinois, parents and their physician were indicted for attempted murder when they decided against feeding (and keeping alive) horribly malformed Siamese twins. In another case, parents, who had agreed in writing that life support for their premature infant be stopped, later sued the doctors for their baby's death. Citing these and other cases, some doctors fear legal repercussions if they give in to parents' wishes to remove an infant from life support.

On the other hand, neonatologists are often criticized by others in the medical profession for intervening too aggressively to save babies doomed to prolonged suffering or to severe handicaps. Dr. Raymond Duff objects to the "costly, sometimes abusive, use of technology to ensure biological existence with little regard for the quality of child and family life." Pediatrician William Silverman, one of the founders of neonatology and a critic of what he views as its current excesses, refers to "the thoughtless benevolence" of physicians who are "obsessed by a rescue fantasy" and to "the modern intensive care unit with its panoply of rescue machinery [which] blares out the nonverbal message of life prolongation [and drowns out] any murmurings concerning the idea of natural death!" A nurse who left intensive care to become a midwife exclaimed bitterly, "I've seen doctors willing to do anything as long as there was a living cell left in a baby's body. They want to be the first in the country to salvage the tiniest or sickest baby. What they don't worry enough about in my opinion is what this does to the families involved!"

The families involved are pretty much at the mercy of the philosophies and motives of the doctors and nurses treating their child, and of the policies of the nursery and hospital. Some physicians like Drs. Duff and Silverman feel that the parents, who must live with the consequences, should have the major voice in life-and-death decisions concerning their child. Writes Dr. Silverman, "Parents must decide whether they have the emotional and physical resources needed for a life-long commitment to the victim of biologic error who must suffer the miseries that attend, say, deformity, blindness, or brain damage." Other doctors, like pediatrician Norman Fost, suggest that giving parents or physicians the right to stop life support on a brain-damaged infant is in effect advocating that "equal justice under the law" should be amended to read ". . . except for the retarded."

When parents' wishes clash with a physician's philosophy, the parents' tragedy is compounded. In an article in the *Atlantic Monthly,* Peggy and Robert Stinson recounted the ordeal they and their 800-gram infant son, Andrew, suffered at the hands of neonatologists who disagreed with their desire that Andrew be allowed to die a natural death. The Stinsons were accused of being "bad parents" and wanting to return to the law of the jungle. Despite the doctors' "heroics," baby Andrew died anyway—many painful and expensive months later.

Wrote the Stinsons: "We believe there is a moral and ethical problem of the most fundamental sort involved in a system which allows complicated decisions of this nature to be made unilaterally by people who do not have to live with the consequences of their decisions."

When physicians respond sensitively to parents' wishes and needs, the inevitable tragedy is mitigated. Said one couple, "Our doctors gave us the bleak prognosis and encouraged us to speak openly about our feelings on the baby's continued survival. No one pressured us one way or the other, and they did their best to alleviate any guilt we might be feeling. We decided together that it was best to stop treatment, and the doctors were with us by our baby's bedside when the respirator was turned off."

## Paul's Story

### By Susan Wick

It took a year of trying, and surgery to remove an ovarian cyst, before I was able to conceive. I remember the exultation I felt on learning I was pregnant. No baby could have been more wanted. I was the model expectant mother—a good diet, no alcohol, cigarettes, or coffee. I even took a pre-prenatal class.

Then one day at work when I was scarcely six months' pregnant, my membranes began to leak. I drove myself 50 miles to the community hospital close to our home. Perhaps if I'd gone instead to the medical center near work, the premature birth could have been averted. But in my panic I wasn't thinking clearly. Now, like so many other mothers of premies, I continue to beat myself with the baseball bat of guilt.

I spent three days in the community hospital listening to my unborn child's monitored heartbeats and watching the pens chart out contractions I couldn't even feel. I imagined my 26-week baby as one of those transparent jelly-like fetuses pictured in my prenatal books. Our obstetrician told us that the baby, if born now, could not survive an hour on his own. My husband Steve, the doctor, and I, with the consultation and agreement of a high-risk obstetrician, decided that the baby would be born in bed at our community hospital and allowed to die a natural death. We did not want our baby's dying prolonged by machinery. Our decision to spare our child from needless suffering was made with love and sorrow.

I could not bring myself to watch the birth. I didn't want to become more attached to this baby than I already was. As our newborn son was taken away, the doctor consoled us. We had made the best decision, he said, and there was no reason we couldn't try again for a baby within a year.

Sedated with Demerol, I fell asleep while Steve went home to call our families and inform them of the baby's birth and death.

Hours later, a pediatrician awakened me with the news that my baby boy was being transported to Children's Hospital for treatment. I was in shock. Surely he was in the wrong room. This had to be a mistake.

Later, from fragments of information I was given, I pieced together the story. Despite our wishes and the doctor's orders, one of the nurses present at our baby's birth took it upon herself to resuscitate him. Someday I would like to find this nurse and ask her why.

The next day Steve went to Children's Hospital to see the baby. But it took me four days to work up my courage. Then, with a tranquilizer churning in the pit of my stomach, I walked into the ICN—table after table of naked babies wrapped in tubes and wires. And there was our son. His head was shaved. His skin looked as though he'd been through a fire. Tubes and wires were randomly stuck into his one-pound, nine-ounce body. Baby Boy Wick—how I loved him and how I didn't want it to hurt anymore for him or for me.

I hated all the people who tried to help. I saw them as prolonging our baby's dying in a cruel, agonizing way. I wished I could somehow unplug his respirator and bring a quick end to his misery. I thought it would be well worth going to jail if that's what they chose to do with me. When Steve and I were asked to sign a form consenting to a PDA ligation, we refused. It seemed the only way we had to control a situation that had gotten out of our hands. The doctors explained to us that our refusal would only cause the baby more suffering, and we gave our consent. Surgery went without complication.

The staff urged us to name the baby and we chose Paul. Steve gave the baby his own name as a middle name—no matter which way things turned out, his son would carry a bit of Daddy with him.

In the months that followed I fell into a depression that I felt I would never overcome. My visits to the hospital were erratic. Sometimes I went every day, sometimes just once or twice a week.

In the nursery I would sit by Paul's bedside, listening to the monitors and the respirator and watching the nurse take his blood. Occasionally he would open his eyes and look at me. I wanted to run away. His stare seemed so accusing. Ironically, it was his eyes that would bear the major scars of his prematurity.

During those long difficult hours I composed this poem:

> I sit in this cold metal room and watch you.
> I stare in anguish as you breathe through
>     spaghetti-tubes.
> I see you through a tapestry of wires.
> I follow the red tracings of your heartbeat on
>     miles of paper.
>
> The probes burn your parchment skin.
> You cry, but the tubes take even that from you.
>
> I sit and watch as though you weren't real.
> Yet I feel your struggle and I breathe deep,
>     dizzying breaths for you.
>
> Then you open your eyes.
> "Please, Mama, no more needles, no more tubes
>     please, no more."
> I want to help you, but I am powerless.
>
> I am ashamed for all of us.

I declined the nurses' offers to help with Paul's care. They all suggested I stroke him and talk to him. It sounds simple enough, but it wasn't, not with all those people walking around and listening. I see now that I was holding back to protect myself from pain, like a person who will not fall in love for fear of being hurt.

Through this ordeal, Steve was my support, my rock. He never pushed, never criticized. He always listened and consoled me. After the PDA surgery, Steve became very optimistic about Paul. He wanted the baby to survive at any cost. He felt we could live with whatever happened. Steve's positive attitude helped me, but I found it hard to agree with him that Paul's survival was "for the best."

At my insistence we consulted a lawyer. I wanted to sue the nurse who'd revived Paul and the doctors who were keeping him alive against our wishes. The lawyer advised against legal action. Before Paul's birth, we, like most people, knew nothing of the extreme measures used to save even the tiniest of prematures. As we explored the legal, moral, and medical issues involved in neonatal care, we came to understand the complexities that surround life-and-death decisions. Suppose, for example, that Paul hadn't been resuscitated. Suppose he'd been horribly brain-damaged from lack of oxygen, but had survived anyway? We might then be wanting to sue for different reasons. I feel strongly that *realistic* discussions of prematurity and its implications should be a part of all prenatal instruction. No parent should have to come into this situation as unprepared as we were.

Although I am not a religious person, I consulted a priest and a minister. I saw this as a moral issue, and I regarded them as moral experts. I asked a lot of questions: "Was it right for babies this premature to be kept alive? What was the point of all this suffering?" I didn't really expect answers, and I didn't get any, but I was helped by their good advice. The minister, who had recently experienced a personal tragedy of his own, said that surviving a crisis is a bit like body surfing—either you ride with the wave or you struggle against the wave and get swept under. He showed me how I was suffering from trying to control events that were beyond my control. While no one could ever totally relieve me of the guilt I felt, the priest and the minister helped me see how unfounded it was. In doing so, they eased my burden.

But in a way it was Paul himself who helped me the most. I came to see such a strength and spirit emanating from his little body. This tiny person we had created had more of a will to survive than I did. He taught me a lesson—to fight against any odds and to give my all no matter what the outcome. How well I have learned this lesson only time will tell.

At one point, in an effort to save what was left of my sanity, I went to spend several weeks with my parents 2000 miles away. Many people saw my taking off like that as an unmotherly thing to do, but it worked. I returned to a much improved baby. I came into the nursery with my sleeves rolled up, ready to go to work.

Paul was finally taken off the respirator, and for the first time I came to believe that he would survive. The day he was extubated I ran out to buy some doll clothes. It's hard to explain the miracle that happens when you put clothes on these kids—but suddenly they look human. Had I known that the expenditure of a mere $20.00 would have such a positive effect on me, I would have done it much sooner.

In the days before Paul came home, we learned

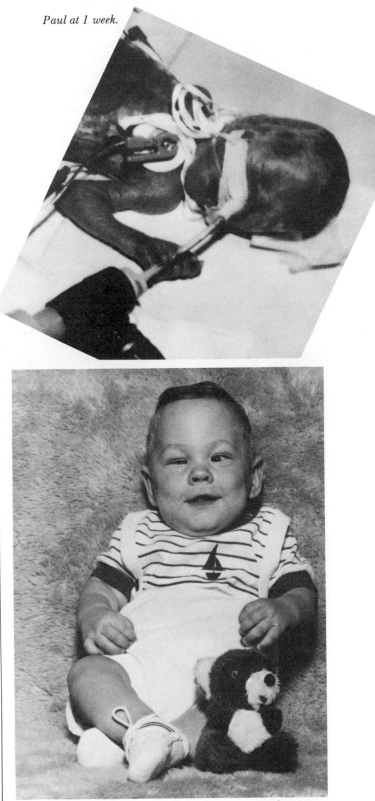

*Paul at 1 week.*

*Paul at 1 year.*

how to care for him, how to measure and give his medicines, how to do CPR and administer oxygen.

No one can go from being pregnant to being

childless and back to motherhood in just 3½ months and do it smoothly. I still had problems feeling like a mother, and Paul was exceptionally hard to care for. Paul came home with two horrendous hernias. His inguinal hernia looked like it weighed at least 2 of his 4½ pounds, and I felt if I pushed on the umbilical hernia it would make his tongue stick out. The hernias were painful and gave him colic. He cried constantly, which only put more pressure on the hernias and made the colic worse. He would also turn blue during his screaming spells, and Steve and I raced from room to room to see Paul in different lights as we tried to tell if he was blue enough to need oxygen.

We'd been told that Paul was in the early stages of RLF (retrolental fibroplasia) when he left the nursery, but no one really explained to us what that meant. And as we dealt with his hernias and constant crying, we didn't pay much attention to Paul's eyes.

Shortly after his surgery to repair the hernias, Paul's former nurse visited us at home and noticed that something was wrong with his right eye. We took Paul to the ophthalmologist, who groped for the words to tell us that Paul was now blind in his right eye and rapidly losing sight in the left eye as well. We were stunned. Immediate surgery was performed to "spot weld" the left retina in an attempt to save a little of Paul's vision.

The surgeon came out of the operation with good news and bad news. The retina had been partially reattached, but the optic nerve in the left eye was found to be badly damaged. Paul would probably be blind.

I tried so hard to be brave, and for several days I succeeded. Then at five o'clock one morning after a sleepless night, I phoned the minister and poured out my despair. He asked if I had talked to Steve about how I felt and I said no. "Then go wake him up and tell him," he said. I told Steve that I just couldn't bear it any longer. We decided to take Paul and leave him with a woman who cares for the ICN babies no one else wants or can care for. I needed time away from my constantly screaming child, to think and figure out what to do.

Again, the "time out" was just what I needed. Steve and I spent three days together talking, going for drives, going out to dinner—we even went roller-skating. When we went to take Paul back, I was glad to see him.

A woman who teaches blind children and counsels their parents came to talk to us. She explained to me that Paul cried so much because he couldn't see

and was bored. She gave me a number of books and pamphlets, but made me promise not to read these books exclusively. "Go to the library and get a good novel to read, too," she advised. "It's good to take action but don't make this your entire life."

Several weeks later as I leaned close to Paul and silently smiled, I saw him smile back at me. I called Steve at work: "Paul sees me!" Steve thought it was time to send for the men with the straight jackets. So did the friends I told. But I wasn't imagining things. The ophthalmologist confirmed it. Paul did have some degree of central vision in his left eye. How much vision he has we won't know until he is older.

Recently, Steve and I attended a weekend workshop for parents of blind and visually impaired children. Everyone we met was so friendly and open. We all felt drawn together by our common bond. A panel of blind adults discussed how blindness had affected their lives. Doctors spoke on RLF, optic nerve damage, and other causes of blindness. While I attended a class on stimulating low vision, Steve went to a pre-braille workshop. He came away highly impressed, enthusiastic, and ready to get involved with helping Paul.

Now, at 11 months, Paul is becoming an easier child. His crying has tapered off. He's learning to play by himself. He smiles a lot and generally seems happier.

I have my good days and bad days. I'm really beginning to enjoy my baby, but the shocks aren't over yet. At a recent doctor's visit, Paul was diagnosed as having partial paralysis of his right arm and cerebral palsy. A CAT scan revealed damage to the left side of his brain. The costs of Paul's care are constantly mounting. He used up his maximum lifetime allowance of insurance coverage in the first few weeks following his birth, so we no longer have insurance to help with his expenses. We are receiving state aid to assist us in meeting these costs, but our share is still so high that we've considered declaring bankruptcy.

My existence before Paul's birth seems unreal to me now, and I talk about my life as "before" and "after." I am still dealing with a lot of anger. I find it hard to relate to parents and babies who have not been through struggles similiar to ours.

I am now helping to start a parents group at Children's Hospital. It's been good for me to see I'm not the only one with problems. While I've basically accepted what has happened to us, I know I will continue to need the support of others who have been there too.

# 6

# The Death of a Baby

All parents of a sick premature infant, in some way, on some level, must come to terms with the death of their baby. The stages of coping with a birth crisis—shock, denial, anger, bargaining, and acceptance—are, in fact, adapted from the stages of grieving described by Elisabeth Kübler-Ross in her book *On Death and Dying*. They are appropriate responses to the premature birth situation whether or not the baby physically dies, for the parents of a premature infant must grieve for the loss of the full-term, healthy baby they expected. In addition, most parents of a sick premature baby fear their child's actual death, and they grieve for that death in advance. In most cases, the anticipated death never becomes a reality.

However, despite the recent dramatic increase in infant survival rates, thirteen to fourteen infant deaths still occur in the United States for every thousand live births. This means that of the approximately 3.5 million infants born in the United States each year, between 45 and 49 thousand die. Of those infants who die, nearly 70% die from causes related to prematurity.

## When a Baby Dies at Birth or Soon Afterward

The death of a child has been called the ultimate tragedy, the most unnatural of disasters. These words apply to the death of a child of any age, but they apply with special force to the death of a newborn. The death occurs just as the family is happily anticipating the arrival of their new baby. Suddenly, the parents are robbed of the future they had planned with their child, and they are plunged into a limbo of private sorrow and emptiness. In today's world of medical miracles, babies are not supposed to die. Parents, caregivers, relatives, and friends do not know how to deal with this unexpected violation of the natural order. As a result, many of the emotional aspects of the infant's death may simply not be dealt with at all. This gives the loss of a newborn an added dimension of tragedy, for the parents may deny themselves (or be denied) the opportunity to acknowledge their child's life and death, publicly mourn their loss, and fully experience the healing process of grief.

When an older person dies, we can grieve openly and intensely for someone whose long life was a reality to us and to those around us. But parents who lose a baby at birth, or soon afterward, must first accept the fact that their child existed at all before they can begin to grieve properly. And there are many factors besides the brevity of the child's life that can make such an acceptance difficult.

At some hospitals, when a baby dies at birth or shortly after birth, the body is removed and disposed of before the parents have seen or touched their child. "The rationale for this procedure," says psychologist John Golenski, counselor to bereaved parents, "is that it spares the parents further pain. What it does, however, is condemn them to a long period of ambiguity and anguish." "I knew I had lost *something*," said the mother of a stillborn premature, "but I didn't know what. My husband had a brief glimpse of the baby after the delivery, and I've cross-examined him over and over again about what the baby looked like, the baby's hair color, complexion, anything I can think of to help me piece together a picture. But it hasn't worked. It's been three years now, and I've been in and out of therapy, but I still can't finalize it."

Seeing and holding the baby's body is an important first step in accepting the infant's reality, and the reality of the loss. It is a painful step, writes Harriet Schiff, author of *The Bereaved Parent*, "much in the same way that cauterizing a wound is painful . . . [But] healing may not begin without that very painful procedure; psychiatrists believe the same principle applies to viewing the body."

Many parents, at the death or anticipated death of their newborn, feel a natural first impulse to escape the pain they fear would accompany a knowledge of their baby. "When I learned during the labor that the baby was dead," a mother recounted, "I asked for general anesthesia for the delivery. I told the doctors and nurses that I wanted to know nothing about the baby. When I woke up, a nurse who had been with me during the labor pleaded with me to see and hold my daughter's body. The nurse had lost a newborn the year before, and she had never seen or held her baby. She said this had been one of the greatest mistakes of her life. At her insistence, I agreed to hold my dead baby, and I'm so glad I did. Although my eyes were so full of tears I could hardly see her, my daughter became a person to me and I became a mother. In those moments as I held her, I felt my entire perspective on life shift. I learned a valuable lesson: face reality, even painful reality, and live it while it happens."

The attitudes of others also compound the parents' problem of accepting the infant's existence and properly mourning the death. Friends and relatives may find the death awkward to acknowledge and the parents' sorrow difficult to comprehend. Obstetricians and maternity ward nurses who have chosen life-promoting professions often feel uncomfortable, professionally and personally, with the "failure" implicit in an infant's death. They may also try to play down the parents' loss, implying in the process that the baby was somehow not important, better off dead, or less than real.

One mother was told by her obstetrician that it was easier to lose a baby at birth than to lose a child who was known and loved. "But I loved that baby from the moment I knew I was pregnant," the mother insisted, "and the fact that I hadn't come to know him as a child made it even worse. I'll always be left to wonder what he would have been like if. . . ."

Another mother told of friends and medical staff who kept telling her it was for the best, that the baby would have had terrible problems if he had lived. "I suppose this should have helped console me," she said, "but somehow it never did."

"You're young, you can try again," is another unhelpful comment people often make. Said one mother, "When the obstetrician told me I could always have another baby, I yelled at her, 'But I want *this* baby, not some other one!'"

Often the doctors and nurses are too ill at ease to respond at all: "My OB who had been my doctor for *years* suddenly became very distant. My postpartum checks were as abrupt and short as possible. He never once looked me in the eye." Said another mother, "My doctor did not even acknowledge that one of the twins had died, as if it were enough to have one living baby."

Under the circumstances, the maternity ward can be an uncomfortable place for a mother whose baby is dead or close to death. "I was given a private room at least," said a mother whose prematurely born son was dying, "but I could still hear babies crying and see the new mothers shuffling around out in the hall, laughing and happy. And with every change of shift, there was a new nurse who hadn't been told, who would come in my room and ask why my baby wasn't with me. Once a nurse mistook my tears for postpartum depression and said in a very patronizing way, 'We can't have our new mothers crying now, can we?'"

On the other hand, some mothers resent being taken to other wards of the hospital since this, in effect, denies their maternity: "I was put on a surgical ward to recover from my cesarean. When my breasts suddenly became engorged, no one knew how to deal with it and it took a very painful day before I was able to get someone to wheel me down to Maternity to use the breast pump. I felt being on the surgical ward was medically and psychologically wrong. No matter what had happened to my baby, I was still a mother!"

Mothers who have strong preferences on this matter should not hesitate to make their wishes known to the staff.

An additional problem for the mother who loses her newborn is that she must deal with her grief as she copes with the physical aftermath of birth—the episiotomy or cesarean incision, postpartum bleeding, and, for women who did not receive "drying-up" shots, engorged breasts. "I felt doubly betrayed by my body," said one woman, "first by allowing the baby to be born prematurely, and, now that the baby was dead, by refusing to recognize that fact, by continuing to produce milk. It seemed so stupid and cruel." Poet Marion Cohen, whose daughter died two days after birth, expressed different feelings in "How I Live with Three Children and Die with a Fourth:"*

I wanted my milk to come in.
It wasn't practical, but I wanted it anyway.
First I wanted it so I could express it for the nurses to feed her through a tube when her condition improved; then I wanted it just so the experience of having a baby wouldn't be gone so soon.
I wanted that fullness; I wanted that milk. . . .
[It] flowed continuously onto the bed, along with the blood and tears. I'd think of her and

*Poetry by Dr. Marion Cohen, mathematician, poet, and bereaved mother, can also be found in *After a Loss in Pregnancy* by Nancy Berezin, a book we highly recommend to grieving parents. See p. 246.

that milk would keep coming. Maybe I believed she'd get it somehow.

One of the most difficult situations in early newborn death occurs when a transported baby dies in a nursery far from the hospitalized mother. "We do everything we can," said an intensive care nurse, "to keep the baby alive until the mother can see and touch her living child, but unfortunately that is not always possible."

"When an infant dies and the mother is in another hospital," says Dr. John Golenski, "we feel she should see her infant as soon as she is medically able to do so. This may mean transporting her to the baby's hospital on a stretcher. It is very important for her to see her baby's body, to see where her baby died, and to talk to the doctors and nurses who cared for her baby. Sometimes this involves keeping the baby's body in the hospital morgue for a number of days, but it is worth doing."

A mother who sees her baby's body should realize beforehand that the body may be ashen or discolored, cold and stiff, and that viewing, touching, and holding her baby can be an emotionally wrenching experience. Nevertheless, parents who have done this are almost always grateful later to have had the opportunity. In the words of bereaved mother Harriet Schiff, "facing life's harshest reality is what we need in order to go on with life."

Even a baby who is stillborn, or who lives only briefly, should be given a name. Parents may not wish to give the baby the name they had chosen during pregnancy. Some professionals feel that this name rightly belongs to the baby whether or not he survives. Dr. John Golenski disagrees: "If parents do not wish to give the name they had previously selected, then it is wise that they not do so. After all, this is not the baby they had expected. Nevertheless, the baby should have a name." A name allows the parents to talk about their child more easily and to discuss the baby's birth and death more naturally with others. A name confers human status upon the baby and provides further evidence that a baby existed who died and must now be mourned.

## Death in the Nursery

While parents live in fear of the midnight phone call informing them that their baby has died, this is more the exception than the rule. The medical staff usually knows ahead of time when a baby is losing his fight for life, and the parents can be informed in

advance, giving them the option of being with their baby at the time of death.

Not all parents are physically or emotionally able to be with their dying baby, and some stay away, saying that they prefer to keep intact the memory of their living infant. Nevertheless, an intensive care nurse notes that, in her decade of experience, *all* parents whose infants died, even those parents who refused to be present at the death, returned to the nursery within a year's time asking for the nursery photograph taken after the child had died. Despite attempts to deny and forget, these parents seemed to have a need for a realistic understanding of their baby's death.

Mothers and fathers who choose to be with their baby at the time of death find their initial grief quite intense, but easier to resolve in the long run. "It was emotional and sad," said a mother who held her son as he died, "but at least I had a chance to know and love my baby. A friend of mine had a baby who died shortly after birth of a congenital defect. She never saw her child and now she has nightmares about it. At least I have a real baby to mourn." "Before our baby died," another mother said, "they put a screen around her heating table to give us privacy. The clergyman was unavailable, so our baby's nice Jewish nurse performed the baptism and signed the baptismal documents. And we held our daughter at last without any tubes or wires—a peaceful, sleeping baby."

Some parents find it helpful to bring family members or friends to see the baby before, during or after the death: "The nurses encouraged us to bring our other children in to see their little sister before she died. I'm glad we did because it made the experience real to them." Said another mother, "I wish now that I had brought a friend to the hospital to see my daughter. That way I would have had someone who was close to me who knew what she was like. Now, when I feel like I have to talk about it, I go back to the hospital. The nurses are the only ones who really understand."

When a baby dies in the nursery, it is often following a decision to stop life support (see page 102): "I came into the unit that morning, and I could tell by looking at Andrew that his condition had worsened and that he was about to die. I sat down beside him and refused to leave. 'It could be a matter of hours or a matter of days,' said the doctor, 'and you can't sit here like this forever.' He suggested that Andrew's respirator be stopped. At first I was shocked. We had done so much to preserve the pregnancy and to fight for Andrew's life that I didn't want to give up, even though I realized that it was just a question of time.

On the other hand, I didn't want to prolong my baby's agony. Finally, with my husband's encouragement, I agreed. The doctor took out the tubes and put Andrew in my arms for the first time. I held Andrew as he died and looked into his eyes, and I felt that we communicated on some level, that we touched each other, and that he could feel my love. If I had missed those few minutes to be his mother I could never have forgiven myself."

Andrew was the smaller of twins, and his mother faced the difficult emotional task of grieving for her dead infant while becoming attached to the living twin. "After I had given Andrew's body to the doctors, I automatically began walking toward Eddie's warming table. One of the nurses stopped me and gave me the wise advice to go home and let the experience of Andrew's death sink in and then, when I felt ready, to come back to the nursery and begin a relationship with my surviving child on a new basis."

"When a mother loses one of twins," says Dr. Golenski, "her attachment to the remaining twin is almost always affected; often the mother becomes overly attached." A mother who lost one of her premature twin daughters recounted: "After Christine's death, my relationship with Megan became intensely overprotective. I literally stayed in the house with her for the first year and a half. During that time, I was obsessed with death. I had nightmares in which I dreamed a baby was suffocating inside the mattress. When my husband would wake me from these dreams, which I had several times a week, I would be dripping with sweat, screaming, and clawing at the mattress. Other times, still in my sleep, I would jump up in a panic and search through Megan's room, believing she had disappeared. Megan is three now, and finally, after a year of therapy, I'm beginning to accept the fact that she is going to live and has to be allowed to enter the world."

Many parents, at some time during a critically ill infant's intensive care, have wished for their baby's death and an end to the suffering. Although these wishes are common and natural, they are very difficult for most parents to acknowledge, and they can become a conscious or unconscious source of guilt, especially if the baby dies. A mother who *was* able to express this wish, who had, in fact, argued unsuccessfully with the doctors to have her terminally ill son removed from the respirator, was surprised by her strong and contradictory feelings of guilt at her child's eventual death: "It was a Catch-22 situation. On the one hand, I felt guilty because I had been powerless to stop my child's months of suffering. But now that it was finally over, I also felt guilt because I had wished for his death, even though I knew it was the only merciful outcome."

## Practical Decisions

After a baby dies there are decisions that must be made. Some decisions, such as whether or not to perform an autopsy, should be made as soon as possible after death. Others, such as funeral, burial, or cremation arrangements can wait for several days.

The decision about the autopsy is usually left to the parents. However, in certain circumstances an autopsy is required by law. An autopsy may be required, for example, if a physician was not in attendance for 24 hours before the death (as might occur with a baby who dies after a home birth, or a baby who dies soon after admittance to the hospital.) Parents may always request that an autopsy be done whether or not the physician suggests one.

Before parents sign an Autopsy Permit to authorize the procedure, they should be fully informed about what an autopsy involves. They should know where and when the autopsy is to take place. Parents may wish to inquire about limitations that can be placed on the extent of the autopsy, and they should specify in writing on the Autopsy Permit any such limitations they wish to impose. Sometimes, for example, parents request that incisions not be made on the baby's head. However, limitations on the extent of the autopsy also limit the information that the autopsy can reveal. The autopsy should also be conducted within a day or two following the death in order to yield the best understanding of the cause of the baby's death.

"I always advise that there be an autopsy," says Dr. Golenski, "*not* for the sake of medical science, *not* for the sake of future babies, but for the sake of the *parents*. Several weeks or months after the death, parents inevitably have questions about why the baby died. An autopsy frequently provides answers that would be otherwise unavailable."

The preliminary results of the autopsy are usually known within a day or two of the procedure, but the more detailed tissue studies may take several weeks to complete. Usually, three to six weeks after the baby's death, the parents meet with the baby's doctors to discuss the autopsy report. These conferences are an opportunity for parents to ask any unanswered questions—medical or otherwise—that they have about the baby's death. Because these conferences can be emotionally difficult, parents should write down their questions in advance so that they can remember what they wish to ask. They may also want to make a tape of the conference that they can listen to at home under calmer circumstances. Parents should never hesitate to contact their baby's caregivers to pursue additional questions or concerns that occur to them later.

After the autopsy, a decision must be made concerning the burial or cremation of the baby's body. "Each alternative has its advantages and disadvantages," says Dr. Golenski. "If you bury a child in a town where you live and then later move away, it may be difficult for you to leave your buried child. A second problem with burial is that it allows parents to postpone the acknowledgment that the child has died, since the body has been placed in a specific location. However, some people benefit from having that postponement." In some counties, a baby can be buried on the parents' own land if they wish, although a burial permit will be required. Parents who wish to explore their options on burial, embalming, cremation, caskets, or transporting their baby's body should contact the hospital social worker or the agency that issues the death certificate. "Most funeral directors," says Dr. Golenski, "tend to give incomplete answers to these questions."

Cremation, as opposed to burial, is a more emphatic ending. "Nevertheless," says Dr. Golenski, "cremation has its own awkwardness. If parents keep the baby's ashes in their home they can become a haunting presence." The ashes may also be buried or left at a mortuary, but again this perpetuates the feeling that the child still physically exists somewhere. Dispersing the ashes is another alternative. One family had their child's ashes mixed with wildflower seeds and scattered in a beautiful nature preserve.

If there is to be a funeral in which the body is viewed in an open casket, parents may wish to have their baby's body embalmed. Embalming is a procedure in which preservatives are added to the body. It is done for sanitary and cosmetic reasons. In most cases, it is *not* mandatory. It may be required, however, if the baby died from an infectious illness or if the body is to be viewed in a public building. It may or may not be required if the body is to be viewed at the parents' home. Contact your local health department for more information. Embalming is done at a mortuary or a funeral home. Although mortuaries and funeral homes used to provide different services, their functions today are virtually identical. They embalm the body, prepare it for viewing, sell caskets, provide a place for the funeral, and perform a variety of other services for the bereaved family. If you do not have a funeral home that your family has used before, you may wish to get a referral from the hospital social worker. Social workers generally know those funeral homes that offer their services at a reasonable price.

Depending on hospital regulations and local ordinances, you may be able to transport your baby from the hospital to the mortuary. If you are taking your baby to a funeral home far from the hospital, it may save you considerable expense if you transport your baby yourself. You will need your baby's death certificate, and, if you are crossing state lines, you may need a special permit. Discuss this with your social worker and the health department.

Many parents, in the numbness of grief, or under pressure from well-meaning relatives or hospital staff, forgo the usual funeral rituals when a baby dies. Sometimes they regret these decisions later. "While I convalesced from the difficult delivery," one mother said, "my mother and my husband arranged everything. They named the baby without consulting me; they had his body cremated. No funeral. That was that. I am still very resentful at having been denied my rights to grieve for my baby in my own way."

Many professionals who counsel bereaved parents now advise some kind of ceremony to mark the baby's death. The funeral or memorial service can take any number of forms. Some parents opt for the standard religious rites. Harriet Schiff found the traditional service "with its set and ancient guidelines easier to cope with than decision making in a new direction would have been." Other parents, especially those without a religious affiliation, may prefer a non-traditional ceremony that has personal meaning for them. One couple, whose child died after months in intensive care, held the memorial service at the hospital, where it was attended by those on the staff who had been closest to their daughter during her life. Dr. Golenski recalls the way in which another family mourned and commemorated their child's death: "After the autopsy, the father took his son's body, wrapped in a quilt, to the mortuary for embalming. A friend who was a woodworker carved a beautiful cedar chest for a casket. The parents placed their son's body in the chest, and held a wake in their front yard for two days. They stayed with their son's body, sleeping beside him at night in sleeping bags. During this time, friends came and went constantly to mourn with the parents. After the two days, they buried their son in a local cemetery. During the service, the adults threw flowers on the casket, and, as the child was buried, the other children at the service released helium-filled balloons."

Not every parent wishes to have a service. "I dislike funerals," said one mother. " I don't want one when I die, and I didn't want one for my baby."

Instead of the usual cards and flowers, mothers and fathers may prefer that contributions in their child's memory be made for some helping purpose. "Flowers were just going to die," one mother said. "But the nursery never had enough rocking chairs. We asked our friends to contribute to a memorial fund for the purchase of a comfortable rocker."

Parents may also wish to make and send birth

and death announcements to friends, relatives, and anybody else they might encounter. The announcements can give the baby's name, the date of birth and death, and can include a poem or other inscription. Such announcements avoid awkward questions that might otherwise arise, and they signal to your acquaintances that it is all right for them to talk to you about your baby and your baby's death.

"After the baby has died," says Dr. Golenski, "I also advise that parents gather together any keepsakes they have of their baby and put them in a baby book. These might include such items as the birth certificate, death certificate, cards they received, the baby's footprints, handprints, a lock of hair, mementos from the pregnancy, especially photographs taken of the mother while pregnant. Not every couple is ready to do this immediately. Some may begin the project a month after the baby's death, others may wait a year or longer."

"It is a mistake to erase all evidence of the baby," Dr. Golenski continues. "The mother of one woman in our support group dismantled the nursery and removed all the baby things before her daughter came home from the hospital. The baby's mother reports that she has gone to her mother's house when she isn't home and has spent time going through the items her mother stored away. She says this is the closest she can come to 'playing' with her baby."

# A Special Grief

Psychiatrist Erna Furman feels that a mother who grieves for her dead baby is coming to terms not only with the loss of her child, but also with the loss of a part of herself. Mothers, she writes, often describe "the bodily experience of a hole inside that nothing can fill; sometimes a feeling of aching arms, like the phantom limb of an amputee." Said a mother whose premature infant died during delivery, "I remember waking up after delivery, touching my still-bulging stomach, but realizing the baby was gone, dead. It gave me the most incredible sense of emptiness." (These sensations are common among mothers who deliver prematurely whether or not the baby dies. See page 4.) A mother who lost her daughter to SIDS, sudden infant death syndrome, exclaimed, "It's been over a year now, and my breasts still ache!"

There is no more intimate physical relationship than the one a pregnant woman has with her unborn baby, and the grief a mother feels at the loss of her baby can be quite intense, prolonged, and complicated—a fact that is often poorly understood by those around her: "For well over two years I would have crying jags for no apparent reason. I would be driving down the freeway and suddenly I'd burst into tears. It took me lots of time and therapy to realize that I was crying about the baby. Meanwhile, my husband and my friends all thought I was going crazy."

Husbands and wives rarely grieve for their dead infant in the same way. Although some couples we interviewed felt they had been drawn together by their common grief, the majority expressed resentment over the way their partner had dealt (or not dealt) with their child's death. "My husband's way of coping," said one mother, "was to immerse himself in his work and not discuss the baby. He couldn't understand why I wanted to go to parent group meetings. He accused me of wallowing in grief." "I've really tried to understand what she's going through," said one father plaintively, "but whatever I say or do, it seems like it's the wrong thing."

Sexual tensions, as well as individual grieving styles, can severely stress the marriage. Many couples feel guilty about enjoying a sexual relationship during a time when they think they should be feeling sad. Sexual problems often arise after a birth crisis, but after the death of an infant, an aversion toward sex in one or both partners can be very strong. "Sex reminded me of babies," said one mother, "and babies reminded me of death." Unfortunately, the disruption of their sexual relationship denies a couple the consolation of physical closeness at a time when they need it most.

"I advise any couple who has lost a child to get counseling immediately," said one bereaved mother. "The strains on the marriage may seem small at first, but they build and build and build." Finding a good therapist is not always easy. "The first person we saw," one mother said, "couldn't understand how the dying of a premature infant could so seriously affect a healthy marriage. We wasted a lot of time and money with this man while he tried to discover what was 'really wrong' with our marriage. Finally, we changed therapists and found someone who gave us good, constructive counseling."

Another problem couples frequently face is the lack of support from family and friends. "Most of the people we thought were our friends didn't even call," said one mother, "and those who did were at such a loss for words that we ended up comforting them." "In my grandfather's family," said one father, "only two out of seven children survived infancy. Almost every family back then lost a child. But among all our friends, we know of no one else who has been through this." It seems that society has forgotten how to deal with what was once a common experience. To help parents cope with this problem, groups have formed in many parts of the country where bereaved parents can meet and share their special grief. Some of these groups specifically provide support to parents who have lost newborns. They include such groups as A.M.E.N.D. (Aiding a Mother Experiencing Neonatal Death), S.H.A.R.E. (A Source of Help in Airing and Resolving Experiences), and H.A.N.D. (Helping After Neonatal Death). For referrals to groups in your area, contact the hospital social worker or the Pregnancy and Infant Loss Center, a national clearinghouse for resources on miscarriage, stillbirth, and newborn loss. (See page 247.)

With a counselor, or in groups of others who have lost newborns, parents can more easily come to terms with the complicated emotional process of mourning their dead infant.

"One of the watersheds of grieving," says Dr. John Golenski, "is the parents' acknowledgment of the anger they feel toward the child that died. This is a hard feeling to recognize and understand because it isn't rational. You don't get angry at a baby who dies. The child, after all, didn't choose to die. But on some level parents still feel angry because the child they wanted, prepared for, and expected, has left them. Suppose, for example, that you had planned a big party, decorated your house, prepared all sorts of food and entertainment. Then, the guest of honor arrives at your doorstep, turns around, and leaves. Wouldn't you feel rejected and angry? Anger is the number one unacknowledged feeling parents have. Often it is misdirected toward others—toward friends who can't say the right thing, for example, or toward the nurses and doctors.

"Health care professionals do what they can to mitigate parental feelings of anger and guilt by providing medical explanations and simple reassurances. These are helpful, but no matter how many reassur-

---

## Saying Good-Bye

In the grief you feel following your baby's death, you may not think to ask for:

*Time alone with your baby to say good-bye.* Ask for a private place where you can hold your baby. The amount of time you spend should be limited only by your own feelings of comfort. Some parents stay with their baby only a few minutes after death; others choose to do so for a day or longer. You may wish to have family members, your clergyman, or friends stay with you during this time.

*Keepsakes of your baby.* You can ask for such items as your baby's birth certificate; death certificate; a lock of your baby's hair; footprints and handprints; photographs; your baby's nursery bracelet; a record of your baby's weight, length, and other measurements; paper from the fetal monitoring machine or from the nursery monitors with tracings of your baby's heartbeat; blankets, clothing, and other items used in your baby's care.

*Further opportunities to see and hold your baby.* Even after your baby's body has been taken to the morgue, you may ask to have your baby's body brought to you if you feel the need to see your child again.

*The opportunity to take your baby from the hos-* pital to the mortuary or funeral home, and from the funeral home to the cemetery. Ask the social worker and the public health department about any special permits that may be required.

*The opportunity to dress your baby yourself in a special burial gown and bonnet.* Infant burial gowns and bonnets, and patterns for gowns and bonnets are available in several small sizes from the Pregnancy and Infant Loss Center, 1421 E. Wayzata Blvd., Wayzata, Minnesota 55391, (612) 473-9372. The Center also offers baby books for infants who died, information on funeral planning, caskets for tiny babies, infant-loss announcements and comfort cards, "Loving Arms"—a quarterly newsletter, and supportive materials for the entire family.

*Consultations with the nurses and doctors who were with your baby before, during, or after death.* This may be especially important to you if you were unable to be there yourself. Never hesitate to contact these people later, even years later, to answer questions and help resolve concerns you may have. Even years after your baby's death, the hospital may have photographs and other mementos of your baby. If you would like them, be sure to ask.

## Telling Your Children About the Baby's Death

It may seem easier to avoid the subject entirely, especially if your children have never seen the baby or do not know that a baby was expected, as might happen with a premature stillbirth. However, psychologists feel this is a mistake. Even the youngest child will sense something is terribly wrong and will be less upset by an honest explanation than by no explanation at all.

What you say to your other children will depend on the age level of the child and upon your own religious and philosophical views of death. In discussing death with your children, there is no harm in admitting there are many aspects of death and dying that no one fully understands.

Jerri Oehler, R.N., and Katherine Shelburne have designed the story-coloring book *The Frog Family's Baby Dies* to allow parents to discuss death more easily with their children, and to address some of the fears and concerns young children commonly have about death. The 13-page, 8½- × 11-inch book is available for $1.50 from Jerri Oehler, R.N., Ph.D., Box 3362, Duke University Medical Center, Durham, North Carolina 27710.

**Three sample pages from *The Frog Family's Baby Dies*, by Jerri Oehler, R.N.**

ances parents receive, on a nonrational, emotional level they still feel that they and their baby are responsible for what happened.

"To help cope with guilt and blame, I suggest to the mother and father that separately, together, or with a counselor, they communicate with their dead child—out loud or in writing—to express the anger, guilt, and sorrow they feel. Once this is done, I further suggest that the parents express forgiveness to their baby and ask for their baby's forgiveness. As in any relationship in which there has been a disruption, the very important relationship between the parents and their dead baby benefits from the granting of and the requesting of forgiveness. Parents who have allowed themselves to undergo this experience usually find that they have passed a major milestone in the healing process we call grieving. Many describe a physical sense of relief and find that they are able to get on with life and are better able to allow subsequent children their rightful individuality."

## Back to Life

"Reentering the world is a battle," writes Harriet Schiff, "one that is all the more difficult because we are entering it battered and limping. Start small," she advises. "Begin with everyday tasks." Pay the bills, balance the checkbook, clean out the closets, and begin to make small but pleasant changes in your life—a new hairstyle, a bottle of wine with dinner.

The recovery process is rarely a straightforward one; relapses and setbacks are bound to occur. Some of these problems are obvious and expected. Others may come as a surprise.

Among the expected difficulties are the feelings of jealousy a parent may have toward other parents and infants—especially if the infant is the same age as their child would have been. Some parents feel a strong resentment toward babies in general or anything that reminds them of babies. "I'd turn off the television whenever ads for baby products came on," said one mother, "and I still go out of my way to avoid the antique store with the cradle in the window that I'd hoped to buy."

Family holidays are often filled with distressing memories, and so are the sad anniversaries: the baby's birthdate, the baby's due date, and the day the baby died. Parents may find it helpful to observe these occasions in some special way. One couple lights their wedding candle every year on the day of their premature son's birth and death.

In trying to return to a normal life, many couples take up a challenging new activity. Some mothers or fathers return to school or start a new career. One father began jogging and lost 75 pounds. Some bereaved parents go on trips, trying to recapture the feeling of life before the baby. (One unfortunate couple arrived at their resort hotel only to find it was hosting a convention of neonatologists!)

Often the bereaved parents begin to think of having another child, and it is during the subsequent pregnancy that surprising relapses of grief can occur. "During the next pregnancy," says Dr. Golenski, "many mothers and fathers feel their greatest need for the bereaved parents' support group. It sounds strange, but there is often an unspoken fear that the child who died, if not publicly acknowledged, will harm the pregnancy. In West Africa, there is a tribe that makes a doll of the infant who has died. During the subsequent pregnancy, the doll is offered food to placate it so that it will not wreak vengeance on the new baby. Many parents have said that the only place where they feel comfortable and happy about the new pregnancy is in the parent support group. That is because here the child who died can be openly acknowledged."

The birth of the new baby may also be clouded by grief for the baby who died. "It really surprised me," said one mother, "but the time of my greatest sadness was right after my healthy full-term was delivered. I suddenly realized that in the 45 minutes after his birth, I knew more about Jonathan than I had ever known about his brother who died after months of intensive care."

The pain of a baby's death never entirely vanishes, but it does diminish. Life does go on. Slowly, imperceptibly at first, the balance between sorrow and happiness begins to shift in favor of the latter. A parent who has survived the ultimate tragedy is often braver and stronger for it, and the recovery process is often helped by this new-found strength and the accomplishments that may accompany it. After her son's death, Harriet Schiff became a professional writer. She was no longer frightened of facing an unknown editor. After all, she had known the worst fear—"waiting for a doctor to tell you whether your child will live or die." To other bereaved parents she offers these encouraging words: "The fear of the unknown is behind us . . . for we have already taken a long look at hell. Understand and accept that, for you, there is still a future and one that can be as bright and good as you choose to make it."

## Rachel's Story

### By Linda Zeichner

Alan and I were expecting our first baby in 1976. I was having a normal pregnancy. Our lives had always been without crisis—we never expected otherwise. Then my water broke nine weeks early and our lives changed in one minute.

Our baby girl Rachel was not only premature, she also had an omphalocele, a congenital defect of the intestines. All I remember is a blur as she was hurried out of the delivery room. By the time I actually saw her, she had already had intestinal surgery. She weighed two pounds, nine ounces.

She went through the usual premie problems, but her recovery from RDS was very slow. Her color remained blue even after her lungs improved, and the doctors soon diagnosed a congenital heart defect, one that would eventually need surgical correction.

Rachel's three months in the hospital were filled with ups and downs. Every doctor we talked to gave us a different story about her condition. We would go back and forth from utter despair at the thought that our child might die, to optimism when doctors assured us all her problems could be overcome.

One day when we were feeling especially optimistic, we went to interview a pediatrician who'd been recommended to us. I guess we looked too happy when we entered his office and he decided to give us a dose of reality. He delivered a long lecture about how children like Rachel can ruin their parents' lives and destroy marriages.

Alan and I had come in separate cars, and as I drove home that evening, sobbing and shaking with rage, a policeman pulled me over on the freeway. I'd forgotten to turn on my lights.

But there were moments of laughter as well as tears. We became close to the couple whose tiny son was in the incubator next to Rachel's. They understood our need to break the tension with jokes that may have seemed cruel to outsiders. Together we planned a wedding for Freddy and Rachel—how they'd walk down the aisle with oxygen blowing from Freddy's boutonniere. There we'd be—parents of the two sickest babies in the nursery—laughing away. Occasionally we'd get some strange looks from the nurses, who surely must have thought we'd gone mad.

We sometimes felt distant from our friends outside the nursery, the ones who would call and talk and talk about everything except Rachel. They, too, were shocked by our affectionately humorous attitude toward "Blueberry," as we nicknamed our daughter. They were unable to understand how we could find her so precious and exquisitely beautiful; they could see her only as horribly ill.

We brought Rachel home weighing four pounds. Our job was to fatten her up so that she could withstand heart surgery. But her weight gain was slow, only an ounce or two a week. We added supplements to her feedings and eventually had to gavage feed her. We followed doctors' orders to the letter. It was difficult work, but we received lots of support from the doctors, our families, and others who praised our efforts with Rachel and gave us a feeling of competence as parents.

During this time Alan and I felt a wonderful sense of closeness as we shared a common love and worked toward a common goal. Nevertheless, we handled our emotions differently. Although I was the one who was often in tears, Alan seemed even more deeply attached to Rachel than I was. He found it difficult to gavage-feed her because he feared she would come to dislike him. While he never ran from her or her problems, I was usually the one who dealt with the practical aspects of her care.

We tried to stay optimistic, but Rachel was not improving. After a serious bout of diarrhea, she was rehospitalized. Her doctors felt immediate heart surgery was necessary. "Rachel the Lion-hearted" read the sign Alan made for her bed.

After surgery, Rachel continued to deteriorate. She was bleeding everywhere, and Alan gave his own blood for her transfusions. We began to talk about her possible death, wondering if it might not be for the best, but also desperately wanting her to live.

One day when I just couldn't face going to the hospital, Alan went alone. Usually his role had been to comfort me, but without me there he broke down himself and sobbed. He needed that time alone with her to express his emotions, and, as it turned out, to say good-bye.

Rachel died two days later.

We are not religious people, but when a friend gave me the name of a rabbi, we went to talk to him. He was wonderful, totally in tune with our feelings. He cried with us and laughed with us. He helped us end things the way we wanted. We picked out a stone for Rachel. We planned the service and burial. We brought the little formula-stained terry cloth outfit we'd always loved for her to wear. All of this gave us a feeling both of completion and continuity.

We had worked hard and loved hard and now it was over. We kept Rachel's belongings and her pic-

*Rachel, summer 1976.*

tures. It was important for us to talk about her, to laugh and remember her in our own way. We are not certain what we believe about an afterlife, but we were comforted by a sense of her presence long after she died, by the breeze we felt from our little angel's flapping wings.

But the central place she had occupied in our lives was gone. I tried to keep as busy as possible. I went back to work and to school at night. We had genetic counseling, and a month after Rachel died, I became pregnant again.

I was poorly prepared for this pregnancy, physically and psychologically. I denied that I could ever have a healthy baby. I remained emotionally uninvolved. In the sixth month my cervix effaced and began to open. I was put on complete bed rest, with all the more time to think and brood. I felt it was not in my stars to have a baby, and I kept my distance even after our full-term daughter, Lauren, was born.

Alan and I were disappointed with her—she didn't look like Rachel. She fussed and screamed, and we resented the fact that this normal, healthy baby was so demanding—Rachel had never been like that. Although I gave Lauren a lot of attention, a real emotional connection was missing. I was still too

frightened. I didn't want to get too close to her. What if something terrible were to happen?

We have since had another daughter, Lindsay, and I love her intensely with normal motherly feelings. My mourning for Rachel must finally be over because now I feel close to *both* my children and am able to love them with the abandon that is essential to the relationship. I know that tragedies happen in life, but I don't live each day expecting them.

Alan and I have also learned some valuable lessons about parenting. With Rachel we simply followed doctors' orders. Having our two children to raise—alone—is far more difficult.

As we cared for Rachel, we had often thought that normal, healthy children must be a cinch to bring up. We were in for a rude awakening. We are still realizing that the parenting of any child is the most challenging job there is.

Our marriage has changed too. We can't possibly still feel the same singleness of purpose we felt during Rachel's life, now that we must cope with the normal problems of two strong, demanding children striving to grow up. Our romantic illusions are gone, but we are rebuilding our relationship on a new reality.

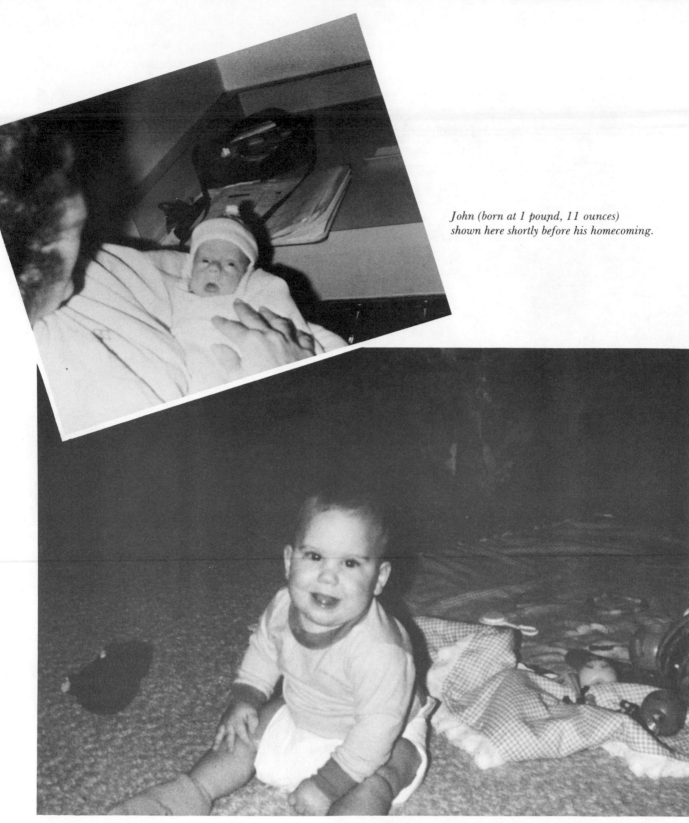

*John (born at 1 pound, 11 ounces) shown here shortly before his homecoming.*

*John at 11 months.*

## John and Michael's Story

### By Paulette Barry

It was to be very simple, really. A second child. We already had one perfect child, our two-year-old daughter, Paula, so why not another?

My husband and I had been married nine years before the first pregnancy. My biological clock was running down, so I wasted no time getting pregnant again. I discovered I was pregnant in April 1980.

By June an ultrasound test confirmed my suspicions—I was carrying twins. We had so much fun at first telling everyone our wonderful news. I remember the jokes, the laughs. Then came the apprehension. I was growing very large, changing visibly almost every day. It was no longer funny. Early in August I was diagnosed as having an excessive bag of waters or polyhydramnios, also known as a severe case of "big."

The doctor told me my condition would get worse. It would be painful. My organs would be jammed against my upper body. I would have the bag of waters tapped several times if necessary.

My due date was December 5. By August I was declared disabled, and was I ever! I won't describe the sleepless nights, the pain, the anxiety. Suffice it to say that six months into my pregnancy I had gained over 60 pounds, and I'm only five feet, two inches tall. My husband watched me as if I were a time bomb ready to go off. My job was to rest, relax, and hold on past September—when the babies' lungs would be better developed.

On September 10 I arrived at Children's Hospital 15 minutes before my bag of waters blew—and blow it did! The babies were born five minutes apart an hour after I got to the hospital.

The delivery was incredibly easy. I was so relieved not to hurt any more. I felt so physically good I could scarcely believe it. In recovery, my husband and I shared a few wonderful hours, happy that the babies were alive and that I was feeling well again. Had I not felt so well, the weeks and months ahead would have been much more difficult.

That evening we were told that the first twin, who weighed 1 pound, 11 ounces had a "fighting chance"; but the doctors were not optimistic about the second baby, who weighed only 14 ounces, the smallest live birth ever at Children's Hospital.

The next morning we were overwhelmed by fear and sorrow. We were told it was important to see the babies and name them. We named the firstborn John Charles and the "little one" Michael Patrick—two wonderful names.

I can still see us in my mind's eye during that first visit! Our shock at the babies' smallness, especially 14-ounce Michael, but also our wonder at seeing them as "mini-people" complete in every detail.

Those early visits were all the same: a pause at Michael's Isolette, a longer stay with John.

Two days later, Michael Patrick died. He was just too small to survive. It was remarkable that he had lived as long as he had. As he was dying, the doctors unhooked him from the tubes and wires and put him in my arms. Michael's nurse, who had been physically closer to him since birth than I, shared in

holding him. I couldn't exclude her from sharing this experience because her grief was as great as mine. My decision to be with Michael then, to hold him and rock him as he died, is one I'll never regret. I flew to the family homestead in Maine two days later and buried Michael Patrick.

We wanted to protect ourselves from more hurt, but we had to support John 100%. We did. But it was not always easy. The staff had warned that there would be good days and bad days; instead, there were bad weeks and not so bad weeks. John was on a respirator for two months. When he was 11 days old, he had surgery to close his patent ductus. He was pokey. He'd get stuck at one weight and refuse to budge for a week.

Those daily visits were a drain. They became almost ritualistic: locate the Isolette, check the weight, convert the gram weight to "English," peer into the Isolette, perhaps touch, and confer with the nurse. All this was done, I hoped, with great aplomb, great confidence, masking great fear. Throughout the 99 days John was in the NBICU, I never left without crying. But I wanted, needed, to appear very strong, very sure. The staff was wonderful—alert, sensitive to our moods during those difficult days.

Although no one ever told us that John would make it, we could see the positive changes for ourselves as John came off the respirator, onto CPAP, off the IVs, and into the "feeding pens" as my husband called the less intensive side of the nursery.

Finally, early in December, the "spurt" began. John gained almost an ounce a day. Soon the doctors were saying that he might be home for Christmas.

On December 17, weighing four pounds, nine ounces, John Charles came home. John has been home two months now. He weighs 10 pounds, 12 ounces. He is an easy baby to care for (he began sleeping through the night almost immediately), and his development is normal, even a bit precocious for his corrected age of two and a half months. We have a beautiful son. We'll never forget the NBICU days, but we are ready to go forward.

*Update:* At age 11 months John is a delight. If all babies were this easy, no one would need books. Three weeks before his first birthday, he weighs 21 pounds. His development is normal. He sits up, pulls to standing, feeds himself, and calls his father "Da." He's been phenomenally healthy—only one mild cold since leaving the nursery—and he's never been to the pediatrician except for well-baby checkups.

# 7

# *The Premature Nursery, Past and Present*

## Premature Care Through the Ages

Premature babies, their frailty and high mortality, have been discussed in medical and nonmedical literature since the beginning of recorded history. In 460 B.C., Hippocrates declared that no infant born before the seventh month could survive. Ancient Hebraic law did not recognize the legal survival of a premature born in the eighth month (as opposed to the seventh or ninth month) until that individual reached the age of twenty. The myth of the special vulnerability of the eight-month premature persists to this day and is often repeated by nursery personnel who should know better.

Quite early, the association was also made between prematurity and various handicapping conditions. Shakespeare's Richard the Third blamed his limping walk on the premature birth that had sent him "unfinish'd . . . before my time into this breathing world, scarce half made up."

However, it was not until the end of the nineteenth century that physicians could offer the prematurely born baby anything more than a box by the stove or hearth. Not surprisingly, most premature babies died. Then, in the 1870s, French doctors, hoping to rebuild a population decimated by the Franco-Prussian War, began serious efforts to improve infant survival. In 1878, the Parisian obstetrician Tarnier asked a keeper at the Paris Zoo to design an incubator, like the one used at the zoo to hatch chicks, that could accommodate one or more prematurely born infants. By 1880, the first warm-air incubators were in successful use at the Paris Maternité Hospital. Tarnier and his associate, Pierre Budin, were acclaimed for "saving a battalion from the slaughterfield of infancy."

At the turn of the century, Pierre Budin, considered by many to be the father of premature care, began a study of the special needs and problems of the premature baby. In his lectures and book, *The Nursling* (1907), he outlined the premature's three basic problems: (1) poor temperature control, (2) feeding difficulties, and (3) vulnerability to disease. For temperature control, Budin advocated use of the Tarnier incubator, complete with an electric alarm bell to warn of overheating. For feeding, he advised breastmilk supplied by the mother or a wet nurse. The baby too weak to suck was fed breastmilk by spoon or gavage tube. To prevent infection, he suggested strict cleanliness, sterility, and refrigeration of the babies' milk in summer. Sick babies were isolated from well babies. The incubators were supplied with air from the street or garden, considered healthier than the air in the poorly ventilated hospital wards.

Budin was keenly aware of the importance of a mother's early attachment to her baby. He encouraged mothers to come to the hospital to help care for their infants. He designed glass walls for the incubators to allow mothers to see their babies easily. He encouraged breast-feeding, and suggested that mothers of prematures also nurse a full-term infant to help keep up their milk supply.

---

### Prematures Who Made Their Mark on History

Although the fate of prematurely born babies used to be rather bleak, a list of some who survived reads like a historical Who's Who:

| | |
|---|---|
| Voltaire | Napoleon Bonaparte |
| Rousseau | Daniel Webster |
| Sir Isaac Newton | Mark Twain |
| John Keats | Anna Pavlova |
| Charles Darwin | Pierre Renoir |
| Charles Wesley | Winston Churchill |
| Victor Hugo | Albert Einstein |

---

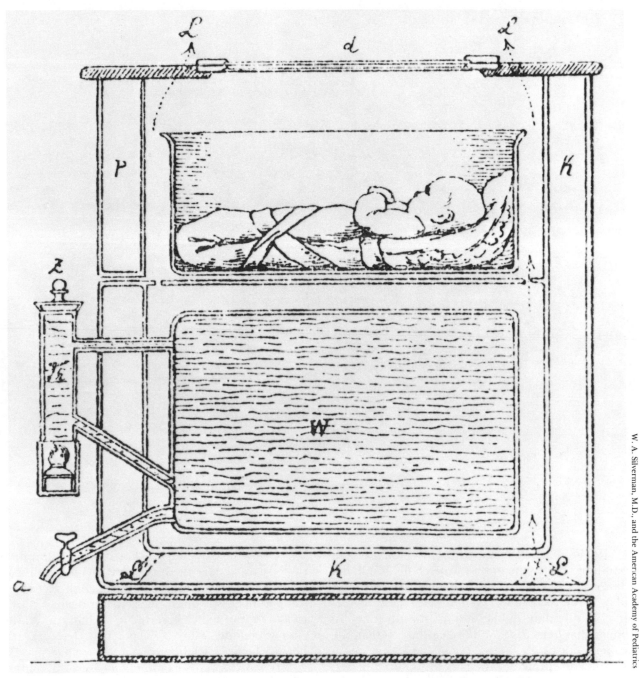

*The incubator designed by Dr. Tarnier and zookeeper M. O. Martin for the Paris Maternité Hospital, 1880.*

One of Budin's pupils, Martin Couney, exhibited incubators and premature care techniques at fairs and expositions throughout Europe and the United States. Doctors and parents readily handed over their premature infants whom they considered too small to save to be displayed in Dr. Couney's "Kinderbrutanstalt" or "child hatchery." Tended in the incubators and gawked at by the public whose admission fees supported their care, many of these babies did, in fact, survive.

Couney came to the United States in 1901 for the Pan-American Exposition in Buffalo. For the next 39 years he traveled across the country caring for and exhibiting over 5000 babies. Wherever they went, Couney's premature baby shows ("Infant Incubators with Living Infants") were a huge success. Public enthusiasm was undampened by the occasional criticism that it was in poor taste to exhibit tiny newborns alongside wild animals, clowns, freaks, and penny peep shows. At Chicago's Century of Progress Expo-

W. A. Silverman, M.D., and the American Academy of Pediatrics

*The Premature Baby Exhibit at the Pan-American Exposition in Buffalo, N.Y. 1901.*

sition (1933–34), the Premature Baby Exhibit was in the building next to the one in which Sally Rand, the fan dancer, performed. The two shows were the most popular of the Exposition. (When Sally Rand was arrested for offending public morals, she protested to the police that her girls had more clothes on than the babies next door.)

Couney eventually settled in the United States, appropriately enough on Coney Island, where he opened a permanent Premature Baby Exhibit. His own daughter, Hildegarde, was born prematurely and kept in an exhibit incubator for three months. Hildegarde later became a nurse and was closely involved with her father's work.

Despite Couney's commercialism and dubious taste, he did manage to interest the world in the care of premature infants, saving the lives of many babies in the process. He met and greatly influenced Chicago physician Julius Hess, who later became one of the leading American authorities on premature care. Couney's exhibits also led to the establishment of premature nurseries in hospitals around the country—the first, at Chicago's Sarah Morris Hospital, opened in 1923.

Couney, unlike his teacher Pierre Budin, did little to involve parents in the care of their infants-on-display. And Couney, who "never took a cent from the parents," was often puzzled and dismayed by the lack of gratitude he perceived in mothers and fathers, who sometimes had to be persuaded to take their healthy babies back home again.

It was Couney's example, not Budin's, that most of the new premature nurseries followed. Parents were excluded. This was done in hope of preventing the lethal respiratory and intestinal infections that routinely swept through hospitals in the pre-antibiotic era. The practice of separating parents from their newborns—full-term as well as premature—continued in most hospitals until the early 1970s.

Although doctors from the time of Budin had used oxygen on occasion to help a poorly breathing premature, it was not until 1931 at the Sarah Morris Premature Infant Station that oxygen use began in a routine, regulated way. In concentrations of 40 to 55%, the gas was piped into "oxygen beds," special incubators designed by Dr. Julius Hess. Supplemental oxygen, which was used for as long as six weeks with some infants, was credited with improving premature survival rates in the 1930s.

The 1940s and 1950s were decades sometimes referred to as the "dark ages of premature care." Physicians with the best of intentions often did more harm than good in their attempts to help prematures with oxygen therapy, antibiotics, and new feeding and caregiving techniques. Many prematures developed a mysterious form of eye damage—even blindness—from a condition that came to be called retrolental fibroplasia (RLF). In the 1950s it was suspected that RLF was related to the use of oxygen. But when oxygen use was restricted, more babies died, or survived with cerebral palsy.

Antibiotics offered new hope to the infection-prone premature. But the unmonitored use of the "mycin" antibiotics left many infants deaf or hearing-impaired. Babies were often not fed for days after birth in hope of preventing digestive and respiratory complications. But the metabolic derangements that resulted permanently damaged a large number of infants. A "hands off" attitude prevailed toward premature infants, and they were left alone in their droning incubators and rarely touched or handled. The deprivation of human contact these infants experienced may have contributed to later problems.

The rate of serious handicaps among the under-1500-gram prematures well exceeded 50%, and many hospitals felt it was useless even to try saving babies that small.

Major breakthroughs in the care of pre-term babies began in the 1960s, when respirators were first devised for tiny infants. The treatment of respiratory distress syndrome (RDS) was revolutionized by University of California physician George Gregory's development of CPAP (continuous positive airway pressure), a therapy that prevents the premature's lungs from collapsing. Now over 85% of infants with RDS survive this disease, which once had a 70% fatality rate.

New techniques were also developed for quickly analyzing the oxygen and carbon dioxide content of small amounts of blood. More recently, transcutaneous blood gas monitors, CAT scans, and ultrasound tests have been providing physicians with valuable diagnostic information on their tiny patients.

Early feeding for prematures was reinstituted. In the late '60s, intravenous hyperalimentation was first used in an attempt to meet the nutritional needs of babies too immature for oral feedings.

Obstetrical advances have also brightened the outlook for the premature, or potentially premature,

*Inside the Buffalo exhibit: eight incubators, each containing a "live babe."*

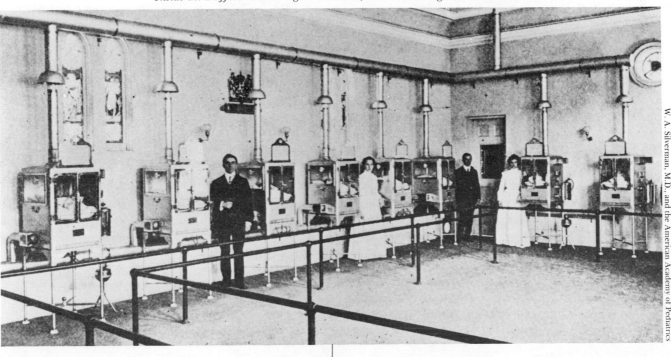

infant. Ultrasound and amniocentesis can diagnose many problems in utero. Since the mid-'70s, the steroid betamethasone, given to mothers before a pre-term delivery, has prevented many cases of RDS. And new labor-stopping drugs are allowing many threatened pregnancies to go to term.

These innovations in perinatal care have greatly contributed to the declining U.S. infant mortality rate, which in the last decade has dropped by nearly 40%.

But as smaller and sicker babies are being saved, new problems and diseases have emerged. The serious intestinal affliction necrotizing enterocolitis was first discovered in prematures in 1964. Bronchopulmonary dysplasia, a complication of respirator therapy, was described in 1967. As younger babies survive, with their greater oxygen needs and greater vulnerability to eye damage, retrolental fibroplasia is once more on the rise. And the verdict is still not in on the long-term effects of the newer treatments and medications.

The ethical questions that have been asked since prematures were first given special care are being debated again with a new intensity. Should the *very* tiny babies, so vulnerable to handicaps and so expensive to treat, be saved, or as some put it, "salvaged?" How small is too small? Is it 900 grams? Or 750 or 500 grams? Not so long ago this question was asked about the under-1500-gram baby; but, according to follow-up studies, the majority of these infants now survive to be normal. The focus of the ethical debate constantly shifts as today's "heroic measures" become tomorrow's "standard practice." But is there a limit? Many neonatologists think so, at least for the foreseeable future. Babies below the gestational age of 25 weeks, they say, almost always have lungs and nervous systems too immature for survival even with the best modern care techniques.

In the '70s, the breakthroughs in neonatal care were accompanied by the development of regionalization, a new system for providing that care. In the days when doctors merely kept the premature warm and hoped for the best, it mattered little where the baby was treated. But now the pre-term infant has a much better chance of normal survival if treated at a nursery equipped and staffed for intensive care. These nurseries are generally located in large, urban medical centers. To maintain quality care, and avoid duplication of services, hospitals offering this care are designated tertiary, or third-level, centers. They accept sick or premature infants born throughout a given geographic region. High-risk mothers about to give birth, or newborn babies with problems, are transferred from outlying hospitals to the tertiary centers. Relatively healthy prematures are cared for in the secondary centers, or regular premature nurseries of community hospitals. Primary centers, or regular newborn nurseries, care for the biggest, healthiest "borderline" prematures.

Paradoxically, as the nurseries mechanized and centralized, they have also "humanized." Beginning in the late '60s, premature nurseries, previously off-limits to parents, began opening their doors. This was done in response to studies suggesting the importance of early mother-child attachments and to experiments showing a *decrease,* not an increase, in infections when parents were allowed to enter the nursery.

One of the most promising trends in neonatology is the attention now being paid to the human side of newborn care. Those who work with premature infants are coming to respect these babies' unique capacities and vulnerabilities. Efforts are being made to modify the nursery environment in ways that enhance the child's ability to recover, grow, and develop. Nurseries are becoming more family-centered—parents are actively encouraged to play a major role in their baby's care. Physicians have once more come to realize what Pierre Budin sensed a hundred years ago—that the relationship parents form with their premature baby is every bit as important as their child's medical treatment.

# The Premature Nursery Today

## Who Does What in the NBICU

"Despite the machines and technology," says neonatologist Roderic Phibbs, "infant intensive care is essentially provided by people, a lot of people, who all care intensively. There is no more personal form of medicine than that which is practiced in the newborn ICU."

True enough. But the personal element may be lost on the parents, confronted as they are by a baffling, ever-changing multitude of neonatal specialists. One doctor counted 483 caregiver changes for a single infant during a three-month nursery stay.

For the parent who is justifiably puzzled over who's in charge, who does what, and where to go with questions and complaints, we offer the following guide to the nursery personnel and power structure.

Not every hospital works in exactly the same way—policies, personnel, and procedures vary—but the staff hierarchy and routine found in many NBICUs is described in the following pages. First, we should note that there are two different types of hospitals: teaching hospitals (where medical students learn to become doctors and doctors learn to become specialists) and nonteaching hospitals. A nonteaching hospital NBICU is staffed primarily by neonatologists and nurses. The teaching hospital—and most NBICUs are in teaching hospitals—has medical students, interns, residents, and fellows, who provide much of the baby's care.

A *neonatologist* is a doctor who has specialized in pediatrics, and then further subspecialized in newborn (neonatal) care, a process that involves at least nine years of medical training and the passing of a rigorous examination. Since 1975, when the subspecialty of neonatology was officially recognized by the American Board of Pediatrics, intensive care nurseries (tertiary care centers) have been required to have at least one certified neonatologist on the staff—most nurseries have more.

One neonatologist serves as *director of the nursery*, with ultimate responsibility for the unit's policies, procedures, budgets, teaching, research, and community relations. The director of the nursery is accountable to the director of the entire hospital.

All the neonatologists, including the director, take turns, usually for a month at a time, as the *attending physician*—the neonatologist who is actually present in the nursery and responsible for what happens during his time on duty. The attending physician usually works a regular nine-to-five, Monday through Friday schedule. At nights and on weekends, another neonatologist is *on call* in the nursery or close by. Before the "attending" leaves at night, and again when he arrives in the morning, he and the "on call" physician make "attending rounds" together to discuss each baby. This way a neonatologist fully informed about every infant is available around the clock. The attending physician is also responsible for training others in the unit. Several times a week he makes "teaching rounds" to review each baby's case with the medical students, interns, residents, nurse specialists, and fellows. When neonatologists are not "attending," they may work on teaching or research projects, or perform other nursery-related tasks.

A *fellow* is a licensed pediatrician who has received at least seven years of medical training and is completing a two-year training fellowship before taking the exam to become a certified neonatologist. A fellow generally spends more time in the unit and personally performs more procedures than does the neonatologist. The fellow also supervises, teaches, and carries out research. A fellow is on duty during regular working hours. In addition, once or twice a week he works a grueling 36-hour nonstop shift.

*Interns* and *residents* are doctors training to become pediatricians, although not necessarily neonatologists. The intern is in his first year of specialty training, the resident is in his second or third year. Pediatric interns and residents spend one or two months each year working a "rotation" in the nursery. The rest of the year they work in other areas of the hospital. During their time in the unit, interns and residents serve as "primary physicians" for a certain number of babies. They work nine-to-five, except for the two or three times a week, when they, too, work a 36-hour shift. During the day, they are in the nursery, or attending classes or lectures. (Third- and fourth-year medical students, under a doctor's close supervision, occasionally take part in a baby's care.)

A *neonatal nurse practitioner* is a registered nurse who has received extra training either in the hospital or through a master's degree program. The nurse practitioner is qualified by this extra training to provide some aspects of a patient's care normally provided by a physician. The nurse practitioner must legally work under a doctor's supervision; in other words, a doctor must sign all medical orders. Along with the interns and residents, the neonatal nurse practitioner may be referred to as one of the *house staff* or *house officers*.

A *clinical nurse specialist* is a registered nurse who has received extra training usually through a master's degree program. The function of the clinical nurse specialist varies from hospital to hospital. In some units, the clinical nurse specialist's role is identical to that of the neonatal nurse practitioner's. Usually, however, the clinical nurse specialist's job is to review nursing procedures and to provide education to the staff and to the parents.

The intern, resident, nurse specialist, or nurse practitioner is considered the *physician* or *staff officer on first call*, the fellow on duty is the *physician on second call*, the attending neonatologist is the *physician on third call*.

Although the director of the nursery is ultimately responsible for everyone working in the unit, there is a separate subhierarchy for the nurses.

The *head nurse* or *nursing care coordinator* for the unit decides policies, budgets, staffing, hiring, and firing. The head nurse is accountable to the director of the nursery and to the *director of nursing* for the entire hospital. The head nurse usually works a regular nine-to-five, Monday through Friday week.

The *charge nurse* is responsible for the overall

nursing care in the unit during a specific shift.

The *staff nurses* are the ones who actually care for the babies. Depending on the hospital, they work 12- or 8-hour daily shifts. *Registered nurses* (*RNs*) have had two to five years of medical training and have passed a state examination to become certified. In addition, all nurses in the NBICU have received special training in newborn intensive care. They do most of the minute-to-minute, hands-on care of the baby. They may perform such procedures as intubation, resuscitation, and stabilization of a baby for transport. They start IVs and, in some hospitals, insert chest tubes and umbilical catheters. "They are the ones who actually run the unit," concedes one physician, "the rest of us here are sometimes thought of as para-nursing professionals."

Working in the nursery under the supervision of the RNs are *licensed vocational* or *practical nurses* (*LVNs* or *LPNs*). These nurses have had at least 18 months of training. Occasionally, *nurse's aides*, who have completed a 6-month program, also help out in the unit.

Nurses may be assigned arbitrarily to the care of a different baby each shift. Many hospitals, however, try to have the same group of nurses care for the same infant throughout his nursery stay. Some hospitals also designate a *primary nurse* to oversee the baby's care and become a friend and advocate for the parents. Even when such arrangements are not part of official nursery policy, parents often find a nurse who is special to them and who helps them cope with life in the nursery.

*Respiratory therapists* may be involved in the care of the infant with breathing problems. These individuals have completed six months to two years of special training and are responsible for maintaining the respirators and other breathing equipment. In some hospitals, they may do suctioning and postural drainage, draw blood and perform blood gas tests, and, under a physician's guidance, adjust respirator settings.

*Laboratory technicians* with one to two years of special training often do the heel sticks and perform the baby's many laboratory tests.

*X-ray technicians* who have completed at least six months of training take and develop x-rays ordered by the physician. A medical doctor, either a *radiologist* (an x-ray specialist) or a doctor in the unit, interprets the x-rays.

*Developmental specialists, physical therapists, occupational therapists,* or *infant educators* may evaluate development and provide appropriate stimulation and activities for the infant who requires long-term hospitalization.

Doctors with different pediatric specialties may be called upon to diagnose and treat certain medical conditions.

A *pediatric cardiologist* evaluates and treats ductus and heart problems, short of performing surgery. Ductus and heart surgery are usually performed by a *pediatric thoracic (chest) surgeon*. A *general pediatric surgeon* performs "cut downs" for the insertion of central lines and does surgery on other parts of the body— bowel surgery, for example.

A *pediatric anesthesiologist* is skilled at anesthetizing tiny infants for surgery.

A *pediatric neurologist* identifies, evaluates, and manages nonsurgical treatment of neurological problems, such as seizures or hydrocephalus. A *pediatric neurosurgeon* does surgery involving the brain or nervous system, such as installing shunts for hydrocephalus.

A *pediatric nephrologist* deals with an infant's kidney problems.

A *pediatric hematologist* may be brought in to evaluate the child with blood disorders or to help manage such procedures as exchange transfusions.

The *pediatric ophthalmologist* screens babies who receive oxygen to diagnose any vision problems. This doctor usually continues to see the child after he has left the nursery to diagnose and treat any problems that may arise later.

Last, but not least, is the baby's own *private pediatrician*. If the baby is in a nursery far from his home, the pediatrician may not become actively involved in his care until the baby returns to a nearby community hospital. But the pediatrician should be in regular contact with the neonatologists so that he or she is fully informed of the baby's medical course in the nursery.

## Transitions

Before and after the baby leaves the NBICU there are still others who may be involved in his care.

In the beginning, there is the *transport team*— usually a doctor and a nurse—who stabilize the baby after birth and accompany him to the tertiary care center. The baby is transported in a specially equipped ambulance or aircraft—a sort of portable intensive care unit complete with incubator, oxygen, respirator, intravenous equipment, monitors, medications, and even provisions for minor surgery. En route, the transport team members are aided by *paramedics*, who are familiar with the equipment and

Dorothy Larimer Boyd, courtesy of Children's Hospital Medical Center of Northern California

*Transport team bringing a newborn premature to a tertiary center.*

techniques used in the emergency care of newborns.

When the baby returns to the secondary nursery in his community, he makes the trip back in an ambulance or ambulance plane accompanied by a nurse and paramedics.

At the *secondary* or *regular premature nursery*, the recovering, growing baby is cared for by his regular pediatrician instead of a neonatologist. Here, closer to home, in more intimate and peaceful surroundings, parents can learn to care for their baby before the time of discharge.

Not every parent is pleased with the move to the regular premature nursery. There is a new staff to contend with and a new set of regulations—rules that are often more conservative than those of the NBICU. Sibling visits might not be allowed. Parents might no longer be able to dress their baby in clothes of their choice. Visiting hours might be limited. This is not the case with *every* secondary nursery. Nevertheless, parents may wish to check the policies of their local hospital before consenting to a transfer. If par-

ents wish, their child may usually be kept in the NBICU until discharged to go home.

Once the baby is home, his association with the NBICU often continues through the nursery *follow-up clinic.* In theory, all tertiary care centers should have these clinics; in fact, economic reality does not always permit it.

The primary purpose of most follow-up clinics is to collect data on the long-term outcome of babies who have suffered certain perinatal problems or who were given certain drugs or therapies. At clinic visits, which may be annual or more frequent, the infant is seen by professionals such as pediatrician specialists in child development, psychologists, neurologists, physical therapists, nutritionists, social workers, and vision and hearing specialists. Although research is generally the clinic's main function, clinic staff members are usually available to help parents concerned about their child's development. The staff can diagnose problems, suggest remedial help, and refer parents to useful community services and programs.

### The Million Dollar Baby
### or
### If I'd Known You Were Coming I'd Have
### Robbed a Bank

When we asked parents for tips on dealing with medical costs, their responses ran the gamut from the illegal to the unprintable.

The following suggestions are from Cathy Elias, who has ten years' experience in the field of medical insurance and three years' experience as mother of a premature baby.

**1.** *Immediately* check your insurance to determine its coverage for a newborn. If you have group insurance, notify your personnel office of your baby's birth as soon as possible. If you have an individual policy, notify your insurance company directly. *Be sure your baby is added as a dependent on your policy!* Failure to do so within a certain amount of time (usually 30 days after the birth) could make your child ineligible for coverage. While many policies do not cover routine newborn care, virtually every policy covers a sick baby if notification is made soon after birth.

**2.** Contact your hospital business office to give them your insurance information if this was not done prior to delivery. Discuss your situation with the financial counselor, and determine your baby's eligibility for various federal, state, and local financial aid programs. Then, work out a timetable for paying the balance of the hospital bill. By establishing a good working relationship with the business office, a satisfactory payment schedule can usually be arranged.

**3.** Learn how your insurance works. If claim forms must be submitted with the bills, be sure to make out the forms fully and correctly to avoid delays in benefits payments.

**4.** While the hospital directly bills the insurance company, some health care providers, like doctors and ambulance companies, bill *you* directly. Make copies of their bills which you keep. Send the originals to the insurance company.

**5.** Look at the forms you sign. Most claim forms have a blank which you sign to allow the release of information to the insurance company. You *must* sign this blank for your claim to be processed. Another blank on the form is for assigning benefits. If you sign this part of the form the insurance company will pay the health care provider directly. Do not sign this blank if you plan to pay the health care provider yourself. People often sign this blank without understanding what it means. They then receive a bill from the doctor which they pay. Meanwhile, the doctor is paid a second time by the insurance company, and the insured person may have a long wait to be reimbursed by the doctor. To avoid this hassle, do not sign the assignment-of-benefits blank. Pay the doctor yourself, and arrange to receive reimbursement from the insurance company.

**6.** Learn how to take medical deductions on your income tax. Keep good records of your medical and hospital related expenses. Certain expenses, such as mileage to and from the hospital, meals in the cafeteria, and babysitting for your children, may also be tax deductible. If your budget allows, contact a tax consultant.

**7.** Develop a consistent, workable system for organizing and paying your bills. (One uninsured couple we interviewed, parents of twins, papered their kitchen wall with $700,000 worth of unpaid medical bills. They used the dart board method to determine which bill they would tackle next.)

**8.** Contact *all* your creditors and let them know your situation. Inform them when payments are going to be late. By demonstrating good faith, you can usually avoid having your account turned over to a collection agency. However, if this happens, first talk to your creditor and try to straighten things out. If this fails, contact the collection agency and outline your situation. Indicate a willingness to cooperate as fully as possible. Remember, collection agencies are legally barred from such harassing tactics as phoning you at work or late at night. If you are being threatened or illegally bothered by a collection agency, consult a lawyer.

## Help for the Parents

The role of certain members of the staff is primarily to help the family of the hospitalized child.

*Social workers* can help parents cope with the emotional and practical problems surrounding their child's birth and hospitalization. They are aware of community resources that can help when the child is in the unit and later at home.

Most hospitals have a *chaplain* for parents in need of spiritual counsel or comfort.

Though not a formal part of the hospital staff, *parent-group members,* who themselves had children in intensive care, may be available by telephone or in personal meetings or group sharing sessions to give new parents advice and moral support. Some parent groups also provide practical services for new NBICU parents—babysitting for other children while parents visit the nursery, breast-feeding counseling, and even lodging for out-of-town parents.

A *financial counselor* or *advisor* helps parents who have enough on their minds without the additional worry of bankruptcy. The financial advisor knows the eligibility rules for financial aid programs and is skilled at working with insurance companies to extract maximum benefits.

## Parent-Staff Problems: Communication and Complaints

Conflicts are bound to arise when distraught parents and overworked staff interact amidst the chaos of the nursery. Personality clashes can be expected even in the best of circumstances. Not every parent is going to like every staff member and vice versa. When so many care for (and about) a single infant, power struggles and rivalries are inevitable. And these feelings of possessiveness can arise in the "surrogate parents"—the nurses and doctors—as well as in the biological parents. Mothers and fathers, angry about their baby's premature birth and difficulties, sometimes direct that anger irrationally at the staff. But parents may also have justifiable grievances against insensitive or inept nurses and doctors.

The social worker, who is not involved in the baby's care, is often a good person to help arbitrate disputes. Parents can also take their complaints to the offending staff member's superior. If parents want a nursing change for their baby, they should talk to the charge nurse or head nurse. If they have problems with the baby's primary physician (intern, resident, or nurse specialist), they should consult with the attending neonatologist or the director of the nursery. Major problems with the neonatologists or nursery policies can be discussed with the director of the hospital or, if necessary, with the parents' lawyer. When parents are in serious conflict with the nursery staff, they might arrange to have their child transferred to a different hospital.

Problems with communication are a frustration for parents and staff alike. In the nursery's frantic atmosphere, informative conversations are next to impossible. Upset parents are poor listeners. Doctors who haven't slept for days are often poor communicators. The helpful doctor or nurse who was here today may well be gone tomorrow. What to do?

Parents offered several suggestions for communicating with the hospital staff:

"When you begin a relationship with a doctor or nurse, find out first how long that person is going to be around and involved with your baby."

"Let the neonatologists know you would like regular, frequent meetings with them on your baby's condition and care. *Don't* have these meetings in the nursery. Go somewhere where you can sit down, talk privately, and take notes. Write down your questions before you talk to the doctors. Write down their answers. Then, before you leave, put those answers in your own words and ask the doctors if you have understood them properly."

Many parents suggested taping the conferences (with the doctors' permission, of course).

"Sometimes," said one couple, "we brought along a psychologist who worked in the unit. She had become a friend, and we felt at ease with her. Before the conference with the doctor, we'd outline our questions to her; then during the meeting, she'd remind us what to ask and give us moral support."

The social worker or a trusted nurse could also accompany parents during their conferences with the doctors.

## The Baby's Caregivers

We've looked at the job descriptions and the chain of command, but just who are these people who take care of premature babies? Why did they choose their professions? What are the personal drawbacks and the rewards?

The neonatologists we talked to gave varying answers to these questions, but all were unanimous on one point: neonatology is, quite simply, the most exciting area of medicine today.

"It's never boring," says neonatologist Sally Sehring.

Intellectually, I enjoy the way each medical problem is so intensively explored. And when you treat these babies, what you do makes such a difference. Everyone wants to make people better, and the immediate gratification that comes from understanding a problem in depth, and then fixing it, is enormous. And I like doing things with my hands—catheterizations, intubations are very easy for me; I get technical satisfaction out of performing procedures well.

The hardest part was becoming a neonatologist in the first place. I would never advise anyone to live the way I did as an intern, resident, and fellow: to go for days without sleep, skip meals, live on coffee, work 105 hours a week in an atmosphere of constant crisis. . . .

And it wasn't easy for me to develop the "professional veneer," which means: doctors don't cry. I went through an interesting emotional progression during those years. As an intern, I cried every night in the car on the way home. As a resident, I waited till I got home to cry. As a fellow and a neonatologist, I didn't cry that often, but sometimes at home I'd get upset over some trifle and then realize that I was really crying about one of the babies.

I've also come to view life, and especially birth, from a rather unusual perspective. The only deliveries I've ever seen have been ones where disaster was expected. I want to have children of my own some day, though quite frankly, I'm terrified.

Nevertheless, I find the work emotionally rewarding. I like working with families, even in stressful situations. And when things turn out well, it's such a wonderful feeling!

What about the nurses, the front-line workers whose jobs are far more stressful than air traffic controllers', but whose salaries are lower than check-out clerks'? What's in it for them?

"It's one of the few areas of nursing," says intensive care nurse Ann Kositsky,

*Nurses are the front-line workers in premature care.*

Dorothy Larimer Boyd, courtesy of Children's Hospital Medical Center of Northern California

where nurses work in a true partnership with the doctors. We are expected to know a lot about medicine and to perform a lot of difficult procedures. It's intellectually and emotionally challenging—a constant rush of adrenalin. This is both a reward and a drawback. The high stress level is why so many nurses and doctors "burn out" and leave the unit. A human being can only tolerate so much—that's also a reason for the constant shift and rotation changes.

I think people choose their professions, in part, to meet certain needs in themselves or to help resolve certain emotional issues. For me, it was a fear of death and life's difficulties, which I've never yet had to experience personally. Here in the nursery, I've watched parents cope with disaster and I've learned from them. I think I've become a stronger, more compassionate person. I'm much more aware of life's problems and ambiguities.

And then I love babies, especially tiny, premature babies. They amaze me with their strength, their will to live. Even at that age they are complete human beings with very distinct personalities. I respect them. I respect their parents, too, and enjoy for a brief time being part of their families.

# 8

# Nursery Parenting

To thrive, a premature baby needs his parents' loving attention just as much as he needs food, warmth, and oxygen. But physical affection should be given with the same care and sensitivity used to provide him with proper amounts of oxygen, heat, and nutrients.

The premature's nervous system, like his respiratory or digestive tract, is not quite ready for extrauterine life. And the world of the premature in intensive care is radically different both from that of the fetus in utero and that of the normal newborn. Before birth a baby is gently rocked and massaged in the dark liquid enclosure of the womb. After birth, the *full-term* baby comes home to a dimly lit nursery and his parents' gentle rocking and soft lullabies. A hospitalized premature lies on hard motionless surfaces and is bombarded with bright lights, loud noises, and uncomfortable handling. His immature nervous system, in fact his entire body, can be stressed both by overstimulation and by the absence of soothing sensations.

Parents can do much to protect and comfort their baby. Together with the doctors and nurses, they can find ways to modify the baby's environment to makes it less stressful. Slowly and cautiously, they can introduce their baby to the types of love and nurturing appropriate for a newborn. *Caution is the key,* however, for when the baby is overwhelmed by stimulation, even loving stimulation, his vital physical functions can be disrupted.

Nevertheless, even the sickest, tiniest baby can benefit from the sight, voice, and affectionate touch of his parents. In his study of premature behavior, Dr. Peter Gorski has consistently observed that mothers, with their heightened sensitivities, are the ones best able to reduce their premature babies' physical distress. When offered carefully, a parent's love can be a powerful positive force in the baby's recovery.

But the first encounters between parents and their baby are rarely smooth or trouble-free. Mothers and fathers beset by feelings of guilt, anger, or fear do not make relaxed and confident new parents. And the baby—for whom all of this is new and unsettling—may respond poorly to his first handling. These early interactions take place, not at home and in private as they do with parents and full-term babies, but in a crowded noisy nursery. The parents' "successes" and "failures" are on public display. It is hardly surprising that the early relationship between the parents and their baby has its tense and awkward moments. But despite these difficulties, parents can go on to develop a relationship with their baby that is uniquely rich and rewarding. In this chapter we offer information and suggestions to make nursery parenting easier.

## Understanding Your Baby

Go slowly at first. Take time to observe your baby. Learn what upsets him and what soothes him and how he shows distress and comfort. Watch your baby's responses to various types of stimulation. Notice the length of time it takes him to regain his equilibrium after a stressful procedure—a heel stick, for example. A premature may not cry when he is uncomfortable the way a full-term does. Instead, his distress signals often involve subtle (and not so subtle) physical changes such as

1. shifts in skin color from pink to gray (especially around the lips)
2. abrupt variations in muscle tone—either sudden limpness or flailing, startle-type motions
3. a rapid change in heartbeat and breathing rate, often followed by
4. apnea and bradycardia.

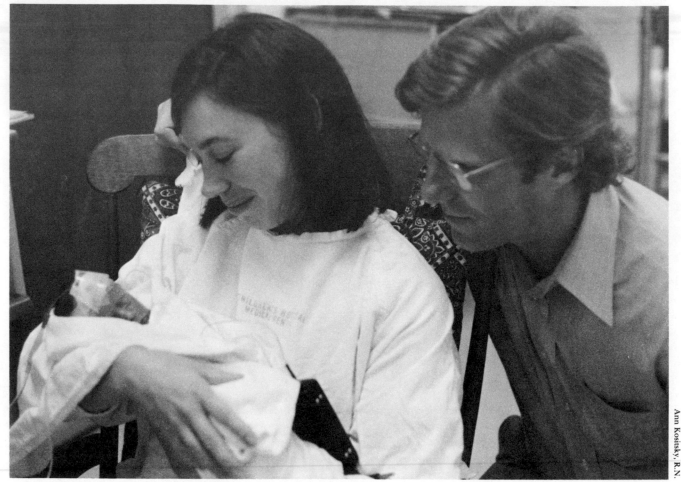

*To thrive, a premature baby needs his parents' loving attention.*

A baby on a respirator cannot have apnea, since his breathing is controlled by the machine, but he can show the other physiological signs of stress. A sudden drop in blood oxygen is one indication of stress easily observed if the baby is on a transcutaneous oxygen monitor.

The baby may also show discomfort or fatigue through gestures and facial expressions. A stressed baby may

1. look exhausted
2. grimace (a crying expression without sound or tears)
3. avert his eyes, or
4. cover his face with his hands as if to say, "Enough!"

The *contented* premature, by comparison, is physically stable. His color is even; his heart and breathing rates are relatively steady and within nor-

mal limits. The baby may be quietly alert and able to focus on the people or objects around him. The contented baby may drift off slowly into a relaxed, quiet sleep.

Interactions with the baby will be easier if they coincide with his natural periods of alertness. Notice your baby's sleep-awake cycles and see if there are predictable periods during the day when he seems ready for you. Ask the nurses if they have noticed times when the baby seems especially active or alert.

A very tiny or sick baby has few periods of alertness, and the types of interactions his parents can have with him are limited at first. A baby given curare or Pavulon is unresponsive while on these medications. Nevertheless, he can hear and feel and is aware of a parent's voice and touch.

As the baby matures and recovers, his alert periods lengthen and his tolerance for stimulation increases. What the baby once found stressful, he may soon come to enjoy. On the other hand, a premature, like the rest of us, has good days and bad days. The maturation of the baby's nervous system can follow the familiar two steps forward, one step backward pattern. The baby who cuddled happily for an hour yesterday may not want to be held at all today.

Good parenting involves *protecting*, and protecting the baby means respecting his need to rest even when it conflicts with your strong desire to hold him.

A premature may find it hard to cope with more than one type of "socializing" at a time. He may only tolerate being touched, or being talked to, or being looked at, but not all of these together. When your baby seems ready, try touching alone, or talking alone, or just making eye contact. Experiment to see what the baby can handle before combining different forms of stimulation. If the baby seems stressed, stop, wait, and try again later.

No two prematures are alike. One may love to be rocked for hours, while another is overwhelmed by the briefest touch. Babies who are smaller than normal for their gestational age (whether full-term or premature) and babies with bronchopulmonary dysplasia are often hypersensitive, with low tolerance for social stimulation. These babies must be handled with special care.

Each baby, regardless of his medical complications, has his own individual ability to cope with stimulation. The baby's reaction to handling while he convalesces in the nursery does not necessarily predict his later personality (see Kiyomi, Kiedi, Kenichi, Toshi and Tadashi's Story, page 148).

Dr. Gorski tells of an infant who would not take his bottle unless he was placed in his incubator and fed by a nurse who did not touch or look at him. Being held, eating, and making eye contact all at once were just too much for this baby. "I had grave concerns about the child's social development," said Dr. Gorski, "but on follow-up he seems happy and well-adjusted."

# Your Loving Touch

When so much of your baby's early handling is painful or uncomfortable, your consistent loving touch can help him discover that there really is something nice about being alive.

Before birth, the baby was enveloped and massaged by the muscular walls of the womb. Prematures seem to miss that feeling of containment. They seem insecure out in the open and unrestrained. An agitated baby can often be calmed by being covered or swaddled in a pair of warm hands. Prematures may be soothed by a firm whole-hand touch or massage, which they tend to prefer to light finger-tip stroking.

Massaging the baby with oils or creams is one of the first caretaking procedures parents can assume. Even the smallest, sickest baby needs this skin care. It is a wonderful way to begin a relationship with the baby. It is an expression of affection that may also contribute to the healing process, for a number of studies have shown better growth and development among prematures who received regular touching and stroking.

Psychologist Ruth Rice, the author of one of these studies, divided 30 prematures into two groups. As the babies were discharged from the nursery, mothers in the control group were only instructed in normal home care for their infants. Mothers in the experimental group were taught a special massage technique. Four times a day, for 10 to 15 minutes at a time, each of these mothers undressed her baby and massaged the infant's entire body, beginning at the head and working down. Afterward the mother wrapped her baby snugly and rocked him for 5 minutes.

At age four months, the 30 babies were all examined by doctors who did not know which babies had received the stroking and which had not.

The babies who had been massaged were significantly ahead of the control group in weight gain and neurological development.

Dr. Rice feels that touching and stroking produce these effects by stimulating the nerve pathways and aiding the process of myelination (see page 95), by increasing the activity of the hypothalamus (a gland that serves as a general arousal center), and by stimulating the production of the growth hormone somatotrophin.

While Dr. Rice's study was conducted with prematures *after* they had left the hospital, other studies have shown enhanced growth and development among prematures who were regularly stroked during their nursery stay.*

Even when opportunities are limited for "social" handling of the baby, there are many necessary "hands-on" medical or caretaking procedures that you can perform. You can change and weigh the baby's diapers. You can take the baby's temperature.

You can help "position" the baby. Frequent

---

*Dr. Rice has assembled a kit for home use by parents that contains a chart and a tape, which both describe her massage techniques. The "Loving Touch" kit for premature infants is available for $21.95 from Cradle Care, P.O. Box 801548, Dallas, Texas 75380-1548. (Texas residents must add sales tax.) A video is also available for $30.00. For more information call (214) 363-7244.

Professionals who wish instruction in the clinical use of Dr. Rice's techniques (Rice Infant Sensorimotor Stimulation) should write to Ruth D. Rice, Ph.D., R.I.S.S., Inc., 6455 Meadow Road, Dallas, Texas 75230; or, call (214) 363-7244 for further information.

changes in position are important for the baby's comfort and for prevention of skin problems and asymmetrical bone growth. Many babies prefer to lie on their stomachs. They breathe better in this position (even on a respirator) and absorb more oxygen into their blood. (Babies with umbilical catheters or chest tubes *cannot* be placed on their stomachs, but they can sometimes be propped in side-lying positions.) Babies are usually more comfortable with their arms and legs bent. If their hands are brought close to their mouths, they can learn to soothe themselves by sucking on their fingers. When repositioning your baby, try to contain his arms and legs in your hands as you turn him slowly and gently.

You can help with the baby's daily sponge bath or tub bath. Bathing is usually done on the night shift, so it may be necessary to request ahead of time that the bath be rescheduled to take place during your visit.

You can do mouth care—cleaning and lubricating your baby's mouth with water or glycerin swabs.

You can help your baby develop his feeding skills by offering him one of your fingers to suck on.

The baby may enjoy tiny pacifiers fashioned from premie nipples or doll nipples stuffed with cotton, or made from the rubber tip of a medicine dropper. The pacifier can be taped to a rolled-up towel or a stuffed toy and positioned so it doesn't fall out of the baby's mouth.

If the baby rejects the pacifier, try tasting it yourself. Some rubber or plastic products have an unpleasant taste. It may also help to moisten the pacifier with water.

Though babies vary in their need and desire to suck, many find it a pleasant, soothing activity. Doctors have found that prematures who suck on pacifiers during gavage feedings digest their food better, gain more weight, and go home earlier.

## Your Baby Is Listening

A premature baby usually prefers human sounds to the mechanical noises that bombard him in the nursery. The baby is familiar with his parents' voices, especially his mother's voice, which he has heard from his earliest months in the womb.

Although many parents feel self-conscious talking or singing to a seemingly unresponsive infant, the

*Your loving touch.*

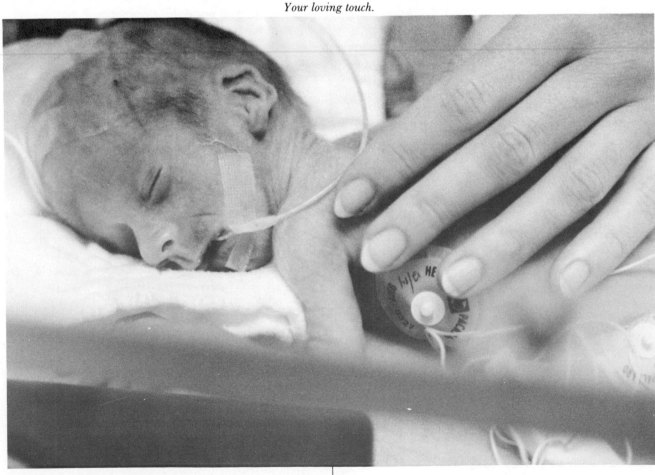

Bill Laurie

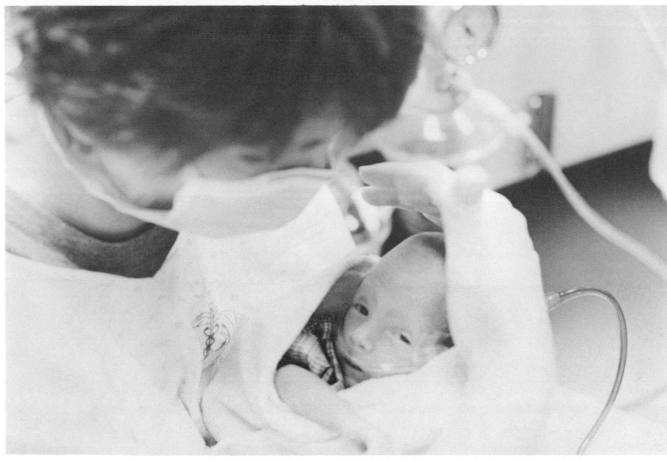

Bill Laurie

*To encourage your baby to open his eyes, try shielding his face from the light with your hand.*

baby *is* listening. Studies have shown better development and attentiveness among hospitalized premies who regularly heard recordings of their mothers' voices. Using combined stimulation (rocking, heartbeat sounds, recordings of the mother's voice), researchers have improved weight gain and development of premature infants.

Both pre-term and full-term babies are soothed by sounds they heard in the womb—the mother's heartbeat and the churning noises of the placenta. Most crying newborns quiet within 60 seconds of hearing the familiar womb sounds. These recorded sounds are available in battery-powered teddy bears at a price of $40 to $50. "Lullabye from the Womb," a Capitol Records LP of heartbeat and placental sounds, is available for about a fifth of the price of the bear. The record can be taped along with your voice and played for the baby in the nursery on a small battery-powered cassette player.

*A note of caution:* Sounds reverberate loudly in the enclosed incubator. This can be very distressing to the baby. Before putting sound toys or tapes into the incubator, check the volume and the baby's reaction to the sounds.

# Eye to Eye

The baby's first look into his parents' eyes is an important moment in early attachment; and because eye contact *is* so important, it can also be stressful. It may take time before the premature baby is comfortable with more than the briefest periods of eye contact.

A premature baby shows he is not yet ready for eye contact by averting his eyes when looked at. Or he may become so locked into looking that he cannot break the stare, even when stressed to the point of apnea and bradycardia. You may need to help your baby break his fixed stare by passing your hand in front of his eyes or by shifting positions. Even if the baby makes eye contact easily, he may not be able to handle additional stimulation such as talking or rocking at the same time.

In the brightly lit nursery the baby may find it unpleasant to open his eyes at all. He may keep his eyes closed even when he is awake. To encourage your baby to open his eyes, try shielding his face from the light with your hand.

# Holding and Rocking

Once the baby's condition has stabilized, the momentous occasion arrives at last, and the tiny baby, in a tangle of tubes and wires, is placed in his parent's arms. The first holding experiences are often interrupted by buzzing alarms. The baby's apnea and bradycardia is not a rejection of his parents, it is just his way of saying, "This is new. I'm overwhelmed!"

It is quite common for a premature to show some degree of physical instability (changes in color, breathing, and heart rate) as he is transferred from the incubator into his parent's arms. But once the baby settles in and becomes comfortable, he usually returns to normal. In his mother's or father's arms, the baby may drift off to sleep. Parents sometimes interpret this as a lack of responsiveness in their baby, when, in fact, the baby is responding to their comforting embrace by "blissing out."

The baby should be warmly dressed in hat, shirt, and booties, and wrapped in preheated blankets when he is out of the incubator. An overhead lamp can provide an additional heat source, but a well-bundled baby cuddled close to his parent's body is unlikely to become chilled.

Even a baby on a respirator (if his condition is stable) can spend some time in his parents' arms. However, seriously ill babies, babies on curare or Pavulon, babies with chest tubes or precarious IVs cannot be held.

The baby in utero moves back and forth whenever his mother moves. These rocking motions are thought to stimulate the development of the vestibular system, a center chiefly located in the brain stem that is important for proper coordination and, some think, for emotional stability.

Several researchers have demonstrated that prematures who are given vestibular stimulation (irregular rocking motions from oscillating water beds or motorized hammocks) show better growth and development along with a reduced incidence of apnea. Rocking your baby in a rocking chair also provides this stimulation.

*Always close the incubator door gently.*

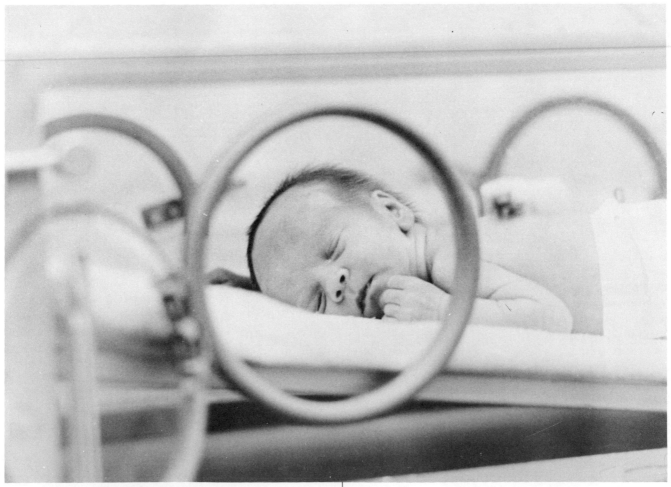

Al Thelin

But while rocking is soothing and beneficial for some babies, others find it too much to handle. As with every other form of stimulation, each baby reacts differently. If you watch your baby closely and learn to read his cues, he will let you know what is right for him.

## Your Baby's Comfort

"While we on the staff look and listen to alarms," says Dr. Gorski, "parents look at and listen to their baby." Mothers and fathers are often the first to notice changes in their baby's condition, and their suggestions to the staff frequently lead to improved care. As a parent, you are the most consistent and motivated observer of your child. Never hesitate to share your observations and suggestions with the doctors and nurses.

Sometimes a simple change in the baby's environment—a reduction of noise or light—can make an enormous difference in the baby's comfort and health. Infants in intensive care are rarely treated with the same respect as seriously ill adults. Loud rock music blares from the PA system in far too many infant ICUs. Raucous conversations take place as nurses and doctors shout to be heard above the buzzing alarms, ringing telephones, rock music, and crying babies. Compare this to the hushed tones and calm atmosphere of an adult intensive care unit. Because the babies cannot complain for themselves, their parents must do it for them. Always feel free to request (politely) that the staff turn down the music, tone down the conversation, and lower the volume of nursery telephones.

The baby in the incubator is especially vulnerable to noise pollution. The decibel levels of incubator motors are high. Add to this the amplified clatter a baby hears when clipboards or medical instruments are thoughtlessly banged against the incubator walls or when the incubator door is slammed shut. A folded up gown or towel on top of the incubator provides a space where objects can be quietly placed. And always close the incubator door gently.

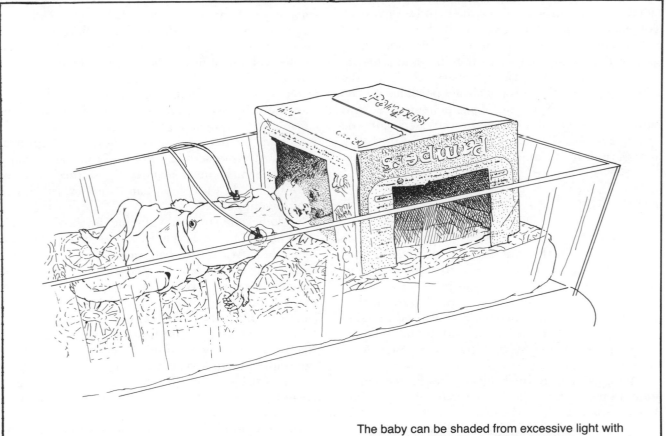

The baby can be shaded from excessive light with a cardboard box that has been cut in half.

The gown on top can serve a double purpose by shielding the baby from the constant bright overhead lights. A great deal of light penetrates through the baby's thin eyelids, even when his eyes are shut. Babies find the light irritating and generally will not open their eyes unless shaded from the overhead glare. While a certain amount of light is necessary for the staff to observe the baby, it is still possible to protect the baby's eyes from light. A baby on a warming table, for example, can be shaded by a cardboard box cut out on two or more sides and placed around his head. Once the baby is stable, you might suggest that the incubator be shaded during the night to help the baby adjust to normal day and night cycles. In one experiment at the Child Development Unit of Boston's Children's Hospital, doctors began covering the babies' incubators at night to simulate the normal cycle of day and night. Four days later, the babies in the experiment were eating better and gaining more weight.

Medical and caretaking procedures are generally done at the staff's convenience, not the baby's. But when the baby's level of fatigue or alertness is considered, procedures are more likely to be successful. For example, neonatologist Lula Lubchenco found that prematures will take nearly twice as much by gavage if they are fed when they become *active* instead of according to rigid nursery schedules. Rescheduling procedures is not always possible, but you can always try requesting a postponement if your baby seems especially fatigued or stressed, and you can suggest that the staff take advantage of the baby's alert periods for feeding or other necessary handling.

# Dressing Up

At Hershey Medical Center in Pennsylvania, one of the doctors in the infant intensive care unit suggested dressing the babies as a way to improve parent-infant attachment. The parents were enthusiastic and so, it seems, were the babies. With clothes on they gained more weight. Later the doctor tried dressing the babies on alternate weeks and found that the babies gained better during the weeks they wore clothes.

With clothes on, the baby appears more human. Many women tell of first feeling like a mother when they were able to dress their babies (full-terms as well as prematures) in clothes *they* had chosen.

Finding clothes for a tiny baby is no longer the problem it once was; parents no longer need to turn to doll clothes to outfit their tiny infant. Many manufacturers of children's wear now offer special lines of clothing for premature infants (see box, page 141). "Premie Boutiques" are springing up in major department stores across the country. Premature garments are sold in many hospital gift shops.

Parents may also select from a wide variety of homemade premature baby clothes (see box, page 141). In addition to the items offered in their brochures, most of the manufacturers of these clothes accept custom orders from parents and will use fabrics the parents themselves have chosen.

Mothers who wish to make their own premature baby clothes can find patterns in this book and elsewhere (see box, page 139).

In the nursery, light-weight, front-opening outfits are the most comfortable and convenient. Velcro closures are often recommended for premature baby clothes because they make it easier for the nurses to dress and undress the baby. We advise *against* the use of Velcro, however, because it can scratch the baby's delicate skin. Velcro also has a tendency to snag everything else in the wash. Tie closures or buttons are less convenient for the nurses, but more comfortable for the baby. Parents and nurses sometimes express concern that metal fasteners might overheat in an incubator and burn the baby. However, nurses who have actually dressed babies in clothes with metal fasteners have not found this to be a problem. Nevertheless, caution is advised. Metal fasteners, if used, should not come into direct contact with the baby's skin as long as the baby is in an incubator or on a warming table.

When buying or making clothes for your premature baby, avoid scratchy fabrics, trims, and seams. Check the garment or material for softness, not just by touching it with your hand, but by rubbing it against your cheek.

Clothes for the baby should be easy to wash. They should be washed at least once before the baby wears them. Wash your baby's clothes by hand or machine using Ivory Snow, or according to directions on the label. Be sure to rinse well—soap or detergent can irritate the baby's delicate skin. Mark the baby's clothes with a laundry marker or name tag to be sure they are not sent to the hospital laundry and lost. Keep a laundry bag by your baby's bedside so that you can collect his laundry and wash it yourself.

Tiny babies grow quickly, and some parents prefer to invest in newborn-size clothes rather than premie outfits that will soon be too small. Regular newborn terry-cloth sleepers with sleeves rolled up and feet tied in knots may not be beautiful, but they serve the purpose. Nightgowns with drawstring bottoms need only fit in the sleeves, which can be rolled up for the tiny baby.

The very first clothes the hospitalized premie can wear are a cap and booties. A simple cap can be made from two-inch-diameter Stockinette (tubular elastic bandage), tied at the top with brightly colored yarn or ribbon.

Below are knitting instructions for premie booties, cap, and sweater. They can be made with synthetic baby fingering yarn. Fingering yarns can vary in thickness and texture. Choose the softest, finest brand available. Do not use wool or other scratchy yarns. Test for softness by rubbing yarn against your cheek. Two 25-gram or one-ounce balls will make the sweater, booties, and cap. Either circular (round) or straight needles can be used. Check the gauge before knitting.

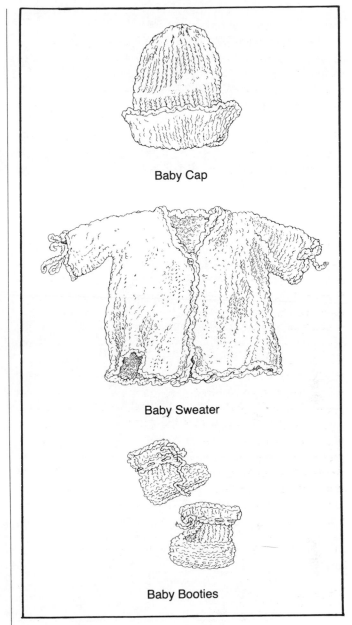

Baby Cap

Baby Sweater

Baby Booties

## Premie Baby Bootie Pattern

Materials: Synthetic baby fingering yarn; #3 needles for small (up to three pounds), #4 needles for "large" (three to five pounds)—don't knit too tightly.

Gauge: 7 sts = 1 inch; 12 rows = 1 inch

Cast on 32 sts loosely.

Knit 11 rows in garter stitch (i.e., K all sts each row).

Row 12: K 14 sts, K 2 tog, place marker, K 2 tog, K 14.

Row 13: P 13, P 2 tog, slip marker, P 2 tog, P 13.

Continue in stockinette (K 1 row, P 1 row) with 2 sts tog before *and* after marker until there are 10 sts each side of marker (20 sts total).

K next 2 rows, discarding marker.

Next row: K 1, * YO, K 2 tog. Repeat from *, end YO, K 1 (21 sts total).

Next row: K across.

Next row: K 1, * inc in next st, K 3 (that includes the stitch you increased in). Repeat from *, end K 2 (28 sts total).

Next 3 rows: K 1, P 1.

Cast off in stockinette loosely, so cast off row stretches with ribbing.

Sew bootie together. Insert 12-inch drawstring (can be made by crocheting a chain with a small crochet hook, using same yarn as for bootie).

## Premie Baby Cap Pattern

Materials: Synthetic baby fingering yarn; #3 needles for small, #4 needles for large.

Gauge: 12 sts = 1 inch. (Measure with knitting flat; 6 knit sts per inch will be visible.)

Cast on 74 sts.

K 1, P 1 (ribbing) for 5 to 8 inches (better too long than too short; edge can be rolled up).

Decrease row: K 2 tog, P 2 tog to end.

Next 3 rows: K 1, P 1 (ribbing).

Repeat decrease row.

Cut yarn, leaving 10 inches, and pull through remaining sts. Gather. Sew seam. With small crochet hook and single strand of contrasting color yarn, do one row of single crochet and then one row of shell stitch for decorative trim. The crocheting must be able to stretch with the ribbing, so make plenty of stitches, somewhat loosely.

## Premie Baby Sweater Pattern

Materials: Synthetic baby fingering yarn; #3 needles.

Gauge: 8 sts = 1 inch; 10 rows = 1 inch.

*Note:* The sweater is knit from the shoulder down to the bottom hem. The numbers given are for small babies, up to three pounds. The numbers in parentheses are for larger babies, from three to five pounds.

*(Baby's) Right Front:*

Cast on 30 (38) sts.

P 1 row, K 1 row.

Neck increase, rows 3 through 31: continue in stockinette with the following increases for approximately 2¼ inches (2¾ inches).

Purl rows: P 2, increase in next st, P to end.

Knit rows: K across.

*Note:* On a knit row, when you have 40 (48) sts on needles, bind off first 16 (24) sts for arm, K to end. This will occur at about row 22. Then continue increases until there are 28 (28) sts on needle.

Continue in stockinette on 28 (28) sts for 4½ inches (6½ inches) or to desired length.

Bind off remaining sts on K side.

*(Baby's) Left Front:*

Cast on 30 (38) sts.

K 1 row, P 1 row.

Neck increase, rows 3 through 31: continue in stockinette with the following increases for approximately 2¼ inches (2¾ inches).

Knit rows: K 2, increase in next st, K to end.

Purl rows: P across.

*Note:* On a purl row, when you have 40 (48) sts on needle, bind off first 16 (24) sts for arm, P to end. This will occur at about row 22. Then continue increases until there are 28 (28 sts on needle).

Continue in stockinette on 28 (28) sts for 4½ inches (6½ inches) or to desired length.

Bind off remaining sts on K side.

*Back:*

Cast on 80 (96) sts.

K 1 row, P 1 row for 2¼ inches (2¾ inches).

Next row (Knit side): bind off first 16 (24) sts; K to end.

Next row (Purl side): bind off first 16 (24) sts; P to end.

Continue in stockinette on 48 (48) sts for 4½ inches (6½ inches) or to desired length.

Bind off remaining sts on K side.

*Finishing:* Using single strand of yarn and blunt tapestry needle, sew side seams from bottom up through underarm seams. Sew shoulder seams from sleeve toward neck. With one strand of yarn in contrasting color and small crochet hook (Boye #1 or "B"), do one row of single crochet along exposed edges, including sleeve edges. Then crochet one row of shell stitch for decorative trim. For a continuous line, start at neck, go down front, around bottom, and up other front to neck. (If left-handed, start at top of *baby's right* front; if right-handed, start at top of *baby's left* front, so crochet stitches show on outside of sweater.) Iron edges if necessary. Attach buttons or ribbons for closures. Crochet an 8-inch chain to thread through knitted stitches at sleeve end to gather it snugly.

---

### Patterns for Prematures

**Special Patterns**

Patricia A. Silvers
1401 34th Street
Anacortes, Washington 98221
(206) 293-0200
Patterns for a cap, gown, sleeper, long- and short-sleeved t-shirts. Patterns fit the 3–4 pound baby and can be easily adjusted to fit the 4–5 pound baby. Pattern packet is available for $5.95. (This price includes first class postage.) Washington residents must add sales tax.

**Parents of Prematures**

Houston, Texas (See page 251 for address.)
Patterns for an ICU gown to fit the under-3-pound baby and a kimono to fit the 3- to 6-pounder. Available free with self-addressed stamped envelope.

**Ellen Smith of NICUF**

Lansing, Michigan (See page 249 for address.)
Pattern for a kimono, and instructions for crocheted or knitted booties and hats. Free with self-addressed stamped envelope.

## Premature Baby Clothes by Major Manufacturers

(For wholesale purchase.
Contact for catalogs or
lists of local distributors.)

### Premie Line by Carter's

The William Carter Company
Needham Heights, Massachusetts 02194
(617) 444-7500
Line includes side-snap short-sleeve shirt, side-snap long-sleeve shirt with mitten cuffs, drawstring gown with mitten cuffs, bonnets, bootees, Jamakin stretch coveralls, and "swifty change." Selection of colors, prints, and styles for boys and girls. Fits 0–5 pounds.

### "Little Me," Preemie Group

S. Schwab Co.
Cumberland, Maryland 21502
(301) 729-4488
Line includes stretch terry sleepers, hats, drawstring gowns, creepers, matching blankets. Selection of colors, prints, and styles for girls and boys. Fits 0–5 pounds.

### The Zona Lee Preemie Line

Zona Lee, Inc.
986 Mission Street
San Francisco, California 94103
(415) 664-4619
This particularly elegant line of premature apparel includes gowns, sleepers with mittens, hooded bags, caps, bonnets, booties, receiving blanket and hood, and quilted pram bags. Most outfits come in either brushed nylon or batiste. Selection of colors, prints, appliques and styles for boys and girls. Fits 0–8 pounds.

### Infant Clothes in Premature Sizes

The Warren Featherbone Company
Box 383
Gainesville, Georgia 30503
(404) 535-3000
Line includes tie or pull-on t-shirts and matching diaper covers, sleepers, rompers. Selection of colors. Fits 3–8 pounds.

### Paty Preemie Garments

Paty, Inc.
4800 W. 34th, Suite A-9
Houston, Texas 77092
(713) 688-7686
Pull-over or tie short-sleeved t-shirts, diaper covers, one-piece shirt and diaper cover set. White with choice of color trim. Fits 3–5 pounds.

### Toddle Tyke Premé Collection

Toddle Tyke
440 Armour Place, N.E.
Atlanta, Georgia 30324
(404) 875-8953
Coveralls, rompers, bubbles, hats. Lovely selection of trims, colors, and styles for boys and girls. Fits 2½–5 pounds.

J. C. Penney and Sears may carry premie clothes in their stores or through their catalogs.

## Homemade Premature Clothes

### Anne's Preemie Wear

% Anne Long
208 Fairview Drive
Greenville, South Carolina 29609
(803) 244-7835 (Call after 5 P.M.)
Elegant dresses trimmed in lace or decorative stitching, shirts and matching diaper covers, front-closing gowns and shirts. Selections of colors, prints, trims and styles for boys and girls. Fits 0–5 pounds. A $2.00 charge for the catalog is applied to the first order.

### Early Arrivals

Margaret Price
3875 Telegraph Road
Suite A-150
Ventura, California 93003
(805) 684-2189
Gowns, sleepers, coordinating tops and bottoms (with long or short pants or sleeves), jogging suits, dresses, custom hand-painted shirts, special orders. Variety of fabrics, styles, colors and prints. Sizes available for babies 2 through 8 pounds. Each stretchable outfit can be worn an average 4–6 months.

## Homemade Premature Clothes

**Oh, So Small**
by JoAnne Bock
6432 Pacific Avenue
Tacoma, Washington 98408
(206) 474-0840
Gowns, sleepers, hooded gowns with mittens, short-sleeve and long-sleeve undershirts with side ties, booties, dresses with matching tights or panties, coveralls, jogging suits, many one- and two-piece dress-up outfits, and pull-on white vinyl plastic pants. Styles fit babies 17 to 21 inches, and from 4 to 8 pounds. When ordering, be sure to specify whether baby is a boy or girl. Pay by check or money order. Phone orders can be shipped UPS, COD. Send 50¢ for the catalog. Orders sent day after receipt of order.

**The LAMBi Collection**
Lact-Aid Moms and Babes International
P.O. Box 1066
Athens, Tennessee 37303
(800) 228-1933
In Tennessee, (615) 744-9090
Featuring items from JoAnne Bock's Oh, So Small line of premie outfits, the LAMBi Collection also includes premie-sized Snugli infant carriers, toys for the isolette, a washable Rock-A-Bye Lamb that plays sounds of the womb, a hospital-tested "Baby Go To Sleep" cassette with heart-beat sounds, and lullabies to calm fussy babies. A variety of baby-care, breastfeeding, and relactation products are also available. Call toll-free number to receive catalog or to place orders. Payment by credit card, check, or money order.

## Diapers and Plastic Pants

### Disposables
Premature Infant Pampers can be ordered from Procter and Gamble by calling their toll-free number (800) 543-4932, in Ohio (800) 582-2623. The diapers must be ordered by the case (180 diapers) at $27.20 a case COD or $25.00 if charged by Visa or Mastercard. UPS delivery takes 5 to 7 working days. Premature Infant Pampers may also be available from certain hospital pharmacies or large children's stores. These disposables fit the up-to-6-pound baby. Call for list of local distributors.

### Cloth Diapers
The Dexter B-29 Brand is a t-shaped diaper that can be folded to fit the tiniest bottom. It can be used until the baby is ready for toilet training by varying the folding and pinning configuration as the baby grows. Dexter B-29 Diapers are available in some department stores. They can also be ordered directly from the factory:

> The Dexter Diaper Factory
> 236 W. 17th, P.O. Box 7367
> Houston, Texas 77248
> (713) 861-1382.

Inquire for current prices. The factory promises "quick delivery by mail anywhere in the world."

Soft flannel, hour-glass-shaped diapers to fit the 4- to 8-pounder are available by the dozen from:

> Premie Pals
> Nancy Nelson
> 1313 Harrington Avenue, S.E.
> Renton, Washington 98058
> (206) 271-0423.

Contact Nancy Nelson for current prices and ordering instructions.

You can also make your own cloth diapers by cutting regular diapers to the required size.

### Plastic Pants
Plastic pants to fit the 4- to 8-pound baby are available from Nancy Nelson at Premie Pals (see address given above). They are machine washable, with tricot around the edges for softness.

Pull-on white vinyl plastic pants for prematures are also available from JoAnne Bock of Oh, So Small (see address given above).

Although some major lines of premature wear offer lined diaper covers, they must generally be purchased as part of a shirt and diaper cover set.

## Playtime

Once your baby is having regular periods of alertnesss, he may enjoy toys to look at and listen to.

A premature baby, like a full-term, is more interested in primary colors—bright reds, blues, yellows, and greens—than in the softer pastels. The premature, like the full-term, seems to be more responsive to curving lines (like the lines of the human face) than he is to straight lines or other geometric configurations. The baby sees objects best when they are between 9 and 20 inches from his face.

The baby may like looking at a brightly colored paper plate, a cutout of the Pampers baby, or a picture of Mom, Dad, or other family members. Put these pictures on the outside of the incubator—they may get too moist inside. And watch the baby's response when he looks at them. Just as eye contact can be stressful to the baby, so might looking at a picture that constantly looks back. Your baby may also have preferences for certain colors or shapes. Experiment and carefully watch his responses. Once the baby is in

This is a good mobile for a baby who is lying down and looking up. In the nursery, mobiles can be suspended from IV poles, as shown here.

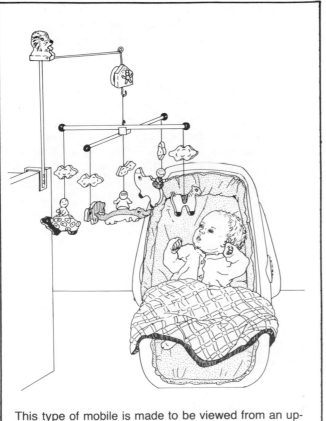

This type of mobile is made to be viewed from an upright or semi-upright position.

an open bassinet, he may enjoy a mobile.

One of the first toys nurses tend to suggest is a music box. But some babies are stressed by mechanical noises like ringing bells or music boxes; observers have noted drops in blood oxygen levels among some babies exposed to these sounds. If you wish to give your baby a music box, be sure it is well muffled inside a stuffed animal or pillow, and begin by playing it at some distance from the baby until he is used to it. *Be cautious about putting the music box inside the incubator—sounds become amplified and distorted in the enclosed space.*

Remember, the most interesting sight and sound you can offer your baby are your own face and voice.

# Ready to Go Home

If you are like most parents of prematures, you anticipate your baby's homecoming with a mixture of joy and panic. On the one hand, no more hospital; on the other, no more doctors and nurses to turn to for help. You will be on duty for all three shifts.

The homecoming of a baby who has had health problems and who still requires special care is a difficult and frightening time for mothers and fathers. It is not at all uncommon for parents to find excuses to leave the baby at the hospital just a little bit longer. "We were asked if we wanted to take the baby home on Friday," said one mother. "I thumbed through my appointment book and said, 'Oh no, that's impossible. We have theater tickets that night.' The doctors understood and let us have that extra time. It's probably the most expensive night of baby-sitting we'll ever have, but it was worth it."

Both parents and staff tend to put off discharge planning until the last minute, when suddenly there are a million procedures to learn, a million purchases to make, and later, at home, a million questions still unanswered.

Some hospitals ease the nursery-to-home transition by allowing one or both parents to room in with the baby for several days and slowly assume total care of their child. This can be especially valuable to the mother who is trying to establish breast-feeding. Other hospitals let the baby go home on passes (accompanied by a nurse) so that parents can learn how to care for the baby at home. If either of these arrangements interests you, find out if your hospital offers it. If not, suggest to the doctors that you be allowed to try it. You might just start something.

To help make homecoming easier on everyone, begin planning early. Here is a list of procedures to learn, things to buy, and questions you may wish to ask in the days or weeks before your baby leaves the hospital.

## *Things to Learn*

1. Learn to bathe your baby. Babies come in two varieties: those who love water and those who hate it. Watch the nurse bathe your baby and find out which type of child you have before trying it yourself. Then bathe the baby on at least four or five occasions or until you are comfortable giving your baby a bath.

2. Learn to feed your baby. If you are breast-feeding, total nursing can only begin at home or during rooming in; but try putting your hospitalized baby to the breast for at least one feeding a day so it won't be an entirely new experience. If bottle-feeding, learn how to mix your baby's formula, learn any special feeding techniques, and find out how much formula the baby normally takes in a 24-hour period. This is also the time to stock up on free samples from the nursery. Those four-ounce glass bottles used for sterile water or formula make good baby bottles for a premie, who usually will not take more than four ounces at a feeding at first. Many babies take much less. You might also want to collect the plastic 45-milliliter premie bottles that many nurseries use.

3. Learn to diaper your baby. Notice the normal frequency and consistency of your baby's stools so that you can recognize constipation and diarrhea. Notice how often the baby wets his diaper and observe the color of his urine. If the baby wets less at home or the urine color is darker than normal, it may be a sign that he is not getting enough breastmilk or formula. Learn how to care for diaper rash.

4. Learn to take an axillary (under the arm) and rectal temperature. Be sure you know how to read a thermometer correctly. You can take your baby's hospital thermometer home.

5. Learn to use a bulb syringe to unclog your baby's stuffed nose. There will be a bulb syringe among the equipment at your baby's bedside; this is also yours to take home.

6. Learn what medicines and vitamins your baby will need. Find out when and how they should be given, how they should be stored, why they are necessary, and how long they should be continued. Ask what to do if the baby spits up his vitamins or medication (a common problem). Find out if larger than normal doses of these vitamins or medications could be dangerous.

7. Learn cardiopulmonary resuscitation—CPR. Although it is unlikely that you will ever need to use CPR on your baby, it is a skill *every* parent should know. Doctors are often reluctant to instruct new parents in CPR for fear of frightening them. But parents who have seen their child stop breathing in the hospital are frightened anyway. Knowing CPR makes

most mothers and fathers feel more, not less, secure. In our questionnaires, parents frequently mentioned that they wished they had had CPR instruction before bringing their baby home. For emergency use, we are including an outline of the CPR technique. (See page 190.) Simple instructions for reviving an infant can also be found in the front of your telephone directory. But no written instructions can replace a CPR training class. The Red Cross offers courses in adult and infant CPR. Sign up early if you wish to take a class. Call the Red Cross now.

8. Learn your baby's normal breathing patterns. Watch his chest as he breathes. Count his normal number of breaths per minute. Listen to the normal noises he makes when breathing. Notice if he has spells of periodic breathing, retractions, or rapid breathing. Observe him many times during the day. Crying or excitement may alter his breathing pattern. If your child has an abnormal chest x-ray, be sure that you and/or your pediatrician have a copy of it, so that any changes can be noted in the event of respiratory problems.

9. If your baby is a boy, carefully consider the pros and cons of circumcision, and do so well before it's time for him to leave the nursery. Circumcision is the cutting away of the foreskin, the tissue that normally surrounds the sensitive end of the penis. Since anesthetizing the infant poses unacceptable risks, this surgery is performed without anesthesia. The baby *does* feel the surgery. Approximately 2 out of every 100 infants experience complications from circumcision, including bleeding severely enough to require transfusion, local or bodywide infection, and improper removal of the foreskin or excessive scarring of the penis resulting in deformity or the need for further surgery.

The American Academy of Pediatrics recommends *against* routine circumcision. While male infants in many parts of the world (including Europe) are not routinely circumcised, the surgery is still widely performed in the United States. Some parents have their male infants circumcised for religious reasons. Others have it done because they've heard it will help prevent cancer. (Actually, keeping the penis clean is just as effective in preventing cancer as circumcision.) Most parents have their sons circumcised because "everyone else does it" or because they "wanted the baby to look like his father."

The majority of parents who responded to our questionnaire *did* have their premature baby boys circumcised. Said one couple, "We figured things were going to be hard enough for him without having him look different from the other kids, too." The minority of parents who decided against circumcision said they felt it was too much to subject their premature baby to another risky, painful procedure. Some parents took advantage of later surgery (for hernias or for strabismus) to have their babies circumcised under anesthesia.

If you have your baby circumcised, you must take special care of the incision for the three days following surgery. Your pediatrician will instruct you in the specifics of this care. Be sure to call him if you notice any bleeding.

If you choose not to have your baby circumcised, learn how to keep the penis clean. Some time during the latter half of the first year, you might try to pull back on, or retract, the baby's foreskin. If the foreskin retracts *easily*, wash the end of the penis and *be sure to return the foreskin to its normal position*. If the foreskin does not retract, do not worry. Approximately half of all male infants do not have retractable foreskins during the first year. By the age of 3, 90% have retractable foreskins, and by age 17, 99% do. In rare cases, the foreskin does not retract sufficiently for cleaning even when the child is older. If this becomes a problem, the older child can be circumcised under anesthesia.

## Twenty Questions

Many of these questions will be considered in the following chapters, but ask your doctor anyway. There is no one answer that is right for every baby.

1. How warm should we keep the house?
2. How should we dress the baby?
3. When can we take the baby out or have visitors?
4. When can we take the baby in an airplane?
5. How can we tell if the baby is getting enough to eat?
6. When should we start to increase his feedings?
7. When should we start solids?
8. Can the baby have water or juice as well as breastmilk or formula?

9.  What should we do if the baby sleeps through a feeding?
10. What, if anything, do we need to sterilize?
11. Can we allow our pets around the baby?
12. What if we or one of our children get sick?
13. What about smoking around the baby?
14. When should the baby first visit the pediatrician? The follow-up clinic?
15. (If your baby received oxygen.) What were the results of my baby's hospital eye checkup? When should the baby next see the ophthalmologist? (Some doctors feel that all prematures, especially those born weighing less than 1500 grams, should have follow-up examinations by an ophthalmologist, whether they received oxygen or not. Discuss this with your neonatologist and pediatrician.)
16. Has my baby had a complete hearing evaluation while in the nursery? If not, may I have a referral for a thorough audiologic evaluation to be done in the next three months? (Babies who weighed less than 1500 grams at birth, and many others who required intensive care, are at risk for hearing loss. See page 210 for a complete list of risk factors.)
17. When should my baby get his immunizations?
18. How much should the baby sleep?
19. Should we let the baby cry? For how long?
20. What are some good toys and activities for the first few months at home?

And remember, the intensive care nursery is open 24 hours a day. Feel free to call them with your questions once the baby is home.

## A Shopping List

Use the time while your baby is in the hospital to buy the items you will need during the first months at home. Once the baby is home, shopping trips will be difficult, so plan ahead. Your baby will need:

*A car seat.** Even the tiniest baby should come home in a car seat. Parents often wrongly assume that a young infant is safe in his mother's arms to too small for a car seat, but automobile accidents take more children's lives each year than any single disease, and the highest fatality rate is among babies under six months. Safe car seats for infants face the back of the seat, and some of them can later be converted to a front-facing seat for older babies and toddlers. Car seats like the Infant Love Seat and the Bobby-Mac come with accessories that allow the seat to be used in a stroller frame. This is a particularly convenient feature for babies who come home with oxygen. (While a car seat can sometimes double as an infant seat, it is important to note that infant seats are not safe car seats.)

A baby in a bunting fits more easily into a car seat than a baby wrapped in receiving blankets. A tiny baby will need extra support; rolled-up blankets on either side of his head will prevent excessive motion. For car seats that do not have adjustable positions, a rolled-up blanket under the seat may be needed to increase the reclining angle and prevent the baby from sliding down.

*An infant seat.** If your car seat does not serve double duty, you will probably want to purchase one.

*A crib and/or bassinet.* The baby will need a crib eventually, and there is no really good reason not to start him out in one. Buy a good quality firm mattress and crib bumpers. Some parents (and babies) prefer the coziness of a bassinet at first. Try to find one on sturdy casters or wheels. The bassinet can then be pushed back and forth to soothe a fussy baby to sleep. A large baby carriage can also be used as a bassinet.

*An infant swing* is optional.*

*A cool mist vaporizer.* "No premie household should be without one," said a mother of twins. "I turn mine on at the first sneeze or sniffle." Avoid steam vaporizers; they are less efficient and are dangerous for use around children.

---

*Some premature babies experience oxygen deprivation if placed in an upright or semi-upright position. Discuss your choice of car and infant seat with your neonatologist. Monitoring your baby's oxygen levels in the seat before leaving the nursery can indicate if there is a problem.

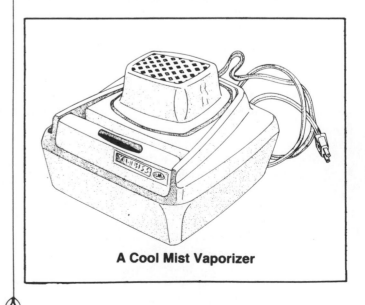

**A Cool Mist Vaporizer**

## Fitting Your Baby into a Car Seat

Even the tiniest baby should come home in a car seat. For extra support the baby may need rolled-up blankets on either side of his head to prevent excessive motion. The support roll shown here (Fig. A) was made from a fabric strip 10 inches wide and 30 inches long. The fabric was sewn into a tube, stuffed with Fiberfill, and stitched together at each end. It is machine washable, can be dried in the dryer, and can be used in infant seats and swings. When using such head supports, be sure that the baby's nose and mouth cannot be obstructed by them. Watch the baby closely.

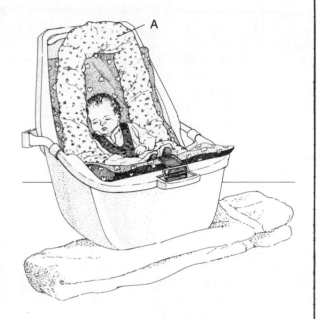

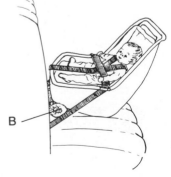

A rolled-up towel or blanket under the front of the car seat can increase the reclining angle to give the baby better head support. [B]

## An Infant Swing

Although this is an optional item, some parents feel the swing is a necessity, believing it is the only way they ever eat a meal in peace. A good swing should have a sturdy, broad base. Some swings come with a bassinet attachment as well as a swing seat. Some wind up for as long as 45 minutes of swinging. (The winding mechanism on certain models is quite loud. Wind it when the baby is out of the room.) To slow the swing or bassinet, put books under the seat or mattress for added weight. The tiny baby may need to be secured with rolled blankets at first to prevent him from slipping around.

A note of caution: child development specialists warn that a swing can be overpowering to some babies and may actually increase their irritability. The swing, specialists also advise, should be used sparingly since the baby is prevented from interacting normally with his environment during the time he is in it.

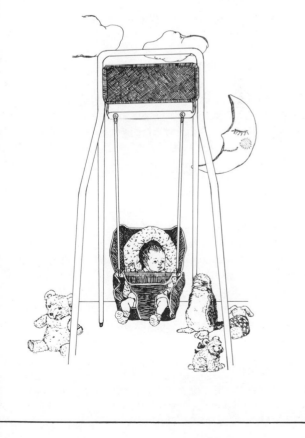

*A good comprehensive book on regular baby care* such as Dr. Spock's *Baby and Child Care,* or Penelope Leach's *Your Baby and Child: From Birth to Age Five.*

*Baby clothes.* Your baby will spend most of the early months asleep, so warm, comfortable sleepwear is what he will live in. A basic wardrobe should include at least:

6 nightgowns or terry-cloth sleepers
6 t-shirts
1 or 2 sweaters
2 or more caps, preferably pull-on knit caps (Head coverings are a must for prematures in cool weather. A great deal of heat is lost from the baby's head.)
2 or 3 pairs of booties
A bunting or pram suit (for cold weather)
4 dozen diapers if you are using cloth and 3 to 4 pairs of waterproof pants (Even if you are using disposables, buy at least a dozen cloth diapers for general clean-up purposes.)
(See pages 138–42 for information on premature clothes, diapers, and plastic pants.)

*Bath, toiletry, and health care items.*
portable baby bathtub
6 to 10 baby washcloths
3 or 4 towels
lotion
moist towelettes for diaper changes
lubricated sterile gauze for circumcision care
rectal thermometer
bulb syringe for suctioning a stuffed nose
nail scissors
baby hairbrush
mild infant soap
petroleum jelly and diaper rash ointment
*Avoid* powder. It is bad for babies with breathing problems.

*Bedding.*
4 to 6 fitted crib or bassinet sheets
6 or more waterproof pads
6 or more receiving blankets
1 or more heavy blankets, quilts, or comforters
A portable baby bed or basket
A night light
*Do not* buy a pillow for your baby; little babies should not sleep on them.

*Feeding items.*
8 bottles (The 4-ounce formula bottles used in hospitals work very well for the first few months.)
10 to 12 nipples, caps, and covers
bottle brush
nipple brush
(Even if you are breast-feeding you might want to have bottles for giving your expressed milk when you are out.)

*Miscellaneous.*
a baby carrier, such as the Snugli or Gerry Cuddle Pack
a diaper bag—the roomier the better
a musical mobile or two for the crib

# Taking Care of Yourself

Your baby's early birth has been as hard on you as it has been on him, perhaps more so. Take time now to plan for outings and recreation once your baby comes home. Ask your social worker, your baby's nurses, or your pediatrician about babysitting or respite resources in your community. If you have a close friend or relative who will help with the baby, ask if you can bring that person into the nursery with you to help learn to care for the baby before you go home.

Although you probably will want to spend most of your time with your baby at first, try to avoid the tendency of so many new parents of premature babies of becoming so devoted that you "burn out." Plan a regular night out each week, just for you and your husband. And when your doctor says it's all right, begin a program of regular strenuous exercise. Many mothers feel that their calisthenic classes, afternoons of jazzercise, or jogging have been real lifesavers. "There is nothing more demoralizing," said one mother, "than delivering a 2-pound baby and coming home from the hospital 15 to 20 pounds overweight. I started jogging and lost my pregnancy weight gain in three months. Now I can eat as much as I want. I'm also a much calmer, happier person." Taking care of yourself is an indirect but vital contribution to taking care of your baby!

# *Kiyomi, Keidi, Kenichi, Toshi, and Tadashi's Story*

## By Kathie Noguchi

My husband, Nao, wanted one child, I wanted three, we compromised at two, and ended up with five. All of them were premature.

Our first daughter, Kiyomi, was just over three

weeks early, making her technically a premie, even though she weighed nearly seven pounds. Aside from a brief period of temperature instability, she was a normal, healthy baby.

We were planning a home birth for our second child. Nao would be the first to hold the baby. I would nurse the baby before the cord was cut.

Then, 11 weeks before term, my membranes ruptured. I wondered what I had done wrong, if it was my fault. The books say that if you take care of yourself, you will have a healthy baby; that prematurity is the result of poor nutrition, drugs, or alcohol. But I was in excellent health and following the Adelle Davis pregnancy diet. So what went wrong? I wondered how a baby could spend its first weeks and months in an incubator. It seemed so unnatural. Wouldn't it be better to let the baby die?

Attempts to delay my labor were unsuccessful, and our daughter was born a few hours after I arrived at the hospital—much too early for the betamethasone injection I'd been given to take effect. Before the birth, the doctor told us our baby had a mere 20% chance for survival. Nevertheless, 2-pound, 10-ounce Keidi escaped RDS and amazed everyone by her strength. The night she was born she sucked vigorously on a pacifier. The next morning she was crying loudly and doing much better than the huge full-term baby next to her who was seriously ill from meconium aspiration. Size isn't everything.

Keidi was a responsive baby right from the start She soothed down and stopped crying whenever I placed my hand on her back. Her first attempt at nursing at age four weeks was a great success. She knew exactly what to do. I nursed her for a year and a half.

Keidi's main problem during her six weeks in the hospital was apnea, but a little extra oxygen in her Isolette seemed to help her out. (When I nursed her, I tied the oxygen tube to my gown so it would blow past her face.)

Keidi's birth and hospitalization were especially hard on 2-year-old Kiyomi. She began to stutter and would become hysterical at the sound of an automobile engine, a sound she associated with my trips to the hospital. When Keidi came home, we paid extra attention to Kiyomi, and her fears and stuttering soon went away. She accepted her new sister very well.

At home, Keidi continued to have dusky spells at the end of feedings. Like many premies, she sometimes forgot the "breathe" part of the "suck-swallow-breathe" sequence, and she would be very tired by the end of the meal. For the first few

months, I had to watch her closely while she nursed and give her a gentle pat to remind her to breathe. She also turned gray once during a bout of pneumonia, but stimulation started her breathing again. As far as we can tell, Keidi's susceptibility to bronchitis and pneumonia (which she used to get with virtually every cold) is her only ongoing problem from prematurity, a problem she finally seems to be outgrowing at age four. Otherwise, she is a very sweet-natured child who is developing quite normally.

Although Nao and I decided on two children, we'd postponed taking any permanent birth-control measures until we were certain Keidi was going to be all right. Then in February 1980 I discovered I was pregnant once more.

From the second month on I knew there was something different about this pregnancy. I was having frequent contractions and spotting. I was quite large for my dates. I was certain it was twins, and I began eating a doubly nutritious diet. At six months, my doctor did a sonogram. "Are you sitting down?" he asked when he phoned me with the results. "Yes," I answered, wondering why he was being so melodramatic about it. He knew that I knew I was carrying twins.

"There are three of them," he said. "You're going to have triplets."

It's a good thing I *was* sitting down. I was nervous enough about twins with my history of premature delivery, but triplets! On doctor's orders I went straight to bed. My husband, still in a state of shock, began shoveling more food into me.

The very next day, the doctor discovered that I was completely effaced and four centimeters dilated. Again, I was 11 weeks from term. At our community hospital I was given my first shot of betamethasone and rushed 60 miles to a San Francisco medical center.

During the next few days my labor was slowed with terbutaline in hope that delivery could be delayed at least 72 hours—the time needed for the betamethasone to mature the babies' lungs. The terbutaline made my heart race; I was tilted in bed with my feet up. The weight of the babies and the side effects of the terbutaline made it hard for me to breathe. From time to time I was given oxygen. I remember how awful I felt during those three days as I struggled for each breath. Meanwhile, Nao was constantly urging me to eat: "The babies are hungry. You've got to feed the babies!"

The delivery room was a blur of lights and noise. There was a team of doctors and nurses for each baby and some for me. An anesthesiologist

150

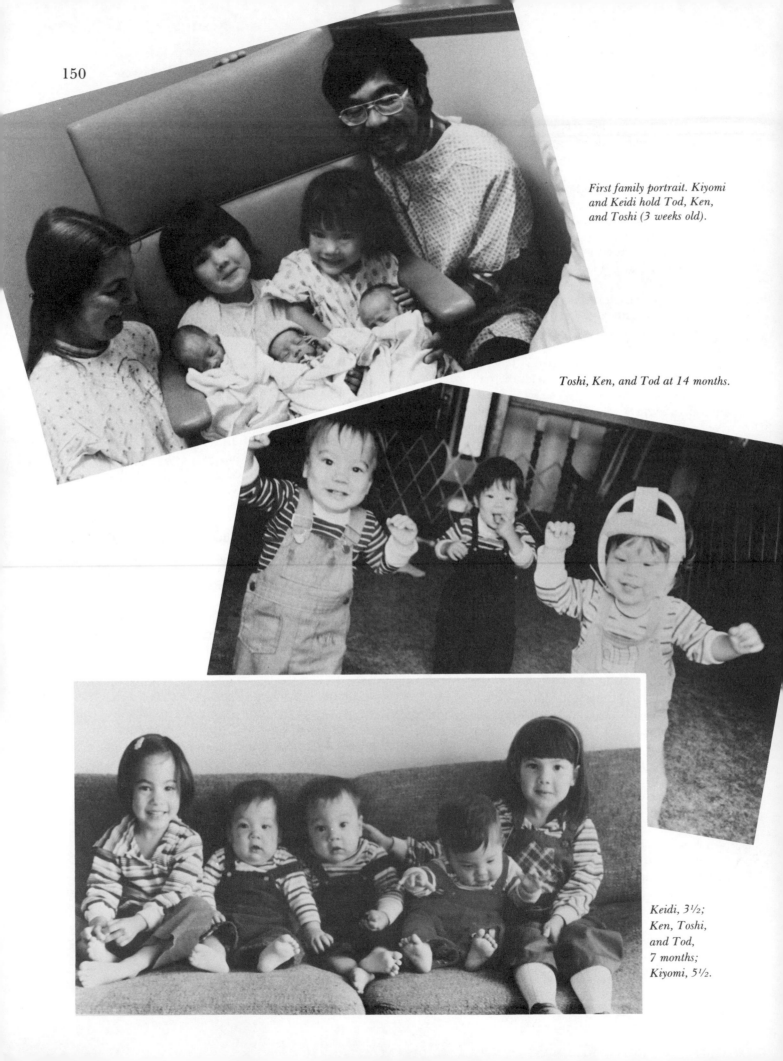

*First family portrait. Kiyomi and Keidi hold Tod, Ken, and Toshi (3 weeks old).*

*Toshi, Ken, and Tod at 14 months.*

*Keidi, 3½; Ken, Toshi, and Tod, 7 months; Kiyomi, 5½.*

stood by in case an emergency cesarean became necessary. I was terrified. The doctors expected 1½-pound babies. We'd been *very* lucky with Kiyomi and Keidi. We knew this time it would be different.

Our first son, 2-pound, 14-ounce Kenichi (Ken) was born crying. The doctor felt around inside me to see which baby would be next, since neither seemed eager to fall into place. He chose the one on the left, and 3-pound, 5-ounce Toshi was pushed into the world. He seemed paler than Ken, but he cried, too. The third was a breech—the doctor gently pulled the baby out by the feet. Another boy! He was smaller (2 pounds, 10 ounces), but pink and crying. We hadn't yet chosen a third boy's name, so this one became "Baby C." Keidi hadn't had a name her first few days either, and it had bothered me, a little person without a name. As soon as we could, we named "Baby C" Tadashi (Tod, for short).

Right after delivery I was taken to surgery for a tubal ligation.

Although I had been given betamethasone, all three boys developed respiratory distress syndrome and were intubated. We were pleased that the boys were so much bigger than expected (thanks to my hearty diet), but we also knew weight wasn't the most important factor. After all, Keidi had been as small as Tod, the smallest triplet, and she hadn't had the benefit of betamethasone, but she never got RDS and never needed a respirator, and Toshi, the largest of the triplets, had the most severe RDS.

During the next few weeks the boys experienced RDS, apnea, jaundice, ductus problems (corrected by indomethacin), numerous septic workups (all false alarms), and a suspected brain bleed (another false alarm). All three developed anemia severe enough to require transfusions. We were familiar with infant intensive care from Keidi's birth, but nothing can really prepare you to see your babies the way we saw the triplets—IVs in their heads, umbilical catheters, respirators, and monitors. I did most of my crying in the car on the way home from the hospital. It didn't take much to make me cry, either. I even remember watching Mr. Rogers with Keidi and being moved to tears by one of his songs.

Before Keidi's birth, I read a lot about bonding, and I had worried about the effects of our separation during her time in the hospital. But we bonded eventually, so I wasn't worried about forming an attachment to the triplets. Still, it was hard on me not to be able to hold them. I wanted to wrap them in soft blankets and cuddle them.

I was able to touch the babies, however. Ken and Tod loved to be stroked; Tod would even wrap his tiny fingers around my finger. But Toshi completely fell apart whenever he was touched. He thrashed around so much that his arms and legs needed to be restrained. I soon stopped trying to touch him at all. I just sat beside him, talked to him a little, and cried inside. It helped me to remember how I'd felt gasping for breath during the terbutaline treatment. I hadn't wanted to be touched either. The nurses all predicted Toshi would have a terrible temper, but once his medical problems went away, he became an easygoing baby who enjoyed being held.

Nao was a proud father, pleased that the boys were "big" and doing better than expected. When he visited his home in Japan several months later, he was the toast of the town. Three boys all at once!

We brought Kiyomi and Keidi in to see their brothers. When I was in labor with the boys, Keidi had been asked where I was. "She's having lots of babies," three-year-old Keidi replied. When Keidi came into the ICU and was introduced to the triplets, she seemed puzzled: "Where's another brother?" Apparently, she thought *all* the babies in the nursery were ours! When we explained that some of them belonged to other families, she replied, "I hate boys." Kiyomi was also disappointed that there were *only* three. She thought we should have had one more baby so we would all have a baby to hold.

I had nursed both girls, and I was determined to nurse the triplets, too. At first, they received my milk by gavage. Then, when they were a month old, I tried to nurse them for the first time. It was disappointing. With Keidi it had been so easy, but none of the boys had the slightest idea what to do. It took several days of trying before Toshi figured it out. From then on, he was a terrific nurser (yes, antisocial Toshi!). Ken and Tod took much longer to learn to nurse, but they eventually got the hang of it. I nursed all three for almost 14 months.

Toshi was the first one home. Ken and Tod were still having problems with anemia, apnea, and ductuses that wouldn't stay closed. Both boys improved after receiving blood transfusions, and soon they were home too.

We settled into a routine of nurse, nurse, nurse. The books make it sound easy. Let the hungriest one set the schedule and wake the others up. But they don't tell you how to wake up a soundly sleeping baby and make him eat. Although I tried to establish a three-hour feeding schedule, the boys all had their own very different ideas of when they should eat and nap. Ken and Tod were still poor nursers. I began weighing them before and after each feeding and expressing milk into bottles for them if they hadn't nursed enough. For one feeding each night, Nao would give the boys a bottle of my milk or formula so that I could have at least four hours of uninterrupted sleep.

Although we were able to get some help with the housework and laundry, and my parents came to our rescue on weekends, it was an exhausting, difficult time for me. I felt like I was constantly juggling. I put my mind "on hold" that first year—it was the only way to survive. When I did think, it was to remind myself that they're babies only for a short time. It seems an eternity as you live through it, but it actually goes very quickly. And despite the fatigue, I found nursing to be a real joy. It was my time to get to know and enjoy each baby.

We had worried about the three boys sharing Keidi's vulnerability to pneumonia, but they've not had this problem. In fact, they've been quite healthy.

Except for Tod. He had only been home a week when, on an impulse, I peeked in as the three boys were sleeping in their buggy (all three fit in one buggy). Tod was an awful gray color. He revived with stimulation but continued having apnea. The pediatrician readmitted him to the hospital for observation and tests. He was severely anemic and needed a transfusion. The apnea stopped once his anemia was corrected. Then when he was six months old, I removed some cradle cap from Tod's scalp before putting him to bed. The next morning the entire top of his head was oozing blood. Testing revealed that Tod's platelet count (the number of cells that help the blood to clot) was abnormally low. Tod was started on medication for this not-too-unusual problem. But nothing seemed to help. Tests for diseases that can cause this condition all proved negative. The hematologists at Stanford where Tod was seen suggested that the clotting problem might have resulted from cytomegalovirus contracted from a blood transfusion. No one knows for sure, however, and this problem may have nothing at all to do with his prematurity. Tod must now wear a helmet to protect his head. A normal toddler fall that would not even bother Ken or Toshi could cause Tod to have serious internal bleeding. And there is nothing we can do except hope that he eventually outgrows this problem.

The boys are now 15 months old, walking and starting to talk. They are exuberant and active. All the children enjoy playing together (most of the time), and our home is a very lively place. I'm beginning to feel more like a human being now that the boys are sleeping 11 to 12 straight hours a night. There are still times when I wonder why all this has happened to us. We seem to have had more than our share of trials and burdens. Of course we'll never know why, and it really doesn't matter. We are just thankful for our five beautiful children and the gift and miracle of their lives.

# 9

# *Feeding Your Baby*

"If you wish to nurse, get help from someone who had trouble getting started herself. Mothers who never had problems nursing assume that if it was easy for them, it should be easy for you."

\*

"Sebastian would nibble weakly at my breast, then fall asleep, but I had to hang on to the tiniest progress. I gave him supplemental bottles after most feedings in the beginning. Then I got it down to one or two a day. After seven weeks he was completely on the breast."

\*

"She was doing so well, I was afraid to try taking her off the formula."

\*

"I pumped while Katie was in the hospital, but my supply never materialized to meet her demand. I felt some guilt at first. I wanted so much to breast-feed her. I feel my supply was hindered by the emotional state I was in."

\*

"My son was on a respirator for so long (three months) that I just didn't have the energy to keep pumping and still make all the trips to the hospital. I chose to be with him every day touching and talking to him. I don't feel less close to him because I didn't nurse and I don't feel guilty."

\*

"There are women whose chief claim to fame in life is that they've nursed a baby. Despite pressure from people who feel breast-feeding is the *only* way, I chose to bottle-feed my children. One was full-term, the other a premie. Both are normal, healthy, well-adjusted kids."

\*

"For months my life revolved around feeding, around cc's ingested, and grams lost or gained. Whenever I called the nursery I had my cookbook open to the metric conversion tables. At home I weighed my son daily and worried constantly. Now that he's outgrowing his clothes faster than I can buy them, it amazes me that I agonized so much over his growth in the beginning."

\*\*\*

There are probably more anxieties about feeding than about any other aspect of the parent-baby relationship. How and how much the baby should be fed are major concerns of all new mothers and fathers. For the parents of a tiny premature these issues take on heightened importance.

Of 100 mothers we interviewed, 47—nearly half—eventually breast-fed their premature babies. But almost every mother, whether she fed by breast or by bottle, reported problems, at first, getting her baby to feed. In this chapter we provide information to help you make knowledgeable decisions about feeding methods; we also offer suggestions on ways to make the feeding experience easier, no matter which method ultimately works out best for you and your baby.

## Breast-feeding the Premature Baby

If you had decided during your pregnancy that you would nurse your new baby, there is no reason to abandon those plans just because your baby is premature. If you have not made a decision about how to feed your baby, you might wish to consider breast-feeding in view of the nutritional, health, and emotional benefits it can offer. Even if you were given medication to dry up your milk supply, it can be brought in again through a regular program of breast pumping or expression. It will take time, effort, determination, and the support of those around you for you to maintain a milk supply while separated from your baby. But as so many stories in this book demonstrate, it can be done.

Breast-feeding a premature baby is almost always divided into two stages. During the first stage, the milk is pumped or expressed and fed to the baby by gavage or bottle. During the second stage, the baby nurses directly at the breast. Usually there is also a transitional stage in which the baby is fed from both breast and bottle.

It is a mistake to think that the second stage alone constitutes real breast-feeding, while the first stage is a mere preliminary. *Any* milk you supply your baby is important. Even if your baby receives your milk only by gavage or bottle, you are successfully breast-feeding. You are providing your child at a critical time in his life with a naturally nutritious, healthful food that no one else can duplicate.

## Breastmilk and Nutrition

The ideal food for a premature baby is one that allows him to grow at the most rapid rate while imposing the least amount of stress on his immature digestive tract, kidneys, and other organs.

Whether or not breastmilk constitutes this ideal nutrition has been debated for some time. Breastmilk is certainly the food that is most easily handled by the baby's immature body. But some researchers have found it to be too low in protein, calories, and minerals such as calcium, phosphorus, and sodium to meet the tiny premature's *estimated* requirements for growth. Studies have also shown faster growth in formula-fed babies.

However, no one really knows what rate of growth is actually desirable in a premature baby. Most tiny pre-term infants do not grow as rapidly as they would have in the womb no matter what they are fed, and there is no evidence to indicate that this slower rate of growth harms the baby.

In addition, the experiments that suggested human milk might be inadequate for prematures were carried out using sterilized, pooled donors' milk taken from mothers of *full-term* infants. The sterilization process may have destroyed some of the milk's nutritional benefits. And recent studies show that the milk of a mother who delivers *prematurely* is quite different in composition from the milk of a mother who delivers at term.

The premature mother's milk during the first weeks after delivery is significantly higher in protein, sodium, chloride, and potassium. It provides a form of fat that is easier for the baby to digest and assimilate than the fat found in formula or sterilized donor's milk.

One investigation in which premature babies were fed their own mothers' milk, formula, or sterilized donors' milk found that the babies who received their mothers' fresh milk were the *best nourished;* the formula-fed babies were a close second, and the donor-fed babies came in third.

The nutritional content of breastmilk varies widely from feeding to feeding (or expression to expression). Fat, for example, is usually more abundant in late morning feedings (or expressions). Most of the fat comes at the end of the feeding or expression as a sort of dessert. Because of the variations in nutrient content over a 24-hour period, your baby should receive at least a sample of all the milk you express during the day and night in order to receive maximum nutritional benefits.

Breastmilk averages 17 to 20 calories per ounce.* However, because of the fluctuation in fat content, a given sample of breastmilk may contain anywhere from 11 to 30 calories an ounce. The fat content of a sample of milk can be roughly determined by placing a few drops of milk in a small tube and spinning it in a centrifuge. The fat rises and forms a visible layer at the top of the tube. This test, similar to the red blood cell count, or hematocrit, is called a "cream-atocrit."

If a breastmilk-fed baby is gaining too slowly, his feedings may be supplemented with formula, with medium-chain triglyceride oil (MCT oil), or with Polycose, a type of sugar. In addition, a premature baby, whether breast- or bottle-fed, may be given vitamins, iron, and other mineral supplements throughout the first year because of his special growth needs and his susceptibility to anemia.

## Breastmilk and Health

Your breastmilk contains many types of disease-fighting cells and antibodies that you custom-make to meet your baby's special needs. Through close physical contact with your baby, you become exposed to the same germs to which your baby is exposed. Your

---

*By contrast, formula given to prematures in the nursery generally ranges from 20 to 24 calories per ounce.

body manufactures immunities against those germs, and the immunities are passed on to your baby in your milk.

Whenever possible, give your baby your *freshly expressed* milk, since it is the richest in disease-fighting substances. Freezing breastmilk destroys some, but not all, of the disease-fighting cells; however, antibodies and other anti-infective substances in the milk are thought to be unaffected by the freezing process. Sterilization of the breastmilk (even overheating the milk when thawing or warming it) also reduces the milk's disease-fighting properties.

Studies of breast-fed children have found them to be healthier as a group than formula-fed children. One investigation of 253 full-term babies revealed that the infants who were formula-fed (about half of the sample) had twice as many ear infections, 16 times more lower respiratory tract infections, 2½ times the incidence of vomiting and diarrhea, and 8½ times as many hospital admissions as the breast-fed group. Others studies indicate a reduced incidence of allergies in breast-fed babies. Animal experiments also suggest that breastmilk may help protect against necrotizing enterocolitis. It is important to point out, however, that breast-feeding does not *guarantee* good health. As the stories in this book show, there are exceptions to virtually every rule. Breast-fed Ami Everett developed necrotizing enterocolitis (see page 84). Colin (see page 14), Keidi (see page 148), Steven and Timothy (see page 71)—all breast-fed—suffered from frequent respiratory infections.

## The Emotional Aspects

The acts of supplying breastmilk and, later, of nursing can offer many emotional benefits to a mother whose baby was born prematurely. The regular expression of milk helps provide a focus and routine to a mother's life at a time when she tends to feel lost and disoriented. She can experience the sense of accomplishment that comes from providing a food her body has custom-made to meet her baby's special needs. Later, she enjoys the physical closeness of nursing her baby at her breast. Above all, she can have the satisfaction of offering her child a bit of natural mothering despite the unusual circumstances of a premature birth and separation.

A mother who developed toxemia in her seventh month recounted: "I was given an emergency cesarean section under general anesthesia. The baby was transported before I woke up, and I didn't see her for a week. I had never experienced labor or seen the baby. As far as I was concerned, I'd had an operation and that was all. Then my milk came in. It was hard to believe that something normal was actually happening to me. Meanwhile, the baby was having a very difficult time. She developed hydrocephalus and required shunt surgery. Throughout, she received my milk; and a week after her surgery, I was able to nurse her. With all that had gone wrong with both our bodies, it was wonderful and amazing to me that one thing—the nursing—was going right."

But what happens when nursing doesn't go right? Breast-feeding has its emotional lows as well as its highs. This is true even for mothers of hearty full-terms, and the mother of a premature must contend with special problems. It is hard to have warm feelings about a breast pump. Round-the-clock milk expression is a tiring business. Weak, neurologically immature pre-term babies are often poor nursing partners, and nursing *is* a partnership.

The support a mother receives in her attempts to nurse is often ambivalent at best. Doctors and nurses tend to feel more comfortable giving the baby a formula they know to be sterile, one that has a precisely determined calorie and nutrient content. Often a physician, nurse, even a well-meaning husband or relative may discourage the mother of a premie from trying to breast-feed for fear of putting her through additional difficulties and the risk of disappointment. And it is true that a mother who invests a great deal of her ego into total breast-feeding and who views the feeding experience in rigid terms of success or failure may be setting herself up for unnecessary disappointment and guilt. But does that make it better not to try at all? A mother who approaches the feeding of her baby with an open-minded, relaxed "let's-try-it-and-see-if-it-works" attitude, is likely to develop a good feeding relationship with her child, whether she ultimately feeds by breast or bottle.

## How Breastmilk Is Made

Each breast is composed of 15 to 20 lobes, or groups, of glandular tissue surrounded by fat and separated from the ribs and chest muscles by a layer of connective tissue. Only the milk gland lobes are involved in the production of milk. The fat, muscles, and connective tissue that determine breast size play no role. *A woman's ability to produce milk, therefore, has nothing at all to do with the size of her breasts.*

Doug Edwards

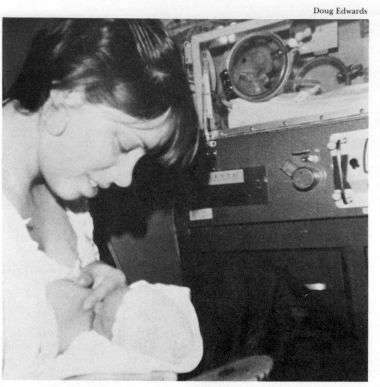

*Gayla Edwards found breast-feeding to be a "beautiful closeness."*

The breasts begin to change quite early in pregnancy as increased circulation and hormonal stimulation cause swelling and tenderness. In the early months of pregnancy, drops of *colostrum* (the clear yellowish milk meant to nourish the baby after delivery) may be secreted by cells in the milk glands, but full milk production does not begin until after the baby is born.

Sometime during the second or third day following delivery, most new mothers experience a sudden increase in breast size as their milk "comes in." This first engorgement represents not only the accumulation of milk, but also increased blood flow and tissue swelling as the breasts prepare for full-scale milk production. Breast size declines after a week or two. *This is normal and does not mean the milk has disappeared. As long as the breasts are regularly emptied, milk continues to be produced.*

The lobes of glandular tissue where milk is made resemble stalks of broccoli. At the end are tiny bud-like clusters called *alveoli.* The alveoli are in close contact with the capillaries in the breast. When stimulated by the milk-producing hormone *prolactin,*

*For Kathy Swinbank Laurie, breast-feeding was "uncomfortable, exhausting, and generally a nuisance."*

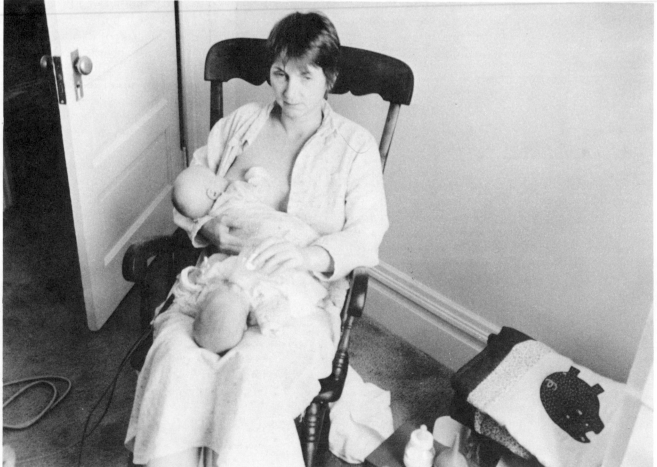

Bill Laurie

the cells in the alveoli extract nutrients from the mother's blood and turn them into milk. Muscle-like *contractile cells* squeeze the milk down into a channel of ducts that lead to collection areas behind the nipple. Each collection area opens into the nipple.

The first type of milk to be produced is the yellowish colostrum, rich in nutrients and antibodies. Within a week or two the milk changes and takes on a watery, bluish-white color, although the color may vary from time to time depending on the mother's diet. Green vegetables, for example, may give the milk a greenish cast. These color variations are normal.

The breasts produce milk in response to regular stimulation and emptying. Sucking-type stimulation to the nipple sends nerve impulses to the pituitary gland in the brain, which releases prolactin. When no stimulation or emptying of the breasts occurs, milk production generally stops within two to four weeks. Nevertheless, some women who have never pumped, expressed, or nursed are able to relactate (bring the milk back in) months after delivery. There are even women who have never been pregnant who have been able to induce lactation through a regular program of sucking-type stimulation. During the Middle Ages, grandmothers, well past childbearing age, often worked as wet nurses. To maintain their milk supply between jobs, they nursed newborn puppies!

The amount of milk the breasts produce is directly related to the amount demanded. Mothers of twins and other multiples may be reassured to know that centuries ago a single wet nurse often breast-fed as many as six babies. The limiting factor was the time involved, not the woman's milk supply. Extra sucking, expressing, or pumping (even when no milk is coming out) encourages the breasts to produce more next time. Adequate rest,* a good diet (at least 300 more calories than you needed during pregnancy), and plenty of fluids also help produce abundant, high-quality milk. Antihistamines can interfere with milk production and should be avoided while you are nursing. Birth control pills also decrease your milk supply and they should not be taken during the time you are expressing or breast-feeding. However, be sure to use another reliable form of birth control. Contrary to the popular myth, you *can* get pregnant while nursing.

*While most mothers we interviewed said that stress and fatigue interfered with their milk supply, there were two mothers who found just the opposite to be true. Said one mother, "Maybe I'm wired backwards or something, but the days when I was sick with worry or exhausted from lack of sleep were the days when I pumped the most. Everyone said it was impossible, but that's how it happened."

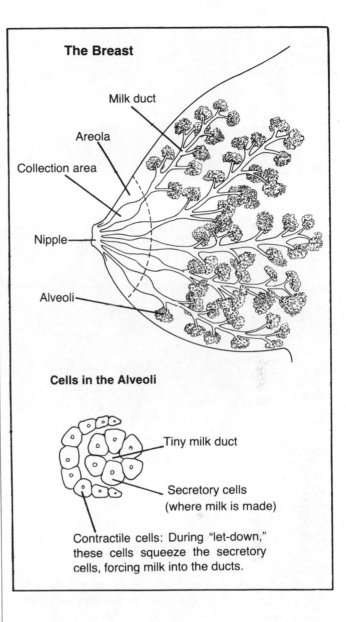

Some mothers find that brewer's yeast, imported beer (made with brewer's yeast), or B and C vitamin supplements help improve their milk supply. Nevertheless, mothers who are pumping or hand-expressing often find that their supply temporarily drops off. No matter how good the pump, or how well the mother expresses, nothing can empty the breasts as efficiently as a strongly sucking baby

A few mothers we interviewed nursed a friend's full-term baby to help keep up their supply or simply to become familiar with the process of nursing. If you wish to "cross-nurse" a friend's baby, check with your neonatologist and be sure both your friend and her baby are in good health. Since nursing is such a personal relationship, cross-nursing does not appeal to everyone. "Although I was glad to have the experience," one mother said, "I felt I was being unfaithful

Nao Noguchi

*Kathie Noguchi with the triplets at mealtime. Mothers of multiples may be reassured to know that wet nurses centuries ago produced milk for as many as six babies at once.*

to my baby." Some women have their husbands suck at their breasts to stimulate milk production. In *The Nursling,* written in 1907, Dr. Pierre Budin reported that mothers at his nursery successfully used this technique to keep up their milk supply.

The method you choose to express your milk—hand expression or the use of the various types of breast pumps—may influence the amount of milk you produce. Experiment to see what works best for you.

Pumping schedules also affect milk production. Again, this varies with the individual. Some mothers we interviewed pumped every 3 to 4 hours day and night. Others found that a full night's sleep made them more productive during the day. Some mothers who went on to total breast-feeding pumped only 3 times during a 24-hour period; others needed to pump 6 to 8 times a day to maintain a good supply.

## The Let-Down Response

In order for the breasts to be properly emptied, the milk must first "let down." Let-down occurs when the hundreds of contractile cells squeeze the milk-producing cells to force the drops into the ducts and down into the collection areas behind the nipples. The mother feels this squeezing as a tingling, tightening, needles-and-pins sensation in her breasts. As the tingling begins, the milk may let down with such force that it drips rapidly or sprays from both nipples.

The let-down reflex is caused by the hormone *oxytocin,* which is released by the pituitary gland in the brain in response to stimulation. The stimulation can be physical (sucking, expressing, pumping) or it can be psychological. Some women experience the let-down reflex just by thinking about their baby or by hearing a baby cry.

The let-down response can also be slowed or stopped by physical or psychological means. Some women find the use of mechanical breast pumps to be "a real turn-off" and their let-down responses are much harder to elicit than if they were nursing a live, warm baby. Stress, fatigue, pain, and anxiety can all interfere with let-down. Since these physical and emotional discomforts are facts of life for mothers of premature infants, it is hardly surprising that many have problems getting their milk down and out. Some mothers erroneously feel that their milk has dried up when the let-down reflex has been inhibited by stress: "After a month of pumping I was finally told I should pump milk to be given directly to Michael. I was so freaked out that I dried up completely that same night."

Several mothers told of psychological strategies they used to get their milk flowing freely. Some would call the nursery before expressing or would look at their baby's picture as they pumped. Said one mother, "When I was especially tired and upset and getting only drops of milk, I would think of Emily and imagine her little tongue lapping up the drops. Before I knew it, the drops became streams."

Following a fixed routine before and during expression also helps a mother to establish the let-down reflex. Kittie Frantz, nurse practitioner and lactation counselor, tells of advising an actress on expression techniques following the birth of her premature baby. The actress was filming on location and had to express quickly during her breaks. She and Kittie worked out a ritual that involved the drinking of a large glass of apple juice before expressing. The technique was so successful that the actress began having a let-down response whenever she so much as looked at a bottle of apple juice. To her embarrassment, this would happen even in the middle of a crowded supermarket!

A back rub before expressing may help. Some people claim that there are nerve endings located between the shoulder blades that can stimulate the let-down response when massaged. (This point on the back is well known to acupuncturists.)

A mother who is having real problems establishing a let-down response should ask her doctor for a prescription for oxytocin nasal spray. Although the spray does not directly increase milk production, it does encourage the let-down reflex, allowing the mother to empty her breasts; this in turn stimulates the production of more milk. The spray does not harm the milk, the mother, or the baby, although some women experience nausea if they use too much. Short-term use of the spray—several days to a week— can help a woman break the cycle of failure and frustration by demonstrating that her milk really can let down. The danger comes in relying on the spray as a crutch. Use of the spray for longer than the recommended period may diminish its effects and actually interfere with let-down and milk production.

A warm bath before expressing or pumping, a glass of wine or beer can also help a woman relax and experience let-down more easily. However, large quantities of alcohol can interfere with the response, as can tobacco.

## Expressing Your Milk

As soon as possible, notify your baby's neonatologist that you wish to supply your child with *your* milk. Discuss with the neonatologist (not with the obstetrician, regular pediatrician, or nurse) any health problems you have and *any* medications you are taking—anything from aspirin to antibiotics. Some drugs will have no effect on the baby, others may. Let the neonatologist determine this. If you must take medication, the medicine you take can sometimes be switched to a type that will not adversely affect the baby. Review your diet with the neonatologist. Certain substances such as caffeine or chocolate may not be good for your baby.

Each nursery has its own set of guidelines on expressing, collecting, storing, and transporting milk to be given to a premature baby. The goal is to provide the baby with the freshest, most sterile milk possible. The suggestions given in this chapter should be modified, if necessary, to conform to your neonatologist's recommendations.

Milk is generally sterile when it leaves the breast, and precautions should be taken to avoid contaminating the milk with bacteria. Contamination can come from several sources—from the external breast, from your hands, from the collection container, and most importantly, from the breast pump.

We strongly suggest that you try hand expression (rather than a breast pump) for the following reasons:

1. done properly, hand expression is the most sterile method of breastmilk collection
2. it dispenses with cumbersome equipment that must be constantly sterilized
3. it is easy, costs nothing, and can be done anywhere
4. it is much less painful for most women than the use of pumps.

## Breast Pumps

Although we feel that hand expression is the best method for supplying milk to a premature baby, many women prefer breast pumps. There are a variety of types, brands, and models for sale or for rent. We have tried the pumps listed below and evaluated them for comfort, convenience, cost, and efficiency. Note: The manufacturer's instructions on cleaning or sterilizing the pump may not be sufficient to achieve the level of sterility necessary when supplying milk to

## How to Hand Express Your Milk

Assemble:

a) a warm, wet towel (optional)
b) a stack of clean paper towels
c) soap
d) a nail brush (which you buy and use only for this purpose)
e) a sterile container of the type recommended by your nursery
f) a sterilized funnel (optional)

1. Place the warm, wet towel over your breasts for five minutes. This may help open the ducts and allow the milk to flow more easily. Next, massage your breasts by firmly pressing with the heel of your hand beginning on the chest wall surrounding each breast and pushing toward the nipple. The warm towel and massage are optional. Use only if they work for you.
2. Wash your hands thoroughly with soap and hot running water. Scrub your nails with the nail brush.
3. Wash your breasts with warm water and pat dry with a clean paper towel.
4. Wash your hands again, and rewash whenever you touch anything other than your breast.
5. Remove the lid from the sterile container, touching only the outside of the container and the lid. Place the lid upside down on a clean, dry paper towel. Rewash your hands. If your milk has a tendency to spray, you may wish to place a funnel (which you have sterilized) into the container to help catch stray droplets. Touch only the outer rim of the funnel. Rewash hands.
6. Supporting the breast from below with your fingers, place your thumb above the areola (the brown area surrounding your nipple) and squeeze with a gentle scissor-like motion. Some women get more milk using massage movements (see step 1) or by rolling their fingers behind the areola. Experiment. Avoid touching the areola or nipple as you express directly into the funnel or container. Reposition your hands frequently around the areola as you express so that you exert pressure on all the milk ducts. At first, you may just get drops, and it may take time (as long as ten minutes) before the let-down reflex occurs. Relax and try not to be discouraged.
7. After you have emptied one breast, express from the other. Then return to the first breast for a second time. Changing back and forth like this gives the milk more time to come down the ducts. It also stimulates further milk production. Total expression time should not exceed 30 minutes; 15 to 20 minutes is often sufficient.
8. Put the lid on the container. Label the container with your name, date, and time of expression. Refrigerate or freeze the milk immediately.

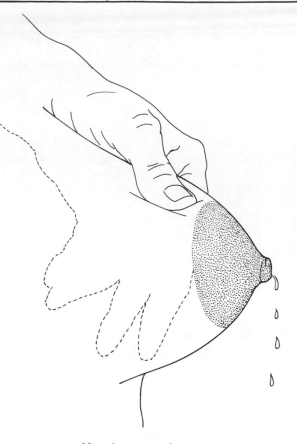

**Hand expression**

## Sterilizing Collection Utensils

Utensils that come into direct contact with your milk such as containers, funnels, or breast pump parts must be sterile. To sterilize:

1. Wash and rinse utensils thoroughly. Place them in a large pot of cold water. To prevent breakage, wrap glass utensils in clean cloths.
2. Place a pair of tongs in the pot to sterilize. Prop the tongs so that the top is out of the water and you can retrieve them without touching and contaminating the water. The tongs will be used to remove the sterilized utensils. *Or:* Place the utensils in a large strainer or colander, which you put in the pot of water in a double-boiler arrangement. (Be sure all utensils are submerged in the boiling water.) You may then lift the strainer or colander to remove the utensils easily once they are sterilized.
3. Cover the pot if possible. Heat water and boil for 15 to 20 minutes.
4. Remove pot from heat. Keep covered and allow to cool. Using tongs, remove the utensils and allow them to drain on clean paper towels. *Or:* Remove strainer or colander from the water and allow utensils to drain.
5. You may use the sterilized utensils immediately (any water on them should be sterile) or you may allow them to air dry.

## How to Store and Transport Your Milk

1. Whenever possible pump or express in the nursery to supply your baby with your fresh milk.

2. At home, mark all milk containers with the date and time the milk was expressed. If the milk is to be given to your baby within 24 hours, refrigerate it immediately; otherwise, freeze it immediately.

3. Frozen milk must stay *frozen solid* until the time it is used. In a deep freeze or a separate freezer compartment on your refrigerator, your milk can be stored (if frozen solid) for 2 to 3 months. An ice cube compartment inside your refrigerator may not be cold enough to freeze your milk for long-term storage. If your ice compartment is not cold enough to keep ice cream frozen and hard, discuss how to store your milk with the neonatologist.

4. Do not freeze your milk in layers. That is, do not add freshly expressed milk to milk already frozen. This may cause the previously frozen milk to thaw. It increases the risk of contamination.

5. See if your nursery permits the storage of milk in plastic nurser bags or baggies. Plastic bags are manufactured under such high heat that they are considered to be sterile when first opened. You may express directly into the bag or pour your milk into the bag from the sterile container in which you collected it. Be sure the bag is fastened securely with a twist-tie and labeled with a piece of tape giving time and date of expression. Plastic bags take up much less room in the freezer than bottles.

6. Bring refrigerated or frozen milk to the nursery well packed in ice in an ice chest. Cool the ice chest in advance. Reusable freeze packs, available in most hardware or camping goods stores, are helpful. Stuff any empty spaces in the ice chest with newspaper for extra insulation. If the milk thaws or becomes slushy en route, it should be given to the baby within 24 hours.

7. If bringing in a large amount of milk, notify the nursery first. One mother, who learned this lesson the hard way, wrote: "I would send my milk to the nursery only to find that they had no place to store it all. The excess was poured down the drain. Talk about crying over spilt milk!"

8. When thawing the milk, do so slowly in lukewarm water. The use of hot water to thaw or warm the milk quickly can destroy some of the milk's disease-fighting properties.

a premature baby. Discuss your choice of breast pump with your neonatologist and review cleaning and sterilizing procedures. In general, any part, or surface of a part, that comes into contact with your milk must be thoroughly scrubbed, rinsed, and sterilized before each use. Prices listed for breast pumps and other items are subject to change. Contact the manufacturer before ordering.

### Fully Automatic Electric Breast Pumps

*The AXicare Automatic Breast Pump CM 10*
distributed by:
Neonatal Corporation
One Blue Hill Plaza
Pearl River, New York 10965
(914) 735-5075

*The Egnell Electric Breast Pump*
distributed by:
Egnell, Inc.
765 Industrial Drive
Cary, Illinois 60013
(800) 323-8750

*The Medela Breastpump*
distributed by:
Medela, Inc.
457 Dartmoor Drive
P.O. Box 386
Crystal Lake, Illinois 60014
(800) 435-8316

Automatic electric breast pumps are often available for use in the hospital. Although many women use the same pump, each woman is supplied with her own glass or plastic accessories. These are the only parts of the pump that come into direct contact with her milk. If they are cleaned and sterilized before each use, the sterility of the milk can be well maintained.

Mothers can rent electric pumps for home use through special rental depots—medical supply companies, hospital pharmacies, La Leche League chapters or from individual suppliers. Call the pump's national distributor for the rental depot nearest you. Rental fees vary from supplier to supplier, so call around. Generally, there is an initial charge of $10.00 or more for the purchase of an individual accessory kit, plus *daily* rental fees for the pump that may range from $1.50 to $3.00. Some insurance policies cover this expense.

Fully automatic pumps work by creating a natural suck-relax-suck-relax rhythm that closely approximates the sucking action of a nursing baby. When

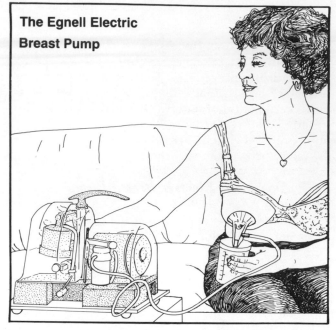

The Egnell Electric Breast Pump

using the pump, the mother need only hold the breast cup over her nipple. Otherwise, she is free to relax, read, watch television, or close her eyes and think about her baby.

*Comments:* Because they are comfortable, effective, easy to use and sterilize, we consider *fully* automatic breast pumps to be the best choice for supplying milk to a hospitalized premature infant. A major drawback to these pumps is the high rental cost. The pumps are also heavy and not easily portable. They all require a 3-pronged electrical outlet or an adapter. We found the AXicare, the Egnell, and the Medela equally comfortable and effective. Our personal favorite is the AXicare CM 10, which, at 11 pounds, is the lightest of the automatic pumps. It is also the most compact and attractive (similar to the Axicare CM 6 pictured on page 163).

## Semi-Automatic Electric Breast Pumps

*The AXicare CM 6*
distributed by:
Neonatal Corporation
One Blue Hill Plaza
Pearl River, New York 10965
(914) 735-5075

*The GOMCO Breast Pump*
distributed by:
GOMCO Division
Allied Healthcare Products, Inc.
878 East Ferry Street
Buffalo, New York 14211
(716) 894-6678

These pumps create suction that the mother controls by sliding her finger over an air hole on the collection container. There are settings on the pumps to allow variations in the level of suction. Use of these pumps requires somewhat more effort and concentration than the use of fully automatic pumps, but they are still easier to operate than most non-electric pumps. They require 3-pronged electrical outlets or adapters. Semi-automatic pumps are also available at rental depots at prices similar to those of the fully automatic pumps. The AXicare CM 6 can be purchased for around $235.00.

Of the two semi-automatic pumps we tried, we definitely preferred the AXicare CM 6. At 4½ pounds, it is easily portable. It is a very attractive pump and it is comfortable to use. The GOMCO semi-automatic we tested created an uncomfortably strong suction even at the lowest pressure setting. (GOMCO will soon offer a new pump—model 218—with the option of automatic or semi-automatic control.)

### Cylinder Pumps

Cylinder pumps are hand-operated. Suction is created by sliding the pump's two cylinders back and forth. These pumps are sold under such brand names as *Kaneson, Marshall,* and *Happy Family.* We tested the Happy Family Breast Milking and Feeding Unit from Happy Family Products, 12300 Venice Blvd., Los Angeles, California 90066. Call (800) 228-2028 to order the pump and charge it to your Visa or Mastercard. The pump costs $25.70 for orders outside California. Inside the state, the price is $27.14. Cylinder-type breast pumps are also available in some pharmacies for prices ranging from $25.00 to $30.00.

*Comments:* We found this to be an effective, comfortable pump. Suction pressure is easy to control. Parts are easy to clean and sterilize. The pump is light and portable. About 4 ounces of milk can be collected before the cylinder must be emptied.

### The Loyd-B Pump

The *Loyd-B pump,* a hand powered pump with glass parts, is available from certain medical supply houses and from the manufacturer, Lopuco, Ltd., 1615 Old Annapolis Road, Woodbine, Maryland 21797, (301) 489-4949. The pump can be ordered by mail—enclose check for $40.00 payable to Lopuco, Ltd.—or by phone. The pump is $43.00 COD. It is shipped the day the order is received.

*Comments:* The pump applies powerful suction that is difficult for a woman with small hands to regulate properly. Result: sore hands, sore nipples. The

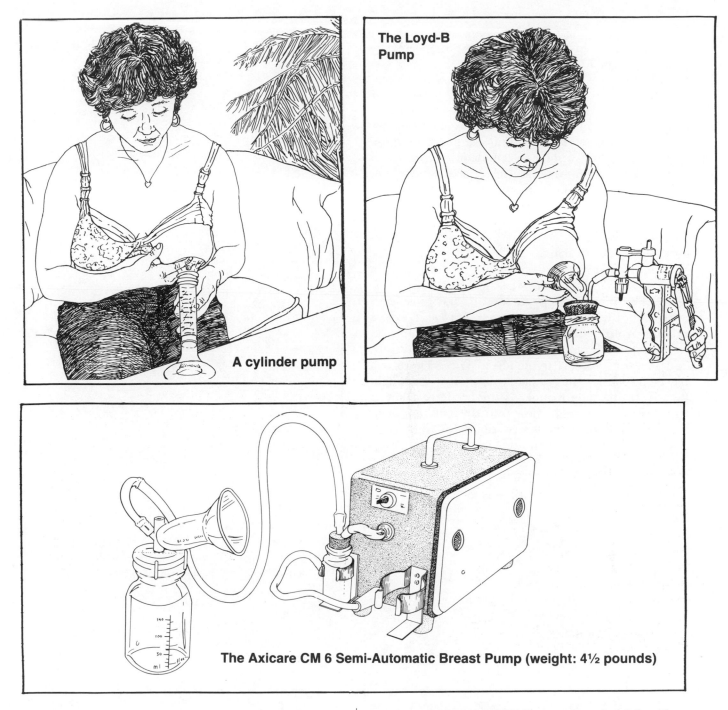

**A cylinder pump**

**The Loyd-B Pump**

**The Axicare CM 6 Semi-Automatic Breast Pump (weight: 4½ pounds)**

rubber stoppers on the models we used began to disintegrate rather rapidly, leaving flecks of rubber in the collected milk. Nevertheless, many women use this pump successfully.

### Bulb Pumps

These are hand-operated pumps. Suction is created by squeezing and releasing a bulb.

*Le Pump breast pump and infant nurser* is available for around $20.00 from drug stores and medical supply companies. Contact the distributor, Scientific Cor-

poration, 855-D Conklin Street, Farmingdale, New York 11735, (800) 645-9066, for the stores in your area that carry Le Pump.

*Comments:* We found Le Pump to be effective, comfortable, easy to use and to clean. Although it is more expensive than the other bulb pumps, we feel it is far superior to them in quality.

The *Evenflow Natural Mother Breast Pump* is a hand-operated bulb pump attachable to a bottle or baby food jar. It is widely available in drug and department stores for around $5.00.

*Comments:* Although some mothers use this pump

successfully, we found it virtually impossible to achieve proper suction.

*"Bicycle horn"–type breast pumps* are widely available in drug and department stores for around $5.00.

*Comments:* We do not recommend this type of pump. Only ¼ ounce of milk can be collected before the pump must be emptied. This is a nuisance. More importantly, the constant manipulations involved in emptying the pump increase the risk of contaminating the milk. The milk also has a tendency to flow back into the bulb and become contaminated. The pump is difficult to clean properly.

### The Ora'Lac Pump

The *Ora'Lac Pump* is available for $30.00 from Ora'Lac, Box 137, Sitka, Alaska 99835, (907) 747-3434. The mother sucks on one of the tubes connected to the plastic collection bottle to create a vacuum around the nipple. We found this pump awkward to use. It is quite flimsy. The bottle tipped easily, and the tubes had a tendency to kink. There is a plastic trap inside the bottle to collect saliva that might flow from the mouth tube. If the bottle tips, and it easily can, saliva might flow into the milk and contaminate it. Because of the possibility of contamination, we do not recommend this pump.

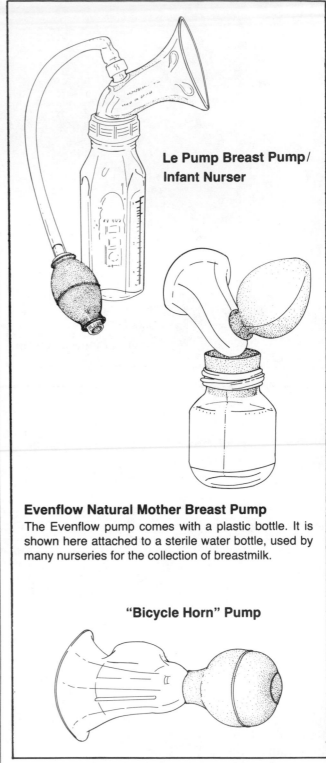

**Le Pump Breast Pump/ Infant Nurser**

**Evenflow Natural Mother Breast Pump**
The Evenflow pump comes with a plastic bottle. It is shown here attached to a sterile water bottle, used by many nurseries for the collection of breastmilk.

**"Bicycle Horn" Pump**

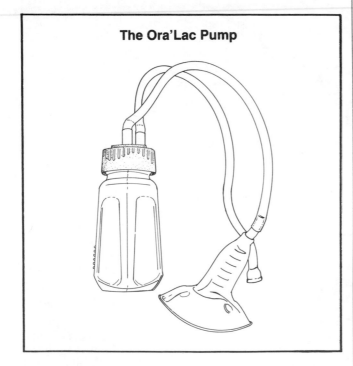

**The Ora'Lac Pump**

*Note:* The purchase or rental of a breast pump can be very expensive. Ask your doctor to write a prescription for the pump so that your insurance can help with the cost.

## Special Problems

There are certain problems, most of them temporary, that may keep you from being able to supply milk to your baby or that may interfere with your ability to nurse comfortably and easily.

### High Bacteria Count in the Milk

Although milk is theoretically sterile when it leaves the breast, it can become contaminated by bacteria on the skin (you can't sterilize your breasts) and from other sources. Doctors sometimes culture a mother's milk to see if the bacterial count is too high to be safe for the baby. Every nursery has its own ideas about what bacterial count is too high. Some nurseries do not do cultures on the assumption that the baby has already been exposed to the mother's bacteria, and that bacteria ingested by the baby are probably killed by acids in his stomach.

If your milk has a high bacteria count, review with the neonatologists the procedures you are using to express, collect, store, and transport the milk. You might also try discarding the first ¼ ounce you express from each breast, since most skin bacteria will be in these first drops of milk.

If the bacteria count of your milk is still high (or if you have an actual breast infection), you can be treated with antibiotics.

If none of these suggestions work, remember that this is a temporary problem resulting from the doctors' wish to be extra cautious with a tiny baby. It does not mean your milk is bad for your baby. Keep pumping. Once the baby is home, you can nurse.

### Breastmilk Intolerance

Whenever a breastmilk-fed baby develops digestive upsets, doctors tend to blame the mother's milk. If your baby's doctor asks you to stop bringing in your milk, ask him to check for other causes of the baby's problem first. If the doctor insists, rest assured that this intolerance is temporary. Keep pumping. Your baby will eventually tolerate your milk, and you can still breast-feed.

### If You Are Ill or Taking Medication

If you become sick while supplying milk to your baby, it is possible to transmit the illness to the baby in your milk. Inform the neonatologist of your illness, and of any medications you are taking for it. And keep pumping your milk. Once you have recovered, you can supply milk to your baby.

If you are taking magnesium sulfate for toxemia, or pain medication following a cesarean section, do not supply milk to your baby until you have been off the medication for 24 to 48 hours, but keep pumping anyway.

Diabetic mothers who wish to breast-feed may need special monitoring during lactation to help keep their insulin levels properly regulated. While fluctuating insulin or blood sugar levels will not harm the quality of the milk, they may harm the mother. But with special attention to diet and insulin needs, diabetic mothers can nurse.

### Breastmilk Jaundice (See Chapter 5, page 86)

### Clogged Ducts and Breast Infection (Mastitis)

Breast infection (mastitis) and clogged milk ducts that are not infected can produce red, inflamed, very painful lumps in the breast. Fever may or may not be present. Hot compresses and aspirin or Tylenol help alleviate the pain. Antibiotics are prescribed for mastitis. *Emptying the breasts regularly* is important to help open the ducts and relieve pain and pressure. If you are supplying milk to your premature in the hospital, tell the neonatologist. Your milk may need to be cultured. If you develop a breast infection at home while you are nursing, there is no need to stop nursing. The baby has probably been exposed to the infectious organism already. In fact, *he* probably gave the infection to *you*.

### Thrush (See Chapter 5, page 91)

If your baby develops thrush, it may spread to your nipples and cause extreme tenderness. The baby whose mouth is very sore from this fungus infection may not want to suck. Thrush is common among intensive care graduates who have received antibiotics. It can be treated—both you and your baby must be treated—with applications of nystatin (Mycostatin), an anti-fungal drug. During the treatment, you must be very careful to sterilize any pacifier or bottle nipples the baby is using, or any other objects the baby puts in his mouth, to avoid reinfection.

### Sore Nipples

Many mothers who express and/or nurse have sore nipples in the beginning. This problem can even afflict those mothers who have carefully prepared and "toughened" their nipples. One mother, who breast-fed her first child right up until the delivery of her second child, found that she developed sore nipples anyway, once her new baby began to nurse. Sore nipples usually go away in 4 to 6 weeks.

Meanwhile, exposing the nipples to air and sunlight helps some mothers. Plastic nursing cups, such as the Netsy Milk Cup or the AXicare Nursing Shell, that cover the nipples without touching them, help alleviate the pain caused by clothing rubbing against the nipples. However, plastic nursing cups should be used for this purpose only when absolutely necessary, and then only briefly. This is because moisture from leaking milk accumulates in the cups, and *sore, cracked nipples do not heal properly if they are kept overly moist.* Therefore, *do not* slather your sore nipples with breast creams. In fact, never use anything on your breasts that you must wash off before you nurse. Anhydrous lanolin, vegetable oil, or pure vitamin E (from capsules) may be used in moderation to keep the skin on your nipples supple. These substances do not need to be washed off before nursing. When using vegetable oil or vitamin E oil, be sure the oil is fresh. Rancid oil could make your baby sick. Smell the oil. Fresh oil does not have a strong odor. If you use vitamin E, buy the capsules in small quantities from a drug store that has a rapid turnover. Keep the capsules refrigerated. Before applying the oil to your nipples, prick a capsule with a sterile needle, squeeze out a few droplets, and smell the oil to be sure it is not rancid. When in doubt, do not use it. If the oil seems fresh, squeeze the contents of the capsule directly onto your nipple.

Breast pumps—especially hand pumps or semiautomatic electric pumps—can cause soreness by applying too great a suction pressure to the nipples. Try switching to a fully automatic breast pump, or, better yet, try hand expression.

Lactation counselor Kittie Frantz has found that a baby's improper sucking technique is a major cause of nipple soreness. She suggests that mothers be sure the baby's gums are coming down on the areola, and not directly on the nipple itself. (However, it is not necessary, or always possible, for the baby to take the entire areola into his mouth.) If the baby is sucking on his tongue or on his lower lip while nursing, this too can create a painful type of suction on the nipple. If the baby's tongue is not where it should be (below the nipple, and between the nipple and the lower lip) or if the baby is sucking in his lower lip as he nurses, take the baby off the nipple, reposition the nipple correctly in his mouth and try again. (For more information, see "Managing Nipple Problems" by Kittie Frantz, R.N., C.P.N.P., La Leche League Reprint No. 11, March, 1982.)

### Flat or Inverted Nipples

It is thought that flat or inverted nipples are caused by shortened connective tissue within the nipple. The nipples usually stretch out if they are frequently pulled or rolled. A strongly nursing baby usually pulls the nipple out; so can an electric breast pump. Some mothers use plastic nursing cups or breast shells that apply gentle pressure around the nipple and encourage the nipple to stand out.

# Bottle-feeding in the Hospital and at Home

At about 34 weeks' gestational age, a premature who is healthy (or recovering) may show signs of readiness to nipple-feed. By now the baby may have a strong rooting reflex—if his cheek is touched, he turns and "roots" around in search of a nipple. The baby may gag on the gavage tube and he may suck on the tube while he is being fed. The appearance of the gag reflex and a strengthening suck are indications that the baby is ready to try a nipple.

Occasionally, a premature is ready to nurse directly at the breast as soon as gavage feedings are stopped. Usually, however, there is a lag between the time the baby has aquired his gag reflex—and can no longer be comfortably fed by gavage—and the time the baby is strong enough to meet his nutritional needs at the breast. For this reason, although the baby may receive his mother's milk, his first nipplefeedings are usually given by bottle.*

Parents who wish to give their baby the first nipple-feeding should inform the staff well in advance so that the feeding can take place during their visit.

The baby's first nipple-feedings of breastmilk or formula are usually given in small 45-milliliter plastic bottles equipped with special soft blue or red premie nipples. The baby often reacts to his first pull on the nipple with a combination of shock and pleasant surprise. As he gets his first real taste of milk, his eyes may widen as if to say "so this is what it's all about!" He may be so delighted or startled by the experience that he forgets to breathe. Or he may forget to swallow, allowing the milk to drool down his chin or go down the wrong pipe. If the baby turns dusky, gags, or chokes, stop the feeding and give him time to recover. It takes time and practice for the suck-swallow-breathe sequence to become automatic to him.

While the baby is still developing these skills, his sessions with the bottle (or breast) are supplemented by gavage feedings. Slowly, over a period of days or weeks, as the baby begins to suck well and gain weight, the gavage feedings are phased out until the baby is totally nipple-feeding.

Nipple-feeding a premature baby takes time and patience. It is not at all unusual for a tiny baby to take half an hour or longer to drink as little as 15 cc's (½ ounce). He may suck several times, stop, and need to

*Mothers may also try using the Lact-Aid Nursing Supplementer (see page 170) that allows a weakly sucking baby to nurse at the breast while still receiving adequate nourishment. (A few nurseries gavage-feed babies up until the time they are ready to feed from the breast.)

be coaxed into resuming his efforts with a gentle upward push on the bottom of his chin or by slowly rotating the nipple in his mouth.

Calm handling and a peaceful environment help the baby devote his full attention to the business at hand. In the hospital, you might want to take your baby to the breast-feeding room or to another private area. At home, a quiet, semidarkened room may be the best place to feed. This is not the time to talk to the baby or play with him. Even full-term babies stop sucking if they are talked to; most are not ready to eat and socialize at the same time until they are well past four months of age.

The baby will be easier to feed if his meals take place when he is awake and active. Although many nurseries awaken babies for regularly scheduled feedings, doctors have found that when prematures are fed on demand (i.e., when they become active), they take more food, digest it better, and gain more weight.

Another factor to consider is the type of nipple you are using. Some babies prefer the very soft, short

*Nippling.*

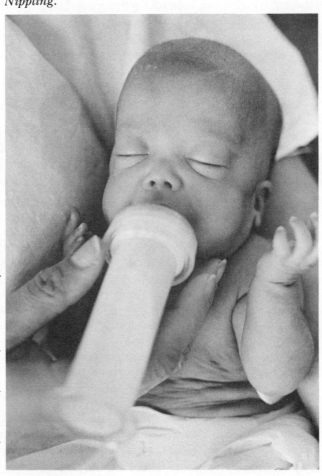

Dorothy Larimer Boyd, courtesy of Children's Hospital Medical Center of Northern California

blue premie nipple. Others do better with the longer red nipple; still others may like the regular firm yellow nipple. Once the baby is home, you can experiment with the variety of differently shaped nipples that are commercially available to see which he prefers. The baby who has a weak suck may also want a larger hole in his nipple. To enlarge the nipple hole, heat a large sewing needle over a flame and pass it through the nipple hole. To keep the nipple hole widened, put toothpicks in the holes after the nipples have been washed. When enlarging nipple holes, do not overdo it. Too fast a flow may cause the baby to choke.

The temperature of the milk can also make a difference. While many babies happily take formula or breastmilk straight out of the refrigerator or at room temperature, others may prefer their bottles slightly warmed.

When bottle-feeding your baby, try to offer the bottle with your left hand at one feeding and with your right hand at another. This way the baby alternates positions the same way he would if breast-feeding, and he is encouraged to use both sides of his body.

Sometime during the middle of the feeding and again at the end, the baby needs his back rubbed or patted to help bring up any air he may have swallowed. A good way to "burp" a tiny baby is to sit him up in your lap so that he leans slightly forward, supported by one of your hands. With the other hand, rub or pat his back firmly. But be careful; too vigorous patting can bring up his meal as well as the air.

In the hospital, prematures are usually fed every two or three hours, with feedings timed from the beginning of one meal to the beginning of the next. Feedings should not last longer than 40 minutes. Otherwise, feedings start to overlap. Don't worry if the baby takes much less at one feeding than he does at another. This is normal. The baby's *total* calorie intake and weight gain matter more than what he takes at any one meal. Let the baby decide how much he wants. A baby who is forced to eat more than he can handle often vomits.

If the baby is on a special formula such as SMA 24 or PM 60-40, he is usually switched to a commercially available formula like Similac or Isomil several days before discharge. This is to be sure that he is doing well on the new formula before he goes home. Many formulas require the addition of water. Discuss with the neonatologist your use of tap water to make the baby's formula. Usually plain tap water is safe. But if you live in a rural area and your water comes from a well, you may need to have the water tested by the Public Health Department for bacteria and other contaminants (especially nitrites) before you use it in the baby's formula. Boiling the water for 20 minutes kills any bacteria present.

Unless your doctor advises differently, bottles and nipples need not be sterilized once the baby is home. Wash these items in a dishwasher or by hand in hot soapy water. Rinse and dry thoroughly.

Do not give your baby any bottles of formula (or breastmilk) that have been out of the refrigerator longer than four hours. Bacteria grow very rapidly at room temperature.

## How Much Does the Baby Need?

The number of calories a baby needs to grow depends on his health, activity level, and individual metabolism. Some babies grow well on as few as 90 calories per kilogram (2.2 pounds) of body weight per day; others may need as many as 180 calories per kilo. Generally, babies require between 120 and 150 calories per kilo per day. This means that a baby who weighs one kilo—approximately 2 pounds, 3 ounces—needs about 6 or 7½ ounces of formula or breastmilk (at 20 calories per ounce) every day. A baby who weighs two kilos—close to 4 pounds, 7 ounces—usually needs double that amount of breastmilk or formula, or 12 to 15 ounces per day.

Once the baby is nipple-feeding, doctors like to see an average daily weight gain of 14 to 28 grams (½ to 1 ounce). The baby seldom gains weight at this rate every single day. There may be several days of no weight gain at all followed by a great leap forward. This ½ to 1 ounce per day *average* weight gain should continue for the first two to three months after the baby's due date. After that, weight gain generally occurs at a slower pace.

When a premature baby in the nursery is not gaining well on nipple-feedings, doctors often add high-calorie supplements to the milk (or switch to a higher-calorie formula) rather than increase the *volume* of the feedings. This is because too much fluid volume can create circulatory overload, which can cause the baby's ductus to reopen. Except for babies still recovering from bronchopulmonary dysplasia, such restrictions are generally not necessary once the baby is ready to go home.

At home, parents sometimes find that the baby wants a much different feeding schedule from the one established in the nursery: "My (four-pound, six-ounce) daughter was awake all night nursing every half-hour. Then she slept without nursing most of the day. I didn't know how long I could let her go at a stretch without feeding her."

Parents often wonder if the baby should be awakened for feedings. There is no one recommendation that applies to every baby. If the baby is gaining well (and this little girl was gaining a hefty two ounces a day!), the baby probably does not need to be awakened for extra feedings. However, *many physicians feel that a baby under seven pounds should not go for longer than five hours without being fed and that the baby should have only one such five-hour stretch during a given 24 hours.* Discuss this with your neonatologist and your pediatrician.

In general, babies eat and gain better if they are fed when they want to eat—according to demand. But compromises must be made with the parents' need to sleep at night. Waking the baby a half-hour to an hour earlier than usual from long daytime naps may increase the baby's awake time during the day and ease the baby into a more reasonable routine.

A breast-feeding baby usually increases his feedings automatically by sucking longer at each feeding or demanding more frequent feedings to build up his mother's milk supply. When a bottle-fed baby finishes his bottle quickly (in 10 rather than 20 to 30 minutes) and still seems willing to eat, start adding an extra ounce or two to his bottles.

## From Bottle to Breast

Many physicians feel that when the baby is sucking well enough to take most of his feedings by bottle (rather than by gavage), the baby is also strong enough to begin having sessions at the breast. A baby who has become used to the bottle is sometimes reluctant to make the switch. Sucking from the breast requires a different mouth action and a good deal more effort than sucking from a bottle, and the premature baby may approach this new challenge the same way he approaches other novel events in his life—by turning dusky or falling asleep. Many prematures take days, even weeks, before they finally learn how to nurse. Meanwhile, patience and frequent practice are advised.

Relaxed surroundings are important. Most nurseries have a breast-feeding room where you can nurse your baby in privacy. If the baby is still on monitors, IVs, or oxygen, you might ask that a screen be put around your baby's bed for privacy. Sit in an armchair or rocker in a position comfortable to both of you.

The "football carry" often works well for holding a tiny baby at the breast. In this position, the baby lies slightly on his side, cradled by your forearm. His head, supported by your hand, is in front of the breast with his mouth directly at the nipple. (You may need to use pillows to raise your arm and the baby to the right height.) With your free hand, try to express a bit of milk from your nipple so that the baby has an immediate taste of milk and so that your nipple is firm and easy for the baby to take in his mouth.

Hold your breast, with your thumb well above the areola and your fingers underneath for support. Gently tickle the baby's lips with your nipple and wait patiently until the baby opens wide. Then pull the baby close to you, so close that the tip of his nose touches your breast. The baby's gums should come down on the areola behind the nipple; however, the *entire* areola does not need to fit into the baby's mouth. As the baby nurses, continue to support your breast with your hand. The baby may not be strong enough yet both to hold the breast in his mouth and suck too. You may also need to use your thumb to depress the skin around the areola so that the baby's nose isn't buried. If the baby needs encouragement to suck, apply gentle upward pressure on the baby's chin, using one of the fingers you have positioned below your breast. Do not be discouraged if the baby sucks weakly, seems uninterested, or falls asleep. This often happens at first. Just relax, cuddle, and enjoy the closeness.

Only a vigorously nursing premature (or a premature whose mother is using a Lact-Aid) can meet his nutritional needs solely from the breast. After nursing, the baby may be given a supplemental bottle, or, if the baby is very tired from his efforts at the breast, he may be gavage-fed.

Unless your hospital has a rooming-in program that allows you to establish full breast-feeding before discharge, you will be taking home a baby who is still at least partially bottle-feeding.

The transition from bottle to breast may involve several problems. Your milk supply may not be high enough to meet your baby's needs at first. Even if your supply is abundant, the baby may still suck too weakly to empty the breasts efficiently. The baby may prefer to drink from the bottle because it is easier. But with time, patience, perseverance, and *help*, many mothers and babies are able to overcome these difficulties.

While you are trying to establish total breast-feeding, arrange to have someone help with the household chores and care for your other children.

**The Football Carry**

Spend your time nursing, drinking lots of fluids, and relaxing. Put the baby to your breast every two to three hours, or more frequently than that if he is awake and interested. After 20 minutes at the breast, offer the baby a bottle of formula and/or your expressed milk. Do not hold the baby close or cuddle while you give him the bottle; this may help make bottle-feeding less attractive to him. After nursing and bottle-feeding, express your breasts to obtain milk for the next bottle and to help your supply build up. Refrigerate the milk at once and use within 24 hours.

As your supply builds and the baby becomes stronger, he will take fewer and fewer supplements until he is totally breast-feeding. The transition period when the baby takes both bottle and breast may last only a few days or it may take a month or longer. (Some mothers find that combined breast- and bottle-feeding is a satisfactory compromise that allows them to experience the closeness of nursing and some degree of rest and personal freedom, with husband or babysitter providing an occasional bottle-feeding.)

Breast-feeding counselors often tell mothers of prematures not to offer the baby any supplemental

### The Lact-Aid Nursing Supplementer

To establish breast-feeding without the use of supplemental bottles, try a Lact-Aid Nursing Supplementer. This device, designed by a family for nursing their adopted baby, allows your baby to suck at your breast (and stimulate your milk production), while he receives supplemental formula or breastmilk through a soft tube placed next to your nipple. The supplement is contained in a sterile, disposable bag worn between the breasts. The bag can be attached to a nursing bra or it can be worn with a neck cord. Hairsetting tape may help hold the tube in place on your breast. By slightly raising or lowering the bag, you can adjust the amount of suction the baby must apply to receive the supplement. For a weakly sucking premature the supplement can also be pre-warmed to allow for an easier flow. As your baby's suck strengthens, and your milk supply increases, lower the bag so that milk flows more easily from your breast than from the tube. You will know that your baby is ready to give up the Lact-Aid when he nurses, seems satisfied, is gaining well, but is taking very little of the supplement. Many mothers of premies, as well as adoptive mothers, have used the Lact-Aid successfully to relactate or to induce lactation.

The Lact-Aid Nursing Supplementer is available through the mail from Lact-Aid, P.O. Box 1066, Athens, Tennessee 37303, or by phone (800) 228-1933. The Lact-Aid Kit costs around $33.00 plus shipping. It can be ordered for next-day delivery. All orders must be pre-paid. Payment can be made by Visa or Mastercard. The Kit includes an instruction book, 2 complete Lact-Aid Nursing Supplementers, 1 roll of Lact-Aid bags (each with a 4-ounce capacity), 1 funnel, an adjustable neck strap and a cleaning syringe.

*Note:* The Lact-Aid *is* expensive. Ask your doctor to prescribe it so that your insurance can cover part of the cost.

**The Lact-Aid Nursing Supplementer**

bottles or to "cut" the supplemental feedings with water. *This is very dangerous advice!* A 4½- or 5-pound baby needs a steady, constant intake of fluids and nutrients. He does not have the reserves of a larger baby. Although some mothers have successfully used the "cold turkey" treatment with their prematures, others have had their babies rehospitalized for dehydration or illness as a result of malnutrition. The starvation treatment is often counterproductive, anyway. Depriving the baby of needed food, even for brief periods, often leaves him too frantically hungry or too weak to nurse properly.

Mothers may also be told to administer supplemental feedings to their baby by spoon or medicine dropper to avoid the nipple confusion that results from switching back and forth from breast to bottle.

This, too, is bad advice because a young infant is not ready to take food except by sucking. Liquid introduced into the front of the baby's mouth is likely to be ejected by the baby's tongue thrust—an automatic reflex of young infants in which the tongue pushes out material placed in the front of the mouth. If the liquid is spooned or injected into the back of the mouth, the baby is likely to choke. Feeding an infant an entire meal by this method is bound to be an unpleasant experience for mother and baby, as anyone who has administered medicine drops to an infant will readily understand. The practice is also potentially dangerous.

An excellent way to establish breast-feeding without the worry of malnutrition, dehydration, or choking is with a Lact-Aid Nursing Supplementer, a device that allows the baby to receive supplemental breastmilk or formula through a soft tube beside the mother's nipple as he sucks at her breast. (See page 170.)

While making the switch to total breast-feeding, many mothers worry about whether or not the baby is getting enough milk. Note the baby's output of urine. If he is urinating at least every 3 hours, or 8 to 10 times a day, and he is not being given extra water or juice, then he is getting enough milk to keep him from being dehydrated. (See page 192 for other signs of dehydration.) Over the long term, the baby's weight gain is the best indication of whether or not he is getting enough to eat.

## The Decision to Bottle-feed

Slightly over half of the women we interviewed (53 out of 100) bottle-fed their babies. A few women decided to bottle-feed before the baby was born. Others assumed (or were told by their doctors) that they should not try to breast-feed because the baby would be in the hospital too long or because the baby might die. In several cases, mothers were discouraged from supplying breastmilk because they were on medications or because their babies were not "tolerating" breastmilk.

Most women who switched from breastmilk to formula cited lack of support, a diminishing milk supply, and the burdensome pressure to pump and produce at a time when they were already physically and emotionally exhausted. "My daughter was on a respirator for seven months," said one mother, "and she was going to come home in oxygen. I had another child to care for and we lived far from the hospital. After six months of pumping, it just got to be more than I could deal with and I stopped." Another mother wrote, "No one taught me how to express my milk or gave me any help or advice (except to quit). There was no comfortable place in the hospital where I could go and express my milk and I had the choice of staying home and pumping or staying with the baby. My milk supply went down quickly. When I brought in what little milk I had, half the time the nurses didn't even give it to him. After three months, I tried putting my baby to the breast, but my supply was so low and his suck so weak that nothing much happened. Meanwhile, the pediatrician kept telling me not to bother. Finally I gave up."

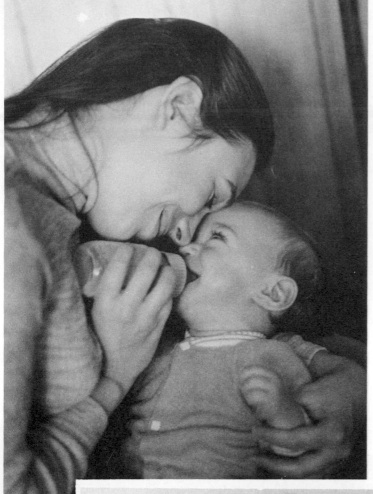

*A bottle-fed baby can be held and cuddled.*

*Bottle-feeding has its advantages.*

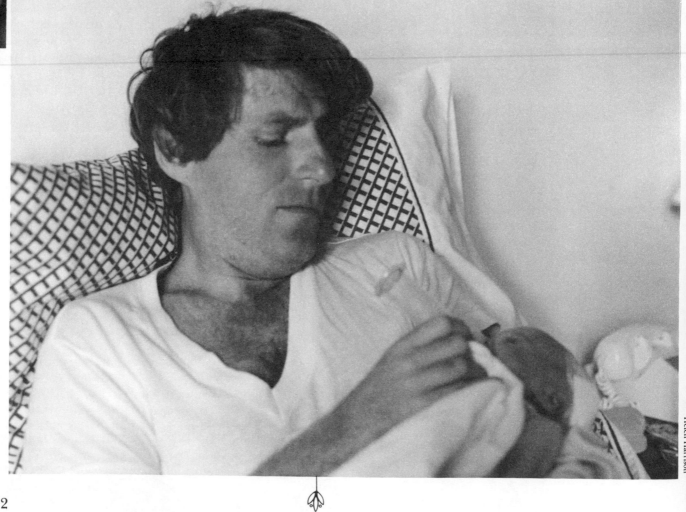

Sometimes it is the baby rather than the mother who makes the decision not to nurse. Certain babies—full-terms and prematures alike—prefer the bottle so strongly that they absolutely refuse to switch.

Weaning a baby frequently involves feelings of loss and sadness no matter when or why it takes place. If the weaning occurs earlier than the mother had hoped, especially if the baby never "totally" nursed at the breast, these feelings are often more intense. While a few mothers we interviewed expressed unmitigated relief when they abandoned their efforts to nurse, many felt varying degrees of regret and guilt. Some experienced the premature birth and their baby's inability to nurse as a double blow to their femininity. These feelings of guilt, inadequacy, and disappointment were sometimes reinforced by overzealous breast-feeding counselors: "After three months of pumping," said one mother, "I'd had enough. The women at La Leche League, where I'd rented the pump, were very intimidating. The pressure put on me to nurse was probably the most stressful aspect of my daughter's premature birth."

When the frustrations of breast-feeding clearly outweigh the benefits, when attempts to continue have a negative, rather than a positive, effect on a mother's life and her relationship with her baby, the mother's decision to stop nursing deserves support. It is sad that so many women we interviewed, who were given inadequate help and information in the beginning, felt (or were made to feel) guilty when "total" breast-feeding did not work out. "I had always thought bottle-feeding was unnatural and unhealthy," stated one mother. "I couldn't help feeling that if I'd tried harder maybe my baby wouldn't have had so many colds and perhaps we would have been closer."

Breast-feeding *is* natural, but so are breast-feeding problems. Throughout history, babies unable to nurse have been fed by alternate means. Infant feeders have been found in archeological sites dating back to 2500 B.C.

And while evidence is strong that breast-feeding promotes health in infancy, it must also be noted that many babies born during the '40s and '50s (when breast-feeding was out of fashion) were brought up on formula without apparent ill effects. Also, the infant formulas available today are much closer in composition to mother's milk than were the formulas of past decades. Breast-feeding, as was noted earlier, does not *guarantee* good health. On the other hand, bottle-feeding does not necessarily make a baby sickly and allergic. John Barry (see page 118), one of the healthiest babies in our survey, was entirely formula-fed. Edward Harrison (see page 219), who was bottle-fed after initial breastmilk feedings in the nursery, has been relatively healthy, unlike his full-term sister Amy (entirely breast-fed for eight months) who suffers from allergies.

As for closeness, a bottle-fed baby can be held and cuddled just as closely as a breast-fed baby. A mother who wishes to have skin-to-skin contact can hold her baby against her bare breast while she feeds him. Instead of a pacifier, she can offer her baby her nipple to suck on for comfort.

Bottle-feeding also allows the baby's father to have a fuller share in his child's care and feeding, and gives the mother more personal freedom.

## Offering New Foods

Unless the weather is quite hot, most breast-fed babies do not require additional fluids. They may want to nurse more often than usual, but unless they are showing actual signs of dehydration (see page 192) they do not need to be given water. (If your baby shows signs of dehydration, consult your physician!) If your baby is formula-fed, check with your pediatrician about the amount of water you use to mix the formula and about any extra water the doctor feels the baby might require. Giving a tiny baby unneeded extra water may cause poor growth and other problems.

Fruit juices provide the baby with little more than sugar, water, and a little vitamin C. They may spoil the baby's appetite for more nutritious formula or breastmilk feedings. Citrus fruit juices should be avoided in the first six to nine months post-term, since they can cause the baby to develop allergies.

The American Academy of Pediatrics advises that solids be started *after* the first 4–6 months. Some nutritionists and neonatologists feel that premature babies should be started on solids *not* according to real age, but according to their age corrected for prematurity. A baby born three months early would then start solids around nine months real age. Beginning solids earlier than this is not recommended, because the baby's digestive tract is not mature enough to properly digest foods more complex than formula or breastmilk. While most of the food remains undigested, the additional calories can still lead to obesity. Allergies are also associated with the early introduction of certain solids. Solids also greatly interfere with the absorption of iron from breastmilk.

When the baby *does* begin solids, the foods he is offered should be rich in iron but unlikely to provoke allergic reactions. Rice or barley cereals fortified with iron are the first solids for many babies. Some pediatricians start babies on ground meat, especially ground liver, which is rich in iron and other nutrients but non-allergenic.

During the first year, avoid giving plain cow's milk, which is hard for the baby to digest and may cause allergies. Never give the baby skim milk. He needs the fat in whole milk to absorb vitamins A and D, and for the proper development of his nervous system. Another food to avoid is honey. Samples of honey have been found to contain botulism spores that may be fatal to an infant though harmless to an older child or adult. The American Academy of Pediatrics recommends that honey be omitted from the baby's diet during the first year.

Remember that breastmilk or formula is your baby's most important food during the first year. Do not allow juices or solids to spoil your baby's appetite for breast- or bottle-feedings.

---

### Beginning Solids

#### Why?

To introduce your baby to a variety of tastes and textures, and to begin to develop his spoon-feeding skills.

*Comments:* Breastmilk or formula, along with vitamin supplements, meet most of your baby's nutritional needs in the first year.

Contrary to popular belief, solids *do not* help a baby sleep through the night.

#### When?

Usually between the 4th and 6th month post-term, but this is highly variable and depends more on the baby's level of maturity than on actual age. A baby is ready for solids when:

1. He sits well with support and is able to lean forward toward the spoon to indicate a desire to eat, or lean back and turn his head away when he has had enough.
2. He is losing the tongue thrust reflex of early infancy in which the tongue automatically pushes foreign material (like solids) out of the baby's mouth.

*Comments:* Introducing solids before the 4th to 6th month post-term may lead to food allergies and kidney stress. Solids offer the very young baby no nutritional benefits and may, in fact, interfere with his ability to absorb iron from breastmilk. For this reason, physicians at the 82nd Ross Conference on Pediatric Research (1980) recommended *against* the early introduction of solids for premature or low-birthweight babies, especially if these babies are breast-fed.

#### How?

Slowly, with patience and good humor. This is a social and learning experience for your baby, not a nutritional necessity.

*Comments:*

1. Introduce only one new food each week, and observe your baby carefully for such symptoms of food allergy as rashes or diarrhea. Avoid combination-of-ingredients foods. If your baby has an allergic reaction, you won't know which ingredient caused it.
2. Use a spoon, not one of those infant feeders that passively injects food into the baby's mouth.
3. Offer very small amounts at first—no more than a teaspoon or two. Mix infant cereals to the desired consistency by adding formula or breastmilk.
4. Do not add salt or sugar. Do not purée regular canned foods; they may be too high in salt and sugar for your baby. Commercial baby foods no longer contain these or other harmful additives.
5. Refrigerate baby food carefully, and discard after it has been opened 48 hours. Do not spoon-feed the baby directly from a container you plan to store and reuse, since the baby's saliva in the food causes rapid spoilage.

# *10*

# *The First Year*

"I had no idea what I was doing in any respect. I was frightened to have the twins alone. I needed someone to talk to about the difficult adjustments the mother and father must make. I mean, all I ever heard from nurses, friends, and everyone was how great and exciting a new baby is. *Now* I know that almost everybody goes through great emotional turmoil. The babies' crying was horrible, totally overwhelming. These are things no one admits to, or they forget."

*

"Parents should be prepared for the baby's distress at new surroundings. Our daughter needed lights and noise 24 hours a day at first. But later, stimulation bothered her. She was fretful the whole first year."

*

"He settled right in and was no more difficult than our full-term daughter had been."

*

"I washed my hands a great deal, limited visitors, kept the baby in numerous blankets. Our son was difficult to care for because I made it so. I was paranoid that something would go wrong. In actuality, the baby was fine but *I* was a wreck."

*

"When we brought our 4½-pound son home, we thought we were bringing home a normal newborn. Not so! He was difficult and demanding. It took half an hour to get one to two ounces down. He vomited frequently and had a colic-like condition for the first few months."

*

"Developmental milestones were hard to identify. When my baby left the nursery he was 36 weeks' gestational age, but had had 10 weeks of extrauterine experience. When he got colic, it took me a long time to realize it was colic. He was too old on the one hand, and not old enough on the other."

"We could never figure out where necessary sheltering ends and overprotection begins."

*

"I thought I wanted nothing more than to have my baby home. But when I walked into the house, everything was so quiet. It was just me, my husband, and the baby. I felt very frightened. I missed the nursery."

## The Post-Nursery Letdown

With your baby home at last, you may be surprised to feel a sort of post-nursery depression. The excitement of the baby's hospitalization is over, and no matter how horrible it was, it was still exciting. High anxiety levels do not recede overnight. It takes time to get off the emotional roller coaster and settle into something resembling normal life.

New babies are difficult, and prematures have an especially bad reputation in this regard. Your baby's frequent feedings, fussiness, and nighttime wakefulness may keep you in a state of chronic fatigue. There is no longer a night shift to take over.

This can be a lonely time. The nurses, doctors, and social workers who once played such a large role in your life are no longer around. You may have been cautioned to limit visitors and to avoid taking the baby out. Your chief social activity may be pediatrician visits, but after your baby has been cared for by teams of neonatologists, you may find it hard to relate to a "regular" pediatrician.

And now the bills come pouring in. Even couples who are well insured may find their share of the medical costs overwhelming.

Marital stresses may build. The previously supportive father may be finding excuses to stay away from the house, or he may *have* to stay away working overtime to help pay the bills. "Rod was hardly ever home," one mother recounted," and when he was, we never talked. He spent his time sulking or banging his fist against the wall. I spent my time mentally dividing up our possessions. The only thing that kept us together was the realization that no matter how difficult our life together was right now, it would be even worse if we split up."

The post-nursery period is a time when the support of parents who have shared and survived similar experiences can be most valuable. If no support groups exist in your area, consider starting one yourself. Your pediatrician may be able to put you in touch with other interested families, or you might try putting an ad in a local newspaper. One successful group began when two mothers met through a notice in a diaper service newsletter. (See page 247 for more information on parent support groups.)

This is also the time to become involved in some pleasant *non-baby-related* activities that can help you maintain contact with the outside world. Find a reliable babysitter and plan to spend a few hours each week out of the house and away from your baby. It will be good for you both.

# Getting Organized

Since most prematures come home around their due date, parents tend to assume that they are bringing home the equivalent of a full-term baby. But a prematurely born baby at 40 weeks (term) still has some catching up to do. The baby is generally not as neurologically mature or "organized" as a newborn full-term. He may not give easy-to-read, reliable signals to indicate that he is hungry, sleepy, or overstimulated. He may still be weak and difficult to feed. He may spend his time either sound asleep or screaming, and he may go from one state to the other with little transition. Even a full-term baby may take weeks to get into reasonable sleeping and eating routines. The premature tends to have an even longer and more difficult period of adjustment.

The premature baby's "disorganization" disorganizes his parents as well. "After a couple of weeks," one mother exclaimed, "I was so out of it that I couldn't remember when I last fed the baby, *what* I fed the baby, where the baby was, where *I* was, *who* I was or why!"

It may help you and your baby get organized if you keep a round-the-clock chart of what the baby did at various times of the day and night—when the baby slept, for how long, when he seemed active and alert, when he was fussy, when you changed his diaper, when and how much he ate or how long he nursed, and when you gave him his vitamins or other

medication, along with any other information you feel is relevant. Try keeping the chart for two or three consecutive days every week or two. You may begin to see patterns emerging that you might otherwise not have noticed. The baby may be unusually fussy at certain times of the day; certain feedings may go better than others. Perhaps the baby's easy or difficult behavior can be associated with other events in the household. Perhaps he is fussy when there is a lot of activity around him. Maybe his good feedings take place at calm, quiet times. By keeping a regular chart of your baby's days and nights, you may begin to see signs of progress and organization as the weeks go by, and that can be heartening.

You might also be able to use this chart to establish a regular caretaking routine with baths and other activities taking place when the baby seems most alert. Some babies respond well to a regular schedule, others do not; but it is worth the effort to help you both get organized.

# Getting Some Sleep

Newborn babies generally sleep 16 to 18 hours a day. Prematures at or before term may sleep even more than this. It sounds like a lot, but the baby's sleep times are rarely arranged to suit his parents' need for nighttime rest.

Prematures, like other newborns, often come home from the hospital with their days and nights mixed up. Certain nursery procedures, bathing for example, take place on the late-night shift, and the baby may come to expect activity at this time. In the nursery there was always a freshly rested nurse to indulge the baby who thought 3 A.M. was a terrific time to start the day.

While some babies just out of the nursery thrive on the peace and quiet of home, others miss the familiar lights and noises. If your baby seems fretful in a dark, quiet room, turn on a night light and place a softly playing radio, a ticking clock, or a recording of nursery noises nearby. As soon as possible, cut back on the extra light and noise, so that your baby learns to adapt to your way of life. Keep nighttime feedings as businesslike as possible and resist the urge to play with your baby at this time.

It is impossible for you to feed your baby every two to three hours day and night and still feel like a human being. Have the baby's father take over one or more late-night feedings so that you get at least five hours of sleep at a stretch. If you are breast-feeding, you will need to nurse your baby at *every* feeding until your milk supply is established. Then begin expressing your milk into bottles for those late-night feedings. The extra rest you get as a result may help you produce more milk.

# Coping with a Difficult Baby

Crying is communication. Try to learn what your baby's cries mean and respond to his crying whenever possible. By answering your baby's cries you help him develop a feeling of trust and a sense that he has an influence on his environment. Do not worry about spoiling the baby with lots of attention. No baby in the early months is spoiled by being held. However, there is no need to pick the baby up at the first whimper. Left alone for a few minutes, the baby may drift back to restful, *needed* sleep. And if you absolutely cannot pick up your crying baby, do not feel guilty. No one has all of his needs met all of the time. A certain amount of crying is inevitable and possibly beneficial. For many babies crying seems to act as a necessary release of tensions.

Full-term newborns may cry two to three hours a day during the early months of life and a disorganized premature sometimes cries more than that. Some prematures, especially those born smaller than normal for gestational age, are highly irritable. They may cry six hours a day or more. However, if your premature does *not* cry this much, do not worry about it. Be grateful!

Babies are normally fussy during the first three months after term. Their crying may occur in several different patterns. *Periodic irritable crying* may take place at random or regular intervals of the day or night. Irritable crying may be a discharge of excess energy, an expression of boredom or of overstimulation. *Colicky crying* usually begins right after feedings. It seems to be caused by gas pains or intestinal spasms. The baby may stiffen his legs, scream piercingly, pass gas, or vomit.

Frequent burping may help prevent colic. A warm towel or blanket under the baby's stomach may ease his distress. If the colic is severe, you might discuss a change of formula with the pediatrician. If breast-feeding, keep a record of *your* diet and review it with the pediatrician. Certain foods that you eat

*Coping with crying.*

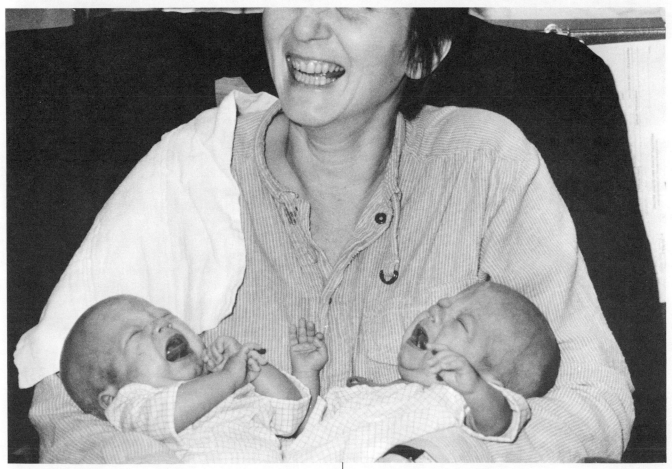

Bill Laurie

*Kathy Swinbank Laurie demonstrates a soothing technique learned in the NBICU.*

may make your milk hard for the baby to digest. Often no cause for the baby's colic can be identified. Colicky babies, it seems, are just colicky babies. There is no *reliable* cure but time and patience.

Prematures often have a low tolerance for stimulation, and they may become quite irritable when a lot of activity is going on around them. The natural impulse of most mothers trying to cope with a squirming, fussy baby is to step up efforts to entertain him—to bounce him a bit more vigorously or talk to him in a louder, more animated voice. This may make a "hyper" baby even more irritable. He may squirm and look away, trying to avoid stimulation that has become too much for him. Psychologist Tiffany Field has found that when the mother of a squirming, fussing, gaze-averting baby quiets down and looks away herself, the baby often stops fussing and becomes more attentive. One of the mothers we interviewed discovered a similar technique: "When my son had his screaming fits and I was getting rattled, I would

stop and ask myself, 'Now *who* is the adult here?' Then I would take deep breaths and try to disengage myself. Instead of becoming upset and feeding into his craziness, I tried to offer him calmness."

Some irritable babies are soothed by swaddling. With their arms and legs firmly contained in a blanket, they are better able to relax and regain control. Other babies are calmed by rhythmic motion or vibrations—swinging in a baby swing, riding in a car or baby carriage. One mother put her baby's basket on top of the dishwasher, washing machine, or dryer whenever she ran these appliances. (If you try this, be sure the basket cannot be knocked off!) Whenever possible, encourage the baby to calm himself by sucking on a pacifier or, better yet, his fingers or thumb. Thumb or finger sucking is not bad for the baby. In fact, thumb-suckers are generally better sleepers than babies who have not discovered this self-calming technique.

When all else fails, you may just have to put the baby down and let him cry it out. Sometimes just being left alone in a darkened, quiet room is enough to calm a hyper baby. Before you put the crying baby down, be sure nothing obvious is wrong—that he is fed, dry, and not ill. Then try for 5 to 10 minutes to soothe him. If this is unsuccessful, put him down and let him cry for 20 to 30 minutes. If he hasn't stopped crying by then, pick him up. Try again to soothe him for 5 or 10 minutes, then put him down and let him cry again.

If your baby's crying suddenly becomes unusually intense or seems abnormal for him, talk to your pediatrician. Usually nothing is wrong, but it is always wise to check.

And remember, it is always darkest before the dawn. A baby's increased irritability often precedes the acquisition of some new skill or the reaching of a developmental milestone: "One day when I was at the end of my rope from the crying, I picked the baby up (rather roughly, I admit) and his mouth flew open. There it was—his first tooth."

Your baby's crying is probably much harder on you than it is on him. A number of parents we interviewed said that they had felt close to losing control on occasion as they tried to deal with their frantic howling infant. One harassed father exclaimed, "The only thing I don't understand about child abuse is why there isn't more of it!"

The mother of an especially irritable premature described her method for coping: "I used to have nothing but contempt for parents who hit or abused their children, but after a few months of my baby's screaming I was close to the breaking point myself. I learned what my limits were and how to provide my-

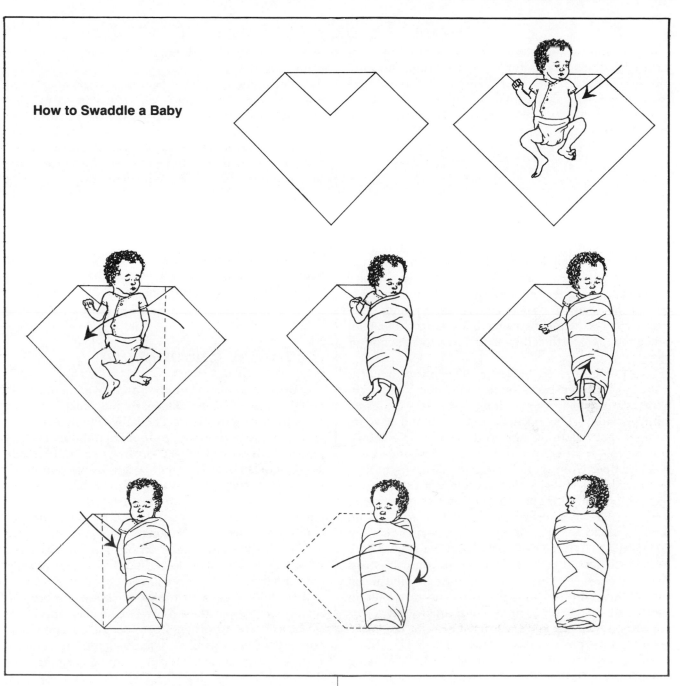

**How to Swaddle a Baby**

self with outlets. I'd check the baby to make sure he was otherwise all right. Then I'd put him in his room and do something active and noisy so I couldn't hear him. I'd take a shower, run the vacuum cleaner, or go outside and garden."

Said another mother, "When I'd start to lose control, I'd put the baby down, go into my room, close the door, and scream into my pillow."

Some communities have parental-stress hotlines that mothers and fathers can call for advice and support in handling the difficulties of parenthood. Par-

ents Anonymous is a national organization for parents who wish help to avoid abusing or stop abusing their children. (See page 243.)

## Taking Precautions

The premature baby just home from the hospital is usually smaller than the full-term newborn and more susceptible to infections. And he may need several weeks or months of special care. Here are some general recommendations for the early home care of a tiny premature. Since every baby is different, however, check with the neonatologists and your baby's pediatrician for any other special precautions you might need to take.

## Keeping the Baby Warm but Not Too Warm

The under-eight-pound baby has difficulty coping with temperature extremes. He doesn't have much insulating fat yet. The surface area of his skin (which loses heat) is still proportionately high compared to his heat-conserving body core; he cannot shiver or sweat efficiently at this age to generate or give off heat.

There is no need, however, to keep your house as warm as the intensive care nursery. A low- to mid-70s temperature is sufficient as long as the baby is dressed appropriately. This means the baby should have on slightly more clothing than you need to be comfortable at that temperature. Because babies lose a great deal of heat from their heads, one item of clothing your baby should wear for a while is a pull-on knit cap—especially at night. Thin decorative bonnets are not as effective at preventing heat loss as a pull-on knit cap. Clothes that fit close to the skin are more insulating than loose clothing. Sleepwear should have feet or a tie closure at the bottom so the babies legs are not exposed. Unless the weather is quite warm (mid-80s or higher), do not dress the tiny baby in clothes that leave his arms and legs uncovered.

Keep the baby out of drafts. The crib should not be placed next to a window—this can be a cool, drafty area. In chilly weather, preheat the car before taking the baby out. Bathe your baby in the warmest room of the house, possibly a bathroom with a heater or a living room or kitchen with a sunny exposure. Sponging the baby quickly and drying him immediately will keep heat loss to a minimum. As long as the baby's diaper area, face, and neck are kept clean, thorough daily baths are not necessary.

Overheating and overdressing the baby should also be avoided. An overheated baby must struggle to lower his body temperature. He may also be more susceptible to apnea. Never leave the baby in direct sunlight. In very hot weather, 90s or above, dress the baby lightly in a diaper and t-shirt. Offer the baby an extra ounce or two of fluids. Sponge him off occasionally with lukewarm water. But avoid placing him close to a fan or air conditioning duct where he may become chilled.

The best way to tell if your baby is too hot or cold is to look at him and touch him. If his hands and feet are cool, pale, mottled, or blue, the baby is trying to preserve his central body temperature by reducing circulation to his extremities. Warm him up. If he feels quite warm and appears flushed, remove some of his clothing or blankets—he is too hot. You might also check your baby's axillary temperature, but some babies maintain a normal temperature even if under- or overheated. But they use up many calories to do so, calories they need for growth.

After the baby reaches 8 to 10 pounds, he will be better able to adjust to temperature changes, and you won't need to be so careful.

## A Healthy Environment

Do not smoke around your baby. Children exposed to smoke have a higher than normal incidence of respiratory infections. The baby who had respiratory distress syndrome or bronchopulmonary dysplasia needs special protection from such pollutants as cigarette smoke. If you must smoke, go outside or smoke in a room far away from the baby. Do not smoke in the baby's room even when he isn't there. Smoke residues that accumulate in carpets, curtains, and blankets are also irritating.

Try to keep the baby's room free of dust, and *avoid* baby powders and cornstarch. Inhaled powder particles irritate the baby's lungs.

It's a good idea to wash your hands before you feed the baby, but there is no need to be compulsive about it. If you or others in your family become sick, your baby will probably become sick too; some illnesses are inevitable. But frequent hand washing may help avoid passing an illness on to your baby. It is worth a try. Always wash your hands thoroughly after gardening, feeding the dog, or emptying the cat box. And for the first month or so, it might be wise to keep your household pets away from the baby.

Unless you have been expressly told to sterilize your baby's bottles, there is probably no need to do so. But be sure that everything you use to feed the baby has been thoroughly cleaned in hot, soapy water and is well rinsed and dried. Washing bottles in a dishwasher is usually sufficient. If you have been told to sterilize certain items, do so by putting them in boiling water for 15 to 20 minutes. Remove the items from the boiling water with clean tongs and allow them to air dry on clean paper towels.

## Having Visitors and Going Out

There is no reason why healthy visitors cannot come into your home, but do try to limit their handling of the baby, both to cut down on the risk of infection and to avoid overstimulation. Have your friends visit quietly with you while your baby naps in another room. Of course, no one with a cold, cough, fever blister, or other illness should be allowed into your house or near the baby.

As for taking the baby out, you took him out when you brought him home from the nursery, and you'll take him out again soon to see the pediatrician.

When you do take the baby out, it is wise, at first, to avoid crowds and places or situations in which you have little control over the baby's exposure to germs. One such place is the pediatrician's crowded waiting room. To avoid exposing your baby to other sick children, call ahead and arrange to be shown into an examining room as soon as you enter the office.

It is best not to take the baby out unnecessarily for the first three months. Afterwards, with the pediatrician's okay, you can start taking the baby with you on an occasional trip to the store or to visit a friend. If the baby is not overstimulated by these outings and if his resistance to illness seems good, there is no reason to keep him at home all the time.

Parents sometimes avoid taking the baby out because they fear the reactions and rude questions of strangers on the street or at the supermarket: "How old is that baby, anyway? Good heavens! What are you feeding him?"

One mother coped with the so-called "supermarket syndrome" this way: "Whenever strangers asked me about the baby I told them—*everything!* I told them about how the baby was nine months old but was three months early, so he was really only six months old. And I always told them about the struggles he had as a newborn and how proud we were that he had made it. People really reacted positively. I'll always remember the clerk in the supermarket who told me he'd been premature himself. 'It really set me back,' he laughed. 'Here I am at age 25 with the mind of a 23-year-old.'"

## Your Baby's Health

Your baby should see the pediatrician within two weeks after coming home. Ask your pediatrician about the checkup schedule he would like to establish for your child.

The American Academy of Pediatrics recommends that prematures receive immunizations at the same schedule and dose as full-term infants. Some neonatologists, however, feel that the premature should be given immunizations according to *corrected age* rather than *actual age,* since a young premature's immune system might not be mature enough to respond properly to the immunizations. Discuss your baby's immunization schedule with your pediatrician.

The normal immunization schedule proceeds as follows:

| | |
|---|---|
| DPT 1 (diphtheria, pertussis, tetanus) | 2 months |
| Oral polio 1 | 2 months |
| DPT 2 | 4 months |
| Oral polio 2 | 4 months |
| DPT 3 | 6 months |
| Oral polio 3 | 6 months |
| Measles, mumps, and rubella | 15 months |
| DPT booster and oral polio booster | 18 months |
| DPT booster and oral polio booster | 4½ years |

If your child has an illness with a fever at immunization time, the pediatrician may wish to reschedule the shot after the child recovers. Because of the confusion over real age and corrected age, and because of frequent illnesses in babyhood, prematurely born children tend to be an under-immunized group. Be sure your child receives all his immunizations.

Antibodies to a number of diseases pass from mother to baby during the final weeks of pregnancy. Premature babies miss receiving these antibodies. Lack of immunity, combined with continuing weakness from health problems at birth, leave many prematures unusually susceptible to infection during the first years of life. Colds, pneumonia, bronchitis, ear infections, and gastrointestinal infections and upsets are more common among prematures than among full-term babies. Prematures are also vulnerable to anemia, breathing disorders, hernias, neurological disturbances, and eye problems. It is not uncommon for a premature to need rehospitalization at some time during infancy for the treatment of one or more of these conditions.

However, while prematurity increases the *likelihood* of these health problems, it does not make them inevitable. Some prematures, even those who were very tiny and sick at birth, have remarkably healthy infancies once they are out of the hospital.

## Bathing Your Baby

In a warm room, a sunny kitchen, for example, or a bathroom with a space heater, assemble:

1. a baby bathtub
2. a pad for changing and dressing the baby
3. a mild soap, such as Neutrogena Baby Soap (avoid perfumed soaps or deoderant soaps—they are too harsh and may cause allergic reactions)
4. a stack of towels that you have pre-heated in the dryer or in an oven set at 200°
5. cotton balls and/or baby wash cloths
6. clean clothes

Avoid scented oils or creams—they can cause allergic reactions. If you wish to use oil, use *small* amounts of fresh olive oil. Also avoid powders; they are irritating to the lungs if inhaled.

To keep the baby warm, clean as much of him as possible without undressing him.

### Cleaning the Baby's Eyes and Ears

1. Wet a cotton ball in warm, running water and gently wipe the eye beginning at the nose and wiping outward. Clean the other eye using another freshly moistened cotton ball.
2. Use a stiffly twisted cotton ball or the edge of a thin baby wash cloth to wash the folds of the baby's outer ear. Do not use cotton-tipped wooden swabs. A cotton ball moistened with olive oil can help remove dry skin and dirt from behind the baby's ears.

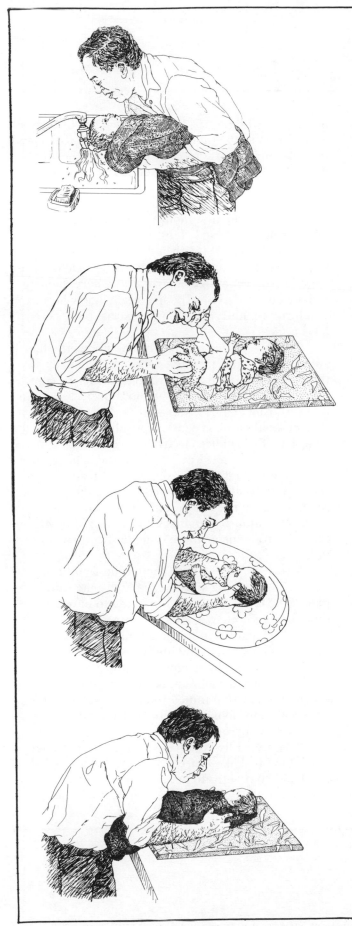

### Washing the Baby's Hair

1. Do not undress the baby. Bundle him in a warm towel to keep him dry.
2. Moisten his scalp with a warm, wet wash cloth. Using a small amount of soap (not shampoo) massage his scalp gently, but firmly, even over the soft spot—it is quite sturdy.
3. Sponge baby's head with fresh water to rinse, or, as shown here, rinse under fresh tap water. Be sure to check the water temperature first.
4. Pat the baby's head dry with a warm towel.

### Washing the Baby's Diaper Area

1. Remove the baby's diaper but leave his shirt on. Soap, rinse, and dry the diaper area.
2. Wrap the baby in a warm towel and put him in a safe place while you fill his tub with warm water. The water temperature should be about 100°, or just warm enough to feel pleasantly warm on your wrist.

### In the Tub

1. Place the baby in the tub, holding him securely. Wash the rest of him using a small amount of soap. Rinse well. Be sure to wash, *thoroughly* rinse, and dry those hard-to-get-at skin folds around the neck and under the arms.

### After the Bath

Wrap your baby in a warmed towel. Dry him quickly and dress.

### Tips

1. If your baby has just been circumcised, be sure to follow your pediatrician's instructions about cleaning the diaper area and bathing.
2. Your baby does not need a daily bath as long as his diaper area is cleaned with every change and his neck and face are washed after meals. In fact, dermatologists recommend that young babies be bathed with soap only two or three times a week, since soap can be very drying to the skin.
3. For diaper rash, change the baby frequently. Keep his bottom as clean as possible. And, when possible, take his diaper off and let his skin dry. (Do this in a warm room.) A severe or persistent diaper rash may be caused by the fungus monilia (yeast, Candida albicans). Such a rash is especially likely to occur after the child has been treated with antibiotics. Consult your pediatrician. Your baby may need prescription ointment to treat this type of diaper rash.

# A Homecoming Diary

## by Nancy Samson

Rachel was born 10 weeks early on February 27, 1982, after I went into pre-term labor. She was delivered by cesarean and immediately transported to an intensive care nursery 30 miles away. She weighed 3 pounds, 1 ounce at birth. Her problems included RDS, patent ductus, jaundice, and an intraventricular hemorrhage, but she made a good recovery and was soon back at our community hospital to grow. On April 18, a month before her due date, Rachel weighed 5 pounds, 1 ounce and was ready to go home. Three days before her homecoming, Rachel had a sleep study test that showed she was still having long, frequent spells of periodic breathing (see page 74). We would have to take her home on a monitor. What a disappointment! After two months of intensive care we were hoping to leave all our troubles behind at the hospital door, but this was not to be.

### April 18, 1982

*9:00* A.M.: Rich and I arrive at the hospital for an hour of CPR instruction with Marty, the nursing care coordinator. She is very supportive and reassuring. She gives us a booklet "At Home with a Monitor" by Anne Barr that relates other parents' experiences. I find it especially helpful.

*10:00* A.M.: At the nursery, I dress Rachel for the first time in clothes of her own—a little pink gown knitted by a woman who designs clothes for premies. We take photographs, pick up the monitor we ordered yesterday from a medical supply company, and drive to the sitter's to get David, our two-year-old.

*12:15* P.M.: We pull into the driveway. A friend has decorated our house with crepe paper and a banner that says "WELCOME HOME RACHEL." What a lovely surprise!

*12:30* P.M.: I put Rachel in her cradle and watch her closely while trying to keep David out of the way as Rick installs the monitor. We test the machine and find that the alarm is too soft to hear in other parts of the house. We call the company for a remote alarm. A representative arrives within the hour. We are told we must make an immediate $250.00 payment to cover the first month's rental or they will take the machine away. Most customers just hand over their Medi-Cal (Medicaid) stickers, the representative tells us, and the alarms are sufficiently loud to be heard in the small apartments where they are usually installed. These people really know how to add insult to injury. Don't middle class babies ever have apnea?

*2:15* P.M.: After much climbing under the house and running wires through windows, we finally have the monitor in place and working. Rachel is beginning to stir. I try to attach the monitor belt—a foam pad with rubber electrodes—around her chest. Rachel squalls and wriggles. I put the belt next to my own skin. The rubber electrodes are icy cold. No wonder she is upset. I put the belt under my blouse so it can warm next to my skin while I feed her. In the hospital I nursed her twice a day and this is her regular time at the breast. She nurses drowsily for about 10 minutes, then takes 35 cc's of PM 60-40 formula from one of those little plastic nursery bottles.

*3:00* P.M.: Rachel is on the monitor and fast asleep. The nursing sessions really tire her out. I play with David. In a way, I'm going to have more time for him now. With Rachel home and on a monitor, I can't be on the go anymore. At first, the idea of being stuck in the house really bothered me, but I think it will do me good to slow down.

*6:30* P.M.: Rachel is awake and hungry. She takes 50 cc's in 10 minutes and stays awake for the next half hour, looking around wide-eyed, checking out her new surroundings.

*7:30* P.M.: I fix lasagna for dinner. It's strange but I don't feel like I just brought home a new baby. I've had two months to get my energy back and to get used to Rachel's routines. During the time

Rachel was in the hospital I held back my tears, promising myself a good cry once I got her home, but I don't feel like crying now. It seems anti-climactic somehow.

*10:00 P.M.:* Rachel wakes and nurses, then takes 35 cc's of formula and goes back to sleep. I wonder if she'll wake up at 2:00 and if I'll hear her.

*2:00 A.M.:* Just like clockwork, Rachel is up to be fed. She takes 50 cc's of formula.

*5:00 A.M.:* Rachel is up for another 50 cc's. David slept through the night, thank heavens (he doesn't always). I even managed to get some sleep.

*10:00 A.M.:* Rick left for his Saturday morning tennis game an hour ago. I am alone with the two children, feeling overwhelmed. Finally, I put Rachel in her car seat and drive David to the tennis club to stay with Rick. I need time alone with Rachel. It is a warm day. I take off all her clothes and look her over with a critical eye. Is she sickly or healthy looking? Is she cute? I find the only things that bother me are the bald patches where her hair was shaved. I consider shaving her entire head so the hair will grow in evenly. But no, I'll just keep her in bonnets for a while.

I touch Rachel and hold her very close to me. I almost want to consume her. Although I had become used to her in the hospital, this is the first time that I've had a *physical* sense of her as my daughter.

## Afterthoughts—One Month Later

*Family adjustments:* After Rachel came home, Rick and I began drifting further and further apart. He was working extra-long hours, and I had very little time away from the kids. We weren't communicating. Finally, I suggested dinner out, just the two of us. I taught a neighbor CPR and how to use the monitor. She stayed with Rachel while we left David with another friend. With all the babysitting preparations, getting dressed up, etc., I was exhausted by the time we got to the restaurant. Nevertheless, Rick and I accomplished a lot. We worked out a schedule of specific times when we would be together as a couple, and we arranged some free time for me. None of this is new to us. We went through a similar adjustment after David was born.

*Monitoring:* This hasn't been as hard as I feared. Rachel rarely trips the monitor and we've never needed to revive her. We take her out frequently without the monitor. We just watch her closely.

*Reactions of others:* A few friends and family members pitched right in, like my brother-in-law who took a CPR course so he could help babysit. Others are frightened of Rachel because of her prematurity and especially because of the monitor. When I take Rachel out, I'm always asked her age. I'm so tired of explaining, that sometimes I lie and say she's two or three weeks old.

*Nursing:* A month after Rachel's homecoming, my milk supply has really built up. I get a let-down response just thinking about her. She nurses well (still every three to four hours), and sometimes when she is offered a supplemental bottle, she refuses it because she wants to nurse. I'm sure I could establish total breast-feeding, but I must admit I find occasional bottles very convenient.

*My feelings toward Rachel:* I was surprised by my angry feelings towards Rachel that surfaced soon after her homecoming. I felt resentment if she cried or didn't eat right. I didn't feel madly in love with her the way I did with David. I think this has less to do with her being a premie than with her being a second child. The novelty isn't there, but the hassles are. I also found Rachel's cry irritating. I believe that by being aware of these feelings, and allowing myself to have them, I helped clear the way for re-establishing good feelings for Rachel. Now, a month later, I actually find that some of her little cries are cute and touching. I enjoy holding her and soothing her when she's upset. I find that I really love her. Rachel weighs over nine pounds now and suddenly, like a flower that has just blossomed, she looks like a real baby. I have a fantasy of taking her back to the hospital and putting her in the regular nursery to be admired along with all the full-term babies.

## Upper Respiratory Infections (URI): Colds

It has been estimated that the average small child spends 10 to 20 weeks a year with colds—the susceptible premature may be sniffling and coughing even more than that.

Call the pediatrician when your baby has his first cold. If your baby was ever on a respirator for RDS, BPD, or other breathing difficulties, he is at increased risk for developing lower respiratory tract complications (pneumonia or bronchitis) when he has a cold. Your pediatrician may want to examine your baby for these problems.

Always feel free to call your doctor with any concerns about your baby's colds or other illnesses. If you hesitate to disturb the doctor in the middle of the night, remember the intensive care nursery is open 24 hours a day. You can always call there with your questions.

When your baby has a cold, check his temperature once or twice a day. If the baby develops a fever of 100° F or above, he should be seen by a pediatrician. To take your baby's rectal temperature, hold him face down across your lap. That way, he cannot break the thermometer if he moves suddenly. An axillary (under-the-arm) temperature can be just as accurate as a rectal temperature, and it is much easier on you and the baby. Be sure to hold the thermometer (a rectal or oral thermometer) snugly under the baby's arm for a full five minutes. When reporting your baby's temperature to the doctor, specify that it was an axillary temperature, since under-the-arm temperatures are normally somewhat lower than rectal temperatures. *When your baby has a fever, dress him the way you usually do. Don't overbundle him. He needs his temperature lowered, not raised.*

At your baby's first sniffle, turn on the *cool mist* vaporizer. This helps loosen secretions so they can drain more easily. When you run the vaporizer, check frequently to make sure the baby's clothes and blankets are not becoming damp from the moisture.

The baby breathes and drains more easily in an upright or semi-upright position. Hold your baby up on your shoulder whenever possible. Place folded towels or blankets under one end of the baby's mattress so that his upper body is *slightly* elevated when he sleeps. The baby can also nap in his infant seat in a semi-upright position. Do *not* put the baby on a pillow.

Tiny babies have difficulty breathing through their mouths. A stuffy nose makes the baby especially frantic when he tries to sleep or eat. Since your baby cannot blow his nose, you may have to remove the mucus with a bulb syringe. Suctioning with the bulb syringe alone may relieve the baby's congestion, but your pediatrician might also recommend salt water (saline) nose drops to help loosen the mucus when you suction. To make the nose drops, add a half-teaspoon of salt to one cup warm water. Before giving the drops, suction mucus from the front of the baby's nose like this: Close one of the baby's nostrils with your finger. Squeeze the syringe. Insert the syringe into the open nostril and release the pressure. Squirt out suctioned mucus onto a piece of tissue, then repeat with the other nostril. After the first suctioning, instill two or three drops of salt water solution in each nostril, using a clean medicine dropper. For several minutes, hold the baby with his head down and back, and slowly tilt his head from side to side so the drops can reach the back of his nose and his sinuses. Then repeat the suctioning.

Clean the syringe well after each use. Babies hate nose drops and suctioning; you may need someone to help you hold the baby during this procedure.

Your baby may not eat well while he has a cold. Suctioning his nose before feedings might help. Also try offering small, frequent feedings. If he absolutely refuses to nurse or take a bottle for eight hours or longer, call the pediatrician and watch the baby for signs of dehydration (page 192).

Do not give your baby cold medications, aspirin, or Tylenol unless your doctor has specifically recommended them, and then be sure to follow directions carefully. *There is a very small difference between the safe and dangerous dose of medicine for a tiny baby.*

Antibiotics are *ineffective* against colds or other viruses. Your doctor will not prescribe them unless the baby develops (or threatens to develop) a complicating bacterial infection, such as an ear infection, bronchitis, or pneumonia. When antibiotics are prescribed, it is important that they be stored properly (many must be refrigerated) and given according to direction. *Never* give your child (or anyone else) expired, outdated antibiotics left over from another illness. In fact, there should never *be* any leftover antibiotics. Unless your doctor tells you differently, you must give the entire amount of the prescribed antibiotic. *Even if your child recovers after a few days of treatment, continue the medication until it is used up.* Failure to do this allows the stronger, more drug-resistant germs to survive and cause an even worse infection later.

Administering medicine to an unwilling infant is

one of the major challenges of early parenthood. If your baby recoils at a spoon or at those plastic test-tube-spoon devices often given out with liquid medication, you might try putting the medicine in a nipple. First place the nipple in the baby's mouth. Then quickly pour in the medicine. The baby may start sucking and drink the whole dose before he realizes just what it was he was drinking. You might also try drawing up the medicine in a medicine dropper or in the top of a large hypodermic syringe (the part without the needle)—both are available from your pharmacist. Hold the baby's chin firmly so that he cannot turn to the side and spit the medicine out. Squirt the medicine slowly into the side of his mouth. Syringes and medicine droppers are marked in cubic centimeters (cc's) or milliliters (ml's). A teaspoon equals 5 cc's or 5 ml's.

Whenever your baby has a cold, watch him during and afterwards for signs of ear infection (see below). Always consult with your pediatrician before taking a baby with a cold in an airplane or to a different elevation, since pressure changes can damage the congested baby's ears.

## Ear Infections and Inflammation

*Otitis media,* an infection of the middle ear, is probably the most common bacterial illness seen in children. The infection usually begins with a blockage of the Eustachian tubes—tubes connecting the middle ear with the throat to provide drainage and equalization of pressure. (See page 209.) When the Eustachian tubes are blocked, an environment is created in the middle ear that promotes the growth of bacteria. The Eustachian tubes become easily clogged with mucus and bacteria when a baby has a cold. Milk and bacteria can also accumulate in the Eustachian tubes if the baby's head is not kept raised during feedings. Keeping the child's ears warm does nothing to prevent ear infections, since the problem originates in the Eustachian tubes.

Typically, ear infections develop on or after the third day of a cold, although they can also occur in a child who is otherwise healthy. The child with an ear infection may (or may not) have a fever. He may pull or rub at his ear or suddenly become very irritable. He may refuse to nurse or take a bottle. He may become dizzy and vomit, since the middle ear is close to structures that control balance and prevent dizziness. If the infection is quite severe, it may break the

child's ear drum and release a discharge.

If you suspect that your child might have an ear infection, contact your pediatrician *immediately.* Have the baby seen in a hospital emergency room if necessary. Untreated ear infections can lead to more serious infections and hearing loss. Early treatment with antibiotics and decongestants prevents these complications.

Children who suffer frequent ear infections may also develop a chronic middle ear inflammation known as *serous otitis.* Serous otitis is a collection of fluid behind the eardrum. This fluid is not infected and does not cause the child pain. It does produce a rumbling sound in the ears, causing a temporary partial hearing loss.

Repeated ear infections and bouts of serous otitis can permanently damage the delicate bones of the middle ear, resulting in permanent conductive hearing loss (see page 209). A baby should always have his ears examined at each visit to the pediatrician so that this common and insidious problem does not go unnoticed.

Serous otitis can be treated with decongestants that open the Eustachian tube and allow the ear to drain. Sometimes children with chronic ear infections and serous otitis have tiny plastic tubes surgically implanted through the eardrum to provide drainage and pressure equalization in the middle ear.

Any child prone to ear problems should be checked by the pediatrician before riding in an airplane or traveling to a different altitude. The pediatrician may prescribe a decongestant to be given before the trip. During changes in altitude (takeoffs and landings), the baby should be awake and sucking on a bottle or pacifier to help his ears "pop" to equalize the pressure. Crying serves the same purpose.

## Lower Respiratory Infections (LRI)

Pneumonia and bronchitis usually develop as a complication of a cold, but they occasionally occur in a child who has no cold-like symptoms. Children who sustained lung damage from RDS or BPD are especially vulnerable to these infections. Sometimes the symptoms resulting from their original lung damage are hard to distinguish from those of a lower respiratory tract infection. If you are familiar with your child's normal breathing patterns, you will be better able to detect the changes that indicate lower respiratory infection. Your pediatrician should also have a copy of your baby's most recent chest x-ray so that changes indicating a new disease can be distinguished from abnormalities caused by RDS and BPD.

Any of the symptoms listed below, alone or in combination, may indicate lower respiratory problems.

1. *Tachypnea* (rapid breathing). Breathing rates in tiny babies can vary from 30 to 60 breaths per minute. The baby's breathing rate normally speeds up and slows down at times, depending on his mood and activity level. But if a baby who normally breathes around 40 times a minute begins to breathe 60 times or more a minute and continues to breathe at this rate when he is calm, then this breathing pattern is abnormally fast for him. It may be a sign of respiratory distress.

2. *Retractions* (a sucking in of the chest while breathing; see page 61.) Retractions indicate that the baby is making unusual efforts to breathe. Some babies retract by sucking in below the center of the breastbone. Others may show a pulling in around the ribs or a sucking in of the hollows above the collarbone on either side of the neck. Watch your baby breathe with his shirt off and learn what his chest normally looks like when he breathes. An occasional retraction when the baby takes a deep breath is nothing to worry about. Some babies still recovering from RDS or BPD have mild retractions and tachypnea for several months after leaving the hospital. If this is your baby's normal breathing pattern, it, too, is nothing to worry about. An exaggeration of his "normal" retractions should be cause for concern.

3. *Wheezing.* The baby recovering from RDS or BPD might normally make wheezing sounds when he breathes. Listen to your baby's breathing (in a quiet room) so you will know what his breath sounds are like. An increase in wheezing can be a danger sign.

4. *Duskiness.* A bluish or grayish cast around the baby's lips or eyes may indicate poor circulation as a result of breathing difficulties.

5. *Cough and/or fever.* A very young baby may not have a cough with a lower respiratory infection; older children usually do. The baby may or may not have fever.

If your baby shows these signs of lower respiratory problems, contact the pediatrician immediately.

## What to Do If Your Baby Stops Breathing

First of all, be prepared. *Every* parent should have emergency numbers—ambulance, rescue squad, fire and police departments—taped to every phone extension in the house.

Prematures may continue to have breath-holding spells once they are home. Most often this is simply periodic breathing, a pattern of respiration common among newborns, in which the baby fails to take a breath for 10 to 15 seconds. This temporary cessation of breathing is *not* accompanied by a color change, the baby does *not* turn dusky, and *he begins breathing again on his own.*

A common breathing difficulty in prematures occurs during or after a feeding. The baby may become so intent on sucking, or so tired from his sucking efforts, that he forgets to breathe or breathes very shallowly. He may turn slightly dusky, but he usually remembers to breathe again on his own. If your baby tends to turn dusky during feedings, give him frequent rests. Watch him closely during and after his feedings. Keep a light on for nighttime feedings so you can observe his color. Report this problem to his pediatrician.

If your baby stops breathing for 10 to 15 seconds or longer and turns gray and *does not start breathing on his own,* shake him gently and call his name. Most babies will start breathing again with gentle stimulation. Once the baby is breathing, call the pediatrician immediately or take the baby to a hospital emergency room. The baby should be observed in a hospital setting and tested for underlying conditions that may be causing the apnea.

If your baby should ever stop breathing and *not* respond to stimulation, yell for the help of anyone nearby, then immediately try to revive your baby using the cardiopulmonary resuscitation (CPR) technique (see page 190).

Any baby who has required vigorous stimulation or resuscitation to restart his breathing should be re-hospitalized and tested for possible causes. The baby may be given a *pneumogram* or a *sleep study* test in which his breathing patterns are monitored during sleep. Levels of oxygen and carbon dioxide the baby receives may be altered during the test to see how the baby breathes in response to these changes. A baby with abnormal breathing patterns may need electronic monitoring at home or treatment with stimulants such as theophylline until he outgrows the problem.

Virtually every new parent worries about the possibility of crib death—that their baby might stop breathing and die during sleep. The incidence of crib death, also known as sudden infant death syndrome (SIDS), is about .2 to .3% among *all* infants. In other words, out of every 1000 babies, 2 to 3 can be expected to die from SIDS. Sudden infant death syndrome occurs more frequently among low-birthweight babies, and the smaller the baby, the higher the risk. SIDS is reported to strike 1.5% of babies who weigh between 1500 and 2000 grams at birth (15 babies per thousand) and 2.2% of infants with birthweights between 1000 and 1500 grams (22 babies per thousand). Prematures who suffered from bronchopulmonary dysplasia (BPD) seem to be especially vulnerable. At Harvard Medical School, researchers recently reported an 11% incidence of SIDS among a group of 53 BPD babies studied. Because of the increased risk of SIDS among intensive care graduates with BPD, some hospitals conduct sleep studies or pneumograms on these babies before discharge to help determine the babies who would benefit from home monitoring or other treatment.

## Seizures and What to Do About Them

Seizures can occur as a result of underlying neurological problems, high fevers, and many other causes. If your baby had seizures in the newborn period, he may continue to have them later, especially when he has a high fever.

Symptoms of seizures can be subtle (see page 96) or dramatic. The baby may move an arm or leg on one or both sides of his body in a jerky, rhythmic way. If gently touching the affected limb or limbs stops the motion, then it probably was not a seizure. If gently restraining the baby does not stop the rhythmic activity, it probably *is* a seizure. The baby may also vomit and/or turn dusky and/or roll his eyes so that only the whites show and/or blink rapidly and/or lose consciousness. The seizure may not include all these symptoms. Another form of seizure involves a stiffening of the body. The baby may become very rigid, with head back, back arched, and arms and legs straight out.

Seizure symptoms usually abate in two to three minutes. In the meantime, stay calm. Be sure the baby is protected and does not injure himself Do not put anything in the baby's mouth. He cannot bite or swallow his tongue. *Do* check his mouth after the seizure to clean out any milk, mucus, or vomit. The baby will probably be very sleepy after the seizure. Let him rest. Notify your doctor immediately. He will probably want to rehospitalize the baby for observation and tests to determine the cause of the seizure. The baby may be put on a seizure-controlling medication such as phenobarbital if he is having regular seizure activity. If your child should ever have a seizure that lasts longer than fifteen to twenty minutes, take your child to the nearest hospital as quickly as possible. *Prolonged* seizure activity may result in permanent brain damage.

## Anemia

Anemia is a common problem among all children during the first year. Twenty percent of all newborns are affected, and prematures are especially vulnerable. Any baby who received a transfusion is susceptible to anemia six to eight weeks later when the transfused red cells suddenly die off. Parents and pediatricians should be alert to this potential problem.

Iron is essential to the formation of red blood cells, but most prematures are born with extremely low stores of this element. Supplemental iron drops or iron-fortified formula may be given to the baby throughout the first year.

Anemia can have a dramatic effect on the baby's health and behavior. Anemic, iron-deficient babies tend to have low attention spans, irritable behavior, and poor toleration of feedings. One study showed that these symptoms of anemia disappeared in a week when iron-deficient infants were given supplemental iron injections. *Caution:* Never give your child more than the recommended dosage of iron. Too much can be toxic.

Do be sure that your baby's hematocrit (red cell count) is checked frequently during the first year.

When your baby starts solids (usually at six months *corrected age*), be sure to include iron-fortified cereals in his diet.

## Hernias

Hernias are openings or weak places in the muscular abdominal wall through which a bit of intestine protrudes. Inguinal hernias (in the groin area) and umbilical hernias (around the navel) are common in both male and female prematures because of weakness in their abdominal muscles. The hernia is visible as a lump that bulges out when the baby coughs or cries. When the baby relaxes, the lump of intestine

## Cardiopulmonary Resuscitation (CPR)

If your baby stops breathing and does not respond to stimulation, remember A, B, C—Airway, Breathing, Circulation.

### AIRWAY

1. To clear the baby's airway: Place the baby flat on his back on a firm surface, a table top or, if need be, the floor. Wipe away any milk, mucus, or other material that you can see in his mouth.

2. Straighten the baby's head so that the chin is very slightly tilted back and so that the tip of the nose points straight up. Proper positioning is important. If the head is tilted too far back or too far forward, the baby's windpipe will be blocked.

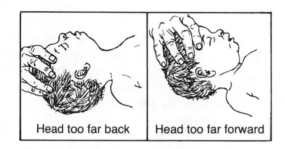

Head too far back      Head too far forward

### BREATHING

3. Cover the baby's *nose and mouth* with your mouth and try blowing in five quick puffs of air. Puff just hard enough to make the baby's chest rise. (If the baby's chest *does not rise* when you puff in the air, turn the baby over your arm so that his head and chest are lowered. Strike him firmly 4 to 5 times between the shoulder blades to dislodge anything that might be blocking his windpipe.)

### CIRCULATION

4. Feel for the baby's pulse on the inside of his arm opposite his elbow. (If it is easier for you, check the baby's pulse by feeling on either side of his neck right below the jaw.) Check carefully for 10 seconds. Even if the baby is not breathing, his pulse and heartbeat will continue for several minutes.

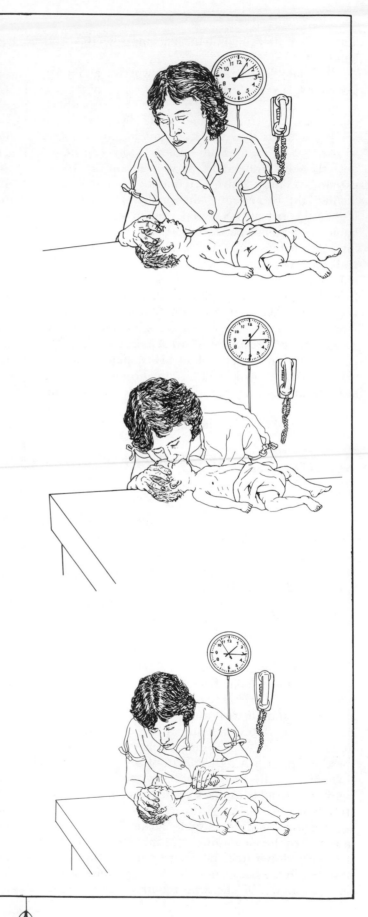

5. *If you do not feel a pulse, or if the pulse is as slow as yours is normally,* try to restart circulation by pressing rhythmically on the baby's chest. Using your first two fingers, push down on the breast bone just between the two nipples. This squeezes the heart between the breast bone and the back bone and forces the blood to circulate. Push just hard enough to depress the chest ½ to ¾ of an inch. Compress the chest five times, then cover the baby's nose and mouth with your mouth and puff in enough air to make the chest rise. Be sure to lift your face slightly to allow the baby to exhale, but keep your face close to his so that you are ready to give the next puff.

Continue in this rhythm: Compress, compress, compress, compress, compress . . . puff. (It may help you to count: 1 and 2 and 3 and 4 and 5 puff.) Repeat the compressions and puffs at a rate of approximately 100 compressions per minute and 20 puffs per minute. After several minutes, stop briefly to see if the baby's heart and breathing have started. If the heart is beating, but the baby is still not breathing, continue blowing in puffs of air at a rate of 1 puff every 3 seconds. Stop again after several minutes to see if the baby is breathing on his own.

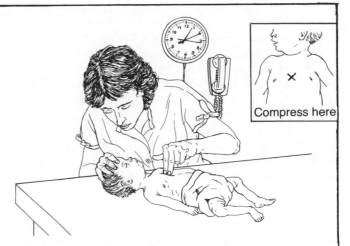

Compress, compress, compress, compress, compress . . .

6. As soon as possible, carry your baby to the telephone and phone the ambulance or rescue squad. As soon as you have completed the call, place the baby on a table or on the floor and resume CPR until the baby's heartbeat and breathing have started again or until help arrives.

puff

These instructions are no substitute for the actual hands-on training you will get in a CPR class. The American Red Cross offers these classes. So do some intensive care nurseries. *Every* parent should have this training. Instructions for reviving an infant (or adult) using artificial respiration techniques can also be found in the front pages of your telephone directory.

*Important:* When practicing CPR techniques, *always* use a doll or mannequin. *Never* practice on your baby, or on anyone else.

*Notice:* The information given here is true and complete to the best of our knowledge. All recommendations are made without guarantee on the part of the author or the publisher. The author and the publisher disclaim all liability in connection with the use of this information.

goes back inside the stomach's muscle wall. Bands or tight clothes do not help to repair a hernia. Keeping the child from crying is not necessary either, and may be next to impossible anyway, since hernias can increase the baby's irritability. If an inguinal hernia does not go away on its own, it is repaired as an elective surgical procedure once the baby weighs 8 to 10 pounds. Emergency surgery is performed before that point if the hernia becomes incarcerated—that is, if the intestinal lump is caught outside the stomach's muscle wall.

If the hernia becomes caught (incarcerated or strangulated), the baby suffers excruciating pain. He may vomit or faint. Take him to the doctor immediately. Do not try to push the lump back in yourself if it causes the baby pain. Simple surgery to repair the hernia will be performed if the doctor cannot make it retract. Umbilical hernias are usually not repaired unless they become incarcerated. They generally disappear by age two.

# Digestive Problems: Vomiting, Diarrhea, Constipation

### Spitting Up, Vomiting, Projectile Vomiting

Almost all new babies occasionally spit up a small amount of milk after they have eaten. Prematures are especially likely to spit up for several reasons. First of all, the muscle surrounding the esophagus (the tube that leads from the mouth to the stomach) is generally quite weak in a premature baby. It does not always close off properly to keep the stomach contents down. Secondly, spitting up or vomiting may be one way the neurologically disorganized premature reacts to overstimulation. Finally, the premature, like any other baby, may swallow air while sucking or he may try to eat more than his tiny stomach can hold.

If your baby tends to spit up, feed him slowly and burp him frequently. Try to keep mealtimes as calm and quiet as possible. Hold the baby upright (at your shoulder) after meals. *Never* place him on his back right after he eats; if he spits up he may choke. A certain amount of spitting up is quite normal. As long as the baby gains well, it should not cause concern.

Vomiting, as opposed to spitting up, is a more thorough emptying of the stomach contents. It is usually a sign of illness or food intolerance. If your baby vomits most of his meal, check his temperature. If you are giving him formula, check the expiration date. Be sure the bottle was not left unrefrigerated too long (more than four hours). If the vomiting con-

tinues, call the doctor. Be sure to call the doctor if the baby vomits greenish or bright yellow bile, since this may indicate an obstruction of the digestive tract.

Projectile vomiting is vomiting that is forceful. The stomach's contents can be propelled several inches to a foot or more away from the baby. "Hyper" babies who tend to be air-swallowers sometimes projectile vomit when accumulated air in the stomach forces the milk up and out of the baby's mouth. Projectile vomiting also occurs with a condition called *pyloric stenosis* in which the outlet from the stomach to the small intestine narrows and impedes the passage of food. Eventually, the stomach muscle ejects the food. Projectile vomiting should always be reported to the pediatrician. It is not normal. However, a number of parents we interviewed reported that their premature babies had projectile-vomited during the early months at home, yet none of these children had any serious underlying digestive problem.

### Diarrhea

Diarrhea is difficult to define except in terms of what is normal for a given baby. If the number of stools increases greatly, the amount of the stools increases, or the stools become much looser in consistency, this may be diarrhea. If the stools seem quite watery (if a water ring is visible around the stool on the diaper), this too is a sign of diarrhea.

Diarrhea can be a symptom of illness or food intolerance. Check your baby's temperature, check the expiration date on his formula, and call the pediatrician. A baby with diarrhea can lose a great deal of fluid from his body very quickly. Offer the baby additional formula or breastmilk. The baby with diarrhea loses not only fluid, but also important minerals (electrolytes) that must be replaced. For this reason, your pediatrician may recommend that you also give the baby a special water and mineral formula such as Pedialyte.

Observe the baby for signs of dehydration:

1. Dry mouth or thick saliva.

2. Scanty amounts of dark urine. Normally the baby urinates *at least* every three hours (8 to 10 times a day or more). The urine should be clear or pale yellow. When a baby is dehydrated, he voids a smaller amount of concentrated dark yellow urine.

3. A sunken fontanel (soft spot) when the baby is held upright.

4. Loss of skin elasticity. When a fold of skin is lifted, it does not spring back quickly.

### Constipation

Constipation is common among prematures. Perhaps their low activity levels or their neurological immaturity causes food to pass through the intestinal tract more slowly. If the baby is sick and not eating well, he may become constipated from low fluid intake. The iron supplements that most prematures receive can also cause constipation. Formula-fed babies are more vulnerable to constipation than are babies fed breastmilk, which has a natural laxative effect.

Constipation is not determined by how often a baby has a bowel movement. Some babies have a bowel movement at every feeding. Others may go two or three days without having a stool. Both patterns can be normal.

The consistency of the stool is what determines constipation. If the stools are harder and drier than normal, this is constipation.

Call your pediatrician for advice. An increase in fluids may help. A teaspoon to a tablespoon of dark Karo syrup in water may ease constipation. Prune juice works well for some babies; so does Maltsupex mixed with formula or water. Check with your pediatrician before giving any of these to your baby.

Rectal stimulation with a rectal thermometer or an infant glycerin suppository often helps the baby have a stool. Again, check first with the pediatrician.

If your baby has infrequent stools but is eating well, gaining well, and does not seem uncomfortable, do not worry. This is just a normal pattern for your child.

## Teething

Your baby will cut his teeth according to his age corrected for prematurity. Teething schedules are genetically determined. If you or the baby's father cut a first tooth at six months, start looking for your baby's first tooth around six months after his due date.

Prematurity, and the illnesses that often accompany it, may affect the quality of the baby teeth. The enamel on the teeth may be softer than normal or discolored as a result of poor nutrition and illness in the immediate newborn period. When your baby's teeth come in, have the pediatrician check them carefully. You may also want to see a pediatric dentist before the usual first checkup at three years of age. Be sure to find a dentist who has had experience with other intensive care graduates. Ask your neonatologist or follow-up clinic staff for a referral.

## Cosmetic Problems

For reasons no one understands, prematures are more likely than full-terms to have *hemangiomas*, birthmarks sometimes referred to as strawberry marks. Hemangiomas are soft, red raised areas composed of swollen capillaries. They grow during the first year and then slowly begin to disappear. Usually the birthmark is gone entirely by age four, leaving a slightly paler than normal area of skin.

Other cosmetic problems may result from nursery treatment. A premature may acquire an elongated head when his soft skull bones are molded by the flat surfaces on which he must lie. His head begins to round out and assume its genetically determined shape once the baby is able to hold his head up for long periods. Although the child's head shape may always be *very slightly* longer and narrower than it would have been had he not been premature, when his hair grows in, this characteristic should be virtually unnoticeable.

Babies who had a tube inserted in a nostril for a long period of time may develop an enlargement of one nostril and a constriction of the other. This disfiguration can be permanent unless the smaller nostril is widened. The doctor can do this by placing tubes of increasing diameter into the narrowed nostril to slowly enlarge the opening and return the nose to its normal appearance.

Repeated heel sticks may cause small, usually painless, raised cysts to form on the baby's heels. These cysts may appear and disappear, recurrently, up to two years of age. If they cause the child any discomfort, the pediatrician can lance them, but they usually disappear on their own.

Scars from nursery surgery can be large and un-

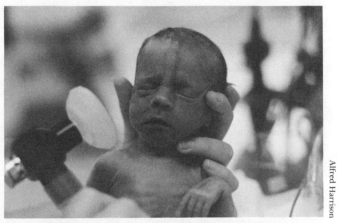

Alfred Harrison

*Nostril constriction from intubation is a reversible cosmetic problem.*

sightly on some children, who may later benefit from cosmetic surgery. Discuss this with your pediatrician.

Whenever your baby is seen by a new doctor—in a hospital emergency room, for example—be sure to explain that your child is an intensive care graduate, and inform the doctor of any scars or bone fractures your baby acquired in the nursery. Several parents we interviewed had been falsely accused of child abuse by hospital personnel who misinterpreted abnormal x-ray results and scars from cut-downs or transcutaneous monitors.

## Growth

The premature baby, like other newborns, generally loses several ounces after birth, largely due to fluid loss. A very premature or sick baby may then take a month or longer just to regain his birthweight.

Once the baby recovers from illness and is given adequate nutrition, his growth rate accelerates as he attempts to fulfill his original growth potential. The head circumference measurement is usually the first to show a spurt in growth. Next, the baby makes a rapid increase in length, and then he begins to fatten up until he approaches the size he would have been had prematurity not set him back. Generally, this growth spurt occurs sometime in the first six to nine months after birth.

Some babies catch up very quickly. Slightly or moderately premature babies who experienced few complications after birth may, by their due date, already be the size of a full-term newborn.

Smaller, sicker, more prematurely born infants take much longer to achieve their original growth potential. Although some tiny babies do grow amazingly fast (John Barry, for example, in John and Michael's Story, see page 118), most very small infants remain small and underweight for their corrected age throughout infancy and childhood. Nevertheless,

*It is unfair to compare your premature child with children his same age who were conceived months earlier. Shown here are two 6-month-old babies, one born 3 months prematurely.*

Alfred Harrison

prematures who were appropriate in weight for their gestational age at birth (AGA) are thought to have an excellent chance of eventually achieving normal stature.

Babies who were small for gestational age (SGA) at birth—both full-terms and prematures—have a tendency to remain small throughout life. Although some SGA babies grow normally, others do not—especially those whose growth slowed early in pregnancy as a result of fetal alcohol syndrome, the TORCH viruses, or chromosomal abnormalities.

On the pediatrician's growth chart, your premature baby may be compared to full-term babies born at the same time. This hardly seems fair. It is not. As long as your child is healthy and growing steadily, ignore the percentiles. It is his rate of growth that matters, not how he compares to children conceived months before he was.

# Development

When considering your baby's development, think in terms of his due date, not his birth date. A five-month-old baby who was born three months early is a two-month-old from a developmental point of view. And prematures who were quite early or sick often lag well behind their *corrected* age in development during the early months of life as they recover from their postnatal illnesses. This lag is especially evident in their physical or motor skills. As with all babies, prematures have peaks of rapid development followed by long plateaus when nothing much happens. Do not be discouraged by occasional periods of slow development; this is normal.

You cannot stimulate or otherwise push your child to develop before he is neurologically ready. Attempts to do so will just leave both of you frustrated. What you *can* do is offer your baby companionship, encouragement, and the time and opportunity to experiment and practice. Never force your baby into activities when he is tired or actively resisting. A calm, easygoing approach toward your child's development usually gets the best results. As long as your baby keeps making progress, a decade from now it will not make the slightest difference if he began walking at 12 or 22 months.

In the following pages we describe some of the physical, social, and intellectual skills your baby will be working on during the first year after his due date, along with suggestions on ways to encourage his emerging abilities.

# Physical (Motor) Skills

## Body Awareness

During the first year your baby will become increasingly aware of his body and what it can do. To help the baby discover his body, touch him, cuddle him, tickle him, and massage him as you dress, change, and bathe him. Speak to him as you touch him and describe what you are doing: "Now I'm going to tickle your toes." Expose your baby to a variety of pleasant textures—silky, velvety, furry fabrics or toys.

Play with him in front of a mirror so he can watch himself move.

Encourage him to use both sides of his body by nursing him at both breasts at each feeding. If bottle-feeding, switch feeding positions from time to time; offer the bottle with your right hand at one feeding, your left hand at the next. If one side of the crib is against a wall, do not always put the baby in the same position in his crib. Put him with his head facing in one direction half the time and in the opposite direction the other half, or put the crib in the middle of the room. That way he will be encouraged to look out on both sides.

## Gross Motor Skills

Gross, or large, motor skills involve the coordination of large parts of the body—skills like rolling over, sitting up, and walking. A baby acquires control over his body beginning with the head and working downward, and beginning at the center, or midline, of his body and working out. For example, the baby learns head control before he learns to roll over or sit; he learns to control his arms before he is able to use his hands and fingers well.

You can help your baby develop head control by holding him up at your shoulder (hold him high enough to see above your shirt). Slightly release your support of the baby's head to give him a few seconds practice holding his head up himself. If he holds his head up well, gradually increase the time you leave his head unsupported. But do not let his head flop. If he is not ready to support his head yet, wait a few days and try again.

Find a warm spot on the floor, spread out a blanket, and put the baby down on his stomach so that he can practice raising his head. If he objects to lying on his stomach, get down on the floor and sing or talk to him. If he still objects, do not leave him on his stomach for more than a brief period, but continue to offer him some time on the floor each day. You might also lie on your back with the baby lying face down on your chest. Talk to him to encourage him to raise his head and look at you. Try not to leave him in an infant seat for more than half an hour to 45 minutes at a time, since he cannot practice head and trunk control in a supported, semi-reclining position.

Once the baby is able to lift and turn his head, he is ready to learn to raise his head and chest by supporting himself with his arms. Lots of practice on his stomach will help him master this skill. You might also place a rolled-up towel or blanket under the baby's chest so that his chest is slightly raised and he is resting on his forearms. After a while, remove the support and see if he can maintain this position on his own.

Once the baby is lifting his head and chest well, he can begin to roll over. At first, he rolls from his side onto his stomach or back. Help him learn to roll by placing him on his side and gently bringing his arm and leg over until the rest of his body follows. Once he gets the idea, encourage him to try it himself by offering a toy that he must reach for. He may roll over in the process. Alternate sides. Next, the baby learns to roll from his stomach to his back. Tuck the arm and leg on one side under his body to give him leverage and see if he flips over on his own; if he does not, encourage him with a gentle push. Rolling from back to stomach is harder and takes more time to learn. With the baby on his back, encourage him to reach up and to the side for a toy. Give him a gentle boost over.

When the baby has mastered rolling over, he begins to develop the strength and coordination needed for sitting up unsupported, standing, and eventually walking.

To help the baby learn to sit, hold him in a supported sitting position on your lap, with your hands under his arms. Slowly lower your hands to his waist; if he continues to support himself, lower your hands to his hips. Once the baby has learned to sit well unsupported on your lap, help him develop control and balance by gently elevating one of your legs to throw him *slightly* off balance (be ready to catch him). See if he learns to correct his balance by shifting his body position or extending his arms to catch himself. Once the baby can maintain a sitting position without slumping over, take two sofa cushions, place them in a V on the floor so that the baby can sit between them, gently supported.

Later in the year, you can help your child learn to pull to standing by holding him upright in your lap so that he bears his own weight on his feet. Encourage him to pull himself up on low, sturdy objects by placing enticing toys on top of them.

Give him large boxes to push and use as "walkers."

### Fine Motor Skills

Fine motor skills involve the use of small muscle groups such as those in the hands, or the coordinated use of small muscle groups in the hands and eyes.

The baby learns to use his eyes before he uses his hands and eyes together. In the early months of life he begins tracking, or following moving objects with his eyes. Encourage your baby to follow your face with his eyes as you lean over him and slowly move your face up and down, from side to side, and around in a circular motion. Offer your baby brightly colored mobiles to look at.

A very young baby keeps his hands tightly closed. If you pry open his fingers and place an object in his hand, he may hold it briefly, and then drop it. By the third or fourth month after term, the baby begins to relax his hand and keep it open at least some of the time. He may start to grab and hold toys with a sort of clumsy "mitten grasp." To encourage the baby's grasp, stroke his palm softly and place an object in his hand. Once he is holding the object, tug at it gently to help strengthen his grip.

During the first six months after term, the baby begins to reach and bat at dangled objects. Place the baby in a semi-upright position in his infant seat. Using sturdy string, suspend a mobile so that it is within batting distance of the baby's hands. Show him how to reach out and strike at it. (Be sure the baby cannot become tangled in the mobile.) Change the mobile every few days. Babies get bored, too.

During the second six months post-term, the baby begins passing toys from one hand to the other. He learns to bang two objects together. Play pat-a-cake games with him. Put objects in his hands that make interesting noises when banged against each other.

Toward the end of the first year the baby begins working on his pincer grasp—picking up small objects between his thumb and index finger. To encourage the baby to use the pincer grasp, try putting a Cheerio for him to retrieve in each section of an empty egg carton. (Hold the carton. An enterprising baby will get the Cheerios the easy way—by turning the carton over!) Your baby might also enjoy boxes and puzzles with small knobs that he must lift with a pincer grasp.

During the second half of the first year, babies enjoy container play. Offer your baby an old purse filled with small (safe) objects—blocks for example. Putting objects in containers and taking them out again helps the child become more skilled at using his hands.

Around the end of the first year post-term, your baby might like creating with edible fingerpaint, such as chocolate custard or whipped cream. Tape a piece of paper to his high chair tray and let him experiment.

## Social, Language, and Intellectual Skills

One of your baby's first and most rewarding accomplishments is responsive or social smiling, which begins around two to three months post-term. To encourage your baby to smile, smile at him. Respond to your baby by smiling, talking to him, or picking him up when he smiles at you.

Although your baby cannot understand words in the early months of life, he is getting used to the rhythms and the give and take of conversation. He is learning the meaning of different tones of voice. Talk to your baby and sing to him. As you bathe, change, and dress him, describe in short simple sentences what you are doing. Don't be embarrassed to use baby talk—babies seem to prefer the high-pitched tones and exaggerated intonations of baby talk. During the second half of the first year, begin reading to your baby. Begin simply by pointing to animal or car pictures, identifying them, or imitating their noises.

Your baby should begin making cooing or babbling sounds of his own during the first six months post-term. Imitate his sounds. Talk to him when he "talks" to you. As the year proceeds, his babbling will begin to sound more and more like speech, and he will understand much of what is said to him. By 12

---

### "You're Overprotecting that Child!"

What parent of a premature hasn't heard those words from a "helpful" friend or relative, even from the pediatrician? The stereotype of the over-anxious, over-indulgent "premie parent" is widespread, and this bit of advice is often handed out whether it is appropriate or not.

Nevertheless, it is a real problem for the parents of *any* child to know when necessary precautions end and overprotection begins, or to know when a child is being appropriately challenged, but not pushed too hard. Making such judgments is especially difficult for the parents whose prematurely born child began life with health and developmental problems. Child care books about full-terms are of little help. So are friends and relatives who have had no experience with a premature. Other parents of premies can offer only limited guidance, for pre-term babies can be as different from one another as they are from full-terms. What is right for one premature may be wrong for another. It may be wise, for example, to keep a pneumonia-prone toddler out of large play groups where he would be exposed to other children with colds. However, such precautions with a relatively healthy premature are unnecessary. The "hyper" premature who falls apart when over-stimulated needs protection from situations that upset him. Shopping trips, restaurant meals, even nursery reunions—excursions other children enjoy—may be too much for the "hyper" child, at least for a while. There are no answers on caregiving that fit the needs of every child. Pediatricians have been known to give widely conflicting recommendations even on the care of the *same* child. What's a parent to do?

1. Remember that some pediatricians have had little experience with intensive care graduates. If your pediatrician (or any other professional) advocates care for your child that you feel is inappropriate, do not hesitate to seek a second opinion. You may wish to consult your baby's neonatologist for further advice.

2. Find a babysitter whose judgment you value to spend some time each week with your child. Discuss with the babysitter any areas of your child's care or development that concern you. While you are under no obligation to follow the babysitter's advice, it is still helpful to have feedback from someone outside the family who knows your child well. Your child may also benefit from his time with the babysitter and his exposure to a different style of caregiving. A child will sometimes develop or reveal new skills for an outsider more readily than he will for his own parents. (Your child *knows* you think he is wonderful, but he may have to make extra efforts to impress the babysitter.)

3. When friends and relatives give unsolicited advice, listen politely, give careful consideration to what they have said, then trust your instincts and do what *you* think is best for you and your baby. To quote Dr. Benjamin Spock: "You know more than you think you do."

months post-term he may be using an identifiable word or two like "ma-ma," "da-da," "up," or "bye."

During the first year a baby also learns a great deal about how the world operates. He learns about object permanence: that a toy does not vanish just because he dropped it under the high chair and cannot see it, that Mom has not really disappeared behind the blanket in a peek-a-boo game. Hide-and-seek, peek-a-boo, and covering a toy for the baby to find are favorite games during the first year.

The baby is also learning about cause and effect and about the ways he can cause things to happen. When he cries, for example, he is picked up. When he bats at a mobile, it moves. He learns to do things on purpose, and toward the end of this first year and throughout the second year, he constantly tests his new sense of power. "If I cry loud enough I won't have to go to bed . . . If I throw my food on the floor, Mom will have to come clean it up."

Now is the time to set, and consistently enforce, limits on your child's behavior. This is, of course, much easier said than done. Finding the right balance between leniency and strictness is a problem for every parent. It is an issue that requires constant reappraisal as the child grows, develops, and changes. Parents of prematures who may still feel a certain degree of guilt or pity toward their child have special difficulties in this regard. One couple we interviewed told of being unwilling to impose a (very reasonable!) 9 P.M. bedtime on their prematurely born toddler because she had been through so much. But it is just such a child (one who may be neurologically disorganized as a result) who benefits most from limits, structure, and consistent, firm guidance. Another couple, increasingly tyrannized by their willful toddler (an intensive care graduate), remarked, "It finally dawned on us that our daughter was an essentially happy (if spoiled) little girl and that *we* were the ones who had suffered and were suffering the most. Once we realized that, we stopped feeling guilty every time we told her 'no.'"

## Cause for Concern

While normal prematures can show wide variations in their developmental patterns, there are certain delays and abnormalities that should cause concern.

If the baby is not smiling responsively by three months corrected age, this could be a sign of problems. By three months post-term, the baby should also be able to follow a moving object with his eyes.

By four months after term, the baby should be relaxing and opening his hand at least some of the time. By the corrected age of seven months he should be using his arms and hands to reach, grab, and hold an object.

By four months after term, the baby should *not* be showing noticeable asymmetry—a consistent favoring of one side of his body over the other. During the first year, the baby should *not* show a consistent preference for one hand over the other.

By seven months corrected age, the baby should be able to roll over, and by eight to nine months corrected age he should be able to sit when placed.

The absence of cooing and babbling by seven months corrected age may also indicate problems.

If you have questions or concerns about your child's developmental progress, never hesitate to discuss them with your pediatrician or with the developmental specialists listed in Chapter 11.

## Anthony's Story

### By Katherine Degher

When I was three months pregnant, Tony, my baby's father, decided to end our relationship. He would continue to be around, but he needed his "space." I considered an abortion, but decided against it. I was 29 and single, and I wanted a baby, with or without a father in residence.

I'd work every day until the baby was born, pay off all my debts, save enough money to live comfortably for a while, then go on welfare. I had no options. My baby would need a full-time mother for at least a year.

Tony wasn't around much during the pregnancy. I ached for someone to feel my belly grow and bring me pickles and tell me I was beautiful. I ached, and tried not to, for the baby's sake. I went to work, kept up a cheerful facade, and tried to relax, for the baby's sake.

I had been talking to my baby ever since I knew he was there (I was sure it was a boy). As I felt him moving, the bond became very tight. Perhaps because I didn't have his father there to share my attention, my unborn son filled my life. I considered us "us."

During my 24th week of pregnancy, I began having contraction-type pains every 20 minutes, along with a fever. I asked some friends, a nurse, and my obstetrician—who all dismissed my symptoms as the flu. Several times a day I called the OB to tell him that the pains were worse. Finally, on the third day, he told me to go to Labor and Delivery and have the nurses check me. He then admitted me to the hospital for "the flu," gave me Demerol for the "intestinal spasms," and put me on a medical ward. The pains worsened all night, but since I wasn't thought to be in labor, no one bothered to check me until the following morning, when I was completely effaced and 3 centimenters dilated.

Finally, I was officially considered to be "in labor." I was immediately put on terbutaline. I was already sick and frightened. The terbutaline intensified my terror: pounding heart, shortness of breath, dizziness. A sonogram showed a 24-week baby and possible abruption. An amniocentesis was negative. A half-hour later, I began to leak fluid. And lose hope.

But within a few days the leaking slowed, my fever resolved, the labor stopped. Because of the fluid leak, the doctor said I'd never make it to term. The best I could hope for was four more weeks—the baby might stand a chance then. Right now he had no chance. After a week in the hospital, I was sent home with instructions to stay in bed. I was home only four hours when my membranes totally ruptured and I went into hard labor.

Tony and a girlfriend of mine were with me at the hospital that night. I tried to freeze my emotions and concentrate on the pain. I tried to block out the fact that it was all for nothing. When it came time for the delivery, I wanted to be alone, but Tony insisted that my friend go with me. He was too "squeamish" to go himself. My friend was cheerful and supportive—the last thing I needed. I wanted to know *nothing* about the baby I was miscarrying; she told me it was a boy.

It was a difficult breech delivery. Anthony's head got stuck, and the doctor finally yanked him out of me. He was badly bruised. He wasn't breathing and his heart was barely beating. He weighed exactly two pounds. As he was taken to the nursery, the pediatrician told Tony, "It doesn't look good." Despite all of this, I was ecstatic that my baby was alive at all. I was a mother. I refused a shot to dry up my milk.

The transport team wheeled Anthony into the recovery room. I reached down from my gurney and touched my son. I was crying, and it seemed everyone else was too.

I called my father and my friends. No one knew what to say. One friend asked me not to call her until the baby either came home or died. She didn't want to hear the details. I couldn't help feeling that the people I cared about thought that Anthony's

death would be the best solution to a bad situation.

My roommate in the maternity ward had a nine-pound, healthy baby boy who roomed in with us. She was as uncomfortable with me as I was with her.

Two days after his birth, Tony and I went to Anthony's hospital to visit him for the first time. He looked like a little old man, literally skin and bones. He was flailing both of his arms the way that premies do. I was so overcome with the joy of merely having a living baby that I blocked out the fact that his life was in serious danger.

Ant's problems? I'll start at the top: intracranial hemorrhage, the beginning stages of RLF, patent ductus, RDS and BPD, hyperbilirubinemia, hypocalcemia, hyperglycemia, severe anemia, osteopenia (rickets), two bouts of pneumonia. When he was four days old, the day after an IV had been taken out of his left arm, I noticed that he wasn't moving it at all. It took three days for me to get anyone to pay attention to it. The arm turned out to be paralyzed as a result of nerve damage. At the time, it was the least of his problems.

My biggest problem? Being cheated out of my Lamaze-LeBoyer birthing and bonding ceremony. I tried my best to compensate. The nurses allowed me to take over as much of Anthony's care as possible. I touched him, held him, sponged him, changed him, and greased his cracked skin. I took pictures, played music boxes, and talked to him constantly. I continued singing a song that I'd made up and sung to him while I was pregnant. I wanted him to know that I was still there, that there was something sweet about extrauterine life, something besides the beeps, the lights, and the pain.

Since the nursery was his home, it became my home, too. I moved in and redecorated. I filled his bed with tiny stuffed animals and hung scrolls and cards to celebrate his one-week, one-month, two-month birthdays. I pasted up Pilgrims and turkeys for Thanksgiving, and decked the warming table (and later the incubator) with paper chains at Christmas. People thought I was obsessed, spending all day, every day with my baby. I was offered well-meant suggestions about better ways to spend my time. They fell on deaf ears.

My brother came for Thanksgiving. He was allowed to see Anthony for an hour, and was overwhelmed—especially by the "intensity" of the ICN. He took me out to dinner and couldn't understand the agony I felt during those two hours. All I wanted to do was "go home" to the nursery.

Another aspect of the natural birth experience that escaped me was breast-feeding. I froze my initial two-week "gush," which was eventually gavage-

*Anthony at 1 month (2 pounds, 6 ounces).*

*Anthony (watching "Sesame Street") at 18 months.*

fed to my son. Then I promptly dried up. I tried everything: an electric breast pump, beer, brewer's yeast, wine, all manner of weird herbs. For 2½ months I massaged, pummeled, and otherwise mangled my breasts, then decided that Anthony had his whole lifetime to have wonderful experiences—nursing was one he could do without.

After a month of uncertainty, the neonatologist finally gave me a prognosis of fair to good, despite the fact that Ant possibly would have permanent brain and lung damage, and probably would have permanent paralysis in his arm.

Once he was extubated, Anthony took off. The brain hemorrhage resolved, he started gaining weight. All of a sudden, his main problem was his arm. As we left the hospital 2½ months after Anthony's birth (and a month before his due date), I was instructed in range-of-motion exercises to keep his arm from becoming atrophied. He weighed 4½ pounds, and I was the proudest of mamas.

The next six months were a blur. Anthony ate every 2½ hours. He got four different medicines at different times. I gave him range-of-motion exercises three times a day. I did the interminable wash and housework during his 2-hour naps. I really don't know when I slept.

I took him to surgeons, neurosurgeons, ophthalmologists, pediatricians, follow-up clinics, and therapists. I also took him to *my* doctor visits, the grocery store, and anywhere else I had to go. I took him out in the stroller once he reached six pounds. I had no choice. There was no one to keep him.

I was determined not to become an overprotective mother, and aside from a ban on smoking in my apartment, I took no special precautions. And in the first year Ant only had two colds, neither of which turned into the pneumonia I'd been prepared for. His lungs improved, his eyes improved, his anemia (slowly) improved, and after months of therapy to his arm, it also improved.

This isn't to say that the first year was easy. It was hell. After Anthony had been home for several weeks, he began screaming every evening. It never occurred to me that he could have something as ordinary as colic. For six weeks, every day at four o'clock he began to cry and he didn't stop until eight o'clock, when he fell asleep from exhaustion. I tried any and everything to stop his crying (and save my sanity), but nothing worked.

The lowest point in the first year came about a week before Ant's birthday. He developed severe diarrhea. If I had any leftover romantic notions about motherhood, they were completely erased by five days and five nights of constant clean-up. Anthony was rehospitalized, mainly to give *me* a rest. He came home on his first birthday.

Ant's second year was no improvement. He had three nasty ear infections. He didn't cut his first tooth until he was 15 months old. He didn't start walking until 20 months, and we had two physical therapy sessions a week for what seemed like forever. It was either teething or an ear infection or a temper tantrum, all designed to try the patience of a saint, which I'm not.

Once he started walking, however, everything changed. He entered the realm of *normal*. Now, at 26 months, Anthony is a very small (21 pounds), adorable, happy child. In some areas his development has sped along. He knows his numbers to 20, his alphabet (upper and lower case), and can "read" about thirty words. His social skills are fine. His motor development, however, has always been delayed, partly due to problems with his arm. Even though things look fairly good, I'm still waiting for the other shoe to drop. To have been as small and sick and early as he was, and to escape all permanent damage seems unlikely to me. While I feel very fortunate that he's doing so well thus far, I don't know when I'll be able to really relax.

Raising a child alone on welfare has been a true challenge. There have been times when Anthony and I have been up in the middle of the night, me with only two pennies to rub together and him with a 105° fever. I'd look at my son and say, "Well, Ant, I've heard that God takes care of fools and babies, so I guess we're covered." I know I'd have to be crazy to want to try this again, but I wouldn't trade my child for all the gold in Fort Knox. The best part of all this is that we have each other.

# *11*

# *Will My Baby Be Normal?*

Once a baby's survival seems certain, the question most parents ask (or are afraid to ask) is: "Will my baby be normal?" Since half of all neurological handicaps in infants result from prematurity, this is a valid concern.

## Follow-up Studies

### *The Under-1500-Gram Baby*

With the advent of newborn intensive care in the 60s and 70s, tiny prematures were being saved in record numbers, and hospitals around the world launched follow-up studies to look at the quality of life among this new group of survivors. Most of these studies focused on babies who weighed less than 1500 grams, or 3½ pounds, at birth, since the most dramatic improvements in survival were occurring among these infants.

How many of these babies have problems? How many are normal? Statistics vary from study to study. The population of babies included in a follow-up investigation can influence the outcome statistics. Prematures from low socioeconomic backgrounds, for example, tend to have poorer outcomes than middle-class prematures. Those studies that include transported babies often report a higher percentage of problems than do studies limited to inborn babies—babies born and treated at a tertiary center where expert care is available to them during the critical periods before, during, and immediately after birth. The duration of the study also affects the statistics. Studies that follow infants only for the first year or two tend to declare more babies normal than do studies in which nursery graduates are followed into childhood, when more subtle problems become apparent. On the other hand, long-term studies of school-age prematures evaluate children who were born and treated six or more years earlier. Changes in neonatal care may improve the outcomes of babies born more recently.

One of the oldest ongoing studies of under-1500-gram babies is being conducted at the University of California, San Francisco. The study is limited to inborn babies with no known prenatal problems—such as congenital abnormalities (Down's syndrome, for example) or intrauterine infections—that might adversely affect development. While babies from a wide range of social and ethnic backgrounds are included in the study, the tiny babies are predominantly from white middle-class families.

"We now have good data on 200 of these children who are six years of age or older," says Dr. Jane Hunt, a psychologist with the UCSF clinic. "By the end of the first year we are finding problems in about 12%* of these children. Only a handful, fewer than 5%, are *seriously* disabled with blindness, *profound* retardation, or *severe* cerebral palsy. The rest have lesser degrees of retardation—mild to moderate cerebral palsy, visual or hearing impairments, or combinations of these handicaps. Then, by age six an *additional* 28% of the children begin showing evidence of milder problems, problems that mean these children will need extra help in school or special schooling."

These milder difficulties may include learning disabilities, behavior disorders, problems with physical coordination, or a somewhat lower than normal IQ.

Some prematurely born children exhibit a combination of characteristics referred to as *minimal brain dysfunction* or *hyperactivity*. These children tend to be-

---

*By comparison, a 1979 study of under-1500-gram, inborn babies at Hammersmith Hospital, London, revealed a 13.7% incidence of major handicaps. Another study that year from Rainbow Children's Hospital in Cleveland, Ohio that included inborn *and* transported babies showed an 18% handicap rate.

202

Will My Baby Be Normal? 203

have impulsively, have a low tolerance for frustration, and have poor emotional control. They may have short attention spans and be easily distractable. They may be hypersensitive to sights, sounds, and other sensory stimulation. On the positive side, one researcher has observed that the premature's great sensitivity to sound and color often gives him considerable pleasure as a child and may lead to creative pursuits in later life.

Prematures are also vulnerable to learning disabilities, problems that often involve hand-eye coordination or visual perception. These learning problems are not generally caused by defects in the eye, but rather by disorders in the part of the brain that processes visual information. Drawing, copying a design, and later on, reading and writing may present special challenges. Some children also have problems with speech and self-expression. They may mispronounce words or find it hard to use words to express ideas.

Learning disabilities and minimal brain dysfunction are not limited to prematurely born children. They afflict over 10% of the entire population—boys are more often affected than girls. They exist in children of all IQ levels, from retarded to genius. Although learning and behavior problems are troubling to the child and his family, they are not necessarily disabling and do not rule out a successful or productive life.

John Zimmer, born a three-pound premie, was hyperactive and learning-disabled. In the introduction to the book *Living with Our Hyperactive Children* (see page 245), he tells what it was like to grow up with these problems. As a small child he was constantly in motion. He needed to be eating a cookie to hold still long enough to have his picture taken. His favorite pastime was unrolling toilet paper. School was difficult. "Upon entering first grade," he writes, "I found it easier to spell backwards than forwards. My mother finally taught me to spell forwards but only after a solid year of working with me . . . It took me an hour to do a fifteen-minute lesson because I could not concentrate . . . Tests became a problem when I read the wrong words in questions." He was clumsy at games, the last to be chosen for a team. His mother was told her son was not college material. Nevertheless, he managed to finish college and medical school, graduating in the top half of his class. "I am still not a speed reader," Dr. Zimmer admits, "and I find taped lessons and lectures easier to understand than written matter." Dr. Zimmer is now a successful pediatrician who is held in special esteem by parents of hyperactive children in his practice.

Thomas Edison, Nelson Rockefeller, and Winston Churchill (also a premie) are others who achieved success despite minimal brain dysfunction and learning disabilities. Comedian Joey Bishop (another three-pounder) had academic problems beginning in kindergarten when he "flunked sandpile." Prematurely born Albert Einstein was developmentally delayed, learning-disabled, and considered to be a hopeless student.

However, Dr. Jane Hunt emphasizes: *It is important to keep in mind that 60%—the majority of the tiny premies we see—do not even have mild problems. They are, as best we can determine, completely normal.*

And contrary to the fears of some parents and doctors, the tiny prematures do not seem to have been emotionally scarred by their difficult beginnings. "We have not seen mental illnesses such as autism or schizophrenia among the children we've followed," states Dr. Hunt.

At the UCSF follow-up clinic and at similar clinics around the country, prematurely born babies are periodically evaluated during infancy and childhood. Their developmental progress is followed: When does the baby reach certain milestones such as rolling over, sitting, crawling, and walking? When does the baby begin to talk? The older child is also tested for IQ and given special tests to evaluate visual-motor integration (hand-eye coordination), use of language, and academic achievement.

The prematurely born child has his age adjusted for prematurity, and his test scores are compared to normal values for a child of that age. In other words, a baby born three months early would be compared at age 15 months to a one-year-old baby. Correcting for prematurity is important in infancy, when a few months can make a great difference in a child's development. Later in childhood, the weeks or months of prematurity become less significant.

"During the first year," says Dr. Hunt, "we also look at the baby's general appearance, posture, and body tone. We look at how he uses his hands and how he plays with toys. We listen to the way he vocalizes and cries. We note his level of alertness and attention span, his mood swings and social responses.

"It is difficult, however, to make predictions from what is seen in the first year. Some infants who appear to be developing normally will be among those children with educational problems later on. (Predicting their problems at earlier ages is an important research goal, and one of the reasons for follow-up studies of premies.) On the other hand, certain infants who develop more slowly than average during the first year turn out to be all right. Some of these delayed infants may be showing the residual effects of illness and hospitalization. Although these babies have been declared ready to go home, they may still

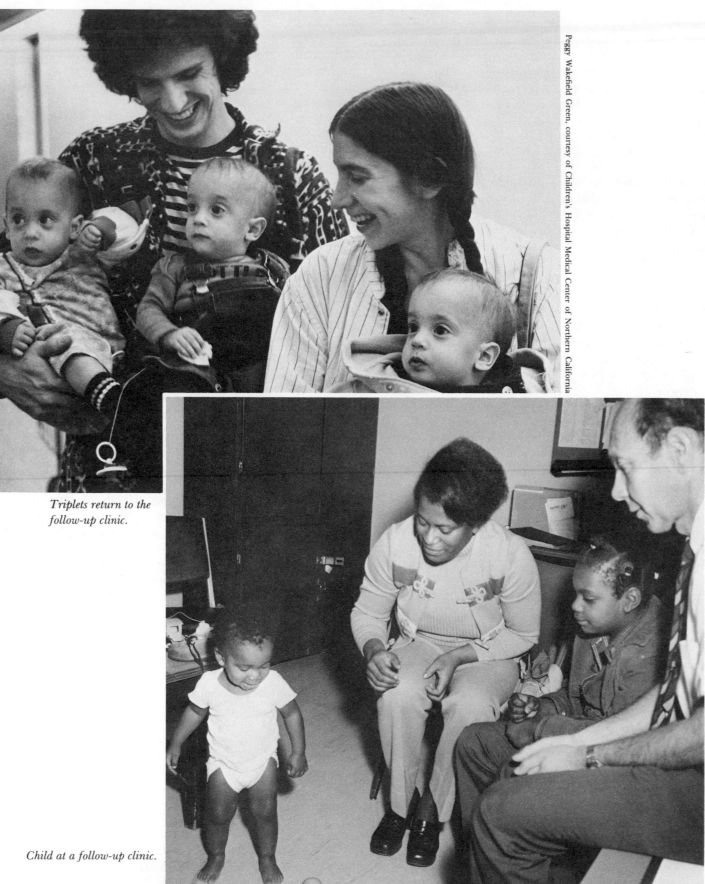

Peggy Wakefield Green, courtesy of Children's Hospital Medical Center of Northern California

*Triplets return to the follow-up clinic.*

*Child at a follow-up clinic.*

Dorothy Larimer Boyd, courtesy of Children's Hospital Medical Center of Northern California

be weak and convalescing. It is possible, too, that some have suffered a brain injury or disturbance that isn't permanent—one that will be compensated for during the further process of growth and development."

Other researchers have noted abnormalities during the first year in prematures who were later normal. Dr. C. M. Drillien of Edinburgh, Scotland, has found abnormally stiff muscle tone and jitteriness in half the under-1500-gram birthweight babies she examines. In the majority of cases, she reports, the stiffness goes away.

Says neonatologist Sally Sehring, "I often see young babies in follow-up who are sitting very rigidly in their mothers' laps, shoulders tightly back. Then the minute I hold out a cookie the suspicious-looking muscle tone disappears and the baby makes a smooth, coordinated grab. If the stiff muscle tone doesn't interfere with the baby's functioning, I don't worry so much about it."

Many doctors have observed uneven development in premature babies during the first year of life. Typically, the baby acquires intellectual and social skills appropriate for his corrected age well before he develops the motor skills normal for that age.

During the first year of the premature baby's life, only the most severe problems can be diagnosed with certainty. "But by ages two and three," says Dr. Hunt, "we can tell much more about the child. We can begin to test hand-eye coordination, paper and pencil tasks. We look at the way the child is using speech—how he understands what is said to him and how he expresses himself. We look at his level of emotional control. Is he highly distractable? How does he interact with his mother and with the examiner?"

"At ages four, five, and six, we begin to test for what we call 'language tracking and processing'—how well the child listens and responds to specific questions or directions. This is different from social chatting—and some of these kids are great social chatters. They may also be strong at rote learning and memorizing. They may get high scores on certain tests, but they still have trouble organizing and expressing ideas."

At age eight, the children are tested for their ability to deal with abstract concepts and for their level of scholastic achievement.

Among the 900- to 1500-gram children, birthweight has less of a relationship to outcome than do the medical complications the child experienced before, during, and after birth. While 40% of *all* the very low-birthweight babies seen at the UCSF follow-up clinic have some form of problem, nearly two-thirds of those who had RDS are affected.

Some follow-up studies also show a higher incidence of handicaps among prematures who were born smaller than normal for their gestational ages (SGA).

Still, it can be difficult to predict a baby's outcome just on the basis of his perinatal problems. "When we try to do this," says neonatologist Ronald Clyman of Mt. Zion Hospital, San Francisco, "we only have a 50-50 chance of being right." In Dr. Clyman's opinion, many very sick prematures probably do suffer brain injuries, but most learn to compensate as they grow, eventually recovering much better than would an adult with similar brain damage. What the brain-injured child has in his favor, states Dr. Clyman, is "the entire lifetime he has ahead of him."

Even babies with the most serious medical problems sometimes turn out amazingly well. Dr. Hunt gave several examples. One was a child who had been hospitalized for nearly two years with "one of the worst cases of bronchopulmonary dysplasia we've ever seen." At age six, the child has some speech and coordination problems, but a normal IQ. Another child—two pounds at birth—suffered an intracranial hemorrhage and developed hydrocephalus. Going into the first grade, this child has mild hand-eye coordination problems, but an IQ over 120. In both cases, sensitive and concerned parents helped their children develop far beyond the expectation of the medical experts.

## Very, Very Low-Birthweight Babies

Very, very low-birthweight babies, those who weigh less than 1000 grams at birth, are now being studied as a special subgroup. Until quite recently, few of these babies survived. Now they have a 50% or better chance to live.

Studies show, however, that these very, very tiny babies are at higher risk for handicaps than the slightly bigger babies—and the lower the birthweight, the greater the risk of severe problems. Follow-up studies done on babies with birthweights below 1000 grams reveal that up to 30% of these children have handicaps serious enough to be diagnosed in the first years of life.

By school age, a high incidence of more subtle problems become apparent. Of the under-900 gram babies followed at the UCSF clinic, most, according to Dr. Hunt, display some problem that causes them significant difficulty in school. However, Dr. Hunt notes, the children currently being studied were born

# Testing Your Baby

In the nursery, and later at the follow-up clinic, your baby may be given tests or assessments of development such as those described below.

### The Brazelton Neonatal Assessment Scale (BNAS)

The "Brazelton" is a physical and behavioral assessment which may be made on a full-term baby around the third day after birth and repeated on day 9 or 10. It may also be given to a recovering premie around his due date and repeated a week or so later.

The test is an observation of the baby's responses to his environment. It assesses the baby's interactions with people and objects. How cuddly is the baby? How easily consoled? How alert to sights and sounds? The test evaluates the baby's motor responses and physical reflexes, his ability to maintain muscle tone and control his movements. It looks at the infant's "organization"—his capacity to make smooth transitions from the various states of deep sleep, light sleep, drowsiness, alertness, active awakeness, and crying. It evaluates the baby's ability to "habituate," or tune out, annoying stimulation. It assesses the baby's responses to stress, his irritability level and his self-comforting skills.

Although the test includes a rating scale from 1 to 9 for different categories of behaviors, there is no "normal" or "abnormal" score. The test merely describes the baby's capabilities during the early days of life. The assessment is used for research purposes, for helping to identify infants at risk, and for giving parents an understanding of their baby's individual behavior style.

### Assessment of Pre-Term Infant Behavior (APIB)

This assessment is a recently developed adaptation and expansion of the "Brazelton" to be used with premies. It evaluates a premature baby's range of behaviors from the time he is medically stable until his responses to his environment are similar to those of a full-term newborn.

During the assessment the baby is observed for his reactions to light, sound, and handling, and for his "social" responses to the face and voice of the examiner. The baby's reflexes are checked and his ability to regulate such bodily functions as heartbeat and breathing are also noted.

As with the "Brazelton," the baby may be given scores on certain groups of items. Again, there is no "normal" or "abnormal" score. The purpose of the test is to describe the baby's current abilities and vulnerabilities so that recommendations on appropriate handling of the baby can be given to his parents and the nursery staff.

### The Denver Developmental Screening Test (DDST)

The "Denver" is an easily administered test used to screen children from birth to age six for possible developmental problems. The test can be given by pediatricians, nurses, or others who have had no special training in psychological testing.

The test consists of a list of skills in four areas—personal-social, fine motor, large motor, and language. Depending on a child's ability to accomplish tasks in each area appropriate for his age, he is given an evaluation of "normal," "abnormal," or "questionable." During the examination the child is also tested for skills *above* his age level. No child is expected to accomplish every item on the test.

The "Denver" is not an intelligence test. It merely indicates what a young child is able to do at a given age. The test is a rough screening device that can reveal areas in a child's development that need further evaluation. It does not pick up subtle problems or delays. Prematures and other infants at risk benefit from more comprehensive testing than that provided by the "Denver."

### The Bayley Scales

The "Bayley" is the most highly standardized, widely used infant test. It can be given to children from the 2nd to the 30th month post-term. Administering the "Bayley" properly is an art as well as a science. It is given by specially trained professionals who use a variety of toys and play activities in testing the child. During testing, the child may be asked to perform certain tasks requiring skills above his age level. No child is expected to accomplish everything asked of him on the test.

The "Bayley" consists of three sections:

1. *The Mental Scale* examines the child's ability to sense and perceive the world. It tests for the development of memory, problem-solving ability, the beginning of abstract thought, vocalization and early speech. The score on this part of the test is termed the MDI or Mental Development Index.
2. *The Motor Scale* evaluates the child's control of his body, his general coordination, and his fine motor skills (the use of his hands). The score given is the PDI or Psychomotor Development Index.
3. *The Infant Behavior Profile* consists of the examiner's subjective impressions about the child's temperament, attention span, activity level, and reactions to people and objects. No score is given.

An overall score or DQ (Developmental Quotient) may be computed from the MDI and PDI. The DQ has only a very limited ability to predict a child's later IQ or Intelligence Quotient. Normal DQ scores on the Bayley range from 86 to 115.

Often a child's performance is expressed in terms of age equivalency. For example: "Johnny is at the 14 month level in mental development and at the 12 month level in motor development."

Since children normally have developmental lags and spurts, and since a child's response to the test may be very different on any given day, the "Bayley" is repeated throughout infancy. Over time, the child's pattern of strengths and weaknesses emerges, and early intervention, if necessary, can be directed toward those areas where special help is needed.

6 to 8 years ago. Subsequent improvements in neonatal care may brighten the outlook for very tiny babies born more recently.

## The "Big" Healthy Premature

And what about those prematures who weigh over 3½ pounds at birth, babies who only need extra time in the hospital to grow and develop? Studies conducted in the 30s and 40s showed that although these children were likely to have a "developmental lag" in infancy, they usually appeared normal later in childhood.

Recently, researchers have tested a group of healthy, middle-class, slightly premature children to see if their early birth made any difference in later life. These were children with birthweights between 1400 and 2500 grams who had not suffered RDS or any other major health problem in the newborn period. They were given a variety of tests at 7 to 9½ years of age and compared to their full-term counterparts. The prematurely born children showed no significant difference in their personal or social development in middle childhood. Their school achievement was also similar to the term-born children. However, on tests of special skills, especially those involving visual processing of information or visual-motor integration, the prematures scored significantly lower *as a group*. It seems likely that although these children are functioning well, some of them have subtle problems that make certain types of academic work more difficult.

# Ongoing Problems

## Cerebral Palsy

Although the words conjure up visions of wheelchairs and braces, cerebral palsy is a catch-all term used to describe virtually any difficulty with coordinated movement caused by a brain injury. Anything from clumsiness to complete paralysis can fit this definition. Close to 500,000 people in the United States have some degree of cerebral palsy—about one-third of them were born prematurely.

The term "cerebral palsy" includes several quite different neuro-muscular disorders. *Athetosis* is a form of cerebral palsy characterized by involuntary writhing motions. This type of cerebral palsy can be caused by oxygen deprivation or more often by the toxic effects of bilirubin. Since levels of bilirubin in most newborns are so carefully controlled, athetosis is now relatively uncommon.

*Ataxia,* another form of cerebral palsy, results from damage to a part of the brain called the cerebellum. With ataxia, functions controlled by the cerebellum such as balance and depth perception are impaired; muscle tone may also be limp and floppy.

The most common type of cerebral palsy, and the type most often seen in prematures, is *spasticity,* an abnormally increased or stiff muscle tone. To perform an act, muscles receive messages both from nerves that initiate action and from nerves that limit or control the act. In the spastic form of cerebral palsy, there is impairment in areas of the brain that help modulate and control certain motions. As a result, movement can be stiff and poorly coordinated.

Spasticity is described in terms of the body parts involved. When the arm and leg on one side of the body are affected, it is called *hemiplegia. Diplegia* refers to the involvement of both legs. When both arms and both legs are affected, it is termed *quadriplegia.* Although the suffix "plegia" literally means paralysis,* it is used to refer to any degree of spasticity from mild clumsiness to major impairment.

A child with mild or moderate spasticity in his legs may walk stiffly or bounce along on his toes. Because many of these children keep their feet extended and toes pointed, their heel cords (Achilles tendons) may shorten from constant contraction. Exercises that bend the ankle help keep the heel cord supple, but occasionally surgery to lengthen the heel cords is recommended.

If the arms are affected, the child may have trouble coordinating the motions necessary for fine motor skills, such as buttoning buttons, tying shoelaces, and eating well with utensils. The child later has difficulty drawing and writing.

If the muscles of the mouth are involved, the child may mispronounce words. Chewing and swallowing are sometimes difficult, and parents may need to experiment with some special food textures and feeding techniques. Children with cerebral palsy may also need extra-rich diets to replace the calories their overly contracted muscles expend and to fuel the extra efforts they must make to control their actions.

Some children with cerebral palsy have poor control over their eye muscles. Strabismus (crossing of the eyes) is a common problem, but one that can be helped with glasses, patching the strong eye to exercise the weak eye, and simple surgery to readjust the eye muscles.

*Sometimes the more correct *paresis,* meaning weakness, is used.

Hearing disabilities are also frequently seen in the cerebral-palsied child. And while cerebral palsy occurs among children of all IQ levels, approximately half of those afflicted are also to some degree mentally retarded.

It is difficult to diagnose cerebral palsy in a premature during early infancy. A premie is normally limp (hypotonic) after birth. Then slowly, over a period of months, he begins to gain muscle tone. During this period even the baby who will later be spastic may appear normal. On the other hand, some infants who appear stiff and possibly spastic during the first year are later found *not* to have cerebral palsy.

When a baby consistently holds or moves one side of his body very differently from the other side, it may be an early indication of cerebral palsy. Children who are later found to have cerebral palsy often have feeding difficulties and highly irregular sleep patterns in infancy (but then so do many normal premies). Extreme listlessness or irritability can also be early warning signs.

Cerebral palsy is caused by an injury to the brain from asphyxia (lack of oxygen and blood flow), meningitis, or toxins such as bilirubin. The nature of the brain injury does not change, that is, it does not get better or worse as the child grows. However, children with cerebral palsy often show improvement in their ability to function as they grow and develop. Many children with mild cerebral palsy learn to compensate so well that as they get older their problems are virtually unnoticeable.

## Mental Retardation

Over six million people in the United States (roughly 3% of the population) are mentally retarded. Since the great majority of these individuals live at home, it is estimated that retardation touches the lives of over 20 million people.

Premature babies are among those at risk for mental retardation. The same types of brain injuries (from asphyxia, meningitis, and so on) that cause cerebral palsy may lead to mental retardation as well. Many premature babies who are mentally retarded also have some degree of motor impairment or cerebral palsy.

A person's mental ability is evaluated by his score on an intelligence test. His IQ (Intelligence Quotient) is then derived by taking his mental age (as determined by his test score) and dividing it by his actual or chronological age and multiplying by 100. For example, a six-year-old whose test score was similar to that of most other six-year-olds would have an IQ of 100 (mental age/chronological age = 6/6 × 100 = 100). A six-year-old whose test score was that of an average three-year-old would have an IQ of 50 (mental age/chronological age = 3/6 × 100 = 50).

Based on the Stanford-Binet IQ scales, scores from 84 to 116 are within the normal range.

*Borderline retardation* includes IQ scores from 68 to 83. A borderline retarded child may be developmentally normal in early childhood but a slow learner in school. As an adult he is usually self-supporting and able to marry, care for children, and lead an independent life. He may be virtually undistinguishable from people with normal IQs.

*Mildly retarded* individuals, sometimes referred to as "educable," score between 52 and 67 on IQ tests. The mildly retarded infant is usually slow in his early development, eventually achieving the academic abilities of an 8- to 12-year-old. Many mildly retarded adults are self-supporting; some are able to marry, but few are capable of caring for children.

*Moderately retarded* persons (with IQs of 36 to 51) are sometimes referred to as the *trainable mentally retarded*. These individuals show marked developmental delays in infancy, especially in the acquisition of speech. They eventually achieve a mental age of three to seven years. While they can perform simple tasks in a sheltered environment, they are not capable of an independent life.

The *severely* or *profoundly retarded*, those with IQs below 35, never reach a mental age beyond that of an infant or toddler. They have few, if any, self-help skills and require complete care and supervision throughout life.

But IQ scores never tell the entire story. What matters most is how well a person actually functions in his environment, and many important adaptive characteristics—creativity, mechanical ability, and social skills, for example—are not measured by these tests. Many people with subnormal IQs perform very well in society and are not considered by those around them to be retarded. And others with very high IQs may adapt so poorly to the world that they do not function much at all.

IQ test scores may not accurately reflect the intelligence of people with learning disabilities or other handicaps, simply because these people cannot take the tests properly. One youngster with visual-motor and reading problems had always tested in the retarded range until he was given the test aloud. His actual IQ was found to be 135. IQ tests have also been criticized for a cultural bias that favors the white middle-class test-taker.

Tests given during the first four years of life are not necessarily predictive of the child's later IQ. (During infancy, tests measure DQ, or Developmental Quotient, which refers to the developmental tasks a child has mastered at a given age.) Even later, scores may vary widely each time the child has his IQ tested.

A child's IQ score may improve greatly over time depending on the intellectual stimulation he receives from the world around him. This is as true for the retarded child as for the genius. The brain-injured child's eventual ability for intellectual achievement depends on a combination of variables—the child's original genetic potential, the extent of his brain injury, his own will and determination, and, above all, the amount of support and encouragement he is given by the important people in his life.

## Hearing Impairment

Hearing impairment is the most common handicap in the United States, affecting some 3 million children and 13 million adults. Prematurely born individuals make up a high proportion (about 17%) of the hearing-impaired population. Somewhere between 2 and 10% of prematures who weighed less than 1500 grams at birth have a hearing impairment. Because of the high incidence of hearing loss among these babies, it is recommended that they receive a thorough audiologic evaluation within the first three months of life.

### Types of Hearing Loss

If sound impulses are not properly transmitted across the ear drum and through the bones of the middle ear to the cochlea, the resulting impairment is called a *conductive hearing loss*. This type of hearing impairment is most often caused by frequent ear infections or inflammations (and prematures are highly vulnerable to ear infections). Many cases of conductive hearing loss could be prevented by prompt treatment of middle ear problems. People with a conductive hearing impairment cannot hear low-volume or low-frequency sounds. They often benefit from the sound amplification of a hearing aid.

If hearing problems result from damage to the cilia (the microscopic hairs in the cochlea) or from damage to the nerves that receive and transmit sound

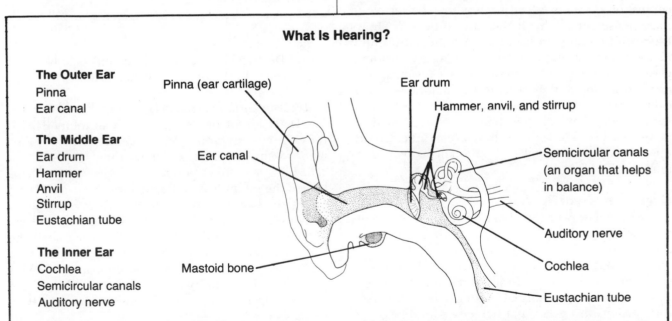

**What Is Hearing?**

**The Outer Ear**
Pinna
Ear canal

**The Middle Ear**
Ear drum
Hammer
Anvil
Stirrup
Eustachian tube

**The Inner Ear**
Cochlea
Semicircular canals
Auditory nerve

Pinna (ear cartilage)
Ear drum
Hammer, anvil, and stirrup
Ear canal
Semicircular canals (an organ that helps in balance)
Mastoid bone
Auditory nerve
Cochlea
Eustachian tube

When sound waves enter the ear they cause vibrations in the ear drum, the membrane that stretches across the back of the ear canal and separates the outer ear from the middle ear. Vibrations from the ear drum pass along a chain of tiny bones in the middle ear called the hammer, anvil, and stirrup. The last of these bones, the stirrup, partially extends into a small organ in the inner ear called the cochlea. The cochlea, a fluid-filled structure shaped like a snail's shell, is lined with thousands of nerve cells and microscopic hairs, or cilia. When the stirrup bone vibrates, it sends ripples through the cochlear fluid. Different areas of cilia sway back and forth in response to the different frequencies of the vibrations. The motion of the cilia generates electrical impulses that are carried along the auditory nerve to the brain. There, special areas of the cerebral cortex interpret these impulses as meaningful sound.

impulses to the brain, the impairment is called a *sensory-neural hearing loss*. Damage to these delicate structures may be caused by lack of oxygen before, during, or after birth; by certain congenital infections such as cytomegalovirus or rubella; by meningitis; and by large doses of drugs such as kanamycin or gentamicin. (When these antibiotics must be given to an infant, his blood is checked frequently to be sure the drugs do not accumulate in toxic levels.) Sensory-neural hearing loss does not affect the volume of sounds a person can hear. Instead, certain frequencies of sound—usually high frequencies—cannot be perceived. Sounds may also be distorted. High-frequency consonant sounds like *s, sh, t, th* are not heard, and the child can distinguish only parts of words. Rhyming words—cat, sat, that—may sound identical. Some people with sensory-neural hearing impairment are helped by hearing aids, others are not.

A *central* or *perceptive hearing loss* results when those areas of the brain that process sounds have been damaged. Since sound impulses still reach the brain, this is not so much a hearing impairment as a listening and understanding impairment. Meningitis or asphyxia can cause such damage. A person with a central or perceptive hearing loss may be unable to make sense out of what he hears, as if he were always listening to a foreign language. People with central hearing loss may suppress sounds that are meaningless to them and may sometimes, as a result, appear deaf even though they react to startling noises. Children with central hearing loss can usually learn to speak, but their speech tends to be limited to memorized responses. They have great difficulty with the normal give-and-take of spontaneous conversation.

## Degrees of Hearing Loss

Another way of classifying hearing impairments is according to the volume of sound that can be perceived. Sound is measured in units called decibels: normal conversation is around 30 to 45 decibels; street noises, 70 to 80 decibels; a train, 90 to 100 decibels; and a jet taking off, 140 decibels. A person with a *mild hearing loss* can't perceive sound below 30 to 45 decibels. A person with *moderate hearing loss* (no perception below 45 to 60 decibels) can hear only loud speech. A person with *severe hearing loss* can't hear below 60 to 80 decibels. With *profound hearing loss*, only noises above 80 to 90 decibels can be heard. Mild hearing loss may cause a child problems in school and require special seating so that he can hear properly. Children with moderate to profound hearing loss usually need special instruction in learning to

---

### Babies at Risk for Hearing Impairment

According to the Joint Committee on Infant Hearing (a group composed of members from the Academy of Pediatrics, the Academy of Otolaryngology, and the American Speech-Language and Hearing Association), infants are at risk for hearing impairment if they manifest *one or more* of the following risk criteria:

1. A family history of childhood hearing impairment.
2. Congenital perinatal infection (e.g., cytomegalovirus, rubella, herpes, toxoplasmosis, or syphilis).
3. Malformations involving the neck or head.
4. Birthweight below 1500 grams.
5. Hyperbilirubinemia (jaundice) exceeding the level at which an exchange transfusion is indicated.
6. Bacterial meningitis, especially H. influenzae.
7. Severe asphyxia, which may include infants with Apgar scores from 0–3 or those who fail to breathe on their own by 10 minutes of age, or those with hypotonia (very limp muscle tone) persisting to 2 hours of age.

According to the Committee's 1981 recommendations, infants who meet one or more of these risk criteria should receive expert audiological screening before leaving the intensive care nursery or within the first 3 months of life.

---

speak. Deafness is hearing so impaired as to be of no use—even with the help of a hearing aid.

## Detecting and Treating Hearing Problems

Detection of hearing loss early in infancy helps the child and his family make the best possible adjustment. Some hospitals are now using a special test called a *Crib-O-Gram* to screen for hearing problems before the infant leaves the nursery. A device placed under the baby's mattress detects his movements in response to sound. The Crib-O-Gram can reveal deafness, but not subtle degrees of hearing loss. The baby may also have his hearing more thoroughly evaluated by *brainstem evoked response audiometry*. This procedure involves placing monitor pads on the baby's scalp to pick up his brain wave responses to various sounds.

At home, parents can observe the way their baby reacts to a sudden loud noise. Usually the child will wake up if asleep, startle if awake, or at least blink or widen his eyes when he has heard a loud, unexpected sound. Even a normally hearing infant will ignore some loud noises; only a *consistent* lack of response should cause concern. Other signs of possible hearing impairment are a lack of cooing and babbling by seven months of age (corrected for prematurity) or lack of some intelligible speech by the age of two. Certain behavior patterns are also common among children with impaired hearing. The child who hears poorly may seem inattentive and withdrawn, but also given to irritability and tantrums because of his frustration at not understanding or being understood.

When parents suspect something is wrong, they should first consult their pediatrician. "However, the pediatrician is often the *last* person to admit that there is a problem," says Harriet Eskildsen, a teacher of deaf and hearing-impaired children. "If parents think their child hears poorly, they should follow their gut instinct and pursue the matter. They should take their child for an evaluation by an *otologist*, a

doctor who specializes in hearing problems, and by an *audiologist*, who can evaluate the nature of a hearing loss. Most large hospitals, such as those with intensive care nurseries, have the staff and facilities to test an infant's hearing."

The earlier the problem is detected, says Mrs. Eskildsen, the more there is that can be done about it. Many hearing-impaired infants benefit from hearing aids, though, she adds, designing a hearing aid for an infant is an inexact science. Finding the proper device may be an expensive trial-and-error proposition. "How the baby responds to the hearing aid is the only reliable indication of whether or not it is helping," Mrs. Eskildsen continues. "If the baby objects to the

*Baby being tested by brainstem-evoked audiometry.*

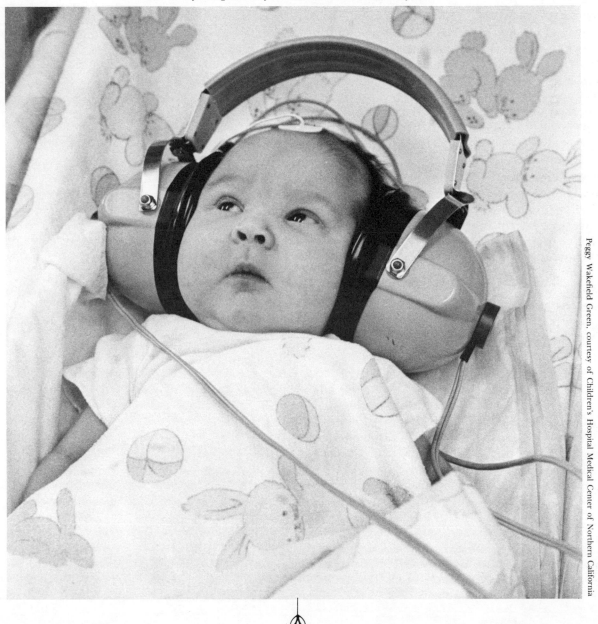

hearing aid, then it is probably not the right one for him." Despite the difficulties involved, the earlier the baby receives the proper hearing aid, the greater his chances are of eventually achieving good oral speech.

Mrs. Eskildsen further advises parents of hearing-impaired infants: "Talk to your baby as much as possible, and sing to your baby. Hold the baby close so that he can feel the vibrations from your body when you speak. Talk to the baby when he is looking at you and repeat the names of objects that the baby sees or touches. Don't exaggerate your voice or shout. Let your baby get used to what normal speech *looks* like. And encourage your baby to vocalize. When he coos and babbles, light up, smile at him." Aside from speech, which will come only with time and special training, the development of the hearing-impaired child should proceed normally unless other handicaps are also present. Mrs. Eskildsen adds that some parents can become so absorbed with the child's problem that they neglect the other aspects of his development. "As much as possible," she says, "the hearing-impaired child should be included in normal activities."

## Visual Impairment

Visual impairment is one of the most frequently encountered problems among prematures, especially the smaller prematures. Many of these vision problems are the aftereffects of retrolental fibroplasia (RLF). But even prematures who never get RLF (or those whose early RLF resolves) still have more than their share of errors of refraction (focusing difficulties such as nearsightedness or farsightedness), strabismus (crossing of the eyes), and damage to the optic nerve or to the part of the brain that processes visual information.

### Errors of Refraction

Abnormalities of the eye structure itself may cause errors of refraction or poor focusing of visual images onto the retina. If the lens is too thin or too thick or if the eye is too long or too short, light waves may focus before they hit the retina—causing nearsightedness (*myopia*)—or they may focus at a theoretical point behind the retina—causing farsightedness (*hyperopia*). Another error of refraction, astigmatism, results from irregularities in the lens or outer eye that distort entering light waves. An ophthalmologist, on simple examination of the eye, can diagnose errors of refraction even in the youngest of infants. Corrective lenses—glasses or contact lenses—can then be prescribed to alleviate these problems.

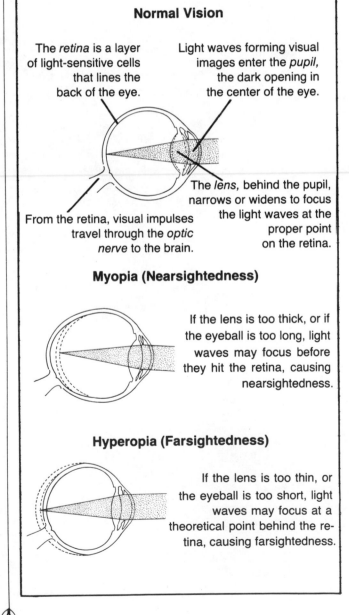

### What Is Vision?

Vision is a complex process involving the eye, the muscles that support and move the eye, the nerves that carry visual impulses to the brain, and the areas of the brain that interpret visual information.

Light waves from an object enter the eye through the pupil, the dark opening in the center of the eye. Behind the pupil is the lens, which focuses the light waves through the fluid-filled center of the eye—called the vitreous body—and on to the back wall of the eye, the retina. Nerve fibers in the retina pick up the projected image and carry it along the optic nerve to the brain, where it is interpreted as a meaningful picture.

Our two eyes receive light waves from an object at slightly different angles. The brain combines these two slightly different images to give us a picture of three dimensional reality.

#### Normal Vision

The *retina* is a layer of light-sensitive cells that lines the back of the eye.

Light waves forming visual images enter the *pupil*, the dark opening in the center of the eye.

From the retina, visual impulses travel through the *optic nerve* to the brain.

The *lens*, behind the pupil, narrows or widens to focus the light waves at the proper point on the retina.

#### Myopia (Nearsightedness)

If the lens is too thick, or if the eyeball is too long, light waves may focus before they hit the retina, causing nearsightedness.

#### Hyperopia (Farsightedness)

If the lens is too thin, or the eyeball is too short, light waves may focus at a theoretical point behind the retina, causing farsightedness.

Alfred Harrison

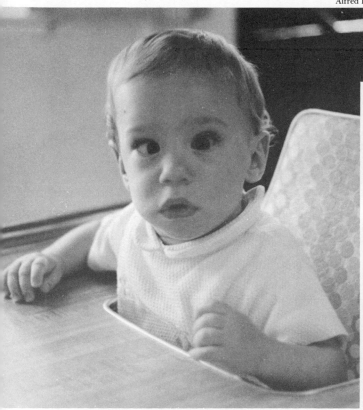

*Before strabismus surgery.*

*After strabismus surgery.*

Alfred Harrison

### Strabismus

Each eye is controlled by six muscles working in pairs. One muscle contracts while its partner lengthens to move the eye and keep it in alignment with the other eye. The eyes must be properly aligned and working together for three-dimensional vision to occur. If one eye tends to drift up, down, in or out, this condition is called strabismus.

During the first six months of life, the baby's eyes do not always move or focus together, and a certain amount of eye-crossing is normal. However, if the eyes are persistently out of alignment during the first six months, or if the misalignment continues into the second half of the first year, the child should be evaluated by an eye doctor (an ophthalmologist).

When a child's eyes do not work together, they send pictures to the brain that are too different from each other for the brain to combine properly. At first double vision occurs. But after a while the brain compensates by suppressing the weaker image and accepting impulses only from the stronger eye.

A child does not outgrow strabismus. The earlier in infancy that it is detected and treated, the better the prospect of restoring the child's proper vision and appearance. In fact, if the problem is not corrected before the age of six, the brain will permanently suppress the visual impulses from the weak eye, leaving the child effectively blind in that eye. This brain-centered vision loss is called *amblyopia*.

Glasses or contact lenses may be prescribed for infants with strabismus to reduce eyestrain. In addition, the strong eye may be patched or medicated to force the weak eye to work. Simple surgery may be necessary to shorten or lengthen certain muscles that control the eyes.

**The Aftereffects of Retrolental Fibroplasia.** During the early stages of RLF, abnormally growing blood vessels can leak fluid into the eye structures, causing scars to form. Over a period of weeks or months as the scar tissue contracts, it can stretch, tear, and partially or entirely detach the retina. The scar tissue may also block the normal passage of light through the lens to the retina. (See page 68.)

Depending on the extent and location of the scarring and retinal damage, varying degrees of vision loss result. If the retina detaches entirely, the child becomes blind. A child with healthy bits of tissue near the center of his retina often has enough useful vision for tasks like reading, though he may have poor peripheral (side) vision. If the retina is stretched, the macula—the point on the retina where visual images are focused—may be pulled off-center, and the child may need to turn his eye out to the side in order to focus properly, a condition called *exotropia*.

Myopia and strabismus are also common aftereffects of RLF.

Children who received oxygen in the nursery should be seen by an ophthalmologist before leaving the hospital and again during the early weeks or months at home.

Any child with permanent eye changes from RLF should be seen regularly throughout childhood by an eye doctor, since retinal detachment can occur later, especially in children who are quite nearsighted as a result of RLF. However, surgery to reattach the retina and preserve vision is often successful in such cases.

## Optic Nerve Damage

Infection, lack of oxygen, birth trauma, or pressure in the brain can all cause damage to the optic nerve, the cable of nerve fibers that leads from the retina to the brain. The amount of visual impairment that results depends on the number and type of fibers that are damaged. The child may be blind or have partial sight that one ophthalmologist likened to poor reception on a television set.

## Brain-centered Visual Impairment

Even with normal eyes and optic nerves, some children cannot see properly because of injury to the part of the brain that processes visual information. Visual impressions may be jumbled and confused. The child may be unable to perceive distances or judge the speed of moving objects. He may have difficulty distinguishing up from down, big from little, left from right. A child who cannot trust what his eyes tell him is slow to develop motor skills, since he cannot tell when to stop, how low to duck, or when to get out of the way. He may be able to focus on visual details but not perceive a picture as a whole. He literally cannot see the forest for the trees.

The child may have a hard time combining or integrating what his eyes see with what he hears and feels. He may be unable to associate a word written on a page with the same word spoken aloud. Each sense may seem to operate independently with little interconnection. If his visual-motor skills are poor, the child may be unable to duplicate with his hands an image that he sees with his eyes. He may have trouble copying a design, drawing, or writing. Many learning disabilities result from some degree of visual (or auditory) imperception.

## Degrees of Visual Functioning

Visual acuity refers to how well the eyes see a given object at a certain distance. Normal vision is 20/20, meaning that a person sees at 20 feet what is *normally* seen at a 20-foot distance. If his vision is 20/200, he can only see an object at 20 feet that a normal-sighted person could see 200 feet away.

A person who has 20/70 vision or worse after correction is considered partially sighted, or able to use vision to some degree as a part of his educational process. A person who has 20/200 vision or worse, even after his vision has been corrected by glasses, is considered legally blind, despite the fact that he often has some useful eyesight.

The field of vision is also important in determining the usefulness of eyesight, and a person is also considered legally blind if the width of his field of vision has been narrowed to less than 20 degrees in his better eye. (The normal field of vision using both eyes is 180°.) Children who have been shunted for hydrocephalus sometimes have an impaired vertical field of vision, that is, they may not be able to see things that are above them. This is because the shunt is generally placed through an area of the brain that controls the vertical, upward gaze. There are about 500,000 blind or partially sighted people in the United States. Of those who are considered legally blind, about 20% see nothing at all, but approximately 40% see well enough to read large print.

Raising a baby who is blind or partially sighted is a challenge that requires special parental sensitivity. One mother of a blind premature infant told of her early difficulties interacting with her child. "Without having eye contact, I found it very hard to understand Michael at first. I had to learn to 'read' his hands, how he would make open and shut types of grabbing motions when he wanted something. And when I talked to him, he'd often become very still. I had to learn that this was intent listening—an involvement and not a withdrawal or a rejection of me. I held him a lot and talked to him a lot, always telling him what I was doing. He's become quite a responsive, cheerful baby with a beautiful smile and laugh. He can distinguish most of the people he knows just by touching their faces."

Because the child who is blind or visually impaired cannot perceive depths, barriers, or alluring objects in his environment, he may be slow to develop motor skills—a result of both insecurity and a lack of interest. Typically, a blind child learns to walk between 13 and 22 months of age. Earlier in infancy he may be slow to reach out for things. Toys a blind baby can hear do not elicit the same desire to grab as do toys that the sighted baby can see. The blind baby generally sucks well, because sucking is an inborn reflex. But chewing, which is partially learned by imitating others, may not come easily to the visually impaired or blind child. Unless the blind child has additional problems, his speech should develop on schedule as long as his parents talk to him frequently. Motor development can be enhanced by carrying the baby as much as possible, placing him in different locations and positions, giving him interesting toys to touch and listen to, and helping him safely reach out and explore the world around him.

Partially sighted children should be encouraged to practice using the vision that they have. Despite poor visual acuity, many of these children, given proper motivation and training, can develop relatively high levels of visual functioning.

## Professionals Who Can Help

There are various medical specialists and therapists who are available to help the handicapped child and his family. If your baby's development is being evaluated by a hospital follow-up clinic, these professionals may be available through that clinic. However, many tertiary centers do not have follow-up clinics,

and those that do rarely provide services to every intensive care graduate.

If you feel your child would benefit from special evaluations and developmental help, ask your pediatrician for referrals to the appropriate specialists, and to early intervention programs in your community. If your pediatrician cannot make satisfactory referrals, contact the National Health Information Clearinghouse, P.O. Box 1133, Washington, D.C. 20013, phone: (800) 336-4797. The National Health Information Clearinghouse is a national referral organization that helps direct health care consumers to needed services. The Clearinghouse could, for example, put you in touch with your state council on developmental disabilities. Such groups exist in each state under various names. They are required by the terms of the Developmental Disabilities Act (PL95-602) to coordinate state services for the disabled or those at risk for disabilities. The state council should be able to inform you of resources in your area.

Other organizations that may help are your local chapters of the United Way, United Cerebral Palsy, Association for Retarded Citizens, or the Easter Seal Society.

Listed below are professionals who may be involved in the screening, diagnosis, and treatment of the ongoing problems of prematurity.

A *neurologist* is a medical doctor who diagnoses and treats disorders of the brain and central nervous system.

A *psychologist* can administer tests, diagnose developmental or learning problems, as well as behavioral and emotional difficulties, and recommend special programs or therapies. He or she can offer direct personal counseling to parents and children. There are many different types of psychologists, but the ones most likely to work with young children who have delays or special problems are *clinical psychologists, educational psychologists,* and *developmental psychologists.*

A *social worker* can provide a variety of services for parents and children with special problems. He or she can help parents find and take advantage of appropriate programs, schools, clinics, agencies, and sources of financial aid. A social worker may also give personal counseling.

A *physical therapist (PT)* evaluates a child's physical functioning, and plans and carries out a therapy program to help the child achieve self-sufficiency in large motor skills such as rolling over, sitting, walking, and maintaining balance.

An *occupational therapist (OT)* provides services similar to those of a physical therapist but with a greater emphasis on the fine motor skills, the use of

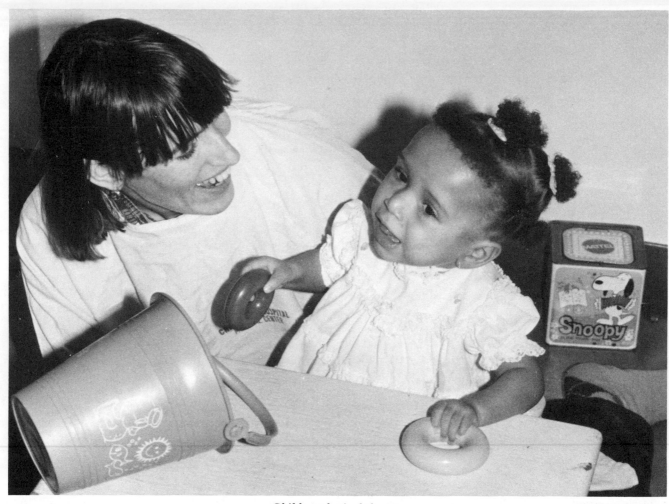

*Child at physical therapy.*

Peggy Wakefield Green, courtesy of Children's Hospital Medical Center of Northern California

hands, and hand-eye coordination. The occupational therapist is more likely to work on the child's self-help skills, and play or school-related activities.

An *orthopedist* is a medical doctor who can diagnose and treat disorders of the bones, muscles, ligaments, and tendons.

A *nutritionist* can evaluate eating habits, design a diet for the child with special nutritional needs, and suggest ways to cope with feeding problems.

An *ophthalmologist* is a medical doctor who diagnoses and treats diseases, injuries or defects that affect visual function. He or she can prescribe glasses and medication and can perform surgery.

An *optometrist* (not a medical doctor) can evaluate vision and prescribe corrective lenses, but he or she cannot prescribe medication or perform surgery.

An *optician* makes corrective lenses (glasses or contact lenses) prescribed by an ophthalmologist and adjusts the frames of glasses so that they fit properly.

A *vision therapist* conducts remedial activities to help the visually impaired child learn to use his remaining vision most efficiently.

An *otolaryngologist* (also known as an ENT) is a medical doctor who specializes in the diagnosis, treatment, and surgery of disorders of the ear, nose, and throat.

An *otologist* is an otolaryngologist who has subspecialized in disorders of the ear.

An *audiologist* (not a medical doctor) administers tests to determine the nature of hearing loss. He or she can recommend hearing aids when appropriate and refer families to special programs and services for hearing-impaired children.

A *speech-language pathologist* (also called a speech clinician or speech therapist) can diagnose speech problems and devise a program of speech therapy.

# When a Child Has Ongoing Problems

Parents of a premature who know that their child may be vulnerable to later problems must cope with difficult uncertainties as the child grows and develops. But should they suspect that the child has a problem, they have one big advantage over other parents with similar suspicions: they are likely to be taken seriously. Pediatricians are notorious for dismissing parental concerns about their child's development, delaying needed help for the child (and his parents) in the process. Doctors are less likely to do this when a child is known to be at risk. In addition, many intensive care graduates are seen regularly by developmental specialists at a follow-up clinic associated with the nursery. As a result, if the child does have problems, they are usually diagnosed early, when treatment and remedial therapy are most effective. And an early realistic awareness of a child's disabilities leaves parents better equipped, both practically and emotionally, to cope with them.

Although the parents of a premature baby have been alerted to possible future difficulties, this does little to lessen the blow if a problem is actually diagnosed in their child. Nevertheless, the diagnosis, by resolving uncertainties, can sometimes bring a sense of relief. "I'd suspected that something was wrong with my son by the way he moved and the way he felt when I held him," one mother said. "But the doctors were very noncommittal about making a diagnosis. Then we moved to a different county. The new doctor took one look at my son and said, 'Your child has cerebral palsy.' I went home and walked around the house in a daze, saying over and over to myself: 'My son has cerebral palsy. My son has cerebral palsy.' Mixed in with the shock, though, was a feeling of relief that my son's condition had a name, that it was a problem that other children had, and, now that I knew what it was, I could begin to deal with it."

Following the diagnosis, some parents go through the same cycle of grief responses they experienced following the baby's birth. Denial may include a search for a different diagnosis, or a miracle therapy or cure. Parents may devote themselves to an overly ambitious therapy routine as a form of bargaining: "If I sacrifice myself for my child, maybe that will make him normal." Ambivalent or negative feelings toward the child may reemerge—feelings of resentment, shame, guilt, and pity. The parents may feel on constant public display and resent the therapists and other professionals who sometimes become an intrusive part of their lives. Once again, their parental role is compromised. Said one mother, "First he was the neonatologists' baby, now he's the therapists' baby. I wonder if he'll ever just be *my* baby?"

Honest discussions of these concerns and emotions with each other, with a counselor, and *especially* with other parents of handicapped children can help a mother and father adjust to their child and his problems in a healthy and constructive way. "What keeps me sane," said one mother, "is the companionship of other parents with handicapped children. In our support group we share information on everything from how to make a baby wear his glasses to which disposable diaper comes large enough to fit a six-year-old. We talk about the stresses on our marriages, on our children, and on ourselves. We cry together in the difficult times, and we laugh together about aspects of our situations that others just wouldn't understand or find humorous. It's a marvelous release for me, a real life-saver."

Once a child's problem is diagnosed, the question becomes: What to do about it? Special therapies and developmental programs can be highly valuable, but parents need to be careful, critical consumers of these services.* Professionals often give conflicting advice, and parents must come to trust their own good judgment about what is best for them and their child. Therapy programs that seriously disrupt family life or interfere with the child's emotional well-being certainly do more harm than good, and parents should feel comfortable about rejecting them.

A good therapy program *helps the parents*. It gives them moral support, practical advice on caretaking, feedback on their child's progress (valuable information for parents whose child is not developing according to the books), and suggestions for helpful activities that they can enjoy together with the child. Above all, a good therapy program encourages parents to become sensitive observers and teachers of

---

*Many parents are curious about the widely publicized "patterning" therapy used to treat everything from learning disabilities to severe handicaps. The treatment involves as many as five people working day and night to move the afflicted child in patterns claimed to enhance neurological development. Several parents have written accounts of how patterning helped their brain-injured child recover. But every doctor and health professional we consulted expressed a negative opinion with the possible exception of a physical therapist who said, " 'Patterning' makes no sense to me but I believe in faith healing. If you have that many people laying hands on a kid, something's bound to happen." A recent study found no significant differences between a group of retarded children who had been "patterned" and another group who had not.

their child, for in the final analysis, it is they, the parents, and not the therapists who can best help their child. And it is from experience in the real world, not in the clinical setting, that a child learns the most. A child with cerebral palsy, for example, probably benefits as much from regular family outings to a park or playground as from weekly sessions with a physical therapist.

When concerned parents set out to help their child they naturally want to make every possible effort. But too great an emphasis on remedial activities can be counterproductive. The parents may focus so intently on the child's problems that they lose sight of the child himself and his normal emotional needs. They may spend countless hours on therapy, doing lots of things *to* their child but not very much *with* him. While chauffeuring him from one special program to the next, they may leave the child with little time alone to practice his skills or merely play and have fun. While devoting their lives to their child, they may harm their marriage and relationship to their other children.

For the child's sake, the parents' sake, and the sake of the other children, necessary special care and therapy should be integrated as unobtrusively as possible into the family's normal routines. Each family member should share in the inevitable extra work so that no one person becomes overburdened. Each family member, including the child with the problem, should have time to himself for fun and recreation. This is, of course, easier said than done, and it is the rare family that makes a perfect adjustment. "Physically, financially, and emotionally," said one mother, "we do what we can to shore up each other's strength. But sometimes there is nothing to do but try to laugh and share a supporting word. There is no magic formula."

Parents often wonder about the effect a child with problems has on his siblings. A study of adolescents and young adults who had grown up with an afflicted sibling found that half felt they had been harmed by the experience. They expressed shame and embarrassment about their sibling (and guilt for having these feelings). They resented having been neglected by their parents, and they felt guilty about their own good health.

On the other hand, half of those interviewed felt that they had benefited from life with their handicapped brother or sister. These young people tended to be more understanding of and compassionate toward others and more thankful for their own good health. Those who had interacted with their handicapped sibling on a daily basis showed a greater interest in contributing to worthwhile causes, achieving success in family and business activities, and learning not to take life too seriously.

Parents can help determine whether or not their children find life with a handicapped sibling destructive or maturing. By encouraging (but not forcing) the other children to participate in the handicapped child's special care and therapy, parents allow their children to share a sense of pride in their sibling's progress—and handicapped children often learn much more from interactions with other children than they do from adults. But the afflicted child must not always be the center of family life. Whenever possible, the other children should also have time away from their handicapped sibling to enjoy activities, outings, or vacations alone with their parents. Above all, the other children need the opportunity to discuss negative feelings they may have toward their handicapped brother or sister, and they need parental reassurances that such feelings toward a sibling (handicapped or otherwise) are entirely normal and nothing to be ashamed of.

Once a child reaches school age, his attitudes are shaped as much by his peers as by his parents, and even the wisest mother or father can do little to alleviate the social stresses on a child whose sibling is different. School-age children, like their parents, may benefit from contact with others who are coping with similar problems. A peer support group for children with handicapped siblings, or contact with such children on an informal basis, may help the child with an afflicted brother or sister realize that his problems are far from unique.

The reactions of grandparents are another special concern. While some grandparents form an easy attachment to their afflicted grandchild, it is not unusual for older people who grew up in less tolerant times to have difficulties accepting handicaps in others, especially in a family member. The grandparents may be more likely than the parents themselves to engage in denial, dismissing or exaggerating the child's problems, or searching for miracle cures. It may help to include such grandparents in some aspect of the child's special care. For instance, they can be invited on a visit to the therapist or pediatrician. In time, with the parents' own accepting attitude as an example, most grandparents do come to understand, love, and enjoy their special grandchild.

Beyond the immediate family there is the question of how the rest of society will accept the child with problems. During the '70s, attitudes toward the handicapped population changed in dramatic and positive ways. This new awareness of the problems and potential of handicapped people has been reflected in the passage of the federal Education For

All Handicapped Children Act (PL94-142) and the Rehabilitation Comprehensive Services and Developmental Disabilities Amendment (PL95-602), which acknowledge the rights of the handicapped to receive education and services in the least restrictive environment so that they can come to function as normally as possible. Although these rights still exist more on paper than in practice, an important first step has been taken. People with handicaps are at last beginning to take their rightful place in the social mainstream—in the school system, the labor force, and in society at large.

## *Edward's Story*

### By Helen Harrison

Tonight I am staffing the parents' coffee room down the hall from the intensive care nursery. Few parents are here this evening, and I am taking advantage of this time to myself and of the memories this place stirs in me to begin Edward's story. The neonatologist now attending in the nursery is the same one who seven years ago told my husband Alfred and me that our newborn son was going to die.

"Don't even hope," he said, pointing to the lengthy problem sheet taped to Edward's warming table, "any *one* of these problems could be fatal, but all of them together . . ."

I was scarcely seven months into my first and long-awaited pregnancy when I developed a high fever and back pains. The obstetrician diagnosed "flu" and sent me home with the usual instructions about fluids and bed rest. A week later the baby stopped kicking and I went into labor.

At the hospital the nurses assured me that I was in false labor. My cervix wasn't effaced or dilated, but after 17 hours of this false labor my membranes ruptured, and the baby was born so quickly that my obstetrician, who'd stepped out for coffee, missed the whole thing.

The pediatricians present at the delivery encouraged me to see and touch our son as they stabilized him for transport. They pointed out the petechiae, the pinpoint rash that covered his body, indicative of sepsis from an intrauterine infection and a very grave prognosis. But in my post-delivery euphoria I hardly noticed the rash or the horrible bruising the baby had received during his rapid breech delivery. He looked beautiful to me. At two pounds, 13 ounces he was bigger than I had expected.

I was put in a private room in the maternity ward because I was ill with a contagious infection, later diagnosed as listeriosis, a disease with flu-like symptoms that afflicts pregnant women, often killing or damaging the unborn baby. I was grateful to be alone. I was heartbroken by the end of my pregnancy—the seven happiest months of my life. I knew that our baby's chances of living and being normal were almost nonexistent. I was terrified that our son would die and even more terrified that he might somehow live.

When the nurse brought me a birth certificate to complete, I was outraged. Name a baby who was dying, perhaps already dead!? Nevertheless, Alfred and I conferred. We chose the name "Edward" after my brother and father. But we were also thinking of my late grandfather, a wealthy family tyrant (called "Big Ed" behind his back) who for years had amazed his doctors and disappointed his eager heirs by surviving a number of seemingly fatal illnesses. Despite my misgivings about the baby's survival, a part of me hoped that our son had inherited his great-grandfather's fighting spirit.

Alfred never shared my ambivalence about Edward's survival. He wanted Edward to live no matter what. He cheered him on the way he cheered for his favorite underdog hockey and football teams. So did the nursery staff, who marveled at "Big Ed" Harrison's incredible will to live. At Edward's bedside I, too, was caught up in the drama of fluctuating blood gases; I, too, cheered him on. As I cradled Edward in my hands for the first time and looked into his newly opened eyes, I was overwhelmed by maternal feelings. When I left the nursery that day the entire front of my shirt was soaked. My milk had just come in. But at home, my rational side took over. Edward's death, I felt, was in everyone's best interest and I tried to resign myself to it. I wondered whether Alfred, with his optimistic attitude, was a better, braver person, or whether I was simply more realistic.

A week after Edward's birth, the neonatologists called us in for a conference. Edward had suffered a massive brain hemorrhage. His brain waves were "grossly abnormal." The time had come to stop the respirator and let Edward die. "Quite frankly," said one of the doctors, "we don't think he has enough brain left ever to breathe on his own." This was September 1975. The Karen Ann Quinlan case was in the news, and I had been haunted by visions of court orders, of Edward's tiny chest mechanically expanding and contracting for months or years. I left the conference both heartsick and relieved.

That evening we were with Edward when the respiratory therapist came and turned the dials. To everyone's amazement, Edward kept on breathing. He was still breathing on his own when we left the nursery at midnight. Edward was going to live.

Now the doctors began saying things like, "Aren't you lucky Edward was born when he was? Only a year or two ago we probably couldn't have saved him."

Somehow I didn't feel very lucky to be at the cutting edge of this new technology. Our child could breathe, but what else could he do? No one would venture a guess. It distressed me to realize that behind the impressive nursery hardware were fallible human beings who were as puzzled by our baby as I was.

Edward's problem list soon doubled. He was, as one of the nurses graphically phrased it, "a real train-wreck of a kid." Edward had frequent seizures, he developed hydrocephalus as a result of his brain hemorrhage, and he was taken to shunt surgery weighing 2½ pounds. He had numerous exchange transfusions. He barely escaped surgery for an open ductus and NEC. Then his shunt became infected and the infection went into his brain. Again, he nearly died. We were sent from the nursery as doctors pounded on his chest to restart his heart. "This is the worst thing that could possibly happen," said the neurosurgeon. "Have you ever seen a baby this sick turn out to be normal?" I asked. "Very few," he replied, "and normal is a damned big category." (I am grateful to this man, and to the other doctors who told us the truth, even when the truth was painful.)

Edward's infected shunt was removed, and there was hope, at first, that he wouldn't need a new one, that his hydrocephalus had "arrested." We would have to wait and see.

As we took Edward home from the hospital, we were given contradictory instructions to "treat him like a normal baby but bring him in if he becomes irritable or lethargic or if he starts to vomit (signs of increasing hydrocephalus)." Since every baby I'd ever known was alternately lethargic, irritable, or vomiting, I figured we'd see a lot of the doctors. And we did.

I remember that first year as one long doctor's appointment—exhausting, anxious hours in waiting rooms and ERs, at radiology, in hospital wards, therapists offices, and the follow-up clinic. We spent our nights awake, coaxing our reluctant baby to eat, watching him for danger signs, checking to see if he was breathing.

We rebounded from crisis to crisis. A CAT scan revealed Edward's hydrocephalus was worsening and he underwent shunt surgery again. At the first eye appointment, the ophthalmologist told us Edward had no functional vision. At the second follow-up clinic, his cerebral palsy was diagnosed. At each subsequent checkup a new developmental delay was discovered. He would almost certainly be retarded. At age one Edward underwent surgery to correct his badly crossed eyes, and glasses were prescribed to help him use his remaining vision. Throughout, there were constant false alarms about his shunt. It was a source of terror to me that my baby's life and what was left of his brain depended on a thin plastic tube that could clog, dislodge, or become infected at any time.

Our lives were totally centered around Edward. I was afraid to leave him with a babysitter (the first time we did, to go out to dinner, I came home and promptly threw up). I was frightened that if I let down my guard and enjoyed myself, something dreadful would happen. The tension was such that when I began having severe chest and stomach pains, I dismissed them for months as psychosomatic. (They were actually gallbladder attacks.) There were many days and nights when I was too depressed, exhausted or sick to function, and Alfred took over. His optimism, which had puzzled and irritated me in the beginning, was now my greatest source of strength. He was, and is, a wonderful father to Edward.

The gallbladder surgery was my first vacation from my son. As I recovered, I realized that I had to find some way of dealing with the tensions that were ruining my health and sapping my energy. I began a program of strenuous exercise. After running two or three miles a day, I had little adrenalin left over for Edward.

We found babysitters who loved Edward and worked well with him. They became virtually a part of our family. I forced myself into activities that got me out of the house, and slowly I began to lose my fear of leaving my baby. I planned a trip to visit friends in Eastern Europe. Alfred agreed to stay with Ed; we were nervous about both leaving him at once. I remember the exhilaration of the flight halfway around the world and the shock when Alfred called me in Budapest, only 12 hours after I'd arrived, to tell me Ed had just undergone emergency shunt surgery. I sobbed my way through various European airports, looking for a flight home. My worst fear had been realized. I'd enjoyed myself and was being punished for it. Determined to overcome this irrational fear, I planned a new trip several months later. A girl friend and I spent a glorious week in Hawaii. I called home several times each day, but Ed was fine.

I became involved with a group for parents whose children required intensive care at birth. I found I had much more in common with these mothers and fathers than with my friends, whose main parental concerns were teething, diaper rash, and enrolling their toddlers in the right college preparatory nursery school. By meeting other parents of premature babies, I soon lost the feeling that I had been struck by lightning or singled out by a malevolent fate. I came to realize that my emotions were shared and normal. The bravery of these parents was an inspiration to me.

I had always been suspicious of the glowing accounts parents write about life with their special children, but life with Edward (once the horrible first year was over) was not the grim martyrdom I had expected. Despite his developmental problems, our son was a healthy, happy child. His loving, exuberant nature was a delight. We worked very hard with him, and he rewarded us with slow but steady progress. We were amazed at his perseverance and will to succeed. By age two he had learned to sight-read 50 word cards—not bad for a baby with "no useful vision" and "not enough brain left to breathe."

Still, Edward's development was highly uneven. While he could read, he could not identify the simplest picture unless he had memorized it. He rarely used words in a meaningful way. He had problems eating: he chewed poorly, gagged easily. With dim vision, no depth perception, and spasticity in his legs, he had difficulty navigating and walking. He reacted to unfamiliar or overstimulating surroundings by throwing tantrums.

Little by little, we introduced him to the outside world through trips to the supermarket, the drugstore, the zoo, the park. We tried to keep these excursions as brief and controlled as possible—to push him just a little, but not so much as to bring on tantrums. I walked with Edward for miles through the hills around our house and he became steadier on his feet. I put a harness on him so that he could walk without holding my hand while I could catch him if he tripped. In liberal Berkeley, where leashing a dog is considered inhumane, I got some hostile stares, but I soon learned to ignore them. Ed was making progress and that's what mattered.

Dealing with the reactions of others is a problem for many parents of handicapped children. We found a straightforward, honest approach worked best. When children at the park would ask me why Edward walked "funny," talked "funny," or wore glasses, I'd tell them that he'd been very sick as a baby and things that were easy for them to do were hard for Edward. Usually the children then became quite interested in him and tried to include him in their games, taking him under their wings. Adults were also curious. When I told Edward's story, they too became interested and helpful. It was people we met at the park, at the grocery store, or through other chance encounters who directed us to the resources—schools, parent groups, etc.—that ultimately were the most valuable to us.

Unfortunately, the "helping" professionals (with a few wonderful exceptions) did little to help us or our son. As parents of a high-risk baby we were often treated as specimens of pathology, rather than as normal people coping with a difficult situation. If Alfred held Edward at a clinic appointment while I talked to the doctor (our usual roles since I was the medical one in the family), I was labeled a "non-nurturing" mother. If I took Edward to a therapy by myself, I was solemnly questioned about whether the father was involved. Once a doctor who'd kept the three of us waiting for an hour and a half noted our agitation and suggested we receive psychological counseling to help us adjust to parenting a handicapped child. We had to bite our tongues not to offer the counter-suggestion that counseling might help the good doctor keep to his schedule.

When we first consulted developmental specialists we hoped for answers about Edward's condition and suggestions for helping him. What we got, instead, was confusion. Yes, Edward was ready for toilet training. No, he wasn't. Yes, heel cord surgery would help him walk better. No, it was the worst thing we could do. We soon learned that there was no right answer to any question about Edward's care and upbringing. We began to rely more and more on our own judgment. We continued to seek professional insight, but we tried to find doctors and therapists with whom we felt compatible, people whose advice made sense to us. When parents of a handicapped child switch specialists or look for new opinions, doctors call it "shopping around." They disapprove of it. But it was through shopping around that we finally discovered the small day school where Ed is now making excellent progress.

And what is Edward like today? At age 7 he is a peculiar mix of abilities and disabilities. He reads at a first-grade level, but his speech is that of a two-year-old. He walks stiffly, but he can run, jump, stand on his head, climb and go down the highest slide at the playground. He writes his name and many other words on the board at school, but he can't unscrew a lid, turn on a faucet, or button a button. After years of heroic effort, he is almost toilet trained. He still indulges in occasional tantrums, but he is easier to take out in public. He is beginning to

222

Edward, approximately 1 week old, after extubation.

Alfred Harrison

Edward at 3, with favorite book.

Alfred Harrison

Edward at age 6.

Alfred Harrison

interact socially with other children and is developing a healthy sibling rivalry with his little sister, Amy (born April 10, 1980, two weeks *after* her due date).

Edward has brought great happiness into our lives, something I never would have thought possible in those bleak months after his birth. As Alfred and I struggled with every facet of our son's development—from the acquisition of his rooting reflex to his learning to write—we became extraordinarily close to him. When I was pregnant with Amy we often wondered if we could bond with a normal child whose progress was predictable and effortless.

I no longer have any ambivalence about Edward's survival. I'm very glad he lived. I *do* feel lucky, extremely lucky. I feel lucky that with all the brain damage our son sustained, he still turned out to be a fun-loving, affectionate, "bright" child. Alfred and I are lucky that our marriage has survived, that we have found the physical, emotional, and financial resources to cope. Not everyone is so lucky.

But even with everything Ed has going for him, I'm still worried about his future. A doctor recently told us Edward would never live independently. I know that life outside the family can be a dismal one for seriously handicapped children and adults. State hospitals, where these people usually end up, are often brutal and brutalizing places. What will happen to Edward when we are unable to take care of him?

I can only hope, unrealistically perhaps, that the doctor is wrong about Edward, that some day our son will manage on his own. Or, perhaps, some day our society, which puts such enormous resources into the saving of high-risk babies, will develop a similar commitment for providing the handicapped survivors with a decent life.

## Rosie's Story

### By Kathleen Vasek

My husband Jerry sped through all the stoplights that July morning, and we made it to the hospital just in time. Our three-pound, seven-ounce daughter, born minutes after our arrival (and 2½ months before my due date), needed life-saving techniques immediately. She was transferred to the Neonatal Intensive Care Unit at Loyola Hospital that same day. She had severe hyaline membrane disease.

I insisted on being discharged the next day, and Jerry and I went straight to Loyola. As I stroked my tiny newborn hooked up to tubes, monitors, and respirator, the reality of the situation began to sink in. The doctors did not know whether she would live or die.

I obtained an electric breast pump from La Leche League. After nursing my first daughter, Polly, I knew there could be no other way. This critically ill baby needed mother's milk even more than a healthy full-term.

The hot, sticky summer days passed slowly. I sat at the kitchen table and pumped my breasts, crying when I was alone, laughing when I was solemnly observed by 2½-year-old Polly and her playmates.

Incredibly, Rosie began to improve. After a month she started to get partial-strength breastmilk through the gavage tube. Soon she was getting my milk from a bottle with a premie nipple. She was gaining weight, and her apnea spells were becoming less frequent.

I became increasingly anxious to nurse Rosie, and when she was eight weeks old, the happy day arrived at last. For the first few minutes, Rosie didn't seem to understand. I asked the nurse to bring me a bottle of my milk so I could put a drop or two on my nipple. But before the nurse even returned, Rosie was nursing vigorously. It was just as I had imagined so many times during those long weeks.

When Rosie came home she was still so tiny that she had to nurse every two hours around the clock. And I had to watch her carefully while she nursed because she'd get so intent on feeding that she'd forget to breathe and turn blue. But despite those early problems, we persevered. Rosie nursed happily for two years.

When I talk to other mothers with premature babies in the hospital, mothers who are discouraged and sick of the breast pump, I remember those hot summer days sitting at the kitchen table without my baby. I try to encourage them to keep at it because I know how they will eventually tell themselves a thousand times over that it was worth it.

It was not a good time for us. At eight months Rosie had been diagnosed as having mild cerebral palsy. Now she was 16 months old and still not walking. Her physical therapist at Easter Seals said she definitely *would* walk and she was *ready* to walk, but Rosie just wouldn't take those first steps. By this time we also knew she'd need surgery for crossed eyes. Meanwhile, we were patching her good eye, waiting for the bad one to get equal vision. It was a constant battle to keep the eyepatch on, to say nothing of the

*Rosie at 4 weeks.*

*Rosie at age 4.*

glasses. The crises of her birth and early hospital days were long over, and the drudgery of physical therapy twice a week, vision therapy twice a week, and all the trips to the eye doctor and pediatrician was wearing us down. Our marriage was in bad shape. Communication was at an all-time low. I was trying to deal with feelings of my own that had been pushed down for well over a year.

My main source of support was the Loyola Parents' Group. So far, I'd received little understanding from my relatives. They could not fully comprehend what we had been through or what lay ahead. It was at this time that I had the dream.

My sister Janet and I were small girls again. We were at Sunday school and a movie was about to be projected on the wall. Janet did not want to watch, but it was important to me that she see it. I turned her toward the wall and held her by the shoulders so she'd have to watch.

The movie began. First buildings, then a whole town appeared. The town was on fire; flames and smoke were everywhere. A hollow tube emerged from the burning town into the foreground. Attached to the tube was a box. The box, to my horror, was an incubator and inside was a baby. The flames were traveling through the tube to the incubator. The baby would die! I woke up—fast—with one thought pounding in my head. It would have been better if Rosie had died right then—when she was so sick in the hospital. Our lives had gone in such an awful direction since her birth. Nothing had worked out as we planned.

The dream was a turning point for me. Once I could allow that terrible thought into my conscious mind and admit that I *did* have such a feeling, things were never again quite so difficult in our efforts to help Rosie reach her full potential. When I talk to other parents about this dream, I find that these feelings are common among mothers and fathers with babies in intensive care.

Rosie's fourth birthday is next week. It will be the first time she's had a "real" birthday party with *her* choice of friends invited, and she's crazy with excitement!

After Rosie was born we received a bill from an unknown doctor who, coincidentally, became our pediatrician two years later. Rosie was a great favorite of his. It was not hard to tell she was special to him. I suspected that he had been the doctor who intubated Rosie, although I could never bring myself to talk to him about it.

Then one day in his office—impulsively—I asked: "Were you the one who had intubated her?"

He was. Four years later it was still vivid in his mind. He would always remember that baby lying in the incubator almost black from asphyxia. She was, as the neonatologists say, a "bad baby," a terrible baby.

And now I ask myself—how is it that she has done so well? People who meet Rosie today, knowing nothing of her past struggles, see her as a perfectly normal little girl. A bit klutzy at times, somewhat cross-eyed when she forgets to wear her glasses, but a delightful child with a terrific sense of humor.

Is she a wonderful example of early intervention? God knows we worked with her from the time she was first diagnosed as having cerebral palsy. We helped her learn to roll over, sit up, stand, and walk. We worked with her vision teacher going over colors, matching, and hand-eye coordination activities until at last Rosie understood and got it right.

Or was it the prayers? Although we are not religious people ourselves, there were many, many others who prayed for Rosie. I guess we did too, in our own way.

I haven't cried about Rosie in a long time. But in these days before her fourth birthday the tears come easily again. The hot summer weather brings back to me those long, desperate weeks she spent in the neonatal ICU. And now I have the clear image (which I didn't want to have before) of what my baby was like in the hours after she was born when I couldn't be with her. Four years later I cry for that "bad baby." And mixed in are the tears of joy and relief for the beautiful little girl she has turned out to be.

*Update: 1982.* Rosie enters regular kindergarten this fall. Although she is being watched by a physical therapist and a learning disabilities specialist, Rosie no longer shows any special problems and seems to be a happy, well-adjusted, normal, child.

# 12

# *Another Baby?*

"When the neonatologist told me that my son would need at least nine months of intensive care, I said, 'Then I'll have another baby while I wait.' The doctor was horrified, but it made perfect sense to me. Here I was with all these maternal hormones and no baby to take home."

\*

"I decided to have my tubes tied. I felt I could no longer trust my body."

\*

"I wanted a second child, but I was terrified of another disaster. After three years of trying, I still wasn't pregnant. I went to a doctor who practices hypnosis. She made a tape for me with positive suggestions about my next pregnancy. I played the tape every day. Three months later I conceived. Nine months later my eight-pound, healthy baby was born."

\*\*\*

Once you have had a premature baby, your view of pregnancy and birth is never again the same. The normal pregnancy and healthy baby other women take for granted now seem nothing short of miraculous. During the postpartum period especially, you may have very strong feelings about a future pregnancy. Some mothers, fearing the ordeal of another pre-term birth, immediately opt for sterilization. Others become obsessed with the idea of conceiving again as a way of completing their "unfinished" pregnancy.

Whether your feelings lie at either extreme or somewhere in the middle, it is best to wait a year before making any irrevocable decisions. Use this time to recuperate emotionally and physically and to explore your options with your family and physician. Be sure to seek family-planning advice soon after your baby's birth. Even if you are nursing, you can still become pregnant, and a baby conceived within a year of a previous birth is at increased risk to be born prematurely.

## Am I a High-Risk Mother?

To help identify those women at greatest risk for pre-term delivery, some obstetricians use a risk-scoring system. The one shown here was devised by Dr. Robert Creasy for the University of California's Preterm Labor Clinic. Points for each item pertaining to an expectant mother's life and current pregnancy are added up. If the total is 10 points or more, the woman is considered to be at risk and is seen weekly at the clinic for prevention, early detection, and treatment of pregnancy complications. According to the scoring sheet, any mother who has had a premature baby is a high-risk mother. But, says Dr. Creasy, some women seem to be at greater risk than others. The mother whose pregnancy was interrupted by a one-time occurrence—an emergency appendectomy, for example—has a better chance for a normal subsequent pregnancy than does the woman who went into pre-term labor for unknown reasons and who may have a physical tendency to begin labor early.

While many high-risk women can be identified by the risk-scoring chart, Dr. Creasy emphasizes that the chart is only a screening tool, one with its deficiencies. *Some women with no apparent risk factors may still have premature babies, and many women classified as high-risk have normal pregnancies.*

A study conducted in New Zealand showed a 30% incidence of pre-term delivery among women designated at high risk by the scoring chart. (By comparison, only 2% of the low-risk women delivered prematurely.) However, the high-risk women in the New Zealand study received no special prenatal care. At the UCSF Clinic, when high-risk women

# Risk of Pre-Term Delivery

This chart is adapted from the scoring sheet compiled by Dr. Robert K. Creasy for use at the UCSF Preterm Labor Clinic. To determine if you are at risk, check each item that pertains to your life and current pregnancy and add up the risk points for those items. If your score is 10 or higher you are at risk for a pre-term delivery.

| RISK POINTS | SOCIOECONOMIC | PAST HISTORY | DAILY HABITS | CURRENT PREGNANCY |
|---|---|---|---|---|
| **1** | —2 or more preschool children at home, no domestic help<br>—low socioeconomic status (1)* | —one first-trimester abortion or miscarriage<br>—less than one year from the last birth to the conception of this pregnancy | —work outside the home | |
| **2** | —age less than 20 years<br>—low socioeconomic status (2)*<br>—age more than 40 years<br>—single parent | —two first-trimester abortions or miscarriages | —more than 10 cigarettes per day | —weight gain below 12 pounds by the 32nd week<br>—protein in urine<br>—high blood pressure<br>—bacteria in urine |
| **3** | —low socioeconomic status (3)*<br>—height below 5 feet<br>—weight below 100 pounds at the time of conception | —three first-trimester abortions or miscarriages | —heavy work**<br>—long, tiring commute, riding or driving over 1 hour | —fibroids<br>—baby in breech position at 32 weeks<br>—weight loss of 5 pounds or more<br>—illness with fever<br>—baby's head low in the womb (engaged) at 32 to 34 weeks |
| **4** | —age less than 18 years | —pyelonephritis (kidney disease) | | —bleeding after the 12th week<br>—shortening and opening of the cervix (effacement and dilation)<br>—uterine irritability (frequent contractions) |
| **5** | | —DES exposure<br>—cone biopsy of the cervix<br>—uterine malformation<br>—one second-trimester miscarriage or abortion | | —placenta previa<br>—hydramnios (too much or too little amniotic fluid)<br>—uterine tumor |
| **10** | | —previous pre-term labor<br>—previous pre-term delivery<br>—two second-trimester miscarriages or abortions | | —twins<br>—abdominal surgery (during the pregnancy) |

*The degrees of socioeconomic status are determined by the father's occupation and the mother's education.

| | Box 1 | Box 2 |
|---|---|---|
| father's occupation | semi-skilled laborer<br>laborer<br>student | farm laborer<br>unemployed |
| mother's education | Box 3<br>grades 10 through 12 | Box 4<br>less than 10 years |

Socioeconomic status:
| | | |
|---|---|---|
| Box 1 only | = | 1 |
| Box 3 only | = | 1 |
| Box 1 & Box 3 | = | 2 |
| Box 1 & Box 4 | = | 2 |
| Box 2 & Box 3 | = | 2 |
| Box 2 only | = | 2 |
| Box 4 only | = | 2 |
| Box 2 & Box 4 | = | 3 |

**Heavy work is that which involves strenuous physical effort, standing, or continuous nervous tension. Nurses, doctors, sales people, cleaning staff, punchcard operators, and hairdressers all perform heavy work by this definition.

were given the special prenatal care described in this chapter, the incidence of pre-term delivery among these women fell below 7%.

## Choosing an Obstetrician

Ask your baby's neonatologist for a list of obstetricians in your area who specialize in high-risk pregnancies. Then, *before* you conceive, interview several of these doctors until you find one with whom you feel especially comfortable, a doctor who listens well and takes your observations seriously. Your family should also meet with the doctor. They must understand and be willing to make the extra efforts required of them should you develop complications and need bed rest or hospitalization. They should realize the importance of keeping your pregnancy as stress-free as possible.

When you interview a prospective physician, here are some questions you may wish to ask. If the doctor is part of a group, be sure to ask these questions of any others who might handle your prenatal care and your delivery:

1. If I go into pre-term labor or develop other complications, what drugs or medical techniques might be used (drugs to stop labor, drugs for toxemia, drugs to mature the baby's lungs, etc.)? What are the known side effects to me and the baby? What alternative methods are available?
2. If I go into pre-term labor very early, at, say, 25 weeks, how would the delivery be handled? Would an all-out effort be made to save the baby, efforts that may involve a cesarean section, or would you not intervene aggressively to save a baby whose prospects for normal survival are poor? Would my feelings on this matter be considered in the decision-making process?
3. (If you have had a delivery by cesarean.) Many doctors no longer believe "once a cesarean, always a cesarean." Could I have a vaginal delivery this time if all goes well?
4. If my pregnancy is uncomplicated, would my high-risk status automatically exclude me from a natural delivery in an alternative birth center?
5. Follow-up studies indicate that babies treated in the hospital where they are born do better than babies who must be transported. What arrangements will you make to assure that I deliver at a hospital with a good intensive care nursery?

## Choosing a Hospital

If you live in or near a large city, you may be able to comparison shop for a hospital with a good intensive care nursery. Nurses who work in the unit and parents whose children were treated there are often good sources of information. You may also wish to interview the neonatologists about nursery policies. Here are some questions to ask:

1. To what extent does the nursery include parents in major caretaking decisions?
2. What is the policy concerning parental visits? Sibling visits? The visits of friends and family members?
3. What types of practical and emotional support are available to mothers who wish to nurse? (Ask to see the breast-feeding room, pumps, etc.)
4. Can I room with my baby for a day or two before discharge to help establish breast-feeding and caretaking routines?
5. Will my baby be sent to another unit to convalesce?
6. Is there a program of home follow-up after the baby is discharged?
7. Is there a follow-up clinic to evaluate my baby's developmental progress?
8. If this nursery is filled when I deliver, where might my baby be sent instead?

## Preparing

Although you may never need to take special precautions during your pregnancy, you and your family should be prepared. What sort of babysitting and housekeeping arrangements could you make if you should require bed rest or hospitalization? Do you have relatives nearby, a church group, a parent support group, or friends and neighbors who can help? Consult with these people ahead of time and work out contingency plans.

If you *do* show signs and symptoms of pre-term labor, you will have to avoid all sexual stimulation. (This includes the nipple-toughening exercises done in preparation for breast-feeding.) Are you and your husband willing to go through months of sexual absti-

## Tocolytic (Labor-stopping) Drugs

The betamimetic drugs (ritodrine, terbutaline, isoxsuprine), magnesium sulfate, and alcohol are the most common medications used to treat pre-term labor. These drugs, given alone or in combination, can be highly effective at stopping pre-term labor if they are administered early in the labor process—before the membranes rupture, before the cervix has totally effaced, and before the opening of the cervix has dilated beyond 4 centimeters. Not all premature births, however, can or should be stopped. A baby who is infected *in utero* must be delivered immediately and treated, and early delivery is vital for the mother and baby whose lives are threatened by severe diabetes, toxemia, or placental bleeding.

### Betamimetics

Betamimetics, also called betasympathomimetics or beta-adrenergic agents, include the drugs ritodrine (Yutopar), terbutaline (Brethine), and isoxsuprine (Vasodilan). These drugs, which may be given intravenously or orally, imitate the action of the hormone adrenalin. Like adrenalin, these drugs have a stimulating effect on the body. It may seem strange that stimulants would stop labor contractions, but these drugs work by stimulating beta receptors, areas in the cells of the uterus that cause the uterine muscle to relax.

In the mother, these drugs may cause such side effects as rapid or irregular heartbeat, flushing of the skin, nervousness, and tremors. A rare, but potentially serious, side effect is pulmonary edema, fluid accumulation in the lungs. Pulmonary edema is treated by stopping the drug and administering diuretics. Betamimetics may also cause changes in blood sugar and insulin levels. For this reason, they are generally not used with diabetics. Others who cannot be treated with these drugs include women with toxemia, heart disease, or hyperthyroidism.

In the baby, the drugs cause a slight increase in heart rate, which is not thought to be harmful. Studies conducted in Europe, where the drugs have been in use for over a decade, have reported no long-term adverse side effects among treated infants. There is also evidence indicating that betamimetic drugs may actually help protect the baby from RDS in those cases in which the drugs fail to stop the pre-term labor.

### Magnesium Sulfate

Magnesium sulfate is a drug that controls high blood pressure in pregnant women with toxemia. It also increases blood flow to the unborn baby. In addition, the drug can stop uterine contractions, possibly by blocking nerve transmissions to the uterine muscle. It is usually given intravenously.

Unlike the betamimetic drugs, magnesium sulfate can be used with women who have toxemia, diabetes, or heart disease. Side effects include sedation, a feeling of warmth, and flushing of the skin. In rare instances it may cause maternal respiratory problems, low blood pressure, even shock. These side effects can be reversed by stopping the drug and giving calcium.

Magnesium sulfate also sedates the baby. At birth the baby may be limp and he may have problems breathing. Again, the administration of calcium helps reverse the side effects.

### Alcohol

Alcohol has been used for decades, both orally and intravenously, to help stop pre-term labor. It is thought that alcohol works by blocking the release of oxytocin, a hormone that induces uterine contractions. Alcohol may also have a directly relaxing effect on the uterine muscle.

The large doses of alcohol used to stop pre-term labor may cause extreme drunkenness and a bad hangover for the mother. Although women have been given the drug in large doses for many years with no apparent long-term ill effects on their offspring, the discovery of fetal alcohol syndrome raises new fears about the safety of alcohol for the fetus. And in those cases in which alcohol fails to stop pre-term labor, the premature infant seems to be unusually vulnerable to respiratory distress syndrome. Because the other labor stopping drugs seem safer and more effective, alcohol is no longer used as widely as it once was. However, alcohol may be given in combination with other labor stopping drugs to enhance their effects. It is still used for those women who cannot tolerate the other tocolytic drugs. Alcohol is also an easily available home remedy for a woman in pre-term labor to use (with her physician's approval) until she can get to a hospital.

---

nence if it becomes necessary? You and your husband should discuss this matter thoroughly and honestly with your doctor. Counseling beforehand may help you avoid the emotional alienation that afflicts many couples during a high-risk pregnancy.

If it is likely that you will need bed rest, plan ahead. Make a list of all those interesting, non-

strenuous activities that you have never had time to pursue. Have you ever wanted to crewel-embroider a bedspread? Learn a foreign language? Teach your toddler to read? Knit Christmas presents for the entire family? Read the complete works of Tolstoy? Polish up your artistic skills? Well, now is the time. Stock up on all the materials you might need—books, tapes, records, patterns, yarn, sketching pads and pencils. And take out subscriptions to every magazine that might remotely interest you. Remember, there can be more to high-risk pregnancy than day-time television.

Before your confinement, try to make your surroundings as attractive as possible. Redecorate the bedroom. Install a telephone extension close to your bed. Ask your obstetrician or nurse practitioner to put you in touch with another high-risk mother. You and your telephone friend can cheer each other on.

Lay in a supply of morale boosters like fancy soap, cologne, make-up, glamorous maternity nightgowns, robes, and loose but attractive housedresses (maternity nightgowns that open at the breasts, and dresses or shirts that open at the front can be worn later when you are nursing your baby.) You don't need to look like an invalid.

There is also no need to spend all your time in bed unless those are your doctor's specific orders. You can be just as inactive on the living room sofa, in a hammock, or on a chaise lounge outdoors.

If you are one of those busy people who cannot cope with unstructured leisure, make a schedule of your daily activities—for example, 9:00 A.M.–9:30 practice relaxation techniques (see page 233), 9:30–10:30 needlepoint, 10:30–11:30 sketching, and so forth.

And be sure to schedule time for your other children. Set up a card table by your bedside for special games or toys, a toy train or a doll house, for example, that your child plays with only in your room. Keep a supply of children's books, paper, crayons, flash cards, playing cards, and board games handy. Several mothers have said that they actually became closer to their other child(ren) during their high-risk pregnancy, that the enforced bed rest gave them the opportunity to relate to their child(ren) in new ways.

Your physical well-being during pregnancy is enhanced by your psychological well-being, and you will feel better psychologically if you keep busy. So don't just lie there, do something!

## Giving Your Baby the Best Chance

Your most important job during the pregnancy will be to observe the basics of good prenatal care.

## Stop Smoking

If you are a smoker, stop—preferably well before you try to get pregnant. This is probably the single most important thing you can do to improve your chances for a healthy pregnancy. Cigarette smoke contains over 1000 chemicals, many of which are known to be hazardous both to you and your baby. Carbon monoxide in cigarette smoke lowers the level of oxygen in your blood. Other substances in tobacco smoke interfere with your body's ability to use certain nutrients. Just one cigarette, for example, robs your body of 25 mg of vitamin C, the amount present in one orange. Smokers deliver low-birthweight infants almost twice as frequently as nonsmokers. Premature labor, premature rupture of the membranes, placenta previa, and abruption are all more likely to occur to smokers.

Your local chapter of The American Lung Association can give you a list of programs in your area for people who want to quit. If you have tried in the past to stop smoking and failed, try again. This time it may work. Concern for your unborn baby can be an excellent motivating factor.

If you absolutely can't quit, try to cut down to fewer than five cigarettes a day. Pregnancy complications caused by smoking are dose-related; the less you smoke, the greater your chances for a healthy pregnancy.

## Eat a Healthy, Balanced Diet

Barbara Abrams, nutritionist for the UCSF Preterm Labor Clinic, offers the following suggestions for your diet during pregnancy. Examine your eating habits *before* you try to conceive. Then, make any necessary improvements in your diet so that your pregnancy gets off to a good start. Before and during pregnancy, you need a variety of foods daily from each of the following groups: (1) protein foods, (2) milk and dairy foods, (3) grains, (4) vitamin C-rich foods, (5) green vegetables, (6) other fruits and vegetables, and (7) fats and oils.

Emphasize whole, natural ingredients. Read labels and avoid processed convenience foods high in sugar, fats, and salt. They often contain additives that may not be good for your baby, such as artificial colorings, flavorings, or preservatives. Avoid empty-calorie foods like soft drinks, cakes, pies, chips, fried foods, cookies, and candy.

You need extra nutrients during your pregnancy, but don't overdo a good thing. Do not overdose on vitamins A and D—through pills or fortified foods. Excess amounts of these vitamins can harm you and your baby. Megadoses of other vitamins and minerals can also be toxic or cause nutritional imbalances. And recent studies suggest that *unbalanced*

## Tests and Procedures That May Be Used in High-Risk Pregnancy

| Procedure | Purpose | Description | Side Effects |
|---|---|---|---|
| Ultrasound (Sonogram) | • To view the position of the fetus and placenta (often done before an amniocentesis).<br>• To diagnose a multiple pregnancy. | • A device called a transducer is passed over the abdomen. The transducer bounces high frequency sound waves off the baby and the placenta. The echoes from these sound waves produce a picture on a screen. The procedure is painless. | • No adverse side effects on mother or fetus have yet been documented. |
| Amniocentesis | • To examine the fluid surrounding the baby. Cells and other substances in the fluid can be analyzed to detect certain chromosomal abnormalities and birth defects in the unborn baby.<br>• The fluid can also be analyzed to determine the baby's lung maturity (see L/S ratio, below). | • A needle is inserted through the mother's abdomen and into the womb to withdraw a sample of amniotic fluid for testing. Local anesthesia may be used, but even without anesthesia, the test is relatively painless. | • Slight possibility of introducing infection into the womb.<br>• Slight risk of rupturing the membranes.<br>• Slight risk of inducing pre-term labor.<br>• Slight risk of striking the baby with the needle (usually this causes the baby no permanent harm). |
| L/S Ratio | • To analyze amniotic fluid for the presence of lecithin (L) and sphingomyelin (S), components of surfactant. (See page 58.) An L/S ratio of at least 2 to 1 generally means the baby is mature enough to escape respiratory distress syndrome. The test is performed before carrying out an elective cesarean section to be sure the baby is mature enough for safe delivery. | • See amniocentesis. | • See amniocentesis. |
| Non-Stress Test | • To evaluate the baby's heart rate pattern as he moves in the womb and as he responds to spontaneous Braxton-Hicks contractions. Abnormal heart rate patterns may mean the baby is in distress, usually from improper placental functioning. | • An external monitor is wrapped around the mother's abdomen and the baby's heart rate is recorded for up to an hour. The test is painless. | • None. |
| Stress Test | • To assess the baby's heart rate patterns in response to induced uterine contractions. As in the non-stress test, abnormal patterns of heart rate may indicate poor placental functioning and resulting fetal distress. This test is more reliable, but also more risky, than the non-stress test. | • An external monitor wrapped around the mother's abdomen records the baby's heart rate for one to two hours to note the heart's response to induced uterine contractions. Contractions are usually induced by the administration of IV oxytocin (Pitocin.) The procedure involves some discomfort from the induced contractions. | • Because of the risk of inducing actual pre-term labor, this test is not used with women who have a history of pre-term labor. It is also not used in multiple pregnancies. The stress test may be used in pregnancies complicated by diabetes, high blood pressure, heart or kidney disease, as long as the mother does not have a history of premature labor. |
| Estriol Levels | • To check blood or urine for levels of estriol, a hormone produced by the mother, baby, and the placenta. A drop in estriol levels may indicate placental malfunction and fetal distress. | • When blood is checked for estriol, samples may be drawn daily.<br>• When urine is being examined, *all* urine voided over a 24-hour period must be collected for analysis. The test is repeated every few days so that samples can be compared and changes noted. | • None. |

diets very high in protein may adversely affect pregnancy outcomes. Do not take special protein supplements unless directed to do so by a physician or a nutritionist.

Drink plenty of fluids—four to six glasses of water a day *in addition to* the other liquids in your diet. Extra fluids aid in the digestion and assimilation of food, in circulation, and in the removal of wastes from your body and your baby's body.

Your need for salt increases during pregnancy. However, the average American diet provides far more salt than necessary to meet this additional requirement. Since the excessive consumption of salt contributes to high blood pressure and associated problems, it is best to use salt *in moderation.* If you crave salt, salt your food to taste but limit your consumption of foods that are already highly salted—foods like potato chips, salted nuts, soy sauce, cured meats, and pickled foods. When you use salt be sure it is *iodized* salt, which provides iodine, an important nutrient during pregnancy.

Use of alcohol, coffee, and sodas should be moderate. If you drink alcohol, limit your intake to an occasional glass of wine with dinner. Do not drink more than this except on doctor's orders. (Some physicians may recommend the use of alcohol to help calm an "irritable" uterus.)

A slow, steady weight gain of 25 to 35 pounds is desirable during pregnancy, but the precise amount of weight you gain is an individual matter. Some women following good diets gain more or less than this and have healthy term babies. However, *very* rapid weight gain should be reported to your physician. The weight gain may be caused by excessive fluid retention, a possible symptom of toxemia. If water retention is not the problem, cut back on fats and sweets but forgo other attempts at weight control until after your baby is born and weaned. If you have trouble gaining, remember that the pregnancy nutrition guidelines listed here represent a *minimum* daily intake. Feel free to add nutritious high-calorie foods to your diet.

If you have questions about pregnancy diet, consult a nutritionist (a registered dietitian, or R.D.)—unfortunately, most physicians are not trained in nutrition. To find a good nutritionist, ask for a recommendation from your physician, the dietitian at your local hospital or university medical center, the state or county health department, or the March of Dimes.

Although an excellent diet cannot guarantee a perfect outcome, it can help make you and your baby stronger and healthier, and this is beneficial to any pregnancy.

## Nutrition Tips

**Protein**

1. The recommended four servings of protein—80 to 100 grams a day—seems like a lot. But you may be eating this much already. Eight ounces of meat, a quart of milk, and four slices of whole grain bread add up to 88 grams of protein.
2. Vegetable proteins should be combined to insure complete protein. Some sample combinations: beans and rice; cereal and milk; bread and peanut butter; tofu, rice, and vegetables; lentil soup and crackers. If you are a vegetarian who uses *no* animal products, be sure to consult a nutritionist.

**Iron**

Many women suffer from iron-deficiency anemia, and pregnancy increases the need for iron. Dietary sources of iron include liver and other organ meats; lean beef or pork; beans; prune juice; whole grain, enriched hot and cold cereals; enriched whole grain pasta or bread; spinach and other greens; broccoli; eggs. Iron is absorbed better if the iron-rich food (or iron supplement pill) is taken with a source of vitamin C, a glass of orange juice for example. Cooking in cast iron also adds iron to your foods. Tea and milk may bind iron, making it unavailable to your body. Do not take iron pills with these liquids.

**Milk/Dairy**

1. Hate the taste of milk? Substitute cheese, yogurt, and other foods for milk (see the guide on page 233) or try a fruit smoothie: In a blender combine ⅔ cup powdered instant nonfat milk or ½ cup non-instant milk with l cup fluid milk, blend with 1 banana and ¼ cup chopped almonds or with 1 cup fresh fruit and vanilla extract to taste. This drink equals three servings of milk, one-half serving of protein, and one serving of fruit.
2. If you cannot digest milk sugar (lactose), stick to cultured milk products like yogurt, buttermilk, kefir, and cheeses.
3. If you can't tolerate dairy products, have six to eight servings of protein and ask your physician for a calcium supplement.

**Fruits and Vegetables**

1. Eat fresh and raw whenever possible. Many valuable nutrients are lost through cooking and improper storage. If you cook your vegetables, use a vegetable steamer so nutrients are not washed away in cooking water. Store foods and juices in covered containers to help retain nutritional value.
2. If you dislike greens, try steaming them until just tender, then purée in a blender and add to gravies, dips, soups, or juices. Suggested recipe: Steam until bright green 1 cup spinach or chard or broccoli, purée in blender with tomato or vegetable juice. Blend, chill, and add lemon juice to taste.

## Pregnancy Guide*

| Food Group and Serving Size | Number of Servings to Have Each Day | Why? |
|---|:---:|---|
| PROTEIN FOODS: Meat, poultry, fish (2 oz.) eggs (2); beans (1 cup cooked); nut butters (¼ cup), or nuts and seeds (½ cup); tofu (1 cup) or cottage cheese (½ cup). | **4** | To build tissues in your baby and in yourself. These foods contain iron, protein, zinc, and many other nutrients. |
| MILK/DAIRY FOODS: Nonfat, low-fat or whole milk (1 cup); plain yogurt (1 cup); soymilk or tofu (1 cup); cheese (1½–2 oz); nonfat milk powder (⅓ cup). | **4** | Calcium builds healthy bones and teeth. The vitamins A and D and protein also make your baby healthy. |
| GRAINS (Whole grains are best!): Bread, rolls (1 slice); macaroni, rice, noodles (½ cup); hot cereal (½ cup); cold cereal (1 oz.); wheat germ (1 tablespoon). | **4+** | B vitamins for strong blood and nerves. Iron and trace minerals. Natural fiber to keep your digestive system regular. |
| VITAMIN C-RICH FOODS: Orange or grapefruit juice (½ cup); 1 orange or ½ grapefruit; bell peppers, greens, tomato, cantaloupe, broccoli, cabbage, cauliflower (1 cup). Don't use fruit drinks. | **2+** | Vitamin C (ascorbic acid) is for connective tissue and resistance to infection and disease. You need to eat it daily. Especially important if you smoke. |
| GREEN LEAFY VEGETABLES: Broccoli, brussels sprouts, asparagus, cabbage, greens, red leaf or romaine lettuce, bok choy, watercress (1 cup raw or ¾ cup cooked). | **1–2+** | Folacin and iron for blood. Vitamin A for soft skin and good eyesight. Also vitamins E, C, and K and natural fiber. |
| OTHER FRUITS AND VEGETABLES: All the others and their juices: apples, carrots, bananas, sweet potatoes, green beans, etc. (about ½ cup). | **2+** | Lots of different, healthy nutrients in various amounts. |
| FATS AND OILS: Butter, margarine, salad dressing, cream cheese, cooking fats, fatty cheeses. | **3 tsp.** | For energy and healthy skin. Good foods in *moderation.* Fats contain a lot of calories. |

*Note:* Use the empty-calorie foods (soft drinks, cakes, pies, chips, fried fast foods, cookies, candy, etc.) infrequently. Choose the foods that offer nourishment to your baby and to yourself. If you don't like milk or meat, the nutritionist can help you plan a good diet without these foods.

*This chart appears courtesy of Barbara Abrams, R.D., M.P.H., Obstetrics Clinic, University of California, San Francisco.*

## Learn to Relax

The months of a high-risk pregnancy can be stressful. Once you know the things that can go wrong, it is hard not to worry. And if your activities have been limited, you have few diversions and no opportunity to exercise and work off your tensions. If you must spend time in the hospital or at home in bed, you will soon discover that the experience is anything but relaxing and restful.

However, through simple techniques of controlled meditation you can achieve the deep relaxation so important to your mental and physical well-being during pregnancy.

Two times a day, for at least 20 minutes at a time, lie down on your left side, a position that increases circulation to the womb. Place a pillow under your head and another one under your right leg. Use additional pillows for support if necessary. Once you are comfortable, begin a series of mental suggestions to relax each part of your body beginning at your head and working down. Many people find it easier to follow taped instructions. Your recorded suggestions might go something like this (in a calm voice):
"The muscles of my forehead are loose and relaxed."
(Repeat slowly three times, pause.)
"My jaw is loose and limp." (Repeat slowly three times, pause.)

"My neck and shoulders are relaxed and comfortable." (Repeat three times, pause.)

"My right arm (left arm) is heavy and warm." (Repeat three times, pause.)

"My heartbeat is calm and regular." (Repeat three times, pause.)

When you have relaxed each muscle group down to your feet, you may turn off the tape and take a nap or you can continue the meditation exercise by mentally repeating a single word or phrase after each slow, regular breath you take. In your relaxed state try to imagine your baby being nurtured by the increased blood flow to your womb.

When you are ready to wake up, turn on the following taped instruction: "At the count of 5, I will return to my normal level of awareness feeling awake, alert, and full of energy: 1 . . . 2 . . . 3 . . . 4 . . . 5."

Regular practice of relaxation techniques has been shown to reduce blood pressure and lower the levels of stress hormones in the bloodstream. Some people find the relaxation experience even more refreshing than sleep.

If you wish to learn more about this technique and its benefits, read *The Relaxation Response* by Herbert Benson, M.D., Avon Books, 1975. Available in paperback for $1.95.

---

## How to Eat Well When You Must Rest in Bed

By Barbara Abrams, R.D., M.P.H., Obstetrics Clinic, University of California, San Francisco.

Many women find that eating can be a problem when they must restrict their activity during pregnancy. Eating well can be difficult because:

It is difficult to buy, prepare, and eat food while in bed.

Some medications, such as those used to treat preterm labor, may decrease the appetite.

Some women find that inactivity can cause constipation, which is uncomfortable and may also make eating seem less appealing.

Some women find that the combination of constant bed rest, along with anxiety about whether the baby will be all right, decreases appetite and weight gain.

Some women not only have a normal appetite, but find that the combination of less activity and boredom of lying in bed all day increases food cravings and intake so that too much weight gain occurs.

These are very real problems, yet it is important to remember that your baby is depending on you for nourishment. The quality of your baby's growth, both physically and mentally, can be affected by what you eat now.

### You Should Eat

A variety of dairy products, protein foods, whole grain breads and cereals, fruits and vegetables. If you have not received a prenatal diet guide, be sure to ask your health care provider to give you one. Vitamin pills can help supplement your diet, but pills *do not* contain everything you need.

It is important that you eat well now, especially if your baby may come early. These weeks are a critical growing period for your baby who needs nutrients to do a good job.

### Food Purchase and Preparation

List the foods that you need bought—be specific. Plan menus consisting of foods that:

1. are nongreasy, not messy
2. need little or no refrigeration
3. need little or no preparation
4. could be included in a "bag lunch"

Some simple nutritious foods are:

| | |
|---|---|
| hard-boiled eggs | fruit |
| yogurt | cheese slices |
| nuts | vegetable sticks |
| cottage cheese | cream soups |
| sandwiches on whole grain breads | milk shakes |
| crackers and peanut butter | bran muffins |
| | small cans of juice |

Try nongreasy take-out foods like pizza, Chinese and Japanese foods, burritos, barbeque chicken. When possible, eat take-out foods that are *not* fried.

### Food Storage at Bedside

Keep a pitcher of water for fluids. *Remember,* you need at least four to six cups of liquids per day.

Use a thermos for soups, milk shakes, fruit-yogurt drinks.

Have an ice chest for cottage cheese, milk, sandwiches, cheese slices, vegetable sticks, and yogurt.

A TV tray by the bed is handy for keeping food within reach.

The **room atmosphere** may improve your spirits and help you eat better! Consider plants, flowers, fresh air, music, pictures, and window view.

**Poor Appetite: Low Weight Gain**

Try to relax.

Eat at regular times.

Eat small frequent meals.

Choose foods that give the most nutrition for the calories, e.g., milk, hard-boiled eggs, milk shakes, yogurt.

Drink fluids between rather than during meals.

Write down what you eat. Try to identify when and what you could add throughout the day, e.g., peanuts, trail mix, milkshakes.

Schedule visitors at mealtime for company.

Call your nutritionist for advice on diet.

**Milk Shake**

¾ cup milk

1 cup ice cream

1 tbsp. chocolate syrup

½ ripe banana

⅓ cup dry milk

Blend together.

Other nutritious, high-calorie snacks are:

ice cream blended with orange juice

peanut butter and jelly on whole wheat

pudding and custard

dry-roasted nuts

shakes with varied ingredients

**Excessive Appetite: High Weight Gain**

Eat at regular times.

Eat more low-calorie, high-nutrient foods: e.g., raw vegetables, fruit, low or nonfat milk, low-fat yogurt, diluted juices.

Write down what you eat. Try to identify when and what you could delete throughout the day, e.g., cookies.

Call your nutritionist for advice on your diet.

**Lo-Cal Shake**

1 cup nonfat milk

4 frozen strawberries

Blend together.

Other nutritious, low-calorie snacks are:

plain yogurt and fruit

hard-boiled eggs

celery and peanut butter

fruit juice popsicles

unbuttered popcorn

mineral water

**Nausea**

Eat five or six small meals a day. Never go for long periods without food.

Drink fluids between rather than with meals.

Eat lightly seasoned foods. Avoid foods cooked with pepper, chili, and garlic.

Avoid greasy and fried foods.

When you feel nauseated between meals, drink small amounts of apple juice, grape juice, or carbonated beverages.

Get plenty of fresh air.

**Constipation**

Eat high fiber grains, e.g., bran and wheat germ.

Drink a lot of fluid, e.g., water and fruit juices.

Drink hot water with 1 tsp. lemon juice three times a day.

Eat more raw fruits and vegetables.

Eat at regular times.

Ask for a stool softener if dietary measures are not producing results.

**Bran Muffins**

2 cups whole wheat flour

1½ cups bran

1¼ tsp. baking soda

½ tsp. nutmeg

2 tbsp. grated orange rind

½ cup raisins

½ cup orange juice or pineapple juice

2 cups milk

2 tsp. oil

1 20-ounce can of pineapple in its own juice (drained)

Preheat oven to 350°.

Toss flour, bran, soda, and nutmeg together with a fork. Stir in orange rind and raisins. Pour the juice, milk and oil together, mix well. Mix wet with dry ingredients. Stir in pineapple. Pour into muffin tins two-thirds full.

Bake 25 minutes. Makes 24 muffins.

# Stay in Touch with Your Body

Be aware of the warning signs of pregnancy complications. If you feel something is not right, do not hesitate to report it to your doctor. Be persistent; have the problem checked out. EARLY DETECTION OF PREGNANCY COMPLICATIONS IS THE KEY TO THEIR SUCCESSFUL TREATMENT. Call your doctor at once if you experience one or more of the following symptoms:

## Symptoms of Pre-Term Labor

1. any low backache, continual or rhythmic, that is different from what you've experienced in pregnancy so far
2. menstrual-like cramps
3. intestinal cramps and/or diarrhea
4. rhythmic pelvic pressure that feels different from what you've normally felt during your pregnancy
5. an increase in vaginal discharge, or change into a mucousy, watery, or blood-tinged discharge

Note: Because pre-term labor can begin without any obvious warning signs and because many of the early symptoms of premature labor are hard to distinguish from the normal sensations and discomforts of pregnancy, expectant mothers are urged to learn and use the self-monitoring technique given in the box on page 237.

## Symptoms of Toxemia (Pre-Eclampsia, Eclampsia)

1. persistent headaches or dizziness
2. visual disturbances, the sensation of flashing lights before your eyes
3. rapid weight gain (three pounds or more a week) accompanied by puffiness of the hands, face, or feet
4. infrequent urination or inability to urinate
5. stomach pains

## Symptoms of Placental Detachment

1. any vaginal bleeding after the first three months of pregnancy
2. severe stomach pain, rigidity and uterine tenderness (may indicate concealed bleeding behind a partially detached placenta)

## Symptoms of Infection

1. fever, especially in the absence of cold symptoms
2. severe back pains
3. pain with urination
4. increase in vaginal discharge, vaginal irritation

## Symptoms of Gestational Diabetes

1. excessive thirst or hunger
2. unusual frequency of urination

At the University of California's Preterm Labor Clinic, high-risk expectant mothers are taught the early warning signs of pregnancy complications. They are urged to call in day or night to report any suspicious symptoms. In addition, the women are seen weekly at the clinic so that potential problems can be quickly discovered and treated.

The clinic, partially funded by the March of Dimes, is directed by Dr. Robert Creasy and Marie Herron, R.N. This program of intensive prenatal care has reduced premature births at the hospital from 6.75% in 1978 to 2.43% in 1979. Through a combination of early detection and prompt treatment, close to 70% of the women who begin labor prematurely are brought to term.

Special programs for high-risk pregnant women now exist or are being established at many perinatal centers around the country. Dr. Creasy estimates that if programs similar to the one at UCSF were available to all high-risk pregnant women nationwide, the number of premature births in this country could be cut in half.

## Detecting Premature Labor

At the UCSF Preterm Labor Clinic, this simple technique to detect the regular uterine contractions of premature labor is taught to all high-risk expectant mothers. It is a self-monitoring method that every pregnant woman should know.

1. Twice a day—once in the morning and again in the afternoon or evening—lie on a bed or sofa with pillows behind your back to prop you toward your left side. (The flat-on-your-back position should be avoided during pregnancy, since it allows the heavy uterus to compress major blood vessels and disrupt circulation.) Have a clock or a watch with a second hand close by.
2. Place both of your hands on top of your uterus and feel for contractions with your fingertips. Contractions begin at the top of the uterus, causing your abdomen to become hard—like the tip of your nose or harder. You may even see your abdomen move up slightly. The tightness increases, then reaches a peak, then relaxes. This is a contraction. The contraction may be entirely painless.
3. If you detect tightening and relaxing of the uterus, note the time when each contraction begins, how long it lasts and how much time elapses from the beginning of one contraction to the beginning of the next one. If contractions are occurring, time them for one hour like this.

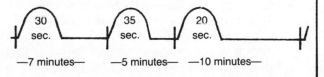

—7 minutes—    —5 minutes—    —10 minutes—

4. If you are having contractions every 10 minutes (or more frequently) for an hour, notify your doctor, clinic, or delivery room.

*Remember,* these contractions may be painless. Nevertheless, report them promptly. Premature labor can only be stopped if detected in its early stages!

# Diary of a High-Risk Pregnancy

## By Kathleen Vasek

After one late miscarriage and one premature baby, the decision to try for another child was the hardest my husband and I ever had to make. It had been only 2½ years since Rosie's premature birth—2½ years of pain, doubt, and disillusionment. But Rosie and her 5-year-old sister Polly had also brought us much happiness and joy; otherwise we would never have considered more children.

At first, everyone, including my husband, thought I was crazy even to think of another baby. Jerry couldn't understand my desire to become pregnant again, my great need to "do it right." It took a period of marriage counseling for us to sort out our feelings on the matter.

Meanwhile, I saw Dr. Yaqub, a high-risk OB at Loyola. He thought that with surgery to correct my problem of incompetent cervix and medication to control the early uterine contractions, my chances of having a healthy full-term baby were good. At age 37 I became pregnant for the fourth time. Here are excerpts from the diary I kept of that high-risk pregnancy.

*14 weeks*

Things are going beautifully today—makes it seem that high-risk pregnancy is a snap! Polly and the babysitter are at the swimming pool. Rosie is napping. I'm lounging in the hammock. The Vasodilan seems to be working; I've had very few crampy feelings since I started taking it. The only nagging worry I have is about Down's syndrome. Maybe I should reconsider and have amniocentesis—but no, I'll just have to hope and pray the baby is normal.

*16 weeks*

The cerclage surgery is over. The worst part was the nausea I felt coming out of the anesthesia and the sore throat from being intubated. If I had it to do over again, I'd choose to have a spinal. Otherwise, I had some light bleeding and cramping—nothing out of the ordinary. Now the hard part starts. The bed rest.

*18 weeks*

I'm trying to emphasize the positive and keep busy writing letters, organizing photo albums, reading, knitting, and watching television. I'm on modified bed rest—no exerting myself and only an occasional outing to the yarn store or a Parents' Group meeting.

All my planning is paying off. Polly and

Rosie are happy going to different people's homes and they are always invited back. The babysitters take the girls swimming and help with the housework.

The main problem is with Jerry and his attitude. He's crabby and tired most of the time. He feels too many demands are being made of him. He doesn't understand how hard it is on me to have to depend totally on others or why I might find it difficult to sympathize with his tiredness. I asked him to visualize the nice little baby we'll have, a baby who'll have a better start in life than Rosie did. This seemed to work—for a day, anyway.

*20 weeks*

The novelty of my restful pregnancy is wearing off. I'm becoming very bored and irritable. I'm mad because there's nothing good on TV. And the house is filthy. Half the laundry is still in the basement. Pillows and blankets are strewn all over the floor, and there's the mess Jerry left after painting the windows and trim. I'm making an effort to stay off his back and not let the messes upset me. But it's hard to sit here in the middle of it all, to see it constantly, and not be able to clean it up.

Last week we were told that there wasn't a place for Rosie in the Special Ed Preschool. We finally straightened it out, but the upset and hassle were not good for me. I was definitely having more contractions. Dr. Yaqub told me to take more Vasodilan and it worked.

The pregnancy is half over now, probably more than half, since 36 weeks is all we're hoping for. I still can't think in terms of an actual baby, even though the baby's moving a lot now. I can't bring myself to think about a port-a-crib and all the other things we need. I want to wait until the baby is actually *here* and *OK*.

*22 weeks*

Today is the first school day for Polly and Rosie. They looked so cute in their dresses, white socks, and sandals. I really have my heart set on another girl!

Jerry wanted me to go to dinner with some customers of his. But Dr. Yaqub has not been pleased with all my recent activity. I called him for definite instructions. He said I could *not* go out to dinner or anywhere else and I was *not* to drive unless it was absolutely necessary. We have too much invested in this pregnancy to take risks. I'm glad to have explicit doctor's orders. Jerry sometimes thinks I could be doing more than I am. Now he knows. I can't do anything.

*23 weeks*

Today is the first time I felt really frightened about the baby being born too soon. Polly threw a tantrum that lasted an hour. Then she and Rosie started their obnoxious brat stuff while I was on the phone. Jerry was out mowing the lawn and couldn't hear what was happening. I had three hard, painful contractions in half an hour. I called the doctor. He asked (hopefully) if I was 26 weeks along. He said not to worry if I had more contractions. I could come to the hospital and a Vasodilan IV would take care of it.

But I'm sick I'm so worried. Just the thought of another baby in the NICU . . . I'm praying to get to 28 weeks. I must talk myself into staying calm. I'm close to hysteria.

*25 weeks*

I feel more positive now: Dr. Yaqub says the baby is good-sized and that he's sure I'll go to 36 weeks (five days before Christmas).

My sister Peggy called Friday to say that she'd just had her baby, a little boy. Was I ever excited! Peggy seemed so calm about the birth, I don't know if she was tired or trying to keep it low-key for fear of sending me into contractions. She talked about the baby shower and all the gifts, but I didn't care about that. I wanted to know how *she* felt and what baby Andrew is like.

There's a difference between a mother who's had a normal pregnancy and a high-risk mother. High-risk mothers know what a miracle it is for a baby to be born without problems. Lately I've been having flashbacks to when Rosie was a baby—all the terrible times, like when she'd turn dusky and when she was home on the apnea monitor to wean her off theophylline. I will *never* take a normal baby for granted.

*26 weeks*

Talked to Peggy again this afternoon. She sounds so happy and contented. The baby nurses beautifully then goes back to sleep. Just the way I remember it was with Polly—I was never so happy in my whole life as I was after she was born. It is in motherhood that I find the contentment I've always searched for. But why does it have to be so difficult for me? I feel the resentment rising as I think back on the surgery I needed before conceiving Polly, the baby boy we lost at 18 weeks, our three years of upset after Rosie's premature birth, and now this horrible pregnancy that has turned me into an invalid and practically wrecked my marriage. Jerry makes me feel so selfish for wanting this child. How much longer, I wonder, can I stand to be the cause of everyone else's work and worry? I'm so tired of "thinking positive." I'm so sick of staying in this house I could scream! It is important for me to write this all down so I'll *never, never* be tempted to become pregnant again.

*28 weeks*

I walked to the mailbox Saturday and had lots of contractions the rest of the day, so no more of that. I've been feeling faint and out of breath. Dr. Yaqub thinks it's because I've been taking too much Vasodilan. He also told me that my cervix was effacing around the stitch—not too terrific. It was at 30 weeks that I went into labor with Rosie and Dr. Yaqub wants me to stay strictly in bed until we pass this critical time. The good news is the baby is big—3 pounds already, he estimates.

*30 weeks*

A milestone. This was when Rosie was born. But I feel good and not at all worried. Staying down is the key. As soon as I get up I have a contraction.

Grandma and Grandpa were here to visit. What a help! Mother brought food and made casseroles. We aren't living on MacDonald's and Brown's Fried Chicken like I'd feared.

*32 weeks*

Felt very depressed since my last doctor's appointment. I wait two weeks for this "big outing," then it's over in one hour and I'm back in bed for another two weeks. It does seem to drag on forever.

Polly has been having terrible tantrums lately. Whenever there is something on TV about mothers and babies she runs out of the room with her hands over her ears. She says she's scared the baby will be early, or blind, or deaf. Guess it's not just me who worries!

Rosie, too, knows the birth is approaching. She and Polly play "babies" all the time now. She constantly asks when the baby is coming out.

*34 weeks*

Not a good weekend. I didn't feel well all day Friday, couldn't eat but felt extremely full. By evening I was feeling the way I had when I was in labor with Rosie but didn't realize it. I began having contractions and we went to the hospital. I was put in the labor room, hooked to monitors, and started on a Vasodilan IV. The contractions stopped quickly. I was 70% effaced but not dilated. I stayed in the hospital till Sunday noon, but had no more problems, thank goodness!

*36 weeks*

I still can't bring myself to get out the baby clothes or do anything to prepare. Jerry and I decided we wouldn't bother going over the Lamaze breathing. We'll do it the old-fashioned way—he'll pace and smoke cigarettes in the waiting room and I'll yell and scream.

We went to visit Peggy and baby Andrew. While I was holding him he started to cry, and I began to get that old feeling of my milk letting down. That was the closest I've come to acknowledging that we'll soon have a baby.

We went to Jerry's company Christmas party Friday night and to the Loyola reunion Sunday afternoon. Everyone was open-mouthed at how big I am. We had a wonderful time, but by Sunday evening I was having painful contractions. Jerry made me a Rob Roy and that did the trick. By the second drink the contractions had stopped.

My due date is exactly a month away now. I sit in bed looking out the window at winter and realize I've been here through summer and fall. Already I'm thinking, "Well, that wasn't so bad." How soon we forget!

*37 weeks*

Dr. Yaqub took out the stitch yesterday—not the most pleasant experience. Everyone said it wouldn't hurt, which was not true. But once it was done I felt quite elated.

Jerry took me to the store and *I* went in and got the groceries while he waited in the car. Came home and cleaned up the kitchen. Made 10 trips upstairs!

With the stitch out, the contractions have stopped and that pressure feeling has gone away. Evidently, I have a lot of scar tissue from the suture, which may mean I won't have a fast labor like I'm used to. I hope it doesn't mean other complications. I didn't like all the frowns on Dr. Yaqub's face as he was examining me.

*39 weeks, 5 days*

Went to bed at 11:15 P.M. after the late news on TV. I was just about asleep when the contractions began for real. I packed, wrote out instructions, and called the friend who'd promised to stay with the kids.

When we arrived at the hospital there was scarcely time to listen to the kindly nurse who saw I was in need of a Lamaze refresher course. After two contractions I felt the baby coming—so much for long labors!

Our third daughter was born at 1:57 A.M. as I was being wheeled toward the delivery room. From the very first glance there was no doubt that this was a big, healthy baby.

Was it worth going through those long, worrisome months? No one would even ask that question had they seen this precious baby girl nursing in the first hours of her life with her exhausted but happy parents taking turns holding and kissing her.

# Appendix A

## Resources for Parents

Many of the resources listed here have been useful in writing and updating *The Premature Baby Book*. Others were recommended by parents, professionals, and support organizations. Prices are given for unusually expensive or inexpensive items. *These prices are approximate and/or subject to change.* PLEASE VERIFY CURRENT PRICES BEFORE ORDERING.

Books marked with the initials *BLB* can be ordered (for as long as they are in print) from:

Birth and Life Bookstore
7001 Alonzo Avenue, NW
P.O. Box 70625
Seattle, WA 98107-0625
800/736-0631

To place orders, call the toll-free number. For information or to request a sample copy of *Imprints*, the bookstore's review newsletter and catalog, call 206/789-4444.

Books marked with the initials *SNS*, or a catalog, can be ordered from:

The Special Needs Selection
Boston University Bookstore
660 Beacon Street
Boston, MA 02215
617/236-7461

Publications marked with the initials *ACCH* can be ordered from:

Association for the Care of
  Children's Health
3615 Wisconsin Avenue, NW
Washington, DC 20016
202/244-1801

ACCH is a parent and professional organization promoting family-centered, supportive children's health-care services through education, networking, research, and advocacy. Call or write for their catalog of resources.

Materials marked with the initials *CC* can be ordered from:

The Centering Corporation
P.O. Box 3367
Omaha, NE 68103-0367
402/553-1200

Centering Corporation booklets on prematurity include *Low Birth Weight, Baby Talk* (an illustrated introduction to preterm behavior), *Daddy: NICU* (conversations with fathers of premies), and *Special Beginnings* (for parents with a baby in the NICU). Call or write for a catalog of publications and products.

Books in print not available from these sources can be ordered directly from the publisher by using the customer service number included with the entry. A few books listed here are no longer in print but may be found at your local library, through library exchange, or through a local parent-support group.

A book or periodical marked with an asterisk is oriented toward professionals and can be found in most medical libraries. Your pediatrician can direct you to a medical library in your area and help you to locate medical texts and articles.

Inquiries about topics covered in *The Premature Baby Book* can be addressed to Helen Harrison c/o St. Martin's Press, 175 Fifth Avenue, New York, NY 10010.

## PREMATURITY AND NEWBORN INTENSIVE CARE

### Organizations

**Parent Care, Inc.**
101½ South Union Street
Alexandria, VA 22314-3323
703/836-4678

An international organization of parents of premature and high-risk infants, Parent Care helps form and maintain local support groups, encourages communication between parents and professionals, produces publications and videos, holds annual conferences and seminars, and promotes public awareness of the special needs of high-risk infants and their families. Three membership categories at $25, $50, and $100 offer a variety of benefits.

**The National Perinatal Association (NPA)**
101½ South Union Street
Alexandria, VA 22314-3323
703/549-5523

An organization of regional and state perinatal associations with membership open to all perinatal health professionals and consumers (NICU parents). Contact the NPA for current information on membership, dues, and benefits.

### Periodicals

*Intensive Caring Unlimited*
(Bimonthly newsletter produced to share information and resources with parents and professionals caring for premature and high-risk infants.) $8/year for parent subscriptions, $12 for professionals, from the Intensive Caring Unlimited Support Organization of Philadelphia, 8 Haycroft Avenue, Springhouse, PA 19477; 215/646-6643.

*\*Journal of Perinatology*
(Official quarterly journal of the NPA with articles on all areas of obstetrics and neonatal care.) $25/year for NPA members, $45 for nonmembers, from the National Perinatal Association (see address under Organizations).

*News Brief*
(Quarterly newsletter with informative, supportive articles for parents and professionals, a benefit of membership in Parent Care.) From Parent Care, Inc. (see address under Organizations).

*\*Perinatal Press*
(Current research and trends in obstetrics and neonatology. Commentaries, articles, reviews in a lively, readable style.) Six issues a year for $19 from The Perinatal Center, Sutter Memorial

Hospital, 52nd and F Streets, Sacramento, CA 95819; 916/733-1750.

*Your Premature Baby: Parenting in the First Year*
(A series of 15 magazines to help parents cope with the special stresses of premature birth.) $25/set from Valencia Community College, Center for Family Education, P.O. Box 3028, Orlando, FL 32802; 407/299-5000, ext. 3150.

## Books for Parents
Avery, M. E.; Litsack, G. *Born Early: The Story of a Premature Baby*. Boston: Little, Brown and Company, 1983. BLB.

Henig, R. M.; Fletcher, A. B. *Your Premature Baby: The Complete Guide to Premie Care During that Crucial First Year*. New York: Rawson Associates, 1983.

Hynan, M. *The Pain of Premature Parents: A Psychological Guide to Coping*. Lanham, Md.: University Press of America, 1987 ($10 from the publisher 301/459-3366).

Jason, J.; van der Meer, A. *Parenting Your Premature Baby*. New York: Henry Holt and Company, 1989. BLB.

Kitchen, W. H.; Ryan, M. M. *Premature Babies: A Guide for Parents*. Emmaus, Pa.: Rodale Press, 1983. BLB.

Lieberman, A.; Sheagren, T. *The Premie Parent's Handbook*. New York: E. P. Dutton, 1984.

Nance, S. *Premature Babies*. New York: Arbor House, 1982. BLB.

Pfister, F.; Griesmer, B. *The Littlest Baby*. Englewood Cliffs, N.J.: Prentice-Hall, 1983.

Sammons, W. A. H.; Lewis, J. M. *Premature Babies: A Different Beginning*. St. Louis: The C. V. Mosby Company, 1985. BLB.

## Books for Siblings
Althea. *Special Care Babies*. London: Dinosaur Publications, 1986. (From England, an illustrated story of a young boy with a premature baby sister. For ages 3 to 8.) $5.45 from ACCH.

Hawkins-Walsh, E. *Katie's Premature Brother*. Omaha: Centering Corporation, 1985. (A story/coloring book for ages 3 to 8.) $2.45 from CC, BLB.

Oehler, J. *The Frogs Have a Baby, A Very Small Baby*. (See page 37.)

Pankow, V. *No Bigger Than My Teddy Bear*. Nashville: Abingdon Press, 1987. (An illustrated story for ages 3 to 8 of a boy's reactions to the birth of a premature brother.) $5.95 from BLB.

## NICU Cards and Baby Books
*Footsteps* (To record milestones of growth and recovery in the NICU.) Free from Wyeth-Ayerst Laboratories Professional Services, P.O. Box 8299, Philadelphia, PA 19101-1245; 800/321-2304 or, in PA, 800/342-2401.

Kards by Kristin (Birth announcements for premies and premie multiples, personalized printing, NICU graduation announcements, diplomas, and more.) P.O. Box 9116, Fountain Valley, CA 92728-9116; 714/432-7282.

"Little Feats" Greetings (Birth announcements for premies and multiples, NICU graduation announcements and diplomas, cards of introduction from support parents to new parents, support group buttons, logos, and more.) 1004 Horseshoe Drive, Nashville, TN 37216; 615/227-2610.

*Small Wonders* (A 16-page book to record milestones for hospitalized and discharged premies, $2.50.) Small Wonders Birth Announcements (in pink or blue with mother and baby bunny in a rocking chair, $2.50 for a set of ten). From Parents of Prematures, P.O. Box 3046, Kirkland, WA 98083-3046; 206/283-7466.

## NICU Art and Poetry
Erling, S. *Newborn Intensive Share*. Omaha: Centering Corporation. (Poems by a mother of premature twins.) $2.45 from CC, BLB.

Gunther, K. *The Babies: Portraits of Fragile Lives*. Milwaukee: Main Street Publishing, 1986. (Forty-eight charcoal drawings of prematures in the NICU.) $8.75 from BLB.

Spears, H. *Drawings from the Newborn: Poems and Drawings of Infants in Crisis*. Port Angeles, Wa.: Ben-Simon Publications, 1986. (A lyrical depiction of prematures in a Copenhagen NICU.) $39.95 from BLB.

## NICU Videos
*A Joyful Tear* (Fears, stresses, strengths, and insights of NICU parents.) Free loan to hospitals and support groups, $90 to purchase from Ross Laboratories, Educational Services Depart-

ment, 625 Cleveland Avenue, Columbus, OH 43216; 614/227-3557.

*Breastfeeding the Premature Infant: Delivery to Discharge* (Set of three videos.) Rental, $120, purchase, $350 from PGG Associates, Care Video Productions, P.O. Box 44132, Cleveland, OH 44145; 216/835-5872.

*Incubator Loving Touch* (Dr. Ruth Rice's massage technique in the NICU, see p. 133), *The Loving Touch* (massage at home), and *The Kangaroo Method* (caregiving techniques in which premies have extensive skin-to-skin contact with their mothers). $30 each, prepaid; no credit cards; from Cradle Care, P.O. Box 801548, Dallas, TX 75380-1548; 214/363-7244.

*Prematurely Yours* (behavior of premies, guidance for parent-infant interactions) and *To Have and Not to Hold* (parents discuss the stresses of having a baby in the NICU). In video or slide/tape, $40 each to rent; to purchase, $295 each in video, $200 each in slide/tape from Polymorph Films, 118 South Street, Boston, MA 02111; 800/223-5107.

*Special Delivery: Understanding Your Premature Infant* (protecting premies from NICU stress, enhancing recovery and parent-infant interactions). In video, $75 to purchase; in slide/tape, $130 from Education Programs Associates, 1 West Campbell Avenue, Bldg. D, Campbell, CA 95008; 408/374-3720.

## Bonding and Attachment
Brazelton, T. B. *On Becoming a Family*. New York: Delacorte Press, 1981. BLB.

Klaus, M. H.; Kennell, J. H. *Parent-Infant Bonding*. St. Louis: The C. V. Mosby Company, 1982. BLB.

Sims, C. I. "Kangaroo Care." *Mothering* (Fall, 1988). (In South American and European hospitals, medically stable prematures breastfeed right after birth, keep warm by skin-to-skin contact with their mothers, and go home soon after birth. Babies thrive and bonding is enhanced. For more information contact:
Gene Anderson, R.N., Ph.D., College of Nursing, J-187, Health Science Center, University of Florida, Gainesville; FL 32610, 904/392-3531.

## Preterm Behavior and Developmental Care
Flushman, B.; VandenBerg, K. *Developmental Steps: A Guide for Parents to Infant Development in the Intensive Care*

*Nursery,* 1984. (Parenting premies and protecting them from stress in the NICU and at home.) $7.50 plus tax and shipping from Education Programs Associates, 1 West Campbell Avenue, Bldg. D, Campbell, CA 95008; 408/374-3720.

*Gardner, S. L. et al. "The Neonate and the Environment: Impact on Development." *Handbook of Neonatal Intensive Care, 2d Edition,* edited by Merenstein and Gardner, 1989 (See *Neonatal Care,* below). (Health and developmental consequences of NICU stress; how to comfort and protect hospitalized premies.) BLB.

Goldberg, S.; DiVitto, B. A. *Born Too Soon: Preterm Birth and Early Development.* San Francisco: W. H. Freeman and Company, 1983. BLB.

Healy, T. *Guiding Your Preterm Infant Through Development,* 1985. (Calming and handling techniques, avoiding overstimulation, beginning interactions.) $3.50 from Parent Care, Inc., 101½ South Union Street, Alexandria, VA 22314-3323; 703/549-5523.

Infant Sensory Enrichment Education (Educational materials and sensory enrichment products for families and professionals caring for high-risk infants.) 422 Sierra Trail, Coralville, IA 52241; 319/337-4868.

*Lawhon, G.; Melzar, A. "Developmental Care of the Very Low Birthweight Infant," *The Journal of Perinatal and Neonatal Nursing* (July 1988). (See *Neonatal Care,* below). (Improving health and developmental outcome through individualized caregiving.)

Rice, R. D. *The Loving Touch* (The Premature Version—chart and cassette to instruct in the massage technique described on page 133. Also available in Spanish, French, and German.) $21.95 prepaid; no charge cards; from Cradle Care, P.O. Box 801548, Dallas, TX 75380-1548; 214/363-7244.

### Neonatal Care

*Cone, T. E. *History of the Care and Feeding of the Premature Infant.* Boston: Little, Brown and Company, 1985. (Fascinating historical information and illustrations.) $36 from the publisher; 800/343-9204.

*Guthrie, R. D. *Neonatal Intensive Care.* New York: Churchill Livingstone, 1988. (Current treatment of RDS, BPD, apnea, and more. Excellent

*(handwritten: Out of Print ✓)*

chapters on the outcomes of prematurely born children and on complications of NICU treatments.) $46 from BLB.

*Marshall, R. E. et al. *Coping with Caring for Sick Newborns.* Philadelphia: W. B. Saunders Company, 1982. (Staff and parents describe pressures and rewards of life in the NICU. Good information on parent support groups.) $24.95 from BLB.

*Merenstein, G. B.; Gardner, S. L. *Handbook of Neonatal Intensive Care, 2d Edition.* St. Louis: The C. V. Mosby Company, 1989. (Comprehensive neonatal text oriented toward humane infant care and family concerns. New information on alleviating pain and stress in the NICU, coping with nutritional and feeding difficulties, breastfeeding and more.) $27.95 from BLB.

*Prematurity and Premature Birth. *The Journal of Perinatal and Neonatal Nursing,* Vol. 2, No. 1 (July 1988). (Articles on developmental care, breastfeeding premies, nutrition, RDS, preventing prematurity and more.) $14.95 from Aspen Publishers; 800/638-8437.

### Ethical Issues

Barthel, J. "Jimmy: Should He Have Been Allowed to Live?" *McCalls* (November 1985). (One family's experience with a severely handicapped prematurely born child saved against their wishes.)

Guillemin, J. H.; Holmstrom, L. L. *Mixed Blessings: Intensive Care for Newborns.* New York: Oxford University Press, 1986. (Sociologists study the impact of NICU care on babies, families, and society.) BLB.

Gustaitis, R.; Young, E. W. D. *A Time to be Born, A Time to Die: Conflicts and Ethics in an Intensive Care Nursery.* Reading, Ma.: Addison-Wesley, 1986. (Case histories from an NICU show the technological imperative in conflict with the medical principle "Do no harm.") BLB.

Lyon, J. *Playing God in the Nursery.* New York: W. W. Norton & Company, 1985. (NICU in the era of "Baby Doe," implications of treatment vs. nontreatment. Excellent information on the problems and outcomes of prematurity.) BLB.

Scully, T.; Scully, C. *Playing God: The New World of Medical Choices.* New York:

Simon and Schuster, 1987. (Practical family guide to ethical decisionmaking, "Baby Doe" legislation, informed consent, experimental treatment, malpractice, and more.) BLB.

*Silverman, W. A. *Human Experimentation: A Guided Step Into the Unknown.* New York: Oxford University Press, 1985. (See following entry.) $29.95 from BLB.

*Silverman, W. A., *Retrolental Fibroplasia: A Modern Parable.* New York: Grune & Stratton, 1980. (Both Silverman books describe how prematures can be harmed by poorly evaluated treatments and how randomized controlled clinical trials provide an ethical alternative.) $32.00 from BLB.

Stinson, R.; Stinson, P. *The Long Dying of Baby Andrew.* Boston: Atlantic–Little, Brown, 1983. (Parents' account of their battle with physicians to stop intensive care for their dying baby.) BLB.

### Financial Coping

Gaylord, C. L.; Leonard, A. M. *A Guide to Health Care Coverage for the Child with a Chronic Illness or Disability,* 1988. $20 prepaid from the Center for Public Representation, 520 University Avenue, Madison, WI 53703; 608/251-4008.

IRS Publications: #17 *Your Federal Income Tax;* #502 *Deductions for Medical and Dental Expenses;* #503 *Child Care and Disabled Dependent Care;* #933 *Major Tax Law Changes Enacted in 1987.* Free from 800/424-FORM.

McManus, M. A. *Understanding Your Health Insurance Options: A Guide for Families Who Have Children with Special Health Care Needs,* 1988. $3.75 from ACCH.

*Meeting the Medical Bills.* (25-minute video discusses private insurance, SSI, Medicaid waivers and more. Free informational brochures and background reading packet included.) $10.95 from NCCIP/Med Video, P.O. Box 1492, Washington, DC 20013; 703/893-6061.

### Emotional Coping

Kushner, H. S. *When Bad Things Happen to Good People.* New York: Schocken Books, 1981. (Creative, healing insights into coping with life's inevitable difficulties.) BLB, SNS.

# BREASTFEEDING

## Organizations

**Lact-Aid International** and **Lact-Aid Moms Network**
Box 1066
Athens, TN 37303
800/228-1933
(In TN) 615/744-9090

Support, information, and products for nursing, relactation, and premie care; national support network for mothers using the Lact-Aid (p. 170).

**Lactation Associates**
254 Conant Road
Weston, MA 02193-1756
617/893-3553

Educational materials at nominal cost include *Breastfeeding Your Premature or Special Care Baby, Breastfeeding Your Twins, The Slow Gaining Baby,* and *Expressing, Storing and Transporting Breastmilk.*

**La Leche League International (LLL)**
P.O. Box 1209
Franklin Park, IL 60131-8209
312/455-7730

Support, information, pump rentals; free catalog of products, publications; free directory of LLL representatives.

## Books and Pamphlets

Danner, S. C.; Cerutti, E. R. *Nursing Your Premature Baby.* Rochester, N.Y.: Childbirth Graphics Ltd., 1984. 50¢ from BLB.

Grams, M. *Breastfeeding Source Book.* Sheridan, Wy.: Achievement Press, 1988. (Resources and information for nursing in special circumstances; evaluations of breast pumps and nursing products.) BLB.

Huggins, K. *The Nursing Mother's Companion.* Boston: The Harvard Common Press, 1986. (Good information on breastfeeding problems and special circumstances.) BLB.

*McCoy, R. et al. "Nursing Management of Breastfeeding for Preterm Infants." *The Journal of Perinatal and Neonatal Nursing* (July 1988). (See *Neonatal Care* p. 243). (Discusses recent research showing that breastfeeding is easier for premies than bottle feeding; tells how to express, handle, and store breastmilk; how to position the baby and more.)

# AFTER THE NICU: HEALTH AND DEVELOPMENT

*Ballard, R. A. *Pediatric Care of the ICN Graduate.* Philadelphia: W. B. Saunders Company, 1988. (Health, growth, development, well-baby care; apnea, anemia, cosmetic problems, sensory and motor problems, seizures, hydrocephalus, infections, endocrine disorders; home care for babies with monitors, ventilators, shunts, and ostomies; follow-up, early intervention, community resources.) $45 from BLB.

*Bennett, F. C. "Neurodevelopmental Outcome in Low-Birthweight Infants: The Role of Developmental Intervention," in *Neonatal Intensive Care* by Guthrie, 1988 (See *Neonatal Care* p. 243). (Behavior and development of prematurely born children, birth through school age.) BLB.

*Guidelines and Recommended Practices for the Individualized Family Service Plan, P.L. 99–457,* 1989. (Guide to the new law providing family-oriented early intervention services for high-risk infants, birth to age two.) $15.50 from ACCH.

Schwartz, S.; Miller, J. *The Language of Toys: A Guide for Parents and Teachers.* Kensington, Md.: Woodbine House, 1988. (Using toys to teach communication skills to high-risk infants and children, birth to age five.) SNS.

Segal, M. *In Time and With Love.* New York: Newmarket Press, 1988. (For families of high-risk infants in the first three years. Over 100 tips on coping, feeding, dressing, discipline, social skills, games and activities.) BLB, SNS.

# TWINS AND SUPERTWINS

## Organizations

**The Center for Study of Multiple Birth**
333 Superior Street, Suite 476
Chicago, IL 60611
312/266-9093

Information, research, support and referrals; "twin" bookstore.

**National Organization of Mothers of Twins Clubs, Inc.**
12404 Princess Jeanne, NE
Albuquerque, NM 87112-4640
505/275-0955

Call or write for referral to a club in your area.

**The Triplet Connection**
P.O. Box 99571
Stockton, CA 95209
209/474-0885

Information, resources, and networking for families with (or expecting) triplets or more.

**Twin Services (formerly TWINLINE)**
P.O. Box 10066
Berkeley, CA 94709
415/644-0863

Information, advice, publications, and services for multiple-birth families and professionals.

## Books

Alexander, T. P. *Make Room for Twins: A Complete Guide to Pregnancy, Delivery and the Childhood Years.* New York: Bantam Books, 1987. BLB.

Clegg, A.; Woollett, A. *Twins: From Conception to Five.* New York: Van Nostrand Reinhold, 1983. BLB.

Friedrich, E.; Rowland, C. *The Parents' Guide to Raising Twins.* New York: St. Martin's Press, 1984. BLB.

Gromada, K. *Mothering Multiples: Breastfeeding and Caring for Twins.* La Leche League publication #267, 1985. BLB.

Novotny, P. P. *The Joy of Twins.* New York: Crown Publishers, 1988. BLB.

## Periodicals

*Double Talk* (A quarterly newsletter.) $8/year. P.O. Box 412, Amelia, OH 45102; 513/753-7117.

*Twins* (A bi-monthly magazine with a regular column on prematurity.) $18/year. P.O. Box 12045, Overland Park, KS 66212; 800/821-5533 ext. 30.

# CONTINUING HEALTH AND DEVELOPMENTAL PROBLEMS

## Organizations

**Association for the Care of Children's Health (ACCH)** and **ACCH Parent Network**
(See p. 241.)

**The Federation for Children with Special Needs**
312 Stuart Street
Boston, MA 02116
617/482-2915

Parent group coalition promoting parental involvement in the care of chronically ill or disabled children; access to medical, legal, financial, and educational information and resources; advocacy; parent/professional collaboration; and the development of national and regional support networks.

**National Information Center for Children and Youth With Handicaps (NICHCY)**
P.O. Box 1492
Washington, DC 20013
800/999-5599 or 703/893-6061

National clearinghouse providing free information to parents and professionals.

**SKIP (Sick Kids Need Involved People)**
216 Newport Drive
Severna Park, MD 21146
301/647-0164

Information, support, referrals, and training for families with chronically ill and technology-dependent children.

**Periodicals**
*The Bridge* (Quarterly journal published by Parent Resources on Disabilities.) $10/year. P.O. Box 14391, Portland, OR 97214; 503/234-2644.

*The Exceptional Parent* (Supportive, informative magazine for parents of disabled children, published eight times a year. Free issue on request.) $16/year. P.O. Box 3000, Dept. E.P., Denville, NJ 07834; 617/730-5800.

**Coping with Chronic Illness**
*Ahmann, E. *Home Care for the High Risk Infant: A Holistic Guide to Using Technology.* Frederick, Md.: Aspen Publishers, 1986. (Home care for children with apnea, BPD, tracheostomies, feeding problems, hydrocephalus, seizures, neurological and sensory handicaps; family issues; financial aid.) $48.95 from BLB.

*Ballard, R. *Pediatric Care of the ICN Graduate* (see After the NICU: Health and Development, p. 244). BLB.

Goldfarb, L. A. et al. *Meeting the Challenge of Disability or Chronic Illness—A Family Guide.* Baltimore: Paul H. Brookes Publishing Co., 1986. (Problem-solving techniques to help families cope.) SNS.

Jones, M. L. *Home Care for the Chronically Ill or Disabled Child: A Manual and Sourcebook for Parents and Professionals.* New York: Harper & Row, 1985. (A comprehensive, empowering guide to emotional and practical coping.) BLB, SNS.

Shelton, T. L. et al. *Family-Centered Care for Children with Special Health Care Needs*, 1987. (Resources for parents of chronically ill children.) $7.50 from ACCH.

**Coping with Handicaps**
Batshaw, M. L.; Perret, Y. M. *Children with Handicaps: A Medical Primer, 2d Edition.* Baltimore: Paul H. Brookes Publishing Co., 1986. (Prematurity; birth defects; sensory, learning, and behavior disorders; cerebral palsy; seizures; retardation; autism. Nutrition; special health and dental care; ethical, legal, and family issues. An excellent resource.) SNS.

Dickman, I.; Gordon, S. *One Miracle at a Time: How To Get Help for Your Disabled Child—From the Experience of Other Parents.* New York: Simon and Schuster, 1985. SNS, BLB.

Featherstone, H. *A Difference in the Family: Life with a Disabled Child.* New York: Basic Books, 1980. (Honest, eloquent account of family life with a handicapped child. A classic.) SNS, BLB.

Simons, R. *After the Tears: Parents Talk about Raising a Child with a Disability.* New York: Harcourt Brace Jovanovich, 1987. SNS, BLB.

**Apnea**

**National Sudden Infant Death Syndrome Foundation**
Two Metro Plaza, Suite 205
8240 Professional Place
Landover, MD 20785
301/459-3388

Handbooks on home apnea monitoring at nominal cost.

**Bronchopulmonary Dysplasia (BPD)**
Hanson, J. *Parent Guide to Bronchopulmonary Dysplasia, 1987.* (Emotional,

practical, financial coping; nutrition; medication and side effects; home oxygen and nebulizer use; chest physical therapy; aiding development; when to get medical help; medical and developmental follow-up.) $1 from The American Lung Association of New Mexico, 216 Truman, NE, Albuquerque, NM 87108; 505/265-0732.

Johns, N.; Harvey, C. *Home Care of Babies with BPD: A Workbook for Parents*, 1986. (Use of oxygen, humidifiers, aerosols, nebulizers; tracheostomy care; gavage and gastrostomy feeding; medications and more.) About $6 from Philadelphia Parenting Associates, 127 Birch Avenue, Bala Cynwyd, PA 19004; 215/668-8616.

*Merritt, T. A., et al. *Bronchopulmonary Dysplasia* (from the series Contemporary Issues in Fetal and Neonatal Medicine, Vol. 4) Boston: Blackwell Scientific Publications, 1988. (Causes, treatments, and complications; home respiratory care; health and developmental outcomes.) About $65 from BLB.

**Cerebral Palsy**

**Organizations**

**National Easter Seal Society for Crippled Children and Adults**
70 East Lake Street
Chicago, IL 60601
800/221-6827

Information, referrals, equipment loan, evaluation, recreation, and rehabilitation.

**Rhizotomy Network**
20321 122d Avenue, SE
Kent, WA 98031
206/631-2677

Parents and professionals share information on rhizotomy, a new surgical procedure to relieve spasticity. Membership and newsletter subscription $15/year.

**United Cerebral Palsy Association**
66 E 34th Street
New York, NY 10016
800/USA-1UCP

Information, referrals to local affiliates and infant programs.

**Books**
Finnie, N. R. *Handling the Young Cerebral Palsied Child at Home.* New York: E. P. Dutton, 1975. SNS, BLB.

Palmer, F.; Steelman, V. A. *A Parent's How-To Book of Ideas for Special Needs Children*, 1988. (Parents tell how to make or adapt furniture and play equipment for children with motor impairments.) $15 from Fran Palmer, 645 N. Wrightwood Drive, Orange, CA 92669; 714/538-2720.

Schleichkorn, J. *Coping with Cerebral Palsy: Answers to Questions Parents Often Ask*. Austin, Tex. Pro-Ed, 1983. (Well-researched guide to medical, developmental, legal, social, and family issues.) SNS.

Thompson, C. *Raising a Handicapped Child: A Helpful Guide for Parents of the Physically Disabled*. New York: Ballantine Books, 1986. BLB, SNS.

## Hearing Loss

### Organizations

**Alexander Graham Bell Association for the Deaf**
3417 Volta Place, NW
Washington, DC 20007
202/337-5220

Information, referrals, financial aid, advocacy, conferences, and publications. Promotes the oral approach to communication.

**American Society for Deaf Children**
814 Thayer Avenue
Silver Spring, MD 20910
301/585-5400

Parent organization offering information and empowerment to parents of deaf, hard of hearing, and multiply involved children. Promotes understandable communication including sign language.

**National Information Center on Deafness**
Gallaudet University
800 Florida Avenue, NE
Washington, DC 20002
202/651-5051

Clearinghouse for information on hearing loss, parenting, education, and all approaches to communication.

### Books

Adams, J. *You and Your Hearing Impaired Child*. Washington, D.C.: Gallaudet Press, 1988. SNS.

Ferris, C. *A Hug Just Isn't Enough*. Washington, D.C.: Gallaudet Press, 1980. SNS.

Freeman, R. D. et al. *Can't Your Child Hear? A Guide for Those Who Care About Deaf Children*. Baltimore: University Park Press, 1981. SNS.

Ogden, P. W.; Lipsett, S. *The Silent Garden*. New York: St. Martin's Press, 1982. SNS.

Schwartz, S. *Choices in Deafness: A Parent's Guide*. Kensington, Md.: Woodbine House, 1987, SNS.

Spradley, T. F. *Deaf Like Me*. New York: Random House, 1978. SNS.

## Hyperactivity/Learning Disabilities

### Organizations

**Association for Children and Adults with Learning Disabilities**
4156 Library Road
Pittsburgh, PA 15234
412/341-1515

Free information packet and resource directory. Referrals to local affiliates.

### Books

Bittinger, M. L. *Living with Our Hyperactive Children: Parents' Own Stories*. New York: BPS Books and Two Continents Publishing Group, 1977.

Ingersoll, B. *Your Hyperactive Child: A Parent's Guide to Coping with Attention Deficit Disorder*. New York: Doubleday, 1988. SNS.

Osman, B. B. *Learning Disabilities: A Family Affair*. New York: Random House, 1979. SNS.

Smith, S. L. *No Easy Answers: The Learning Disabled Child at Home and at School*. New York: Bantam Books, 1981. SNS.

Wender, P. H. *The Hyperactive Child, Adolescent, and Adult: Attention Deficit Disorders Through the Life Span*. New York: Oxford University Press, 1987. SNS.

## Intraventricular Hemorrhage (IVH), Hydrocephalus, Seizures

### Organizations

**Epilepsy Foundation of America**
4351 Garden City Drive
Landover, MD 20785
800/332-1000

Information packet for parents; library; advocacy and legal services; referrals to local affiliates.

**Hydrocephalus Foundation of Northern California**
2040 Polk Street, Box 342
San Francisco, CA 94109
415/776-4713

Parent-run organization providing quarterly newsletter, resource guide, extensive bibliography on hydrocephalus, national conferences, and referrals to local support groups. Membership $15/year.

**IVH Parents**
P.O. Box 56-1111
Miami, FL 33156
305/232-0381

International network of parents whose children suffered IVH and of professionals who care for these children; quarterly newsletter; medical and psychological data compiled. U.S. membership $10/year.

### Books

Edwards, M. S. B.; Derechin, M. *About Hydrocephalus: A Book for Parents*. San Francisco: University of California, 1986. $1.50 for single copy from the Hydrocephalus Foundation of Northern California (see address under Organizations).

*Just Like Any Other Little Beagle*, 1988. (A coloring book about shunting for young children with hydrocephalus and their siblings. Also available in Spanish, French, and other languages.) Free from Cordis Corporation, P.O. Box 025700, Miami, FL 33102; 305/824-2595.

## Ostomies

### Organizations

**United Ostomy Association, Inc.**
36 Executive Park, Suite 120
Irvine, CA 92714
714/660-8624

Information, support, referrals, publications, quarterly magazine.

### Books

Filipek, J. *Caring for Your Baby with a Trach Tube*. $2.50 from The American Lung Association of Alameda County, 295 27th Street, Oakland, CA 94612; 415/893-5474.

Jeter, K. F. *These Special Children: The Ostomy Book for Parents of Children with Colostomies, Ileostomies, and Urostomies*. Palo Alto, Calif.: Bull Publishing Company, 1982. SNS.

## Vision Loss

### Organizations

**American Foundation for the Blind, Inc.**
15 W. 16th Street
New York, NY 10011
800/AFBLIND
(In NY) 212/620-2147

National consulting agency with regional offices. Free pamphlets on parenting blind infants and children. Publications include directory of agencies providing services to preschool blind children.

**Blind Children's Center**
4120 Marathon
Los Angeles, CA 90029-0159
800/222-3566
(In CA) 800/222-3567

Free booklets in English and Spanish including *Talk to Me* (language acquisition and concept formation), *Move with Me* (motor development), *Learning to Play,* and *Heart to Heart* (parents' feelings).

**Blind Children's Fund**
230 Central Street
Auburndale, MA 02166-2399
617/332-4014

Information and services for parents and professionals. Newsletter; national, international symposiums; advocacy. Publications available at nominal cost include *Get a Wiggle On* and *Move It* (enhancing development birth to school age), *Watch Me Grow* (English/Spanish guide to developmental activities, birth to age 3), and *Learning to Look* (stimulating low vision).

**Hadley School for the Blind**
700 Elm Street
Winnetka, IL 60093
800/323-4238

Free correspondence courses for parents such as *Reach out and Teach* (teaching developmental skills to blind or multiply involved children, birth to school age).

**National Association for Parents of the Visually Impaired, Inc. (NAPVI)**
P.O. Box 562
Camden, NY 13316
800/562-6265

Parent-to-parent support, referrals,

quarterly newsletter, publications, national and regional conferences.

### Books

Kastein, S. et al. *Raising the Young Blind Child.* New York: Human Sciences Press, 1980. SNS.

Rogow, S. M. *Helping the Visually Impaired Child with Developmental Problems.* New York: Teacher's College Press, Columbia University, 1988. SNS.

Scott, E. P. et al. *Can't Your Child See?* Baltimore: University Park Press, 1977. SNS.

*Silverman, W. A.; Flynn, J. T. *Retinopathy of Prematurity.* Boston: Blackwell Scientific Publications, 1985. $35.00 from BLB.

Ulrich, S. *Elizabeth.* Ann Arbor: University of Michigan Press, 1972. (A mother's account of her blind premature daughter's first five years.) SNS.

## DEATH OF A BABY

### Organizations

**The Compassionate Friends, Inc.**
P.O. Box 3696
Oak Brook, IL 60522-3696
312/990-0010

An international self-help group for bereaved parents. Free informational brochures, complimentary newsletter, referrals to local chapters.

**National Sudden Infant Death Syndrome Foundation** (see under Apnea, p. 245)

Information, support, and referrals for parents who have lost a child to SIDS.

**Pregnancy and Infant Loss Center**
1421 E. Wayzata Boulevard, Suite 40
Wayzata, MN 55391
612/473-9372

Clearinghouse for resources on miscarriage, stillbirth, and newborn death. Infant-loss announcements, burial gowns and patterns, infant caskets, funeral planning, quarterly newsletter.

### Booklets

Most of the following materials are available at nominal cost from Preg-

nancy and Infant Loss Center (PILC), CC, and/or BLB.

Cohen, M. *She Was Born, She Died* (poems on the death of a newborn). CC, BLB.

*Explaining Death to Children.* PILC.

Gryte, M. *No New Baby: For Boys and Girls Whose Expected Sibling Dies.* CC, BLB.

Isle, S. *Empty Arms* (the book that changed the way we deal with infant death). PILC, CC, BLB.

*Ocaso Sin Aurora* (for Spanish-speaking parents). CC.

Oehler, J. *The Frog Family's Baby Dies* (see p. 114).

*Our Forever Baby* (a memento book). PILC.

*Planning a Precious Goodbye* (funeral, burial, cremation, a sample service). PILC.

Schwiebert, P.; Kirk, P. *When Hello Means Goodbye* (emotional and practical tasks facing parents after the death of a newborn) and *Still To Be Born* (options for future pregnancy). CC, BLB.

Webster, B. *Letters to Geoffrey* (a father's letters to his premature son from birth to burial). CC.

### Books

Borg, S.; Lasker, J. *When Pregnancy Fails: Families Coping with Miscarriage, Ectopic Pregnancy, Stillbirth and Infant Death.* New York: Bantam, 1989. BLB.

Cohen, M. *The Limits of Miracles: Poems About the Loss of Babies.* South Hadley, Mass.: Bergin and Garvey, 1985. BLB.

Friedman, R.; Gradstein, B. *Surviving Pregnancy Loss.* Boston: Little, Brown and Company, 1982. BLB.

Limbo, R. K.; Wheeler, S. R. *When a Baby Dies: A Handbook for Healing and Helping.* La Crosse, Wis.: Resolve Through Sharing, 1986. BLB.

Peppers, L. G.; Knapp, R. J. *How To Go On Living After the Death of a Baby.* Atlanta: Peachtree Publishers, 1985. BLB.

Schiff, H. *The Bereaved Parent.* New York: Penguin Books, 1977. BLB.

*Woods, J. R.; Esposito, J. L. *Pregnancy Loss: Medical Therapeutics and Practical Considerations.* Baltimore: Williams & Wilkins, 1987. BLB.

# HIGH-RISK PREGNANCY

## Organizations

**March of Dimes Birth Defects Foundation**
1275 Mamaroneck Avenue
White Plains, NY 10605
914/428-7100

Information, research, and services for prevention, diagnosis, and treatment of perinatal problems.

**DES Action U.S.A.**
2845 24th Street
San Francisco, CA 94110
415/826-5060
   and at
Long Island Jewish-Hillside Medical Center
New Hyde Park, NY 11040
516/775-3450

Information and support for those exposed to DES.

**Resolve, Inc.**
5 Water Street
Arlington, MA 02178
617/643-2424

Information and support for those with problems related to infertility.

For multiple pregnancy, see organizations and resources listed under Twins and Supertwins (p. 244).

## Books

*Creasy, R. K.; Resnik, R. *Maternal-Fetal Medicine: Principles and Practice*, 2d Edition. Philadelphia: W. B. Saunders, 1989. $95 from the publisher; 800/545-2522.

Hales, D.; Creasy, R. K. *New Hope for Problem Pregnancies*. New York: Berkley Publications, 1984. BLB.

Institute of Medicine, *Preventing Low Birthweight* (summary), 1985. $5 from National Academy Press, 2101 Constitution Avenue NW, Washington, DC 20418.

Johnston, S. H.; Kraut, D. A. *Pregnancy Bedrest: A Guidebook for the Pregnant Woman and Her Family*, 1986. Send $10 check, made out to Pregnancy Bedrest, to P.O. Box 7304, McLean, VA 22106-7304.

Katz, M. et al. *Preventing Preterm Birth: A Parent's Guide*. San Francisco: Health Publishing Company, 1988. BLB.

Robertson, P. A.; Berlin, P. H. *The Pre-*

*mature Labor Handbook: Successfully Sustaining Your High-Risk Pregnancy*. New York: Doubleday, 1986. BLB.

*[handwritten: Yes $9.95 paperback]*

# PARENT-TO-PARENT SUPPORT

## Organizations

The following list of support groups for parents of premature and high-risk infants is current for 1989. For additional information on groups in your area, contact Parent Care, Inc. (p. 241), your local March of Dimes chapter, or a hospital social worker. To add your group to this list, or to change a listing, write to Helen Harrison, c/o St. Martin's Press, 175 Fifth Avenue, New York, NY 10010.

## Alaska

Parents Sharing Together
Providence Hospital Social Work Department
Box 196604
Anchorage, AK 99519-6604
907/261-3175

## Arizona

ICU Care Parents
Laura Shockley
19820 N. 13th Avenue, #215
Phoenix, AZ 85027
602/582-5661

## Arkansas

St. Vincent Parents Support Group
Betty Diehl, RN, CNS
St. Vincent Infirmary Medical Center
2 St. Vincent Circle
Little Rock, AR 72205-5499
501/660-2910

## California

Good Beginnings
Dorothy Williams
Cedars-Sinai Medical Center
8700 Beverly Boulevard, Room 4310
Los Angeles, CA 90048
213/855-4431

Infant/Parent Support Network of Orange County
Johanna Downs, Program Coordinator
1100 N. Tustin, Suite G
Santa Ana, CA 92705
714/836-5511

Parent Share
Linda Cole, RN
Intensive Care Nursery
Alta Bates Hospital
3001 Colby
Berkeley, CA 94705
415/540-1626

Special Care Parents
Kate Judson
P.O. Box 22322
Sacramento, CA 95822
916/395-2338

UCSF Parent Support Group
Laura Repke
Room U587-G
San Francisco, CA 94143
415/476-8354
(North Bay Chapter, Cindy Woolley, 707/255-1094)

Valley Parents Support Group
Judith Sultan
P.O. Box 5973-272
Sherman Oaks, CA 91413
818/902-1616

## Colorado

Parent Resource Group
Ellen Keckler
University Hospital
University of Colorado Health Sciences Center, C-300
4200 E. 9th Avenue
Denver, CO 80262
303/399-1211

Parent to Parent
Susan Rudd, MSW
Children's Hospital
1056 E. 19th Avenue
Denver, CO 80218
303/861-6887

## Connecticut

Parents Available to Help (PATH)
Yale-New Haven Hospital
789 Howard Avenue
P.O. Box 91
New Haven, CT 06504
Donna Levine 203/785-2318
   or Sandy Balayan 203/272-4245

Parent Sharing
Anne Parker
Hartford Hospital
80 Seymour Street
Hartford, CT 06115
203/282-0280

## Florida

Neo-Care
Julie Busch

P.O. Box 160683
Altamonte Springs, FL 32716-0683
407/774-1754

Parent to Parent of Florida
Susan Duwa
3500 E. Fletcher, Suite 225
Tampa, FL 33612
813/974-5001

Veteran Intensive Parents (VIPS)
Leigh Ware
P.O. Box 2700
Pensacola, FL 32513-2700
904/474-7656

### Georgia

The Preemie Fund-Raising
  Committee, Inc.
Debbie Hunter
P.O. Box 1583
Buford, GA 30518-1583
404/932-5546

Premie Parents Support Group
Anne Weiner
P.O. Box 71953
Marietta, GA 30007-1953
404/973-3295

### Hawaii

Kamali'i leo Hauoli'i
(Children with Happy Voices)
Lori Meyers-Cannon
P.O. Box 10517
Hilo, HI 96721-5517
808/935-4490

### Idaho

NICU Parents for Parents
Judy Cross, RNC, MSN
St. Luke's Regional Medical Center
190 E. Bannock Street
Boise, ID 83712
208/386-2661

Parents for Parents Support Group of
  Blaine County
P.O. Box 1594
Hailey, ID 83333
Reggie Swindle 208/788-3084
  or Kathy Walker 208/788-4893

### Illinois

Concerned Parents Organization for
  High Risk Infants and Mothers
NICU Office
Lutheran General Children's Medical
  Center
1775 Dempster Street
Park Ridge, IL 60137
312/696-5313

Loyola Premature and High Risk
  Parents Association
Fran Tobias
3 South 306 Shagbark Lane
Glen Ellen, IL 60137
312/858-2847

Parent Education and Support
  Meetings
Jane Turner, CSW
St. John's Hospital
800 East Carpenter
Springfield, IL 62669
217/544-6464 ext. 4480

Parent to Parent Support Group
Ann Newkerk, RN
Evanston Hospital ISCU
2650 Ridge Avenue
Evanston, IL 60201
312/492-3907

### Indiana

Neo-Fight
Darla Cohen
4363 Idlewild Lane
Carmel, IN 46032
317/843-0850

Special Care Parents
Department of Neonatology
St. Mary's Medical Center
3700 Washington Avenue
Evansville, IN 47750
812/479-4000

### Iowa

The Parent Support Group
Bev Lessman
2505 South Lyon
Sioux City, IA 51106
712/276-7845

Pilot Parents of Prematures
Carla Lawson
33 N. 12th Street
Fort Dodge, IA 50501
515/576-5870

Special Care Parents
Jule Reynolds
P.O. Box 938
Des Moines, IA 50304
515/263-9247

### Kansas

Parents & Friends of Special Care
  Infants
Shannon Scholler
602 South Chatauqua
Wichita, KS 67211
316/689-8849

### Kentucky

Neo-Life, Inc.
Patricia Hays Evans
3217 Breckenwood Drive
Lexington, KY 40502
606/277-0008

### Louisiana

NICU Parents, Inc.
Kelly Amirkhani
Woman's Hospital
% Social Services
P.O. Box 95009
Baton Rouge, LA 70895-9009
504/293-3562

We(e) Care
Terry Harkey
7815 Lotus Lane
Shreveport, LA 71108
318/686-8558

### Maryland

Reliance
Sallie B. V. Dunkle, Coordinator
Department of Pastoral Care and
  Counseling
Memorial Hospital
Memorial Avenue
Cumberland, MD 21532
301/777-4297 or Sacred Heart
  Hospital, 301/759-5158

### Massachusetts

NICU Parent Support, Inc.
Linda Sternberg
18 Lovett Road
Newton Center, MA 02159
617/698-1172

### Michigan

NICU Friends (NICUF)
Ellen Smith
% RNICU
Sparrow Hospital
P.O. Box 30480
1215 E. Michigan Avenue
Lansing, MI 48909
517/649-8317

Parents of Premature Infants of
  South East Michigan
Karen Angell
1680 Washington
Birmingham, MI 48009
313/258-6753

Perinatal Positive Parenting (PPP)
Judy Levick, MSW
Butterworth Hospital NICU
100 Michigan Street, NE
Grand Rapids, MI 49503
616/774-1675

**Minnesota**

NICU Pilot Parents
Addie Jesswein
201 Ordean Building
Duluth, MN 55802
218/726-4725

Parents for Parents
Sue Lamoureux, ACSW
Child and Family Services
Children's Hospital
345 North Smith Avenue
St. Paul, MN 55102
612/298-8720

Parents Share
Karen Osmundson
Medical Social Services
Mayo Clinic
Rochester, MN 55905
507/284-8137

Parent Support Group
Mary Bergs, MSW
Minneapolis Children's Medical
  Center
2525 Chicago Avenue South
Minneapolis, MN 55404
612/863-5878

**Missouri**

HOPE (Helping Other Parents
  Endure)
Violetta L. Niesen
3921 Regalway Drive
St. Louis, MO 63129
314/894-8636

**Montana**

NICU Parent Support Group
Sherry Zimmerman
2955 Custer Avenue
Billings, MT 59102
406/656-4137

**Nebraska**

Parent to Parent
Shari Lyons, RN
University of Nebraska Medical
  Center
42d and Dewey
Omaha, NE 68105
402/559-4441

**New Hampshire**

Caring and Coping for Preemies
Diana Perry
204 River Bank Road
Manchester, NH 03103
603/625-2214

Parents of Premies
Kathy Teeple, RN
Nashua Memorial Hospital Nursery
8 Prospect Street
Nashua, NH 03061
603/883-5521 ext. 2565

**New Jersey**

Intensive Caring Unlimited
Carol Randolph
740 Carter Hill Drive
W. Deptford, NJ 08066
609/848-1945

Microtots
Eileen and Josh Saks
17 Ellsworth Avenue
Morristown, NJ 07960
201/539-3427

**New Mexico**

Parents Reaching Out (PRO)
Debra Garcia
1127 University, NE
Albuquerque, NM 87102
505/842-9045
(In NM) 800/524-5176

**New York**

Intensive Care Nursery Parents'
  Group
Cynthia Dubois or Sharon Wall,
  Family Service Coordinators
Children's Hospital
219 Bryant Street
Buffalo, NY 14222
716/878-7410

Parents For Parents, Inc.
(serving the New York Metropolitan
  Area and Westchester County)
Christina Fox
P.O. Box 121
Yorktown Heights, NY 10598
914/962-3326

Parents Helping Parents
Mary Kilpatrick or Carol Marsella
% March of Dimes
5858 E. Molloy Road, Suite 115
Syracuse, NY 13211
315/455-2451

**North Carolina**

Family Support Network of North
  Carolina
Division of Community Pediatrics
Campus Box 7340, Trailer 31
University of North Carolina
Chapel Hill, NC 27599-7340

916/966-2841
(In NC) 800/TLC-0042

**Ohio**

Family First
Cindy Norwood
360 South 3d Street, Suite 101
Columbus, OH 43215
614/228-4333

Parents Available to Help (PATH)
Barbara Ensign
24161 Smith Avenue
Westlake, OH 44145
216/779-7880

Parent-to-Parent
Sue El Shafie, RN
The Toledo Hospital
2142 N. Cove Boulevard
Toledo, OH 43606
419/471-4227

PIN-Pals (Parents in Need) of Central
  Ohio, Inc.
Nancy Nelson
Department of Clinical Social Work
Children's Hospital
700 Children's Drive
Columbus, OH 43205
614/461-2630

**Oklahoma**

Parent to Parent
Carol Barnes
9726 Lakeview
Edmond, OK 73034
405/340-6397

**Oregon**

Parents Supporting Parents, Inc.
Linda Hawley, RN
Emanuel Hospital NICU
2801 N. Gantenbein
Portland, OR 97227
503/280-4511

**Pennsylvania**

Intensive Caring Unlimited, Inc.
910 Bent Lane
Philadelphia, PA 19118
Lenette Moses 215/233-4723 or Page
  Gould 215/667-7496

Parents Helping Parents of NICU
  Infants
Lisa de Angelis, MSW
Medical Social Work Department
Magee Women's Hospital
Forbes and Halket
Pittsburgh, PA 15213
412/647-4255

## South Dakota

Parents Supporting Parents
Gail Jamison, Social Worker
Sioux Valley Hospital
1100 S. Euclid Avenue
Sioux Falls, SD 57105
605/333-7205

## Tennessee

Graduate Parents
Lynn Jackson
University of Tennessee Newborn
   Center
853 Jefferson
Memphis, TN 38163
901/575-8424

Parents Reaching Out
4-C NICU
Vanderbilt University Medical Center
Nashville, TN 37232-2410
615/322-5000

Wee Care
Charlotte Ward-Larson, RN, MSN
Baptist Memorial Hospital, East
6019 Walnut Grove Road
Memphis, TN 38119
901/766-5023

## Texas

Our Special Children
Emma Ramirez-Bell
1922 Westview Terrace
Arlington, TX 76013
817/265-6009

Parent Care of Austin, Inc.
Brenda Vaughan
12808 Sherbourne Street
Austin, TX 78729
512/331-5512

Parent Care Support Group
Yvonne Acosta, RN, MSN or Sheryl
   Buchanan, RN
Providence Memorial Hospital
El Paso, TX 79902
915/542-6622

Parent Helpline
Ann C. Harper, RN, MS
Project Any Baby Can
519 West Houston Street
San Antonio, TX 78207
512/228-2222

Parents of Prematures of Houston,
   Inc.
Mary Moore
P.O. Box 440094
Houston, TX 77244-0094
713/524-3089

## Utah

Parent to Parent
Becky Hatfield
University of Utah Health Sciences
   Center
50 N. Medical Drive, Room 2187
Salt Lake City, UT 84132
801/581-7052

## Vermont

SPIRIT
Evelyn Sikorski, MSW
Medical Center of Vermont
Burlington, VT 05401
802/656-2370

## Virginia

NICU Grad Parents
Sandy Koval
11701 Wiesinger Lane
Midlothian, VA 23113
804/794-8222

Special Parents of Special Newborns
NICU Social Worker
University of Virginia Medical Center
Charlottesville, VA 22901
804/924-2335

Time Out for Parents
Tony Haymaker
2107 Deauville
Richmond, VA 23235
804/272-2797

## Washington

Parents of Prematures
P.O. Box 3046
Kirkland, WA 98083-3046
206/283-7466

## West Virginia

Parent to Parent
Peggy Morris
Easter Seal Rehabilitation Center
1305 National Road
Wheeling, WV 26003
304/242-1390

## Wisconsin

Parenting Premies
Teresa Wolding
P.O. Box 530
Stevens Point, WI 54481
715/824-2596

## Wyoming

Parents Helping Parents, Inc.
Candy Cook
924 Divide Street
Rock Springs, WY 82901
307/362-2390

## Books

Boukydis, C. F. Z. *Support for Parents and Infants: A Manual for Parenting Organizations and Professionals.* New York: Routledge and Kegan Paul, % Methuen, 1986. $30 from BLB.

Cansler, D.; Mastrianni, M. A. *Parent to Parent Support in North Carolina: A Manual for Program Development,* 1987. $5 plus postage from the Family Support Network of North Carolina (see p. 250).

*Directory of National Self-Help/Mutual Aid Resources.* (Key facts about more than 500 self-help organizations; list of clearinghouses and health-related toll-free hotlines.) $25 from the American Hospital Association, 800/242-2626, or, in Ill., 800/527-6850.

Duwa, S. *Leader's Guide for Developing a Parent to Parent Support Program* and *Parent to Parent Training Manual.* $25 plus postage from Parent to Parent of Florida (see p. 249).

*Guide for Organizing Parent Support Groups.* Free from the March of Dimes (see p. 248).

*Parent Resource Directory,* 3d Edition, 1989. (List of 425 parents of children with special needs in the U.S. and Canada interested in networking and improving the quality of care for children.) $6.50 from ACCH.

Pizzo, P. *Parent to Parent.* Boston: Beacon Press, 1983. (An empowering book on the rationale for parent-to-parent support. Out of print at present. Look for it in your library.)

# Appendix B

# Glossary

**ABO incompatibility:** see **blood group or type.**

**a.c.:** the abbreviation for the Latin words meaning "before meals."

**acidosis (acidemia):** an excess of acid in the blood and body tissues. See page 62.

**AGA (appropriate for gestational age):** a baby who weighs between the 10th and 90th percentiles for his gestational age at birth. See page 53.

**alternative birth center (ABC):** a hospital room with a homelike atmosphere where a woman can have a natural childbirth.

**alveoli:**
1. tiny sacs in the lungs where oxygen and carbon dioxide are exchanged with the bloodstream.
2. tiny sacs in the milk glands of the breast where cells extract nutrients from the mother's bloodstream and convert them to milk.

**amblyopia:** a loss of vision, centered in the brain, that develops over a period of years when the brain fails to receive proper signals from a weak eye. See page 214.

**amniocentesis:** a procedure for withdrawing amniotic fluid by inserting a needle through the mother's abdomen and into the womb. The fluid can be analyzed to detect certain abnormalities in the baby and to assess the maturity of the baby's lungs. See page 231.

**amniotic fluid:** the fluid surrounding the baby in the uterus.

**amnionitis:** an infection of the amniotic fluid.

**ampicillin:** an antibiotic.

**anemia:** an abnormally low number of red blood cells, the cells in the blood that carry oxygen to the tissues. See page 89 and page 189.

**anomaly:** a malformation of a part of the body.

**anoxia:** a lack of sufficient oxygen.

**antepartum:** before birth.

**antibiotics:** drugs that kill bacteria or interfere with their growth.

**antibodies:** proteins produced by the body to combat specific harmful substances like bacteria or viruses that have entered the bloodstream.

**aorta:** the artery leading from the heart that supplies the body with oxygenated blood.

**apnea:** lack of breathing for longer than 15 or 20 seconds. See page 74 and page 188.

**Apgar score:** a score ranging from 0 to 10 indicating a baby's physical condition immediately following birth. See page 57.

**areola:** the dark area on the breast surrounding the nipple.

**arterial blood gas (arterial stick):** a sampling of blood from an artery for its oxygen, carbon dioxide, and acid content.

**arterial catheter (indwelling arterial catheter):** a thin plastic tube placed in an artery to give nutrients, blood, and medications, and to withdraw blood for testing. Arterial catheters are most commonly placed in the umbilical artery (an umbilical artery catheter or UAC), but they may also be inserted into the radial artery on the arm (a radial artery catheter or RAC), or into the temporal artery on the scalp (a temporal artery catheter or TAC).

**artery:** any blood vessel that leads away from the heart. Arteries carry oxygenated blood to the body tissues (except for the pulmonary artery that carries non-oxygenated blood from the heart to the lungs).

**asphyxia:** lack of proper oxygen and blood flow. At birth, an Apgar score of 5 or lower indicates asphyxia.

**aspiration:**
1. breathing a foreign substance such as meconium, formula, or stomach contents into the lungs; may cause aspiration pneumonia.
2. withdrawal of material from the body by suctioning.

**Assessment of Pre-Term Infant Behavior (APIB):** a test given to prematures to assess their physical and behavioral strengths and vulnerabilities. See page 206.

**atelectasis:** a collapsed condition in a part of the lungs. See page 61.

**attending physician:** the physician in charge of the nursery at a given time.

**audiologist:** a trained professional who can assess hearing loss and determine the nature of the hearing loss. An audiologist is not a medical doctor.

**audiometric testing:** tests for hearing loss. See **Crib-O-Gram** and **brain stem evoked response audiometry.**

**Baby Bird:** a type of respirator used with infants.

**bacteria:** one-celled organisms that can cause disease. See page 91.

**bagging:** pumping air and/or oxygen into the baby's lungs by compressing a bag attached to a mask that covers the baby's nose and mouth.

**Bayley Scales:** tests given to infants and toddlers to assess their level of development. See page 206.

**beta-adrenergic drugs:** see **betamimetics.**

**betamethasone (Celestone):** a steroid drug given to a mother before a threatened pre-term birth to help the baby's lungs mature. See page 17 and page 60.

**betamimetics (also called beta-adrenergic drugs or betasympathomimetic drugs):** a category of drugs used to stop labor. See page 17 and page 229.

**betasympathomimetics:** see **betamimetics.**

**bicarbonate (bicarb), (sodium bicarbonate), (NaHCO₃):** a substance that may be given the baby orally or intravenously to help neutralize excess acid in the blood.

**b.i.d.:** the abbreviation for the Latin words meaning "twice a day."

**bililights (phototherapy):** bright lights used to treat jaundice. See page 87.

**bilirubin:** a yellowish substance produced when red blood cells break down. May cause jaundice, a yellowing of the skin, and, in large amounts, kernicterus, a form of brain damage. See page 86.

**bladder tap:** a way to withdraw urine from the bladder under sterile conditions by inserting a needle through the abdominal wall directly into the bladder.

**blood gas:** a test to determine the oxygen, carbon dioxide, and acid content of a sample of blood. See page 62.

**blood pressure:** the pressure the blood exerts against the walls of the blood vessels. It is this pressure that causes the blood to flow through the arteries and veins. The blood pressure measurement is given in the form of two numbers. The top number, the systolic pressure, is the measurement of the pressure exerted when the heart contracts and sends blood to the body. The lower number, the diastolic pressure, is the measurement of the pressure exerted during the relaxation between heartbeats.

**blood group or type:** a classification of blood according to the presence or absence of certain proteins. Each person belongs either to type O, A, B, or AB. Differences in blood type between mother and baby (ABO incompatibilities) can lead to anemia and jaundice in the baby.

Blood is also categorized as Rh positive or Rh negative by the presence or absence of the Rh factor. When an Rh negative mother carries an Rh positive child, antibodies in her blood may cross the placenta and attack her baby's red blood cells. The resulting condition, called erythroblastosis fetalis, is characterized by severe anemia and jaundice in the newborn. See page 89.

**bonding:** the process by which parents and baby become emotionally attached. See Chapter 3, page 28.

**BPD:** see **bronchopulmonary dysplasia.**

**bradycardia ("brady"):** a slower than normal heartbeat rate; in an infant, below 100 beats per minute. See page 74.

**brain bleed:** bleeding or hemorrhaging into some part of the brain. See page 96.

**brain death:** an absence of electrical impulses from the brain.

**brain stem evoked response audiometry:** a method of detecting hearing loss in infants in which the baby's brain wave responses to various sounds are measured.

**Braxton-Hicks contractions:** normal "practice" contractions of the uterus that occur at irregular intervals during pregnancy and do not lead to effacement or dilation of the cervix.

**Brazelton Neonatal Assessment Scale (BNAS):** tests of a newborn's reflexes, behavior, and responses to his environment. See page 206.

**breastmilk jaundice:** a very rare type of jaundice thought to be caused by a substance in the mother's milk. See page 86.

**breech delivery:** when a baby is born bottom or feet first.

**BRM:** the abbreviation for "breast-milk."

**bronchial tubes:** the tubes that lead from the trachea (windpipe) to the lungs.

**bronchioles:** smaller tubes that branch off from the bronchial tubes.

**bronchiolitis:** an inflammation or infection of the bronchioles.

**bronchitis:** an inflammation or intection of the bronchial tubes.

**bronchopulmonary dysplasia (BPD) or chronic lung disease (CLD):** damage to the lungs and bronchioles caused by the respirator. See page 66.

**BUN (blood urea and nitrogen):** a blood test for liver and kidney function.

**calcium (Ca):** a chemical necessary for the normal functioning of the nerves, the heart, and other muscles, and for the growth of bones and teeth.

**Candida albicans (monilia):** the fungus that causes thrush and other "yeast" infections. See page 91.

**capillaries:** tiny blood vessels that come into close contact with the body cells to supply the cells with oxygen and nutrients, and to remove waste products.

**carbon dioxide (CO₂):** a waste product of bodily processes that is carried by the blood to the lungs where it is exhaled.

**cardiology:** the branch of medicine dealing with the heart and circulation.

**cardiopulmonary resuscitation (CPR):** a method of reviving a person whose breathing and heartbeat have stopped or slowed abnormally. See pages 190–91.

**catheter:** a thin tube used to administer fluids to the body or to drain fluids from the body.

**CAT scanner or CT scanner (computerized axial tomography):** a computerized x-ray machine that can take pictures of cross sections of body tissues. Sometimes used to diagnose bleeding in the brain or hydrocephalus, an excess of fluid in the brain.

**CBC:** see **complete blood count.**

**Celestone:** see **betamethasone.**

**central line:** an intravenous line that is threaded through the vein until it reaches a position as close as possible to the heart. See page 79.

**central nervous system (CNS):** the brain and spinal cord.

**cerclage:** a procedure sometimes used to correct an incompetent cervix, which involves stitching the cervix closed during pregnancy. Types of cerclage include the Mac-Donald stitch and the Shirodkar. See page 17.

**cerebral palsy (CP):** brain damage that results in difficulty with coordinated movement. See page 207.

**cerebrospinal fluid (CSF):** fluid produced in the ventricles of the brain that circulates around the brain and spinal column.

**cervix:** the lower section of the uterus that shortens (effaces) and opens (dilates) during delivery.

**charge nurse:** the nurse in the unit who is in charge of nursing care for that shift.

**chest tube (ct):** a tube surgically inserted between a collapsed lung and the chest wall to suction away air and allow the lung to re-expand.

**chronic lung disease (CLD):** see **bronchopulmonary dysplasia.**

**CLD:** abbreviation for "chronic lung disease." See **bronchopulmonary dysplasia.**

**clinical nurse specialist:** a registered nurse who has received special training, usually through a master's degree program. The clinical nurse specialist may carry out special medical procedures, or may be involved with education of parents and staff.

**CMV:** see **cytomegalovirus.**

**CNS:** see **central nervous system.**

**colostomy:** a surgically created opening to allow the colon, the lower section of the large intestine, to empty directly through the abdominal wall.

**colostrum:** breastmilk produced in late pregnancy or in the days following delivery. The milk is yellowish in color and is especially rich in nutrients and antibodies.

**complete blood count (CBC):** tests to determine the number and types of cells in the blood. The CBC is part of the septic work-up, a

group of tests to check for infection. See page 92.

**conductive hearing loss:** a temporary or permanent hearing loss caused by problems with the middle ear. See page 209.

**cone biopsy:** a surgical procedure in which tissue from the cervix is removed to check it for malignancy. The procedure is associated with an increased risk for later preterm delivery.

**congestive heart failure (CHF):** the failure of the heart to perform efficiently because of a circulatory imbalance, as might occur in a baby with an open ductus. See page 70.

**corrected age:** the age a premature baby would be if he had been born on his due date. For example, a baby born 3 months early is, at the actual age of 7 months, only 4 months old according to his corrected age.

**CP:** see **cerebral palsy.**

**CPAP (continuous positive airway pressure):** pressurized air, sometimes with additional oxygen, that is delivered to the baby's lungs to keep them expanded as the baby inhales and exhales. See page 62.

**CPR:** see **cardiopulmonary resuscitation.**

**Crib-O-Gram:** a test to screen for hearing loss. See page 210.

**CSF:** see **cerebrospinal fluid.**

**cultures and sensitivities:** tests performed as part of the septic work-up in which samples of fluid or other material from the body are placed in special cultures that encourage the growth of any infectious organisms present. Organisms that grow are then tested for their sensitivity to various antibiotics.

**curare:** a drug sometimes given to an infant to keep him from breathing against the respirator. The drug causes a temporary paralysis of the baby's muscles.

**cyanosis:** a blue or "dusky" color of the skin caused by a lack of oxygen.

**cytomegalovirus (CMV):** a type of virus that may infect an unborn baby causing severe illness and

birth defects. The virus can also infect a baby after birth. See page 92.

**dc:** medical abbreviation for "discontinue," i.e. "stop."

**Decadron:** the trade name for dexamethasone.

**Denver Developmental Screening Test (DDST):** a screening test to help identify infants and children with developmental delays. See page 206.

**DES (diethylstilbestrol):** synthetic estrogen, formerly thought to prevent miscarriage. Daughters of women who were given DES during pregnancy are now vulnerable to certain types of cancer and to reproductive problems, including the tendency to deliver prematurely.

**dexamethasone:** a steroid drug that may be used to help reduce swelling in the brain following a brain injury.

**Dextrostix:**
1. a simple blood test to assess sugar levels.
2. the chemically treated plastric strip used in the test.

**DIC:** see **disseminated intravascular coagulation.**

**Dilantin (phenytoin):** a drug used to control seizures.

**disseminated intravascular coagulation:** a condition in which the platelets and clotting factors of the blood are consumed because of infection, hypoxia, acidosis, or other diseases or injuries. Without sufficient platelets and clotting factors, there is a tendency to bleed excessively. Transfusions of platelets or exchange transfusions may be given to correct this condition. See page 90.

**diuretic:** a drug that increases the excretion of body fluids in the urine.

**Doppler:** a monitoring device attached to a special blood pressure cuff to give intermittent blood pressure measurements.

**Down's syndrome:** a chromosomal abnormality, sometimes referred to as mongolism, characterized by physical malformations and varying degrees of mental retardation.

**DPT (diphtheria, pertussis, tetanus):** used to refer to the immunizations against these diseases.

**Dubowitz assessment:** an assessment of a newborn's appearance, behavior, and activity to determine the baby's gestational age at birth.

**ductus arteriosus:** a blood vessel in the fetus that joins the aorta with the pulmonary artery in order to divert most blood away from the fetal lungs. This blood vessel must close after birth so that blood can flow properly to the lungs to receive oxygen. See page 70.

**dx:** the medical abbreviation for "diagnosis."

**dysmature:** refers to a baby whose weight gain stops in the weeks before birth as a result of poor placental functioning.

**dyspnea:** difficult breathing.

**echocardiogram (echo):** a picture of the heart produced by the echo of ultrasound waves directed through the chest. This is a painless, non-invasive procedure.

**edema:** fluid retention in the body tissues that causes puffiness or swelling.

**EEG (electroencephalogram):** a tracing of the electrical impulses of the brain.

**EKG (electrocardiogram):** a tracing of the heart's electrical activity.

**electrodes:** devices attached to adhesive pads that are placed on the baby's body to conduct the electrical impulses of his heartbeat and breathing motions to a monitoring machine.

**electrolytes:** chemicals that, when dissolved in water, can conduct an electrical current. The main electrolytes in the human body are sodium (Na) and Potassium (K). They play important roles in the proper functioning of the cells.

**endotracheal tube (ET tube):** a thin plastic tube inserted into the baby's trachea (windpipe) to allow delivery of air and/or oxygen to the lungs.

**epilepsy:** a disorder of the nervous system that results in periodic convulsions or seizures.

**episiotomy:** an incision made to widen the vaginal opening during childbirth.

**ER:** emergency room.

**erythroblastosis fetalis:** see **blood group or type.**

**erythrocyte:** a red blood cell.

**esophagus:** the tube extending from the mouth to the stomach that carries food to the stomach.

**estriol levels:** a series of tests to check the mother's blood or urine for the hormone estriol. The tests are done to assess fetal well-being over a period of time. See page 231.

**ET tube:** see **endotracheal tube.**

**exchange transfusion:** a type of blood transfusion in which the infant's blood is removed in small amounts and simultaneously replaced with the same amounts of donor blood, often to dilute harmful concentrations of bilirubin. See page 88.

**extubation:** the removal of the endotracheal tube.

**fellow:** a neonatology fellow is a physician who has finished his or her residency in pediatrics and is training to become a specialist in neonatology.

**fetal circulation:** the special pattern of blood flow in an unborn baby in which the blood flows to and from the placenta to receive oxygen and nutrients, and to discharge wastes. See page 56.

**fetus:** the developing unborn child from the end of the embryonic stage (the 12th week of pregnancy) until the date of delivery.

**fibroids:** benign (noncancerous) growths in the uterine wall. See page 18.

**fine motor skills:** skills involving the coordination of the small muscles such as those in the hand.

**fontanel:** the "soft spot" on the top of the baby's head between the unjoined sections of the skull.

**fraternal twins:** twins formed when two eggs are simultaneously released and fertilized.

**full-term (FT):** infant born between the 38th and 42nd weeks of gestation.

**gastrostomy:** a surgically created opening in the abdominal wall to provide nutrition directly to the stomach when the esophagus is blocked or injured, or to provide drainage after abdominal surgery.

**gavage feeding:** feedings given through a tube passed through the nose or mouth and into the stomach. See page 81.

**gentamicin:** a type of antibiotic.

**gestation:** the length of time between the first day of the mother's last menstrual period before conception and the delivery of the baby.

**gestational age:** a baby's age in weeks from the first day of the mother's last menstrual period before conception until the baby reaches term (40 weeks).

**glucose:** the type of sugar that circulates in the blood and is used by the body for energy.

**gram (GM, gm, G):** the basic unit of weight in the metric system. There are 28 grams in one ounce.

**Gram stain:** a technique in which certain types of dyes are used to stain bacteria so that they become easily visible under the microscope.

**HA (hyperalimentation):** see **total parenteral nutrition.**

**heel stick:** the procedure of pricking the baby's heel to obtain small amounts of capillary blood for testing.

**hematocrit (hct., "crit"):** the percentage of red blood cells in the blood.

**hematology:** the medical specialty dealing with blood disorders.

**hemoglobin (hgb., hb.):** a substance in red blood cells that contains iron and carries oxygen.

**hemolysis:** the rupture of red blood cells.

**hemolytic:** pertaining to hemolysis.

**hernia:**

1. inguinal, a lump under the skin in the groin caused by a portion of the intestine protruding through a weak place in the abdominal muscle wall. See page 189.
2. umbilical, a lump under the skin at the navel caused by a portion of the intestine protruding through a weak place in the abdominal wall. See page 189.

**herpes:** a virus that produces sores on the mouth or genitals. In infants, it can cause a severe body-wide infection often leading to death or neurological damage. See page 92.

**high-risk (at-risk):** refers to persons (e.g., high-risk newborns) or situations (e.g., high-risk pregnancies) needing special intervention to prevent illness, damage, or death, or to keep illness or damage from worsening.

**HMD:** see **hyaline membrane disease.**

**house officer (HO):** intern, nurse specialist, nurse practitioner, or resident. A house officer is usually the person on first call; in other words, he or she is the first person to be consulted on medical aspects of the baby's care.

**house staff:** another term used to refer to the house officers.

**hyaline membrane disease (HMD or RDS):** respiratory distress that affects premature babies. It is caused by a lack of surfactant, the substance that keeps the lungs' air sacs from collapsing. See page 58.

**hydramnios:** see **polyhydramnios** and **oligohydramnios.**

**hydrocephalus:** an abnormal accumulation of cerebrospinal fluid in the ventricles of the brain. See page 98.

**hyperactivity:** see **minimal brain dysfunction.**

**hyperalimentation:** see **total parenteral nutrition.**

**hyperbilirubinemia:** excess bilirubin in the blood, a condition common in newborns. See page 86.

**hypercalcemia:** an excessive amount of calcium in the blood.

**hypercapnia (hypercarbia):** an excess of carbon dioxide in the bloodstream.

**hyperglycemia:** abnormally high sugar levels in the blood.

**hyperkalemia:** excessive amounts of potassium in the blood.

**hypernatremia:** excessive amounts of sodium in the blood.

**hypertension:** high blood pressure.

**hyperthermia:** abnormally high body temperature.

**hyperventiliation:** abnormally rapid breathing.

**hypocalcemia:** abnormally low levels of calcium in the blood.

**hypoglycemia:** abnormally low blood sugar levels.

**hypokalemia:** too little potassium in the blood.

**hyponatremia:** too little sodium in the blood.

**hypotension:** abnormally low blood pressure.

**hypothermia:** abnormally low body temperature.

**hypovolemia:** an abnormally low volume of blood in the body.

**hypoxia:** a lack of sufficient oxygen.

**hysterosalpingogram:** a test in which dyes, visible on an x-ray, are injected into the womb and Fallopian tubes. X-rays are then taken to detect any structural abnormalities of the reproductive organs.

**IAC:** abbreviation for "indwelling arterial catheter." See **arterial catheter.**

**IAL:** abbreviation for "indwelling arterial line." See **arterial catheter.**

**I and O:** abbreviation for "input and outflow." It refers to the amount of fluids given by oral feedings or by IV, and the amount of fluid excreted in the urine or stools, as well as blood removed for testing, over a given period of time.

**iatrogenic:** an injury or disease caused by medical treatment. For example, bronchopulmonary dysplasia, a disease caused by the respirator, is an iatrogenic illness.

**ICH:** see **intracranial hemorrhage.**

**ICN:** abbreviation for "intensive care nursery." See **newborn intensive care.**

**identical twins:** twins that result from the accidental division of a single fertilized egg.

**IDM:** abbreviation for "infant of a diabetic mother."

**IL:** see **Intralipid.**

**ileostomy:** a surgically created opening to allow the ileus, the part of the intestine above the colon, to empty directly through the abdominal wall.

**IM:** see **intramuscular injection.**

**inborn:** a child born and treated in the same hospital, a baby who was not transported to receive intensive care. See **outborn.**

**incompetent cervix:** a cervix that opens in mid to late pregnancy, often causing a miscarriage or premature birth. See page 17.

**indomethacin:** an aspirin-like drug sometimes used to close the patent ductus arteriosus.

**infiltrate:**
1. the slipping of an intravenous needle out of the vein, allowing IV fluid to accumulate in surrounding tissues.
2. fluid or other foreign substances in the alveoli of the lungs, seen as fuzzy areas on a chest x-ray.

**informed consent:** permission that a patient or the guardian of a patient gives for a specific medical procedure after the risks, benefits, and alternatives have been fully explained by the physician. See page 101.

**infusion pump:** a pump attached to an intravenous line to deliver IV fluids to the baby in tiny, precisely measured amounts.

**intern:** a doctor just out of medical school who is in the process of completing his or her first year of specialty training.

**intracranial hemorrhage (ICH):** bleeding in or around the brain. See page 96.

**Intralipid (IL):** a white solution of fatty acids that may be given to an infant intravenously along with hyperalimentation.

**intramuscular injection (IM):** an injection into the muscle; in a premature baby, injections are usually given into the thigh muscle.

**intravenous (IV):** a tube or a needle placed into a vein to allow the infusion of fluids into the blood stream.

**intraventricular hemorrhage (IVH):** bleeding within the ventricles of the brain. See page 96.

**intubation:** the insertion of a tube into the trachea (windpipe) to allow air to reach the lungs.

**in utero:** within the womb.

**IRDS (ideopathic respiratory distress syndrome):** a type of respiratory distress in newborns. The term is sometimes used synonymously with RDS.

**Isolette:** a brand of incubator, an enclosed, heated bed.

**IUGR (intrauterine growth retardation):** refers to a baby who is smaller than normal for his gestational age at birth. See **dysmaturity** and **small for gestational age.**

**IVC:** indwelling venous catheter. See **umbilical catheter.**

**IVH:** see **intraventricular hemorrhage.**

**IVL:** indwelling venous line. See **umbilical catheter.**

**jaundice:** the yellowing of the skin and the whites of the eyes caused by excessive bilirubin.

**jugular veins:** large veins on either side of the neck that return blood to the heart from the head and neck.

**K:** chemical symbol for potassium. See **electrolytes.**

**kanamycin:** a type of antibiotic.

**kernicterus:** damage to nervous system caused by very high levels of bilirubin in the blood.

**kilogram (kg):** unit of weight of the metric system that equals 1000 grams or 2.2 pounds.

**labor:** process by which the cervix shortens (effaces) and opens (dilates) to allow the baby to pass from the uterus through the vagina into the outside world.

**lactation:** production of milk by the breasts.

**lactose:** sugar found in milk.

**lanugo:** fine, downy hair that covers the body of the fetus.

**large for gestational age (LGA):** newborn infant who is above the 90th percentile in weight at birth for his gestational age. See page 53.

**large motor skills:** skills such as crawling and walking that involve the coordination of large muscle groups.

**laryngoscope:** tool with a long, lighted, hollow metal tube and handle. Used in intubation to see the vocal cords and guide the tube between them.

**Lasix:** type of diuretic.

**LBW:** see **low-birthweight infant.**

**lead wires:** wires that lead from the electrodes to a monitor.

**lecithin:** one of the components of surfactant.

**let-down reflex:** flow of milk into the nipple characterized by a tingling sensation. See page 158.

**leukocyte (white blood cell):** a type of blood cell that protects the body against harmful substances such as bacteria and viruses.

**LGA:** see **large for gestational age.**

**LPN:** licensed practical nurse.

**LVN:** licensed vocational nurse

**low birthweight infant (LBW):** baby who weighs less than 5½ pounds at birth; can be premature or full-term.

**lower respiratory tract infection (LRI):** an infection affecting the larynx (voice box), trachea (windpipe), bronchial tubes, the bronchioles, or the lungs. See page 187.

**LP:** see **lumbar puncture.**

**LRI:** see **lower respiratory tract infection.**

**L/S ratio:** the ratio between lecithin and sphingomyelin (components of surfactant) in the amniotic fluid. The ratio indicates the maturity of the unborn baby's lungs. See page 231.

**lumbar puncture (LP, spinal tap):** a procedure involving the insertion of a hollow needle in between the vertebrae of the lower back to withdraw spinal fluid. See page 92 and 97.

**magnesium sulfate:** a drug used in the treatment of toxemia and in stopping pre-term labor. See page 229.

**mastitis:** an inflammation of the mammary gland or breast. See page 165.

**MBD:** see **minimal brain dysfunction.**

**meconium (mec.):** greenish-black material present in the fetal intestinal tract before birth and usually passed during the first days after birth. Sometimes meconium is excreted in utero, especially if the baby is in distress before birth.

**meconium aspiration:** the inhaling by the baby of meconium-stained amniotic fluid. Serious respiratory problems may result.

**meconium staining:** refers to amniotic fluid stained with meconium. In some instances, meconium stained fluid indicates the fetus was in distress before birth.

**meningitis:** inflammation or infection of the meninges, the membranes surrounding the brain and spinal cord. See page 93.

**meningocele:** a birth defect in which there is a protrusion of the meninges (the tissue lining the brain and spinal cord) through an

opening in the skull or spinal column.

**mental retardation (MR):** limited intellectual development. See page 208.

**metabolism:** all the life-sustaining processes carried out by the cells in the body.

**minimal brain dysfunction (MBD):** syndrome in which children experience behavioral problems and/or learning disabilities due to abnormalities in the central nervous system. See page 202.

**monilia:** see **Candida albicans.**

**monitor:** a machine that records signs such as heartbeat, blood pressure, and respiration. See page 75.

**mucus:** a sticky secretion produced by mucous membranes.

**murmur:** sound made by blood flow through the heart or blood vessels; may be normal or abnormal. An abnormal murmur can often be heard when the ductus arteriosus has not closed.

**myopia:** nearsightedness.

**Na:** chemical symbol for sodium.

**narcotic:** a type of drug that relieves pain and produces sleep.

**nasal CPAP:** continuous positive airway pressure administered to an infant through nasal prongs.

**NBIC:** the abbreviation for newborn intensive care.

**NBICU:** the abbreviation for newborn intensive care unit.

**nebulizer:** a device that humidifies oxygen and/or air delivered to the baby.

**NEC:** see **necrotizing enterocolitis.**

**necrotizing enterocolitis (NEC):** a gangrene-like condition of the intestinal tract that can afflict premature babies. See page 82.

**neonatal period:** the first 30 days of life.

**neonatal nurse practitioner:** a registered nurse who has received additional training, usually through a master's degree program, and who is qualified by this training to provide certain aspects of the baby's medical care under the supervision of a physician.

**neonate:** a baby during the first month of life.

**neonatologist:** a pediatrician who specializes in the care of neonates.

**neurologist:** a physician who specializes in disorders of the brain and nervous system.

**newborn intensive care unit (NICU, NBICU, NBIC, ICN):** section of a hospital with trained staff and special equipment to care for critically ill newborns.

**NG tube (naso-gastric tube):** a small, flexible tube inserted through the nose or mouth, down the esophagus, and into the stomach. Used to gavage-feed an infant.

**NICU:** newborn intensive care unit.

**"nippling":** sucking on a bottle filled with formula or breastmilk.

**non-stress test:** a test in which the unborn baby's heartbeat is monitored to detect abnormal patterns indicating fetal distress. See page 231.

**NPO:** the abbreviation for the Latin words meaning "nothing by mouth."

**OB:** the abbreviation for "obstetrician."

**occupational therapist (OT):** a therapist who treats problems involving fine motor skills.

**oligohydramnios:** too little amniotic fluid. See page 19.

**omphalocele:** a congenital defect that allows the intestines to protrude through an opening in the abdominal wall.

**"on call":** physician or nurse specialist who can be summoned at a particular time to make and carry out medical decisions in the nursery.

**ophthalmologist:** a physician specializing in disorders of the eye.

**optician:** a person who makes corrective lenses. An optician is not a medical doctor.

**OR:** operating room.

**orthopedist:** a medical doctor who specializes in disorders of the bones and connective tissues.

**osteopenia:** a condition like rickets, in which the bones lose minerals (demineralize), become weak, and break easily. This condition is sometimes seen in prematures who receive hyperalimentation for long periods. See page 81.

**OT:** occupational therapist.

**otitis media:** a bacterial or viral infection of the middle ear. See page 187.

**otolaryngologist:** a physician who specializes in disorders of the ear, nose, and throat.

**otologist:** a physician who specializes in disorders of the ear.

**outborn:** a baby who is transported after birth to a tertiary care center for treatment.

**oxygen (O₂):** the gas that makes up 21% of the atmosphere. It is essential in sustaining life. The amount of oxygen delivered to an infant can be controlled from 21% to 100%.

**oxytocin (Pitocin):** a hormone that stimulates uterine contractions and the "let-down response" in lactating mothers.

**Pavulon (pancuronium):** a drug that produces temporary paralysis. It may be used to keep a baby from fighting the respirator.

**patent ductus arteriosus (PDA):** an abnormal condition, common in prematures, in which the ductus—the fetal blood vessel connecting the aorta and the pulmonary artery—fails to close after birth. See page 70.

**p.c.:** the abbreviation for the Latin words meaning "after a meal."

**PCO₂ (PaCO₂):** the partial pressure of arterial carbon dioxide; a measure of the carbon dioxide content of the blood.

**PDA:** see **patent ductus arteriosus.**

**perinatal:** describing the period from 28 weeks gestation to one week following delivery.

**perinatologist:** a doctor who specializes in fetal and neonatal care.

**periodic breathing:** breathing interrupted by pauses as long as 10 to 20 seconds. Periodic breathing is common in prematures and in full-term newborns. See page 74 and page 188.

**persistent fetal circulation (PFC):** the persistence, after birth, of a pattern of circulation typical of the fetus in which blood bypasses the lungs through an open ductus arteriosus. See page 70.

**petechiae:** a pin-point rash caused by tiny hemorrhages from the blood vessels close to the surface of the skin. Petechiae usually indicate clotting problems resulting from infection or injury.

**pH:** the symbol for hydrogen ion concentration. It expresses the degree to which a solution is acid or alkaline. The lower the pH, the more acid the solution. See page 62.

**phenobarbital:** a drug used to control seizures.

**phototherapy:** treatment of infants with hyperbilirubinemia by exposing them to bright lights called bililights. See page 87.

**physical therapist (PT):** a therapist who treats problems of coordination and of the large motor skills.

**placenta abruptio:** premature separation of the placenta from the wall of the uterus, usually accompanied by bleeding. See page 19.

**placenta previa:** a condition in which the placenta is abnormally positioned over the cervix; can result in bleeding during middle or late pregnancy. Cesarean delivery of the baby is often necessary. See page 19.

**plasma:** clear, fluid portion of blood (after the red blood cells have been removed).

**platelets:** elements of the blood needed for proper clotting; also called thrombocytes.

**pneumogram (sleep study):** a monitoring of the baby's breathing during sleep to detect any abnormal breathing patterns.

**pneumonia:** an inflammation or infection of the lungs. See page 93.

**pneumothorax:** a collection of air in the chest resulting from a rupture in the lung. See page 67.

**PO₂ (PaO₂):** partial pressure of arterial oxygen; a measure of the oxygen content of the blood.

**polycythemia:** abnormally high number of red blood cells, a condition that causes "sluggish" circulation. See page 89.

**polyhydramnios:** excessive amount of amniotic fluid. See page 19.

**positive end expiratory pressure (PEEP):** on a respirator, the constant amount of pressure exerted on the infant's lungs to keep them expanded during and after breaths.

**postpartum:** after delivery.

**postural drainage (PD):** A method of tilting the baby in various positions to allow mucus to drain easily from his lungs. See page 66.

**pre-eclampsia (toxemia):** a complication of pregnancy in which the mother has protein in the urine, high blood pressure, rapid weight gain, and swelling from fluid retention. The disease can worsen into eclampsia, a life-threatening condition for mother and baby. See page 20.

**premature infant (pre-term infant):** a baby born before the 37th completed week of pregnancy.

**premature rupture of the membranes (PROM):** the breaking of the membranes surrounding the fetus before the beginning of labor; may occur before a term or a pre-term delivery. See page 18.

**prenatal:** before birth.

**progesterone:** a hormone of pregnancy thought to protect the developing fetus.

**projectile vomiting:** extremely forceful ejection of the stomach contents. See page 192.

**prostaglandins:** substances found in body tissues that can cause contractions of the smooth muscles and the widening of certain blood vessels. Prostaglandins are thought to be involved in the process of labor.

**Pseudomonas:** a type of bacteria.

**PT:** see **physical therapist.**

**pulmonary hypertension:** an inability of the blood vessels of the lungs to relax and open up normally after birth. Poor circulation through the lungs and poor oxygenation of the blood result. Respirator therapy and drugs to relax the lungs' constricted vessels may be used to help treat this condition.

**pulmonary insufficiency of the premature (PIP):** a type of respiratory distress afflicting the youngest prematures. It is caused as much by an immaturity of the lung tissue as by a lack of surfactant. The treatment is the same as for RDS. See page 58.

**pulmonary interstitial emphysema (PIE):** a condition, associated with high respirator pressures, in which bubbles of air are forced out of the alveoli and in between the layers of lung tissue. See page 67.

**q.:** medical abbreviation for "every."

**q.d.:** medical abbreviation for "every day."

**q.h.:** medical abbreviation for "every hour."

**q.i.d.:** medical abbreviation for "four times a day."

**q.o.d.:** medical abbreviation for "every other day."

**q.s.:** medical abbreviation for "a sufficient amount."

**q.wk.:** medical abbreviation for "every week."

**rales:** abnormal crackling noises in the chest made by air passing through congested bronchial tubes.

**RBC:** red blood cell.

**RDS:** see **hyaline membrane disease.**

**red blood cell (RBC, erythrocyte):** the type of blood cell that carries oxygen and carbon dioxide to and from body tissues.

**regionalization:** a system for providing appropriate care to all mothers and infants within a specific geographical region. Perinatal care may be provided at primary, secondary, or tertiary centers depending on the risk status of mother and baby. The low-risk pregnancy can be managed at a primary center—a regular hospital delivery room and nursery, where basic emergency equipment and trained personnel are available if needed. A secondary center has trained staff and special equipment to care for a pregnant woman or for an infant with moderate problems. A tertiary, or third level, center has all the staff and technology needed to manage serious medical problems of the mother or infant. Intensive care nurseries are found in tertiary centers.

**resident:** a doctor in his or her second or third year of specialty training.

**residuals:** the amount of undigested food left in the stomach after a reasonable length of time has elapsed for digestion.

**respirator:** a mechanical device used to substitute for, or to assist with, breathing. See page 62.

**respiratory distress syndrome (RDS):** see **hyaline membrane disease.**

**retina:** the lining of the back of the eye that receives visual images.

**retinopathy of prematurity (ROP):** see **retrolental fibroplasia.**

**retraction:** an abnormal sucking in of the chest during breathing, indicating that great efforts are being made to breathe. See page 61.

**retrolental fibroplasia (RLF), retinopathy of prematurity (ROP):** an eye disease of prematures. See page 68 and page 214.

**Rh factor:** a type of protein that may or may not be present in a person's red blood cells. See **blood group or type.** Also see page 89.

**RhoGAM shots:** injections given a mother with Rh negative blood after the birth of an Rh positive baby. These injections prevent the mother from developing antibodies that could harm a future Rh positive baby.

**ritodrine (Yutopar):** one of the betamimetic drugs used to stop preterm labor.

**RLF:** see **retrolental fibroplasia.**

**room air (RA):** the air we normally breathe that contains 21% oxygen.

**rubella:** a virus that causes German measles and severe intrauterine infections. See page 92.

**Rx:** the medical abbreviation for "prescription."

**scalp IV:** an intravenous needle placed in a vein in the infant's scalp.

**secondary center:** see **regionalization.**

**seizure:** a "short-circuiting" of the brain's electrical impulses. Seizures have a variety of causes and symptoms. See page 96 and page 189.

**sensorineural hearing loss:** a hearing impairment resulting from damage to the structures of the inner ear or to the nerves that conduct sound impulses to the brain. See page 209.

**septic work-up:** a series of tests to check for the presence of infection. See page 91.

**serous otitis:** fluid accumulation in the middle ear. See page 187.

**serum:** the clear portion of the blood that remains after the red blood cells and clotting factors have been removed.

**SGA:** see **small for gestational age.**

**SGOT:** a test for abnormal levels of the enzyme serum glutamicoxaloacetic transaminase. Abnormal levels of this enzyme may be present if organ damage has occurred.

**SGPT:** a test for abnormal levels of the enzyme serum glutamic pyruvic transaminase. Abnormal levels of this enzyme may be present if organ damage has occurred.

**shunt:**

1. an artificially created passage between two areas of the body, as in a ventriculo-peritoneal shunt for hydrocephalus, a tube that drains fluid from the ventricles of the brain into the peritoneum (the abdominal cavity.) See page 100.
2. a naturally existing, but abnormal, connection between two areas of the body, as in a right-to-left or left-to-right shunt through the ductus arteriosus.

**SIDS (sudden infant death syndrome):** crib death, the death of an infant during sleep from unknown causes.

**sleep study:** see **pneumogram.**

**small for gestational age (SGA):** newborn whose weight is abnormally low for his gestational age. See page 53.

**sonogram:** a picture produced by ultrasound.

**speech and language pathologist:** a specialist in the treatment of speech problems.

**sphingomyelin:** a component of surfactant.

**spinal tap:** see **lumbar puncture.**

**strabismus:** a misalignment of the eye muscles that may cause the eyes to turn inward (crossed eyes or esotropia) or turn outward (wall eye or exotropia). See page 213.

**stress test:** a test to monitor fetal heart rate changes in response to induced contractions. Abnormal heart rate patterns may indicate fetal distress. See page 231.

**subarachnoid hemorrhage:** bleeding in the subarachnoid space, the area around the outside of the brain. See page 96.

**sudden infant death syndrome:** see **SIDS.**

**surfactant:** a substance formed in the lungs that helps keep the small air sacs, or alveoli, from collapsing and sticking together.

**tachycardia:** an abnormally fast heart rate. In an infant, above 160 beats per minute. See page 76.

**tachypnea:** an abnormally fast breathing rate. In an infant, above 60 breaths per minute. See page 76.

**terbutaline (Brethine):** one of the betamimetic drugs used to stop preterm labor.

**term infant:** an infant born between the 38th and 42nd weeks of gestation.

**tertiary center:** see **regionalization.**

**theophylline:** a stimulant drug sometimes used in the treatment of apnea.

**thermoregulation:** regulation of body temperature.

**thrombocytes:** see **platelets.**

**thrombocytopenia:** abnormal decrease in the number of blood platelets. See page 90.

**thrush:** a fungus infection of the mouth characterized by white patches on a red inflamed surface. See page 165.

**t.i.d.:** the medical abbreviation for the Latin words meaning "three times a day."

**tocolytic drugs:** drugs used to stop labor. See page 229.

**TORCH study:** tests for the viral infections toxoplasmosis, rubella, cytomegalovirus, and herpes. See page 92.

**total parenteral nutrition (TPN, hyperalimentation):** intravenous administration of solution that provides infant with necessary nutrients—protein, sugar, minerals, vitamins. See page 80.

**toxemia of pregnancy:** see **preeclampsia.**

**toxoplasmosis:** an organism that causes intrauterine infection. See page 92.

**TPR:** medical abbreviation for temperature, pulse, respiration.

**trachea:** windpipe; the tube that extends from the throat to the bronchial tubes.

**tracheostomy:** a surgical opening in the trachea, below the larynx (voice box), made to allow air to enter the lungs when the throat becomes obstructed.

**transcutaneous monitor (TCM):** monitoring device placed on the infant's skin that records blood oxygen levels. See page 62.

**trimester:** a period of three months. A 9-month pregnancy is divided into first, second, and third trimesters.

**UAC:** see **umbilical artery catheter.**

**UAL:** umbilical artery line. See **umbilical artery catheter.**

**ultrasound:** a technique in which echoes of high frequency sound waves produce a picture of body tissues.

**umbilical catheter (umbilical artery catheter—UAC; umbilical artery line—UAL; indwelling arterial catheter—IAC; indwelling arterial line—IAL; umbilical venous catheter—UVC; umbilical venous line—UVL; indwelling venous catheter—IVC; indwelling venous line—IVL):** a small, flexible plastic tube inserted through a blood vessel in the infant's navel. If the catheter or line is in an umbilical artery, it can be used to obtain blood samples, provide nutrition, administer blood and medication, and monitor blood pressure. A venous catheter, a tube placed in the umbilical vein, is used to give fluids and nutrients and to monitor blood pressure. See page 79.

**upper respiratory infections (URI):** a cold; an infection affecting any portion of the respiratory tract above the larynx (voice box). See page 186.

**URI:** see **upper respiratory infection.**

**UTI:** abbreviation for urinary tract infection; usually refers to infections of the bladder.

**UVC:** umbilical venous catheter, see **umbilical catheter.**

**UVL:** umbilical venous line, see **umbilical catheter.**

**Vasodilan (isoxsuprine):** one of the betamimetic drugs used to stop pre-term labor.

**vein:** a blood vessel leading to the heart. Veins carry non-oxygenated blood from the body to the heart (except for the pulmonary veins that carry oxygenated blood from the lungs to the heart.)

**ventricle:**
1. a small chamber, as in the ventricles of the heart.
2. small chambers in the center of the brain where cerebrospinal fluid is made.

**vernix:** white, fatty substance that protects the fetus' skin in utero.

**virus:** a tiny infectious organism that lives inside body cells. See page 91.

**vision therapist:** a therapist who helps visually impaired people make full use of their remaining sight.

**vital signs:** temperature, pulse rate, and rate of respirations.

**WBC:** abbreviation for white blood cell. See **leukocyte.**

**wheeze:** whistling, humming, or raspy sound made during breathing, caused by obstructions in the respiratory tract.

**white blood cell (WBC):** See **leukocyte.**

**yeast (Candida albicans, monilia, thrush):** a microscopic fungus that can cause infection; yeast infections are common after antibiotic therapy.

# Appendix C

# Glossary of Trade Names

The following list of trade names includes registered trademarks, trademarks, certification marks, and nonregistered brand names of products or product lines mentioned in *The Premature Baby Book*.

**Anne's Preemie Wear:** Anne Long, Greenville, South Carolina

**Alexis:** The Warren Featherbone Company, Gainesville, Georgia

**AXicare Automatic Breast Pump; AXicare Breast Shell:** Neonatal Division, D.J. Colgate Medical, Ltd., Pearl River, New York

**Baby Bird:** Bird Corporation, Palm Springs, California

**Bobby-Mac:** Bobby-Mac Company, Inc., Scarsdale, New York

**Brethine:** Geigy Pharmaceuticals Division of CIBA-GEIGY Corporation, Ardsley, New York

**Carter's:** The William Carter Company, Needham Heights, Massachusetts

**Celestone:** Schering Corporation, Kenilworth, New Jersey

**Century Infant Love Seat:** Century Products, Inc., Stow, Ohio

**Cheerios:** General Mills, Inc., Minneapolis, Minnesota

**Crib-O-Gram:** Telesensory Systems, Inc., Palo Alto, California

**Decadron:** Merck Sharp & Dohme Division of Merck & Co., Inc., West Point, Pennsylvania

**Dexter B-29:** The Dexter Diaper Factory, Houston, Texas

**Dextrostix:** Ames Company, Division of Miles Laboratories, Inc., Elkhart, Indiana

**Dilantin:** Parke, Davis & Company, Detroit, Michigan

**Early Arrivals:** Jenny Baarstad and Susan Edgar, Ventura, California

**Egnell Electric Breast Pump:** Egnell, Inc., Cary, Illinois

**Evenflow Natural Mother Breast Pump:** Evenflow Products Co., Ravenna, Ohio, A Division of Questor, Los Angeles, California

**Fiberfill:** E. I. duPont de Nemours and Company Incorporated, Wilmington, Delaware

**Gerry Cuddle Park:** Gerico, Inc., Boulder, Colorado

**GOMCO Electric Breast Pump:** GOMCO Division, Allied Healthcare Products, Inc., Buffalo, New York

**Happy Family Breast Milking and Feeding Unit:** Happy Family Products, Los Angeles, California

**Honey Bunnies:** Lora Whitemarsh, Puyallup, Washington

**Intralipid:** Cutter Laboratories, Inc., Berkeley, California

**Isolette:** Narco Air-Shields, A Division of Narco Scientific, Hatboro, Pennsylvania

**Isomil:** Ross Laboratories, Columbus, Ohio, A Division of Abbott Laboratories, North Chicago, Illinois

**Ivory Snow:** Procter & Gamble, Cincinnati, Ohio

**Karo Syrup:** Best Foods, A Division of CPC International Inc., Englewood Cliffs, New Jersey

**Lact-Aid Nursing Trainer:** The Lact-Aid Division of J. J. Avery, Inc., Denver, Colorado

**Lasix:** Hoechst-Roussel Pharmaceuticals, Inc., Somerville, New Jersey

**Le Pump:** Labtron Products, Scientific Corporation, Farmingdale, New York

**Lilletot:** Judy Mickelsen, Wheaton, Illinois

**Little Me by Lois:** S. Schwab Co., Cumberland, Maryland

**Loyd-B:** Lopuco, Ltd., Woodbine, Maryland

**Maltsupex:** Wallace Laboratories, Cranbury, New Jersey

**"Marshall" Kaneson Breast Pump Infant Nurser:** Marshall Electronics, Skokie, Illinois

**MCT Oil:** Mead Johnson Laboratories, Evansville, Indiana

**Medela Breastpump:** Medela, Inc., Crystal Lake, Illinois

**Mycostatin:** E. R. Squibb and Sons, Princeton, New Jersey

**Netsy Milk Cup:** The Netsy Company, Mill Valley, California

**Neutrogena:** Neutrogena Corp., Los Angeles, California

**Oh, So Small:** JoAnne Bock, Tacoma, Washington

**Ora'Lac Pump:** Ora'Lac Pump, Inc., Sitka, Alaska

**Pampers:** Procter & Gamble, Cincinnati, Ohio

**Paty Preemie Garments:** Paty, Inc., Houston, Texas

**Pavulon:** Organon, Inc., West Orange, New Jersey

**Pedialyte:** Ross Laboratories, Columbus, Ohio, A Division of Abbott Laboratories, North Chicago, Illinois

**Petit Bateau:** Petit Bateau, U.S.A., Inc., New Town, Pennsylvania

**Pitocin:** Parke, Davis & Company, Detroit, Michigan

**Polycose:** Ross Laboratories, Columbus, Ohio, A Division of Abbott Laboratories, North Chicago, Illinois

**Premie Pals:** Nancy Nelson, Renton, Washington

**RhoGAM:** Ortho Disgnostics, Inc., Raritan, New Jersey

**Similac; Similac PM 60/40:** Ross Laboratories, Columbus, Ohio, A Division of Abbott Laboratories, North Chicago, Illinois

**SMA 24:** Wyeth Laboratories, A Division of American Home Products Corp., Philadelphia, Pennsylvania

**Snugli:** Snugli Cottage Industries, Inc., Evergreen, Colorado

**Special Patterns by Patricia:** Patricia Silvers, Lopez Island, Washington

**Stockinette:** Tomac, American Hospital Supply Corporation, Evanston, Illinois

**Tiny Mite Premie Fashions:** Tiny Mite Industries, Incorporated, Glendale, California

**Toddle Tyke Premé Collection:** Toddle Tyke Company, Inc., Atlanta, Georgia

**Tylenol:** McNeil Laboratories, Inc., Fort Washington, Pennsylvania

**Vasodilan:** Mead Johnson Pharmaceutical Division, Mead Johnson and Company, Evansville, Indiana

**Velcro:** Velcro U.S.A., Inc., New York, New York

**Yutopar:** Merrill Dow Pharmaceuticals, Inc., A Subsidiary of The Dow Chemical Company, Cincinnati, Ohio

**Zona Lee, Inc.:** Zona Lee, Inc., San Francisco, California

# Appendix D
# Conversion Tables

## Conversion of Pounds and Ounces to Grams

*Ounces*

| Pounds | 0 | 1 | 2 | 3 | 4 | 5 | 6 | 7 | 8 | 9 | 10 | 11 | 12 | 13 | 14 | 15 |
|---|---|---|---|---|---|---|---|---|---|---|---|---|---|---|---|---|
| 0 | — | 28 | 57 | 85 | 113 | 142 | 170 | 198 | 227 | 255 | 283 | 312 | 340 | 369 | 397 | 425 |
| 1 | 454 | 482 | 510 | 539 | 567 | 595 | 624 | 652 | 680 | 709 | 737 | 765 | 794 | 822 | 850 | 879 |
| 2 | 907 | 936 | 964 | 992 | 1021 | 1049 | 1077 | 1106 | 1134 | 1162 | 1191 | 1219 | 1247 | 1276 | 1304 | 1332 |
| 3 | 1361 | 1389 | 1417 | 1446 | 1474 | 1503 | 1531 | 1559 | 1588 | 1616 | 1644 | 1673 | 1701 | 1729 | 1758 | 1786 |
| 4 | 1814 | 1843 | 1871 | 1899 | 1928 | 1956 | 1984 | 2013 | 2041 | 2070 | 2098 | 2126 | 2155 | 2183 | 2211 | 2240 |
| 5 | 2268 | 2296 | 2325 | 2353 | 2381 | 2410 | 2438 | 2466 | 2495 | 2523 | 2551 | 2580 | 2608 | 2637 | 2665 | 2693 |
| 6 | 2722 | 2750 | 2778 | 2807 | 2835 | 2863 | 2892 | 2920 | 2948 | 2977 | 3005 | 3033 | 3062 | 3090 | 3118 | 3147 |
| 7 | 3175 | 3203 | 3232 | 3260 | 3289 | 3317 | 3345 | 3374 | 3402 | 3430 | 3459 | 3487 | 3515 | 3544 | 3572 | 3600 |
| 8 | 3629 | 3657 | 3685 | 3714 | 3742 | 3770 | 3799 | 3827 | 3856 | 3884 | 3912 | 3941 | 3969 | 3997 | 4026 | 4054 |
| 9 | 4082 | 4111 | 4139 | 4167 | 4196 | 4224 | 4252 | 4281 | 4309 | 4337 | 4366 | 4394 | 4423 | 4451 | 4479 | 4508 |
| 10 | 4536 | 4564 | 4593 | 4621 | 4649 | 4678 | 4706 | 4734 | 4763 | 4791 | 4819 | 4848 | 4876 | 4904 | 4933 | 4961 |
| 11 | 4990 | 5018 | 5046 | 5075 | 5103 | 5131 | 5160 | 5188 | 5216 | 5245 | 5273 | 5301 | 5330 | 5358 | 5386 | 5415 |
| 12 | 5443 | 5471 | 5500 | 5528 | 5557 | 5585 | 5613 | 5642 | 5670 | 5698 | 5727 | 5755 | 5783 | 5812 | 5840 | 5868 |
| 13 | 5897 | 5925 | 5953 | 5982 | 6010 | 6038 | 6067 | 6095 | 6123 | 6152 | 6180 | 6209 | 6237 | 6265 | 6294 | 6322 |
| 14 | 6350 | 6379 | 6407 | 6435 | 6464 | 6492 | 6520 | 6549 | 6577 | 6605 | 6634 | 6662 | 6690 | 6719 | 6747 | 6776 |
| 15 | 6804 | 6832 | 6860 | 6889 | 6917 | 6945 | 6973 | 7002 | 7030 | 7059 | 7087 | 7115 | 7144 | 7172 | 7201 | 7228 |
| 16 | 7257 | 7286 | 7313 | 7342 | 7371 | 7399 | 7427 | 7456 | 7484 | 7512 | 7541 | 7569 | 7597 | 7626 | 7654 | 7682 |
| 17 | 7711 | 7739 | 7768 | 7796 | 7824 | 7853 | 7881 | 7909 | 7938 | 7966 | 7994 | 8023 | 8051 | 8079 | 8108 | 8136 |
| 18 | 8165 | 8192 | 8221 | 8249 | 8278 | 8306 | 8335 | 8363 | 8391 | 8420 | 8448 | 8476 | 8504 | 8533 | 8561 | 8590 |
| 19 | 8618 | 8646 | 8675 | 8703 | 8731 | 8760 | 8788 | 8816 | 8845 | 8873 | 8902 | 8930 | 8958 | 8987 | 9015 | 9043 |
| 20 | 9072 | 9100 | 9128 | 9157 | 9185 | 9213 | 9242 | 9270 | 9298 | 9327 | 9355 | 9383 | 9412 | 9440 | 9469 | 9497 |
| 21 | 9525 | 9554 | 9582 | 9610 | 9639 | 9667 | 9695 | 9724 | 9752 | 9780 | 9809 | 9837 | 9865 | 9894 | 9922 | 9950 |
| 22 | 9979 | 10007 | 10036 | 10064 | 10092 | 10120 | 10149 | 10177 | 10206 | 10234 | 10262 | 10291 | 10319 | 10347 | 10376 | 10404 |

## Conversion of Inches to Centimeters

| Inches | Centimeters | Inches | Centimeters | Inches | Centimeters |
|---|---|---|---|---|---|
| 10 | 25.4 | 17 | 43.2 | 24 | 61.0 |
| 10½ | 26.7 | 17½ | 44.4 | 24½ | 62.2 |
| 11 | 27.9 | 18 | 45.7 | 25 | 63.5 |
| 11½ | 29.2 | 18½ | 47.0 | 25½ | 64.8 |
| 12 | 30.5 | 19 | 48.3 | 26 | 66.1 |
| 12½ | 31.8 | 19½ | 49.5 | 26½ | 67.4 |
| 13 | 33.0 | 20 | 50.8 | 27 | 68.7 |
| 13½ | 34.3 | 20½ | 52.1 | 27½ | 69.9 |
| 14 | 35.6 | 21 | 53.3 | 28 | 71.2 |
| 14½ | 36.8 | 21½ | 54.6 | 28½ | 72.5 |
| 15 | 38.1 | 22 | 55.9 | 29 | 73.8 |
| 15½ | 39.4 | 22½ | 57.2 | 29½ | 75.1 |
| 16 | 40.6 | 23 | 58.4 | 30 | 76.4 |
| 16½ | 41.9 | 23½ | 59.7 | 30½ | 77.6 |

## Volume

1 cubic centimeter (cc) = 1 milliliter (ml) = 20 drops
5 cc = 5 ml = 1 tsp.
15 cc = 15 ml = 1 tbs. = ½ oz.
30 cc = 30 ml = 1 oz.

## Temperature

To convert degrees Fahrenheit to degrees Centigrade, subtract 32, multiply by 5, and divide by 9. To convert degrees Centigrade to degrees Fahrenheit, multiply by 9, divide by 5, and add 32.

|  | Centigrade (C.) | Fahrenheit (F.) |
|---|---|---|
| Freezing point of water | 0 | 32 |
| Boiling point of water | 100 | 212 |
| Thermometer readings | 36.0 | 96.8 |
|  | 36.5 | 97.7 |
|  | 37.0 | 98.6 |
|  | 37.5 | 99.5 |
|  | 38.0 | 100.4 |
|  | 38.5 | 101.3 |
|  | 39.0 | 102.2 |
|  | 39.5 | 103.1 |
|  | 40.0 | 104.0 |
|  | 40.5 | 104.9 |
|  | 41.0 | 105.8 |
|  | 41.5 | 106.7 |
|  | 42.0 | 107.6 |

# Index

ABO incompatability, 90
abortions:
 legal time limits for, 44
 life support decisions in, 103
 subsequent pregnancies affected by,
  21
Abrams, Barbara, 230
Abramson, David, 102
abruption, 19, 21, 25, 230
acidosis, 62, 89
"active" sleep, 49–50, 51
adrenalin, 229
*After a Loss in Pregnancy* (Berezin), 108n
AGA (appropriate for gestational age),
  53, 195
airplane travel, ear problems aggra-
  vated by, 187
alcohol, 232
 breast-feeding inhibited by, 159
 fetal growth retardation associated
  with, 53
 as labor-suppressant, 229
 prematurity not associated with, 24
allergies, 173–174
alveoli:
 in breasts, 156–157
 in lungs, 55, 59, 60, 61
amblyopia, 214
A.M.E.N.D. (Aiding a Mother Experiencing Neonatal Death), 113
American Indians:
 jaundice treated by, 87
 prematurity rate of, 23
amniocentesis, 18, 60, 124, 231
amniotic fluid, 18–19, 90
amphetamines, abuse of, 24
anemia, 89, 90, 92, 96, 189
 physiological, 89
 prevention of, 80, 89, 154
 sickle cell, 21, 23, 53
 in twins, 22
anger, as stage of grief, 6, 107, 113,
  129, 185
antibiotics, 91–92, 93, 100, 165, 183,
  186, 187
 side effects of, 80, 83, 91, 123, 210

antibodies, 87, 89–90, 91, 154, 181
antihistamines, 157
Apgar evaluation, 57, 210
apnea, 49, 50, 51, 62, 76, 77, 82, 90, 93,
  95, 96, 131, 135–136, 180, 188
 defined, 61
 drugs for, 76, 189
 in LBW babies, 74
apnea monitors, 27, 73–76, 184
asphyxia, 57, 95, 96, 208, 210
Assessment of Pre-Term Infant Behavior (APIB), 206
asthma, drugs for, 17
astigmatism, 212
ataxia, 207
atelectasis, 61
athetosis, 207
"At Home with a Monitor" (Barr), 184
*Atlantic Monthly*, 103
Auerbach, Kathleen, 171
autopsies, 110

babies:
 books about, 148
 full-term, 55-57
 premature, *see* premature babies
*Baby and Child Care* (Spock), 148
bacteria, 91, 92, 100, 165
bagging, 58, 76
barbiturates, abuse of, 24
bargaining, as stage of grief, 8, 107,
  217
Barr, Ann, 184
barrel chest, 67
Barry, Paulette, 118–119
baths, 134, 144, 148, 180, 182–183
Bayley Scales, 206
Benson, Herbert, 234
*Bereaved Parent, The* (Schiff), 107
Berezin, Nancy, 108n
Berry, Jan, 171
betamethasone, 16–17, 60, 124
betamimetics, 229
beta receptors, 229

bicornuate uterus, 17–18
bilirubin, 70, 83, 84, 86–89, 96, 207,
  208
biorhythms, 50
birth control pills, 22, 157
birth defects, *see* congenital defects
birthmarks, 193
birthweight:
 drug abuse and, 24
 in Holland, 54
 increase from, 39, 41, 52, 83, 154,
  171
 range of, 44, 53
 regaining of, 52, 83
 statistics on, 2n
 as survival factor, 44
 *see also* low-birthweight babies
Bishop, Joey, 203
blacks:
 multiple births of, 22, 23
 premature births of, 23, 44
bladder tap, 92
blame, 1, 6, 7, 16, 25, 113
blindness, 202, 214–215
 RDS treatment and, 68, 123
blood:
 acid imbalance in, 62, 76
 clotting factors in, 87, 89, 90, 152
 composition of, 87
 disorders of, 86–90
blood gas test, 62–65
blood types, 87, 90
blood urea and nitrogen (BUN) test,
  80
body temperature:
 measurement of, 144, 180, 186
 regulation of, 57, 76–77, 180
bonding and attachment, 12, 28–41,
  120
 in animals, 28
 breastmilk and, 33, 34, 39, 40, 41
 defined, 28
 fathers and, 34–35, 42, 71
 hormones and, 3
 nursing and, 33, 34, 41, 86
 obstacles to, 31–33

siblings and, 35–37
touch and, 28, 40, 41, 42
bottle-feeding, 166–168, 171–173, 180
  readiness for, 52, 81, 83–84, 166
bowel movements, 83, 88, 144, 192–193
bradycardia, 49, 50, 51, 66, 74–76, 77, 89, 90, 95, 96, 131, 135–136
brain, minimal dysfunction of, 202–203
brain damage, 102, 103, 208, 214
  in animals, 30
  causes of, 92, 93, 95–101, 189
  meningitis and, 93, 96
  recovery from, 30, 217n
  TORCH syndrome and, 92
brain death, 102
brain edema, 95, 96
Braxton-Hicks contractions, 16
Brazelton, T. Berry, 24, 29, 52
Brazelton Neonatal Assessment Scale (BNAS), 206
breast-feeding, 21, 120, 153–154, 176–178, 228
  bonding and, 33, 34, 41, 86
  first-stage, 151–168
  help available for, 10, 171
  hormones in, 156, 158
  nutrition for, 83
  second-stage, 154, 168–171
  of triplets, 151–152
  of twins, 74, 157
breastmilk, 108
  bonding and, 33, 34, 39, 40, 41
  drugs and, 157, 159, 165
  formulas vs., 81, 82, 83, 86, 154, 193
  hand expressing of, 12, 39, 41, 159–160
  immunity improved by, 94, 154–155
  jaundice and, 88
  nutritional value of, 154
breast pumps, 72, 84, 159–164
Brethine, 17, 229
brewer's yeast, 157
bronchioles, 60
bronchitis, 186, 187
bronchopulmonary dysplasia (BPD), 32, 66–67, 83, 124, 133, 168, 180, 186, 187, 188, 189
Budin, Pierre, 120, 122, 124, 158
burette, 78

caffeine, for apnea, 76
Candida albicans, 91, 183
carbon dioxide:
  apnea and, 76
  in RDS, 61, 62
carbonic acid, 62, 76

carbon monoxide, smoking and, 54, 230
cardiopulmonary resuscitation (CPR), 74, 144–145, 188
  instructions for, 190–191
car seats, 146, 147
CAT scanner (computerized axial tomography), 97–98
Celestone, 17
central line, 79–80
cerclage, 17
cerebral palsy, 96, 97, 123, 202, 207–208, 218
cerebrospinal fluid (CSF), 97, 98
cervix, incompetent, 17, 18
cesarean section:
  for breech births, 58
  for herpes, 92
  for LGA babies, 54
child abuse, 9, 28, 178–179
childbirth:
  breech, 57, 58
  mystical attitudes toward, 7–8
  premature, see premature birth
  stresses of, 55, 57, 60
Chinese-Americans, prematurity rate of, 23
choreoathetosis, 96
chorion, development of, 43
chromosomal abnormalities, 53
chromosomes, female vs. male, 90
chronic lung disease (CLD), see bronchopulmonary dysplasia
Churchill, Winston, 120, 203
circulation:
  fetal, 56
  persistent fetal (PFC), 70, 71
circumcision, 145
clothing, 136, 138–142, 148, 180
clotting factors, 87, 89, 90, 152
Clyman, Ronald, 205
coffee, pregnancy and, 24, 232
Cohen, Marion, 108
Cohen, Marna, 4
Colautti v. Franklin, 44n
colds, 91, 186–187
colic, 177–178
colostomy, 83, 86
colostrum, 156, 157
Compassionate Friends, Inc., 113
"compensatory care," 29
complete blood count (CBC), 92
congenital defects, 92, 109, 116
  as cause of prematurity, 16
  in identical twins, 21–22
  maternal diabetes and, 54
congestive heart failure, 70
conjugated bilirubin, 86
constipation, 100, 193, 234, 235

contractile cells, 157
cortisol, 16
coughing, 188
Couney, Hildegarde, 122
Couney, Martin, 121–122
counseling, importance of, 10, 112, 129, 229
CPAP (continuous positive airway pressure), 62, 66, 123
cream-atocrit, 154
Creasy, Robert, 226–227, 236
creatinine, 80
crib death (SIDS), 112, 189
Crib-O-Gram, 210
crying, 177
cultures and sensitivities in septic workup, 91
curare, 62, 66, 83, 132, 136
"cut downs," 79–80, 126
cyanide, in cigarettes, 54
cyanosis, 76
cysts, 193
cytomegalovirus (CMV), 53, 92, 210

Davis, Adelle, 149
Davison, Martha, 52
deafness, 210
death, 107–119
  brain, 102
  legal criteria for, 102
  see also infant mortality
Decadron, 95
decompression, 82
Degher, Katherine, 198–201
dehydration, 171, 173, 192
denial, as stage of grief, 5–6, 107, 217
dental treatment, 100, 193
Denver Developmental Screening Test (DDST), 206
depression:
  post-nursery, 175
  postpartum, 7
  in siblings, 36
DES (diethylstilbestrol), 17, 101
developmental tests, 206
dexamethasone, 95
Dextrostix, 80
diabetes, 19, 21, 54, 60, 89, 165, 229
  gestational, 21, 236
diapers, 142, 144, 183
diarrhea, 155, 192
  causes of, 83, 90, 93, 100
Dilantin, 96
diplegia, 207
disseminated intravascular coagulation (DIC), 90
diuretics, 67, 70, 229
dizziness, 187

doctors:
  anger at, 25
  communication with, 5, 10–11, 25, 101, 129, 228
  selection of, 228
  specialists, 125–126, 215–217
Down's syndrome, 53
DQ (development quotient), 206, 209
Drillien, C. M., 205
drugs:
  abuse of, 24, 53
  administering of, 186–187
  antifungal, 91, 165
  for apnea, 76, 189
  for asthma, 17
  for BPD, 67
  for brain edema, 95
  breastmilk and, 157, 159, 165
  excretion affected by, 83
  fertility, 22
  for high blood pressure, 40
  pain-relieving, 58, 165
  for PDA, 70
  for RDS prevention, 17, 60, 124, 229
  in RDS treatment, 62, 66
  for seizures, 96, 189
  side effects of, 17, 83, 132, 149, 157, 199, 210, 229, 234
  tocolytic (labor-stopping), 16–17, 124, 149, 199, 229
  *see also specific types*
ductus arteriosus, 55, 56, 70
Duff, Raymond, 102, 103
duskiness, 188, 189

ear infections, 187
echocardiography, 70
E. coli, 91
edema, 45
  brain, 95, 96
  pulmonary, 70, 229
Edwards, Gayla, 39–41, 156
Einstein, Albert, 120, 203
electroencephalogram (EEG), 96, 102
electrolytes, 80
Elias, Cathy, 130
emergencies, defined, 101
endotracheal (ET) tube, 58, 62, 64, 66
enteritis, 93
epilepsy, 96
episiotomies, 58
erythroblastosis fetalis, 89–90
erythrocytes, 87
Eskildsen, Harriet, 211–212
estriol level test, 231
estrogen, 3
Eustachian tubes, 187
Everett, Sandi, 84–86
extubation, 66

eye contact, 135

farsightedness, 212
fathers, bereaved, 112
fathers, expectant, 16
fathers, new:
  bonding and, 34–35, 42, 71
  mothers compared to, 9, 31, 34
  negative emotions of, 4–7
  supportive behavior of, 4, 8, 31, 104, 219, 220
fetal alcohol syndrome, 229
fetuses, fetal development, 42–54
  amniotic fluid and, 19
  circulation in, 56
  cortisol in, 16
  growth retardation in, 53–54, 92
  infected, 21, 53, 60
  legal viability of, 44
fever, 188
fibroids, 18, 19, 20, 23
Field, Tiffany, 178
financial problems, 4, 6, 9, 10, 106, 128, 129, 164, 170, 184
fontanel, 93, 96, 192
"football carry," 169
*foramen ovale*, 56, 57
forceps delivery, 58
formula feeding, 80–81, 167
  breastmilk vs., 81, 82, 83, 154, 193
Fost, Norman, 103
Frantz, Kittie, 159, 166, 171
*Frog Family's Baby Dies, The* (Oehler), 114
*Frogs Have a Baby, a Very Small Baby, The* (Oehler), 37
funerals, 111
funguses, 91, 165, 183
Furman, Erna, 112
furosemide, 67

gag reflex, 52, 81, 83, 166
Garland, Michael, 102
gavage feeding, 52, 81, 83, 120, 134, 166
German measles, 53, 92, 210
germs, 90, 91
gestational age, 42, 46, 53–54, 124
gestational diabetes, 21, 236
Golenski, John, 107, 109, 110, 111, 112, 113, 115
Gorski, Peter, 29, 51, 52, 102, 133, 137
gram stains, 91
grandparents, 6, 38–39, 218
Gregory, George, 123
grief, stages of, 1–9, 107, 113, 217
gripping reflex, 42, 46, 47
Group B "strep" (Streptococcus), 21, 91

guilt, 1, 4, 6–7, 16, 25, 31, 53, 113, 198, 217
  breast-feeding and, 173
  in life support decisions, 102, 110
  in siblings, 36, 218
Guttmacher, Alan, 18

habituation, 51, 206
H.A.N.D. (Helping After Neonatal Death), 113
handicaps, 202, 207–225
Harrison, Helen, 219–223
Harrison, Michael, 82
headaches, 100
hearing impairment, 92, 96, 97, 123, 146, 187, 202, 208, 209–212
heart:
  congestion of, 70
  in full-term babies, 55–57
heartbeat:
  rapid, 76, 90
  slow, *see* bradycardia
heart murmur, 70–71
heel sticks, 50, 65, 90, 193
hemangiomas, 193
hematocrit, 87, 89, 92, 189
hemiplegia, 207
hemoglobin, 87
hernias, 106, 189–192
heroin:
  fetal stress caused by, 60
  low birthweight and, 24
Herron, Marie, 24, 236
Hess, Julius, 122
high blood pressure, 16, 19, 20, 21, 23, 53, 60
  drugs for, 40
Hippocrates, 102, 120
Holland, birthweights in, 54
hormones:
  bonding and, 3
  in breast-feeding, 156, 158
  as cause of prematurity, 16
  in fetal lung development, 60
  in postpartum depression, 7
  in pregnancy, 3, 16, 229, 231
  steroid, 60
  stimulation of, 133
hospitals:
  discharge standards of, 77, 83, 144
  germs in, 90
  limited facilities of, 2
  premature nurseries in, 2, 122–123, 127
  selection of, 228
  *see also* intensive care nurseries
Hunt, Jane, 202, 203, 205

hyaline membrane disease (HMD), *see* respiratory distress syndrome
hyaline membranes, 61
*Hydatoxi lualba,* 20
hydrocephalus, 97, 98–101, 214, 220
hyperactivity, 202–203
hyperalimentation (HA), 80
hyperbilirubinemia, *see* jaundice
hyperglycemia, 80, 96
hypernatremia, 96
hyperopia, 212
hypertension, *see* high blood pressure
hypocalcemia, 96
hypoglycemia, 54, 57, 58, 76, 80, 89, 95–96
hyponatremia, 96
hypothalamus, 133
hypothermia, 57, 58
hypoxia, 76, 82, 95, 207, 214
   in childbirth, 55, 57
   PDA and, 70
   smoking as cause of, 54

ileostomy, 83
immunization, 91, 181
incompetent cervix, 17, 18
incubators, 77, 120
indomethacin, 70
infant mortality, 31
   maternal diabetes and, 54
   meningitis and, 93
   statistics on, 22–23, 107, 124
   toxemia and, 20
infant swings, 146, 147
infections, 90–95, 181, 210
   ear, 187
   intrauterine, 21, 89, 90, 219
   prevention of, 93–95, 122, 155
   shunt, 100
   symptoms of, 236
   types of, 93
   viral, 91–92
   *see also specific types*
infiltration, 79
informed consent, 101–102
infusion pump, 78
inspiratory pressure, 62
insulin:
   betamimetics and, 229
   breastmilk and, 165
   RDS and, 60
insurance, 10, 106, 130, 164, 170, 184
intensive care, ethics of, 101–106
intensive care nurseries, 120–130
   availability of, 2, 39, 95, 186
   environment of, 5, 31–32, 36, 103, 124
   history of, 120–124
   parenting in, 131–143

regular premature nursery vs., 2, 122–123, 127
intracranial hemorrhage, 97–98
intralipids (IL), 80–81
intrauterine infections, 21, 89, 90, 219
intravenous feedings, 77–80, 93, 123
intraventricular hemorrhage, 97
intubation, 58
iodine, 232
IQ (intelligence quotient), 208–209
iron deficiency, iron supplements, 89, 154, 189, 193, 232
isoxsuprine, 17, 229
Japan, multiple births in, 22
Japanese-Americans, prematurity rate of, 23
jaundice, 70, 83, 84, 86–89, 90, 92, 210

Kennell, J. H., 28, 30
kernicterus, 86, 96
kidney disease, 19, 21, 53
Klaus, M. H., 28, 30
*Klebsiella,* 91
Kositsky, Ann, 130
Kübler-Ross, Elisabeth, 107

labor:
   drugs for suppression of, 16–17, 124, 149, 199, 229
   membrane rupture in, 18
   stresses of, 55, 57
   symptoms of, 236, 237
Lact-Aid Nursing Supplementer, 170
lactic acid, 76
*Lactobacillus,* 91
La Leche League, 10, 40, 161, 173
lanugo, 44, 45, 46
laryngoscope, 58
Lasix, 67
latency period, in visual and hearing ability, 50–51
Laurie, Kathy Swinbank, 71–74, 156, 178
Leach, Penelope, 148
learning disabilities, 203
lecithin, 60
left-to-right shunt, 70, 71
let-down response, 158–159
leukocytes, 87
Levdar, Kathleen, 8
LGA (large for gestational age), 54
life support decisions, 102–107, 109–110
Lipson, Juliene, 14–15
*Listeria,* 91
listeriosis, 219
*Living with Our Hyperactive Children* (Bittinger), 203
Lorber, John, 101

low-birthweight babies (LBW), 53–54, 123, 146, 189, 230
   apnea in, 74
   body temperature of, 76
   follow-up studies on, 202–207
   PDA, 70
   pre-term vs., 2*n,* 4, 24
   RDS in, 59
   very, very, 205–207
   *see also* SGA
Lowen, Lauri, 171
Loyola Parents' Group, 224
L/S ratio test, 60, 231
Lubchenco, Lula, 138
lumbar-peritoneal (LP) shunt, 99
lumbar puncture, 92–93, 97
lungs:
   air leaks in, 67–68
   chronic disease of (CDL), *see* bronchopulmonary dysplasia
   collapsed, 68, 101
   compliance of, 70
   congested, 66
   development of, 60
   in full-term babies, 55–57
   immature, 57, 59
lymphocytes, 92

McNamara, Chris, 25–27
magnesium sulfate, 165, 229
malnutrition, 19, 20, 54
malpractice suits, 25, 101
marijuana, prematurity not associated with, 24
marital problems, 5, 9, 112, 175–176, 217, 218
Martin, M. O., 121
massages, 41, 94, 133, 159, 195
mastitis, 165
maternal behavior, *see* bonding and attachment
*Maternal-Infant Bonding* (Kennell and Klaus), 28
meconium, 83, 90
medical ethics, 101–106
medical staff, 125–130
   anger at, 6, 129
   relationship with, 11, 32, 40, 129
meditation, 233–234
membranes:
   amniotic, rupture of, 18–19, 21, 60, 230
   hyaline, 61
meningitis, 93, 96, 208, 210
menstruation, gestational age and, 42
metabolic acidosis, 62
metabolic imbalances, 95–96
minimal brain dysfunction, 202–203

miscarriages:
  causes of, 17, 18
  fear of, 2
  repeated, 18, 21
Monilia, 91, 183
mothers, bereaved, 112–113, 116–119
mothers, expectant:
  advice for, 228–237
  age of, 21, 22
  diabetic, 19, 21, 54, 60, 89, 229
  with high blood pressure, 16, 19, 20, 21, 23, 53, 60
  high-risk, 16, 226–228
  nutrition for, 20–21, 230–234
mothers, new:
  fathers compared to, 9, 31, 34
  negative feelings of, 3–9, 25, 33
  physical problems of, 7
mothers, nursing:
  nipple problems of, 165–166
  nutrition for, 83, 157, 165
Müllerian ducts, 17
multiple births, 16, 21–23, 54, 157
  polyhydramnios in, 18–19
  see also triplets; twins
Mycostatin, 91, 165
myelination, 95, 133
myopia, 68, 212, 214

names, selection of, 3, 4, 11, 31, 71, 109, 151, 219
natural childbirth movement, 7–8
nausea, in pregnancy, 20–21, 235
NBICU (newborn intensive care unit), see intensive care nurseries
nearsightedness, 68, 212, 214
nebulizers, 64
necrotizing enterocolitis (NEC), 82–83, 86, 124
Neifert, Marianne, 171
neonatology, 125
neurological problems, 95–101
nicotine, danger of, 54
Nigeria, multiple births in, 22
Noguchi, Kathie, 148–152, 158
non-stress test, 231
normality:
  prognosis for, 5–6, 202–225
  worries about, 1, 2, 5–6, 202
nurses, role of, 125–126, 130
nursing, see breast-feeding
Nursling, The (Budin), 120, 158
nutrition:
  breastmilk and, 154
  for expectant mothers, 20–21, 24, 54, 230–234
  of fetal twins, 22
  for nursing mothers, 83, 157

  for premature babies, 80–81, 95, 154
  total parent (TPN), 80
nystatin, 91, 165

Oehler, Jerri, 37, 114
oligohydramnios, 19
omphalocele, 116
On Death and Dying (Kübler-Ross), 107
open ductus, 70–71
optic nerve damage, 214
osteopenia, 81
otitis media, 187
overprotection, 197
oxygen, in RDS treatment, 62, 68–69, 122–123, 214
oxygen deprivation, see hypoxia
oxygen hood, 62, 63
oxytocin, 21, 158, 159, 229

pacifiers, 81, 134, 178
packed cells, 89
pancuronium, 62, 83
parasites, 92
Parent-Infant Bonding (Kennell and Klaus), 30
parenting:
  at home, 175–201
  at home, preparation for, 141–148
  in intensive care nursery, 131–143
Parents Anonymous, 179
parents' rights, 101–106
parent support groups, 113, 129, 176, 179, 217, 221, 224
patent ductus arteriosus (PDA), 70–71
"patterning" therapy, 217n
Pavulon, 62, 66, 83, 132, 136
percussion, vibration and suctioning, 66
periodic breathing, 76, 188
persistent fetal circulation (PFC), 70, 71
pessimism, as denial, 5–6
petechiae, 90, 219
pH, 62
phenobarbital, 96, 189
phenytoin, 96
Phibbs, Roderick, 124
photographing of babies, importance of, 11, 39, 40, 71, 72, 109
phototherapy, 83, 87–88
placenta previa, 19, 21, 25, 230
placentas:
  development of, 43
  function of, 56
  problems with, 16, 19, 20, 21, 25, 54, 89, 230, 236
  twins and, 22, 23
plasma, 87

platelets, 87, 90, 92, 152
pneumococci, 91
pneumogram (sleep study), 73, 188
pneumonia, 93, 186, 187
pneumothorax (collapsed lung), 68, 101
polycythemia, 22, 54, 89
polyhydramnios, 18–19, 21, 54, 119
polymorphonuclear cells (PMN), 92
positive end-expiratory pressure (PEEP), 62
postpartum depression, 7
postural drainage, 66
pre-eclampsia, 20, 39, 236
pregnancy:
  complications in, 16, 19–20
  following birth of premature baby, 226–239
  high-risk, 226–228
  high risk, tests used in, 231
  hormonal changes during, 3, 16, 229, 231
  psychological adjustments to, 2–3
  sex during, 21, 228–229
  see also fetuses, fetal development; mothers, expectant
"premature," 2n
premature babies:
  appearance of, 42, 45–46, 51, 52, 131–132, 180, 188, 189
  behavior of, 49–51, 52–53
  blacks vs. white, 44
  borderline (week 37 to week 38), 52, 120
  breast-feeding of, see breast-feeding
  childbirth stresses of, 57–58
  color of, 42, 45, 76, 131, 132, 180, 188, 189
  "compensatory care" and, 29
  death of, see death; infant mortality
  development of, 195–198, 203–206
  feeding of, 77–84, 120, 123, 138, 144, 148, 153–174
  female vs. male, 44, 50, 60, 90
  genitals of, 45–46, 145
  gestational age of, 42, 46, 53
  hearing of, 50–51, 92, 96, 97, 123, 134–135, 137, 143, 146, 187, 202, 208, 209–212
  irritable, 177–178
  LGA, 54
  moderately (week 31 to week 36), 51–52
  monitoring of, 58, 65, 73–76, 96
  muscle tone of, 46–48, 52, 97, 131, 207–208
  negative feelings about, 3–5, 42, 53, 217
  nervous system of, 49–51

nutrition for, 80–81, 95, 154
photographing of, 11, 39, 40, 71, 72, 109
pre-term vs. low-birthweight, 2n, 4, 24
reflexes of, 49–50, 51, 52, 81, 166, 170, 174
responsiveness of, 32–33, 42, 50, 52–53, 132
senses of, 50–51
serious problems of, 55–106
SGA, 53–54, 68
sleep of, 49–50, 51, 53, 132, 176–177
smiling of, 49–50, 51, 197, 198
stereotyped image of, 2
survival changes of, *see* survival
talking to, 28, 41, 51, 134–135, 167, 197, 212
touching important for, 14, 28, 32, 33, 40, 41, 42, 50, 93–94, 133–134, 195
very (week 25 to week 30), 44–52, 59
vision of, 50–51, 68–69, 92, 97, 100, 105–106, 123, 124, 126, 135, 138, 143, 146, 198, 202, 207, 212–215
premature birth:
causes of, 16–25
as crisis, 1–15
disappointment of, 7–8
statistics on, 1, 2, 16, 22–23, 44, 51, 52, 107
suggestions for coping with, 9–12
progesterone, 16
prolactin, 156, 157
prostaglandins, function of, 16
protein:
for babies, 80
in blood, 87
for expectant mothers, 232, 233
pseudomonas, 91
pulmonary edema, 70, 229
pulmonary insufficiency of the premature (PIP), 59
pulmonary interstitial emphysema (PIE), 67–68
pyloric stenosis, 192

Quaaludes, abuse of, 24
quadriplegia, 207
quadruplets, 22, 54
Quinlan, Karen Ann, 219

radial artery catheter, 79n
radiation, safety questions about, 65–66
Rand, Sally, 122
rashes, 90, 91, 92, 183, 219
reflex smiling, 45–50, 51
*Relaxation Response, The* (Benson), 234

REM (rapid eye movement) sleep, 49–50, 51
research:
animal studies in, 3, 17, 20, 54, 155
human studies in, 28–30, 32, 101–102, 155
residuals, 82
respirators, 58, 59, 62, 63, 64
respiratory acidosis, 62
respiratory distress syndrome (RDS), 52, 57, 58–66, 70, 71, 77, 180, 186, 187, 188, 205
blindness and, 68, 123
carbon dioxide in, 61
development of, 60–61
drug therapy in, 62, 66
insulin and, 60
maternal diabetes and, 54
PIP vs., 59
prevention of, 17, 60, 124, 229
retraction in, 61, 67, 188
statistics on, 59, 61, 123
survival rate of, 61, 68, 123
treatment of, 62–69, 93, 123, 126
respiratory infections:
lower (LRI), 186, 187–188
susceptibility to, 67, 180, 186–188
upper (URI), 186–187
responsive smiling, 49–50, 197, 198
resuscitation, 58
retardation, 96, 97, 103, 202, 208–209
retinopathy of prematurity (ROP), *see* retrolental fibroplasia
retraction, in RDS, 61, 67, 188
retrolental fibroplasia (RLF), 68–69, 105–106, 123, 124, 212, 214
Rh incompatibility, 87, 89–90
RhoGAM shots, 90
Rice, Ruth, 133
*Richard III* (Shakespeare), 120
right-to-left shunt, 70, 71
ritodrine, 17, 229
rooting reflex, 52, 166
rubella, 53, 92, 210

Scanlon, John, 70
Schiff, Harriet, 107, 109, 111, 115
Schwartz, Jane, 24
sedatives, 83
"sed" cells, 89
Sehring, Sally, 102, 129–130, 205
seizures, 93, 96, 189
septate and subseptate uterus, 17
septicemia, sepsis, 93, 219
septic workup, 91–93
serous otitis, 187
sexual activity:
grieving and, 112
during pregnancy, 21, 228–229

SGA (small for gestational age), 53–54, 89, 92, 133, 195, 205, 208
SGOT and SGPT tests, 81
Shakespeare, William, 120
S.H.A.R.E. (A Source of Help in Airing and Resolving Experiences), 113
Shelburne, Katherine, 37, 114
shock, as stage of grief, 2–5, 38, 107
shunts, 214
infection or failure of, 100
left-to-right, 70, 71
lumbar-peritoneal, 99
right-to-left, 70, 71
ventriculo-atrial, 99
ventriculo-peritoneal, 99–101
Siamese twins, 103
siblings:
attention demanded by, 27, 36, 149
bonding and, 35–37
explaining death of baby to, 109, 114
guilt in, 36, 218
handicaps viewed by, 218
sickle cell anemia, 21, 23, 53
SIDS (sudden infant death syndrome), 112, 189
*sietemesino*, 22
Silverman, William, 103
skin care, 94
sleep, of premature babies, 49–50, 51, 53, 132, 176–177
sleep study, 73, 188
smiling, of premature babies, 49–50, 51, 197
smoking:
babies endangered by, 180
breast-feeding inhibited by, 159
pregnancy endangered by, 19, 24, 54, 230
social smiling, 49–50, 197, 198
social workers, role of, 6, 10, 129, 215
somatotrophin, 133
Spain, infant mortality in, 22
spasticity, 97, 207–208
sphingomyelin, 60
spinal tap, 92–93, 97
Spock, Benjamin, 148, 197
spontaneous abortions, *see* miscarriages
Stanford-Binet IQ scales, 208
"staph" (Staphylococcus), 91
startle reflex, 50, 51
steroid hormones, 60
Stinson, Peggy and Robert, 103
stopcock, 78
strabismus, 207, 213–214
strawberry marks, 193
streptococcus infections, 21, 91
stress test, 231

subarachnoid hemorrhage, 97
subependymal hemorrhage, 97
sucking:
    breastmilk stimulated by, 157
    functional, 52, 81, 83, 134
    nutritive vs. non-nutritive, 50
sunlight:
    jaundice helped by, 87–88
    overexposure to, 180
"supermarket syndrome," 181
Supreme Court, U.S., on fetal viability,
    44n
surfactant, 55, 57, 58, 60, 61
survival:
    of RDS, 61, 68, 123
    statistics on, 2, 5, 44, 51, 52, 61, 124,
        205
    worries about, 1, 4, 5, 31, 33
swaddling, 178, 179
Sweden, infant mortality in, 23

tachycardia, 76, 90
tachypnea, 76, 90, 93, 188
Tarnier, Stéphane, 120, 121
teething, 100, 178, 193
temperature, *see* body temperature
terbutaline, 16–17, 149, 199, 229
theophylline, 76, 189
thrombocytes, 87
thrombocytopenia, 90, 92, 152
thrush, 91, 165
thumb-sucking, 178
tocolytic (labor-stopping) drugs, 16–
    17, 124, 149, 199, 229
tongue thrust reflex, 170, 174
TORCH syndrome, 90, 92
total parental nutrition (TPA), 80
toxemia, 20, 21, 39, 53, 54, 60, 165, 229,
    232

symptoms of, 236
toxoplasmosis, 53, 92
toys, 143, 196, 198
tracheostomy, 66–67
transcutaneous monitors, 65
transducer, 78
transfusions, 87, 88, 89, 90, 92, 93,
    101, 189
transport team, 126
triplets, 22, 54, 149–152, 158, 204
twins, 16, 20, 21–23, 31, 54, 60
    breast-feeding of, 74, 157
    case histories of, 71–74, 118–119
    death of one child, 108, 110, 118–
        119
    fraternal, 22
    identical, 21–23, 89
    Siamese, 103

ultrasound, 98, 124, 231
umbilical catheter, 58, 78–79
urinalysis, 92
urinary tract infections, 18, 21
urination, 80, 83, 144, 171, 192
uterus:
    abnormalities of, 17–18, 54
    bicornuate, 17–18
    circulation in, 20
    scarring of, 19
    septate and subseptate, 17
    *see also* intrauterine infections

vaginal infections, 18, 21
vaporizers, 146, 186
Vasek, Kathleen, 223–225, 237–239
Vasodilan, 17, 229
ventilators, *see* respirators
ventricles, of brain, 97

ventriculo-atrial (VA) shunt, 99
ventriculo-peritoneal (VP) shunt, 99–
    101
vernix, 44, 45
Vinstein, Arnold, 65
viral infections, 91–92
visual impairment, 68–69, 92, 97, 100,
    105–106, 123, 124, 126, 146, 202,
    207, 212–215
vitamin D, 80
vitamin E:
    for anemia, 80, 89
    for RLF, 69
    for sore nipples, 166
vitamin K, 80, 87
vitamins and minerals, 54, 80–81, 89,
    154, 157, 189, 193, 230, 231
vomiting, 100, 155, 167, 187, 189, 192

weight, *see* birthweight; low-
    birthweight babies
wheezing, 67, 188
Wick, Susan, 103–106

x-rays, 126, 188
    for NEC, 82
    for PDA, 70
    for pneumothorax, 68
    in RDS treatment, 65–66
    safety questions about, 65–66
    *see also* CAT scanner; ultrasound

"yeast" infections, 91, 183
*Your Baby and Child* (Leach), 148
Yutopar, 17, 229

Zeichner, Linda, 116–117
Zimmer, John, 203

You can order extra copies of this book through your local bookstore, or directly from St. Martin's Press by using the order form below. Enclose $15.95 for each copy requested, plus $1.00 postage and handling charge for the first book and 50¢ for each additional copy. New York State residents please add applicable sales tax. Send check or money order to St. Martin's Press, 175 Fifth Avenue, New York, N.Y. 10010.

---

St. Martin's Press, 175 Fifth Avenue, New York, N.Y. 10011

Please send _____ copies of THE PREMATURE BABY BOOK

Name_____

Address_____

_____ Zip_____

Enclosed is my check or money order for $_____

---

Discounts on quantity orders of THE PREMATURE BABY BOOK are available to physicians, clinics, or other organizations. For information on prices for orders of 10 or more copies, call St. Martin's Press, Special Sales Department. Toll free (800) 221-7945. In New York, call (212) 674-5151.